UNIX®

for the

Impatient

Paul W. Abrahams
Bruce R. Larson

ADDISON-WESLEY PUBLISHING COMPANY

Reading, Massachusetts • Menlo Park, California • New York
Don Mills, Ontario • Wokingham, England • Amsterdam • Bonn
Sydney • Singapore • Tokyo • Madrid • San Juan • Milan • Paris

This book was designed and composed by Paul Abrahams. It was typeset using TEX (written by Donald E. Knuth), supplemented by an extensive set of customized macros (written by Paul Abrahams) and the `eplain` macro package (written primarily by Karl Berry). The index was prepared with the help of an auxiliary program written in Icon. The cover was designed by Toni St. Regis.

The main text was set in Bitstream Baskerville. Examples and other program text were set in Computer Modern Typewriter with the hard-to-read hat and tilde characters of that font replaced by larger and clearer typeforms. Section and chapter heads were set in Zapf Humanist (the Bitstream version of Optima, designed by Hermann Zapf).

The book was phototypeset by Type 2000, Inc., Mill Valley, California and printed and bound by Arcata Graphics-Halliday using New Era Matte 45 lb. paper. Preliminary proofs were prepared on a Hewlett Packard LaserJet II printer.

Library of Congress Cataloging-in-Publication Data

Abrahams, Paul W.
    Unix for the impatient / Paul W. Abrahams, Bruce R. Larson.
       p.   cm.
    Includes bibliographical references (p.   ) and index.
    ISBN 0-201-55703-7
    1. Operating systems (Computers) 2. UNIX (Computer file)
I. Larson, Bruce R. II. Title.
QA76.76.063A27   1992
005.4'3–dc20
                             91-31893
                             CIP

Reprinted with corrections May, 1992.

7 8 9 10 MA 959493

Preface

UNIX for the Impatient is a UNIX handbook—a detailed, comprehensive guide to the UNIX system that can serve both as a ready reference and as a means of learning UNIX. We've consciously aimed the book at readers who are comfortable with technical material, presenting the subject as concisely as possible rather than in the gentle steps of a tutorial book. What other authors cover in an entire volume, we cover in a section. We achieve this not by omitting details but by omitting long explanations and numerous examples that illustrate a single point. The tutorial approach may be less demanding, but ours is faster; hence the title of our book.

UNIX has become the standard operating system for computers in scientific, engineering, and research environments. Unlike other major operating systems, it is not irrevocably tied to a particular computer architecture. Designed to be used interactively, UNIX is not bound by inherent memory constraints, handles multiple processes and users easily and naturally, and is well suited as a platform for networking and graphical environments. Commercially supported versions of UNIX are available for most commonly used computers. Existence of an accepted standard for UNIX system calls enables programmers to write portable UNIX programs, and several groups are working to develop standards for other aspects of UNIX.

But UNIX isn't easy to learn. In the early days when UNIX was still a research project, one person could understand all of it. No longer is that true. Today's UNIX user faces great obstacles to mastery: the variety of implementations; the rapid pace of change; the proliferation of related subsystems; the profusion of commands and their options, variables, and subcommands; the sheer volume of material to be assimilated; the historical accretions; and the assumption prevalent in UNIX documentation that the reader is already familiar with what is being described.

Technically sophisticated people often prefer to learn new programs and computer systems by reading the reference manuals. There isn't much hope of learning UNIX that way. The typical UNIX reference manual consists of an alphabetical list of command descriptions, many of which are cryptic, misleading, poorly organized, or erroneous in subtle ways. It fails to provide an overview or explanation of the basic UNIX concepts. UNIX-specific terminology is often used without being defined; terminology is often used inconsistently from one command to another.

The central purpose of *UNIX for the Impatient* is to serve as a better manual for people who like to learn from manuals. Rather than lead you by the hand through UNIX, we assist you in finding your own way. We don't tell you what you can see for yourself, but we do tell you about many undocumented and poorly documented aspects of UNIX commands. If you're seeking an easier but slower route through the subject, using tutorial books (you'll need several) along with *UNIX for the Impatient* can provide that route.

Most of the book consists of command descriptions. These descriptions are usually as detailed as those in your system's manual—but we present them in a way that you can understand. We've organized the book and its parts, down to the level of the command descriptions, logically by function rather than alphabetically so that you can see how different commands and options relate to one another and find the right tools for a particular task. We make it easy for you to look up commands and their options by including an alphabetical summary of commands cross-referenced to the pages where you'll find the full explanations. We also provide a thorough index and a synopsis preceding the table of contents.

We include a chapter covering the common concepts of UNIX and a glossary. When you encounter a technical term that you haven't seen before, you can easily find out what it means. We provide abundant cross-references to help you through the thicket of dependencies among different UNIX commands and concepts. To get you oriented, we provide a discussion of how to use this book in Section 1.2.

We describe UNIX from the standpoint of a user, that is, a person primarily interested in it as a tool rather than as an object of study for its own sake. Therefore we don't generally say much about UNIX internals—those aspects of UNIX mainly of interest to system programmers—although if you're a system programmer, this book can still be helpful for dealing with the external aspects of UNIX.

Nor do we attempt to describe the programming facilities of UNIX such as the C compiler, `lex`, and `yacc`. How to use these tools, particularly C, can occupy a book by itself. We do, however, describe `awk`, which is relatively easy to learn and which provides an easy way of transforming and filtering data while enabling you to carry out fairly complex programming tasks. In a few places such as our discussions of `awk` and of shell scripts, we assume some familiarity with programming methods and terminology— we couldn't avoid it—but most of the book can be understood even if you aren't familiar with programming.

UNIX has become what it is today more through accretion than through conscious planning. There's a principle of programming language design called "orthogonality"—the idea that different aspects of the language interact as little as possible and can be treated independently. UNIX, unfortunately, violates that principle egregiously. Programs are sensitive to the conventions of other programs and interact with each other in complex ways. For example, the `vi` visual editor was built on top of the `ex` extended line editor, so-called because it extended the earlier `ed` editor. Thus to understand `vi` fully you also must know `ex`.

Moreover, many UNIX facilities are someone's improvement or elaboration on an existing facility. The old version persists even when the new version is indisputably better. Programs with overlapping functions are common. Thus there are two incompatible data compression programs, `pack` and `compress`; two incompatible archiving programs, `cpio` and `tar`; at least two different mail programs that call themselves `mail`; two different programs for transferring files from one machine to another, `ftp` and `uucp`; and at least four shells for managing interaction with your terminal (the Bourne shell `sh`, the C shell `csh`, a C shell extension called `tcsh`, and the Korn shell `ksh`). All of these are widely used.

This profusion of variants created a dilemma for us. How many of these programs should we describe? Should we deal with overlapping programs individually or should we follow the UNIX tradition of presuming that a user is familiar with a program's precursors? Individual descriptions create redundancy since the same material appears again and again. But relying on a precursor results in confusion and frustration—why learn A just for the sake of understanding B? We've partly solved this difficulty by collecting common concepts in Chapter 2. Where that was inappropriate, we've usually chosen redundancy as the better course. For example, when presenting the four shells, we describe wildcards, redirection, and quotation in Chapter 2; we provide detailed descriptions for the Bourne and C shells; and we provide descriptive information for `tcsh` and the Korn shell.

Just as there are many different dialects of English, there are many different versions of UNIX. British lorries roll on tyres, while American trucks roll on tires. Versions of UNIX differ analogously. We could not hope to discover, let alone describe, all the differences among them—and even if we could, the resulting book would be so large and full of irrelevant details that few would find it useful. AT&T System V has incorporated the major facilities and implementation methods of other UNIX versions, notably SunOS, which are themselves based on AT&T source licenses. We therefore follow the AT&T System V specifications most of the time, but because of the popularity of the Berkeley Software Distributions, particularly Version 4.3, we also describe the most conspicuous BSD UNIX variations. For example, we describe both the System V `lp` command for sending files to a line printer and the BSD UNIX `lpr` command that does nearly the same thing but does it differently. We avoid dwelling on details peculiar to System V, focusing instead on those features and functions that are common to almost all versions of UNIX. You may find that some commands don't work on *your* system exactly as we describe them, but the differences will usually be minor.

You'll find topics covered in this book that don't make it into most UNIX books. Some examples are the X Window System, archiving files with `tar` and `cpio`, the emacs editor, using communications programs such as `telnet` and `ftp`, and the addressing conventions used for Internet and UUCP electronic mail. Although we hope this book is the first one you take off the shelf, we realize it may not be the last, so we provide a list of printed and electronic resources you can use for additional information or for another view of the same material.

Our approach to UNIX is like Albert Einstein's approach to physics: make it as simple as possible, but no simpler. We explain UNIX as clearly as we can without neglecting difficult or complicated, but nevertheless essential, details. While some of these details may not seem important when you first see them, you're likely to find them indispensable as you read the manuals supplied with your system.

For those who notice such things, we mention that we've adopted the British (logical) treatment of punctuation at the end of a sentence: when a quotation ends a sentence, we place the period outside the quotation. We consider this policy necessary for any book whose subject matter demands great orthographic precision. We appreciate the indulgence of our editors.

We wish to thank our colleagues at Addison-Wesley who made this book possible: Peter Gordon, our editor, who conceived the idea of the book and whose encouragement and helpful suggestions were invaluable; Helen Goldstein, his editorial assistant, who patiently and unfailingly navigated this book past many obstacles; and Loren Hilgenhurst Stevens, our production supervisor, whose energy, good taste, and deep knowledge of everything from the fine points of English grammar and usage to the intricacies of book manufacturing never ceased to impress us. We thank our proofreader, Lorraine Ferrier, for an exceptionally thorough job performed under stringent time constraints. And we especially thank our reviewers, whose comments and feedback made the book far better than it would have been otherwise: Lyn Dupré, Jennifer Knuth, Thomas F. Reid, Bjorn Satdeva, Stephen Stepanek, Gregory Tucker, and Gerald Weiss.

We also wish to thank George Lukas, who helped refine the original plan of the book; Bob Morris, Betty O'Neil, and Rick Martin of the Computer Science Department at the University of Massachusetts, Boston, who generously provided us with access to the Department's computing facilities; Karl Berry, who provided us with access to several UNIX systems and patiently answered many of our questions, both about UNIX and about TeX; Paul English, who provided us with access to a variety of other UNIX systems; Michael Larson, who carefully went through and commented on much of the draft of the book; and Jerry Nowlin of Iconic Software, Inc., John Norden of Amdahl, and John Chambers and Dick Muldoon of UNIX Systems Laboratories, who answered some of our more exotic questions.

Then there are our individual debts of gratitude to those who provided us with support and encouragement and were so patient and understanding with us: from Bruce to his friends and colleagues Susan Kubany, Bob Heinmiller, and Dave Curado of Omnet, Inc. and Mike Gauthier and Henry McAvoy of Artis, Ltd., and to his wife, Cathy, and his children, Elsa and Eric; and from Paul to his daughter, Jodi, his sister, Nan Rubin, and his parents, Al and Evelyn Abrahams.

The two of us have very different feelings about UNIX: Bruce likes it, Paul doesn't. Yet because some use UNIX by choice while others use it by necessity, our different perspectives and opinions have actually been an advantage for us in creating this book. We hope *UNIX for the Impatient* will be useful to you whatever your view of UNIX may be.

Deerfield, Massachusetts   P. W. A.
Milton, Massachusetts   B. R. L.

Synopsis

Contents

Appendixes

1

Introduction

In this chapter we discuss the background of UNIX and offer some advice on how to use this book. We present a summary of the typographical conventions we follow for displaying UNIX syntax and propose a list of the ten most useful UNIX commands and constructs.

1.1   UNIX Background

In this section we describe the history of UNIX and other aspects of its background.

1.1.1
History of UNIX

The first version of UNIX was written in 1969 by Ken Thompson at Bell Laboratories, Murray Hill, New Jersey. Bell Laboratories had been involved, together with MIT and General Electric, in the development of the Multics system, a large, highly capable time-sharing system that embodied a number of pioneering ideas about operating systems design. Thompson and his colleagues admired the capabilities of Multics but felt it was far too complicated. They set out to prove it was possible to build an operating system that provided a comfortable working environment in a much simpler way. In this they succeeded admirably—though UNIX today, ironically, is far more complex than Multics ever was.

The first version of UNIX, called Unics, ran on a Digital Equipment PDP-7 computer. In 1970 Thompson, together with Dennis Ritchie, moved it to a PDP-11/20. Ritchie also designed and wrote the first C compiler in order to provide a language that could be used to write a portable version

1

of the system. In 1973 Ritchie and Thompson rewrote the UNIX kernel, the heart of the operating system, in C.

UNIX was first licensed to universities for educational purposes in 1974 in a version known as the Fifth Edition. (The "editions" refer to editions of the UNIX reference manual.) The Sixth Edition, also known as V6, was released in 1976 and distributed far more widely than the Fifth Edition. The Seventh Edition, released by Bell Laboratories in 1978, was the first to have portability as a specific goal. Implemented on the DEC PDP-11, the Interdata 8/32, and the VAX, the Seventh Edition has served as a common starting point for the entire UNIX world. If there is a single version of UNIX that defines "classical" UNIX, the Seventh Edition is it.

The release of the Sixth and Seventh Editions led to several independent but interacting threads of UNIX development. The three most influential offshoots of the Seventh Edition were the commercial versions developed by AT&T Information Systems as releases of System V (not to be confused with the Fifth Edition), the research systems that Bell Laboratories continued to develop, and the various BSD (Berkeley Software Distribution) systems.

System V was first released in 1983, followed by Release 2 in 1984, Release 3 in 1987, and Release 4 in 1989. System V is now marketed by UNIX Systems Laboratories (USL), a subsidiary of AT&T, which also handles licensing and further development. In 1988 UNIX International, an organization independent of USL, was established for the purpose of enabling interested parties to influence the direction of System V development.

More recent research versions of UNIX from Bell Laboratories, now known as AT&T Bell Laboratories, are the Ninth Edition (1987) and the Tenth Edition (1990). Neither of these has been distributed outside a small group of installations.

The major BSD versions of UNIX, beginning with BSD 3 (1979), were implemented on Digital Equipment Corporation's VAX computer. The most influential of these were BSD 4.2 (1983) and BSD 4.3 (1987). All of the BSD systems have been built under AT&T license.

At the suggestion of Robert Fabry, faculty advisor to the Computer Science Research Group at the University of California at Berkeley, the Defense Advanced Research Projects Agency (DARPA), a U.S. government agency, provided generous funding for the Berkeley developments. A major goal of the BSD project was to support communication over networks using a variety of protocols, not just the direct-line communication provided by the Seventh Edition. DARPA found the Berkeley work attractive because it was immediately applicable to communications over the DARPA-sponsored Arpanet, which later became the Internet. DARPA also saw BSD UNIX as potentially becoming the standard operating system for research projects using the VAX, at that time the most popular computer in research institutions.

A major BSD contribution was the vi visual text editor, which subsequently became the primary text editor for System V. Vi was written by Bill Joy, a central figure in the Berkeley project who went on to become a founder of Sun Microsystems. Other major contributions included the C shell, the support for the TCP/IP communications protocols, a virtual memory system, device drivers for many kinds of peripheral equipment, and libraries of terminal-independent subroutines for screen-based applications.

Although System V and the BSD systems have greatly influenced each other and have shared many of their newer features, the two systems have developed different personalities. System V is more conservative and solid; BSD systems are more innovative and daring. System V is a commercial product; BSD UNIX is not (although some systems based on it are). These different personalities have been reflected in their progeny.

An interesting example that shows how UNIX has changed as it grew is the System V version of the `who` command. In the Seventh Edition,[1] it had two forms, `who` and `who am i` (plus `who are you` and `who am I`, which meant the same thing) and no options. The System V version of `who` sports no fewer than twelve options, including such exotica as when the system clock was last changed and which processes were started by `init` but are now dead.

Descendents of System V include Microsoft's Xenix, Hewlett Packard's HP-UX, Amdahl's UTS, IBM's AIX, Interactive's System V/386, and Silicon Graphics's IRIX. Currently, SCO (Santa Cruz Operation) sells both Xenix and UNIX—SCO Xenix is sublicensed from Microsoft and based on the first version of System V, while SCO UNIX includes more recent developments. Xenix is said to account for more installations than any other version of UNIX, probably because it runs on the Intel 8086 family of computers (though not on the 8086 itself).[2]

Major descendents of BSD UNIX are Sun Microsystems's SunOS and Digital Equipment Corporation's Ultrix. Berkeley itself does not provide maintenance for the systems it develops. Mt. Xinu,[3] a company founded by Douglas Comer, does offer BSD UNIX maintenance commercially and also offers its own version of BSD UNIX.

In 1987 AT&T and Sun Microsystems entered into a joint agreement on UNIX development that led to a partial unification of the System V and BSD UNIX approaches to UNIX. Though the agreement was dissolved by mutual consent in 1991, its unifying effects have survived. Concerned about the competitive effects of this agreement, a number of other vendors including IBM, Digital, and Hewlett Packard established the Open Software Foundation in 1988. The announced aim of the Open Software Foundation was to develop an alternative to the AT&T-Sun version of UNIX, one that would fulfill the promise of open systems. The first version of this system, OSF-1, was released in 1991.

The late 1980's saw a major change in the UNIX world as the introduction into the UNIX environment of the X Window System, called X for short, led to a shift from character-based working environments to graphical user interfaces. X was developed at MIT in 1984 as part of Project

---

1. As documented in the version of the UNIX *Programmer's Manual* published by Bell Laboratories in 1983.

2. This family includes the IBM Personal Computer AT and its successors.

3. Mt. Xinu is UNIX[TM] spelled backwards.

Athena, a project to create a first-rate computing facility for the entire student body. X works particularly well in networked environments, allowing a user to run a program on a remote computer and display it in a window on the user's local computer. Most UNIX workstations nowadays run either X or another compatible windowing system such as NeWS, the Network/extensible Window System offered by Sun Microsystems. The most recent version is X Version 11 (X11), which has been adopted as an industry-wide standard.

UNIX today is a very different system than it was in the early seventies. The typical system then was a single processor serving a set of teletypewriter-like terminals with the terminals connected to the processor by direct or dial-up phone lines. The typical system now is a workstation with a high-resolution bitmapped display, running a windowing system and actively participating in an extensive network of computers. UNIX then was small, simple, noncommercial, and aimed at a small and select audience. UNIX now is large, complicated, an important commercial product, and used in a wide variety of applications, often by people with no programming experience.

1.1.2
Licensing and
Its Effects

All major commercial UNIX systems are based on code covered by an AT&T source license, including the Berkeley-derived systems (up to Release 4.3, that is). Legally speaking, this source code has been unpublished and proprietary—an AT&T trade secret, in fact—ever since the inception of UNIX. Only AT&T licensees may look at it. Yet this code has been examined, analyzed, and modified by thousands of computer science researchers and students. How did this apparently contradictory state of affairs come to be?

On the one hand, the AT&T UNIX licenses given to universities explicitly permit staff and students to examine the source code for educational purposes. For a long time, in fact, AT&T sold educational licenses for little more than the cost of distributing the UNIX media, and even now those licenses are very reasonably priced. On the other hand, AT&T has always been zealous in enforcing its intellectual property rights when necessary. The threat of action by a large corporation with such an awe-inspiring legal staff has been quite sufficient to prevent any significant breaches of AT&T's licensing terms.[4]

Making UNIX and its sources available to students has been very much in AT&T's interest. In earlier days, computer manufacturers provided hardware to universities on easy terms, thus ensuring that generations

---

4. At one time a message was jokingly posted on a public network containing a universal shell script for clearing the screen of a terminal. It consisted of the text

```
#    Copyright (c) 1984 AT&T
#      All Rights Reserved

#    THIS IS UNPUBLISHED PROPRIETARY SOURCE CODE OF AT&T
#    The copyright notice above does not evidence any
#    actual or intended publication of such source code.
```

followed by a line that simply echoed a form feed. Presumably the notice itself isn't proprietary, or at least AT&T doesn't care if it is.

of students—future corporate decision-makers—would become proselytizers for their equipment. Much the same has happened with low-cost UNIX software—people who used UNIX as students have been some of its most enthusiastic and influential supporters.

1.1.3
Non-AT&T Systems

Not all UNIX systems are based on the AT&T licenses. Several vendors have built UNIX clones that don't require them, starting with Whitesmiths Ltd., which built the IDRIS system in the late seventies. A principal of Whitesmiths was P.J. (Bill) Plauger, co-author with Brian Kernighan of the well-known book *Software Tools*. Recent clones include MINIX, a Seventh Edition-compatible UNIX written by Andrew Tanenbaum, and Coherent, developed by Mark Williams Company. Both of these are available at low prices, and MINIX even comes with a complete set of sources and a book describing it. The Intel 8086-based machines are popular platforms for cloned versions such as these. MKS (Mortice Kern Systems) sells a package of UNIX tools that runs under MS-DOS and includes the usual file utilities as well as `vi`, `awk`, and `make`.

An especially interesting non-AT&T system is GNU, which stands for "GNU's Not UNIX". (The 'G' in GNU is pronounced.) GNU is being developed by the Free Software Foundation, an organization founded by Richard Stallman. When it is finished, GNU will be a complete UNIX-compatible software system freely available to all. A GNU product already in wide use is the Emacs editor (see Chapter 7). The Foundation emphasizes that GNU is *not* public domain software. It can be freely copied, modified, or given away, but only under the strict condition that neither it nor its derivatives be sold for more than nominal copying costs and that further redistribution be unrestricted.

1.1.4
UNIX Standards

Different versions of UNIX resemble each other in some respects and differ noticeably in others. The features available in the Seventh Edition, which include most of the user-oriented commands covered in this book, represent the areas of greatest agreement. The areas of greatest divergence are those issues that the Seventh Edition never dealt with or dealt with superficially, such as real-time processing, communication over packet-switched networks, virtual memory, job control, and signalling.

The proliferation of UNIX variants has led to vigorous interest in developing UNIX standards. AT&T has produced its own standard, called SVID (System V Interface Definition). SVID, while enormously influential, has been totally under AT&T's control—a condition that has prevented its adoption as a standard by accredited standards organizations such as ANSI.

For some time a group of industry standards known as POSIX (Portable Operating System Interface for Computer Environments), or P1003, have been under development by the IEEE (Institute of Electrical and Electronics Engineers) and ANSI (American National Standards Institute). POSIX is intended to define an operating system that *behaves* like UNIX whether or not it really *is* UNIX. P1003.1, the standard for POSIX system calls, has already been accepted as the basis of a Federal Information Processing Standard. As of late 1991, other standards within the POSIX project, including the shell interface and programs for system administration, are under development.

Finally, a group known as X/OPEN is developing international standards for UNIX that are intended to be supersets of the corresponding POSIX standards.

1.1.5
The Role of C
in UNIX

The C programming language is often mentioned in the same breath as UNIX, yet it is often unclear to users who don't intend to do any programming why this relationship is important.

- Many UNIX programs follow C's syntactic conventions. For instance, the awk programming language (see Section 8.5) uses many of the same operators and control structures that C does.

- Most publicly available UNIX software is distributed in the form of C programs that must be compiled before they can be used. This UNIX tradition arose from the need to distribute programs in a portable form that would work on many different kinds of computers.

- UNIX system calls, which programs use to request services from the kernel, are defined as C functions. Although these system calls are primarily of interest to programmers, references to them often appear in user documentation. Sometimes the only way to understand how a user-level program really works is to see what the underlying system calls do.

- Most of the UNIX system is written in C; in fact, C was designed to support UNIX. Organizations holding UNIX source licenses can modify the behavior of the UNIX system by modifying and then recompiling the UNIX source programs.

1.2   How To Use This Book

UNIX for the Impatient is both an introduction to and a handbook for UNIX. To gain the most benefit from it, you need to know what is in it and how to find what you're looking for. These are the first steps we recommend:

- Scan the Synopsis that precedes the Table of Contents to get an overview of the material that we cover.

- If you're new to UNIX, start by reading Chapter 2. It explains the concepts and terminology that are essential to any discussion of UNIX.

- Skim one of the main chapters to become familiar with the way that the material in the book is organized.

- Look at the Alphabetic Summary of Commands in Appendix A and at the Index to see how these parts of the book can help you retrieve information.

Don't feel that you have to read the book in order from front to back or that you have to read everything in it. You'll find it easier and more productive to pick and choose your way through it.

UNIX systems have many minor and some not-so-minor variations from one vendor to another. Even systems from a single vendor change significantly from one release to the next. We usually note when a command behaves differently in different systems, but we don't attempt to catalog all the variations. We urge you to experiment to discover the peculiarities of your own environment.

As you work with UNIX you'll have two kinds of questions:

- Here's what I want to do. How do I do it?
- How does this command work?

The first kind of question is best answered by a *functional* organization, the second by an *alphabetical* organization. We provide both, but in different ways.

The body of the book is organized functionally. Commands that do similar or related things are described together; descriptions of the facilities of individual commands are organized similarly. For instance, when we describe the `ftp` file transfer program, we collect all the commands that pertain to transmitting files in one subsection. The UNIX manual pages for `ftp` list the `ftp` subcommands alphabetically, making it difficult to locate and compare those that pertain to transmitting files.

If you have a particular task to perform and you're looking for the command that will help you do it, here are a few ways to find that command:

- Look in the Synopsis to find the chapter that deals with such tasks. Then use the Table of Contents to narrow down your search.

- Look in the Index to see if the task is listed there.

- If you know of a command that does something similar or related to the task, locate its description. The command you're really looking for may be nearby.

- Check the beginning of the chapter or section that addresses your task for a summary that might direct you to what you want.

On the other hand, you may need to know how a particular command, option, or subcommand works. Appendix A contains an alphabetical list of commands and brief descriptions of what they do, followed by a list, also alphabetical, of the subcommands, options, and other features of each command. Each brief description contains a phrase or sentence to remind you of what the facility does and a cross-reference to the page where you'll find the full description. Appendix A is particularly useful when you encounter an unfamiliar construct or command in a shell script or other set of UNIX instructions written by someone else. Generally you won't find the details of commands listed in the Index, since listing every option and subcommand there would be redundant and lead to distracting clutter.

Often you'll encounter a term or concept that you don't understand, particularly if you haven't used UNIX before. The Glossary defines most of the technical terms that appear in the book. The Index can also help you locate information about particular terms or concepts. Pages where terms are defined are printed in italics in the Index.

Occasionally you'll encounter forward references—references to topics discussed later in the book. We've tried to minimize them, but in the interest of keeping all the information about a topic in one place, we haven't tried to eliminate them altogether. By skimming the material at a forward reference you can gain a general understanding of it, returning to it later when convenient.

We recognize that *UNIX for the Impatient* is unlikely to be your only source of UNIX information. To help you find information elsewhere, we've included lists of printed and electronic resources in Appendix C. In addition to anything you'll find in this book, the online manual pages and printed documentation that come with your system provide essential information.

1.3   Typographical Conventions

In this book we observe the following typographical conventions, which correspond to those typically used in UNIX documentation:

- UNIX entities such as commands and file names appear in typewriter type, e.g, `grep` and `/dev/null`. Explicit input and output also appear in typewriter type and are enclosed in single quotes, like this: '`.`'. We usually omit the quotes around a keycap symbol (see the second item below). When a long keyword must be hyphenated at the end of a line, the hyphen appears in ordinary type (-) rather than in typewriter type (-) to indicate that the hyphen is *not* part of the keyword. For example, the hyphens in the names of Emacs commands appear in typewriter type and are actually part of the commands.

- When a sentence starts with the name of a UNIX command, its first letter is capitalized even if the actual name of the command starts with a lowercase letter. `Vi` is an example. Since virtually all UNIX commands have strictly lowercase names, this practice should cause no confusion once you're aware of it.[5]

- Names of special keys on your keyboard are enclosed in boxes:
  - The keys used for certain UNIX functions are shown by using the name of the function as the name of the key. For example, we indicate the "enter" key by ⌷Enter⌷. The actual key you would use for some functions such as ⌷EOF⌷ depends on the settings of your keyboard parameters (see Section 2.1).
  - Control keys such as control-D are shown like this: ⌷Ctrl⌷D . You get this key by holding down the control key on your terminal and pressing '`D`'.

---

5. Some BSD UNIX systems call their mail program '`Mail`'; that is the only exception we are aware of.

○ The Emacs editor uses "meta" keys, which are shown like this: (Meta) x . The method of typing a meta key depends on your keyboard and system.

• A word in italic type, like *this*, represents a variable part of a construct. Usually the word describes the information that you must provide. For instance, in the construct

    source *file*

the variable *file* indicates the name of a file.

• Character names in sans-serif font and angle brackets such as ⟨return⟩ represent ASCII characters or sequences of characters.

• Square brackets around a construct indicate that the construct is optional, as in

    cd [*dir*]

The form of the cd command indicates that you can either specify the directory *dir* or omit it. Square brackets are sometimes to be taken literally. The typeface indicates which sense is intended— literal brackets look like this: '[ ]' rather than like this: '[ ]'.

• Three dots indicate that the immediately preceding construct can be repeated one or more times. If the construct is in square brackets, however, it can be repeated zero or more times. For example, the form

    file . . .

denotes one or more file names, while the form

    [*name=value*] . . .

denotes zero or more repetitions of '*name=value*'.

    Repeated constructs are ordinarily separated by whitespace (a sequence of one or more spaces or tabs).

• Sometimes we refer to special characters by their names. Here they are in alphabetical order:

&	ampersand	:	colon	(	parenthesis, left
'	apostrophe	,	comma	)	parenthesis, right
@	at	–	dash	%	percent
`	backquote	$	dollars	+	plus
\	backslash	.	dot	?	question mark
!	bang	"	double quote	;	semicolon
|	bar	=	equals	/	slash
{	brace, left	>	greater than	*	star
}	brace, right	#	hashmark	~	tilde
[	bracket, left	^	hat	_	underscore
]	bracket, right	<	less than		

1.4   The Ten Most Useful Commands and Constructs

Newcomers to UNIX are often bewildered by the great number of its commands and constructs. Where do you begin?

In this section we provide a list of ten useful commands and constructs that we hope will help, although these are certainly not the only ones you'll need or want. If you're a UNIX aficionado, your list will probably differ from ours.

ls -CF   This form of the ls (list) command lists the files in your current directory in a convenient format. The 'CF' must be in uppercase as shown. On some systems you'll obtain the same result if you type ls by itself. See Section 3.1.

cat   The cat (concatenate) command, among its other functions, displays the contents of a file—just type 'cat *file*'. You can also use it to build a short file; type 'cat >*file*' followed by the text of the file and (EOF).[6] See Sections 2.1 and 3.4.

pwd   This command prints your current (working) directory. See Section 3.15.2.

cd [*dir*]   This command moves you to the directory *dir*. If you omit *dir*, it returns you to your home directory. See Section 3.15.1.

c1 | c2 , > *file*, < *file*
           The form '*c1* | *c2*' connects the standard output of the command *c1* to the standard input of the command *c2* through a pipeline, thus combining their effects. The form '> *file*' following a command redirects its standard output to *file*; the form '< *file*' following a command redirects its standard input from *file*. See Section 2.12.

*   The character '*', used in a file name, acts as a "wildcard" that stands for any sequence of characters. For instance, 'x*c' includes the files xc, xotic, and xebec (if they exist). See Section 2.11.1.

cp   This command copies the contents of one file into another file. For example, typing 'cp banana aper' copies the contents of the file banana into the file aper. See Section 3.7.3.

rm   This command deletes a file.[7] For example, typing 'rm junque' deletes (removes) the file junque from the current directory. See Section 3.9.1.

mv   This command moves a file from one directory to another. For example, typing 'mv hobo Greece' moves the file named hobo

---

6. Watch out—the previous contents of the file, if any, will be lost.

7. More accurately, it deletes a link.

from the current directory to the directory `Greece` (here assumed to be a subdirectory of the current directory). See Section 3.7.2.

grep   The `grep` command extracts from its input the lines containing a specified string.[8] It is often useful in conjunction with the '`|`' operator. For example, typing '`| grep thelma`' after a command filters the output of the command and extracts just those lines containing the string '`thelma`'.[9] The name `grep` stands for "global regular expression print". See Section 8.4.

---

8. This is really a special case; in general, `grep` extracts the lines containing a regular expression (see Section 2.16).

9. On many keyboards the '`|`' character has a little break in the middle.

2

Concepts

In this chapter we explain the underlying concepts of the UNIX system and the terminology associated with these concepts. We also discuss a number of conventions such as the definition of a regular expression that are common to many UNIX commands. The rest of the book relies on your understanding of the information contained in this chapter. Nevertheless, since some of the material discussed in this chapter is highly technical, you may wish to postpone reading advanced topics in detail until the need for them arises.

2.1 Getting Started

We assume for now that you're using a UNIX system that was set up by someone else; Section 2.1.2 explains what to do if that's not the case. To get started you'll need instructions on how to connect to the system (either by dialing into it or by turning on your workstation or terminal), a user name, and an initial password.

When the system detects that you've established a new connection to it, it issues a 'login:' prompt. To respond, type your user name followed by (Enter).[1] The system then prompts you for your password; type it followed by another (Enter). Your password doesn't appear on your screen as

---

1. Although UNIX systems often vary in their use of terminal keys, you can almost always count on (Enter) terminating a line.

you type it, so type it carefully. After you've successfully logged in, you'll receive a confirmation message. You may also see a "message of the day" containing information about the status of the system and newly installed software. Following that, depending on how your system has been set up, you may see some "welcoming mail". You can usually escape from the mailer by typing 'q'.

At this point your interaction with UNIX is controlled by a program called a *shell*. To issue a command to the shell, type the command followed by (Enter). The shell will execute the command and send its output to your terminal (see Chapter 5).

To terminate your session and log out, type 'exit', 'logout', or (Ctrl)D. None of these work on all systems, unfortunately, but at least one of them will work on any system. Exiting via (Ctrl)D is often disabled as a safeguard against logging out unintentionally. You may also be able to log out by breaking the connection with the computer, but this is *not* recommended. Many systems are set up in such a way that the next person to come in on the same phone line will take over your session where you abandoned it, and such rogue access to your account is a serious security hazard.

2.1.1
Logging In for the First Time

When you log in for the first time, you should go through the following three steps:

(1)   Check that your terminal type is correct.
(2)   See what the key assignments for your terminal are.
(3)   Change your password if it was assigned by a system administrator.

Checking Your Terminal Type.   To check your terminal type, type the command

```
echo $TERM
```

If the value indicated for TERM doesn't seem to correspond to the kind of terminal you have, either ask your system administrator to change your terminal type or change it yourself using the methods described in Section 2.19.1.

Viewing the Key Assignments.   To view the key assignments, type

```
stty -a
```

or, on Berkeley-style systems, type

```
stty all
```

You'll get a listing that shows the key assignments. The notation '∧c' in the listing stands for (Ctrl) *c*, i.e., the key that you get by holding down the control key on your keyboard while pressing *c*. The following keys are defined by key assignments:

- The newline (nl) key, which causes UNIX to process the line you've just typed. We denote it by (Enter).

- The erase key, which deletes the most recently typed character. We denote it by (Erase).

- The kill key, which cancels the line you're typing. We denote it by (Kill).

- The interrupt (`intr`) key, which interrupts the program that is currently executing. We denote it by ⟨Intr⟩. The interrupt key may not work if the program you're executing uses the interrupt key for a special purpose.[2]

- The `quit` key, which provides a stronger form of interrupt. The `quit` key works when ⟨Intr⟩ doesn't, but it also produces a (usually useless) file named `core` that records the contents of computer memory. This key is often assigned to ⟨Ctrl⟩\.

- The end-of-file (`eof`) key, which indicates the end of typed input. It may log you out if you type it as a command to the shell.[3] We denote it by ⟨EOF⟩. Normally this key is set to ⟨Ctrl⟩D, which is also used for other purposes by a number of programs. Changing the end-of-file key doesn't change these other interpretations of ⟨Ctrl⟩D.[4]

- The `flush` key, which causes output from the currently running program to be discarded but does not stop that program from executing. It's useful when a program is producing a file in addition to its normal output and you want to ignore the rest of the displayed output while still producing the entire file. Not all systems provide a flush key. The flush key usually defaults to ⟨Ctrl⟩O.

- The suspend key (`susp` or `swtch`), which enables you to suspend the program you're running and do something else. The suspended program is not destroyed, so you can resume it later. Only systems that support job control (see Section 2.7.1) provide this key. The suspend key usually defaults to ⟨Ctrl⟩Z.

- The word erase key (`werase`), which erases the previous word on the line you just typed. This key is a feature of BSD UNIX. It usually defaults to ⟨Ctrl⟩W.

- The `stop` and `start` keys, which control output sent to your terminal. They are also called "Xoff" and "Xon" or ⟨DC3⟩ and ⟨DC1⟩. The `stop` key stops output and the `start` key restarts it. When you use the `stop` key, the program sending the output waits in suspension until you restart it. The `stop` key is usually assigned to ⟨Ctrl⟩S and the `start` key to ⟨Ctrl⟩Q. On some systems these keys cannot be reassigned.

See "Settings for Control Characters" on page 127 for further discussion of these and other special keys.

Changing Your Password.   You can change your password by issuing the `passwd` command. You'll be asked for your current password once and then for your new password twice—the second time to verify that you entered it correctly, since it won't be visible on your screen.

---

2. A program can do this by intercepting the interrupt.

3. If you're in a shell within a shell, only the inner shell is terminated.

4. Some shells provide an `ignoreeof` variable (see p. 195) as a safety measure. If you set this variable within a copy of such a shell, ⟨EOF⟩ won't log you out of that copy.

**2.1.2
Installing a
New System**

You may be in the awkward situation of having to install a UNIX system without yet knowing how to use UNIX. Most modern UNIX systems include a menu-driven installation program that guides you through the installation process. Very few of the decisions you make during installation are irrevocable, although you can't alter the size of the disk partition allocated to the entire UNIX system without rebuilding the system. Once your system is up and running and you know more about what you're doing, you can modify it to suit your needs.

After completing the installation, your first step should be to register yourself as a user if you didn't already do so during the installation:

(1)   Log in as `root`, using the root password you specified (or were given by default) during the installation.

(2)   Use your system administration program to register yourself.

As a general rule you should not use the `root` identity unless you need the special privileges it confers. Using `root` only when necessary is a safeguard against accidental damage to your system.

2.2   The UNIX Manual

UNIX documentation is published in a standard format established by the earliest versions of the UNIX *Programmer's Manual*. Most UNIX systems provide the "manual pages" on-line as well as in printed form. The description of each command, C function, etc., has its own manual page (which may actually be several pages long), divided into more or less standardized sections: "Name", "Synopsis", "Description", "Files", etc. The manual as a whole has a major division for each category of manual pages, traditionally numbered as follows:

1   Commands available at the shell level
2   System calls in the C library
3   Other functions in the C library
4   Devices and device drivers, sometimes called "special files"
5   File formats and file conventions
6   Games
7   Word processing programs
8   System maintenance programs and information

You'll often see references of the form "*stty* (1)" in UNIX literature. The "(1)" indicates that *stty* is in Section 1 of the manual and is therefore a shell-level command. In this book we omit the numbers for two reasons: we find them distracting and redundant, and nearly everything we refer to is in Section 1.

You can use the `man` command to view manual pages on-line. Typing '`man` *cmd*' displays the manual pages for the command *cmd*. Manual pages include page headers and are formatted for a line printer having 66 lines per page—not a convenient format for viewing.[5]

You can use a pager (see Section 3.13.1) to display manual pages one screenful at a time.[6] Using the pg pager, you can display the manual page for *cmd* by typing

```
man  cmd  |  pg
```

You can substitute a different pager such as more or less for pg (see Section 3.13.1).

2.3   System Administration and the Superuser

System administration refers to a collection of tasks whose purpose is to make the UNIX system available to its users in an orderly and secure manner. These tasks include registering and deleting users, configuring the kernel, controlling access to parts of the file system, backing up and restoring files, and installing new software packages. If you're setting up a UNIX system for yourself, you'll need to perform these tasks both when you install the system and later as you use it. We briefly discuss system administration from the standpoint of an individual system proprietor in Section 2.3.1.

The design of UNIX reflects the belief that any facility accessible to users should be protected from accidental or malicious modification by users and that users should be be protected from each other. Therefore the programs and files for system administration are accessible only to a specially designated user called the *superuser*. The superuser has a special user name, root; whoever knows the password for root can act as the superuser.

The initial password for root is set as part of the process of installing the system; like other passwords, it can be changed at any time thereafter. The person who installs the system chooses the initial root password, so that person necessarily can become the superuser. Thereafter the ability to become the superuser is inherited by those who learn the password from someone who already knows it.[7]

Some versions of UNIX restrict the ability to log in as the superuser. For example, they only accept superuser logins from the console or require

---

5. UNIX software distributed in source form usually includes manual pages in the form of input for the nroff formatter (see Section 4.7.1).

6. You can get an even more readable display by filtering out the internal page headers. The following cryptic shell script (see Section 5.1) does both the paging and the filtering:

```
man $1 | nawk 'NR<=8||(NR%66>=8&&NR%66<=60)' | pg
```

It deletes lines 61–66 on the first page and lines 1–7 and 61–66 on all subsequent pages.

7. An intruder who obtains the password for root can lock out the legitimate superuser by changing the password.

that a superuser not at the console belong to a special group, often named 'wheel'.

Anyone who can log in as root should have an ordinary user name as well and should avoid using the superuser privileges except when necessary. Security considerations aside, it is all too easy to make a costly mistake in superuser mode such as deleting a critical system file by accident.

2.3.1
System Administration for Single-User Systems

Administering a large UNIX system is a full-time job. Administering a system for which you're the only user is far easier. A serious discussion of system administration is beyond the scope of this book, but a number of excellent books on system administration such as the one by Hunter and Hunter (see reference [B12]) are available. Your chief source of information should be the manuals that come with your system. However, we can provide a few pointers:

- System V and other systems based on it come with a system administration program called sysadm. Usually this program is menu-driven so that you can use it without any special instruction. Its functions include the following:

  - Assigning passwords.
  - Setting the date, time, and machine identification.
  - Adding and deleting users and groups. (Having extra user and group names is sometimes handy even if you're the only real user of the system.)
  - Installing and removing software packages.
  - Backing up the data on your disks and restoring it when necessary.
  - Configuring your printer.
  - Mounting and unmounting file systems.
  - Formatting diskettes.
  - Tuning the performance of your disk and your memory allocations.

- Knowing how to recover the use of your system if you lose or forget the root password is vital. The procedure varies from one system to another, but generally involves rebooting the system from a removable medium such as a floppy disk. We recommend that you learn about this procedure *before* you need it.

- Under System V, the main programs for correcting printer problems are lpsched, lpshut, and lpmove, which operate on the queue of files to be printed. More permanent adjustments to the printer arrangements should be done using sysadm. The corresponding BSD UNIX program is lpc ("line printer control"). Consult your system manual for instructions on using these programs.

2.4   Users and Groups

In order to use a UNIX system, you must be registered as one of its users. Each user has a login name, a password, and an area of the file system reserved for storing his or her files. In addition, each user belongs to a *group*. Some systems allow a user to belong to more than one group. A group need not have more than one user in it. Your group is established when your UNIX account is created and can be changed at any time by the system administrator. You can specify group permissions for a file that you own (see Section 2.9), thus controlling what kinds of access members of your group have to it.

Information about your user account is stored in a file named /etc/passwd. This file, despite its name, does *not* contain your password, although in most older systems it contains your password in an encrypted form. It does contain your user number, group number, and full name—information that is not considered privileged and is often useful to other users. Anyone can read the /etc/passwd file but only the superuser can modify it (see "The /etc/passwd File" on page 118).

On most systems you can display information about your account by issuing the id command, which displays your user number, user name, group number, and group name (but not your full name). On BSD UNIX systems that don't have the id command, use the groups command to show the groups to which you belong.

2.5   What the Shell Does

When you log into UNIX, your interaction with the system is managed by a program called a *shell* or *command interpreter*. Several shells for UNIX are available (see Chapter 5). When we make a statement about "the shell" without further qualification, it applies to all of the commonly used shells.

The shell called on your behalf when you log in is called your *login shell*. Your /etc/passwd entry (see "The /etc/passwd File" on page 118) can contain a field that specifies your login shell. If this field is missing from your /etc/passwd entry, your login shell is determined by a system-wide default. The system administrator who sets up your user account establishes your login shell and is the only one who can change it. However, you can switch to a different shell once you're logged in by placing the command

> exec *shell*

at the end of your login initialization file. This command transfers control of your terminal to the shell *shell* (see Section 2.18.1).

2.6 The UNIX Kernel

The UNIX kernel is the heart of the operating system. It controls access to the computer and its files, allocates resources among the various activities taking place within the computer, maintains the file system, and manages the computer's memory. Although ordinary users rarely have any explicit interaction with the kernel, the kernel is central to UNIX and is often referred to elsewhere in this book and in UNIX documentation.

A system administrator (see Section 2.3) can adjust the system's operating characteristics by *configuring* the kernel. Configuring the kernel chiefly involves tuning certain internal parameters and providing drivers that control devices attached to the computer. Even a system administrator cannot modify the *structure* of the kernel, since that would entail rewriting the UNIX system itself.

2.7 Processes

When UNIX is running, many activities are underway at the same time. These activities are called *processes*. You can think of processes as working in parallel, although most computers that run UNIX can only support true parallelism for a few specialized activities such as printing.

Minimally, there is one process for the kernel and one process for each user logged into the system. In practice the kernel always has several processes running, and each user may also have several processes running. The ps (process status) command lists the running processes (see Section 4.2.1). To call it, type either

```
ps -ef
```

or

```
ps -ag
```

depending on your system.

The kernel manages the processes, switching back and forth among them according to their needs and priorities. A process can create other processes; the creator is the *parent process* and the processes thus created are *child processes*. Certain system processes called *dæmons* reside in the system more or less permanently and perform ongoing tasks such as handling mail, scheduling tasks that should be performed at regular intervals, and transferring files from the print queue to printers.

By creating multiple processes, you can run several programs at once. For example, suppose you want to execute a program that takes a long time to complete. You can run the program at a low priority in the background and do something else at the terminal while it is running. Some shells, notably most versions of the C shell (see Section 5.3), provide a facility called *job control* that lets you switch back and forth among processes (see Section 2.7.1). All shells at least enable you to run a process in the background and to lower its priority with the `nice` command (see Section 4.2.6).

Sometimes one of your processes may get stuck and you'll need to kill it. If the stuck process is not in control of your terminal, you can use the `ps` command to get its number and the `kill` command to remove it (see Section 4.2.3). Otherwise you may be able to regain control by using the (Intr) key or, if necessary, the `quit` key. If neither key works, you'll need to kill the process from another terminal if you can or, as a last resort, ask someone with superuser privileges to kill it for you.[8]

2.7.1 Job Control

Job control is a facility, introduced by BSD UNIX and supported by the C shell among others, that enables you to create groups of processes called *jobs* and control them from your terminal. At any moment, one job is running in the foreground and the other jobs (if any) are either running in the background or are stopped. The foreground job is in control of your terminal. A stopped job is in a state of suspense; it remains dormant until you take action to resume it.

The job control facilities enable you to move the current job to the background, bring a particular job to the foreground, and stop or kill any job. Killing a job kills all of its processes. If a background job should attempt to read from or write to the terminal, it simply waits until it becomes the foreground job (though it can be programmed to behave otherwise). The C shell facilities for job control are described in Section 5.3.6.

The processes that make up a job are a special case of a *process group*. In the absence of job control, the processes associated with each logged-in terminal form a process group—in effect, a single job. Every process belongs to a process group, although unfortunately none of the UNIX utilities provide for displaying the process groups. It's possible to kill all the processes in a process group at once; killing a job is a special case of killing a process group. As a user, you can't do much with process groups—they're mainly a convenience for systems programmers—but they're often referred to in UNIX documentation.

Each process group is identified by one process in the group, the *process group leader*. Typically the first process in a pipeline (see Section 2.12.1) becomes the process group leader. The leader's process number acts as an identifier for the entire group.

2.7.2 Alternatives to Job Control

There are several alternatives to job control for managing multiple processes. Which ones are available depends on your system.

- The X Window System (see Chapter 11) enables you to run multiple processes in a graphical environment by creating several pseudo-terminals in separate windows and running a different program in each one.

---

8. For a single-user system, the ultimate recourse is to reboot the computer.

- Some AT&T UNIX systems provide a windowing system called layers that is functionally very similar to the X Window System. Layers runs only on specialized multiplexing terminals with built-in hardware support for windows.

- Some recent versions of System V provide a simpler version of layers called shl ("shell layers") that supports a weak form of job control for character-based terminals.

- Some versions of System V for the Intel 80386 architecture provide a *virtual terminal* facility that does not require windowing support. On these systems, pressing a special key combination switches you to a different virtual terminal. For example, pressing [Alt] [Sysreq] followed by [F1] (or [Alt] [F1] for some systems) switches you to virtual terminal #1. The virtual terminals behave logically as independent connections to your computer, but physically they share the same keyboard and screen. Switching to a different virtual terminal restores the contents of your screen to what they were when you previously were using that virtual terminal.

2.7.3
Exit Status of
a Process

Calling a process has three possible outcomes: the process can succeed, fail, or terminate abnormally. The *exit status* of the process is a number that reveals this outcome.

A process can terminate normally of its own accord, returning an exit status to its parent process. By convention, an exit status of zero indicates success—the process has accomplished its assigned task. Any other exit status indicates failure; the actual value acts as a code that indicates the nature of the failure.

A process can terminate abnormally—for example, if you interrupt it—because of a signal sent to it (see Section 2.7.4). In this case the process itself can't return an exit status because it has lost control, so the kernel returns an exit status on behalf of the process indicating why it terminated. The exit status in this case is 128 plus the signal code number, e.g., 142 for an alarm clock interrupt (see "Signals and Their Codes" on page 22).

You can test the exit status of a process and choose what to do next according to the result of the test. You don't have to be a C programmer to do this; for instance, you can test the status in a shell script with if (p. 152) or any other shell construct that does numeric comparisons.

2.7.4
Signals

A *signal* notifies a process of an abnormal external event, such as disconnection of the terminal. With few exceptions, a process has the option of *catching* any signal sent to it. The information associated with a process includes a list of signals that it catches and an action to be taken for each one.

When a signal is sent to a process, the kernel performs the specified action if the signal is caught and a default action (which usually includes killing the process) if it is not. Killing a process causes it to terminate abnormally (see Section 2.7.3). The "hard kill" signal (#9 below), cannot be caught; it always forces termination. The trap command of sh (see p. 171) is an example of how a process can catch signals. You can use the `kill` program (see Section 4.2.3) to send a signal to another process provided that the process is one of yours or you are the superuser.

Signals and Their Codes.   The following signals are implemented on nearly all systems. Each signal is preceded by its numerical code and its name. Both the numerical codes and the names are used in UNIX documentation. For most signals, the default action is to terminate the process (and in some cases to produce a memory dump, storing it in a file named `core`); for the others, the default action is to suspend the process or to do nothing at all.

The following signals are recognized by all systems:

1	SIGHUP	Terminal hangup
2	SIGINT	Terminal interrupt
3	SIGQUIT	Terminal quit (with a memory dump)
9	SIGKILL	Process killed
13	SIGPIPE	Broken pipe (writing when the reader has terminated)
14	SIGALRM	Alarm clock interrupt
15	SIGTERM	Software termination

Programs such as `kill` normally use `SIGTERM` to kill another process (see Section 4.2.3). The receiving process can catch it and choose to continue. `SIGKILL` cannot be caught; a process receiving that signal is always killed. Signals 4–8 and 10–12 indicate various kinds of machine errors, which are usually caused by program misbehavior rather than a computer malfunction.

The `SIGWINCH` signal is used in windowing systems such as X; the other signals in the following group are used only in systems that support job control (see Section 2.7.1). Systems vary in how they number these signals, but the names have the same meanings for all systems.

20	SIGWINCH	Window size has changed
23	SIGCONT	Continue job if stopped
24	SIGSTOP	Noninteractive stop signal
25	SIGTSTP	Interactive stop signal
26	SIGTTIN	Read attempted by a background job
27	SIGTTOU	Write attempted by a background job

Stopping a job suspends its activity but does not terminate it. A stopped job can be resumed later. By default, `SIGCONT` has no effect unless it's sent to a stopped job, in which case it reactivates the job and brings it to the foreground. `SIGSTOP`, like `SIGKILL` above, cannot be caught; it provides a reliable way of stopping a job. By default, `SIGTTIN` and `SIGTTOU` stop the job.

You can usually find a complete list of the signal codes in the file `/usr/include/sys/signal.h`.

2.7.5 Environment Variables

Each process has a collection of *environment variables* associated with it. These variables can be queried or set by the process and are inherited by its subprocesses. An example of an environment variable is `TERM`, which contains your terminal type. You can see the values of the environment variables currently in effect by giving a command such as `env`, which works for most shells. In addition, most UNIX programs that accept commands interactively have a set of local variables that help to define the program's behavior. The relationship between environment variables and local variables can be confusing; we discuss it on page 54.

Whenever you start a new process as a child of another, UNIX sets the environment variables of the child process to a copy of those of its parent. Thereafter the environment variables of the child and the parent are independent, since one process cannot examine or modify the environment variables of another. When a process terminates, its environment variables disappear and any changes to these variables are lost.

Some systems enable you to set environment variables by specifying them after your name when you log in (see "Environment Variables on Login" on page 117). This facility provides a powerful and convenient method of customizing your environment since the commands in your login initialization file (see Section 2.18.1) can test the values of these variables.

2.8   The UNIX File System

The UNIX file system consists of a set of *files*. Each file has one or more names, called *file names*. There are three kinds of files:

- Ordinary files, which contain data
- Special files, which provide access to devices such as terminals and printers and serve other purposes as well
- Directories, which contain information about a set of files and are used to locate a file by its name

Like most modern operating systems, UNIX organizes its file system as a hierarchy of directories. The directory hierarchy is often called a *tree*, although it's almost always drawn as an upside-down tree. A special directory, `root`, sits at the top of the hierarchy. Commands for navigating and modifying the directory tree are described in Section 3.15.

A directory can include both ordinary files and subdirectories. UNIX treats a subdirectory as just a particular kind of file. If you display the contents of a directory, the subdirectories are listed along with the other files.

UNIX views every file as a sequence of bytes. Whatever internal structure a file might have affects only those programs that care about it. Most published descriptions of UNIX make much of this, which can confuse newcomers since it's what they would expect anyway. Historically, the mainframe operating systems that were dominant when UNIX was first built did have file types with different internal structures—regional, indexed sequential, and so forth—but most current operating systems treat files with the same uniformity that UNIX does.

Whenever possible, UNIX programs have been designed to operate on text files, that is, files that can sensibly be printed. Within these files a *newline* character, represented as the ASCII ⟨linefeed⟩ character, indicates the end of one line and the beginning of the next. Text files can include any character except the null character, the character whose binary representation is all zeros. Because C interprets a null character as indicating the end of a string and most UNIX programs are written in C, null characters in text files give many UNIX programs severe indigestion.

2.8.1
File Identifiers

A file identifier[9] names a file in a directory. A file identifier consists of up to 14 characters in most System V systems and up to 255 characters in most Berkeley-derived systems. A file identifier can include any character other than '/', although some characters such as '-' and ⟨space⟩ are troublesome because of their special meanings on command lines.[10] Letters (either uppercase or lowercase), digits, and the special characters (+ = _ :) are usually safe. By convention, a dot at the start of a file identifier identifies an initialization file or other supporting file for a particular program. Directory listings don't normally include files whose identifiers start with a dot. Dot files are also treated specially during wildcard expansion (see Section 2.11.1).

File identifiers are case-sensitive, so `psaltery`, `Psaltery`, and `PSALTERY` name three different files. Some UNIX programs expect the identifiers of their input and output files to consist of a name part followed by a dot and an extension. For example, when the `compress` program compresses a file *file*, the resulting compressed file has the name *file*.`Z`. As another example, the C compiler expects its input files to have file identifiers of the form *file*.`c`.

2.8.2
File Names

A *file name* is a name that designates a file. A file name consists of a sequence of file identifiers separated by slashes (/). The file identifiers are the *components* of the file name. There are two kinds of file names: absolute path names and relative path names. An absolute path name starts with a slash; a relative path name does not.

Absolute Path Names.   You can refer to a file anywhere in the tree by giving its *absolute path name*. The absolute path name specifies the sequence of subdirectories you must traverse in order to get from the root to the file. The '/' that always begins an absolute path name designates the root directory. For instance, UNIX interprets the file name `/usr/humbert/toads` as follows:

(1)   From the root, go to the subdirectory named `usr`.
(2)   From this subdirectory, go to the subdirectory named `humbert`.

---

9. The term "file identifier" is our own creation. File identifiers are variously called file names, filenames, and component names in UNIX literature. We introduce this term because of the inconsistency in UNIX literature with respect to what a file name (or filename) really is: is it a full path name or is it just one component of the path?

10. A file identifier can even contain nonprinting characters such as ⟨backspace⟩. Only under very unusual circumstances would anyone deliberately create a file with a name containing nonprinting characters, but files with such names are sometimes created by accident. These files are difficult to get rid of—see Section 3.9.3 for instructions on how to do it.

(3)   From this subdirectory, pick the file named toads (which could itself be a directory).

Relative Path Names.   Each process has a directory called the *current directory* or *working directory* that can serve as a starting point for file names. The pwd command displays ("print") your working directory, i.e., the working directory of your shell process. A file name that does not start with '/' is called a *relative path name* and is taken as relative to your working directory unless it is a command to execute a program. In that case the rules for searching your path given in Section 2.11.2 apply. Thus if your working directory is /usr/humbert, the relative path name

    travel/city.data/jakarta

corresponds to the full path name

    /usr/humbert/travel/city.data/jakarta

The simplest and most common case of a relative path name is a single file identifier *file* used as a file name. Such a file name refers to the file *file* in your current directory.

The '.' and '..' Notations.   The *parent* of a directory *d* (other than the root) is the directory just above *d* in the hierarchy. The current directory is named '.' and its parent is named '..', so you can use paths to go up the hierarchy as well as down it. For example, if the current directory is /usr/humbert as above, '..' refers to /usr, '../..' refers to the root, and '../tinkerbell' refers to /usr/tinkerbell. The root is a special case in that its parent is itself; thus /.. refers to the root just as / does.

**2.8.3
Home Directories**

Each user has a *home directory*. The path name for this directory varies according to the system, but its last component is usually the user's name. In the first UNIX systems, a user's home directory was an immediate descendant of the root directory; a user named zsazsa had a home directory named /zsazsa. For System V the home directory for user *user* is usually the directory /usr/*user*, while for BSD UNIX it's usually /u/*user*. Some other systems use /home/*u* or /u/*site*/*u*, where *site* is the computer's host name. In this book we follow the convention that home directories are subdirectories of /usr.

   Because home directories are so important, there's a special notation for them recognized by every UNIX shell except, unfortunately, the Bourne shell: the character '~' at the start of a path name refers to the home directory of the current user, while '~*user*' refers to the home directory of user *user*. Thus for user humbert, '~/ice.cream' refers to /usr/humbert/ice.cream and '~zelda/cookies' refers to /usr/zelda/cookies. Referring to other people's directories is often useful when you're working on a cooperative project or just accessing information that someone has made publicly available, and the '~*user*' notation makes it easy.

   A less convenient notation for referring to your home directory is $HOME, which yields the value of the variable HOME that every shell, including the Bourne shell, supports. Thus $HOME/oldcars refers to the file oldcars in your home directory. This notation has no provision for simplifying references to the home directory of another user. Because you can use the $HOME notation anywhere, we use it when we refer to your home directory in this book, even though '~' would be more convenient.

2.8.4
Subsidiary
File Systems

UNIX allows parts of the directory hierarchy, called *file systems*, to reside on separate storage devices or in separate disk partitions. There are two reasons why. First, the disks or other devices that hold the directories and their files may not be large enough to hold the entire hierarchy, so it may be necessary to distribute the hierarchy among several devices. Second, the storage devices may not be permanently attached to the computer. A floppy disk that contains its own directory structure is an example of such a file system. The Network File System (see p. 419) enables computers on a network to have their own file systems; by linking these file systems together, it causes files distributed over the network to appear as though they were all in the same computer.

UNIX accommodates file systems by associating them with *mount points*. A mount point is a directory in a file system that corresponds to the root directory of some other file system. The primary file system is the one emanating from the true root directory and is named '/'. A secondary file system is linked into the primary system by the mount command, which is given the path name of the mount point and the location of the secondary file system. Its effect is to make the root of the secondary file system correspond to the mount point. Once a file system has been mounted, you can refer to any file or directory within it by using a path that passes through the mount point. Unmounting a file system invalidates all the paths that pass through its mount point.

As a user, you need to be aware of file system boundaries for two reasons. First, there are restrictions on connections across file system boundaries (see Section 2.8.5). Second, when a file system is unmounted you lose all access to its files until it is remounted.[11]

UNIX literature, including this book, refers both to "the UNIX file system" and to "file systems". When we talk about "the UNIX file system", we're referring to how UNIX generally handles files. When we use the term "file system" without qualification, we're using it in the sense of this section.

2.8.5
Links

A *link* to a file is a directory entry for that file, consisting of a file identifier that names the file within the directory and an i-node number (see Section 2.8.6). A UNIX file can have multiple links. The links to a file have the same i-node number but different names. The links can reside in different directories provided that they are all within the same file system.

The ln command (see Section 3.7.1) creates a link to an existing file. Because there is only one copy of a file, a change made to a file through one of its links becomes visible through all of its other links. The rm command (see Section 3.9.1) removes a link to a file, not the file itself. A file is not deleted from the file system until its last link is removed. Properly speaking, every file is a linked file because every file has at least one

---

11. The kernel does not allow a file system to be unmounted if any of its files are in use.

link. Unfortunately the term "link" is not always used correctly in UNIX documentation—sometimes you'll see a reference to a "linked file" when what is really meant is a file with *multiple* links.

Some newer UNIX systems provide another form of link, a *symbolic link*, that records the path name of a file rather than its location (i-node number). Symbolic links are not bound by the restriction that all links to a file must originate from the same file system. Symbolic links are often called *soft links* to distinguish them from the more traditional links, *hard links*.

Use symbolic links with caution. If a symbolic link to a file *file* becomes undefined, either because *file* was deleted or because the file system containing *file* was unmounted, the kernel correctly rejects any attempt to use *file*. But if you delete *file* and later create another file with the same name, references to the old file become references to the new one—usually not what you want to happen. Soft links are usually better used as pointers to directories than as pointers to individual files. When we use the term "link" without qualification, we mean a hard link.

2.8.6
How Files are Stored

We generally don't discuss the details of the UNIX implementation in this book. Nevertheless, we make an exception in this section, where we discuss how files are stored in the UNIX file system. UNIX documentation frequently makes reference to this subject, and an understanding of it can help in understanding other aspects of the file system and the UNIX utilities.

The file system stores the essential information about a file in an *i-node* (information node): where the file's actual contents are stored, how long the file is, how many links there are to it, when it was created, and so on. Each i-node has an *i-number* that identifies it. I-numbers are unique *within* file systems but not *among* file systems, which is why links across file systems must be treated specially. In this discussion we consider only hard links, that is, links within a single file system.

Examine a directory with the od command (see Section 3.13) and you'll see the i-number as the first two bytes of the entry for each file in the directory, followed by the name. The same i-number can (and usually does) refer to different files in different file systems. For this reason and because file systems can be dismounted, UNIX doesn't allow a link from a directory in one file system to a file in another unless the file is a mount point.

The actual data in a file is stored as a sequence of blocks, typically but not necessarily 1024 bytes long. Other common block sizes are 512 and 2048. The file system stores files longer than one block in scattered data blocks and uses a smaller set of blocks to keep track of where the data blocks are. The blocks in this smaller set contain pointers to the data blocks and are called *indirect blocks* because they provide access to the data indirectly. For really large files there may be a second level of indirect blocks that point to the first-level blocks. The UNIX utilities that show the size of a file count indirect blocks as well as the blocks containing the actual data of the file.

2.8.7 Space Limitations on Files

The space available in almost any real UNIX system is limited and fills up faster than most people would expect. Nearly every UNIX system therefore places a limit on the file space allocated to users. There are two different approaches:

- In System V systems the maximum size of a file is limited by a parameter called ULIMIT that is part of the configuration of the kernel. The Bourne shell provides a ulimit command (p. 175) for seeing what it is, although only the superuser can raise it.

- In BSD UNIX there is no limit on the size of an individual file, but each user may be limited to a quota of file space.

Programs that write large files may occasionally behave strangely when they encounter one of these limits. For example, some programs will not be aware that the end of the file has been truncated and will simply produce a defective file—leaving it to the next program that uses the file to discover that something has gone wrong.

2.8.8 Buffers

A *buffer* is a region of computer memory that holds a portion of the data in a file after that portion has been read from the file or before that portion is written to the file. The term is used in two very different contexts.

Buffered Input and Output. When a program reads a file using *buffered input*, it reads the file in chunks of, say, 1024 bytes. Each chunk constitutes a buffer. When the program asks for a certain number of bytes from the file, the supporting software takes those bytes from the buffer rather than directly from the file as it would were it using unbuffered input. If there aren't enough bytes in the buffer, the supporting software brings in another bufferload of data from the file. Buffering has two efficiency advantages: it reduces the number of separate reading operations required, and it enables the reading to take place in parallel with other operations. Its disadvantage for some applications is that it provides less control over the reading action.

Buffered output is analogous to buffered input. When a program using buffered output sends bytes to a file, those bytes are put into a buffer rather than written out immediately. When the buffer is full, the supporting software writes its contents to the file.

Editor Buffers. Editors such as vi, ed, and emacs use a buffer to hold the contents of a file while it is being edited. The basic editing cycle is as follows:

(1) Read a file into the buffer.
(2) Edit the file.
(3) Write the contents of the buffer back to the file.

There's lots of room for variation in this cycle—for instance, when you create a file the first step is omitted.

2.9   File Permissions

Permissions specify who can do what to a file. A file's permissions are sometimes called its *protection mode*, which is set by its owner. You can view the protection mode of a file with 'ls -l' (see Section 3.1.2 for a sample output) and specify it with the chmod command (see Section 3.12.1). Since the permissions of a file are a property of the file itself, all links to a file have the same permissions.

**2.9.1
Permissions for
Basic Operations**

The three basic operations on a file are "read", "write", and "execute". The permissions required to perform these operations are denoted by 'r', 'w', and 'x'. The x permission is needed for compiled programs and for any shell script that you intend to use directly as a command. For instance, if the file yodel contains a shell script but lacks the x (execute) permission, you can't give the command

        yodel

by itself. If you try it, you'll get an error message such as

        yodel: not found

Nevertheless you can execute yodel with the command

        sh yodel

even if yodel doesn't have execute permission since this command explicitly passes yodel to the Bourne shell sh.

The r, w, and x permissions can be specified independently for the owner of a file, for those in the owner's group, and for all others. UNIX always checks permissions for the smallest category that applies. For instance, a user in the owner's group (other than the owner) is always given the group permissions even if the permissions for "others" are broader. It doesn't make sense to provide a permission to a category of users but deny it to a smaller category, e.g., to make it available to others but deny it to your group, but UNIX won't stop you.

The protection mode protects a file not only from unwanted access but also from your own errors. For instance, you can protect a file from accidental modification or deletion by cancelling its w permission. Cancelling the w permission doesn't actually prevent the file from being deleted but does usually trigger a warning if you attempt to delete it. Similarly, a file that you don't intend to execute should not have its x permission turned on.

Permissions for Directories.   File permissions also apply to directories.

- The r permission for a directory lets you find out what is in the directory, but is insufficient for accessing the files whose names appear in it. For instance, you can't read the contents of files in a directory if you only have r access to the directory.

- The w permission for a directory is required in order to add files to it or delete files from it. However, w permission for a directory is not required in order to modify a file listed in the directory or delete its contents.

- The x permission for a directory lets you operate on the names in that directory if you know them, but does not let you find out what they are if you don't. Normally r is granted whenever x is; you can get some strange effects if a directory has x but not r. For instance, if a directory has x turned on but not r, you can't list its contents—but if you already know its contents, you can delete files from it.

2.9.2 Other File Permissions

In addition to the rwx permissions, UNIX has other kinds of file permissions used primarily (but not exclusively) by system programmers. We describe these next.

The Set-uid Bit. The *set-uid bit* gives a program the permissions of its owner rather than those of the user who called it. You specify this bit with s when you use the chmod command. In a listing, it is indicated by an s replacing the x in the owner's permissions.

Normally, when you call a program and that program accesses a file, the program's access privileges for the file are the ones associated with your own user id. As an example, suppose the following:

- User adlai owns the executable file ouija.
- The ouija program uses adlai's private data file tarot.
- User ike executes the program ouija.

The permissions that apply to tarot during this execution are those of "others" (since ike doesn't own tarot) rather than those of the owner adlai. Unless adlai grants read permission for tarot to "others", the ouija program can't access it. Yet if that read permission is granted, ike can read tarot directly and do whatever he likes with the information contained there, using it in ways not intended by adlai.

The set-uid bit provides a way around this. Turning on the set-uid bit of an executable file specifies that when the program in the file executes, the permissions that apply are those of the program's owner, not those of the user calling the program. In effect the set-uid bit grants permission to the user to access a file such as tarot indirectly—with ouija as the agent—but not directly. For instance, suppose the following additions to the example above:

- The owner permissions for tarot are rw.
- The "others" permissions for tarot are all turned off.
- The set-uid bit of the ouija file is turned on.

Now when ike executes ouija, the executing process behaves as though its user id is adlai, not ike. The process therefore has the necessary read permission for tarot, yet ike cannot get at tarot by reading or writing it directly.

The classic example of the use of the set-uid bit is the passwd command (see Section 4.3.4). The password file /etc/passwd is owned by root (the superuser) and must be written by the passwd program.[12] Ordinary users must be able to execute the passwd program, yet they must not be allowed to modify the password file. Therefore the set-uid bit is turned on for the passwd program, enabling it to write to /etc/passwd while that ability remains denied to ordinary users.

Some systems recognize the set-uid bit only when it appears among the permissions of a compiled program and ignore it when it appears among the permissions of a shell script. However, use of the set-uid bit is not restricted to the superuser.

The Set-gid Bit.   The *set-gid bit* is like the set-uid bit except that it applies to group permissions rather than owner permissions. When a program accesses a file with the set-gid bit turned on, the program assumes the group privileges of the program file's group rather than those of the user's group. The set-gid bit is also specified by s.

The Locking Bit.   The *locking bit* for a file, if on, allows a program to lock out other attempts to access that file while the file is being read or written. Turning on this bit prevents nearly simultaneous accesses to the file that could corrupt its meaning or leave it in an inconsistent state. The locking bit and the set-gid bit are actually the same bit; if a group-executable file has this bit turned on, the bit is interpreted as the set-gid bit rather than as the locking bit. The locking bit is indicated by a l replacing the x in the group permissions. Not all systems recognize this bit.

The Sticky Bit.   The *sticky bit* provides a means of retaining a program in memory when that program can be shared among many users. A program can be loaded from disk to main memory in shared mode, allowing any number of users to share the memory copy. If the sticky bit of the program's file is set, the text of the program remains in memory even when it is no longer in use. When another user later executes the program, it need not be reloaded. Applied to a directory, the sticky bit prevents files in that directory from being deleted or renamed by anyone other than their owner (or the superuser). Only the superuser can set the sticky bit.

**2.9.3
Octal
Representation of
Permissions**

The permissions of a file can be specified as an octal number (see Section 2.15); UNIX documentation often refers to permissions in this form. The octal number is obtained as the logical sum of numbers from the following list:

4000	Set user ID on execution.
20d0	Set group ID on execution if d is 7, 5, 3, or 1 (execute permission granted); enable locking otherwise.
1000	Turn on the sticky bit.
0400	Set read permission for owner.
0200	Set write permission for owner.
0100	Set execute permission for owner.
0040, 0020, 0010	Set read, write, or execute permission for group.

---

12. That the file and the program are both named 'passwd' is not significant.

0004, 0002, 0001
> Set read, write, or execute permission for others.

2.9.4
Permissions for
Newly Created Files

When a program creates a file, it specifies a set of permissions for that file. Typical sets are `rw-rw-rw-` (octal 666) for data files and `rwxrwxrwx` (octal 777) for executable files. The permissions in this set are then reduced by the *umask* ("user mask") *value,* which you can change with the `umask` command (see Section 3.12.2). The permissions are calculated by logically subtracting the umask value from the value specified by the program (see Section 2.15). Thus if your umask value is 002 (write permission for others), those outside of your group are not be able to write to files that you create unless you later change the mode of those files with `chmod` or change your umask value. A typical default umask value is 022, which denies write permission to everyone but you.

The reduction of permissions by the umask value applies to newly created directories as well as to newly created ordinary files.

2.10   Devices

A *device* is a piece of equipment for storing or communicating data. Printers, disks, and terminals are examples of devices.

UNIX provides access to a device by associating one or more files with it. The files associated with devices are called *special files* (see Section 2.10.2).[13] For example, you can read a line from your terminal by reading from the special file `/dev/tty` associated with your terminal. Similarly you can print a file on printer 1 (assuming you're entitled to) by sending it to the special file `/dev/lp1` associated with that printer. Operations such as these that involve special files are usually carried out by system programs rather than user-level programs, but since UNIX documentation often refers to devices and special files, it's helpful to know what they are.

Special files live in the `/dev` directory, which you can examine to see which devices are attached to your system. When a program performs an operation on a special file, such as asking the kernel to read the file, the operation is actually carried out by a *device driver* associated with the special file. Each kind of special file has its own device driver that translates file-oriented operations into instructions specific to the device's hardware. The device driver is sometimes called an *interface* to its device. A particular device can have several interfaces, each of which treats the device differently.

Device special files, like other files, have read and write permissions. Though execute permission normally has no meaning for a device special file, there are exceptions. For example, Sun Microsystems provides some

---

13. "Device files" would have been a better name.

SunOS programs on compact disks; for these programs to be executable, the disk itself must be made executable by setting the x permission.

2.10.1
Character Devices and Block Devices

There are two kinds of devices: character devices and block devices. They differ in how they transfer data between the device and computer memory.

Character Devices.   A *character device* is one that transfers data character by character. A single data transfer can include any number of characters up to some limit that depends on the device. A character device usually produces a stream of characters (like a keyboard), consumes a stream of characters (like a printer), or does both (like a terminal or a phone line). Most character devices are memoryless—you can't write information to the device and get it back later.

Block Devices.   A *block device* transfers data in batches of characters called *blocks*. Disks and tapes are the most common examples of block devices.[14] UNIX can read from or write to a block device at the hardware level only a block at a time, although higher-level software usually conceals that fact.

All blocks on a block device ordinarily have the same size, with the block size depending on the nature of the device. Typical sizes are 512, 1024, and 2048 bytes. Some magnetic tape units can read and write variable-sized blocks—but even these units read or write a block all at once, not a character at a time.[15] It's unlikely that you'll ever need to deal with the individual blocks on a block device since part of a device driver's job is to provide a more convenient interface to the device.

Block devices, unlike character devices, are chiefly used to store information rather than to produce or consume it. File systems can be stored only on block devices; the structure of a file system depends on that assumption and the many references in UNIX utilities to blocks and block counts reflect it. When you operate on a file, the kernel translates that operation into an operation on a block special file, namely, the block special file associated with the device containing the file system that in turn contains the file.

2.10.2
Special Files and Their Interfaces

Just as there are two kinds of devices—character devices and block devices—there are also two kinds of special files—*character special files* and *block special files*. In a long directory listing the two kinds are indicated by c and b respectively. Each special file has a corresponding interface.

---

14. A more unusual example in UNIX environments is a block terminal such as the IBM 3270. Such terminals, which transmit a screenful of data at a time, are commonly used with mainframe systems. The Amdahl Universal Timeshare System (UTS) has supported them since the late 1970s.

15. Although you can read information from anywhere on a magnetic tape, ordinarily you can write information only at the end of the portion already written. This limitation exists because magnetic tape drives can't position the tape precisely enough to ensure that when the desired portion of the tape is written the rest of the tape is left undisturbed.

The relation between devices and special files can be confusing. A block device can be accessed via either a block special file or a character special file, as explained below, while a character device is always accessed via a character special file. The device driver associated with a block special file is called a *block interface*, while that associated with a character special file is called a *character interface*.

When a block interface reads a block of data from a device, it attempts to save the contents of that block in a *cache* of buffers. If a program asks to read some data that's already in the cache, the interface can provide the data without having to fetch it from the device again.[16] Caching is particularly efficient when a block interface is performing input/output operations on a file system stored on a block device—the activity that probably affects the performance of a UNIX system more than any other.

A character interface, on the other hand, never saves data in a cache. Although some character interfaces may save data in other types of buffers, these buffers are used only once; after the data in a buffer has been read or written, the buffer is discarded.

Under most circumstances the only difference between using a block interface and using a character interface is efficiency; the actual results are the same. A block interface more efficiently supports operations on a file system; a character interface more efficiently supports operations such as copying the contents of one device to another, since in this case the data is used only once and caching merely adds overhead.

Usually the /dev directory contains two entries for a block device: a block special file and a character special file.[17] For example, /dev/mt1 might be the block special file for magnetic tape unit 1 and /dev/rmt1 might be the character special file for the same unit. The 'r' in 'rmt1' stands for "raw"; the character interface is often called the "raw interface" to signify that it passes data directly between the device and the programs that use it.

**2.10.3
Interfaces for
Terminals**

A terminal is a kind of character device. As a character device, a terminal has some special properties. When you communicate with UNIX via your terminal, the sequence of characters you type is not necessarily the sequence that you want the program you're running to see. For instance, if you type ⎡Erase⎤, you don't want your program to see the character you just erased. The interface for a terminal therefore interprets and transforms both the incoming and outgoing streams of characters. Terminals are the only devices whose interfaces perform this interpretation, which you can specify or deactivate altogether with stty (see Section 4.4.2). When the interpretation is deactivated, the terminal is in *raw mode*; otherwise it is in

---

16. Although the block interface carefully ensures the consistency of the data it works with, it provides no protection against changes to the data on the device that result when the device is accessed through a different interface. A device should *never* be accessed through more than one block interface at a time unless all of the accesses are read-only.

17. A disk usually has a pair of entries for each disk partition rather than one pair for the entire disk, making the disk appear to be a set of devices.

cooked mode.[18] Although it's rarely useful for a user to operate a terminal in raw mode, it's often useful for a program to do so.

A terminal operating in cooked mode collects characters until it has a complete line. It must work that way for the kill and erase characters to be effective; otherwise a program reading your terminal would see characters that you didn't intend it to. When a terminal is in cooked mode, the terminal interface performs the following important transformations:

- Processing erase and kill characters
- Echoing characters back to the terminal
- Expanding output tabs to sequences of spaces
- Generating signals for terminal hangups, end of file, interrupt, etc.
- If necessary, deleting ⟨return⟩ characters in front of ⟨newline⟩s in the input and inserting them into the output

2.10.4 Device Numbers

Each device has two numbers associated with it: a *major number* that specifies the type of the device and a *minor number* that specifies a physical or logical unit within the type. Devices with the same major number use the same device driver. For instance, all terminals might have major number 1. A particular terminal, /dev/tty29, would have minor number 29. If you list the devices with ls (see Section 3.1), the major and minor numbers appear in place of the length for a file.

2.10.5 Device Names for Hardware Devices

Device names for hardware devices vary greatly from one system to another, depending not only on the vendor but also on the system's hardware configuration. Device names usually have the form

[r]*type* [*unit*] [*attributes*]

where r indicates a raw interface; *type*, the type of unit (corresponding to the major number); *unit*, a unit number (the minor number); and *attributes*, additional properties of the device. Here are a few examples:

- In most systems the terminals are named '/dev/tty*nn*', where *nn* is a two-digit number. Device names of the form 'pty*nn*' often refer to pseudo-terminals such as those used in X.

- Magnetic tapes are often named '/dev/mt*n*', where *n* is the unit number. The raw interface is named '/dev/rmt*n*'. The device '/dev/nmt*n*' calls upon an interface that does not rewind the tape before accessing it.

---

18. The word "raw" in this context can be confusing because the same word is used to describe the character interface to a block device. The two usages are related since in each case the device and the program operating on it communicate directly—the transmitted data is not processed in any way. For a raw interface, the omitted processing is the storage of the transmitted data in a cache, while for a terminal operating in raw mode the omitted processing is the interpretation of the input and output data streams. For a block device, the raw interface and the block interface differ only in efficiency—you get the same computed results except under unusual circumstances. But for a character device, raw mode and cooked mode differ in effect—you get different computed results when you switch a terminal from one mode to the other.

- In System V, diskettes are accessed via the devices

  ```
  /dev/[r]dsk/fuds[d][t]
  /dev/[r]dsk/fuqs[d][t]
  ```

The notations in this form are as follows:

r   If present, this is a raw interface
u   Drive number
d or q   Double density (512 bytes/sector) or quad density (1024 bytes/sector). Double density is used only for 360KB $5\,1/4''$ diskettes.
s   Sectors per track
d   If present, the disk is double-sided
t   If present, the entire disk, including track 0, can be accessed

For example, a standard 1.44MB $3\,1/2''$ diskette in drive 1, excluding track 0, is referred to as

```
/dev/dsk/f1q18d
```

while a 360KB $5\,1/4''$ diskette in drive 0, including track 0, is referred to as

```
/dev/dsk/f0d9dt
```

Under SunOS, however, a diskette in the first drive is accessed simply as

```
/dev/fd0
```

since SunOS can auto-sense all the other disk characteristics.

- In System V, hard disks can be divided into partitions. The device name

  ```
  /dev/dsk/1s3
  ```

indicates partition 3 on disk drive 1.

2.10.6
Other Devices

Three particularly useful devices are /dev/null, /dev/tty, and /dev/mem.

- /dev/null, the null device, is a "bit bucket". Anything you send to it is simply thrown away; whenever you attempt to read from it, you get an end-of-file. /dev/null is sometimes called a pseudo-device because it doesn't correspond to any actual hardware.

- /dev/tty refers to your terminal, whichever one it happens to be. Your terminal also has a specific designation, e.g., /dev/tty03, which you can find out with the tty command (see Section 4.1.3). Only you can read from your terminal, but anyone can write to it using the write command (see Section 4.6.2) unless you prevent them from doing so with a command such as chmod (see Section 3.12.1) or mesg (see Section 4.6.3).

- The special file /dev/mem is often supported as an image of computer memory. The nth byte of this file corresponds to the nth byte of memory.

2.11   Conventions for Using Files

All shells and other UNIX programs follow certain conventions for referring to files. We describe these conventions in the following subsections.

2.11.1
Wildcards in
File Names

You can refer to a set of files by using a file name containing one or more *wildcards*. A wildcard matches an arbitrary character or sequence of characters. There are three notations for wildcards:

- The character * denotes any sequence of zero or more characters.
- The character ? denotes a single character.
- The construct [*cset*] denotes any single character in the set *cset*. The set *cset* is written as a sequence of characters and character pairs. A character pair has the form '*c1*-*c2*'; it denotes the characters from *c1* to *c2* in the ASCII character set. Three particularly useful character pairs are 'a-z' (the lowercase letters), 'A-Z' (the uppercase letters), and '0-9' (the decimal digits). If you put '!' in front of the sequence, it denotes all the characters *not* in the sequence. (Some shells don't support this use of '!'.) A '/' in the actual file name must always be matched by an explicit '/' in the pattern. Furthermore, a '.' in the actual file name that comes at the beginning or follows a '/' must be matched by an explicit '.' in the pattern.

Here are some examples of wildcards and the files they can refer to:

Name	*Files*
gn*.1	gnu.1, gneiss.1, gn.1
	but not gn/x.1
~/.[a-zA-Z]*	~/.login, ~/.mailrc
	but not ~/login
/doit	one/doit, two/doit.c, three/doit.h
	but not doit
zz?	zz1, zza
	but not zz12
[A-Z]*[!0-9]	A1a, Mary, Joseph
	but not bagel, Bagel0
*.[acAC]	file.a,file.C
	but not .a

The wildcard notation is recognized by the various shells rather than being built into the UNIX file mechanism. When a shell sees a file name containing wildcards, it translates it into a sequence of specific file names, one after another. This process is called *file name generation* in the Bourne shell and *globbing* in the C shell. For example, if you write the filename 'byron?', your shell turns it into something like this:

```
byron1 byron2 byrons
```

assuming that these are the file names that match. Most UNIX programs accept sequences of file names in this form.

2.11.2
The PATH Environment Variable

Programs and other executable files can reside in many different directories. UNIX therefore provides a search path for executable files so that you don't need to remember (and type) the path name of each command that you execute. The search path is recorded in the environment variable PATH (see Section 2.7.5), which you can examine by typing

```
echo $PATH
```

For example, the typical path

```
$HOME/bin:/usr/local/bin:/bin:/usr/bin:.
```

indicates that the shell looks first in your personal bin directory, then in various public bin directories, and finally in your current (working) directory. You could also write this path as

```
$HOME/bin:/usr/local/bin:/bin:/usr/bin:
```

with the final dot omitted, since by convention an empty directory name refers to your current directory.[19] If the command you type is 'hoptoit', the shell examines each directory of the search path in turn, looking for an executable file named 'hoptoit'. It pays no attention to files that are not executable, that is, whose x permission is not turned on, even if they have the right name.[20]

You can set PATH to any search sequence you wish, using the facilities in your shell for assigning values to variables (see, for example, Section 5.2.9). Under the C shell csh, PATH is also available as a shell variable, path; csh ensures that any change to one of these variables is reflected in the other.

2.11.3
Conventions for Naming Directories

In theory, UNIX directories could be named anything. In practice, the names and usage of several top-level and second-level directories of UNIX systems are firmly established by tradition.

/bin   Contains certain programs, available to all users, that are part of the standard UNIX distribution. Generally the /bin[21] directory includes programs such as ls that are essential to starting a system and repairing it when it is broken (see also the /usr/bin directory cited below). Specialized executable files may be found in other directories, most of which have 'bin' in their names.

/dev   Contains files corresponding to external devices such as printers.

---

19. Although the usual default path has the current directory first, we recommend against this practice for security reasons. If your current directory happens to be one created by someone else and it contains a trojan horse version of a common utility, you'll end up executing the trojan rather than the utility.

20. If you add new commands to any of the directories in the path, you'll need to use the sh command hash (see page 167) or the csh command rehash (see page 182) to make the shell aware of them.

21. The name 'bin' stands for "binary".

/etc   Contains files such as the password file /etc/passwd that are required for system administration. Both data files and programs may be kept in this directory.

/lib   Contains libraries of compiled C subprograms that can be called by C programs and linked with them.

/usr   Often contains subdirectories and files belonging to individual users either directly or indirectly (see Section 2.8.3). It also contains the important subdirectories listed below. The subdirectory structure of /usr partly imitates the directory structure of root.[22]

/usr/bin   Contains generally useful executable files, such as the vi editor, that are not essential to your system's operation.[23] Executable files that are local to your installation might be kept in /usr/bin but are more likely to be found in another directory such as /usr/local/bin.

/usr/lib   Contains a variety of libraries as well as subdirectories of specialized libraries for facilities such as X.

/usr/src   Contains the UNIX source files, i.e., the text of the C programs for the UNIX system. These files are only available on systems covered by a UNIX source license; access to them is restricted (see Section 1.1.2).

/usr/include
            Contains header files for C programs.

/usr/adm   Contains accounting information, diagnostic files generated at the time of system crashes, and similar information needed by system administrators.

/usr/spool
            Contains spool files, i.e., temporary files awaiting processing. These include files to be printed, administrative logs, files to be sent to other computers, and files received from other computers that are waiting to be picked up by users. The files in /usr/spool, unlike those in /tmp (described below), are always preserved even when the system is shut down.

/usr/tmp   An alternative to /tmp, described below.

/usr/ucb   Contains Berkeley-specific programs such as vi and Mail (even on some non-Berkeley systems).

/tmp   Contains temporary files created by various programs as they are operating. In some systems the contents of /tmp are lost when the system is shut down.

---

22. At least one system links /bin and /usr/bin to the same directory, and also links /lib and /usr/lib to the same directory.

23. The reason for the distinction between /bin and /usr/bin appears to go back to early UNIX systems, for which a single disk could not hold all of the executable files.

/var   Used in some BSD UNIX systems to store files that change size often and rapidly, such as spooler files and log files. On these systems, /var/adm and /var/spool replace /usr/adm and /usr/spool.

This directory structure is customarily replicated within other directories. For instance, the user named zachary might keep his personal programs in /usr/zachary/bin and the sources for these programs in /usr/zachary/src.

2.11.4
Compressed and
Packed Files

To save space, files are often kept in a compressed or packed form. A *compressed file* is one that was created using the compress program (Section 3.17.2); a *packed file* is one that was created using the pack program (Section 3.17.1). The compress program usually provides greater compression. A particular naming convention is used for these files: a suffix of '.z' indicates a packed file and a suffix of '.Z' indicates a compressed file. For instance, bundle.Z indicates the compressed form of the file bundle. Some UNIX programs recognize these suffixes and automatically unpack or uncompress a file if necessary. If you specify a file bundle to such a program but only the file bundle.Z is present, the program uncompresses bundle.Z and uses the uncompressed file.

2.12   Standard Files and Redirection

By convention, most UNIX commands read from *standard input* and write to *standard output*. When you're working within an interactive shell (which is the usual situation), standard input and standard output are associated with your terminal. When a program looks for input from standard input, it reads that input from your terminal; when it sends output to standard output, it writes that output to your terminal. Another standard file, *standard error*, is used for error messages and other information about the operation of a command. Information sent to standard error is also sent to your terminal. Standard input, standard output, and standard error are all file descriptors associated with each process (see Section 2.12.2).

This convention works well because you can *redirect* standard input and standard output. When you redirect standard input to come from a file named *ifile*, the program reading standard input takes the input from *ifile* instead of your terminal; when you redirect standard output to go to a file *ofile*, the program writing standard output writes the output to *ofile* instead of your terminal. Input redirection is indicated by '<' in front of a file name, while output redirection is indicated by '>' in front of a file name. The space that we use after a redirection operator is optional.

For example, the cat command copies standard input to standard output if it is called with no files specified, so the command

```
cat < felix > fido
```

causes the file `felix` to be copied to the file `fido`. Putting `>>` in front of a file name causes output to be appended to the file rather than written directly. In the previous example the contents of `fido` are overwritten by the contents of `felix`; but if you instead write

```
cat < felix >> fido
```

the contents of `felix` are put after whatever is already in `fido`. Other forms of redirection are discussed in Sections 2.12.1 and 5.2.5.

You can redirect standard error as well as standard input and output; the method is different for different shells.

- For the Bourne and Korn shells, the construct '`2>` *file*' specifies that anything sent to standard error should be redirected to *file*. For example,

  ```
  diff yin yang 2> yerror
  ```

  compares the files `yin` and `yang` with the `diff` command, sending the error output to the file `yerror`. (Do *not* put a space between the '2' and the '>'.)

- For the C shell, the construct '`>&` *file*' sends both standard output and standard error to *file*. The C shell does not provide an explicit construct for redirecting standard output to one file and standard error to a different file.[24]

A valuable and important property of redirection is that a program whose input or output is redirected does not need to know about it.[25] In other words, a program written under the assumption that it reads from standard input and writes to standard output also works for reading from files and writing to files, provided only that the files are specified through redirection. The same property applies to shell scripts. It is because of this property that so many programs are written to use standard input and standard output.

2.12.1
Pipes and Filters

You can use the output of one command as the input of another by connecting the two commands with a *pipe*. The construct that results is a *pipeline*. As with the forms of redirection discussed above, the connected programs don't need to know about the connection.

Syntactically, you create a pipeline by writing two commands with a pipe symbol (|) between them. For example, the command line

```
grep "pest" phones | sort
```

---

24. See page 184 for a method of achieving this effect.

25. The `tty` command (see Section 4.1.3) reveals whether standard input is coming from a terminal, however.

calls the program `grep` (Section 8.4) which extracts from the file `phones` all lines containing the string 'pest' and produces these lines as its standard output. This output is then piped to `sort`, which sees that output as its standard input. The output of the entire command line is a sorted list of the lines in `phone` containing 'pest'.

In a line containing both redirections and pipes, the redirections have higher precedence: first the redirections are associated with commands and then the commands with their redirections are passed through the pipes. For example, the command line

```
grep "pest" phones | sort > hangups
```

extracts lines from the file `phones` as above, sorts them, and stores the sorted lines in the file `hangups`.

Creation of a pipeline implies creation of a pair of processes, one for the command producing the piped information and one for the command consuming the piped information. These processes are created by the shell that interprets the command line.

A *filter* is a program that reads data from standard input, transforms it in some way, and writes the transformed data to standard output. You can construct a pipeline as a sequence of filters; such sequences provide a powerful and flexible way of using simple programs in combination to accomplish many different tasks and are often cited as examples of the UNIX philosophy.

2.12.2
File Descriptors

Each process has a numbered set of *file descriptors* associated with it. When a program reads from or writes to a file, it refers to that file by its file descriptor. Three file descriptors are created when the process starts up:

0   standard input
1   standard output
2   standard error

Every file descriptor is associated with a file; file descriptors 0, 1, and 2 are by default associated with the file `/dev/tty`, which is your terminal. These associations can be modified by redirection (see Section 2.12).

A program can read or write additional files by asking the kernel to open them (the standard files are opened automatically). When the kernel opens a file, it provides the program with a file descriptor for the file and also associates the file descriptor with the program's process. These additional file descriptors have numbers greater than 2, although ordinarily you never see them.

Although you'll rarely need to do it, you can create file descriptors with numbers greater than 2 and associate them with files using the extended forms of redirection provided by the Bourne shell (see Section 5.2.5) and the Korn shell (see Section 5.4).

2.13   Other Facilities for Interprocess Communication

We now describe three facilities that provide more general forms of pipes: named pipes, sockets, and Streams. Sockets and Streams provide more disciplined and sophisticated interprocess communication than named pipes, but named pipes do have one advantage: they are easily constructed at the user level and require no programming.

2.13.1 Named Pipes

A *named pipe* is a kind of pipe that exists independently of any process. Any process with read permission can read from it, and any process with write permission can write to it. Named pipes are also called *FIFO files* because the data passed through them follows a first-in, first-out discipline. A named pipe can be used to connect two processes that are running on different terminals or to implement a dæmon (see p. 19) that collects error notices from any process that issues them. The input processes and the output processes can be completely unrelated. BSD UNIX systems usually don't support named pipes but they do support socket pairs, which can serve the same purpose.

For those systems that support named pipes, you can create a named pipe `corncob` with the command

```
mknod corncob p
```

or with the command

```
/etc/mknod corncob p
```

if the `/etc` directory is not included in your search path. Because named pipes are actually files, they appear in a file listing—if you look at one with the 'ls -l' command (see Section 3.1), its first file attribute will be p.

Now suppose that `devour` is a program that waits for input to appear in `corncob` and processes that input whenever it appears. The command to start up `devour` would be

```
devour < corncob &
```

The `devour` command should be run in the background since it will be blocked until it receives input. Another program `babble` can send input to `devour` via `corncob` with the command

```
babble > corncob
```

The `devour` and `babble` commands can originate from different terminals as long as both terminals have access to `corncob`. It might be desirable to run `babble` in the background as well, since if `corncob` is full—a named pipe usually has a very small capacity—`babble` has to wait for it to be emptied.[26]

---

26. A process that opens a named pipe, or indeed any pipe, for writing is blocked until some other process opens that pipe for reading. This is another possible reason for running `babble` in the background—if `devour` hasn't started, `babble` becomes blocked.

**2.13.2
Sockets**

A socket is an endpoint for data communication. A pair of sockets provides a generalization of a pipe. Data can be sent to a socket or retrieved from a socket just as it can from a file. Sockets were introduced by BSD UNIX and are not part of the earlier AT&T-derived UNIX systems. You won't find them mentioned in the older classic books on UNIX.

A socket can transmit data to any process, even one running on a different computer. Moreover, socket pairs are bidirectional; either process can send data to the other. Certain types of sockets can exist independently of any particular process.

You can't create a socket or socket pair by issuing shell commands. However, a number of commands such as `telnet` (p. 425) and `rlogin` (p. 423) construct sockets implicitly. You can also construct a socket or a socket pair from within a C program.

Because sockets are so much more general than pipes, they require a more complex underlying mechanism. Communicating data through a socket can require all the facilities of packet-based data transmission over networks.

**2.13.3
Streams**

Streams, a facility of System V, are communication channels very similar to sockets. Like sockets, they provide a uniform method of communicating over networks and are bidirectional. The principal difference between a socket and a Stream is that a socket connects one process to another while a Stream connects a process to an entity that logically behaves like an input-output device. Streams were designed to be used by programmers, not by end users, so you won't find any commands for working with them.

2.14   UNIX Commands

A *command* is an instruction to UNIX that tells it to do something. The usual way to issue a command is to pass it to a shell by typing it in response to a prompt. A command consists of a sequence of *words* separated by *whitespace* consisting of one or more spaces, tabs, or (for some shells) escaped newlines (see Section 2.14.2).[27] The first word is the command name and the remaining words are the *arguments* of the command. The command name refers to the program or shell script to be executed. Some arguments specify which files the command operates on while others control or modify what the command does.

---

27. An escaped newline, i.e., one preceded by '\', is treated as whitespace by the C shell but not by the Bourne shell. Typing

```
echo one two\
three
```

reveals how a shell treats escaped newlines. An unquoted and unescaped newline always terminates a command and therefore can never be interpreted as whitespace.

2.14.1
Standard Syntax of Commands

Commands have a standard syntax; we describe it below. Unfortunately not all commands adhere to it, and the manual page for a command rarely indicates whether it does. For instance, the standard syntax allows options to appear in any order; most command descriptions indicate a particular order without stating whether it is required. We note some of the deviations, but experimentation is still called for.

A command consists of a command name followed by its *options*, if any, and its *arguments*, if any. The options control or modify what the command does. The arguments specify file names or similar information. Each argument is a single word.

The options are specified by a sequence of words. Each word is either an *option group* or an *option argument*. Options generally are denoted by single letters. You can write them in any order, and you can combine several of them into a single group provided that they don't have any option arguments of their own (see below). Each group of options is preceded by a dash (-). For example, the commands

```
ls -al
ls -l -a
```

are equivalent and indicate that the `ls` (list files) command is to be called with the options `a` (all files) and `l` (long listing).

The last (or only) option of an option group can be followed by a word that specifies one or more option arguments for it. For example, the command

```
sed -f bluescript heartthrob
```

causes the `sed` script editor to edit the file `heartthrob` using the script `bluescript`; in this case `bluescript` is an argument to the `-f` option and `heartthrob` is an argument to the `sed` command itself.

Multiple arguments of an option are normally separated by commas, but you can separate them by blanks if you enclose the list of arguments in double quotes. In any event, the multiple arguments must form a single word. The following pair of options shows both conventions:

```
prog -o zed1,zed2 -y "are you with us"
```

There are two other common conventions:

- '`--`' indicates the end of the options. When you want to give arguments that start with '`-`' to a command, you can put '`--`' in front of them to ensure that they are interpreted as arguments rather than as options. For example,

```
rm -- -giraffe
```

is one way to remove the file `-giraffe`. If you had simply written

```
rm -giraffe
```

you'd get an error complaint about an unrecognized g option.

- '`-`' by itself indicates standard input in a context where the command expects a file name. For example, the command

```
diff - quince
```

finds the differences between standard input and the contents of the file `quince`. In some BSD UNIX systems, however, certain commands such as `rm`, `rmdir`, and `mv` follow the older convention of using '–' to indicate the end of the options.

In some cases, the indicator character for an option is something other than a dash. For example, in

```
xterm +sb
```

the '+sb' instructs the `xterm` program *not* to attach a scrollbar to the X window that it generates.

The term "command" is also used to refer to the instructions expected by programs such as the `vi` editor or the `mailx` mailer. In this context the term "command" really means "subcommand". You should usually be able to identify the sense in which the term is being used from the context.

2.14.2 Quotation and Command Substitution

All of the standard shells assign special meanings to certain characters, called *metacharacters*. To use these characters as ordinary data characters on a command line, you must quote them. Each shell has its own set of metacharacters and its own quotation conventions, but certain rules generally hold:

- A backslash acts as an *escape* for one or more characters following it, giving those characters a special meaning. If that character is a metacharacter, the special meaning is usually the character itself. For example, '\\' usually stands for a single backslash and '\$' for a dollar sign. In these cases the backslash effectively quotes the character after it, sometimes called an *escaped character*. The backslash itself is called an *escape character*.

- When text is enclosed in double quotes ("), most metacharacters are treated as data characters but those such as '$' that specify substitutions are interpreted as metacharacters. For instance, in a construct such as

```
"<<$1>>"
```

  the '$' character is interpreted but the '<' and '>' characters are not. (The '$1' refers to the first argument passed to a shell script; see Section 5.1.) If the first argument is 'dhoti', the construct becomes

```
<<dhoti>>
```

- When text is enclosed in apostrophes ('), nearly all metacharacters are treated as data characters. Quoting with apostrophes is a stronger form of quotation than quoting with double quotes.

Spaces and tabs are always treated as data characters within quoted text, so you can use quotation to create a single command argument that contains these characters.

A closely related construct is *command substitution*, which enables you to execute a command and then use its output as part of another command. A command substitution is enclosed in backquotes ('). For example, if the current directory is `/usr/jodi`, the command

```
echo The current directory is `pwd`.
```

produces the output

```
The current directory is /usr/jodi.
```

Three commands that are particularly useful in command substitutions are `expr` (see Section 4.6.5), and `dirname` and `basename` (see Section 4.6.6).

Exactly which characters are quoted by the various forms of quotation, the treatment of newlines within quotations, and the way that the various forms of quotation and command substitution interact all depend on the particular shell.

2.14.3
Other Common
Conventions

Most UNIX commands read their input from standard input and write their output to standard output. If standard input and standard output have not been redirected, they correspond to your terminal (provided the command has been called from an interactive shell). Redirecting the input or the output is the usual way of applying UNIX commands to particular files.

Some UNIX commands operate on one or more files and expect those files to be specified by a list of file names, with the names in the list separated by whitespace. If the list is missing, the command takes its input from standard input—so this form includes the previous one. Since this is the form produced by the expansion of wildcards (see Section 2.11.1), you can easily apply these commands to sets of files. For example, the command

```
cat leopard/* > felix
```

causes all the files in the `leopard` subdirectory to be concatenated into a single file and written to the file `felix`. The fully expanded form of the command might be

```
cat leopard/this leopard/that leopard/file1 > felix
```

The `cat` command also handles the case when no input files are specified, so that

```
cat > felix
```

copies standard input to the file `felix`.

You can use the `echo` command (see Section 4.6.1) to show the files that would be produced by a file name containing wildcards. For example,

```
echo leopard/a*
```

shows you all the files in the `leopard` directory whose names start with 'a'.

2.15   Octal and Hexadecimal Numbers

Octal numbers, also known as *base-8 numbers*, are used by a number of UNIX programs. *Hexadecimal numbers*, also known as *base-16 numbers*, are also used by some UNIX programs, though not by as many.[28] The advantage of octal and hexadecimal numbers is that they can easily be converted to binary (base-2) numbers, and binary numbers are the form in which information is actually stored in your computer.

Number Representations.   In general, a base-b number is represented as a sequence of digits $d_n \cdots d_1 d_0$, where each d_i has a value between 0 and $b - 1$. Thus a binary digit is either 0 or 1, an octal digit is between 0 and 7, and a decimal digit (base 10) is between 0 and 9. Hexadecimal digits are represented using the digits 0–9 and the letters 'a'–'f' or 'A'–'F'. Unfortunately there is no agreement as to whether the letters in a hexadecimal number should be lowercase or uppercase; different programs follow different conventions. The value of a base-b number $d_n \cdots d_1 d_0$ is given by

$$d_n \times b^n + \ldots + d_1 \times b^1 + d_0 \times b^0$$

Converting to and from Decimal.   You can use the formula above to convert an octal or hexadecimal number to decimal. For example, the octal number 137 is given by

$$1 \times 8^2 + 3 \times 8^1 + 7 \times 8^0 = 1 \times 64 + 3 \times 8 + 7 \times 1 = 95$$

You can also use this formula to convert decimal numbers to octal or hexadecimal. To convert the number n from decimal to octal, find the largest power of 8 that is less than n. Divide by this power of 8 to obtain the leading octal digit of n, obtaining a remainder r. Then continue dividing r by smaller powers of 8 until you reach 1. Successive quotients give successive octal digits. For the decimal number 207, the procedure works as follows:

(1)   Divide 207 by 64, obtaining a quotient 3 and a remainder 15.
(2)   Divide 15 by 8, obtaining a quotient 1 and a remainder 7.
(3)   Divide 7 by 1, obtaining a quotient 7.

The octal representation of 207 is therefore 317. The procedure for hexadecimal numbers is analogous, with 16 as the divisor. Although this method is not easy to use for large numbers, you're unlikely to need to convert large numbers unless you're debugging a computer program—and in that case, the debugger can do the conversion for you.

Converting to and from Binary.   Converting octal or hexadecimal numbers to and from binary is particularly easy. We first consider the case of converting octal numbers to binary. Each octal number turns into three binary digits according to the following table:

Octal	*Binary*	*Octal*	*Binary*
0	000	4	100
1	001	5	101
2	010	6	110
3	011	7	111

---

28. UNIX is somewhat out of step with the rest of the world in its preference for octal over hexadecimal. The use of octal traces back to the first implementations of UNIX on the PDP-11 computer, for which octal was the customary notation.

For example, the octal number 4726 turns into the binary number 100_111_010_110. In converting from binary to octal, you add zeros on the left if necessary so that the number of binary digits is a multiple of three.

The conversion between hexadecimal and binary is similar; it proceeds in groups of four digits. Here is the conversion table:

Hexadecimal	Binary	Hexadecimal	Binary
0	0000	8	1000
1	0001	9	1001
2	0010	A	1010
3	0011	B	1011
4	0100	C	1100
5	0101	D	1101
6	0110	E	1110
7	0111	F	1111

Logical Operations on Octal or Hexadecimal Numbers. A few UNIX programs such as chmod and umask perform logical operations on octal or hexadecimal numbers. These operations actually apply to the binary forms of these numbers. There are five such logical operations commonly applied to two binary numbers x and y:

- **Logical Addition.** The logical sum of x and y has a one in each position where either x or y has a one. This operation is often called *logical or.*

- **Modulo 2 Addition.** The modulo 2 sum of x and y has a one in each position where x and y differ. This operation is often called *logical exclusive or.*

- **Logical Multiplication.** The logical product of x and y has a one in each position where both x and y have a one. This operation is sometimes called *logical and,* and one of the operands is often called a *mask.*

- **Logical Subtraction.** The logical difference of x and y has a one in each position where x has a one and y does not.

- **Complement.** The complement of x has a one wherever x has a zero and a zero wherever x has a one.

For example, if

$$x = 101\ 011\ 110 \quad \text{(octal 536)}$$
$$y = 010\ 110\ 100 \quad \text{(octal 264)}$$

then the various operations produce the following results:

Logical sum	111 111 110
Modulo 2 sum	111 101 010
Logical product	000 010 100
Logical difference	101 001 010
Complement of x	101 001 011

2.16   Regular Expressions

A *regular expression* defines a pattern of text to be matched. A number of UNIX utilities such as `sed` expect you to specify search patterns as regular expressions. The definition of a regular expression described here is the one assumed by the `ed` editor (see Section 6.4) and followed by many other programs. The `vi` and `ex` editors provide some additional facilities (see Section 6.1.11). The different variants of `grep` (see Section 8.4) also deviate from the description given here.

In general, any character appearing in a regular expression matches that character in the text. For example, the regular expression 'elvis' matches the string 'elvis'. However, certain characters are used to specify variable patterns and are therefore special. The following characters are special anywhere in a string:

> .   *   [\

In addition, other characters are special under particular conditions:

- The character '^' is special at the beginning of a string.
- The character '$' is special at the end of a string.
- The character that terminates a string is special throughout the string. What this character is depends on the context.

If you want to use a special character in a pattern, you must quote it, in effect, by escaping it with a preceding backslash (\). For example, the regular expression 'cheap at $9\.98' matches the string 'cheap at $9.98'. Here the '.' needs to be quoted but the '$' doesn't since it isn't at the end of the string and therefore isn't special.

The character, if any, that terminates a regular expression is also special and must be quoted if you want to use it within the string. For example, the regular expression '/\//' might be used in `ed` to search for a string consisting of a single '/'. The outer slashes enclose the regular expression and aren't actually part of it.

The meanings of the special characters are as follows:

\   The backslash quotes the character after it, whether special or not.[29]

.   The dot matches any single character.

*   A single character followed by an asterisk matches zero or more occurrences of that character. Similarly, a pattern that matches a set of characters followed by an asterisk matches zero or more characters from that set. In particular, '.*' matches an arbitrary, possibly empty, string. The longest possible matching

---

29. The "official" definition of a regular expression appears in the manual pages for `ed`. The definition there is somewhat misleading about the role of the backslash. It states that the backslash quotes special characters but says nothing about the behavior of a backslash preceding nonspecial characters.

sequence is always used, although the matching mechanism is clever enough to consider the whole string when testing for a match. For example, it can discover that '`^a.*b.c$`' matches '`axybbcc`', even though this match requires that the '`.*`' should consume the first 'b' but not the second one.

$ A dollar sign at the end of an outermost regular expression matches the end of a line. Anywhere else in a regular expression, it matches itself.

^   A hat at the beginning of an outermost regular expression matches the beginning of a line. Anywhere else in a regular expression, it matches itself.

[*set*]   A set of characters in square brackets matches any single character from the set. For example, [`moxie`] matches any of the characters (e i m o x). This notation is extended as follows:

- Within the set, the only characters with special meanings are (-] ^). All other characters, even '\', stand for themselves.

- The notation *c1–c2* indicates the set of ASCII characters ranging from *c1* to *c2*. For example, '[`a-zA-Z_`]' matches any lowercase or uppercase letter, or an underscore. A minus sign at the beginning or end of the set stands for itself, however; thus '[`+-`]' matches a plus or a minus.

- A right bracket as the first character of the set represents itself and does not end the set. (Within the set, a left bracket is not special.) Thus '[] []' matches a left bracket or a right bracket.

- The sequence [^*set*] matches any character that is *not* in *set*. (In this case a '-' or ']' following the initial '^' stands for itself, as above.) Thus '^0-9' matches any character except a digit.

Note that a set of characters can be followed by an asterisk. Thus '[`0-9a-f`]*' matches a possibly empty sequence of characters, each of which is either a digit or a letter between a and f.

- You can enclose a portion of a regular expression between the markers '\(' and '\)'. The entire construct is called a *bracketed expression* or a *tagged regular expression*. Later in the expression you can match a bracketed expression by writing '*n*', where *n* is a digit between 1 and 9. Here '\1' denotes the first bracketed expression, '\2' the second one, and so forth. Thus '\([a-z]*\)\&\1' matches the string 'gnat\&gnat'.

A further extension to the notation is also available in some systems:

- You can follow a single character, or a regular expression that denotes a single character, by one of the following forms:

$$\backslash\{m\backslash\} \qquad \backslash\{m,\backslash\} \qquad \backslash\{m,n\backslash\}$$

Here m and n are non-negative integers less than 256. Let S be the set containing either the single character or the characters that match the regular expression.

- ○ The first form denotes exactly m occurrences of characters belonging to S.
- ○ The second form denotes at least m occurrences of characters belonging to S.
- ○ The third form denotes between m and n occurrences of characters belonging to S.

For example, '[0-9]\{2,\}' matches a sequence consisting of two or more digits.

2.16.1
Generalized
Regular Expressions

The `egrep` and `awk` programs recognize generalized regular expressions, which are like those described above with the following additions and changes:

- The '*' operator following a regular expression matches zero or more occurrences of that regular expression. In particular, the form

  \(*expr*\)*

  matches zero or more occurrences of *expr*. (For the regular expressions described in Section 2.16, the '*' operator applies only to one-character expressions.)

- The '+' operator following a regular expression matches one or more occurrences of that regular expression.

- The '?' operator following a regular expression matches zero or one occurrences of that regular expression, i.e., it matches an optional regular expression.

- Two regular expressions separated by '|' or a newline match an occurrence of either of them, i.e., the '|' operator and its newline synonym act as an "or". (Awk does not accept a newline as a synonym for '|'.)

- *Unquoted* parentheses are used for grouping. For example, the pattern '(cat|dog)(fish|fight)' matches any line containing either 'catfish', 'catfight', 'dogfish', or 'dogfight'.

- Awk also recognizes certain escape sequences that start with a backslash (see p. 358).

In an extended regular expression the characters (+ ? | ( )) are additional special characters that need to be quoted with a backslash if they are used to stand for themselves.

The order of precedence from highest to lowest is:

(1) []
(2) * + ?
(3) | newline

When several operators occur in a regular expression they are interpreted in order of precedence from highest to lowest. In other words, the highest precedence operators are applied first.

**2.16.2
Replacements for
Regular Expressions**

In many contexts where regular expressions are used, you can provide a replacement to be substituted for the regular expression. Within a replacement, the following conventions apply:

- A backslash quotes the following character. The special characters within a replacement are '**&**' and '****'; these are the only characters that need be quoted. The construct '**\&**' produces a single '**&**' and the construct '****' produces a single backslash.

- As a special case of the quotation convention, a newline is indicated by inserting an actual newline preceded by a backslash. For example, the replacement text

  ```
  white\
  rabbit
  ```

  produces the text

  ```
  white
  rabbit
  ```

- An ampersand (**&**) indicates the entire matched regular expression. For example, the replacement '**&&**' would consist of two copies of the matched expression.

- The sequence '**\n**', where n is a single digit, indicates the text matching the nth parenthesized component of the regular expression.

2.17   Local Variables

Most UNIX programs that accept commands interactively have a set of *local variables* whose values help to define the program's behavior. For instance, the `mailx` mailer has a variable `keep` that tells it not to remove a mailbox when it becomes empty. Most programs that provide local variables are either shells, such as `sh` and `csh`, or programs that behave like shells, such as the `mailx` mailer. Some of these programs allow the set of variables to be open-ended, enabling you to define your own variables. These new variables augment the ones defined by the program and can be particularly useful when you're writing shell scripts (see Chapter 5).

A variable can have one of three states:

(1)   It doesn't exist.
(2)   It exists, but has an empty value.
(3)   It exists and has a nonempty value.

A variable that exists is *enabled* or *set*, whether or not it has a value; a variable that doesn't exist is *disabled* or *unset*.

A disabled variable may still have a default value. For example, the `toplines` variable of `mailx` is disabled by default, but it still has a default value of 5 (the value assumed by `mailx` if you don't set `toplines` at all).

The programs that provide variables have a `set` command or something similar to it to set and retrieve the values of those variables. The command usually works as follows:

- The command `set` by itself prints a list of all existing variables.
- The command `set` v sets v to an empty value.
- The command `set` $v=s$ sets v to the value s.
- The command `set` `no`v, or its equivalent, `unset` v, removes v.

If a variable has an empty value, you just see its name when you type `set`; if it has a nonempty value, you see its value as well. For example, typing

```
set askcc
```

in the `mailx` program enables the `mailx` variable `askcc`. Typing

```
set SHELL=/bin/csh
```

sets the `SHELL` variable to refer to the C shell. **Note:** the Bourne shell `sh` has different syntax for these commands.

Don't confuse local variables with environment variables (see Section 2.7.5). Local variables belong to a program and are only visible to that program; environment variables belong to a process and are copied to the environment of any program that executes as part of that process. A local variable named `elliott` can coexist with an environment variable named `elliott`. The difference between the two types of variables is obscured by two facts:

- Most programs that have local variables copy some of them from the environment. For example, they usually copy the value of the environment variable `HOME` into a local variable named either `home` or `HOME`.

- Every shell provides some way of inserting its local variables into the environment of commands executed by the shell.

2.18 Initialization Files

Many UNIX programs are set up to look for *initialization files* in your home directory. These files contain commands that the program executes before it does anything else. The names of these files always start with a dot and often end with `rc` ("run commands"). Some programs also look for initialization commands in special environment variables (see Section 2.7.5). Here are some examples:

- The login process looks for initialization commands in the `.profile` file if you're using the Bourne shell, or in the `.login` file if you're using the C shell.

- The C shell looks for initialization commands in the `.cshrc` file.

- The `vi` and `ex` editors look for initialization commands first in the `EXINIT` environment variable and then (if `EXINIT` is empty) in the `.exrc` file.

- The `mailx` mailer looks for initialization commands in the file whose name is found in the environment variable `MAILRC`. If `MAILRC` has nothing in it, `mailx` looks in the file `.mailrc` in your home directory.

**2.18.1
Login
Initialization
Files**

When your login shell starts up, it first looks in your home directory for a login initialization file and executes the commands in it. A "canned" version of this file is usually placed in your home directory when your account is created, which you can modify to suit your needs and tastes. Here are some examples of useful actions you might include in your login initialization file:

- Setting characteristics of your terminal, including the special characters such as Erase and Kill (see Section 4.4.2)
- Setting your path (see Section 2.11.2)
- Reading your mail (see Chapter 9)
- Setting environment variables for programs that you often use (see Section 2.7.5)

Some of these may already be in the canned file.

If your login shell is not the one you prefer, you can usually have your system administrator change it. (BSD UNIX has a `chsh` command that enables you to do it for yourself.) You can also accomplish the same thing by switching shells as the last action in your initialization file:

- If your login shell is the Bourne shell (the System V default), the command

    ```
    exec csh
    ```

    changes your shell to the C shell.

- If your login shell is the C shell (the BSD UNIX default), the command

    ```
    exec sh
    ```

    changes your shell to the Bourne shell.

Calling your new shell via `exec` ensures that it is a top-level shell and that you can log out directly from it. It also ensures that any environment variables that you have previously set retain the values that you gave them.

2.19   Terminal Descriptions

A "dumb" terminal transmits a single character for each character typed at its keyboard and takes a single action—usually to display a single character—for each character it receives. Output simply scrolls down the screen or printed page. Nonprinting actions are generally limited to backspacing or starting a new line. A "smart" terminal, on the other hand, performs far more complex actions such as changing screen colors or moving the cursor to a designated screen position. These actions are specified by special sequences of characters called *control sequences*, which are usually introduced by a nonprinting escape character. In addition, smart terminals usually have special keys such as function keys that transmit multicharacter sequences when they are pressed. Most terminals in use today are smart terminals, but most terminals in use during UNIX's early days were dumb ones.

Unfortunately there's little agreement among terminal manufacturers about the control sequences for smart terminals—and as long as different terminals offer different amenities, there isn't likely to be any. Because an operating system needs to know the control sequences for each kind of terminal that might be connected to it, UNIX systems include a database of terminal descriptions. In System V it's called `terminfo`; in older Berkeley systems it's called `termcap`, for "terminal capabilities". Berkeley systems also provide a separate but similar database, `printcap`, for describing printers.

A typical edition of `terminfo` or `termcap` contains descriptions of hundreds of different terminals. `Terminfo` and `termcap` differ significantly in that `terminfo` is compiled into a compact form while `termcap` is not. Programs can retrieve information faster from `terminfo` than they can from `termcap`, but `terminfo` can only be read by using a special program `infocmp` that can decompile a description.[30] Nearly all of the following discussion of `terminfo` applies to `termcap` as well.

The information in `terminfo` specifies the control sequences that a program must send to a particular terminal in order to perform a particular function such as clearing the screen or displaying the succeeding characters in boldface. Most UNIX programs needing to communicate with terminals or printers use `terminfo` either directly or indirectly. `Terminfo` contains three kinds of information:

- Boolean capabilities, which indicate whether or not the terminal supports some particular feature
- Numeric capabilities, which indicate the size of the terminal or the limits on particular features
- String capabilities, which indicate what control sequence must be sent to the terminal to achieve a particular effect

You'll often see references in UNIX literature to `curses`, a high-level programming interface to `terminfo` developed as part of the BSD UNIX project that enables a programmer to control a terminal efficiently without knowing the particular control sequences it expects.

As a user you'll rarely need to look at the information in `terminfo`, although you might want to look at it to see which terminals it supports. You can find `terminfo` in the directory `/usr/lib`. It's actually a directory, not a file, with subdirectories whose names are single characters. The directory `/usr/lib/terminfo/h`, for example, contains the descriptions of terminals whose names start with 'h', such as 'hp2621'. In System V-style systems you can use the command

```
tput -T name longname
```

---

30. The `tic` program recompiles descriptions.

to see the full name of the terminal in `terminfo` whose description is named *name* (see Section 4.4.3). The `tput` command can help you check whether a terminal in `terminfo` is the one you think it is. More generally you can use `tput` (or `tset` in BSD UNIX systems) to perform functions such as resetting your terminal or changing its mode of operation (see Section 4.4.3 or 4.4.1).

The `TERM` environment variable records the name of your terminal. Using the value of `TERM`, a program can look up the control sequences in `terminfo` that apply to your terminal and transmit them when it needs to. When you log in, you may sometimes get a query

    TERM=

because the port you've logged in on doesn't uniquely determine your terminal type.[31] It's a good idea to know what the "official" name of your terminal is so that you can respond to such a query. You can find it by typing

    echo $TERM

The information in `terminfo` also includes two special strings, the *initialization string* and the *reset string*. The initialization string, when sent to your terminal, makes it behave as described in `terminfo`, assuming the terminal is in a reasonable state such as its power-on state. The reset string, when sent to your terminal, restores it to sanity if it is in an unusable but unknown state. Normally the reset string does everything that the initialization string does, but it may also produce strange flashes of the screen and other unpleasant side effects—so you should only use the reset string if the initialization string doesn't work. The `tput` and `tset` commands each provide ways to issue these strings.

2.19.1 Setting Your Terminal Type

Ordinarily your terminal type is set in your login initialization file (see Section 2.18), but you might need to set it yourself for one of the following reasons:

- For some reason your normal initialization file isn't being called.
- Your original initialization files aren't correct.
- You customarily log in at two different terminals and these terminals have different types.

Setting your terminal entails setting the `TERM` environment variable and initializing the terminal itself. If you're using the C shell, you can set `TERM` with the `setenv` command; if you're using the Bourne shell you can set it with `export` together with an assignment. The best way to initialize the terminal is with `tset` (see Section 4.4.1); if `tset` isn't available you can use the command 'tput init'.

The login program sets certain characteristics of your terminal, such as whether uppercase characters should be mapped to lowercase ones. If any are set inappropriately, you can use `stty` to change them. You should include the command for making the changes in your login initialization file.

---

31. The query comes from the default login initialization file, so you can eliminate it by modifying that file.

3

Basic Operations on Files

A classic tenet of UNIX philosophy is that the way to get a job done is to use simple tools in combination. UNIX therefore provides a large—for many people, bewilderingly large—collection of simple tools for operating on files and directories. We describe many of these tools in this chapter and others in Chapter 8. If you're using the Emacs editor, you can use its directory editor, Dired, for some of the most frequent operations on files.

3.1 Listing Files with `ls`

The `ls` command lists a set of files, the contents of a directory, the contents of a tree of directories, or any combination of these. You can use it to see if files exist or to examine their characteristics. The form of the `ls` command line is

    ls [options] name

This command lists the directories and files specified in name ..., with the style of the listing determined by options or by default. Two particularly useful sets of options are '-CF' and '-l'. The command

    ls -CF names

lists the files in columnar format and indicates which ones are directories or executable files. The command

    ls -l names

provides a "long" listing containing detailed information about the listed files.

Each name in *names* is either a directory or a file; successive names are separated by blanks. If you omit *names*, it is taken as '.' (the current directory). The items to be listed are determined as follows:

- If a name designates a file that is not a directory, that file is listed.
- If a name designates a directory, the files in that directory are listed.
- If there is no file with a particular name, nothing is listed for that name.

Files and directories whose names begin with a dot are excluded unless the -a option is specified.

An example of the `ls` command is

```
ls -Fl -a .. stuart
```

This command lists two sets of files: those in the parent directory of the current directory and those in `stuart`. If `stuart` is a subdirectory of the current directory, it lists the files in that subdirectory; if `stuart` is a file in the current directory, it lists just that file; and if `stuart` is not in the current directory at all, it lists nothing for `stuart`. The listing options that apply are -F, -l, and -a.

The command `ls` by itself lists the files in the current directory, omitting those whose names begin with a dot. If there are no qualifying files, it produces no output.

3.1.1 Command-line Options

The `ls` command can produce two kinds of listings: short and long. A short listing, which is the default, includes the name of each file and any other information you ask for explicitly; a long listing includes file permissions and other information (see Section 3.1.2). The -l, -n, -o, and -g options all force a long listing; if these are absent you get a short listing.

The following options affect the set of files included in the listing:

-a   List all files, including those whose names begin with a dot or are contained in a directory whose name begins with a dot.

-d   If a name on the command line designates a directory, list only the name of that directory, not its contents. You can use this option with -l to display the status of a directory.

-R   List subdirectories recursively. In other words, for each subdirectory that `ls` encounters, list the files in that subdirectory and in every subdirectory contained in it either directly or indirectly. The listing shows how the subdirectories are organized.

-f   This option only applies to directories. It causes `ls` to list all files contained in a directory in the order in which they are actually stored within that directory. This option nullifies the -l, -t, -s, and -r options if they are given and implies the -a option for the files contained in the directory.

The following options affect the information associated with each file in a listing, either short or long:

-p   Put '/' after each file in the listing that is a directory. This option is not available on some systems.

-F	Put '/' after each file in the listing that is a directory and '*' after each file that is executable. (A file cannot be both.)
-i	Show the i-node number of each file.
-s	Show the size of each file in blocks, including indirect blocks (blocks that contain pointers to other blocks).

The following options control the layout of a short listing:

-C	Produce multicolumn output, with the entries sorted down the columns.
-x	Produce multicolumn output, with the entries sorted across the rows.
-m	List the files across the page, with successive files separated by commas. This option is not available on some systems.

The following options force a long listing, one file per line, in the format described in Section 3.1.2. These options may be used in any combination. By default, the owner name and group name of each file are listed; -n, -o, and -g change the default.

-l	List the files using the long format.
-n	List the files using the long format, replacing the owner name and group name in the listing with the user number and group number. This option is not available on some systems.
-o	List the files in the long format, omitting the group. This option is not available on some systems.
-g	List the files in the long format, omitting the owner. On some systems, the default long listing does not include the group name; the -g option then specifies that the group name should be included.

The following options affect the order in which files are listed.

-t	List the files in chronological order, newest ones first (unless the order is reversed by the -r option). For sorting purposes, the time of last modification is used unless the -u option is specified.
-r	List the files in reverse alphabetic order if the -t option is absent and in oldest-first time order if the -t option is present.

The following options affect the time associated with each file. The time affects the order of the files if you've specified the -t option; it also shows up in the long listings even if you haven't specified -t. The default time is the time of last modification.

-u	Use the time when the file was last accessed.
-c	Use the time when the file's i-node was last modified, namely, when the file was created or its permissions were last modified. If -u and -c are both present, -u controls the time.

By default, nonprinting characters in a file name appear without change in the listing output. The following options provide special treatment for these characters:

-b	If a file name contains a nonprinting character, show that character as an octal number using the notation *ddd*.

-q   If a file name contains a nonprinting character, show '?' in place
         of that character.

**3.1.2
Interpreting the
Long Format**

The ls command produces a long listing if you specify the -1 option or
another option in the same group. Here is an example of the contents of
a directory listed using the -1F options:

```
total 7
drwxrwxr-x   3 clio     muses    176 Mar 19 12:06 ./
drwxrwxr-x  13 clio     muses    944 Feb 16 19:39 ../
drwxr-xr-x   2 clio     muses     48 Apr  4 11:54 d1/
-rwxr-xr-x   1 root     other      3 Apr 11 12:05 lookup*
lrwxrwxrwx   1 clio     muses      9 Mar 23 09:38 mark -> tmp/marvin
-rw-r--r--   3 clio     mail       4 Apr  3 11:02 news
prw-r--r--   1 euterpe  muses      0 Apr 11 11:09 tube
```

The listing is interpreted as follows:

- The first character on the line indicates the file type:

  - Ordinary file
  d Directory
  l Symbolic link (see p. 27)
  b Block device (see Section 2.10)
  c Character device (see Section 2.10)
  p Named pipe (see Section 2.13.1)

  The entry for a symbolic link shows both its name in the current
  directory entry and the name of the file to which it is linked.

- The next three groups of three letters indicate the file permissions
  for the user, the group, and others (see Section 2.9). Other letters
  besides r, w, and x are possible.

- The next item indicates how many links this file has (see Section 2.8.5). A directory *dir* often has several links, because each of
  its subdirectories includes an entry for *dir* as the parent directory,
  and that entry counts as a link to *dir*.

- The next two items give the user and group who own the file. The
  group is usually the user's group, but it need not be.

- The next item gives the file size in characters. If the listing was created using the -a option, the total number of disk blocks occupied
  by the listed files is shown at the top; in this case it is 7.

- The next two items give the date and time when the file was last
  modified. If you've used the -u option, the time of last access is
  shown instead; if you've used the -c option, the time of last i-node
  modification is shown instead (see the description of these options
  above).

- The last item gives the file name. A '/' after the file name indicates a
  directory; a '*' indicates an executable file (and corresponds to x in
  the user permissions).

3.2   Classifying Files with `file`

The `file` command attempts to classify a file by examining its first few bytes. The form of the command line is

       `file` [*options*] *file* ...

Types of files recognized by `file` include ASCII text, natural language text,[1] executable binary files, C code, shell scripts, and binary data.

     The System V version of `file` bases its guesses on a list of "magic numbers" recorded in a "magic file". The usual magic file is stored as `/etc/magic`, but you can use a different magic file by applying the `-m` option.

Command-line Options.   The command-line options for `file` are as follows:

`-f` *lfile*	Read a list of files to be classified from the file *lfile*, and classify these files in addition to any in *file* ... .
`-m` *mfile*	Use *mfile* as the magic file instead of the default, `/etc/magic`.
`-c`	Check that the magic file is in the right format.
`-L`	If a file is a symbolic link, test the file that the link refers to rather than the link itself. This option is only available on systems that support symbolic links.

Not all systems support these options.

3.3   Finding Files with `find`

The `find` program searches specified parts of the UNIX file system for files that match a criterion. Be prepared for variations in how this command works on different systems.

     The form of the command line is

       `find` *pathlist criterion*

Here *pathlist* is a list of files and directories (usually just directories). In the simpler case *criterion* is a sequence of primary tests, each indicated by a dash; more generally it is an arbitrary logical combination of tests.

     The *pathlist* specification generates a list of files, formed by appending additional components to the path names in *pathlist* so as to include all files directly or indirectly contained in directories of *pathlist*. Each file in the list is tested against the criterion. The entire criterion is applied to a file before the next file is tested. The tests in a sequence are "and"ed together and

---

1. If the file appears to contain ASCII text, `file` examines its first 512 bytes and tries to guess what language the text is in.

act as filters; if a test fails, the remaining tests are not executed. Certain tests are always satisfied and are executed solely for their side effects. In particular, the -print test has the side effect of sending the path name of the file (relative to the current directory) to standard output.

For example, the command

```
find /usr -name "v*.h" -print
```

sends to standard output a list of all files contained within /usr and its subdirectories whose names start with 'v' and end with '.h'. Each file is shown with its entire relative path name. The list might look like this:

```
/usr/spool/uucppublic/src/vlimit.h
/usr/include/sys/var.h
/usr/include/sys/vt.h
/usr/include/sys/vtoc.h
/usr/include/values.h
/usr/include/varargs.h
```

Without the -print, the files would be found but nothing would be done with their names.[2] Quoting 'v*.h' is essential to ensuring that find, not the shell, interprets the wildcard '*'.

Some BSD UNIX versions of find recognize the simpler form

```
find string
```

This command produces a list of all known files whose names contain *string* as a substring.[3]

3.3.1
Primary Tests
for `find`

The primary tests described below return "true" or "false", depending on the file they are applied to.

Meaning of Numerical Values in Tests.   A numerical value n appearing in a test may be given in one of three ways:

- n by itself indicates exactly the value n.
- $-n$ indicates a value less than n.
- $+n$ indicates a value greater than n.

For example, the test '-size +1000c' is satisfied by files containing more than 1000 characters.

Testing Properties of Files.   The following tests test properties of files:

-name *file* True if the current file matches *file*, with wildcards taken into consideration (see Section 2.11.1). Be sure to quote *file* if it contains any wildcard characters to ensure that the wildcards are interpreted by find rather than by your shell.

-type *c* True if the type of the current file is *c*, where *c* is one of the following:

        f   Ordinary file

---

2. The BSD UNIX version of find assumes -print even if you don't specify it, provided that you don't specify some other action such as exec.

3. The known files are those in a database prepared by the system administrator and typically updated nightly.

      d   Directory
      b   Block device (see Section 2.10)
      c   Character device (see Section 2.10)
      p   Named pipe (see Section 2.13.1)
      l   Symbolic link (see Section 2.8.5)
      s   Socket (see Section 2.13.2)

Most of these letters are the same ones shown by the long listing format of `ls` (see Section 3.1.2). Some of these file types may not be available on your system.

`-links` n True if the current file has n links. For the form and interpretation of n, see the explanation of numerical values at the beginning of this section.

`-perm [-]`p

True if the permissions of the current file (see Section 2.9) are given by the octal number p (see Section 2.9.3). An exact match is required unless p is preceded by '−'. In that case the bits of p must be a subset of the file's permission bits. The '−' enables you to test for the presence of particular bits independently of any others that might be present.

`-user` *uname*

True if the owner of the current file is user *uname*. If *uname* is a number, it is taken as a user number (unless there is a user whose name is that number).

`-group` *gname*

True if the current file belongs to group *gname*. Like *uname*, a numerical *gname* is taken as a group number unless there is a group whose name is that number.

`-size` n
`-size` nc True if the current file is n units long. The units are bytes if c is present and disk storage blocks otherwise. The comparison is with the file size as shown by `ls` (see Section 3.1). For the form and interpretation of n, see the explanation of numerical values at the beginning of this section.

`-atime` n True if the current file has been accessed n days ago.[4] For the form and interpretation of n, see the explanation of numerical values at the beginning of this section.

`-mtime` n True if the current file has been modified n days ago. For the form and interpretation of n, see the explanation of numerical values at the beginning of this section.

`-ctime` n True if the i-node information of the current file (creation time and permissions) has been modified n days ago. For the form and interpretation of n, see the explanation of numerical values at the beginning of this section.

---

4. Find itself accesses directories and therefore affects their access times.

`-newer` *file*

> True if the current file has been modified more recently than a particular file *file*.

`-local`   True if the current file resides on the local system rather than on a remote system. Not all versions of `find` support this test.

`-inum` *n*   True if the current file starts with i-node *n*. This test is useful for locating a file when a diagnostic message identifies it only by its i-node.

Applying Commands to Files.   The following tests produce their results by applying a command to a file:

`-exec` *cmd*

> True if the command *cmd* returns an exit status of 0 (when executed as a child process). The end of *cmd* and its arguments must be marked with a semicolon, escaped or quoted so the shell doesn't interpret it (see Section 2.14.2). Within *cmd* you may use the notation '{}' to designate the path name of the current file.
>
> The **exec** criterion is often used for its side effects rather than for its result. For example, the command

```
find crud -name "*.bak" -type f -exec rm {} \;
```

> removes all files matching '`*.bak`' in the directory `crud` and its subdirectories. Be sure that the '{}' and ';' appear as separate arguments to `find` after all shell quotation has been removed. For example, the following version of the command above won't work:

```
find crud -name "*.bak" -type f -exec "rm {} ;"
```

> The problem is that `find` sees '`rm {} ;`' as a single argument.

`-ok` *cmd*   Like `-exec`, except that the generated command is sent to standard error (normally the terminal) with a question mark after it. If you answer 'y', the command is executed; if you answer anything else, it isn't. An unexecuted command yields "false".

Tests Executed for Their Side Effects.   The following tests are executed only for the sake of their side effects:

`-print`   Always true; as a side effect, sends the path name of the current file (relative to the current directory) to standard output.[5]

`-cpio` *file* True for ordinary files, false for other kinds of files such as directories. As a side effect, appends the current file (if it is ordinary) to *file*, writing it in the format used by `cpio` (see Section 3.18.1). The appended files are blocked as they would be with the `cpio` option `-B`. The output file used here is often a device name. Not all systems support this test.

---

5. Since the side effect takes place before the result is returned, '`\! -print`' sends the file name to standard output and then returns false, disabling any subsequent tests.

-depth   Always true; as a side effect, causes find to process the entries in a directory before processing the directory itself when descending the directory hierarchy. This "test" bypasses an exotic problem that may occur when find is being used to generate file names for 'cpio -pd' and some of the directories involved don't have write permission.[6] The BSD UNIX version of find does not provide this test.

-mount
-xdev   Always true; as a side effect, causes find to restrict the search to the file system containing the current pathname from *pathlist*. This test is called mount in System V, xdev in BSD UNIX.

3.3.2
Logical
Combinations of
Tests

You may form logical combinations of tests in the following ways:

(1) Enclose a combination of tests in parentheses. Because find treats these parentheses as arguments, they must be surrounded by whitespace—and because parentheses are meaningful to the shell, they must be quoted either by writing them as '\(' and '\)' or by enclosing them in a quotation.

(2) Negate a test by preceding it with '!'. Only the files that don't satisfy the test are accepted. As with parentheses, the '!' must be surrounded by whitespace.

(3) Write two tests one after the other. In this case the combination is satisfied only if both individual tests are satisfied ("and"). You may also put '-a' between the tests (with the same effect).

(4) Put -o ("or") between two tests, indicating that the combination is satisfied if either test is individually satisfied. If the first test is satisfied, the second is not performed.

These constructs are listed in order of decreasing precedence, so the combinations are interpreted in the order listed (parentheses first and -o last).

3.3.3
Examples

Here are some examples of find:

- List all files anywhere in /usr or /lib whose names end in '.1':

  ```
  find /usr /lib -name "*.1" -print
  ```

- Copy all files within your own directories that have been modified within the last week to the device /dev/mt0 in cpio format:

  ```
  find $HOME /dev/mt0 -mtime -8 -cpio
  ```

---

6. When cpio creates an implicit intermediate directory during a pass operation, it always gives that directory write permission so that it may insert files into it. When it copies a directory lacking write permission, however, it is unable to insert anything into that directory. The reordering resulting from the -depth option causes cpio to create intermediate directories implicitly rather than explicitly; when the time later comes to copy them explicitly, cpio changes the permission of the target directory, which by this time already exists, to agree with that of the source directory.

- Remove all files within the directories `hold` and `backup` that are larger than ten blocks or have another link somewhere:

```
find hold backup \( -size +10 -o -links +1 \) -exec rm {} \;
```

- List all subdirectories of the directory `$HOME/tmp` that do not belong to you (assuming your user name is `naomi`):

```
find $HOME/tmp \! -user naomi -type d -print
```

3.4   Displaying and Concatenating Files with `cat`

The `cat` command gets its name from the fact that it copies and concatenates files. It has some common applications that don't involve concatenation and that make it one of the most useful UNIX commands.

The general form of the `cat` command line is

```
cat [options] [file] ...
```

The files in *file* ... are concatenated and copied to standard output. The result is a copy of the first file, followed by a copy of the second file, etc. A '–' in place of a file name indicates standard input.

For example, the command

```
cat pebbles boulders
```

copies the contents of file `pebbles` followed by the contents of file `boulders` to standard output, while the command

```
cat pebbles boulders > rocks
```

copies their successive contents into the file `rocks`.

If only one file name appears on the command line, that file is copied to standard output. If no file names appear on the command line, standard input is copied to standard output. These rules lead to the following important special cases:

- To list the contents of *file*, use the command

```
cat file
```

For example,

```
cat snakes
```

displays the contents of the file `snakes` on your terminal.

- To copy one file to another, use the command

```
cat infile > outfile
```

or the command

```
cat < infile > outfile
```

These commands are ordinarily equivalent to

cp *infile* outfile

(see Section 3.7.3).

- To place some text in *file*, type

  cat > *file*

followed by the text and $\boxed{\text{EOF}}$. For short text of just a line or two, that is often faster than using an editor. For example, the input

```
cat > list
echo Listing of file "$1":
cat $1
```
$\boxed{\text{EOF}}$
```
chmod +x list
```

creates a short executable shell script in the file list that lists a file along with its name.

- To append the text of *file$_1$* followed by *file$_2$* to the end of *file$_3$*, type

  cat *file$_1$* *file$_2$* >> *file$_3$*

See Section 2.12 for an explanation of '>>'.

Command-line Options.   These are the command line options for cat:

-s   Don't complain about nonexistent source files.

-u   Don't buffer the output. With this option set, cat reads and writes characters one at a time instead of accumulating input characters in batches and writing an entire batch at once. Buffered output is usually more efficient because it reduces the number of separate output transmissions, but in unusual circumstances it may not give you correct results.[7] Some systems never use buffering when they produce output; they ignore the -u option.

-v   Represent nonprinting characters as sequences of printable ones. The nonprinting characters have ASCII codes less than 32 or greater than 126.

  - The characters from 0 to 31 are shown as '∧*c*' (control-*c*), where *c* has the character's ASCII code plus 64. For example, the character whose ASCII code is 8 (backspace) is represented as '∧H' since H has ASCII code 72.

  - The character 127 (delete) is represented as '∧?'.

---

7. The actual implementation of cat uses the low-level C library routine read to read the input and the library routine setbuf to modify the behavior of read when unbuffered output is requested. We have not been able to construct an example that illustrates the difference between buffered and unbuffered output and uses only standard commands and shell facilities. Kernighan and Pike (reference [B13]) give an example on pages 44–45 showing the difference, but we have not been able to reproduce their results on the systems where we've tried it.

- The characters from 128 to 257 are represented as 'M-*c*' (meta-*c*), where *c* has the character's ASCII code minus 128. For example, the character 140 is represented as 'M-^L' since L has ASCII code 76 and ^L therefore has ASCII code 76 − 64 = 12.

  The exceptions to this rule are tabs, newlines, and form feeds, which are sent unchanged to the output of `cat` (but see the descriptions of the -e and -t options).

-e   Put $ at the end of each line. This option is only valid if the -v option is also present.

-t   Show tabs as ^I. This option is only valid if the -v option is also present.

3.5   Extracting the End of a File with `tail`

You can use the `tail` program to extract the last part of a file. As a special case you can also use it to monitor what is being added to a file. The form of the command line is

    tail [*sign*[*n*][*unit*][f]] [*file*]

`Tail` copies the contents of *file* to standard output, beginning at a position specified by the items preceding *file*. These items, which must be written with no intervening whitespace, are as follows:

sign   '+' or '−'
n   An integer (default is 10)
unit   One of l (lines), b (1024-byte blocks), or c (characters). The default is l.
f   Indicator for continuous monitoring of text added to *file*

The copied portion of the file starts either *n* units from the beginning (if *sign* is '+') or *n* units from the end (if *sign* is '−'). If *sign* and the specifications following it are omitted, all values are defaulted and the last ten lines of the file are copied.

If *file* is omitted, `tail` assumes that its input file is standard input. For example,

    tail -20l lariat

sends the last 20 lines of `lariat` to standard output, while

    tail +200c lariat

sends the contents of `lariat`, beginning with the 201st character, to standard output.

Now suppose that `logfile` is a file used by one or more processes to record their activities. Whenever a process does anything notable, it adds a line to `logfile`. You can see what the processes are doing by issuing the command

    tail -5lf logfile

Tail immediately produces the last five lines of the current contents of logfile; as processes write additional lines to logfile, tail produces those lines. Tail continues to run until you type (Intr) or terminate it in another way.

If you specify -f and omit *file*, tail continues to read from standard input until you interrupt it. However, if standard input is coming from a pipe, tail quits when the process supplying standard input terminates. For instance, suppose you type

```
cat | tail -f
one
two
three
(Ctrl) D
```

When you type (Ctrl)D, the cat process terminates, causing the parent process (the one corresponding to the pipeline) to terminate. That termination in turn causes tail to terminate.

The length of a tail at the end of a file is limited to 4096 characters on many systems.

3.6   Duplicating Input with tee

The tee command provides a way to capture the contents of a pipe in a file without disrupting the flow of information through the pipe (see Section 2.12.1). It gets its name from its similarity to a tee joint in a plumbing installation. The form of the command is:

```
tee [options] [file] ...
```

Tee causes standard input to be copied to standard output and also to the files *file* ... . For example, if you type

```
soundoff | tee transcript | hearken
```

the standard output of soundoff becomes the standard input of hearken and is also recorded in the file transcript. If you specify no files, tee simply copies standard input to standard output.

There are two options for tee:

-i   Ignore interrupts.

-a   Append the output to each file instead of overwriting the file.

3.7   Linking, Moving, and Copying Files with ln, mv, and cp

The commands ln (link), mv (move) and cp (copy) are closely related:

- Linking to a file creates another name for it.

- Moving a file changes one of its names.
- Copying a file replicates its contents under another name.

These commands, unlike most, do not use standard input or standard output by default.

3.7.1
Linking Files with ln

The ln command creates links to one or more existing files. The new links provide additional names for the files. Links are discussed in Section 2.8.5.

The forms of the ln command line are

ln [*options*] *file₁ file₂*
ln [*options*] *file ... dir*

In the first form, a link is created from *file₂* to the file named by *file₁*. If *file₂* already is linked to a file, i.e., is the name of an existing file, the existing link is destroyed when the new one is created. After the new link has been created, both *file₁* and *file₂* are names of the file previously named by *file₁*.

In the second form, a link is created in *dir* to each file in *file ...* . In this case ln creates a link in the directory *dir* for each file, giving that link the same file identifier as the file. As with the first form of ln, an existing link with the same name is destroyed.

For example, suppose mabel and susan are subdirectories of your current directory and mabel contains the two files ron and don. Then the command

ln mabel/* susan

constructs the links susan/ron and susan/don. If either of these names previously existed as links within susan, these old links are destroyed. After ln has executed, mabel/ron and susan/ron refer to the same file, as do mabel/don and susan/don.

When ln creates a link, the target file name has the same set of permissions and the same owner and group as the source file name.

Another way to describe the effect of the command 'ln *file₁ file₂*' is this:

(1)   If *file₂* names an existing file, break the connection between the name *file₂* and the file, i.e., execute the command 'rm *file₂*'.

(2)   Cause *file₂* to be another name for the file named by *file₁*.

Linking does not entail any copying of data and does not destroy any existing links unless they happen to have the same file names as the newly created ones.

You are not allowed to create a link from a directory in one file system to a file in another file system (see Section 2.8.4) unless the link is a symbolic link. You can specify a symbolic link with the -s option if your system supports symbolic links.

By default, ln creates hard links and asks for confirmation whenever it overwrites a link to a file lacking write permission. You can change this behavior with the following two command-line options:

-s   Create symbolic (soft) links rather than hard links. This option is not available on systems that do not support symbolic links.

-f   Don't ask for confirmation even when overwriting a link that lacks write permission.

3.7.2
Moving Files with mv

The mv command moves one or more files from one directory to another. If both directories are in the same file system, mv merely changes their links and does not move any data. If they are not, mv copies the data in the files from the first file system to the second, creates the necessary links in the second file system, and removes the links in the first file system. You can think of moving as a kind of renaming. Moving a file leaves its protection mode and ownership unchanged unless the move is across file systems; in this case the ownership becomes that of the user who executed the mv command.

The forms of the mv command line are

    mv [*options*] *file*$_1$ *file*$_2$
    mv [*options*] *file* ... *dir*

In the first form, a link is created from *file*$_2$ to the file named by *file*$_1$ and the original link from *file*$_1$ is deleted. If *file*$_2$ already was linked to a file, i.e., was a name of an existing file, the existing link is destroyed when the new link is created.[8]

In the second form, each file in *file* ... is moved to *dir*. The move preserves the file identifiers of the files that were moved. For example, suppose mabel and susan are subdirectories of your current directory and mabel contains the two files ron and don. Then the command

    mv mabel/* susan

moves mabel/ron to susan/ron and mabel/don to susan/don. After the move, the mabel directory is empty and the susan directory has the two files don and ron. If either don or ron previously existed in susan, the old version is unlinked (and deleted, unless it had other links).

By default, mv asks for confirmation whenever it overwrites a link to a file lacking write permission. You can change this behavior with the following command-line options:

-i   Ask for confirmation when overwriting any link no matter what its permissions (BSD UNIX only).

-f   Don't ask for confirmation even when overwriting a link that lacks write permission.

3.7.3
Copying Files with cp

The cp command copies one or more files. Unlike ln and mv, cp actually copies data and does not just reshuffle directory entries.

The cp command is not the only way to copy files. The cat program (see Section 3.4) is often an alternative to cp. The cpio program with the -p option (see Section 3.18.1) copies files and directories from one directory to another, reconstructing the original directory structure at the destination.

---

8. This is not the same thing as destroying the file itself, since other links to the file may remain.

The forms of the `cp` command line are:

> `cp` [*options*] *ifile ofile*
> `cp` [*options*] *iname . . . odir*

where *ifile* is an input file, *ofile* is an output file, each *iname* is an input file or directory, and *odir* is an output directory. Input items are called "sources"; output items are called "targets".

- The first form applies when the target is a file. In this case there may be only one source, a file. The input file is copied to the output file.

- The second form applies when the target is a directory.

A copy may be recursive or nonrecursive, although System V versions of `cp` generally support only nonrecursive copying. The `-r` option specifies recursive copying. It affects only the copying of directories.

Nonrecursive Copying.   For a nonrecursive copy, the directory *odir* must already exist and each *iname* must name a file rather than a directory. Each input file is copied to the output directory and given the same base name it had originally. For example, suppose that `/usr/cathy` and `fishes` are both directories, with `/usr/cathy` containing files `trout` and `pike`. Then the command

> `cp /usr/cathy/* fishes`

copies `/usr/cathy/trout` to a file named `fishes/trout` and `/usr/cathy/pike` to a file named `fishes/pike`.

If a target file does not exist, a file of that name is created. If a target file does exist, then the link specified by the target file is removed and a new link is created. The data is then copied from each source file to its corresponding target file. After the copy, the source and target files are independent—a change to one file does not affect the other.

A file created by `cp` assumes the owner, mode, and permissions of the target file if that file existed prior to the copy; otherwise it assumes those of the source file.[9] If a copy operation would destroy an existing link to a file whose `write` permission is turned off, `cp` displays the protection mode of that file (as a three-digit octal number) and asks you to confirm the copy. Typing something that starts with 'y' permits the copy; typing anything else cancels it.

Recursive Copying.   The behavior of a recursive copy depends on whether the output directory *odir* already exists:

- If *odir* does not already exist, the input must consist of a single directory. After creating *odir*, `cp` copies all the files and subdirectories of the input directory to *odir*, thereby making *odir* a clone of the input directory.

- If *odir* already exists, each input file is copied to the output directory as it would be for a nonrecursive copy. Each input directory is reproduced as a subdirectory of the output directory, including both its contained files and contained subdirectories.

---

9. The sticky bit of the target file is not set unless the copying is done by the superuser.

Command-line Options. The BSD UNIX version of the `cp` command has the following command-line options:

-i   Ask interactively for confirmation of each copy.

-p   Preserve the permission modes and modification time of the original file.

-r   Copy subdirectories recursively as described above. Some systems allow -R as an alternative to -r.

3.8   Making Special Files with `mknod`

You can create an ordinary file just by writing to it, but to create other kinds of files you need special commands: `mkdir` for directories and `mknod` for named pipes and device files (see Sections 2.12.1 and 2.10). The `mknod` command is not supported by BSD UNIX; to create the equivalent of a named pipe under BSD UNIX you need to write a C program.[10] The form of the `mknod` command line is

> `mknod` *file option*

where *file* is the name of the file to be constructed and *option* specifies its type as follows:

-p   Named pipe

-b n_1 n_2 Block special file with major number n_1, minor number n_2

-c n_1 n_2 Character special file with major number n_1, minor number n_2

You need superuser privileges to create a block special file or a character special file, but you don't need these privileges to create a named pipe.

3.9   Removing Files

The two commands for removing files are `rm` and `rmdir`. Rm can remove either ordinary files or directories, while `rmdir` can only remove directories. On the other hand, `rmdir` can delete parent directories that become empty as a result of earlier removals, while `rm` can't.

"Removing" a file, whether an ordinary file or a directory, means removing a file name from a directory rather than removing the file itself. If there are other links to the file, those links remain and the file itself remains. A file is deleted only when its last link is removed. Since a directory is a particular kind of file, the same rule applies to directories.

---

10. What you create is a socket pair, using the `socketpair` system request.

**3.9.1
Removing Links
with rm**

The `rm` command removes links to files, either ordinary files or directories. A file is deleted when all its links have been deleted, so removing the only link to a file deletes the file itself.

The form of the `rm` command line is

> `rm [options] file ...`

where each file in *file* ... may include links to directories if the `-r` option is present. By default, `rm` asks you for confirmation if you attempt to remove a link to a file that does not have write permission.[11] The confirmation query indicates the file's permissions as a three-digit octal number (see Section 2.9). You can change this behavior with the `-i` and `-f` options described below.

Rm returns a zero exit code if it succeeds in deleting all the specified links and a nonzero exit code otherwise.

Command-line Options.   These are the command-line options for `rm`:

-i   Ask interactively for confirmation of each removal. A response that starts with 'y' or 'Y' indicates that the file should be removed; any other response indicates that it shouldn't. Rm asks for these confirmations even if standard input is not a terminal.

-r   Remove links to directories recursively, i.e., remove links to the directories and to all files and subdirectories contained in them either directly or indirectly. This option in effect lops off an entire branch of the directory tree. Rm still asks you to confirm the removal of links without write permission, but if standard input is not from the terminal or if you've specified the `-f` option, the query is suppressed. If you reject removal of a link, `rm` won't remove any directory that contains that link either directly or indirectly.

-f   Don't ask for confirmation of removals, even for links that lack write permission. If you specify both `-f` and `-i`, `-f` governs.

Note: You can't remove links from a directory for which you don't have write permission no matter what options you use.

**3.9.2
Removing Links to
Directories
with rmdir**

The `rmdir` command removes links to directories. The form of its command line is

> `rmdir [options] dir ...`

where *dir* ... is a list of directories. For example

> `rmdir denver`

---

11. You may remove a link to a file if you have write permission for the directory containing the link (see Section 2.9). The permissions of the file are irrelevant—the confirmation query is just a precaution.

causes `rmdir` to remove the link to the `denver` subdirectory of the current directory. Unlike `rm -r`, `rmdir` won't remove a link to a directory unless the directory is empty.

Rmdir returns a zero exit code if it succeeds in deleting all the specified links and a nonzero exit code otherwise.

Command-line Options. The command-line options for `rmdir` are as follows:

-p   If removal of a link to a directory causes its parent directory to become empty, remove the link to the parent directory from *its* parent also. `Rmdir` continues to remove links to empty directories, proceeding towards the root, until it finds a directory that isn't empty. `Rmdir` sends a message to standard error announcing each link that it removes and each removal attempt that fails.

-s   Suppress the messages generated by `rmdir`.

Not all systems support these options.

3.9.3
Removing Files with Unusual Names

Once in a while you may accidentally create a file with a name containing characters meaningful to the shell such as '|' and ';' or other troublesome characters such as spaces, dashes, backspaces, and newlines. You can't remove these files with `rm` in the obvious way because you can't type their names on the command line. Sometimes you can remove them by quoting the troublesome characters. For example,

```
rm " "
```

removes a file whose name consists of a single space. A more general method is to type

```
rm -i -- *
```

and select just those files you want to delete. The '--' is needed to handle file names that start with '-', since otherwise those names will be misinterpreted as command-line arguments (see Section 2.14.3).[12] Better yet, use wildcards in combination with legitimate parts of the file name. For instance, to remove a file named a Ctrl H b, you could type

```
rm -i a?b
```

The `-i` in this case is a precaution against unintentionally selecting a different file.

Another method, useful when the file name contains nonprinting characters, is to delete the file by specifying its i-node (see Section 2.8.6). The command '`ls -ib`' lists the files in the current directory, showing all the nonprinting characters in octal notation and indicating the i-node number for each one. If the file you want to delete has i-node number n, you can then delete it using the `find` command (see Section 3.3) as follows:

```
find . -inum n -exec rm {} \;
```

---

12. Some older versions of `rm` use '-' to end the arguments.

3.10   Comparing Files

The two principal programs for comparing files are `cmp` and `diff`. `Cmp` quickly determines if files differ but doesn't give you much information about the difference; `diff`, on the other hand, produces a list of instructions for transforming one file into another and tries to make that list as short as possible.

Some other file comparison programs, not discussed here, are `bdiff`, which is designed to compare very big files, and `diff3`, which performs a three-way comparison.

3.10.1
Comparing Files with `cmp`

The `cmp` command compares two files. The form of the `cmp` command line is

> `cmp` [*options*] *file*$_1$ *file*$_2$

The return code is 0 if the files match, 1 if they differ, and 2 if one or both files could not be accessed. By default `cmp` stops at the first difference and shows the line number and character position of that difference; the `-l` option causes `cmp` to look for all differences. `Cmp` is most useful for determining if two files differ when you don't care what the difference is. It is also useful for comparing binary files.

Command-line Options.   The following command-line options are available:

-l   Show the byte number and the differing characters (as octal numbers) for all differences. This option is nearly useless for text files with varying line lengths.

-s   Show nothing. This option is useful when you're interested only in the exit status.

3.10.2
Finding Differences between Files with `diff`

The `diff` command analyzes the differences between two files such as different versions of the same document. The form of the `diff` command line is

> `diff` [*options*] *file*$_1$ *file*$_2$

The `diff` command computes a list of instructions for transforming *file*$_1$ to *file*$_2$ and sends that list to standard output. If *file*$_1$ is given as '-', the first file is taken to be standard input. The return code is 0 if the files match, 1 if they differ, and 2 if the differences could not be computed. Although `diff` is cleverly programmed to minimize the list of differences, it will break down if the differences are too complex.

Calling `diff` without Options.   When called without options, `diff` generates a reversible list of instructions for transforming *file*$_1$ to *file*$_2$. A pair of numbers indicates a range of lines. When the range consists of a single line, the pair is replaced by a single number. The kinds of instructions are the following:

n_1, n_2 d n_3

   Delete lines n_1 through n_2 of *file*$_1$.

n_1 a n_3, n_4

   Append lines n_3 through n_4 of *file*$_2$ after line n_1 of *file*$_1$.

n_1, n_2 c n_3, n_4

   Replace (change) lines n_1 through n_2 of *file*$_1$ with lines n_3 through n_4 of *file*$_2$.

The output shows all lines involved in the transformation, with '<' indicating lines deleted from *file*$_1$ and '>' indicating lines taken from the original *file*$_2$. Sample output is shown below.

Calling `diff` **with the** `-e` **Option.**   When called with the `-e` option, `diff` generates a set of instructions for `ed` to perform the transformation (see Section 6.4). If you execute the command

```
diff -e file1 file2 > df
```

then you can later reproduce `file2` with the command

```
(cat df; echo '1,$p') | ed -s file1
```

The instructions work from the end of the file back to the beginning so that early changes won't affect the line numbers appearing in later changes.

 Note: If any of the appended lines consist of a single dot, the editing script won't work.

Calling `diff` **with the** `-f` **Option.**   When called with the `-f` option, `diff` generates a list of editing instructions like those generated with `-e` but in forward rather than reverse order. This list is easier to read but generally won't work as an edit script because the instructions early in the list change the line numbers required for later instructions. The actual list doesn't account for this effect.

Other Command-line Options.   The `diff` command has two other options besides the `-e` and `-f` options described above:

`-b`

   When comparing input lines, ignore trailing whitespace and treat sequences of whitespace characters as equivalent to a single blank.

`-h`

   Do a fast but not as effective ("half-hearted") job. This option works only when the changed areas are short and well-separated from each other, but it enables `diff` to process longer files than it otherwise could. The `-h` option conflicts with `-e` and `-f`.

Sample Output.   The following table shows the output produced by `diff` when called in several different ways: with no options, with the `-e` option, and with the `-f` option. The letters d, a, and c indicate `delete`, `append`, and `change` respectively.

File 1	File 2	diff	diff -e	diff -f
one	one	2,4c2,3	8a	c2 4
two	TWO	< two	nine	TWO
three	THREE	< three		THREE
four	five	< four	.	.
five	eight	---	6,7d	d6 7
six	nine	> TWO	2,4c	a8
seven		> THREE	TWO	nine
eight		6,7d4	THREE	
		< six	.	.
		< seven		
		8a6,7		
		> nine		
		>		

This list of instructions can be changed to one that transforms *file₂* to *file₁* by replacing each 'a' with 'd', each 'd' with 'a', and then interchanging the numbers before each instruction letter with those after each instruction letter. For the example above of `diff` without options, the reversed instructions (omitting the text) would be

```
2,3c20A,4
4a6,7
6,7d9
```

The purpose of the mysterious second number on 'd' is to make this reversal possible.

Maintaining Versions of Documents with `diff` **and** ed.   You can use `diff` and `ed` in combination to keep different versions of a document in a condensed form. The method requires that you keep the original version, the latest version, and a set of edit scripts generated by `diff`. To recreate a previous version, you apply the appropriate sequence of scripts to the original version. You can create a Bourne shell script—call it `update`—for this purpose. The text of `update` is

```
(shift; cat $*; echo '1,$p') | ed - $1
```

If `screed` is an original document and `screed.u2`, `screed.u3`, and `screed.u4` are three update scripts, you can reconstruct the fourth version with the command line

```
update screed screed.u2 screed.u3 screed.u4 > screed4
```

3.11   Touching a File with `touch`

The `touch` command touches a file, updating its access and modification times. If the file does not exist, it is created unless you specify otherwise.

The System V version of touch enables you to set the access and modification times to whatever time you wish. Touching a file is an easy way to create an empty file.

The form of the touch command line is

touch [*options*] [*time*]

The time, recognized only under System V, has the form *mmddhhmm*[*yy*], where *mm* is the month, *dd* is the day, *hh* is the hour, *mm* is the minute, and *yy* is the year. If the time is not specified, it defaults to the current time.

Under System V you may choose to update only the access time or only the modification time by using the -a or -m option. Specifing neither of these options is equivalent to specifying both of them and causes both times to be updated.

**3.11.1
Command-line
Options**

These are the command-line options for touch:

-a   Update the access time only (System V only).

-c   Don't create the file if it doesn't already exist.

-f   Force the touch no matter what the file permissions (BSD UNIX only).

-m   Update the modification time only (System V only).

3.12   Controlling File Access and Ownership

Access to a file is controlled by its permissions (see Section 2.9). You can use the chmod command to change file permissions and the chown and chgrp commands to change the owner or group of a file.

**3.12.1
Setting Access
Permissions
with chmod**

You can change the permissions of a file with the chmod command. For this command to work, you need write access to the directories containing the files.

The form of the chmod ("change mode") command line is

chmod *modespecs file* ...

where each *file* is a file name and *modespecs* is either

- a comma-separated list of permission changes or
- an octal number of up to four digits.

Each permission change has three parts: one or more "who" letters, an operator, and one or more permission letters. These are the "who" letters:

u   Permission for the file's user
g   Permission for the file's group
o   Permission for others, i.e., the rest of the world
a   Permission for everyone (equivalent to ugo)

These are the operators:

+   Add these permissions
−   Take away these permissions
=   Set exactly these permissions, removing any others for the indicated
    "who" letters

These are the permissions:

r   Read
w   Write
x   Execute
s   Set user or group id
t   Sticky bit
l   Lock during access (System V only)

Each change modifies the permissions of the files in *file* . . . as indicated.
If you omit the "who" letters, then a is assumed but the permissions are
modified by your umask (see Section 2.9.4).

Specifying Permissions in Octal.   The octal number notation (see Section 2.15) specifies the entire set of permissions at once.   Section 2.9.3
describes how a set of permissions is represented as an octal number.

Restrictions.   The following restrictions apply to chmod:

• Only the owner of a file or the superuser may change a file's permissions.
• Only the superuser may change the sticky bit.
• You may only turn on the s bit for a group if your own group is
  the same as that of the file and group execution of the file is permitted. Thus the permission change g=xs is legal (assuming your group
  agrees with that of the file) but the permission change g=x is not.
• The s bit is not meaningful for o.
• The t bit is not meaningful for g or o.

Command-line Options.   The BSD UNIX version of chmod recognizes the
following command-line options preceding *modespecs*:

−f   Don't complain if the permissions cannot be changed.

−R   If an indicated file is a directory, descend through it recursively
            and change the permissions of all files encountered.

Examples.   Here are some examples of how to use chmod:

• The command

        chmod ug+wx,o+x erato

  grants write and execute permissions for file **erato** to the owner and
  group of **erato** and grants execute permission to everyone else.

• Suppose that your umask has the value 0027. Then the command

        chmod +x polyhymnia

grants execute permission for `polyhymnia` to you and those in your group but not to others, since the umask removes all permissions for others.

- The command

    ```
    chmod o=wx urania
    ```

    sets the permissions of `urania` for others to "write" and "execute". The u and g permissions remain the same.

3.12.2 Reducing Default File Permissions with umask

The `umask` command enables you to set or examine your umask value (see Section 2.9.4). The `umask` command has the form:

```
umask [n]
```

where n is the three-digit octal number specifying the permissions to be denied. If you omit n, `umask` shows you your current umask value. Once set, your umask value remains in effect for the duration of your shell execution or until you change it again.

3.12.3 Setting Ownership with chown and chgrp

The `chown` and `chgrp` commands enable you to transfer ownership and group ownership of a set of files and directories to someone else. The forms of the command line for these commands are

```
chown owner file ...
chgrp group file ...
```

where *file* ... is a list of the files and directories whose ownerships you wish to change. An example of the `chown` command is

```
chown genghis pillagings
```

which makes `genghis` the owner of `pillagings`. An example of the `chgrp` command is

```
chgrp ducks pond/*
```

which sets the group of all files in the `pond` directory to `ducks`.

You may change the ownership (individual or group) of a file only if you own it or are the superuser. Once you've changed the ownership of a file, you can't change it back (unless you're the superuser) since you no longer own it.[13]

The BSD UNIX version of `chown` won't allow you to change ownership of a file unless you're the superuser. The BSD UNIX version of `chgrp` won't allow you to change the group of a file even if you own it unless you also belong to *group*.

3.13 Analyzing Files with od

The `od` command sends a dump of a file to standard output. The dump displays the bytes of the file in one or more selected formats. The let-

---

13. The new owner can give it back to you, however.

ters 'od' stand for "octal dump", although you can use od for decimal or hexadecimal dumps as well. The form of the command line is

od [*options*] [*file*] [*offset*]

If *options* is omitted, od assumes –o and you get an octal dump. If *file* is omitted, od dumps standard input. The *offset* argument specifies where in the file the dump begins, in a manner described below; if you omit it, the dump begins at the beginning of the file.

The options specify the formats of the output. You may get a dump in several formats at once, and you may dump by words (pairs of bytes) as well as by single bytes. The options are as follows:

-b   Interpret each byte as an octal number.

-o   Interpret each word as an octal number.

-c   Interpret each byte as an ASCII character, using the C notations \c and \ddd for nonprinting characters, e.g., newline as \n and the octal character 274 as \274.

-d   Interpret each word as a signed decimal number.

-x   Interpret each word as a hexadecimal number.

The BSD UNIX version of od provides several additional options.

The dump begins at the byte indicated by *offset*, which has the form

[+] *n* [.] [b]

For the simplest form of *offset* in which only the number *n* present, the dump starts at byte *n* of the file, and *n* is interpreted in octal. A '.' indicates that *n* is given in decimal rather than octal; a 'b' indicates that the offset is measured in 512-byte blocks, not single bytes. The '+' has no special meaning, but you must supply it if you omit *file* so that od knows what follows is an offset rather than a file name.

For example, you might dump the short file wabbit with

od -xc wabbit

This command produces the following dump in hexadecimal and characters:

0000000	6854	7461	4020	255e	5c2a	2002	6177	6262
	T h	a t	@	^	*	\ 002	w	a b	b
0000020	7469	0a21						
	i t	! \n						
0000024								

The numbers in the first column are byte offsets in octal. Note the treatment of the 002 (\002) and the newline (\n). The four-digit octal numbers have the characters in reverse order as a result of how bytes are stored in computer words; some computers have the characters in forward order.

**3.13.1
Pagers**

A *pager* is a program for viewing the output of a command at a terminal, one screenful at a time, thereby solving the problem of text flying by on the screen faster than you can read it. For example, you can use the combination 'ls | pg' to view the results of ls with the pg pager.

We describe **pg** is in terms of viewing files, since **pg** works the same way on standard input as it does on a file that already exists. You can also view a file using an editor—in fact, a full-screen editor such as **vi** or **emacs** (see Chapter 6) provides at least as many conveniences as does a pager. If you edit in read-only mode, you don't need to worry about modifying the file by accident. However, you generally can't use an editor to view standard input; an editor expects its input to contain editing commands, not the text to be edited.

3.13.2
Viewing Files
with pg

The **pg** command enables you to examine one or more files at your terminal a screenful at a time. It is not included in BSD UNIX. Unlike more primitive pagers, **pg** allows you to move backwards as well as forwards through a file. The form of the **pg** command line is

> **pg** [*options*] [*file*] . . .

where the *files* are shown in sequence. The file name '-' designates standard input; if you omit the *files*, **pg** assumes that standard input is what you intend.

To advance through a file one page at a time, press (Enter) after you've examined each page. When you advance past the end of a file, **pg** automatically starts the next file or exits if there are no more files. You can use the commands described below to move around the file in a different order, to examine a later file in the sequence, or to return to a previous file. You must end each command with (Enter) unless you've specified the **-n** option on the command line.

Commands.   The following command lists the **pg** commands:

h   Display a help list containing an abbreviated summary of the **pg** commands.

The commands below enable you to move around the file. The variable *n* can be a signed or unsigned integer. An unsigned integer indicates a specific location or value, a negative integer indicates a backward motion, and a positive integer indicates a forward motion. You may abbreviate '+1' as '+' and '-1' as '-'. The default is '+1'.

[*n*] (SPACE)
[*n*] (Enter)   Display the *n*th page.

[*n*]d
[*n*] (Ctrl) D   Scroll down by half a page, or up by half a page if the count is negative. Because **pg** ignores the numeric value of *n*, '-' is the only count useful with this command.

$ Display the last page of the file.

[*k*]/*pat*/   Search forward for the pattern *pat*, where *pat* follows the rules for regular expressions given in Section 2.16 and *k* is an unsigned integer. This command and the next one *must* be ended by (Enter) even if you've specified the **-n** option described below.

[*k*]^*pat*^
[*k*]?*pat*?   Search backwards for the pattern *pat*, using the same rules that apply to /*pat*/. Here *k* is an unsigned integer.

The following commands redisplay the current page and enable you to change the page size:

Ctrl L
.

Redisplay the current page. This command is useful when a transmission error has scrambled your screen.

[*k*]w

Move forward one page (window) and set the page size to *k*. If you don't specify *k*, the effect is the same as typing Enter.

The following commands enable you to move among the files in the file list on the command line. The default for *k* is 1.

[*k*]n

Examine the *k*th next file.

[*k*]p

Examine the *k*th previous file.

The following commands relate to quitting, saving the file being examined, and executing commands in a subshell.

q
Q

Quit the program.

s *file*

Save the file now being examined in *file*. This command is useful primarily when you're examining standard input.

! *cmd*

Execute *cmd* in a subshell. Pg uses the subshell specified in the SHELL environment variable, or the Bourne shell sh if SHELL doesn't have a value.

Command-line Options. The following options enable you to start examining files at a place other than the first line. They affect only the first file that you display. Thereafter, all files are displayed starting with the first line.

+*n*

Start examining the file at line *n*.

+/*pat*/

Start examining the file at the line containing *pat*, using the same rules as for the /*pat*/ command.

The following options affect how files are displayed:

-*n*

Use *n* as the page size, i.e., the number of lines by which the file is advanced when you move down by one page. The default for the page size is the screen size for your terminal, less one line for messages.

-c

Clear the screen before displaying each page instead of simply sending the next set of lines to the terminal.

-e

Don't pause at the end of examining a file, but go on immediately to the next one (if it exists).

-f

Don't split lines longer than the screen width. This option is useful if the file contains control characters that produce effects such as underlining. These control characters can cause pg to think the line is longer than it really is.

The following options pertain to messages and prompts.

-p *str*

Use *str* as the command prompt. You may include '%d' in *str*; it is replaced by the page number when the prompt is displayed.

-s	Show messages in inverse video or the equivalent.
-n	Don't wait for (Enter) at the end of a command.

**3.13.3
Other Pagers**

Berkeley-derived systems usually provide a pager called more. It has a few features that pg doesn't have, but early versions of more don't enable you to move backwards through a file. Typing a space moves you to the next screen of text; typing 'h' gives you a list of all the more commands.

An excellent pager called less is available as public-domain software. We don't describe it further here because it's easy enough to learn how to use it from the help screens, which you can call up by typing h. It resembles pg but has some useful extra features; some of its commands have different names than the corresponding pg commands. You can obtain less electronically from the OSUCIS archive (reference [U3]) or from other sources.

3.14   Printing Files

The following commands relate to printing files:

- The System V command lp requests that files be sent to a printer. The corresponding BSD UNIX command is lpr.
- The System V command lpstat provides status information about printers and printer requests. The corresponding BSD UNIX command is lpq.
- The System V command cancel cancels a print request. The corresponding BSD UNIX command is lprm.
- The pr command formats a file for printing.

A print request may include multiple files. Each request is assigned a request id that you can use when inquiring about the status of the request or cancelling it.

On a system having several equivalent printers, such printers are usually grouped into a named class of printers. It's usually better to send a request to a class of printers than to a specific printer, since you'll get the results sooner when some printers in the class are available but others are busy.

**3.14.1
Printing Files
under System V
with lp**

The lp command causes a set of files to be queued for printing. The files specified in a single call on lp are treated as a single request. When you issue the request, lp returns a request id that you can later use to refer to the request. The -m and -w options cause a notice to be sent to you when the request has been completed.

The form of the lp command line is

    lp [*options*] [*file*] ...

where each *file* is a file to be printed. Some versions of lp allow options and files to be intermixed. If you omit the files, standard input is printed;

using `lp` at the end of a pipeline is the usual way of printing the output of a command. If '-' appears as a file, the contents of standard input are transcribed and printed.

You can use the '-d' option to specify a particular printer or class of printers. Without that option, `lp` takes the destination from the `LPDEST` environment variable if it exists or from a system default if it doesn't. The destination may be either a specific printer or a class of printers.

By default, `lp` does not make copies of files you ask to have printed. Any changes that you make to those files between the time you issue the request and the time the files are printed appear in the printed version. The -c option forces `lp` to make its own copy of a file to be printed.

Command-line Options.   The following options affect what is actually printed.

-n *n*   Make *n* copies of the output. By default, one copy is printed.

-t *title*   Put *title* on the banner page of the output (if there is a banner page). Normally you should enclose *title* in quotes as in the command

       `lp -t "Dining Out in Antarctica" penguins`

-o *printopt*

      Specify a printer option. The names and effects of printer options available to you depend on your system. A typical option for a dot matrix printer might specify letter-quality or draft-quality output. You may include more than one -o option; you must specify '-o' for each one.

The following options affect how a print request is handled:

-c   Make copies of the files when the command is executed. With this option specified, changes to a file between the time you issue the print request and the time it is printed have no effect on the printed output. By default, no copies are made.

-d *dest*   Send the job to the specific printer or class of printers name by *dest*. If you send a job to a class of printers, it is printed by the first available printer in the class.

The following options affect the information produced by a print request:

-s   Suppress messages issued by `lp` itself.

-m   Send a mail message to the requestor when the request has been completed.

-w   Write a message to the requestor's terminal when all files in a request have been printed. If the requestor isn't logged in, a mail message is sent instead.

**3.14.2
Printing Files
under BSD UNIX
with `lpr`**

Under BSD UNIX, the command for sending files to a printer is `lpr`. To examine the printer queue, use `lpq`; to remove a job from the queue, use `lprm`.

The form of the `lpr` command line is

     `lpr` [options] [*file*] . . .

where the *files* are the files to be printed. Standard input is printed if you don't specify any files, so `lpr` at the end of a pipeline prints the output of the preceding programs in the pipeline. The options are described below.

Filtering Options. By default, files to be printed are sent to the printer without interpretation. The following options specify filtering to be applied to each file before it is printed:

`-i` [*n*]	Indent the output by *n* columns. If you don't specify *n*, `lpr` uses 8 as the default.
`-f`	Interpret the first character of each line according to the Fortran conventions for carriage control.
`-l`	Print control characters, suppress page breaks.
`-p`	Pass the files through `pr` (see Section 3.14.5).

The following two options are meaningful only if you specify `-p`:

`-T` *text*	Use *text* as the title passed to `pr`.
`-w` *n*	Pass *n* to `pr` as the page width.

In addition to the options listed above, `lpr` usually has additional system-dependent options for filtering the output of specific programs such as TeX and `troff`.

Job Control Options. The following options enable you to control the printer used for the job, the number of copies printed, and the treatment of the files to be printed. By default, `lpr` makes its own copy of each file to be printed and saves the copy in a spooling directory until it can be printed, so any changes to the file after `lpr` has received it do not affect the printed copy.

`-P` *printer*	Print the job on the printer named *printer*.
`#n` *text*	Print *n* copies.
`-s`	Use symbolic links for the files to be printed. This option saves storage space, but implies that changes made to the file before it is printed affect the printed copy. If you specify this option, take care not to remove a file before it is printed.
`-r`	Remove the file after printing it.
`-m`	Send a mail message to the requestor when all the files in the request have been printed.

Header Page. A header page, called the "burst page" in BSD UNIX documents, precedes each print job and contains identifying information for the job. The following options enable you to change the information on the header page or suppress it altogether.

`-J` *text*	Use *text* as the job name on the header page.

-C *text*   Use *text* as the system name on the header page.

-h   Suppress the header page.

3.14.3
Displaying Printer
Status with lpstat

The lpstat command displays the status of print requests. It also displays information about the printers attached to your system and what they are doing. The BSD UNIX version of this command is lpq.

The form of the lpstat command line is

    lpstat [*options*]

If you omit the options, you'll get the status of your own print requests.

Several options accept a list of items as an argument. You may provide this list either by separating the items by commas with no spaces after the commas or by enclosing the list in quotes and separating the items by spaces. If you omit an optional list, lpstat assumes all applicable items. For instance, the command 'lpstat -o' produces a list of all pending print requests.

Command-line Options.   The following options produce information about the status of print requests.

-o [*list*]   Show the status of each output request in *list*. The request id's are those you receive from lp.

-u [*ulist*] Show the status of each output request for each user in *ulist*. If you don't specify *ulist*, you get the same result as with -o.

-t   Show all status information.

The following options produce information about the status of the printers and the print scheduler.

-p [*list*]   Show the status of each printer in *list*.

-a [*list*]   Show the acceptance status of each printer or printer class in *list*. A printer may be unable to accept requests either because it isn't available or because there isn't enough file space to hold any more print requests.

-s   Show a summary of information about the printers attached to your system. The summary includes the system default destination, the class names and printer names known to your system, and the device associated with each printer.

-r   Show the status of the scheduler that handles print requests.

The -t option described above also shows information about printers and classes.

The following options produce information about the printers themselves.

-d   Show the name of the default printer.

-c [*list*]   Show the names of the printer classes and their members.

-v [*list*]   Show the path names of the devices associated with the printers in *list*.

3.14.4
Cancelling Printer
Requests with
cancel

The `cancel` command enables you to cancel an outstanding print request. Unless you have superuser privileges, you cannot cancel a print request issued by another user. The BSD UNIX version of this command is `lprm`.

The form of the `cancel` command line is

        cancel [*id*] ... [*printer*] ...

Here each *id* identifies a printer request and each *printer* identifies a particular printer. The printer request id's are those announced by `lp`. You can also see the id's of your pending printer requests by using `lpstat`. Cancelling a printer cancels the request that is currently printing on that printer (assuming it's one of yours).

3.14.5
Formatting Files
for Printing
with pr

The `pr` command formats files for printing on a line printer. Although `pr` behaves like a filter such as `cut` or `sed` and is not directly related to the other programs discussed above, it is rarely useful for any other purpose—that's why we discuss it here rather than in Chapter 8. It works best when the destination printer has a single fixed-width font; for other kinds of printers, the output that it produces is likely to be unreadable.

The form of the `pr` command line is

        pr [*options*] [*file*] ...

If you don't specify any files, `pr` formats standard input. It sends its results to standard output, which is usually piped to `lp`. The `pr` program, in violation of the usual conventions for command-line syntax, does not allow any space between the name of an option and its arguments.

Output consists of a sequence of pages. By default, each page contains 66 lines, but you can change the page length with the `-l` option. Each page starts with a five-line header and ends with a five-line trailer, unless the page length is 10 or less or you inhibit the header and trailer with the `-t` option. The header and trailer lines are counted as part of the page length. The header consists of two blank lines, a line of text, and two more blank lines; the trailer consists of five blank lines. The default header text contains the page number, the date and time, and the name of the file; you can replace the file name by other text with the `-h` option.

You can produce either single-column or multicolumn output. For single-column output, `lp` allows a line to have any length. For multicolumn output, it assumes a fixed total line width. That width is divided by the number of columns to obtain the width of a single column, allowing for at least one space between columns. Lines exceeding this width are truncated unless you specify the `-s` option. The default total line width is 72 characters, but you can change it with the `-w` option.

Multicolumn output has three variations:

- If you specify the `-m` option and provide more than one input file, each input file appears in its own column.

- If you specify the `-n` option but not the `-a` option, the input text is arranged vertically into *n* columns. Successive lines of text on a page are placed in the first column until it is filled, then in the second column, and so forth.

- If you specify both the -*n* option and the -a option, the input text is arranged horizontally across the page into *n* columns. Successive lines of text on a page are placed into the columns of the first row, then into the columns of the second row, and so forth.

Command-line Options.   The following options determine the page dimensions.

-l *n*   Set the page length to *n* lines. The default is 66 lines (which is also what you get if you set *n* to 0). If the page length is 10 or less, the header and trailer lines are omitted.

-w *n*   Set the line width to *n* characters. The default line width is 72 characters. This option does not affect single-column output.

-o *n*   Offset each line by *n* spaces so as to produce a left margin *n* spaces wide. The offset is not counted as part of the line width.

The following options define the layout of multicolumn output.

-*n*   Format the output using *n* columns, where *n* is an integer. This option conflicts with the -m option.

-a   Format columns across the page, with successive input lines filling an output line before proceeding to the next output line. This option conflicts with the -m option.

-m   Merge and format files, one file per column. This option conflicts with the -*n* and -a options.

-s [*c*]   Use *c* as the separator character between columns, i.e., place a single *c* between adjacent columns. The default for *c* is ⟨tab⟩. If you specify this option, lines within columns are *not* truncated.

The following options affect the header and trailer areas.

-h *text*   Use *text* as the page header text instead of the file name. The date, time, and page number still appear.

-t   Don't set aside space for top and bottom margins, i.e., omit the header and trailer. This option nullifies the -h option. If the page length is less than 10, the header and trailer are omitted in any case.

The following options affect the treatment of tabs and of consecutive spaces.

-e[*c*][*k*]   Replace each tab character in the input with spaces, assuming tab stops at positions 1, $k + 1$, $2 \times k + 1$, etc. If *c* is specified, it is taken as the tab character. (The character *c* must not be a digit.) If *k* is omitted or specified as zero, a default tab spacing of 8 is assumed.

-i[*c*][*k*]   Replace consecutive spaces with tabs wherever possible, assuming tab stops at positions 1, $k + 1$, $2 \times k + 1$, etc. If *c* is specified, it is taken as the tab character. (The character *c* must not be a digit.) If *k* is omitted or specified as zero, a default tab spacing of 8 is assumed.

The following options produce various other effects on the output.

+*n*   Start formatted output at page *n*. **Note:** This option does not follow the standard rules for options since it does not start with '-'.

-d   Format the output with double spacing.

-n[*c*][*k*]   Provide *k*-digit line numbers followed by the character *c*. In the case of multicolumn output, the line numbers appear on each line, not in each column, and are counted as part of the line width. The default for *c* is a tab; the default for *k* is 5. For example, you could get two-column output of a file, with line numbering corresponding to the input lines, with the command

```
pr -t -n file | pr +2
```

-f   End pages with formfeeds rather than linefeeds. If you specify this option, all trailing empty lines on a page, including the trailer, are deleted.

The following options affect your interaction with `pr`.

-p   Pause before starting each page.

-r   Don't issue messages about files that can't be opened.

3.15   Operations on Directories

In this section we describe a number of commands for operating on directories. The `rm`, `rmdir`, and `ls` commands, which also operate on directories, are described in Sections 3.9.1 and 3.1.

3.15.1
Changing
Directories with `cd`

The `cd` command changes your current directory. The form of the command line is

```
cd [dir]
```

where *dir* is the path name of your new current directory (see Section 2.8.2). Your new current directory is determined as follows:

(1)   If *dir* is omitted, it is taken to be your home directory. Typing `cd` by itself is therefore a fast way to get back to your home directory.

(2)   Otherwise, if *dir* starts with '/' (the root directory), `cd` interprets *dir* as an absolute path name.

(3)   Otherwise, if *dir* exists in your current directory, it is taken as a relative path name.

(4)   Otherwise, *dir* is taken to be relative to the first feasible path in the environment variable CDPATH (see p. 168). In other words, suppose that $p_1, p_2, \ldots, p_n$ are the paths listed in CDPATH. Then `cd` tries

each of the paths p_1/dir, p_2/dir, ..., p_n/dir until it finds one that designates a valid directory. It then switches to that directory.

Cd uses neither standard input nor standard output, but it does send error messages to standard error. Because cd wouldn't work properly if it were called as an ordinary program (the effect of the cd call would be lost when its subprocess terminated), cd is an intrinsic command of every shell.

**3.15.2
Showing the
Working Directory
with pwd**

The pwd command sends the full path name of your current (working) directory to standard output. For instance, if your user name is sissela and your current directory is the subdirectory darts of your home directory, the command

    pwd

produces the output

    /usr/sissela/darts

(assuming that your home directory is /usr/sissela).

**3.15.3
Creating a Directory
with mkdir**

The mkdir command creates one or more new directories. The form of the command is

    mkdir [*options*] *dir* ...

Here each *dir* is the absolute pathname of a directory you want to create. Each newly created directory has two entries: '.' for the directory itself and '..' for its parent directory. The permissions of the directory are set to 777 as modified by the current umask value (see Section 3.12.2), although you can specify different permissions with the -m option. The owner and group of each new directory are set to those of the process under whose auspices the directory was created. Creation of a directory, like creation of a file, requires write permission in the parent directory.

Command-line Options.   The following command-line options apply to mkdir:

-m *n*   Set the permissions of each created directory to *n*.

-p   If a pathname lacks any components, make the necessary intermediate directories. For instance, suppose that /usr/yorick has no subdirectories and user yorick issues the command

               mkdir -p $HOME/gravity/tools

            Then mkdir creates an intermediate directory gravity with the directory tools as an initial entry.

Not all systems recognize these options.

**3.15.4
Comparing
Directories with
dircmp**

The dircmp command compares two directories, sending the results of the comparison to standard output. Not all systems support this command. The form of the command line is

    dircmp [*options*] *dir*$_1$ *dir*$_2$

where *dir*$_1$ and *dir*$_2$ are the directories to be compared. The output includes a list of files that exist in one directory but not in the other and also, by default, a list of files that exist in both directories but differ in their contents. The options for `dircmp` are as follows:

`-d`	Compare the contents of corresponding files and output a list of differences (if there are any).
`-s`	Suppress all messages pertaining to identical files.
`-wn`	Set the width of the output line to *n* characters. The default width is 72 characters.

3.16   Counting Words, Lines, or Characters with `wc`

The `wc` command counts the number of characters, words, or lines in a file or a set of files. A word is considered to be a (nonempty) sequence of characters delimited by whitespace.

The form of the `wc` command line is

    `wc` [*options*] [*file*] . . .

The options are `-c` for characters, `-w` for words, and `-l` for lines, with `-cwl` as the default.

- If no files are specified, `wc` counts items in standard input and sends a list of counts (on a single line) to standard output in the order (lines, words, characters).

- If files are specified, the counts for each file appear on a single line together with the name of the file.

The `wc` command is often useful in conjunction with other commands as a way of counting items in a list. For example, you can display the number of currently logged-in users with the command

    `who | wc -l`

3.17   Data Compression

You can reduce the space occupied by a file by storing the file in compressed form. Data compression programs come in pairs, one for compressing and one for uncompressing. Each pair is associated with a particular compression method. We discuss two of these pairs: `pack–unpack` and `compress–uncompress`. Data compression programs are often used in conjunction with archiving programs (see Section 3.18) since file archives tend to be large.

3.17.1
Compression
with pack

The pack program compresses a set of files by packing them using Huffman coding; the unpack and pcat programs undo the compression. When pack packs a file named *file*, it renames the file to '*file*.z'.

Calling pack.   The form of the command line for pack is

> pack [*options*] *file* . . .

where *file* . . . is a list of files to be packed. Each listed file is replaced by its packed version *file*.z. If a file would not be shortened by packing it is left unchanged. You can force packing in any case by specifying the -f option.

There are two command-line options for pack:

-        Send a report on the encoding to standard output. Additional occurrences of '-' in place of a file name toggle the reporting.

-f   Force packing of a file even if nothing is gained.

Calling unpack.   The form of the unpack command line is

> unpack *file* . . .

where *file* . . . is a list of files to be unpacked. Each file is replaced by its unpacked version. A file to be unpacked must have a name of the form '*file*.z', although you may specify it in the file list either as '*file*' or as '*file*.z'. The unpacked file is renamed to '*file*'.

Calling pcat.   The pcat command enables you to retrieve the unpacked form of one or more packed files without modifying the files. The form of the pcat command line is

> pcat *file* . . .

It unpacks the specified files, concatenates the unpacked forms, and sends the result to standard output.

3.17.2
Compression
with compress

The compress program compresses a set of files using the Lempel-Ziv compression method; the uncompress and zcat programs undo the compression. When compress compresses a file named *file*, it renames the file to '*file*.Z'.

Calling compress.   The form of the command line for compress is

> compress [*options*] [*file*] . . .

where *file* . . . is a list of files to be compressed. Each listed file is replaced by its compressed version *file*.Z. If a file would not be shortened by compression, it is left unchanged. You can force compression in any case by specifying the -f option. If no files are given, standard input is compressed to standard output.

These are the command-line options for compress:

-c   Write the compressed files to standard output, leaving the original files unchanged.

-v   Show the percentage of reduction for each file compressed.

-f   Force compression of a file even if nothing is gained.

-b *n*   Use *n* bits in the compression algorithm. Higher values of *n* slow down the compression but produce better results. The range for *n* is 9–16, with 16 being the default. Values of *n* above 12 may not work on computers with a small address space.

Calling uncompress.   The form of the uncompress command line is

uncompress [*options*] [*file*] . . .

where *file* . . . is a list of files to be uncompressed. Each file is replaced by its uncompressed version. A file to be uncompressed must have a name of the form '*file*.Z', although you may specify it in the file list either as '*file*' or as '*file*.Z'. If no files are given, standard input is uncompressed to standard output. The only meaningful options for uncompress are -v and -c, which have the same meaning that they do for compress.

Calling zcat.   The form of the zcat command line is

zcat [*file*] . . .

It is equivalent to 'uncompress -c'. If *file* is absent, zcat takes its input from standard input. Otherwise zcat doesn't read anything from standard input, although you can specify standard input as a file with '-'.

3.18   Archiving Sets of Files

An *archive* is a collection of files in which each file is labelled with its source. Archives serve two main purposes: backing up a group of files so that the files can be restored in case they are lost or damaged, and packaging a group of files for transmission to another computer.

UNIX has two main archiving programs: cpio and tar. Cpio is the newer and probably much the better of the two but tar is still very widely used, particularly for preparing software distributions. Advantages of cpio are that it can archive device files and create multi-volume archives, although some newer versions of tar can also create multi-volume archives. An advantage of tar is that you can archive all the files contained in a directory just by naming the directory on the command line; cpio requires that you name all the files explicitly in an input list. You can circumvent this limitation of cpio by using find with the -cpio criterion (see p. 65). An archive written with one of these programs must be read by the same program.

Neither of these programs provide data compression; for that you must use a program such as compress or pack (see Section 3.17). Several MS-DOS programs such as PKZip and arc combine the two functions of collecting files and compressing them. UNIX adaptations of these programs may be available on your system.

**3.18.1
Copying Archives
with** cpio

The cpio program provides three functions:

- Creating an archive from a list of files (the -o option)
- Extracting some or all of the files in an archive (the -i option)
- Copying files from one directory to another, recreating the original directory structure at the destination (the -p option)

The name 'cpio' stands for "copy in and out". The forms of the cpio command line are

> cpio [*options*] [*pat*] ...
> cpio [*options*] *dir*

Here *pat* specifies files to be extracted from an archive and is used only with the -i option, while *dir* specifies a destination directory and is used only with the -p option.

An archive created by cpio includes a path name for each file in the archive. The path name may be either absolute or relative (see Section 2.8.2). Relative path names are taken relative to the current directory both when the archive is created and when files are restored from it. The current directory need not be the same at the two times. In fact, reading files from one directory and writing them to another can be a useful operation in its own right and is explicitly supported by the -p option.

Selecting the Archive Operation.   The options that follow specify whether cpio creates an archive, reads an archive, or copies files from one directory to another. You must specify exactly one of them.

-i   Copy in or list the files in an archive. The archive is read from standard input unless the -I option is specified. If any patterns are specified by *pat* on the command line, cpio extracts the files selected by the patterns; otherwise it extracts all the files. The patterns are path names with wildcards permitted. The pattern matching, unlike that in the shell, treats '/' as an ordinary character.

Cpio will not overwrite a file with an older version unless you explicitly ask it to with the -u option. You can list the contents of an archive without extracting anything by specifying the -t option.

When cpio creates a copy of an archived file, the permissions attached to the copy become whatever they were when the archive was created. The owner and group of the extracted file are those of the user calling cpio.[14]

-o   Copy a set of files out to an archive. The list of files, one per line, is taken from standard input; you can often produce it conveniently by piping the output of ls to cpio.[15] The access

---

14. If the user is the superuser, however, the owner and group of the extracted files are whatever they were when the archive was created.

15. If your version of ls produces a multicolumn listing because it's been aliased to something like 'ls -CF', you can call up the single-column version by typing '\ls'.

times of the copied files are updated unless you specify the -a option.

-p   Copy ("pass") a set of files from one directory to another. The list of files to be copied is taken from standard input as with -o; the destination directory is given on the command line.

The following options specify the archive location explicitly instead of using standard input or output:

-I *file*   Read the archive from *file* (with -i only).

-O *file*   Write the archive to *file* (with -o only).

Not all systems provide these options.

File Creation.   The following options affect the files that cpio creates when it reads an archive:

-t   Don't create any files, just show a table of contents of the input. If -v is also specified, the listing is in the long format and shows the file attributes.

-f   Copy in those files *not* matching the patterns.

-r   Interactively rename files. As cpio reads a file, it prompts you for the name under which it should be stored. Pressing (Enter) causes that file not to be stored at all.

The following options affect file creation both for reading an archive and for passing files from one directory to another:

-d   Create subdirectories as needed. Without this option, cpio is not able to store files in subdirectories that don't already exist.

-u   Copy unconditionally, replacing newer files. Normally cpio will not replace a file with an older version.

-m   Retain the previous file modification time, i.e., the one that was stored with the file in the archive.

The following option applies only when files are being passed from one directory to another using the -p option:

-l   Link files when possible rather than copying them.

Directory Entries for Copied or Passed Files.   The following option affects the directory entry for a file that cpio writes to an archive or passes to another directory:

-a   Leave the access time of a file unchanged when writing it to an archive or passing it to another directory.

Status Information.   The following options affect the messages that cpio issues as it runs:

-M *msg*   Issue *msg* when switching media.

-v   List all file names verbosely, i.e., as they would be listed with 'ls -l'.

-V   Display a dot for each file transferred.

Not all systems provide the -M and -V options.

Header Information and Error Control.   The following option affects the form of headers used in an archive:

-c   Read and write header information in ASCII character form as an aid to portability among different versions of cpio. We recommend always using this option. Most versions of cpio can read an archive in either format and ignore the -c option on input.

-k   Attempt to get past bad headers and i/o errors when reading an archive instead of stopping. Not all systems provide this option.

Blocking Factors for Data Transfer.   By default, cpio uses a block size of 512 bytes when transferring data to or from an archive. The block size usually affects how fast the transfer proceeds but does not significantly affect the contents or interpretation of the archive itself. You can write an archive with one block size and read it back with another. Increasing the block size usually speeds up the transfer, which is why the -B option is often recommended. The following two options change the block size:

-B   Use 5120-byte blocks for data transfer.

-C n Use n-byte blocks for data transfer. Not all systems provide this option.

Data Transformations.   The following options provide data transformations for input. They may only be used with the -i option.

-b   Reverse byte order within each word.

-s   Reverse byte order within each halfword.

-S   Reverse halfword order within each word.

-6   Read archive in Sixth Edition format.

Examples.   Here are some examples of cpio:

- The command line

      ls | cpio -ocBv > /dev/fd0

  archives the current directory onto device fd0, presumably a floppy disk. It produces a list of the copied files.

- The command line

      cd wotan; cpio -icBvm < /dev/fd0

  reads the archive created in the previous example into the directory wotan, leaving undisturbed any files in wotan that are newer than the ones in the archive and listing the files. The modification dates of the restored files are the dates recorded in the archive.

- The command line

      find . -depth -print | cpio -pvdm ../galahad

  recursively copies the contents of the current directory and its subdirectories into the parallel directory galahad. The use of find in conjunction with cpio is typical; see Section 3.3 for a discussion of find.

3.18.2
The tar
Tape Archiver

The tar program is primarily intended to read and write archives stored on magnetic tape, although the archives that it works with may also be stored on other media or kept as ordinary files. The details of how to call tar vary greatly, even among System V-style or Berkeley-style systems. What we describe here is a generic form whose options are common to most implementations.

The most common form of the tar command line is

    tar *key* [*arg*] ... [*file*] ...

The *key* consists of a sequence of key letters and is usually *not* preceded by a dash. The number of *args* is equal to the number of letters in *key* that require arguments. The *args* appear in the order of the key letters that require them. The *files* are the files to be written to the archive or extracted. Writing a directory implies writing all its recursively contained subdirectories and files; reading a directory implies restoring all its recursively contained subdirectories and files. For example, the command

    tar rbf 12 /dev/rdsk/mt3 /usr/luigi

specifies that an archive should be written (r) with a blocking factor of 12 (b) to the device /dev/rdsk/mt3 (f) containing all the files in the directory /usr/luigi and its subdirectories. The conventions for associating key letters with arguments are different from what they are for any other UNIX program that we know of.

Because a magnetic tape cannot be positioned precisely, anything written onto the tape must either be written at the very beginning of the tape (making the rest of it unreadable) or appended to what is already there. The archives created by tar are designed with this fact in mind. They are usually written cumulatively, with new files added at the end of the archive. A particular file may appear in the archive a number of times, the latest version being the last one. When files are extracted from the archive, all the versions of each file are read in. Each version of a file overwrites any older version of that file. The versions that are left are thus the latest ones.

Specifying the Operation.   The following key letters specify the operation to be performed. Exactly one of them must be specified.

r   Append the files to the end of the archive.

x   Extract the files from the archive and restore them. If no files are specified, all files on the archive are extracted. The owner, modification time, and permissions of each file are restored if possible.

t   List the contents of the archive. A file that occurs more than once is listed once for each occurrence.

u   Update the archive by adding only those files that are not already there or that have been modified since the archive was most recently written.

c   Create a new archive containing the files. If the archive is on a magnetic tape, this operation implies writing at the beginning of the tape.[16]

In some implementations, if the file list for writing an archive contains a pair

    -C *dir*

then `tar` changes the current directory to *dir* and writes all of the files in *dir*. Any number of such pairs may appear in the list of files.

Archive Characteristics. The following key letters specify where the archive is to be found and how it is to be written:

n   Use drive #*n* for the archive. The interpretation of *n* depends on the system.

f   Take the archive device name from the next argument.

b   Take the blocking factor for raw magnetic tape from the next argument. The tape consists of a set of records, each record containing some number of blocks. The number of bytes in a block is given by a parameter known to your system; 512 and 1024 are typical values. The blocking factor specifies how many blocks are in a record. The maximum value is usually 20.

k   Take the capacity of the archive device in kilobytes from the next argument. This information enables `tar` to know when the device is nearly full. Not all systems provide this capability.

Status Information and Confirmations. The following key letters specify where the archive is to be found and what its characteristics are:

v   Show the name of each file processed.

w   Wait for confirmation of each action.

l   Don't complain about files that can't be found.

Attributes of Restored Files. The following key letters affect the attributes of restored files as indicated in their directory entries:

m   When restoring a file, set its modification time to the current time rather than to the modification time recorded in the archive.

o   Set the owner and group of each restored file to that of the user running the program rather than to that recorded in the archive.

p   Assign the original permissions to restored files rather than the permissions that would be assigned to a newly created file.

Examples. Here are a few examples of using `tar`:

• To make an archive of the files belonging to `imelda` on device `rst0`:

    tar cvbf 20 /dev/rst0 /usr/imelda

---

16. If you specify the tape using a device name that implies "no rewind", however, the archive is written to the tape at its current position.

- To list all the files in that archive:

  ```
  tar tf /dev/rst0
  ```

- To extract the files from `imelda`'s directory `shoes` within that archive and restore them to their original places:

  ```
  tar xvf /dev/rst0 /usr/imelda/shoes
  ```

4

Utility Programs

In this chapter we discuss an assortment of tools for finding out what's going on in your system, controlling your terminal, and managing other aspects of your working environment. We also discuss some programs that don't fall into any other category.

4.1   Information Services

The commands in this group provide information about users and terminals. They also provide other information such as the date, the time, and a calendar. The ps command described in Section 4.2.1 provides related information about the processes running in your system.

4.1.1
Who's Using the
System: who

The who command shows who is currently using the system. The System V version of who has options for obtaining information about processes that are running and events of interest since the system was last restarted. Two related commands are rwho, which lists users on other computers on a network (see Section 10.5.5), and finger, which locates users whether or not they are logged in (see Section 4.1.2).

The usual form of the command line is

who [*options*] [*file*]

where *file*, if given, is the file from which **who** derives its information.[1] Another form of the command line is

    who am i

or equivalently,

    who am I

These forms show your login name and the name of the terminal you're currently using. BSD UNIX also provides a **whoami** command, which is like 'who am I' except that it works even if you have changed your identity with **su** (see Section 4.3.2).

  Who sends its results to standard output. Here is an example of the output of **who**, called without options:

    root   console   Apr 10 09:36
    yorick   tty01   Apr 11 16:59
    bottom   tty04   Apr 11 14:16
    quince   ttyp1   Apr 11 15:02

The first column shows the name of each logged-in user, the second column the terminal where each user is logged in, and the remaining columns the date and time when each user logged in. On some systems you'll get a fourth column giving the network address of each user.

Command-Line Options for System V.   The command-line options listed below apply only to the System V version of **who** and to its derivatives.

  The following option provides the default explicitly:

-s   List only the name, terminal, and login time of each user. In combination with most other options, -s suppresses additional fields of the listing. In no case does it affect which terminals and processes are listed.

  The following options control which terminals are listed:

-u   List the terminals where a user is logged in.

-l   List the terminals where no one is logged in.

The -u and -l options also cause **who** to include for each terminal the time since it last showed activity and the number of its controlling process.

  The following option provides a quick listing:

-q   Display only the number of users currently logged on and their names. If -q is present, **who** ignores all other options.

  The following option provides column headings:

-H   Put a heading above each column.

  The following option causes the write state of each terminal to be shown:

-T   Indicate the *write state* of each terminal, i.e., whether the terminal will accept **write** commands (see Section 4.6.2). The possible states are '+' (writable by anyone), '-' (writable only by the superuser), and blank (writable by no one).

---

1. The default file is /etc/utmp. Occasionally you may want to use the file /etc/wtmp, which contains all logins since it was created. Any file that you use must be in the same format as /etc/utmp.

The following options provide information about the state of the system that is usually interesting and meaningful only to those who maintain your system. We mention them for the sake of completeness.

-r   Indicate the current run level of the `init` process together with its termination status, process id, and exit status.

-b   Indicate the last time the system was rebooted.

-t   Indicate the last time the system clock was explicitly changed.

-p   List all processes started by the `init` process and still active. The listed information is taken from `/etc/inittab`.[2]

-d   List all processes started by the `init` process that are now dead, i.e., have terminated. The exit status in the comments field indicates why the process terminated.

The following option shows you almost everything:

-a   Turn on all other options except `-T`.[3]

4.1.2
Looking Up User Information with `finger`

The `finger` command enables you to look up information about a particular user or about all users currently logged in. It is particularly useful because you can use it to look up users at remote locations and because you can specify just part of a user's full name. The information that you get is system-dependent but typically includes the user's full name, user name, office location, and telephone number. For logged-in users it also includes the time since the user last typed anything and an indication of whether the user's terminal is blocked from receiving messages (see Section 4.6.3).

The form of the `finger` command line is

        finger [*options*] [*name*] . . .

where each *name* indicates a user or group of users to be looked up and has one of the following forms:

(empty)   Provide information about all users currently logged in.

word   Provide information about each user on your computer whose name matches *word*.

word@hostname
          Provide information about each user at remote computer *hostname* whose name matches *word*.

@hostname
          Provide information about all users currently logged in at remote computer *hostname*.

---

2. `/etc/inittab` is a table that lists processes that should be initiated whenever the system's run state changes. Each process in `/etc/inittab` has a list of states associated with it; it is restarted whenever the run state is changed to one of those states listed. In addition, a process may be marked for "respawning". A respawning process is restarted whenever it is found to have terminated.

3. We assume that the omission of `-T` is a bug.

A match succeeds if *word* agrees with a user's user name or with any word in that user's full name (as listed in the /etc/passwd file). For comparison purposes, words are separated by spaces. The comparison is case-insensitive for the full name but not for the user name. For instance, if the user "Hubert van Gogh" has user name 'hvg', you can look him up as 'hvg', 'gogh', or 'Hubert'—but not as 'bert', since 'bert' doesn't match a complete word in the user's name, nor by 'HVG', since the user-name comparison is case-sensitive. If a single *name* matches several users, you see them all.

Finger recognizes two special files if they exist in your home directory: .plan and .project. Any text you put into .plan appears in your finger listing, so .plan is a good place to provide information such as your telephone number, office location, and usual schedule. The .project file is similar, except that finger displays only its first line.

Output of finger has short and long forms. The short form has one line per user and lists only basic information; the long form has several lines per user. The short form looks like this:

```
Login      Name             TTY Idle     When     Where
operator Operator on Console  a  2:12 Mon 10:06
felix    Felix the Cat        p2 3:03 Mon 09:32  cinema.com
```

The long form (for one user) looks like this:

```
Login name: felix                  In real life: Felix the Cat
Directory: /usr/felix              Shell: /bin/csh
On since Jun 24 09:56:16 on ttyp2
3 hours 3 minutes Idle Time
No unread mail
Plan:
Try X2378 or
look for me at the nearest mousehole.
```

By default you get the long form for users specified explicitly and the short form for the list of all users at a site, but you can force a particular form with the -l and -m options.

Command-line Options. The command-line options for the finger command are as follows:

-l   Use the long output format (several lines per user).

-s   Use the short output format (one line per user).

-m   Match each *name* against user names only (and require an exact match).

-p   Don't show the .plan files.

4.1.3
Getting Terminal
Information
with tty

The `tty` command sends the path name of your terminal to standard output. It can also reveal whether standard input is a terminal. The form of the `tty` command line is

    tty [*options*]

The form of the output is a string such as '/dev/tty03'.

   You can use the exit code of `tty` to test if standard input is a terminal. These are the exit codes:

0	Standard input is a terminal.
1	Standard input is not a terminal.
2	Invalid options were specified.

Command-line Options.   These are the options for the `tty` command line:

-l   Show the line number of the terminal if the terminal is on an active synchronous line. Most UNIX terminals are not on synchronous lines, which are primarily used to connect block-style terminals to mainframe systems. If the terminal is not on an active synchronous line, a message to that effect is added to the output. Not all systems support this option.

-s   Don't send the terminal's path name to standard output. This option is useful when you're using `tty` in a shell script to determine whether standard input is indeed a terminal but don't care about its name.

4.1.4
Showing the Date
and Time with date

The `date` command sends the date and time to standard output. The simple command

    date

produces the date and time in a standard default format, shown by the output

    Sat Apr 13 16:25:00 EDT 1991

The System V version of `date` enables you to specify your own format; the command

    date +*format*

produces the date, formatted according to *format*, a format consisting of a string with interspersed format descriptors. Each format descriptor is preceded by '%'; if you want a '%' in the text you must write it as '%%'. These are the format descriptors:

D	Date in the form '*mm/dd/yy*', e.g., '07/04/92'
y	Last two digits of the year
Y	Four-digit year
j	Day of year as three digits ('001'–'366')
m	Month as two digits ('01'–'12')
h	Month as three letters ('Jan'–'Dec')
w	Day of week as one digit ('0' for Sunday, '6' for Saturday)

a	Day of week as three letters ('Sun'–'Sat')
d	Day of month as two digits ('01'–'31').
T	Time in the form '$hh:mm:ss$', e.g., '14:00:00' for 2 PM exactly
r	Time in AM/PM notation, e.g., '4:45 pm'
H	Hour as two digits ('00'–'23')
Z	Time zone, e.g., 'EDT'
M	Minute as two digits ('00'–'59')
S	Second as two digits ('00'–'59')
n	Newline character
t	Tab character

For example, the command

```
date '+It is now %T on %h %d, 19%y% (%a).%nThank you for your interest.'
```

produces output like this:

```
    It is now 10:29:42 on Feb 01, 1992 (Sat).
    Thank you for your interest.
```

Note that the format has been quoted so that blanks within it are correctly reproduced (see Section 2.14.2). The format descriptors vary somewhat from one system to another.

The superuser may use the date command to set the system date. The command

```
    date mmddhhmmyy
```

sets the system date to month *mm*, day *dd*, hour *hh*, minute *mm*, and year *yy*. You may omit *yy*; if you do, date takes it as the current year. **Note:** You must issue this command at an exact minute if you want the time to be correct to the second.

4.1.5
Displaying a Calendar with cal

The cal command produces a calendar for a single month or for an entire year and sends it to standard output. The form of the cal command line is

```
    cal [[month] year]
```

The following rules apply to cal:

- If you omit both month and year you get a calendar for the current month.

- If you specify both a month and a year you get a calendar just for that month.

- If you specify only a year you get a calendar for that entire year. Note that 'cal 11' gives you a calendar for the year 11, not for November of the current year.

For example, the command

```
    cal 7 1776
```

produces the following calendar:

```
    July 1776
 S  M Tu  W Th  F  S
       1  2  3  4  5  6
 7  8  9 10 11 12 13
14 15 16 17 18 19 20
21 22 23 24 25 26 27
28 29 30 31
```

4.2 Shell Facilities for Managing Processes

In the following subsections we describe a number of commands for listing the processes running on your computer, for controlling when they run and with what priority, and for killing them. We describe two versions of the ps (list processes) command: one that is used on System V systems and another that is used on BSD UNIX systems.

**4.2.1
Showing Processes
with** ps
(System V Version)

The System V ps command lists processes running on a System V system (see Section 2.7). Using the ps options, you can select the processes to be listed and can choose between a brief, full, or extended listing.

The form of the ps command line is

ps [*options*]

As befits a command that provides information about the inner workings of your system, the options and the information in the listing vary considerably among systems. The simple form 'ps' should work on all systems, however, and should list in abbreviated form the processes running at your own terminal.

Options for Selecting Processes. The following options specify which processes are listed. By default, the only ones listed are those associated with your terminal. In these options, a *list* is a sequence of items separated by spaces or commas.

-e   Produce information about every process.

-d   Produce information about every process except for process group leaders. A process group leader has a group number identical to its process number. Unfortunately the information produced by ps does not include group numbers, so the only way to tell which processes are process group leaders is to compare this listing with the one obtained from -e.

-a   Produce information about every process except process group leaders and processes not associated with a terminal.

-u *userlist*
          Produce only output pertaining to the specified users. Users are denoted by their user id's.

-t *termlist*
> Produce only output describing processes that are running at the specified terminals. You can identify a terminal by its file identifier, e.g., 'tty02', or by two digits with an assumed prefix of 'tty'.

-p *proclist*
> Produce only output pertaining to the specified processes. A process is specified by its process number (which you would normally derive from a previous listing).

-g *grouplist*
> Produce only output pertaining to the specified process groups. A process group is denoted by its number, which is the process number of its leader.

The following option enables you to list processes when your system has been started up with a kernel other than /unix. It is useful only if you're maintaining a UNIX system.

-n *name*   Assume that the system has been started from the kernel *name* rather than from the kernel /unix. If that is the case and you don't use this option, you won't get any output from ps.[4] This option requires superuser privileges.

Options for Specifying What Is Listed.   By default, ps provides only an abbreviated listing such as the following one:

```
PID TTY      TIME COMMAND
100 console  0:02 csh
236 console  0:00 sh
319 console  0:01 cp
320 console  0:00 ps
```

The options below provide listings with more information.

-f   Produce a full listing such as the following one:

UID	PID	PPID	C	STIME	TTY	TIME	COMMAND
alice	100	1	1	15:12:57	console	0:02	csh
alice	236	100	10	15:27:09	console	0:00	/bin/sh try
alice	274	236	2	15:28:00	console	0:00	cp king court
alice	272	100	8	15:27:59	console	0:00	ps -f

-l   Produce an extended (long) listing. The additional fields in this listing are usually of interest only to system maintainers.

In the next subsection we indicate the items included in each type of listing.

---

4.   The reason is that ps uses information in the kernel file in order to locate the processes.

Interpreting the Output.   Below we describe the items that appear in the listings. A **B** item appears in a brief listing and an **F** item appears in a full listing. Examples of these listings are given above.

UID   (**F**) The user associated with the process

PID   (**BF**) The process number

PPID   (**F**) The process number of the process's parent

C   (**F**) The processor utilization, for scheduling purposes

STIME   (**F**) The starting time of the process. A process started more than a day ago is given in months and days.

TTY   (**BF**) The controlling terminal for the process. A '?' indicates that the process is not associated with a terminal. System processes almost always have a '?' in this field.

TIME   (**BF**) The cumulative execution time for the process in minutes and seconds of central processor time

COMMAND   (**BF**) The command being executed by the process. For the -f option, the arguments to the command are shown as well.

4.2.2
Showing Processes
with ps
(BSD UNIX Version)

The ps command in BSD UNIX, like the one in System V, shows processes running on your system. The BSD UNIX version of ps is compatible with the Seventh Edition version but extends it significantly. Berkeley-derived systems are likely to have their own small variations on this command.

The form of the ps command line for BSD UNIX is

     ps [-] [*options*] [*pid*]

where *pid* is a process id. If *pid* is specified, only information about the process with this id is shown. The command line may contain additional specifications of interest to system maintainers, which we do not describe here.

Options for Selecting Processes.   The following options specify which processes are listed. By default, only those processes associated with your terminal are listed.

g   Produce information about all processes.

a   Produce information about all processes that are associated with terminals.

t*term*   Show only processes running on terminal *term*. You should write *term* in the same form as it appears in the ps listing, e.g., 't3' for 'tty3' and 'tco' for the console. This option must appear last.

x   Show information about processes not associated with a terminal.

Options for Specifying What Is Listed. By default, ps provides only an abbreviated listing like this one:

```
PID TT STAT   TIME COMMAND
15345 co IW   0:00 - std.9600 console (getty)
 8181 p0 IW   0:02 -tcsh (tcsh)
12883 q7 IW   0:00 mail
16899 q5 S    0:00 -h -i (tcsh)
12901 q7 Z    0:00 <defunct>
 7895 p2 TW   0:00 emacs assignment
```

The options below provide listings with more information.

u   Produce information in a user-oriented format. Here is an example of such a listing:

USER	PID	%CPU	%MEM	SZ	RSS	TT	STAT	START	TIME	COMMAND
root	15345	0.0	0.0	56	0	co	IW	20:31	0:00	- std.9600 console (getty)
betsys	12883	0.0	0.0	112	0	q7	IW	17:11	0:00	mail
root	12901	0.0	0.0	0	0	q7	Z	Oct 7	0:00	<defunct>
prancer	16912	7.7	1.7	208	512	q5	R	22:42	0:00	ps -uag
donder	7295	0.0	0.0	152	0	p5	IW	Oct 8	0:00	-tcsh (tcsh)
vixen	5281	0.0	0.0	1248	0	pb	IW	10:19	1:15	emacs

The specific fields may be different on your system.

l   Produce a long listing. This listing is the only one that shows you the parent of each process; the other additional fields in this listing are usually of interest only to system maintainers.

c   Show the internally stored command name rather than the command name gotten from the argument list. The internally stored command name is more reliable but may be less informative.

e   Show the environment of the command.

v   Show virtual memory statistics. These statistics are not likely to be meaningful unless you are familiar with the internals of your system.

w   Use a wide output format of 132 columns rather than 80. Repeating this option causes an arbitrarily wide format to be used.

Interpreting the Output. Below we describe the items that appear in the listings. A **B** item appears in a brief listing and a **U** item appears in a full listing. Examples of these listings are given above.

USER   (**U**) The user associated with the process

PID   (**BU**) The process number

%CPU   (**U**) The percentage of available central processor time used by this process within the past minute (approximately)

%MEM   (**U**) The percentage of available real memory used by this process

SZ	(**U**) The virtual memory size of the process in 1024-byte units
RSS	(**U**) The real memory size of the process in 1024-byte units
TT	(**BU**) The controlling terminal for the process
STAT	(**BU**) The state of the process (see below)
START	(**U**) The starting time of the process. A process started more than a day ago is given in months and days.
TIME	(**BU**) The cumulative execution time for the process in minutes and seconds of central processor time
COMMAND	(**BU**) The command being executed by the process. For the -u option, the arguments to the command are shown as well.

Information on the Process State.   Each ps listing contains an indication labelled 'STAT' of the state of each process in the listing. The state is given by four indicators, denoted by *RWNA*:

R   The runnability of the process:

R	Able to run
T	Stopped
P	Waiting for a memory page
D	Waiting for disk
S	Sleeping for less than about 20 seconds
I	Idle (sleeping for more than about 20 seconds)

W   The swapping state of the process:

(blank)	Loaded in memory
W	Swapped out
>	Memory requirements exceeded

N   The niceness of the process:

(blank)	No special treatment
N	Reduced priority
>	Raised priority

A   The treatment of the process for the purpose of virtual memory replacement:

(blank)	No special treatment
A	LISP garbage collection or similar activity
S	Sequentially addressing large volumes of data

Options for System Maintainers.   The following options are likely to be of interest only to system maintainers. We list them for the sake of completeness.

n	Show information numerically rather than symbolically.
s	Show the kernel stack size of each process.
k	Use the /vmcore file.
U	Update the private database of system information.

4.2.3
Signalling Processes
with `kill`

The `kill` command sends a signal to a process. Its name is misleading since the "kill" signal is not the only one it can send. The form of the `kill` command is

> `kill [-`*signum*`]` *pid*

The signal numbered *signum* is sent to process number *pid*. The default signal is #15 (terminate), which usually kills the process receiving it. See Section 2.7.4 for a discussion of signals and a list of available signals.

4.2.4
Ignoring Hangups
with `nohup`

The `nohup` command executes a command in such a way that the command continues to execute even if you log out or disconnect your terminal (hang up). It is chiefly used to execute a background job that you wish to leave running even after you've ended your session at the terminal.

To execute a command in this manner, type

> `nohup` *command* [*argument* ...]

Any hangup signals (see Section 2.7.4) sent to the process are ignored. The following command shows a typical use of `nohup`:

> `nohup quilting patch38 &`

The command `quilting` with argument `patch38` is executed in the background and does not terminate when you log out.

A job run with `nohup` should not attempt to read from standard input. Standard output is sent to `nohup.out` (in the current directory).

4.2.5
Scheduling Future
Activities with `at`
and `batch`

The `at` and `batch` commands schedule a job to run at a future time.[5] With `at`, you specify when the job should be run; with `batch`, you leave it up to the system to decide when to run it, based on the system load. `Batch` is usually appropriate for long, low-priority jobs. `At` has options for removing jobs and for listing jobs that you've scheduled (with either `at` or `batch`).

Both commands expect the job to appear in standard input. For example, if you type

```
at 3:30am tomorrow
update mailing_list
gen -y mailing_list >labels.3
(EOF)
```

---

5. Under some systems, permission to use `at` may be restricted to certain users. The files `/usr/lib/cron/at.allow` and `/usr/lib/cron/at.deny` determine who may use `at`. If neither exists, only root may use `at`.

the job consisting of the two commands **update** and **gen** will be run at 3:30 am the day after you typed this. When the job is run, the current directory and environment are made the same as they were at the time you created the job.

You can submit a job from a file by redirecting the input of **at** or **batch** from that file. The standard input of the submitted job is taken from **/dev/null**, the empty file. The standard output and standard error of a submitted job are sent to you in the form of a mail message. When you submit a job, the job number and schedule time are written to standard error.

The forms of the two commands are

```
at time [date] [+ increment]
batch
at -r job ...
at -l [job ...]
```

Here is what these forms do:

- The first two forms submit jobs for later execution.

- The form **at -l** lists jobs that you've submitted. If you supply a list of job numbers, you're told about those jobs; if you don't supply that list, you're told about all your jobs.

- The form **at -r** removes jobs that were previously scheduled by **at** or **batch**. You may only remove your own jobs, although the super-user may remove anyone's jobs. The -r option doesn't provide a direct way to remove all your jobs, but you can do it with the line

```
at -r `at -l | cut -f1`
```

Specifying the Time and Date for at.   You specify *time* in one of the following ways:

- As a one-digit or two-digit number specifying an hour.
- As a four-digit number specifying an hour and minute.
- As two numbers (hour and minute) separated by a colon.
- As one of these followed by 'am', 'pm', or 'zulu'. 'Zulu' indicates Greenwich Mean Time.[6] A 24-hour clock is assumed if none of these are given.
- As one of the special times 'noon', 'midnight', or 'now'. 'Now' only makes sense if you also provide an increment.

You specify *date* in one of the following ways:

- As a month name followed by a day number
- As above, followed by an optional comma and a two-digit or four-digit year number
- As a day of the week
- As one of the special forms 'today' or 'tomorrow'

You may write a month name either in full or by using its three-letter abbreviation; the same holds for a day of the week. If you omit *date*, **at**

---

6. We have no idea where 'zulu' comes from.

assumes 'today' if the time is later than the present time and 'tomorrow' otherwise. If you specify a date before the current date (and no year), at assumes the next year.

The increment specifies an amount of time to be added to the time you specify. It should be given as a number followed by one of the intervals 'minutes', 'hours', 'days', 'weeks', 'months', or 'years'. At also recognizes the singular forms of these intervals.

In all of these forms, lowercase and uppercase letters are equivalent. Spaces between elements are permitted but not required.

Some examples of legitimate at calls are the following:

```
at 2200 Sat
at now + 2 days
at now + 1 hour
at 5:50am Feb 28
at 4 AM
at 11
at now+1year
```

4.2.6 Running a Command at Low Priority with nice

The nice command enables you to execute another command at lower priority. It's called 'nice' because lowering your execution priority is a way of being nice to other users. The form of the nice command line is

```
nice [-n] cmd [arg] ...
```

The command *cmd* with arguments *arg* ... is executed with a priority n lower than it otherwise would be. The default value of n is 10; its permissible range is 1 to 19. The superuser may specify a negative value such as −6 for n, thereby raising a command's priority. (You would write that as '−−6'.)

Nice does not by itself cause *cmd* to be executed in the background; to do that you must follow it by '&' or put it in the background by another method.

4.2.7 Suspending Execution with sleep

The sleep command sleeps, i.e., does nothing, for a specified number of seconds. After that time has elapsed, it terminates. The form of the sleep command line is

```
sleep n
```

where n is the number of seconds for which the process should sleep. You can use sleep to postpone execution of a command until after a certain amount of time has passed.

4.2.8 Waiting for a Process with wait

The wait command waits for a specified process to finish. The form of the wait command line is

```
wait [n]
```

where n is the number of the process being waited for. If you omit n, wait waits until all background processes have finished. The exit code of wait is the same as that of the process for which it's waiting, or zero if it's waiting for all background processes. Wait is an intrinsic command of every shell.

4.3   Commands Related to Logging In

The commands in this group relate to logging in, controlling your password, and setting your group.

**4.3.1
Logging In
with** login

Your first step in logging in is to create a new connection to the system. When UNIX detects your connection,[7] it calls the login program on your behalf. After issuing a prompt, the login program awaits a response from you of the form

> *name* [*var-setting*] . . .

where *name* is your user name and the *var-setting*s (recognized only under System V versions) are settings of environment variables as described below. Login then asks for your password, which is not echoed to your terminal. After validating your password, login executes your login shell, which in turn executes your login initialization file, usually either .profile or .login (see Section 2.18). Your login shell is either recorded in the /etc/passwd file or determined by default.[8] The usual default is /bin/sh, the Bourne shell, even for BSD UNIX (which generally favors the C shell). If you have not successfully logged in within a certain time limit, the system may disconnect you as a security measure.

Calling login **Explicitly.**   Once you're logged in, you may call login explicitly at any time in order to replace your login identity by a different one or to reinitialize your environment. To do this you must be executing your login process, so you can't call login from a subshell. You log in again by typing

> exec login [*name* [*var-setting*] . . .]

If you don't supply a name, login asks you for one. Your new login replaces the old one, just as though you had logged in that way originally.

Under BSD UNIX, you may specify a -p option preceding your name when you call login explicitly. If this option is specified, login preserves your environment variables across the login (see Section 2.7.5).

Environment Variables on Login.   When you log in, login automatically sets up certain environment variables for you (see Section 2.7.5):

HOME   The absolute path name of your home directory (see Section 2.8.3).

PATH   The search path for commands, initially ':/bin:/usr/bin' (see Section 2.11.2).

---

7. The connection is ordinarily detected by the getty ("get teletypewriter") program, a copy of which monitors each input line.

8. The login program prefixes the name of the shell with '-' when it calls it; for example, if your shell is sh, it is called under the name '-sh'. This convention enables a shell to determine if it was called as a login shell.

SHELL   The full name of your login shell as it appears in your
          /etc/passwd entry, or /bin/sh if no shell is specified there.
MAIL   The file name of your primary mailbox (see p. 379).
TZ   The time zone in which your system is located.

Assignments to Variables.   Under the System V version of login, you may
use *var-setting* ... to change the settings of the environment variables
listed above, except for PATH and SHELL. You may also assign values to
other environment variables. Each *var-setting* has the form

> [*name* =] *value*

Values without names are assigned to the variables L0, L1, and so forth.
For example, the login

```
fifi HOME=/usr/fifi/startup INIT=qxt 12 b
```

changes HOME to /usr/fifi/startup and sets INIT to qxt, L0 to 12, and
L1 to b. In this example, INIT is a variable whose name you have chosen
for yourself and L0 and L1 are variables whose names are fixed by convention. Setting environment variables on login provides a convenient
way to customize the actions taken by your login initialization file (see Section 2.18.1), since the login initialization file can test the values of these
variables.

The /etc/passwd File.   The /etc/passwd file contains the information
required by the login program to verify that a login is valid and to initiate
the appropriate shell. Other programs also use the information in this
file. Since it contains no actual passwords, anyone is permitted to read it.
A fragment of it looks like this:

```
root:x:0:1:0000-Admin(0000):/:
alice:x:Alice Liddell:/usr/alice:/bin/ksh
qoh:x:Queen of Hearts/usr/qoh:
```

Each line contains information about a single user, and consists of a sequence of fields separated by colons.

- The first field contains the user name as expected by login. The
  first line represents the superuser, named root.

- The second field contains a dummy indicator for the password. In
  most newer systems the actual passwords are stored in a different
  file called the *shadow file*, where they are kept in an encrypted form.
  In older systems, however, the encrypted password is stored here.[9]

- The third field contains the user's full name.

- The fourth field contains the path name of the user's home directory.

---

9. The encryption uses a "trapdoor algorithm" that makes it easy to transform the password
to its encrypted form but prohibitively time-consuming to transform the encrypted form
back to the password. You should avoid using an ordinary word as a password because an
intruder can write a program that runs through a dictionary and computes the password
that would be generated by each dictionary word. If one of these passwords is found in
the /etc/passwd file, the intruder has just learned how to impersonate the user with that
password.

The fifth field contains the path name of the user's login shell. If it is not specified, it defaults to /bin/sh.

**4.3.2
Changing User
Identity with** su

The su ("substitute user") command enables you to take on the identity of a different user. The form of the command is

    su [-f] [-] [*name* [*arg*]]

Here *name* is the name of the user whose identity you wish to assume; if you omit it, root (the name of the superuser) is assumed. When using the su command you must provide a password unless the new user's login doesn't require one.

Su's effect is to start up a copy of the new user's login shell as a child process of the current process and associate that shell with the new user name. The interpretation of '-f' and '-' on the command line is as follows:

- If you specify '-f' (recognized only by Berkeley versions of su), the C shell (csh) does not execute the .cshrc initialization file. Specifying this option causes csh to start up faster.

- If you put '-' after su (the space between '-' and *name* is essential), you get a new environment, the same one you would have gotten had you logged in as the new user.

- If you don't put '-' after su, you continue working in the same environment as before but with the privileges of the new user. In particular, the current directory isn't changed, the shell initialization file isn't executed, and environment variables available before the su call remain available after it. Nevertheless, your shell is the login shell of the new user rather than the shell you were previously using.

In either case, when you exit from this new shell your previous user name is restored. Note the difference in this respect between su and login— exiting from the new shell that you get with login logs you out altogether.

For example, suppose your user name is ishmael and you're working under the C shell. If you issue the command

    su - ahab

it will appear that you have just logged in as ahab, with ahab's login shell and initializations. If you now type exit or EOF, you'll be back to where you were before you issued the su, operating under the C shell again.

The arguments are passed to the new shell when it starts up (see "Parameters (Numbered Variables)" on page 157). As seen by the shell, argument 1 is the first argument following *name* and arguments 2, 3, ... are the following ones. Argument 0 is the name of the shell prefixed by '-', e.g., '-sh' or '-csh'. The shell can use argument 0 to determine if it was called as a login shell.

The principal use of arguments with the su command is to execute a single command while assuming the identity of another user. To execute the command *cmd* with arguments *args*, using the permissions and environment of user *name*, type

    su - *name* -c "*cmd args*"

For instance, if you know the superuser password you may issue the command

```
su - root -c sysadm
```

to call the system administration program sysadm. Su asks you for the root password, and after verifying it runs `sysadm`. When `sysadm` terminates, your normal identity is restored.

4.3.3
Changing Your
Group with newgrp

The `newgrp` command enables you to change to a group different from the one you logged in with, provided you're listed in the `/etc/group` file as a member of the new group.[10] You may then access any file belonging to the new group for which the appropriate group permission has been set. Because BSD UNIX allows a single user to belong to several groups, it neither needs nor supports this command.

The form of the command is

```
newgrp [-] [group]
```

where *group* is the name of the group you wish to join. If you're authorized to join that group, the command changes your group to *group* for the rest of the current session.

- If you omit *group*, your login group (as shown in the password file) is assumed.

- If you specify '-', the effect is as though you had just logged in as a member of *group*. Any initializations associated with your login shell are performed.

In either case a new copy of your login shell is created and given control of your terminal. Environment variables are preserved across `newgrp`, but local variables are not. If you specify '-' in the `newgrp` command, however, you get a fresh environment also, as you would when you log in.

4.3.4
Changing Your
Password
with passwd

The `passwd` command enables you to change your password after you've been registered as a user in your system. For the sake of security you should change your password periodically; some systems require you to.

The form of the `passwd` command is

```
passwd [name]
```

where *name* is a user name. The default for *name* is the name of the user issuing the command. For an ordinary user the default value is the only legal value, so *name* is usually omitted. The superuser, however, may set the password for other values of *name*. Passwd first prompts you for your old password and then prompts you for your new password twice—the second time to make sure that you typed it correctly (since it isn't displayed on your terminal as you type it).

---

10. You may also switch to a group, even if you're not a member of it, if the group has a group password and you know that password. Most UNIX experts consider group passwords a security weakness in UNIX and discourage their use.

Many systems impose security constraints on `passwd` such as the following ones:

- You may not change your password if you've already changed it within the last n days.

- Your password has at least six characters.

- Your password includes at least two alphabetic characters and at least one nonalphabetic character.

- Your password is sufficiently different from your login name.

- Your new password differs from your old one by at least three characters.

None of these requirements apply to the superuser, who may construct user accounts having no password at all. Not using passwords is a dangerous security hazard under most conditions but would be convenient and appropriate for a single-user system in an environment such as a home office where security is not a major concern.

**4.3.5
Showing User and
Group ID's with `id`**

The `id` command, which has no arguments, sends the user id and the group id of the current process to standard output. Both the number and the name of the user and the group are shown. A typical output is

```
uid=145(felix) gid=117(cats)
```

For a process executing a program for which the set-uid bit is on, both the real user id and the effective user id (the one that currently defines file access) are shown. Similarly, when the set-gid bit is on, both the real group id and the effective group id are shown. Some older systems don't support this command.

4.4   Controlling Your Terminal

In order to communicate effectively with your terminal, UNIX has to know what sequences of characters it should send to produce effects such as starting a new line or clearing the screen. The commands described in this section provide UNIX with the information it needs about your terminal. You can also use them to control the terminal yourself, for example to reset it to a sane state when it's become confused by a random sequence of characters sent by accident.

- The `tset` program determines your terminal type, sends appropriate initialization commands to it, and enables you to define your erase and kill characters. Not all systems provide `tset`. For those that don't, you can achieve its effects more laboriously with `stty` and `tput`.

- The `stty` program defines the meanings of control characters sent to your terminal, sets terminal and line characteristics such as the communication speed, and provides information about your terminal. Though the erase nd kill characters may be defined either with `tset` or with `stty`, the other control characters may be defined only with `stty`.

- The `tput` program sends the control sequences (sequences of characters) needed to achieve a particular function such as resetting the terminal or clearing the screen. You can also use it to learn what those sequences are.

- The `tabs` program sets the positions of the built-in tabs on your terminal (provided your terminal has them).

See Section 2.19 for a discussion of terminals, control sequences, and `terminfo` and `termcap`, the two alternate forms of the database that UNIX uses to record information about terminals.

4.4.1
Preparing Your Terminal with `tset`

The `tset` command serves several purposes:

- It determines the type of your terminal and transmits the control sequences needed to initialize it.

- It can produce a sequence of commands that sets the TERM environment variable to your terminal type (see Section 2.19). You can save these commands in a file and issue them later.

- You can use it to set your erase and kill characters.

The form of the `tset` command line is

    tset [*options*] [*term*]

where *term* is the name of a terminal type. If the environment variable TERM contains the name of your terminal, as it usually does, the simple call 'tset' sends an initialization string to your terminal (see Section 2.19 for a discussion of initialization and reset strings). Your login initialization file should include a call on `tset` to initialize your terminal after you have logged in.

Some Berkeley systems include a `reset` program, similar to `tset`, that sends the reset string to your terminal. If your terminal gets into a confused state, typing 'Ctrl J reset Ctrl J' may restore it, though you may not be able to see what you're typing. The equivalent command for non-Berkeley systems is 'tput reset'.

Determining Your Terminal Type. Tset's first task is to determine your terminal type. It uses the following decision procedure:

(1) If you didn't specified any -m options, then

    (a) if you specified *term*, *term* is the terminal type.

    (b) Otherwise, if you specified the -h option, the terminal type is that associated with the port you're using, as recorded in the file /etc/ttytype or /etc/ttys (depending on your system).

    (c) Otherwise, if the environment variable TERM is defined, its value specifies the terminal type.

    (d) Otherwise the terminal type is the one associated with your port, as with the -h option.

(2) If you specified one or more -m options (see below) and one of them applies, then that option determines the terminal type.

(3) If you specified one or more -m options (see below), none of which apply, then

   (a) if you specified *term* (not associated with any option) on the command line, then *term* is the terminal type.

   (b) Otherwise the terminal type is the one associated with your port as with the -h option.

Two options are relevant to this procedure:

-h   Use the terminal type associated with your port rather than the one found in TERM. Not all systems provide this option.

-m   Attempt to determine the terminal type by matching its speed as described below.

Testing Terminal Speed with the -m Option.   The -m option specifies that tset should attempt to determine the terminal type by testing the terminal speed. Its syntax is

   -m [*itype*][*test speed*]:[?]*type*

To prevent shell metacharacters in this specification from being misinterpreted, you should enclose it in double quotes.

   The items before the colon specify two matching criteria:

- The variable *itype* specifies an "indeterminate" terminal type such as 'dialup' or 'network' that characterizes the line rather than the terminal itself. If your port has that terminal type, the criterion is satisfied. If you omit *itype* the terminal type of your port does not affect the match.

- If the test and speed are specified, tset compares *speed* with the actual speed (baud rate) of your terminal port. The permissible speeds are the same as those recognized by stty (see p. 128). The criterion is one of the comparison operators

   = @ < > <= >= != !@ !< !>

   where '@' and '=' both mean equality and '!' in front of an operator negates it (for example, '!=' means "not equal"). If this criterion is omitted, the port speed does not affect the match.

The type following the colon specifies the terminal type to be used if the criterion is satisfied. A question mark preceding *type* instructs tset to confirm the terminal type. If you press (Enter), *type* is accepted; any other response causes it to be rejected.

   For example, the command

```
tset - -m "dialup@2400:?h19" -m "dialup:vt100" ">=9600:sun" AT386
```

---

specifies the following procedure:

(1) If you're coming in on a dialup line at 2400 baud, tset asks if your terminal is of type 'h19'. If you confirm, then tset uses 'h19'; otherwise it goes on to the next test.

(2)   If you're coming in on a dialup line at any speed, tset assumes type 'vt100'.

(3)   If you're coming in at 9600 baud or faster, tset assumes type 'sun'.

(4)   If none of these tests are satisfied, tset assumes 'AT386'.

The '–' option in the command sends the selected terminal type to standard output as described below.

Suppressing the Initialization String.   The following option suppresses the initialization string:

-I   Don't send the initialization string. Depending on the version of tset you've got, this option may or may not cause the reset string to be sent instead. Berkeley versions that provides reset usually don't send it.

Setting the Erase and Kill Characters.   You can use tset to specify the erase and kill characters for your terminal by specifying one or more of the following options:

-e[*c*]   Set the erase character to *c*. The character *c* is normally a control character, specified with a preceding caret as in '^B'. If you omit *c*, '^H' is assumed.

-E[*c*]   Set the erase character to *c* as in the -e option, but only if the information in terminfo or termcap indicates that the terminal can backspace. Not all systems provide this option.

-k[*c*]   Set the kill character to *c*, using the same notation as in the -e option. The default is '^U'.

If the erase and kill characters are anything other than '^H' and '^U', tset sends to standard error a line such as

```
Kill set to ^C
```

This line does not appear unless you've explicitly requested output using one of the options described in the next subsection. You can suppress this commentary with the -Q option.

Controlling the Output.   The output of tset serves two purposes: to inform you of the terminal type tset is using and to provide the text of a sequence of commands for setting the TERM environment variable. The following options affect the output:

-           Produce the terminal type on standard output, followed by a newline.

-s   Produce the shell commands for setting TERM on standard output. Tset looks at your login shell to decide which commands to produce. It recognizes just two cases: csh, the C shell, and everything else, which it takes to be equivalent to the Bourne shell sh. For csh the commands are

```
set noglob;
setenv TERM term ;
unset noglob;
```

and for everything else,

```
export TERM;
TERM=term;
```

You can then set up your terminal, and set TERM as well, with a command such as

```
'tset -s'
```

This command uses the command substitution notation described in Section 5.2.13.[11]

-S   If your login shell is csh, produce the same text as the - option produces, but without the newline. Otherwise produce the same text as the -s option produces. Not all systems provide the -S option.

-r   Send to standard error a message identifying your terminal type.

-Q   Suppress the 'Erase set to' and 'Kill set to' messages that tset normally sends to standard error whenever the erase or kill character has a nondefault value.

4.4.2
Setting Your
Terminal
Characteristics
with stty

The stty command sets certain characteristics of your terminal. It does not send any data to your terminal. The terminal characteristics serve the following main purposes:

- They instruct the terminal driver[12] how to interpret and modify the characters it receives from your terminal or sends to your terminal.

- They describe the port connected to your terminal, for example by specifying its speed.

- If you're communicating over a phone line, they specify when the terminal driver should disconnect the phone line.

The initial values for these characteristics are set by the system during login.

The usual form of the stty command line is

```
stty [options] [setting] ...
```

The options and settings vary considerably among systems. The options specify what information is produced; the settings specify what terminal characteristics are to be changed. Ordinarily a single call on stty specifies options or settings but not both.

---

11. Be careful of how you do this; if the command is executed in a subshell its effects are lost when the subshell exits.

12. The terminal driver is the program that handles the communication between your terminal and the programs that read from or write to it.

The command `stty` without options produces a short listing that shows only the line speed, parity, and the settings that differ from their default values. A typical example is

```
speed 9600 baud; evenp
intr = ^c; erase = ^h; kill = ^u; swtch = ^`;
brkint -inpck icrnl onlcr tab3
echo echoe echok
```

For System V the options are as follows:

-a   List all the settings.

-g   List the current settings in a form that can later be used as input to `stty`.

Although some of the settings also start with a dash, none of them consist of single letters.

Some Berkeley systems use a different form for `stty` in which options are not indicated by a preceding dash. In these systems the form

```
stty all
```

lists all ordinarily used settings, while the form

```
stty everything
```

lists everything `stty` knows about your terminal.

Below we describe many of the settings you may specify with the System V version of `stty`. We omit those that are obscure or rarely used, such as the ones needed only for printing terminals.[13]

A number of settings control the interpretation of the ⟨newline⟩ and ⟨return⟩ characters. They are needed because terminals differ in how they represent and process newlines. By default, the ⟨newline⟩ character is taken to be the ASCII ⟨linefeed⟩ character; a terminal needs to accompany this character by a motion to the left margin in order to achieve the effect of a newline. For some terminals this additional motion is automatic, but for others it isn't. Some terminals use ⟨return⟩ rather than ⟨newline⟩ to indicate a newline. The characters that a terminal emits to indicate a typed newline may also vary.

Other settings are concerned with the interpretation of special control characters such as the erase and kill characters. `Stty` enables you to specify what those characters are, and in addition enables you to turn the interpretation of those characters on or off.

We discuss the settings in several groups:

- The settings for control characters enable you to specify the characters used for special functions such as [Erase] and [Kill].
- The settings for control modes affect the characteristics of the communications line between your terminal and your computer.
- The settings for interpreting input affect how the stream of input characters coming from your terminal is transformed into the stream of input characters seen by the program you're running.

---

13. Printing terminals require that delays be inserted for actions such as returning the carriage so that the next character doesn't arrive before the action has been completed.

- The settings for interpreting output affect how the stream of output characters generated by the program you're running is transformed to the stream of characters sent to your terminal.
- The composite settings are combinations of the other settings.

A '-' in front of a setting disables it or reverses its effect. For example, the command

```
stty hup -echoe
```

specifies that hup should be turned on and echoe should be turned off.

Settings for Control Characters.   The settings below enable you to specify the values of the special control characters. If the character c is a control character—as it nearly always is—you indicate it with a caret, as in '∧D' or '∧d'. The uppercase and lowercase forms are equivalent. For each character we indicate the most common defaults.

erase c Set the erase character to c. This character erases the previous one typed. Its default is (Ctrl)H or '#'.

kill c Set the kill character to c. This character erases the entire current line. Its default is (Ctrl)U or '@'. **Note:** The kill character kills a line of text, not a process.

eof c Set the eof (end-of-file) character to c. This character indicates the end of standard input, and also acts as an exit for the Bourne shell. Its default value is (Ctrl)D.

intr c Set the interrupt character to c. This character interrupts the currently executing process. Its default value is (DEL) or (Ctrl)C.

quit c Set the quit character to c. This character also interrupts the currently executing process, but in addition generates a memory dump in a file in your current directory named core. Its default value is (Ctrl)\.

stop c Set the stop character to c. This character temporarily stops output to your terminal. You resume the output with the start character. Its default value is (Ctrl)Q (ASCII ⟨DC1⟩); many systems won't let you change it.

start c Set the start character to c. This character restarts output to your terminal when it's been stopped by the stop character. Its default value is (Ctrl)S (ASCII ⟨DC3⟩); many systems won't let you change it.

flush c Set the flush character to c. This character causes the rest of the output from the currently active process to be discarded but without interrupting the process. Many systems don't provide a flush character. Its default value is (Ctrl)O.

susp c Set the job suspension character to c. Typing this character suspends but does not kill the currently active process. Its default value is (Ctrl)Z.

swtch c Set the job switch character to c. This character is used by the shell layers facility offered by some versions of System V to switch from one layer to another. Other versions of System V assign it exactly the same function as the job suspension character. Its default value is Ctrl ' or Ctrl Z.

werase *c* Set the word erase character to *c*. Typing this character erases the most recently typed word. Its default value is Ctrl W. The word erase character is a feature of BSD UNIX.

Settings for Control Modes. The following settings affect the communications line between your terminal and your computer:

speed Set the line to the indicated speed (baud rate). The recognized speeds are 110, 300, 600, 1200, 1800, 2400, 4800, 9600, 19200, and 38400.

0 Disconnect the phone line immediately.

[-]hup Disconnect the phone line when you log out.

[-]parenb Enable parity generation and detection. If parity is not enabled, no other parity settings have any effect.

[-]parity
[-]evenp Select even parity and assume seven-bit characters. The −evenp setting turns off parity and assumes eight-bit characters.

[-]oddp Select odd parity and assume seven-bit characters. The −oddp setting turns off parity and assumes eight-bit characters.

Settings for Interpreting Input. These settings affect how the terminal driver transforms the stream of characters received from your terminal into the stream of characters seen by the program you're running.

The following settings affect the treatment of ⟨newline⟩ and ⟨return⟩:

[-]icrnl Map ⟨return⟩ to ⟨newline⟩ on input.
[-]igncr Ignore ⟨return⟩ on input.
[-]inlcr Map ⟨newline⟩ to ⟨return⟩ on input.

The following settings affect the treatment of control characters:

[-]icanon Enable the erase and kill characters. With this option turned off, the erase and kill characters are treated just like data characters.

[-]isig Enable the interrupt, quit, switch, and flush characters.

[-]ixon Enable the start and stop characters. The negation of this option, −ixon, is necessary with programs such as Emacs that give Ctrl Q and Ctrl S special meanings, although Emacs usually makes the necessary change for you.

The following settings affect the treatment of lowercase characters:

[-]iuclc Map uppercase alphabetic characters to lowercase on input. This option is useful for older (*much* older) terminals that have only uppercase characters.

The following settings affect echoing, i.e., sending a copy of a typed character back to the terminal. Most terminals don't display a character as you type it; instead they expect the computer to send it back. With echoing turned on, each character you type is sent back to your terminal to be displayed; with echoing turned off, it isn't. Echoing is not always desirable—for instance, it should be turned off while you're typing your password.

[-]echo   Echo each typed character.

[-]echoe   Echo erase characters as ⟨backspace⟩⟨space⟩⟨backspace⟩.

[-]echok   Send a newline after eack kill character.

   The following setting affects tab characters in the input:

[-]tabs   Replace tabs by spaces when displaying or printing. This setting is effective only if your terminal can interpret tab characters. You can set the positions of the tabs with the `tabs` command (see Section 4.4.4).

Settings for Interpreting Output.   The following settings affect how the terminal driver transforms the stream of characters sent by the program you're running to the stream of character actually sent to your terminal:

[-]opost   Post-process the output. If this setting is disabled, no other output setting has any effect.

[-]ocrnl   Map ⟨return⟩ to ⟨newline⟩ on output.

[-]onlcr   Map ⟨newline⟩ to ⟨return⟩ on output.

[-]olcuc   Map lowercase alphabetic characters to uppercase on output. This setting, like `iuclc`, applies to terminals that can't handle lowercase characters.

[-]xcase   Indicate uppercase characters with a backslash, i.e, transform 'A' to '\A'.

Composite Settings.   The following settings produce combinations of effects:

sane   Set all settings to reasonable values.

term   Set all settings to values appropriate for the terminal *term*. The list of recognized values for *term* depends on your system.

cooked
[-]raw   Disable processing of special control characters. Setting `cooked` is equivalent to setting `-raw`.

ek   Set the erase and kill characters to '#' and '@'. This option is useful for terminals that print rather than display their output.[14]

[-]lcase   Enable conversion of lowercase alphabetic characters to uppercase ones. This setting combines the effects of `xcase`, `iuclc`, and `olcuc`.

[-]nl   Disable special processing of ⟨newline⟩ and ⟨return⟩. When this setting is enabled, all ⟨newline⟩ and ⟨return⟩ characters are transmitted in either direction exactly as received no matter what other settings are in effect.

---

14. In the early days of UNIX, most terminals were printing terminals.

4.4.3
Sending Instructions to Your Terminal with tput

The tput program can retrieve and display the control sequences for a particular terminal, not necessarily the one you're using. These control sequences instruct the terminal to perform operations such as resetting itself or clearing the screen. Tput can also retrieve the full description of a terminal. It extracts all this information from the terminfo data base of terminal characteristics (see Section 2.19). Tput is not available on older Berkeley-style systems.

The form of the tput command line is

> tput [-T *term*] *cmd*

If you specify a particular terminal with -T you get the sequences for that terminal; otherwise you get the sequences for your terminal type as recorded in the environment variable TERM. If tput can't determine the terminal type, it exits with a nonzero exit status (see below). The variable *cmd* specifies the function to be performed:

init   Send the terminal initialization string to standard output.

reset   Send the terminal reset string to standard output.

longname   Produce the full name of the terminal on standard output. Each terminal description in terminfo includes this information.

name [*param*] ...

Retrieve the terminfo capability *name* as indicated by the *param*s. The following are the types of capabilities and the result produced by tput for each type:

- A boolean capability specifies whether or not the terminal has a particular feature. For a boolean capability, the exit status (see below) indicates the presence or absence of the capability.

- An integer capability specifies a size or capacity of the terminal, such as the number of lines on the screen. For an integer capability, the integer value is sent to standard output.

- A string capability specifies the control sequence needed to accomplish a particular terminal operation. For a string capability, the string value is sent to standard output.

An example of this form of tput is

> tput cup 2 10

which moves the cursor to row 2, column 10. To see what characters are sent to your terminal by this sequence, use the command

> tput cup 2 10 | od

See Section 3.13 for a discussion of the od command. The terminfo data base defines a large collection of capabilities, further discussion of which is beyond the scope of this book.

In particular, the commands

```
tput init
tput reset
```

respectively initialize and reset the terminal.

Exit Status.   The tput exit status conveys two kinds of information: whether or not a terminal has a particular capability and whether or not the tput call itself is in the correct form. The exit status codes are defined as follows:

0   String was produced or capability is present.
1   Capability is absent.(This status does not indicate an error.)
2   Call is incorrect.
3   Terminal type can't be identified.
4   Capability is unknown.

**4.4.4
Setting Tabs
with tabs**

If your terminal has tab stops that can be externally set, the tabs command sends it a sequence of characters that sets them. The form of the tabs command line is

tabs *options*

The options for this command vary greatly from one system to another, though support for the $-n$ option, which sets tab stops every n spaces, is nearly universal. Other common options are those that specify a left margin or your terminal type. The simple command tabs without options sets tab stops every eight spaces. If your terminal type is not specified on the command line, tabs retrieves it from the TERM environment variable.

Positioning the Tab Stops.   The following options specify the locations of the tab stops. No more than one of them may be specified. The default for these options is -8, which sets tab stops every eight spaces.

$n_1,n_2, \ldots$ Set tab stops at positions n_1, n_2, etc.

$-n$ Set tab stops every n spaces, with the first tab stop at position 1.

-code   Use the "canned" tabs for the programming language designated by *code*. For example, $-f$ indicates FORTRAN conventions, with tabs at positions 1, 7, 11, 15, 19, and 23. Check your system documentation for the codes recognized by your version of tabs. This option is not useful for most modern programming languages (including C) since programs in these languages are usually written with uniformly spaced tab stops.

--file   Use the tab stops given in the format specification in *file* (see "Format Specifications in Files" on page 132).

Specifying Your Terminal.   The following option specifies your terminal type, which tabs needs in order to issue the correct tab-setting instructions:

-T *term*   Send the tab-setting sequence for a terminal of type *term*.

By default, `tabs` assumes your terminal type is given in the `TERM` environment variable. If `TERM` is not defined and you haven't provided a `-T` option, `tabs` sends a generic sequence that works on many terminals.

Setting a Left Margin.   The following option specifies a left margin:

+m[*n*]   Use a left margin of *n* spaces. All tab stops are moved right by *n* spaces, with the first tab stop set at column $n + 1$. If you omit *n*, it defaults to 10. `Tabs` applies this option last.

Format Specifications in Files.   Several UNIX programs recognize and use format specifications that appear on the first line of a file.[15] A format specification has the form

        <: *spec* ... :>

where each *spec* consists of a key letter followed by a value. Other material such as comment indicators for various programming languages may also appear on the line. Thus you may include a format specification as the first line of a program without having that specification affect the program.

   The key letter `t` specifies the tab settings for the file that follows. (A format specification may also include several other key letters, not relevant here.) The settings have one of the following forms:

- A list of column numbers separated by commas
- A - followed by an integer *n*, indicating that tab stops should be set every *n*th column as above
- A "canned" tab sequence as defined above

An example of a first line following these conventions is

        #   <: t3 :>

Here the `#` makes the line a comment for several languages, including the Bourne shell.

4.5   Disk Usage Statistics

Two programs provide information about disk usage: `df` reports free disk space and `du` reports disk space in use. They are useful on systems in which disk space is scarce. Disk usage is measured in blocks; the size of a block is system-dependent, with 1024 a typical value.

**4.5.1
Reporting Free Disk
Space with df**

The `df` command reports the number of free blocks and free i-nodes in one or more file systems. The form of the `df` command line is

        df [*options*] [*name*] ...

where each *name* refers to a mounted file system (either local or remote) or a directory. If you specify a directory, you'll get the statistics for the

---

15. Except for `tabs`, we don't discuss those programs in this book. An example of such a program is `newform`, which reformats a file.

file system containing that directory. If you omit the names, you'll get a report on all mounted file systems, whether local or remote.

The command-line options described below apply to System V and BSD UNIX. Some other systems have additional options.

Command-line Options for System V. The command-line options for the System V version of df are as follows:

-l   Report only on local file systems.

-t   Report the total number of allocated blocks and i-nodes on the device as well as the number of free ones. The total includes the blocks that contain the i-nodes for the device.

-f   Count the actual blocks in the free list instead of using the count stored in the i-node representing the entire file system. You may get a spurious complaint about a bad block count if you apply df -f to a mounted file system.

Command-line Options for SunOS and BSD UNIX. The command-line options for the SunOS and BSD UNIX versions of df are as follows:

-a   Report on all file systems, even those having no blocks.

-i   Report the number of i-nodes that are free and the number that are in use.

-t *type*   Report only on file systems of type *type*, such as 'nfs' (Network File System).

For BSD UNIX, only -i is supported.

**4.5.2
Reporting Disk
Space in Use with** du

The du command reports the number of disk blocks occupied by a file or by the files in a directory and its descendent subdirectories (including the disk blocks occupied by the directories themselves). The form of the du command line is

    du [*options*] [*name*] . . .

where each *name* is a directory or a file. If you omit the names, you get a report on the current directory.

Du always shows fewer blocks in use within the root directory of a file system than you obtain by typing 'df -t' and subtracting the free blocks from the total blocks to obtain the blocks in use. That's because df includes i-node blocks in its total while du does not. Du does not count i-node blocks because they are not associated with any particular file.

Command-line Options. The command-line options for du are as follows:

-a   Produce an output line for each file. Each line contains the block count followed by a tab and the name of the file.

-s   Report only the total usage for each *name* that is a directory, i.e., don't report on the individual files within the directory.

-r   Produce messages about directories that can't be read and files that can't be opened. By default, these messages are not issued. Not all systems recognize this option.

4.6   Miscellaneous Services

The commands in this group provide an assortment of convenient services that don't fall into any other category.

4.6.1
Echoing Arguments
with echo

The echo command echoes its arguments to standard output. Its uses include producing error messages in shell scripts, displaying the values of shell or environment variables, and constructing short files. For example, the command

```
echo $PATH
```

displays the current value of the environment variable PATH. The command

```
echo 'find $HOME -name $1 -print' >ff
```

puts the text between the quotes into the file ff; the quotes are necessary to prevent the shell from interpreting the '$1' before the text is stored in the file.

You may include the following escape characters in the echoed text:

\c	Cancel implicit newline
\n	Newline
\r	Carriage return
\f	Form feed (new page)
\v	Vertical tab
\b	Backspace
\t	Tab
\\	Backslash
\0*n*	Character with ASCII code *n* (octal)

Normally the echoed material is followed by a newline; '\c' at the end of the material cancels that newline. The backslashes in these escape characters must be quoted so that echo rather than the shell interprets them.

The BSD UNIX version of echo does not recognize the escape characters but provides a -n option that suppresses the newline at the end of the echoed text. Some other versions of echo support the -n option and recognize all of these characters except '\c'.

4.6.2
Sending Messages
with write

You can send messages to other logged-in users (or even to yourself) with the write command. To use it, type

```
write user line
   ...text of the message
  EOF
```

Here *user* is the user name of the person to whom you're sending the message, which may contain any number of lines. You need provide *line* only if the person is logged in at more than one terminal, in which case you must specify the terminal as *line*, e.g., 'tty17'. After you type the command line, *user* receives a message at his or her terminal similar to

> `Message from` *sender* `(ttynn)`

followed by the lines of the message as you type them.

If messages from other users are disrupting your output, you may block them with the command 'chmod -w /dev/tty' (see Section 3.12.1) or with the command 'mesg -n' (see Section 4.6.3).

Under BSD UNIX, an alternative to `write` is the `talk` command.

4.6.3
Turning Off
Messages with mesg

You can block your terminal to incoming messages by issuing the command

> `mesg -n`

Typing 'mesg -n' is useful when you want to prevent your output from being interrupted. To unblock your terminal, issue the command

> `mesg -y`

The BSD UNIX version of `mesg` does not use the dashes preceding 'n' and 'y'.

The command `mesg` by itself simply reports on whether your terminal is currently accepting messages.

You can get the same effect as `mesg -n` with the command

> `chmod -w /dev/tty`

Note: The superuser may write to your terminal even if you've blocked it.

4.6.4
Timing a Command
with time

The `time` command enables you to time a command to see how long it takes to execute. The form of the `time` command line is

> `time` *cmd*

where *cmd* is the command to be timed. `Time` is an intrinsic shell command rather than a separate program. The Bourne and C shell shells require *cmd* to be a simple command (no parentheses); the Korn shell allows it to be anything you can enclose in parentheses.

A sample output from the Bourne shell version of `time` is

```
real       1:48.1
user        45.6
sys          1.8
```

The three times shown here are the elapsed time, the time consumed by the user process, and the time consumed by system processes (all in minutes and seconds). The output of `time` follows the output of *cmd* itself and is sent to standard error rather than standard output. The output produced by the C shell's `time` command has a different form (see p. 201). You can also use the C shell's `time` variable to time a complex command (see p. 196).

**4.6.5
Evaluating
Expressions
with** `expr`

The `expr` command evaluates an expression, which may include arithmetic operations, comparisons, logical operations, and pattern matches. The form of the `expr` command line is

    expr *expr*

where *expr* is the expression to be evaluated. The value of the expression, which may be either an integer or a string, is sent to standard output.

Conventions for Writing the Expression.   The expression consists of a sequence of words, each of which is either a value, an operator, or a parenthesis. Words must be separated by whitespace. A number of the operators contain characters such as '<' that are meaningful to various shells; these characters must be quoted. Parentheses, which usually must be quoted, have their usual mathematical meaning. For example, if you type

    expr '(' 3 + 4 ')' '*' 8

you'll get the output 56. You must also quote null strings and strings containing blanks.

Arithmetic Operators.   An expression may contain the following arithmetic operators:

    + - * / %

The expression 'e_1 % e_2' gives the remainder after dividing e_1 by e_2. The '$-$' operator may be used either as a unary operator or as a binary operator.

Comparison Operators.   An expression may contain the following comparison operators:

    < > <= >= !=

The operator '!=' indicates inequality. If both arguments to an operator are integers, `expr` compares them numerically; otherwise it compares them lexicographically (as strings). The result of a comparison is 1 if the comparison succeeds and 0 if it fails.

Logical Operators.   The logical operators '&' and '|' are useful for combining the results of tests:

expr$_1$ | *expr*$_2$
> If *expr*$_1$ is neither null nor zero, the result is *expr*$_1$; otherwise it is *expr*$_2$.

expr$_1$ & *expr*$_2$
> If neither *expr*$_1$ nor *expr*$_2$ is null or zero, the result is *expr*$_1$; otherwise it is zero.

Pattern Matching Operator.   The expression '*expr*$_1$: *expr*$_2$' yields the result of matching the string *expr*$_1$ against the regular expression *expr*$_2$ (see Section 2.16). The recognized components of the regular expression are as given in 2.16 with one exception: the regular expression may contain at most one parenthesized subexpression (although you may still use the '\1' notation to repeat that subexpression).

The value returned by the match is the number of characters matched, or zero if the match failed. If *expr₂* contains a parenthesized subexpression, however, the result of the entire expression is the substring matched by the parenthesized subexpression. For example, if you type

```
expr Okeefenokee : '.*\(...\).*\1.*'
```

you'll get the output `kee`, representing the first (and only) repeated three-character string in 'Okeefenokee'.

Application to Shell Scripts. Expr is particularly useful in Bourne shell scripts as a way of doing internal arithmetic. For instance, the following line in a Bourne shell script sets the variable `w` to the sum of the variables `w1` and `w2`:

```
w1 = 'expr $w1 + $w2'
```

It is less useful in C shell scripts because the C shell already includes the ability to evaluate expressions (see Section 5.3.14).

**4.6.6
Parsing File Names
with** basename
and dirname

The `basename` and `dirname` commands parse file names to extract their parts. They are used almost exclusively in shell scripts.

The form of the `dirname` command line is

```
dirname string
```

where *string* is a string that represents a file name. The command produces on standard output the portion of *string* that precedes its last '/', or *string* itself if it contains no '/'.

The form of the `basename` command line is

```
basename string₁ [string₂]
```

where *string₁* is a string that represents a file name and *string₂* is an expected suffix of *string₁*. If *string₂* is absent it is taken to be the null string. The command deletes *string₂* from the end of *string₁* (if it is there) and then produces on standard output the portion that follows the last '/' if any.

For example, the command

```
dirname /usr/natasha/borscht.Z
```

produces the output

```
/usr/natasha
```

while the command

```
basename /usr/natasha/borscht.Z .Z
```

produces the output

```
borscht
```

4.7   Document Processing

In the following subsections we briefly describe the major document processors available under UNIX. All of them expect their input to be an ordinary text file prepared with a text editor such as `emacs` or `vi`.

The nroff formatter ("New Runoff", pronounced "en-roff") takes as its input a document with interspersed formatting commands and produces a version of that document suitable for printing on a line printer. The troff ("Typesetter new Runoff", pronounced "tee-roff") formatter is similar, except that its output consists of a set of instructions to a typesetting machine. The original troff only worked with a specific typesetter; more recent versions produce device-independent output that may be piped through another program, the postprocessor, to drive a particular typesetter such as a laser printer.[16] Nroff is very close in spirit to the DEC RUNOFF formatter and to the IBM Script formatter; all three formatters share the same input format as well as a number of specific commands.[17] Nroff and troff were written by Joseph Osanna at Bell Telephone Laboratories. Reference [B9] provides a tutorial on nroff, troff, and the preprocessors described later in this section.

Input to nroff has the form of a sequence of *text lines* with interspersed directives, also called *control lines*. The directives are one-letter or two-letter instructions preceded by a period and possibly followed by some arguments. For example, the directive '.sp 2' instructs nroff to space down by two lines, i.e., to insert two blank lines in the output. Text lines may also include *interpolations* that specify text to be substituted; for instance, an occurrence of '*G' in a text line is replaced by the current value of the string named 'G'.

Nroff enables you to define *macros*. A macro definition defines a new command as a sequence of input lines. The new command can accept *arguments* on the input line; these are made available to the macro definition and may be retrieved as interpolations. A macro may be called either explicitly or by associating it with a *trap*. A trap is a condition such as the end of a page; when the condition is satisfied, the macro is called. A trap may test for three kinds of conditions: reaching the end of the page, reaching the nth line on the page, or reaching the nth line of a *diversion*. Processed output may be diverted into a macro for such purposes as creating a footnote or measuring the dimensions of the output in order to decide whether it is time to start a new page.

Nroff is almost always used with a prepackaged collection of macros. You may specify the macro package with the -m option on the command line. Strictly speaking, the option '-ms' calls the macro package named 's' rather than the macro package named '-ms', but the custom is to call the package 'ms' nevertheless. These are the major macro packages available:

- The ms package is the original collection of macros developed at Bell Laboratories early in the history of nroff. It is no longer supported by AT&T but is still provided with many UNIX systems.

---

16. Some systems are configured with troff linked to the old device-specific formatter and with the newer device-independent formatter available under the name ditroff.

17. The three formatters show unmistakable signs of a common origin. DEC RUNOFF and UNIX nroff are both descendents of the Multics RUNOFF program, but we don't know how Script fits into the lineage.

- The mm package is an enhanced version of ms for formatting techni-
  cal documents, memoranda, and letters. The letters 'mm' stand for
  "Memorandum Macros". This package is provided as part of the
  AT&T Documenter's Workbench.

- The me package is distributed as part of BSD UNIX. It is comparable
  to ms and mm.

Many specialized packages are also available, such as the -man package for
preparing pages of the UNIX manual.

4.7.2
Preprocessors for
nroff **and** troff

Three specialized preprocessors are available for nroff and troff:

- The eqn preprocessor typesets mathematical formulas.
- The tbl preprocessor lays out tables in a document.
- The pic preprocessor draws pictures.

If you use all three of them in a single document, your command line
should be something like this:

    pic *file* | tbl | eqn | troff -mm | *postprocessor*

It's important to call these preprocessors in the order shown.

   Eqn was written by Brian Kernighan and Lorinda Cherry; tbl was written by Michael Lesk; and pic was written by Brian Kernighan. All of this
work was done at Bell Telephone Laboratories.

Typesetting Formulas with eqn.   The eqn preprocessor takes as its input
a troff file containing pairs of the special directives '.eq' and '.en'. The
material between these directives describes a mathematical formula to be
typeset. The output is a troff input file in which this material has been
replaced by troff instructions for constructing the formula on the printed
page. A version of eqn called neqn works with nroff but does not usually
produce satisfactory results because of nroff's limitations. Eqn normally
places a formula on a line by itself; you may typeset a formula within a
line by surrounding the formula with special delimiters. The facilities provided by eqn include the following:

- Greek letters and other special symbols
- Subscripts and superscripts
- Summations, integral, products, and limits that contain upper and
  lower parts
- Enclosing parts of formulas in big brackets, braces, parentheses, or
  other delimiters
- Fractions, arrays, matrices, and vertical piles of subformulas
- Notations for controlling the amount of space between parts of a
  formula and for using different fonts within a formula

Formatting Tables with tbl.   The tbl preprocessor takes as its input a
troff or nroff file containing special table-building instructions between
the directives '.ts' and '.te'. Its output contains the necessary instructions
for producing the tables. For simple tables, each row of the table is given
by a line of input, with '@' or some other defined tab character separating

the column entries. For more complex tables, the input format is modified appropriately. The facilities provided by `tbl` include the following:

- Left justifying, right justifying, or centering data within a column
- Aligning decimal numbers by their decimal points
- Drawing horizontal and vertical rules
- Vertically centering entries that apply to a set of rows
- Allowing entries to span several rows
- Turning blocks of text into table entries

Drawing Pictures with `pic`. The `pic` preprocessor inserts picture-drawing instructions into a document. It requires full typesetting capabilities and cannot be used with `nroff`. Picture-drawing commands are surrounded by the directives '.ps' and '.pe'. The facilities provided by `pic` include the following:

- Drawing boxes, circles, ellipses, arcs, arrows, lines, and splines
- Placing text within graphical objects
- Connecting objects with various kinds of lines
- Placing objects relative to other objects

The notation for describing pictures is essentially verbal; a typical line of `pic` input would be

```
arrow left down from bottom of last ellipse
```

The `pic` preprocessor is not included with BSD UNIX, even though `eqn` and `tbl` are.

**4.7.3
TeX and LaTeX**

TeX is a computerized typesetting system that provides nearly everything needed for typesetting mathematics as well as ordinary text. It was written by Donald E. Knuth at Stanford University. TeX is especially notable for its flexibility, its repertoire of mathematical constructs and symbols, its superb hyphenation, and its ability to choose aesthetically satisfying line breaks. It has become quite popular in the UNIX world as an alternative to `nroff` and `troff`.

A number of UNIX vendors include TeX and LaTeX as part of their standard system distributions. You may obtain TeX and LaTeX over the Internet via anonymous `ftp` from `labrea.stanford.edu`, IP address `36.8.0.47`, in the directory `/pub/tex` (see Section 10.7), or over the `uucp` network from the OSUCIS archive (reference [U3]). TeX is described in references [B16] and [B1]. This book was typeset using TeX.

Input to TeX consists of an ordinary text file. The file contains the text of a document augmented by *control sequences* that provide special formatting instructions. A control sequence starts with a backslash and may appear anywhere, not just at the beginning of a line. A number of other notations are also available; for example, a mathematical formula can be specified by enclosing it in dollar signs if it is to appear in running text and in double dollar signs if it is to be displayed on a line by itself. Serious users of TeX almost always use packages of macros, some quite elaborate, to define useful control sequences. The output of TeX is *not* sent to standard output; instead it is sent to a file named '*file*.dvi' where '*file*.tex' (or simply '*file*') is the name of the input file.

A disadvantage of TeX is that considerable skill is required to use it effectively. The LaTeX document processing system, written by Leslie Lamport of the Digital Equipment Corporation, is a collection of TeX macros that makes TeX easier to use by enabling the user to concentrate on the structure of the text rather than on the particular commands needed to format it (see reference [B17]). LaTeX documents are particularly simple to prepare, and as a result LaTeX has outstripped TeX in popularity. At the same time, LaTeX provides access to all the facilities of TeX. Some notable features provided by LaTeX are its sets of commands for drawing diagrams and for referring to citations in a bibliographic database. The bibliographic database is maintained by another program called BibTeX.

A disadvantage of LaTeX is that it is difficult to customize it except within rather narrow limits. As a result, documents from different sources produced using LaTeX all tend to look the same. Customizing LaTeX is certainly possible but even more difficult than customizing TeX, since you need to know both TeX and the LaTeX implementation very well in order to do it.

5

Shells

A *shell* or *command interpreter* is a program that interprets and executes commands as you issue them from your terminal. A shell requires no special privileges to run; as far as the UNIX kernel is concerned, a shell is like any other program. Typical shell features include interpretation of shell scripts, expansion of wildcards in file names, combination of commands into pipelines, recall of previous commands, looping and conditional constructs, and variables for creating abbreviations. A *shell script* is a file that contain sequences of shell commands just as you would type them; shell scripts enable you to customize your working environment without having to do "real" programming.

We discuss four shells in this chapter: the Bourne shell `sh` and the C shell `csh` in detail and the Korn shell `ksh` and the extended C shell `tcsh` briefly. The Bourne shell is part of Seventh Edition UNIX and is the earliest major UNIX shell; the C shell is the principal shell of BSD UNIX. Most users have found that the C shell is easier to use interactively but that the Bourne shell is easier to use for writing shell scripts;[1] fortunately it is possible to call a shell script written for one shell from within another. The Korn shell, an extension to the Bourne shell, includes most of the best features of the C shell and many useful additions of its own. The Korn shell is not included in many UNIX distributions, but it is probably your best choice if you can obtain it.

Because some shell facilities are intrinsic to the UNIX style of working and are common to all shells, we explain them in Chapter 2 (Concepts)

---

1. `Sh` includes two capabilities, selective trapping of signals and redirection for arbitrary file descriptors, that `csh` lacks. These capabilities, though rarely used interactively, are essential to some shell scripts.

rather than in this chapter. Pipelines, the simpler forms of redirection, and quotation are examples. Although in principle someone could write a shell that provided the functionality of these facilities differently or not at all, no one has and no one is likely to.

5.1   Shell Scripts

Shell scripts, also called *shell procedures*, enable you to customize your environment by adding your own commands. Although writing a shell script does call for some simple programming, it's far easier than writing a C program.

Short shell scripts are easy to compose and install. For instance, suppose you wish to define a `dir` command that produces a nicer directory listing than the one you get by default. We assume that you use a `bin` subdirectory of your home directory for storing your personal collection of programs and shell scripts and that this directory is on your search path (see the discussion of `PATH` in Section 2.11.2). You can create such a `dir` command for yourself by typing

```
cat >$HOME/bin/dir
ls -aCF $@
EOF
chmod +x $HOME/dir
```

Here the `cat` line copies the second line to the `dir` file; the `ls` line defines the meaning of `dir`; and the `chmod` line makes the `dir` file executable (a precondition to executing a shell script).[2] This one-line script follows the Bourne shell conventions; shell scripts are interpreted by the Bourne shell in the absence of any indication to the contrary.

Once you've created this command, you obtain your improved listing by typing `dir` followed by a set of file and directory names. The names can include wildcards. The command also works if you type `dir` by itself; in this case you get the contents of the current directory. A more elaborate version of `dir` might, for example, recognize a variety of options.

Interpretation of Shell Scripts.   When a shell encounters a command that is not intrinsic, i.e., not recognized and executed directly by the shell itself, the shell calls upon the kernel to execute that command. The command can be either a compiled program or a shell script. If it is a shell script, the kernel must then select a shell to execute the script.

How the kernel makes that selection depends on your system. The default case is always some version of the Bourne shell or, in a few cases, the Korn shell (which is almost completely compatible with the Bourne shell). Bourne shell compatibility is essential because historically the Bourne shell

---

2. A shell script must have read permission as well, but a newly created file normally has read permission by default.

was the only shell available in the Seventh Edition; many shell scripts in common use assume without any explicit indication that they are being interpreted by the Bourne shell.

Most systems now honor the BSD UNIX convention that if the first line of a shell script has the form

```
#!  shell
```

where *shell* is the full path name of a shell, that shell is used to interpret the script. The whitespace after '#!' is optional. For instance, if you write a script using the C shell command set, it should start with

```
#! /bin/csh
```

In fact, you can cause a script to be interpreted by any program at all. For instance, suppose you issue a command naming an executable file whose first line is

```
#!/usr/sybil/read.entrails
```

Then the `read.entrails` program in `sybil`'s home directory is given control with the executable file as its input. Naturally, `read.entrails` must be clever enough to recognize the first line as a comment and ignore it.

Some systems that don't honor the '#!' convention provide another way of tagging some shell scripts: if the first character is ':', it is taken to be a Bourne shell script, while if the first character is '#', it is taken to be a C shell script.

Each of the common shells provides a `-v` option for displaying each input line as it is read and a `-x` option for displaying each command as it is executed. These options are very useful for debugging shell scripts.

5.2   The Bourne Shell `sh`

The Bourne shell `sh`, written by Steve Bourne in 1979, is part of Seventh Edition UNIX and is the earliest major UNIX shell. The newer shells are easier to use interactively because they provide conveniences lacking in the Bourne shell such as command-line editing, recall of previously issued commands and aliases for often-used commands. Nevertheless, many UNIX users still prefer the Bourne shell for interactive use. Most shell scripts follow the Bourne shell conventions.

Because `sh` was the only significant shell when it was introduced, UNIX documentation often refers to "the shell" when it specifically means `sh`. Many of these references apply *only* to `sh` and not to any other shell. Statements in this book about "the shell" apply to all major shells; when a statement applies only to `sh`, we name it specifically.

Important facilities provided by `sh` include the following:

- Operators for background or conditional execution of commands.

- Statements for repeated execution of commands, including iteration over a sequence of values that can be assigned to an iteration variable.

- Substitutable variables, both named and numbered. Numbered variables, also called parameters or positional parameters, contain the arguments to a command.

- Export of specified variables to child processes.

- Three forms of quotation.

- Execution of commands in subshells.

- Automatic notification when mail arrives.

- Inclusion of input data for a command in a shell script as part of the script.

- Trapping of signals and execution of specified commands when a specified signal occurs.

- Execution of commands in initialization files before any input is read. These initialization files can be used to customize sh.

These facilities are all described below.

The version of sh described here is the System V version. The version of sh found in some systems, BSD UNIX in particular, is an older one from Seventh Edition UNIX that lacks some of the facilities in the System V version. For these systems the newer version may be available under the name sh5. There is little reason to use the older version if the newer one is available.

**5.2.1
Quick Exit**

You can interrupt most commands executing within sh by pressing (Intr). A few commands, however, take control of the keyboard and assign their own interpretation to the (Intr) key; for one of these you'll have to consult the command's description to see how to interrupt it. When you interrupt a command, sh returns you to its command level and prompts you for another command. You then can exit from sh by typing either (EOF) or exit.

**5.2.2
Syntax of Shell Input**

Sh can read its input from either a terminal or a file. As it reads, sh decomposes its input into a sequence of *words*. Words are separated either by *separators* or by metacharacters (to be described shortly). Ordinarily the separator characters are space and tab, but you can change the set of separators by assigning a different value to the shell variable IFS (see p. 168).

The effect of a newline, which you produce by pressing (Enter), depends on the contents of the line:

(1) If the line satisfies the syntax of a complete command, the newline ends the command (and is equivalent to a semicolon; see below).

(2) If the line contains no words, the line and the newline are ignored.

(3) Otherwise, the newline is ignored and the next line is taken as a continuation of the current line.

In any event a newline acts as a separator in that it ends a word.

When **sh** is expecting input, it displays a prompt: the primary prompt string ('**$**' by default) when it's expecting a new command and the secondary prompt string ('**>**' by default) when it's expecting a command continuation. You can change these prompt strings by assigning other values to the shell variables PS1 and PS2 (p. 168).

Quotation affects the way that **sh** decomposes its input into words (see Section 5.2.12). A character that normally acts as a separator does not act as a separator if quoted. In particular, a quoted blank does not separate words and a quoted newline does not end a command.

The following characters, called *metacharacters*, have special meanings:

```
; & ( ) | ^ < >
```

These characters end a word unless they are quoted.

Comments. The input to **sh** can include comments. A comment starts with a '**#**' at the beginning of a word and extends to the end of the line. A '**#**' in the middle of a word does *not* start a comment. Sh ignores anything in a comment. For example, the input

```
echo Greetings from the under#world
#and points beyond
```

produces the output

```
Greetings from the under#world
```

**5.2.3
Calling Programs
with
Simple Commands**

A *simple command* is either an intrinsic command or a program call. Intrinsic commands are discussed in Section 5.2.16. Syntactically, a simple command consists of a sequence of words, none of which are among the operators listed below in Section 5.2.4 or among the keywords listed on p. 151. Sh takes the first word as the name of the command and the remaining words as its arguments.

A program call causes the program to be executed. A program call can be preceded by one or more assignments to variables. These assignments apply to the environment of the subshell created by the command (see Section 5.2.11) but do not affect any local variables (see "Local Variables" on page 157). For instance, if you type

```
OPS="+-" recalc
```

the `recalc` program (or shell script) is executed with the environment variable OPS set to '+-'. If a local variable OPS exists, it is unaffected; if it does not exist, it is not created.

If a program terminates because of a signal sent to it (see Section 2.7.4), sh assigns the program an exit status of octal 200 plus the signal code.[3] For example, if you interrupt a command by typing (Intr), the command returns an exit status of octal 202. Since the exit status of a command

---

3. When **sh** calls a foreground program on your behalf, it issues a **wait** system call and waits for the program to terminate. The exit status returned by **wait** informs **sh** whether the program terminated normally or as the result of a signal, and if as the result of a signal, what the signal number was.

that terminates of its own accord is by programming convention less than octal 200, you can distinguish termination caused by a signal from normal termination.

5.2.4 Linking Commands with Operators

Sh provides several operators for linking commands. We first explain what each operator does, assuming that just one operator is being used at a time. We then explain what operator combinations do.

| | The '|' operator connects two commands through a *pipe*. The standard output of the first command becomes the standard input of the second. A group of one or more commands connected this way is called a *pipeline*. For example, the pipeline

```
ps | sort  | lp
```

causes the output of ps (Section 4.2.1) to become the input of sort (Section 8.1) and the output of sort to become the input of lp (Section 3.14.1). The result is that a sorted list of the currently active processes is sent to the printer. Sh implements a pipeline as a set of processes, one for each command in the pipeline.

|| If c_1 and c_2 are commands, the combination '$c_1 || c_2$' first executes c_1. If the exit status of c_1 is nonzero (see Section 2.7.3), it then executes c_2. A nonzero exit status usually indicates unsuccessful execution. In other words, c_2 is executed only if c_1 fails.

&&   The '&&' operator is like '||' except that it tests for successful execution rather than unsuccessful execution. If c_1 and c_2 are commands, the combination '$c_1 \&\& c_2$' first executes c_1. If the exit status of c_1 is zero, it then executes c_2. In other words, c_2 is executed only if c_1 succeeds.

;   A semicolon marks the end of a command. When sh sees a semicolon after a command, it executes that command and goes on to the next one. Thus the sequence 'c_1; c_2' has the effect of "execute c_1, then execute c_2". For example,

```
ls; who
```

causes the command ls to be executed, followed by the command who. A newline is equivalent to a semicolon in any context where a semicolon is permitted (see Section 5.2.2).

&   An ampersand specifies that the preceding command is to be executed as a background process. When sh sees an ampersand after a command, it initiates the background process and proceeds immediately to the next command if any. In other words, the sequence 'c_1 & c_2' has the effect of "start c_1 executing in the background, then execute c_2" while the sequence 'c &' has the effect of "execute c in the background". For example, the input line

```
devour & engulf
```

causes the command `devour` to be executed as a background process. As soon as `sh` has started this process, it starts executing the `engulf` command. As another example, the input line

```
sort < elephantine > humongous &
```

causes `sh` to start a time-consuming sort in the background and prompt you for another command.

Sh executes a background command in a subshell (see Section 5.2.14), displaying the subshell's process number in brackets. Some uses of background execution are described in "Uses of Background Execution" below.

When two commands are combined with an operator, the exit status of the combination is that of the second command. A command executed in the background returns exit status 0 when it is initiated.

Combinations of Operators.   The order of precedence of the operators listed above, from high to low, is

(1)   `|`
(2)   `||`   `&&`
(3)   `;`   `&`

In other words, commands are first grouped with '`|`'. The commands thus collected are called *pipelines*. A pipeline can consist of just a single command if it is not adjacent to a '`|`'.

The pipelines are then grouped with '`||`' and '`&&`' into "conditional lists" (our term). When you connect several pipelines with '`||`' and '`&&`', the pipelines are executed in sequence until one of them returns a zero exit status and is followed by '`||`' or one of them returns a nonzero exit status and is followed by '`&&`'. If and when that happens, the rest of the pipelines are ignored.

Finally, the conditional lists are grouped with '`;`' and '`&`' to form *lists*. A list must be ended with a semicolon, ampersand, or newline if its last command is a simple command (see the example under `if` in 5.2.6 below).

For example, the command line

```
tryit | feed && ls -l ; sleep 20 && echo hi &
```

is interpreted as follows:

(1)   Execute '`tryit`' and '`feed`' as a pipeline, with the standard output of `tryit` becoming the standard input of `feed`.
(2)   If that succeeds, execute '`ls -l`'.
(3)   Then, in any case, start a new background process.
(4)   In that background process, execute '`sleep 20`'.
(5)   If that execution succeeds (which it does unless it is interrupted), execute '`echo hi`' within the same background process.

Uses of Background Execution.   Some uses of background execution are the following:

• Suppose you wish to execute some commands that take a long time and your other work doesn't depend on the results of those commands. If you execute the time-consuming commands in the background, you can do your other work without having to wait for them to finish.

- You can schedule a command execution for a later time by preceding the command with a delay and executing the combination in the background. For example, the command list

      (sleep 600; retry) &

  sets up a background process that waits for ten minutes (600 seconds) and then executes retry.

  If you use sleep to produce the delay and log out before the command has finished executing, the process goes away and the command is aborted (or never starts). You can ensure that the command is executed in any case by scheduling it for a specific time with at (see Section 4.2.5). Alternatively, you can use nohup to execute the command with hangups ignored (see Section 4.2.4). For each of these methods, the combination must be set up as a background process.

- In a windowing system such as X (see Chapter 11), you may wish to have several terminal emulations, some of which may be remote logins, active simultaneously. Each emulated terminal has its own window, thereby enabling you to switch back and forth among the emulations. If you start a new terminal emulation as a foreground process, you are blocked from using your current window until the terminal emulation has exited. For instance, if you type

      xterm

  to create a new terminal, your current window sits on this command until the new terminal has gone away. But if you make the new terminal a background process by typing

      xterm &

  you can switch back and forth freely between the new terminal and the old one.

**5.2.5
Redirection**

Using redirection, you can cause a program to take its input from a specified file instead of from the terminal or send its output to a specified file instead of to a terminal. The principal forms of redirection are explained in Section 2.12. The descriptions that follow include these forms as well as more general forms such as redirection for arbitrary file descriptors (see Section 2.12.2). In these forms, the whitespace preceding *file*, *n*, or '-' is optional.

< *file*   Take standard input from the file *file*, i.e, make the file associated with file descriptor 0 be *file*. See Section 2.12 for a further description of this form of redirection.

<< [-] *word*
             Take standard input from the following text, called *here text*. This form of redirection enables you to include here text in a shell script. You can include here text in interactive input, but it is rarely useful to do so.

When `sh` encounters this form of redirection within a command, it reads input until it encounters either a line consisting exactly of *word* or an end-of-file. This input becomes the standard input of the command. The string *word* thus serves as a marker to indicate the end of the input.

If '–' is present, leading tabs are removed as each line is read; otherwise tabs are not treated specially. The tab-stripping happens after any applicable substitutions are performed.

Within the here text, `sh` normally performs certain limited transformations. It applies variable substitution (see Section 5.2.10) and command substitution (see Section 5.2.13). It deletes the sequence \⟨newline⟩ and treats '\' as a quoting character when it precedes one of the characters (\ $ '). (Any other occurrence of '\' is taken literally, i.e., left alone.) However, if any portion of *word* is quoted (according to any of the quoting conventions), `sh` takes the here text literally and does not perform any of these transformations (although tab-stripping can still occur).

> `> file`
> Send standard output to the file *file*, i.e, make the file associated with file descriptor 1 be *file*. If *file* already exists, it is forced to be empty before any output is sent to it;[4] if it does not already exist, it is created.

> `>> file`
> This form of redirection is like '> *file*', except that the new output is appended to *file* if it already exists. The previous contents of the file are not lost.

> `<& n`
> Cause the file now associated with file descriptor *n* to be associated with standard input as well, thus creating another way to read that file.[5] This form and the following ones must be written without whitespace between the '<' or '>' and the '&'.

> `>& n`
> Cause the file now associated with file descriptor *n* to be associated with standard output as well, thus creating another way to write that file.

> `<& -`
> Close standard input, i.e., disassociate file descriptor 0 from its file. Note that it is the descriptor, not the file itself, that is closed.

> `>& -`
> Close standard output, i.e., disassociate file descriptor 1 from its file. Note that it is the descriptor, not the file itself, that is closed.

---

4. If you redirect output to an existing file but don't actually send any output there, the original contents of the file are still lost.

5. More precisely, file descriptor *n* is duplicated and the new copy assigned to file descriptor 1. The other forms below are analogous.

n< file
n<< file
n> file
n>> file
n<& m
n>& m
n<& -
n>& -   These forms are like the ones listed above, except that they use
file descriptor *n* instead of file descriptor 0 or 1. There must
not be any whitespace between *n* and '<' or '>', nor between
these characters and '&'. For example,

```
exper 3>& 1    1>& 2    2>& 3    3>& -
```

interchanges the role of standard output (file descriptor 1) and
standard error (file descriptor 2). The second redirection could
be written as '>&2'. The purpose of the last redirection is to
avoid leaving behind an extra file descriptor.

As the example above illustrates, `sh` acts on file redirections in the order
it encounters them, from left to right.

A redirection applied to a compound command affects all the command's components. For example, the command

```
for f in *.data; do analyze $f; done > gigo
```

causes the `analyze` program to be executed for every file in the current
directory whose name matches '`*.data`' and causes the output of all these
executions to be sent to the file `gigo`.

The `exec` command (p. 170) has a special interpretation when its arguments consist entirely of redirections: the redirections are made effective
for the rest of the execution of `sh` (or its subshell), and execution then
continues with the next command. For example,

```
exec < newinput
```

causes standard input for subsequently executed commands to be taken
from the file `newinput`.

5.2.6
Compound
Commands

A *compound command* is one that contains other commands. Compound
commands provide conditional execution, looping, case testing, grouped
execution, and function definition.

The following keywords are used in compound commands:

```
if   then  else  elif  fi   case  esac
for  while until  do   done
```

`Sh` recognizes them only in a context where a command name can appear,
such as at the beginning of a line, following ';', or following '||'. Because
these keywords have special meaning to `sh`, you can't use them as the
names of shell scripts or compiled programs.

Redirection applied to a compound command affects the input and output of all contained commands (see p. 151). It also forces the command to

be directly executed in a subshell (see Section 5.2.14) and therefore affects the consequences of assignments to variables from within the command.[6]

The compound commands are the following:

if   The `if` command has the form

```
if list
     then list
[elif list
     then list]
  ...
[else list]
fi
```

Each of the keywords in this command ('`if`', '`then`', '`elif`', '`else`', and '`fi`') must appear either as the first word on a line or as the first word following a semicolon. Each *list* represents a list of commands as defined on page 148.

The command lists following '`if`' and '`elif`' act as tests and are tried in turn until one succeeds. Then the *list* following the '`then`' after the successful test is executed. If none of the tests succeed, the *list* following '`else`' (if '`else`' is present) is executed. If all tests fail and no '`else`' is present, the execution of the entire command is complete. In this case the entire '`if ... fi`' construct returns an exit code of 0; in all other cases the entire construct returns the exit code of the last executed *list*.

The `test` command (see Section 5.2.7) is particularly useful as a test in an `if` command. Recent versions of sh allow you to write a call on `test` in the form '`[...]`'.

Be sure that each *list* in this command and the others below are properly terminated. For example, the command

```
if true then echo egad!;fi     # Wrong!
```

produces an error diagnostic because '`true`' is a simple command and therefore requires a semicolon after it. However, the command

```
if { true;} then echo egad!;fi
```

correctly produces the output '`egad!`' (see the description of '`{...}`' later in this section).

for   The `for` command has the form

```
for name [ in word ... ;] do list
done
```

The commands in *list* are executed repeatedly, once for each *word* following '`in`'. Each time these commands are executed the variable *name* (whose value is obtained from $*name*) takes

---

6. In the Korn shell, which is generally compatible with the Bourne shell, redirected compound commands are not executed in a subshell and full visibility of local variables is maintained.

on the value of the next *word*. (See Section 5.2.8 for a discussion of variables.) For example, executing the command

```
for nbr in one two three
do
    echo [$nbr]
done
```

produces the output

```
[one]
[two]
[three]
```

Note that the newline at the end of the first line obviates putting a semicolon there.

If you omit 'in', sh uses the numbered parameters starting with $1 as the *word*s. The number of *word*s in this case is the number of parameters that actually have values.

See "Exiting from Loops" on page 171 for ways to break out of the middle of a loop.

while   The while command has the form

```
while list
do list
done
```

The first *list* represents a test, just as in the if command. Sh repeatedly tests this *list*. If the test succeeds (zero exit status), the second *list* is executed and the cycle continues. If it fails (nonzero exit status), the while command terminates.

until   The until command has the form

```
until list
do list
done
```

It behaves just like the while command except that the sense of the test is reversed: success means "terminate" and failure means "continue". **Note:** Unlike the until construct in some programming languages, the loop here can exit immediately without executing the second *list*.

case   The case command has the form

```
case word in
    casetest
        . . .
    esac
```

where each *casetest* has the form

   pattern [| *pattern*] ...) *list*; ;

You may omit the '; ;' at the end of the last case test, but we recommend you include it as a safeguard in case the script is modified later.

Each *pattern* in turn is matched against the *word* that precedes it until a match succeeds. The *list* in the *casetest* containing the matching pair is then executed. If no match succeeds, none of the *lists* are executed and the entire command returns an exit status of zero.

The *patterns* are matched according to the rules used to match wildcards against file names (see Section 2.11.1), except that the rules are relaxed so that a slash, a leading dot, or a dot immediately following a slash can be matched by a wildcard. (The rules in Section 2.11.1 require that these characters be matched explicitly.)

Here is an example of a `case` command:

```
case $fn in
    *.c | *.cpp ) cppcompile $fn;;
    *.pas       ) pascompile $fn;;
    *           ) echo "Unclassified function $fn!";;
esac
```

The appropriate compilation procedure is selected for the file `$fn`, depending on the form of its name. Using '`*`' as the last case is a general method of catching anything that can't be recognized.

(*list*) This construct causes the commands of *list* to be executed in a subshell (see Section 5.2.14). A separator (space or tab) is not required between *list* and either one of its surrounding parentheses, and a terminator ('`;`' or '`&`') is not required at the end of *list*.

{ *list* ; }
{ *list* & }

These constructs cause the commands of *list* to be executed directly (see Section 5.2.14). The only effect of the braces is to create a kind of grouping, similar to that created by parentheses in mathematical expressions. A separator (space or tab) *is* required between the left brace and *list*, but not between the semicolon or ampersand and the right brace.[7] Braces differ in this respect from parentheses.

name () { *list*; }

Unlike the previous constructs, this one does not cause any commands to be executed. It defines *name* as a function; thereafter the command *name* is equivalent to the sequence

{ *list*; }

For example, the function definition

```
backdate(){ cd ../old;}
```

---

7. The space is required because braces don't act as separators between words.

in effect creates a command backdate that changes the current directory to the parallel one old. Note that this function would not work correctly if function definitions were not executed directly (see Section 5.2.14), since the effect of the cd command would be lost. The space after the left brace cannot be omitted.

It's often useful to load function definitions into your shell when you start it. To do this, include in your .profile initialization file a command such as

```
. funcdefs
```

where funcdefs is a file containing a list of function definitions (see Section 5.2.18). Function definitions load quickly and execute efficiently since sh can execute them without reading any files. Function definitions are also useful in shell scripts as local definitions, (definitions needed within that script but not elsewhere). Function definitions are not recognized by the old version of sh.

5.2.7
The test, true, and false Commands

The test command, which is intrinsic to sh, can be used to compare numbers and strings and to test the existence and properties of files. It has two forms:

```
test expr
[ expr ]
```

The second form is not recognized by the old version of sh. A test returns a zero exit status if it succeeds and a nonzero exit status if it fails. The elements in a test, *including the square brackets*, must be distinct words, separated by spaces or other separators.

An example of test is

```
[ -x buildit -a "$action" = cons ]
```

This test succeeds (is true) if buildit is an executable file in the current directory and the value of the local variable action is the string 'cons'.

String Comparisons.   Test provides the following string comparisons:

s_1 = s_2 True if strings s_1 and s_2 are identical.
s_1 != s_2 True if strings s_1 and s_2 are not identical.
s_1
-n s_1 True if s_1 has at least one character, i.e., is not the empty string.
-z s_1 True if s_1 has no characters, i.e., is the empty string.

Note that a word appearing by itself is treated as a string and tests true. Be careful—the comparisons don't work properly if either string is a null string (which can result from a variable substitution) unless you enclose the string in double quotes. To test the shell variable var for equality with Q, use something like

```
[ "$var" = Q ]
```

Another way to write the same test is

```
[ ${var}0 = Q0 ]
```

The 0 after the first comparand ensures that the comparand can't be empty.

Numerical Comparisons. Test provides the following numerical comparisons. In these comparisons, n_1 and n_2 are integers, i.e., sequences of digits possibly preceded by '+' or '-'.

n_1 `-eq` n_2
> True if $n_1 = n_2$.

n_1 `-ne` n_2
> True if $n_1 \neq n_2$.

n_1 `-lt` n_2
> True if $n_1 < n_2$.

n_1 `-le` n_2
> True if $n_1 \leq n_2$.

n_1 `-gt` n_2
> True if $n_1 > n_2$.

n_1 `-ge` n_2
> True if $n_1 \geq n_2$.

File Tests. Test provides the following tests for the existence and attributes of files:

`-s` *file*   True if *file* exists and its size is greater than zero.
`-f` *file*   True if *file* exists and is an ordinary file (neither a directory nor a device).
`-d` *file*   True if *file* exists and is a directory.
`-c` *file*   True if *file* exists and is a character device file.
`-b` *file*   True if *file* exists and is a block device file.
`-r` *file*   True if *file* exists and is readable.
`-w` *file*   True if *file* exists and is writable.
`-x` *file*   True if *file* exists and is executable.
`-p` *file*   True if *file* exists and is a named pipe.
`-u` *file*   True if *file* exists and its set-uid bit is set.
`-g` *file*   True if *file* exists and its set-gid bit is set.
`-k` *file*   True if *file* exists and its sticky bit is set.
`-t` [*n*]   True if the file associated with file descriptor *n* is a terminal.[8] If *n* is omitted, it is taken to be 1.

The 'c', 'b', 'p', 'u', and 'g' tests are not supported by the old version of sh.

Combinations of Tests. The following operators can be used to combine tests:

`!` *expr*   True if *expr* is false and false otherwise.
expr$_1$ `-a` *expr*$_2$
> True if *expr*$_1$ and *expr*$_2$ are both true.

expr$_1$ `-o` *expr*$_2$
> True if either *expr*$_1$ or *expr*$_2$ is true.

---

8. In this context a "terminal" is a character special file that has an appropriate device driver associated with it.

(*expr*) True if *expr* is true. The parentheses provide a way of grouping subexpressions.

The `true` and `false` Commands.   The `true` and `false` commands do nothing. The only reason for executing them is to produce their exit status: zero for `true` and nonzero for `false`.

**5.2.8
Shell Variables**

Like many other programs, `sh` has a set of variables, called *shell variables*. There are two kinds of shell variables: local variables and numbered variables (usually called *parameters*).[9] You can refer to the value of shell variable *var* as '$*var*' or '${*var*}'.

Parameters (Numbered Variables).   When you call a shell script as a command, `sh` assigns the command name to `$0`[10] and each argument of the command to a parameter (numbered variable): the first to `$1`, the second to `$2`, and so forth. You can then refer to these parameters within the script. For example, if you call the command `whoopee` using the command line

        whoopee food drink merriment

the parameter `$0` receives the value `whoopee` and the parameters `$1` through `$3` receive the values 'food', 'drink', and 'merriment' respectively.   The quotation conventions described below in Section 5.2.12 apply, so for the command line

        whoopee "food drink merriment"

the value of `$1` is 'food drink merriment'. "Indirectly Executing Commands in a Subshell" on page 166 and Section 5.1 explain in greater detail what happens when a shell script is called.

References to parameters can contain only a single digit, so the highest-numbered parameter you can refer to directly is `$9`. You can retrieve higher-numbered parameters with the `shift` command (p. 172).

The assignment construct '*variable=value*' (see Section 5.2.9) does not apply to parameters. However, you can assign a value to a parameter with the `set` command (p. 172), or with the `getopts` command (p. 172) if you're using a recent version of `sh`.

Local Variables.   Local variables can be used to store information within a shell script. Certain predefined local variables have special meanings to `sh` (see Section 5.2.15).

The name of a local variable starts with a letter or an underscore. Unlike variables in most modern programming languages, local variables are not

---

9. The manual pages for `sh` use the term "parameter" where we use the term "variable", the term "positional parameter" where we use "numbered variable", and the term "keyword parameter" where we use "local variable". We don't use those terms in this book because they are inconsistent with the terminology of most other UNIX programs as well as with traditional programming language terminology.

10. A shell script can have several names, each being a distinct link to the script. The script can test `$0` to determine the name by which it was called. Through this device a single script can implement several different commands.

declared; they come into existence when sh starts executing or when you assign values to them. See Section 2.17 for a general discussion of local variables.

When sh starts to execute, it receives a set of environment variables from its parent process (see Section 2.7.5) and copies them into its local variables, adding some predefined variables of its own. When sh terminates, both its local variables and its environment variables disappear, although for different reasons: the local variables disappear because sh itself has terminated, while the environment variables disappear because the process executing sh has terminated.

The values of local variables are visible to commands executed in a subshell only if that subshell is executed directly or if the variables are exported (see Section 5.2.14). The values of environment variables, on the other hand, are always visible to commands executed in a subshell. Export of variables is discussed in Section 5.2.11.

5.2.9 Assignments to Local Variables

You can assign values to one or more local variables with an assignment (single or multiple) of the form

> *variable=value* [*variable=value*] ...

in any context where sh expects a command. You must quote the value if it contains any blanks or other characters that have special meaning to sh (see Section 5.2.12). The assignment sets each *variable* to the corresponding *value* (treated as a string). For example, the assignment

```
CAT=tabby GOAT='the chomper'
```

causes the variable CAT to acquire the value 'tabby' and the variable GOAT to acquire the value 'the chomper'.

You can also precede a call on a program with one or more assignments to variables (see Section 5.2.3). Such assignments don't affect any local variables, but the values of the variables specified in the assignment are available to the called program in its environment. The following dialogue illustrates this behavior:

```
$ var=one
$ var=two sh
$ echo $var
two
$ exit
$ echo $var
one
```

The assignment on the second line makes the value of var available to the called program, which in this case is another copy of sh. When the called program exits, var still has its original value within the outer copy of sh.

5.2.10 Variable Substitutions

A *variable substitution* refers to the value of a shell variable (see Section 5.2.8), a parameter, or one of several other strings tracked by sh. The substitution produces text that is then substituted into the command line. Several forms of variable substitution, as a side effect, set the value of a variable. You can conveniently evaluate a variable substitution for its side effect by writing it after a null command (see "Null Command" on page 171).

Each variable substitution begins with '**$**'. If you wish a '**$**' to be taken literally, you need to escape it by writing it as '**\$**'. However, a '**$**' followed by whitespace need not be escaped.

In the following descriptions of variable substitutions, *var* signifies a variable (either a parameter or a local variable). Where braces are not shown, they are still permitted, though never needed, around the character following the '**$**'.

$*var*
${*var***}** Replace this construct by the value of *var*. The braces are required if the construct is not followed by a separator or metacharacter. The following dialogue illustrates the replacement:

```
$ book=Decameron
$ echo $book
Decameron
```

As another example, suppose that the shell script in the file **vfy** consists of the text

```
diff $HOME/screed1/$1.tex $HOME/screed2/$1.tex
```

and you issue the command

```
vfy oink
```

Then **sh** compares two versions of the TEX file **oink.tex** by executing the command

```
diff $HOME/screed1/oink.tex $HOME/screed2/oink.tex
```

$*
$@ These constructs stand for '**$1 $2** ... **$***n*', i.e., the sequence of all parameters (with a single space between them). They are particularly useful within a shell script when the script can be called with a variable number of arguments.

The difference between the two constructs lies in how they behave within double quotes. The construct '**"$*"**' translates into

```
"$1 $2 ... "
```

which behaves as a single word, i.e., the spaces are quoted. The construct '**"$@"**' translates into

```
"$1" "$2" ...
```

which behaves as a sequence of words, i.e., the spaces are not quoted.

${*var-word***}**
${*var:-word***}** These constructs provide a form of conditional substitution as follows:

- If **$***var* exists and has a non-null value, its value is substituted into the text.

- If $var does not exist, *word* is substituted into the text.
- If $var exists but has a null value, then
    - the '-' form produces an empty string;
    - the ':-' form produces *word*.

The braces are required.

For example, suppose the command `toast` is defined as

```
echo ${1:-skoal}
```

Then the command line

```
toast prosit
```

produces the output

```
prosit
```

while the command line

```
toast
```

produces the output

```
skoal
```

${*var=word*}
${*var:=word*}

These constructs are valid for local variables but not for parameters. They are like '-' and ':-', except that they have a side effect: if *word* is inserted into the text, it is also assigned to *var*. The braces are required. In effect, these constructs create a default value for *var* that you can use in subsequent substitutions.

${*var?[word]*}
${*var:?[word]*}

These constructs are like :- and -, except that if *var* does not exist, `sh` exits and sends *word* to the standard error file. If *word* is omitted, it defaults to the message 'parameter null or not set'. The braces are required.

${*var+word*}
${*var:+word*}

These constructs work like - and :-, but in a nearly opposite sense:

- If $var exists and has a non-null value, *word* is substituted into the text.
- If $var does not exist, nothing is substituted into the text.
- If $var exists but has a null value, then
    - the '+' form produces *word*;
    - the ':+' form produces nothing.

The braces are required.

Sh also sets the following special variables in addition to the numbered variables:

$#   The number of arguments, as a decimal number.

$-   The flags supplied to `sh` when it was called. Alternatively, you can set the value of $- with the `set` command (p. 172).

$$ The process number of the current shell invocation.

$?   The exit code of the most recent executed foreground command.

$!   The process number of the most recent asynchronously executed command.

**5.2.11
Exporting Variables
to a Subshell**

When `sh` indirectly executes a subshell in order to execute a compiled program or a shell script, it creates a set *E* of environment variables for that process (see Section 2.7.5 and "Indirectly Executing Commands in a Subshell" on page 166). Exporting a local variable includes it in *E* (see p. 172); unsetting a local variable excludes it from *E* (see p. 172). `Sh` constructs *E* in three steps:

(1)   It places all exported local variables in *E*, giving them their current values.

(2)   It adds to *E* any environment variables that `sh` has inherited from its own parent but that have neither been exported nor unset. These variables have their inherited values.

(3)   It adds to *E* any variables specified by assignments preceding the command that initiated the subshell.

It follows from these steps that if a local variable *var* was inherited but has not been exported, *var* appears in the environment of an indirectly executed subshell with its original inherited value, not its current value.

The following dialogue shows how exported and inherited variables behave:

```
$ X=1 Y=2 Z=3 sh
$ X=4 Z=5 T=6 U=6
$ export X T
$ unset Y
$ V=7 sh
$ echo "$X;$Y;$Z;$T;$U;$V;"
4;;3;6;;7;
```

The first line starts a copy of `sh` and provides it with three environment variables X, Y, and Z that have the indicated values. The fifth line starts another inner copy of `sh`. The variables and their values as seen by this inner copy are as follows:

X (4)   Modified by the outer `sh`; inherited by the inner `sh`.

Y (no value)
          Modified by the outer `sh` but unset; not inherited by the inner `sh`.

Z (3)   Inherited by the outer sh and modified by it but neither exported nor unset by it; inherited without modification by the inner sh.

T (6)   Created and set by the outer sh and then exported; inherited by the inner sh.

U (no value)
     Created and set by the outer sh but not exported; not inherited by the inner sh.

V (7)   Added to the environment of the inner sh by the outer sh.

5.2.12
Quotation

You can use quotation to cause characters, normally meaningful to sh, to be treated as ordinary characters with no special meaning (see Section 2.14.2). Sh provides three forms of quotation:

(1) You can quote any individual character by preceding it with a backslash. A backslash at the end of a line, however, acts as a line continuation; the backslash and newline both disappear. For example, if you type

```
echo On a sin\
gle line.
```

you obtain the output

```
On a single line.
```

Without the backslash, you'd receive a complaint about the 'gle' command not being found. **Note:** A backslash must itself be quoted if it is to be treated as an ordinary character.

(2) You can quote anything, even a backslash or a newline, by including it in single quotes ('). Single quotes are the strongest form of quotation—within them, every character is taken literally (except for the closing single quote). A newline within single quotes does *not* disappear, even if preceded by a backslash. The quoted text obviously cannot include a single quote, but you can produce a single quote with '"'"'.

(3) You can quote most text with double quotes, but certain characters do have an interpretation within double quotes:

- The double quote character marks the end of the quoted text.
- The two characters ($ ') are given their normal interpretations, so variable and command substitutions are performed even within double quotes.
- A backslash preceding a newline disappears together with the newline.
- A backslash escapes the four characters (\ " $ ') and therefore quotes them.
- A backslash preceding any other character is taken literally.

Unquoted newlines are also taken literally, just as they are between single quotes.

Examples.   An example showing how the three forms of quotation interact is

```
X='this & that'
echo 'He said, "Why isn'"'"'"'"t my cat
doing $X?\""
```

These commands produce the output

```
He said, "Why isn't my cat
doing this & that?"
```

An example that shows the difference among the three forms of quotation is

```
echo ele\
phant "ze\
bra" "gir
affe" 'ti\
ger'
```

This input produces

```
elephant zebra gir
affe ti\
ger
```

**5.2.13
Command
Substitution**

Using *command substitution*, you can execute a list of commands and use the output as all or part of the text of some other command (see Section 2.14.2). You indicate the command substitution by enclosing the list in backquotes.

When `sh` encounters a command substitution of the form ''*list*'', it executes the commands in *list*. It then replaces the command substitution by the standard output that results from executing these commands. The text of *list* can include metacharacters and intrinsic commands; all such constructs are interpreted just as they would be absent the backquotes (see "Metacharacters in Command Substitutions" below).

The output of command substitution, unlike the input, is always treated as a single simple command, either intrinsic or externally defined. The first word on the line is taken as the name of the command and all other words are taken as its arguments—even if they include shell metacharacters such as '|' or ';'. For example, the command line

```
'echo "echo one;echo    two"'
```

produces the output

```
one;echo two
```

Sh treats the sequence 'one;echo' as a single word despite the semicolon. The several spaces following this sequence act as a single separator and therefore produce a single space in the output.

Metacharacters in Command Substitutions.   When `sh` encounters a command substitution, it first scans the command substitution to process any backslashes that it contains. The treatment of a backslash depends on the character that follows it:

- A backslash preceding a newline disappears along with the newline, just as it does outside of any quotation or command substitution.
- A backslash preceding a backquote, a dollar sign, or another backslash quotes that character and then disappears. (Quoting a dollar sign with a backslash turns out to have no effect because the dollar sign is interpreted later in any case.[11])
- A backslash preceding a double quote (") is left undisturbed if the command substitution is contained within double quotes; otherwise it disappears.
- A backslash preceding any other character is left undisturbed.

All other characters are interpreted as part of the command list. For example, if you type

```
echo "There are "`who | wc -l`" users logged in."
```

you obtain an output such as

```
There are 17 users logged in.
```

The '|', being within backquotes, is treated as part of the command list to be executed.

Note: A '$' within a command substitution introduces a variable substitution as usual; to disable it, escape the '$' with a preceding backslash.

Newlines within the text produced by command substitution act as argument separators rather than as command separators, i.e., like spaces rather than like semicolons. This behavior can be useful when the text has been produced by a command having newlines in its output. For instance, suppose that the file junque contains a list of files, one per line, that you wish to remove. (This is the most convenient format for creating such a list.) If you then type

```
rm -i `cat junque`
```

you remove all the files in the list (with confirmation queries). This method works even when some of the file names contain wildcards.

A command substitution can itself be enclosed in a quotation. The general rule that applies here is that outer quotation conventions are applied before inner ones. For instance, in text of the form

```
"  ...  `  ...  `  ...  "
```

---

11. However, you can use an escaped backslash together with eval to effect an indirection within a command substitution, as illustrated by

```
$ actor=ham ham=shank
$ eval echo `echo \\$$actor`
shank
```

sh processes the outer double quotes before processing the inner backquotes.[12] Consequently certain backslashes are removed before the inner backquotes see them. For example, if you type

```
echo "`echo \"eric\"`"
```

you get the output 'eric'; but if you type

```
echo `echo \"eric\"`
```

you get the output '"eric"'.

You can use the fact that backquotes are quotable within command substitutions to specify nested substitutions. For example, the command

```
echo `echo one \`echo two\` three`
```

produces the output 'one two three'. Without the backslashes, the second backquote would end the command substitution.

<table>
<tr><td>

5.2.14
Execution of
Commands

</td><td>

Sh has three methods of executing commands: direct execution, direct execution in a subshell, and indirect execution in a subshell:[13]

- For *direct execution*, sh executes commands as it encounters them. Any changes that the commands make to the state of sh, e.g., changing the values of variables, remain in effect until sh terminates. Intrinsic sh commands and user-defined functions (see p. 154) are always executed directly.

- For *direct execution in a subshell*, sh creates a subshell, i.e., a child process that is a copy of itself. The subshell then executes the commands.[14] The parent process either waits for the child to complete or just continues, depending on whether the child is executing in the foreground or the background. The child process executes the commands and then terminates.[15]

  The subshell inherits a copy of all the local variables of the parent shell. Any changes of state within the subshell—in particular, assignments to local variables—do not affect on the parent shell.

  The following constructs are directly executed in a subshell:

  ○ A list of commands in parentheses

</td></tr>
</table>

---

12. Most versions of sh silently supply a missing backquote in front of a closing double quote, a behavior that can sometimes be confusing. For example, if you type

```
echo '"`echo herring"'
```

you get the output 'herring' without any error messages.

13. The manual pages for sh, as well as most published descriptions, fail to distinguish between the two kinds of subshell execution. Recognizing the distinction is essential to understanding when local variables are visible in subshells and when they aren't. These terms are our invention.

14. The mechanism for doing that is rather interesting. Fork actually creates a copy of the current process. Each process is then in the state of just having completed the fork call. The only difference between the states of the two processes—parent and child—is in the value returned by that call. But that difference is sufficient for each process to know what to do next, since the next action can be made to depend on it.

15. A background grandchild process started by the child process continues when the child terminates and becomes a child of process #1, the system process named 'init'.

    ◦ A list of commands executed as a background process
    ◦ Any compound command whose input or output is redirected

- For *indirect execution in a subshell*, sh creates a subshell as for direct execution and then calls on the exec system routine to execute the commands in that subshell (see "Indirectly Executing Commands in a Subshell" below). Environment variables are inherited by the subshell but local variables are not. Commands not intrinsic to sh, including both shell scripts and commands implemented as compiled programs, are handled by indirect execution in a subshell.

The implications of the differences among the three methods are shown by the following example. Suppose that your user name is abigail and you issue the commands

```
cd $HOME/one
X=1 Y=2 Z=3
export X
```

All of these commands are directly executed. Next, suppose you issue

```
(cd ../two; pwd; Y=7; echo $X $Y $Z)
pwd
echo $X $Y $Z
```

The commands in parentheses are directly executed in a subshell, resulting in the following behavior:

(1)   The first pwd produces '/usr/abigail/two'.
(2)   The first echo produces '1 7 3'.
(3)   The second pwd produces '/usr/abigail/one', since the state of the parent shell remains untouched and that state includes the current directory.
(4)   The second echo produces '1 2 3'.

Next, suppose you put the line

```
cd ../two; pwd; Y=7; echo $X $Y $Z
```

in an executable file tryit (in the current directory) and issue the commands

```
tryit
pwd
echo $X $Y $Z
```

This time sh indirectly executes the commands of tryit in a subshell, resulting in the following behavior:

(1)   The first pwd produces '/usr/abigail/two', as before.
(2)   The first echo produces '1 7'. Z appears not to be set because it was not exported.
(3)   The second pwd produces '/usr/abigail/one', as before.
(4)   The second echo produces '1 2 3', as before.

Indirectly Executing Commands in a Subshell. When sh encounters a non-intrinsic command *cmd*, it indirectly executes *cmd* in a subshell, using the fork system routine to create a subshell. The subshell searches the path as given in the PATH environment variable (see Section 2.11.2), looking for an executable file whose name is *cmd*. It then uses the exec system routine to execute the file.

- If the file is a compiled program, exec loads it into memory and executes it. Exec provides it with an argument list *arglist*, where *arglist* is the list of arguments following the name *cmd*. When the compiled program exits, the subshell terminates.

- If the file is a shell script, exec calls a shell to execute it (see Section 5.1). If the first line of the shell script specifies a particular shell, exec uses that one; otherwise exec uses sh or a shell compatible with it. The precise rules for the choice of shell may vary from one system to another.

In the second case—calling a shell script—sh sees an argument list of the form

   cmd [*arg*] . . .

In other words, *cmd* appears to sh to be its first argument and the subsequent arguments are displaced by one position. Sh makes the arguments available within the script by assigning them to shell parameters as described in "Parameters (Numbered Variables)" on page 157. See Section 5.2.19 below for more details on calling sh directly.

Command Lookup.   Newer versions of sh keep a table of commands and their locations in the file system. When sh executes a non-intrinsic command it uses this table, called the *hash table* or the *command cache*, to obviate a long search through the file system.

   When sh executes a non-intrinsic command, it first looks in the hash table to see if the command is recorded there. If so, it retrieves the command's name and location (absolute path name) from the table. If not, it searches the path to find the command's location and then records this information in the hash table for future use. You can clear the hash table or place additional entries in it with the hash command (p. 173); the -h option of the set command also affects the table entries (see p. 178).

   If you create a new command during a single invocation of sh and that new command has the same name as an existing command but a different location in the directory tree, sh may fail to recognize the new command because it first looks in the hash table. Finding the old command there, it never looks further for the new one. Calling hash with the command name or with -r corrects this problem.

**5.2.15
Predefined Variables**

Below we describe the predefined variables of sh and their effects.

Directory Operations.   The following variables determine how sh interprets the cd command and how it searches through directories:

HOME   HOME normally designates your home directory, e.g., /usr/ hagar for user hagar (see Section 2.8.3). Many UNIX commands look for files in your home directory; they use HOME to find it. If you issue the cd command without an argument, sh uses the value of HOME as that argument.

PATH When sh encounters a command that is not intrinsic, it searches the directories in PATH for a file with the same name as the command. PATH is inherited from the environment; see Section 2.11.2 for further explanation of how it works.

CDPATH The value of CDPATH is a list of directories used by the cd command when it searches for its argument. This value should have the form

path[: *path*] ...

where each *path* specifies a directory. An empty *path* is legitimate and specifies the current directory. For example, suppose that the value of CDPATH is

:$HOME:/usr/lib:..

and that you execute the command

cd dates

while the current directory is $HOME/imports/new. Then cd checks the following directories in turn until it finds one that exists and changes the current directory to that one:

$HOME/imports/new/dates
$HOME/dates
/usr/lib/dates
$HOME/imports/dates

Prompts and Separators. The following variables pertain to prompts and separators:

PS1 This variable contains the primary command prompt, i.e., the prompt that sh issues when it expects a new command. It defaults to '$'.

PS2 This variable contains the secondary command prompt, i.e., the prompt that sh issues when it expects the continuation of a command on a new line. It defaults to '>'.

IFS This variable contains the characters that act as input field separators, i.e., that mark the end of a word. An input field separator can have another meaning as well. For example, you could include '|' in IFS—although it wouldn't make any difference since '|', being a metacharacter, already terminates a word. The default value of IFS is a string containing the three characters ⟨space⟩, ⟨tab⟩, and ⟨newline⟩. The separators in IFS are also used by the read command (p. 174). It's rarely useful to change IFS except to modify the behavior of the read command.

Mail Notification. Sh can automatically notify you when mail arrives (or is waiting for you when you log in). The following variables control this notification:

MAILPATH This variable contains a list of the files that sh checks to see if mail has arrived (indicated by a change to a file's modification

time). It is not available in the old version of sh. The list of files
has the form

> *filespec* [: *file*] ...

Each *filespec* has the form

> *filename* [%*message*]

The indicated *message* is sent to your terminal whenever mail
arrives in the file named *filename*. If *message* is omitted, the default message 'you have mail' is used.[16] For example, setting
MAILPATH to

> `$HOME/mail:$HOME/bills%you are being dunned`

causes the message 'you have mail' to appear whenever mail
arrives in the mail subdirectory of your home directory and
the message 'you are being dunned' whenever mail arrives in
the bills subdirectory of your home directory.

MAIL This variable exists primarily for compatibility with programs
that don't recognize MAILPATH. It is equivalent to MAILPATH except that it accepts only a single file name and no alternate *message*. Sh ignores MAIL if MAILPATH is set. The value of MAIL is
inherited from the environment, where it is set to the file name
of your primary mailbox when you log in (see Section 9.2).

MAILCHECK
This variable, which should have an integer value, specifies
how often sh checks whether mail has arrived. It is not available
in the old version of sh. A value of n greater than 0 specifies
a check every n seconds; a value of 0 indicates that sh should
check for mail after *every* prompt. If MAILCHECK is not set, it
defaults to 600 (check every ten minutes).

Accounting Information.   The following environment variable causes sh
to generate accounting information:

SHACCT If the value of this variable is the name of a file for which you
have write permission (or which doesn't exist but can be created), sh adds an accounting record to that file whenever it executes a shell procedure.[17] Assigning a value to SHACCT without
exporting it is ineffective. This variable is only available in the
System V version of sh.

---

16. Including a colon as part of *message* requires some tricky shell programming.

17. You can use the acctcms program to display this information. For example, the following command line produces a command summary in tabular form:

    `/usr/lib/acct/acctcms -a $HOME/.shacct`

Restricted Shell. The following variable can specify that when sh is called as a subshell, it is to be a restricted shell:

SHELL   When you call sh in a simple command, the value of SHELL is checked to see if it has the form of a full or relative pathname ending in rsh. If it does, the restricted shell rsh (see Section 5.2.21) is called. You might expect that other values of SHELL would have some effect, but they don't. The default value of SHELL is the path name of your login shell. The old version of sh does not use this variable.

5.2.16
Intrinsic Commands

The commands listed in this section are intrinsic to sh; sh interprets them directly rather than executing them indirectly in a subshell.

Special Forms of Command Execution. The following commands provide special forms of command execution:

exec *cmd* [*arg*] ...
exec *redir* ...

For the first form of exec, executes *cmd* with the specified arguments (if any). The execution of *cmd* replaces the execution of sh as the activity of the current process; when *cmd* terminates, the process terminates also.

The second form of exec specifies one or more redirections (see Section 5.2.5). These redirections cause the associations between file descriptors and files to be changed for the rest of the time that sh is in control (unless further redirections change the associations again). This form of exec does not cause any commands to be executed; command interpretation continues as usual afterwards.

. *file*   Executes the contents of *file* directly (not in a subshell). It is useful when *file* contains commands that are intended to affect the state of sh, for example by modifying local variables or changing the current directory. The space after the dot is required. Sh uses PATH to locate *file* just as it does to locate commands (see Section 2.11.2).

Exiting from sh. The following command terminates execution of sh:

exit [*n*]   Terminates sh with an exit status of *n*. If *n* is omitted, the exit status is that of the last command executed within sh. An end-of-file has the same effect as exit.

Exiting from Shell Functions. The following command terminates execution of a shell function (see p. 154):

return [*n*]

Returns from a defined shell function with an exit status of *n*. If *n* is omitted, the exit status is that of the last command executed within the function. The old version of sh does not support this command.

Exiting from Loops.   The following commands enable you to break out of a loop before control has reached the end of it:

break [*n*]   Exits from *n* enclosing `while` or `for` loops. If *n* is omitted it is taken as 1.

continue [*n*]

Exits from *n* − 1 enclosing `while` or `for` loops and continues execution at the beginning of the *n*th enclosing loop. If *n* is omitted it is taken as 1.

Null Command.   The following command acts as a null command:

: [*text*]   Does nothing but parses *text* as usual. You can use this command to execute constructs solely for their side effects by including those constructs in *text*. For example, the command

   : ${TEA_TEMP:=HOT}

conditionally sets the value of **TEA_TEMP**. **Note:** In some systems, a colon at the beginning of a shell script specifies that the script is to be interpreted by the Bourne shell.

Catching Signals.   The following command enables you to intercept signals that occur during the execution of a command and take appropriate action:

trap [[*cmdtext*] *n* ...]

Associates an action with one or more signals. The signal numbers are given by the list *n* ... and the action by *cmdtext*. Thereafter, when `sh` receives one of these signals it executes the commands in *cmdtext*.

Sh actually interprets *cmdtext* twice: once when it processes the `trap` command and once when it takes the actions, so *cmdtext* is usually quoted. The result of the first interpretation can include compound commands and operators.

If *cmdtext* is absent, the listed traps are reset to their original values. If no arguments are given, `trap` lists the commands associated with each signal number. Signal 0 is associated with exit from `sh`. (The kernel does not use 0 as not a signal number.)

The default actions for the various signals are those inherited from the parent process of `sh`, except that `sh` ignores the "interrupt" and "quit" signals (#2 and #3) when they are received from a background process. The latter condition rarely occurs, since these signals by their nature are supposed to originate from a terminal.

If *cmdtext* is the null string '""', the specified signals are ignored. For example, the command

   trap '' 1 2 15

causes sh to ignore signals 1, 2, and 15.

See Section 2.7.4 for an explanation of signals and a list of signal numbers.

Operations Pertaining to Local Variables. The following commands affect the status of local variables:

export [*name*] ...

Exports the variables *name* ... if specified. Exporting a variable places it in the environment of a subshell executed by sh (see Section 5.2.11). For instance, the command

        export olives hides pottery

marks the variables olives, hides, and pottery for export. The export command used by itself lists the variables currently being exported. You can undo the effect of export with unset.

unset *name* ...

Deletes one or more local variables or shell functions (see p. 154). Unset is not available in the old version of sh. If a variable inherited by sh from its parent is deleted with unset, that variable is not included in the environment of any subshell initiated by sh (see "Indirectly Executing Commands in a Subshell" on page 166).

readonly [*name*] ...

Marks the listed variables as read-only. Sh treats an assignment to a read-only variable as an error. If no variables are given in the command, the current read-only variables are listed. Once you've made a variable read-only, you can't undo this action—not only can't you assign to the variable, you can't remove it with unset either.

shift [*n*] Renumbers the parameters so that parameter *n* + 1 becomes parameter 1, parameter *n* + 2 becomes parameter 2, and so on. The first *n* parameters become inaccessible. If *n* is omitted, it is taken as 1. This command is rarely useful outside of shell scripts. The old version of sh does not recognize *n*.

getopts *text name* [*word*] ...

Parses the command line for a shell script as described in Section 5.2.17. The command line may contains options, ordinary arguments, or both. Getopts is rarely useful outside of shell scripts. The old version of sh does not support getopts.

Setting Options and Parameters. The following command can be used to set options and parameters for the shell:

set [*options*] [*word*] ...

Enables or disables the indicated options, or sets the numbered parameters, starting with $1, to the indicated words. The options and their meanings are listed in "Shell Options" on page 177. The usual conventions for the interpretation of options apply (see Section 2.14), except that '-' enables options and '+' disables them. You can specify several '+' and '−' groups in a single command. For example, the command

```
set -en +fhv -- - nguyen
```

enables the e and n options, disables the f, h, and v options, and assigns '−' to $1 and 'nguyen' to $2. The '−−' separates the options from the parameters. As usual, $- contains the flag settings following execution of set (see Section 5.2.10). Executing set without any options or words shows the values of all variables.

Operations Pertaining to Command Names.   The following commands pertain to looking up command names and determining their meanings. They are not available in the old version of sh.

hash -r
hash *name* ...

hash   Examines or modifies the hash table, i.e., the hash table that sh uses to speed up the search for commands within the UNIX directory structure (see "Command Lookup" on page 167).

- If called with a list of names, hash locates the named commands within the tree, using the current value of PATH (see Section 2.11.2).

- If called with -r, hash removes all names from the hash table.[18]

- If called without arguments, hash produces a list indicating the currently remembered commands, the number of times they have been invoked ("hits"), and the cost of looking up each one ("cost").
  A star next to the "hits" count indicates a command that either was found by looking in the current directory or was found by looking in some directory following the current directory in PATH. If the current directory is the first one in PATH, every command has a star; if the current directory is not in PATH, no command has a star.

type [*name*] ...
             Shows how sh interprets each *name* if given as a command. For example, the command

```
type cd ps
```

produces the output

```
cd is a shell builtin
ps is /bin/ps
```

---

18. The manual pages state that if -r is used with a list of names, just those names are removed. We have found experimentally that if -r is present the table is cleared entirely whether names are present or not.

If no *name*s appear, the command does nothing.

Reading Input Interactively. The following command requests user input from within a shell script:

read [*name*] . . .

Reads one line from standard input and partitions it into words, using the value of IFS (p. 168) to separate words within the line. Successive words are assigned to the successively listed names (as local variables). If there are more words than *names*, sh assigns the extra words to the last name, replacing each separator by a single space. For example, if you type

```
IFS="; "
read a b c
one two; three;;four
echo [$a] [$b] [$c]
```

you obtain the output

```
echo [one] [two] [three four]
```

In this example the input field separators are the semicolon and the space.

Within the input text, lines can be continued with '\ Enter '. Other characters can be quoted by escaping them with backslashes; the backslashes are removed before the words are assigned to the names.

This command returns an exit status of zero unless it encounters an end-of-file.

Multiple Evaluations. The following command evaluates the words of a command before executing it, thereby causing those words to be evaluated twice:

eval [*word*] . . .

Evaluates each word by applying the usual substitutions, then treats the sequence of words that results as a command (or list of commands) and execute that command. For example, suppose that a shell script contains the single command

```
eval echo \$$#
```

If the script is called with three arguments (not counting the command name itself), eval yields the command line

```
echo $3
```

Thus the shell script echoes its last argument, an effect that would be difficult to obtain otherwise.

Process Monitoring and Control. The following commands monitor the resources used by sh and its child processes and wait for child processes to terminate:

times   Produces the user time and system time used so far by child processes. For instance, an output of

```
2m47s 0m19s
```

indicates that child processes have so far used 2 minutes 47 seconds of user time and 19 seconds of system time. The listed times don't include any time used by the invocation of sh itself.

ulimit [*n*]

Limits the size of files written by sh and its child processes to *n* blocks. You can lower the limit with ulimit but not raise it. If *n* is omitted, the command shows the current size limit. This command is not available in the old version of sh.

wait [*n*]   Waits for the process with process id *n* to finish, then returns the exit status of that process. If *n* is omitted, sh waits for all background processes that it has spawned to complete. It then returns an exit code of zero.

Utility Commands.   The following commands are intrinsic to sh primarily for the sake of efficiency. We describe them elsewhere in the book. Only cd and umask are built into the old version of sh; the others are provided by external programs.

cd [*path*]   Changes the current directory (see Section 3.15.1).[19]

echo [*word*] ...

Echoes back the arguments (see Section 4.6.1).

newgroup [*arg*] ...

Changes the group identification (see Section 4.3.3).

pwd   Shows ("prints") the current (working) directory (see Section 3.15.2).

[...]
test   Performs a test (see Section 5.2.7).

umask   Reduces the default permissions for file creation (see Section 3.12.2).

**5.2.17
Parsing Command
Lines with** getopts

The getopts ("get options") command, intrinsic to sh, parses options and arguments on a command line according to the standard syntax described in Section 2.14.[20] You can analyze the contents of a command line using ordinary shell programming facilities rather than getopts, but it isn't easy. Getopts is not available in the old version of sh.

Calling getopts.   The form of the getopts command is

getopts *optstring name* [*arg*] ...

Here *optstring* describes the allowable options, *name* specifies a variable for receiving notification of each option that is present, and the *args* specify arguments to be used in place of the arguments appearing in the command line. To distinguish the arguments of options from those of the

19. Were cd to be implemented by executing a child process, its effects would be lost when the child process terminated. Thus cd must be executed by sh itself.

20. An older version of getopts called getopt may also be available on your system. We recommend against using it, but you may find it in older shell scripts that you've inherited.

command itself, we refer to these as "option arguments" and "arguments" respectively.

The option string *optstring* contains a single letter for each allowable option. If the option takes an argument, the letter is followed by a colon. For example, the option string 'ah:q' used in the example below signifies that the command in question expects options 'a' and 'q' without arguments and option 'h' with an argument. **Note:** Arguments to options are never optional. An option either always takes an argument or never does.

Use of getopts. To use getopts you call it repeatedly until it has parsed all the options. Each time you call it, getopts absorbs either one argument or two, starting with the leftmost argument. It returns a zero exit status if one or more options remain and a nonzero exit status if none do. In addition, it sets three local variables: *name*, OPTIND ("options index"), and OPTARG ("option argument"). It sets them as follows:

- The variable *name* contains the name of the option just found, or '?' for an option not in *optstring*.

- The variable OPTIND contains the index of the next unprocessed argument. When getopts returns, it sets OPTIND to the index of the first argument that is not part of the options. The value of OPTIND is ordinarily uninteresting until all the options have been processed. The command

  ```
  shift `expr $OPTIND - 1`
  ```

  is often used after the options have been processed in order to renumber the arguments. Before the renumbering, the first argument ($1) is the first option to the command. After the renumbering, the first argument becomes the one that previously was the first command argument (after the options).

- The variable OPTARG contains the option argument provided for the option in *name*. That argument may contain commas or, if it was quoted, blanks. The presence of commas or blanks indicates that the option argument is really a list of arguments such as file names.

Example of getopts. The following shell script, while not useful in itself, shows how getopts works:

```
while getopts ah:q opt; do
   case $opt in
   a | q)    echo $opt, OPTIND=$OPTIND;;
   h)        echo $opt: \"$OPTARG$\", OPTIND=$OPTIND;;
   *)        echo other: \"$OPT$\";;
   esac
done
for arg do echo [$arg] \\\c; done
shift `expr $OPTIND - 1`
for arg do echo [$arg] \\\c; done
```

If you name this script doit and issue the command line

```
doit -h one,two -qa three four >out
```

you obtain the output

```
h: "one,two$", OPTIND=3
q, OPTIND=3
a, OPTIND=4
[-h] [one,two] [-qa] [three] [four]
[three] [four]
```

5.2.18
Initialization Files
for sh

When sh is called as a login shell, it first executes the commands in the /etc/profile and $HOME/.profile files (if they exist) in that order. It then prompts you for a command. The commands in /etc/profile are intended to apply to all users of sh (not all systems provide this file). The commands in $HOME/.profile are intended to be modified to taste by each user. When your account is set up, a canned version of this file is usually installed in your home directory. Typically, $HOME/.profile includes commands to set PATH to a preassigned search path and to set TERM to the type of your terminal.

Sh determines if it was called as a login shell by looking at the first character of $0, i.e., the first character of the name by which it was called. If that character is '–', sh assumes it was called as a login shell. Should you need to, you can "fake" a login shell by providing another link to sh under a name such as –sh.

The login command on some systems enables you to specify values for certain environment variables on the login line (see Section 4.3.1). On such systems you can set up your .profile file to test these variables, which provides a handy way to control what .profile does when you log in. For instance, some systems set L0 to the first word after your name on the command line if there is such a word. On these systems you can set up .profile to execute the C shell whenever you put CS after your login name by including the following line at the end of .profile:

```
if [ "$L0" = CS ]; then exec csh; fi
```

5.2.19
Calling sh **Directly**

You can call sh directly as you would any other command. The form of the command line is

sh [*options*] [*arg*] ...

Unless the –c or –s flag is given, sh takes its first argument to be the name of a shell script and the remaining arguments to be arguments for that script.

Shell Options.   The following options are available either through the **set** command (p. 172) or when sh is invoked. You can specify that an option should be disabled rather than enabled by replacing its '–' by a '+'. The –v and –x options are particularly useful for debugging shell scripts.

–v   Show each input line as it is read, i.e., be "verbose".

–x   Show each simple command and its arguments as it is executed.

–a   Cause any variable that is modified or created to be exported automatically.

-k	Treat all local variables as exported, so that they become available in the environments of subshells.
-u	When substituting for local variables, treat an unset variable as an error and issue a complaint.
-e	Exit immediately if a command returns a nonzero exit status.
-t	Exit after executing the first command list, i.e., at the point where sh would otherwise issue the primary command prompt.
-n	Don't execute commands, just read them.
-f	Turn off the interpretation of wildcards.
-h	Enter the names of commands used in a function definition into the command lookup table (see "Command Lookup" on page 167) when the function is defined rather than when it is used. Ordinarily sh does not enter these commands into the table until they are actually executed.

The -a, -f, and -h options are not available in the old version of sh.

The following options are available only when sh is invoked:

-c *string*	Cause sh to use *string* as its input.
-s	Cause sh to read its input from standard input and write its own output to standard error (file descriptor 2). Any arguments on the command line become parameters to sh.
-i	Cause sh to expect its input to be interactive. This option affects the handling of certain signals (see "Signals and Their Codes" on page 22):

- "Terminate" (#15) and "quit" (#3) are ignored.
- "Interrupt" (#2) is caught but then ignored, so it can be used to interrupt a wait.

-r	Invoke sh as a restricted shell (see Section 5.2.21). This option is not available in the old version of sh.

**5.2.20
A Sample
Shell Script**

The sample shell script below effectively changes the name of each file in a file list to lowercase if the name contains any uppercase characters. It asks the user to confirm each replacement and asks for further confirmation if the corresponding file with a lowercase name already exists. The script illustrates a number of features of sh and is also useful in its own right.

```
#!/bin/sh
# tolower - replace files by their lowercase equivalents

for i in $*; do
    tmp=`echo $i | tr "[A-Z]" "[a-z]"`
    if [ -f $i -a "$i" != "$tmp" ]; then
        # echo -n "change $i to ${tmp}? [y/n] "  # BSD echo
        echo "change $i to ${tmp}? [y/n] \c"     # SysV echo
        read ans
        if [ "$ans" != "y"  -a "$ans" != "Y" ]; then
            echo $i will not be changed
        else
```

```
        # check to see if a file with the new name already exists
                if [ -f "$tmp" ]; then
        # (BSD echo) echo -n "$tmp already exists. Overwrite? [y/n] "
                    echo "$tmp already exists.  Overwrite? [y/n] \c"
                    read ans
                    if [ "$ans" != "y" -a "$ans" != "Y" ]; then
                        continue
                    fi
                fi
                mv -f $i $tmp
                if [ $? -ne 0 ]; then
                    echo mv failed, $i is unchanged
                fi
            fi
        fi
    done
```

5.2.21
Restricted Shells

A *restricted shell* limits its user to a small, well-understood set of capabilities, thereby allowing the system to accept logins from unknown or untrustworthy sources. Unfortunately the restricted version of sh does not live up to its billing since its implementation is not totally secure.

A shell becomes restricted if it is initiated in any of the following ways:

- By being called under the name rsh. The path preceding rsh is irrelevant—only the last component matters.

- By a call on sh with the -r option.

- By a call on sh when the SHELL environment variable exists and has as its value a file name whose last path component is rsh.

Within a restricted shell, the following actions are disallowed:

- Changing the current directory
- Assigning a value to PATH
- Specifying a path name or a command name containing '/', i.e., one that might not be in the current directory
- Redirecting output with '>' or '>>'

In addition, a restricted shell is often set up so that the only available editor is red, a restricted version of ed.

The restrictions given above don't apply while .profile is being executed. Thus the author of .profile (which resides in the user's home directory) can perform whatever actions are necessary to set up a controlled environment for the user. Usually these actions include changing the current directory so as to deny the user access to .profile, although setting the permissions on .profile appropriately can often achieve the same effect.

Unfortunately the remote shell program related to rlogin (see Section 10.5.3) is also named rsh. If your system provides both programs, the one that you get when you type rsh depends on your default path:

the restricted Bourne shell is usually stored as /bin/rsh, while the remote shell program is stored as /usr/ucb/rsh. The authors of the remote shell program recommend that you provide another link to it under a name such as remsh.

5.3   The C Shell csh

The C shell, available via the csh command, was developed as part of BSD UNIX. Despite its name, the C shell is not significantly more C-like than the Bourne shell. These are some of the features provided by the C shell but not by the Bourne shell:

- The ability to recall previous commands in whole or in part via a "history" mechanism.
- The ability to switch back and forth among several processes and control their progress ("job control").
- More flexible forms of variable substitution.
- Additional operators as they appear in C.
- Aliases for frequently-used commands without using shell scripts.

Many of the commands in csh behave identically to their counterparts in sh. In our description of csh, therefore, we sometimes refer you back to sh for details and examples.

5.3.1
Quick Exit

You can interrupt most commands executing within csh by pressing (Intr). That returns you to the csh command level. There are three ways to exit from csh itself:

- Type logout.
- Type exit.
- Type (Ctrl)D. Typing (Ctrl)D won't work if ignoreeof has been set (see p. 195).

Some versions of csh may not support all of these methods.

5.3.2
Syntax of Shell Input

As csh reads its input, whether from a terminal or from a file, it decomposes that input into a sequence of *words* separated by spaces or tabs. An escaped newline, i.e., a newline preceded by a backslash, also acts as a separator between words. You can use escaped newlines to continue commands from one line to another. Csh issues a prompt whenever it expects another command. The default prompt is '%', but you can change the prompt by setting the prompt variable to a different value (see p. 196).

In addition to spaces or tabs, words are also ended by certain metacharacters that have special meaning to csh:

       ; & | < > ( )

A sequence of one or more of these metacharacters is also a word. For example, the command lines

```
cat marmot\
hedgehog|sort>>rodents
```

are equivalent to the following command line in which words are separated by single spaces:

```
cat marmot hedgehog | sort >> rodents
```

When `csh` is decomposing a command line into words, it treats a string quoted by double quotes (") or single quotes (') as a unit (see Section 5.3.12). If the quoted string is surrounded by separators, it becomes a word by itself; if it is immediately adjacent to another word, it is combined with that word to form a larger word. Any separators such as blanks within the quoted string are treated as ordinary characters.

Comments. The input to `csh` can include comments. A comment starts with a '#' and extends to the end of the line. `Csh` only recognizes comments in shell scripts.

Commands. A *simple command* consists of a command name followed by its arguments. The name and each argument are single words. The command name can name an executable file or a `csh` intrinsic command, either simple or complex (see Sections 5.3.16 and 5.3.17). The operators

```
|  &&  ||  ;  &  (  )
```

are used to form combinations of simple commands and therefore cannot themselves be arguments to simple commands unless they are quoted.

You can combine simple commands to form a full command, usually just called a *command*. `Csh` expects each input line, taken together with its continuation lines, to contain one command (or the beginning of a complex command). It treats the command as an expression built up from the command operators listed above. Here is what they mean:

| | The '|' operator connects two commands through a *pipe*. The standard output of the first command becomes the standard input of the second command. A group of one or more commands connected in this manner is called a *pipeline*.

|& Like '|', except that the standard error and the standard output from the first command are both sent to the standard input of the second command.

|| If c_1 and c_2 are commands, || the combination '$c_1 | | c_2$' first executes c_1. If the exit status of c_1 is nonzero (see Section 2.7.3), it then executes c_2. A nonzero exit status usually indicates unsuccessful execution.[21] In other words, c_2 is executed only if c_1 fails.

&& The '&&' operator is like '||' except that it tests for successful execution rather than for unsuccessful execution. If c_1 and c_2

---

21. A possible source of confusion is the fact that a zero exit status for a command signifies truth but a zero value for an expression signifies falsity.

are commands, the combination 'c_1&&c_2' first executes c_1. If the exit status of c_1 is zero, it then executes c_2. In other words, c_2 is executed only if c_1 succeeds.

;   If c is a command, the construct 'c;' causes csh to execute c and then, when c has terminated, to proceed to the next command if any. Thus the sequence 'c_1; c_2' has the effect of "execute c_1, then execute c_2".

&   If c is a command, the construct 'c &' causes csh to start c executing as a background process and then to proceed immediately to the next command if any without waiting for c to finish. See "Uses of Background Execution" on page 148 for more information about background execution.

(...)   Within a command, parentheses indicate grouping. Syntactically, a parenthesized group of commands plays the role of a simple command. Commands within parentheses are always executed directly in a subshell (see Section 5.3.3).

The order of precedence of these operators is as follows:

(1) |
(2) || &&
(3)   ;
(4)   &

The command operators are applied in order of precedence. Sequences of '||' and '&&' are carried out in order from left to right. For the purposes of these two operators, a background command enclosed in parentheses is assumed to succeed immediately.

    The command operators for csh follow almost the same rules as they do for sh (see Section 5.2.4). You may wish to look at that section since the operators are explained there in more detail than here. Note, however, that for sh the ';' and '&' operators have the same precedence, while for csh the ';' operator has a higher precedence than '&'.[22]

<table>
<tr><td>**5.3.3**
Execution of
Commands</td><td>Csh, like sh, has three methods of executing commands: direct execution, direct execution in a subshell, and indirect execution in a subshell:</td></tr>
</table>

- For *direct execution*, csh executes each command as it encounters it. Any change that the command makes to the state of csh, such as changing the value of a shell variable, remains in effect until csh terminates. Commands intrinsic to csh are always executed directly, as are commands in a file summoned by the source command (p. 200).

- For *direct execution in a subshell*, csh creates a subshell within which the commands are executed. The subshell inherits a copy of all the variables of the parent shell. Any changes of state within the

---

22. This subtle difference can be demonstrated by the command

```
echo one; sleep 3; echo two & echo three
```

For sh the output is in the order 'one', 'two', 'three' while for csh it is in the order 'one', 'three', 'two'.

subshell—in particular, assignments to shell variables—do not affect the parent shell. Csh executes parenthesized commands and background commands in a subshell.

- For *indirect execution in a subshell,* csh creates a subshell as for direct execution and then calls on the exec system routine to execute a command in that subshell. Environment variables are inherited by the subshell but local variables are not. If the command changes any environment variables, the changes affect only the copies and not the originals. Commands not intrinsic to csh, including both shell scripts and commands implemented as compiled programs, are handled by indirect execution in a subshell and are looked up as described in "Command Lookup" below.

See Section 5.2.14 for further details on these three forms of execution.

Command Lookup.   When csh encounters a non-intrinsic command, either a compiled program or a shell script, it searches for that command in a sequence of directories specified by the shell variable path. Csh derives the initial value of path from the environment variable PATH, obtained from the environment within which csh was called. The path variable has a somewhat different syntax than PATH but essentially the same meaning (see Section 2.11.2).

Csh accelerates the command search by means of a *hash table.* The hash table records the names of the executable files in the directories listed in path. Beware: when you create a new executable file, either a shell script or a compiled program, csh will not be able to find it unless you instruct csh to recreate the hash table, which you can do with the rehash command (see p. 200).

**5.3.4
Redirection**

Using redirection, you can have a program take its input from a specified file instead of from the terminal or send its output to a specified file instead of to a terminal. The basic forms of indirection are described in Section 2.12. The following csh constructs for redirection include both these basic forms and additional ones:

<*file*   Takes standard input from the file *file.*

<<*word*   Takes standard input from the following text, called *here text.* The variable *word* indicates the end of the input. When csh encounters this construct within a command, it reads input until it encounters either a line consisting exactly of *word* or the end of the input file. The input thus read becomes the standard input of the command. No substitutions of any kind are applied to *word*; each input line is compared to *word* before any substitutions are made on that line.

           Normally csh carries out variable substitution (see Section 5.3.11) and command substitution (see Section 5.3.13) within the here text. It treats '\' as a quoting character when it precedes one of the characters (\ $ '). Any other occurrence of '\' is taken literally, i.e., left alone. However, if *word* contains any of the characters (\ "' '), csh takes the here text literally and performs none of these substitutions.

>[&][!]*file* Sends standard output to the file *file*. If the file already exists, it is truncated to zero length, thereby erasing its contents;[23] if it does not already exist, it is created. If the `noclobber` variable is set, however, erasure is inhibited and `csh` issues an error message (see p. 195). The presence of '!' overrides the setting of `noclobber` and causes an existing file to be erased in any case. The presence of '&' causes standard error as well as standard output to be redirected to *file*.

You can redirect the standard output of *cmd* to *file₁* and its standard error to *file₂* with a command line such as

$$(cmd > file_1) >\& \ file_2$$

>>[&][!]*file*

This form of redirection is like the previous one except that standard output is appended at the end of *file*. If `noclobber` is set, it is an error for *file* not to exist unless the error test is overridden with '!'.

5.3.5 Command Completion

Most versions of `csh` have a feature for completing file names interactively. To enable this feature, you must set the variable `filec` (see p. 196). The following conventions then apply:

- If you type a file name at the end of a command followed by Esc , `csh` completes the file name if it has a unique completion. For example, if you type the command

      fgrep roc av Esc

  and the only file in the current directory that starts with 'av' is 'aviary', `csh` changes the input line to

      fgrep roc aviary

  If the variable `fignore` contains a list of suffixes, files with those suffixes are not eligible candidates for file name completion unless they are the only candidates. If no unique completion exists, `csh` completes the file name as far as possible and then sounds the terminal bell.

- If you type a file name followed by EOF , `csh` provides a list of all possible completions of the file name and then echoes your input again so that you can complete the file name.

5.3.6 Job Control

A *job* is a group of processes (see Section 2.7.1). Under `csh`, each group of background processes created through the use of '&' is a job. In addition, a foreground process interrupted by a stop signal (usually sent by typing Ctrl Z) is a job.

Of the jobs running at any particular moment, at most one job is the foreground job; all others are either background jobs or stopped jobs. A

---

23. The erasure affects all links to the file.

stopped job will not run until it is resumed. When csh issues a command prompt, there is no foreground job; at all other times the foreground job is the one given by the previous command to csh. Only the foreground job can receive input from your terminal although any job, foreground or background, can send output to it. If several jobs are producing output in parallel, their outputs are intermingled.

When you start a background job, csh displays the job number and the process number associated with the job, e.g.,

    [2] 470

Here the job number is 2 and the process number is 470. A background pipeline containing several processes shows a process number for each one. When a job terminates or changes status in some other way, csh notifies you of the change just before it issues the next command prompt. By setting the notify variable (see p. 199) you can cause csh to issue notice of status changes as soon as they occur, even if a job is running in the foreground.

Listing and Referring to Jobs.   The jobs command (see p. 199) lists all the current jobs. Its output looks like this:

    [1]   Running   grinder
    [2]   Done   grep oboe hobo |
            Running   sort > lobo
    [4]   - Stopped   emacs scrimp.c
    [5]   + Stopped (tty input) collect

The jobs command itself is the foreground job and is not shown. The number in brackets is the job number. The *current job* is the job most recently stopped, or started in the background; it is indicated by '+'. The *previous job* is the job that was current when this one became the current job; it is indicated by '-'. The third column shows the status of each job. Note that a job can be stopped either because it is expecting input from the terminal or because it was stopped explicitly. The last column shows the command associated with each process of a job. If you specify the -l option to jobs, it shows you the process numbers as well.

Several commands expect references to jobs. You can refer to a job in several ways:

%n   Job number *n*.
%*str*   The unique job whose name begins with *str*. If there is only one background job, *str* may be empty and '%' by itself refers to the current job.
%?*str*   The unique job whose name contains the string *str*.
%+
%%
%   The current job.
%-   The previous job.

Some older versions of csh don't recognize the '%%', '%+', and '%-' forms and interpret '%' as referring to the current job only in the case where there is just one job.

Starting and Stopping Jobs. There are several ways you can change the status of a job:

- You can stop the foreground job if there is one by sending it a STOP signal, thereby making that job a background job and changing its status to 'Stopped'. The usual way to send the signal is to type the suspend character (normally Ctrl Z; see "Viewing the Key Assignments" on page 13). To restart a stopped job as a background job, use the **bg** command.

- You can bring a background job '%*job*' to the foreground, giving it control of your terminal, by typing 'fg %*job*' or just '%*job*' at a shell prompt.

- You can cause a stopped job '%*job*' to execute in the background by typing 'bg %*job*' at a shell prompt, provided that the stopped job is not waiting for terminal input. If you try to restart in the background a job that is waiting for terminal input, it becomes the current job but remains stopped.

- You can kill a job '%*job*' by typing 'kill %*job*' at a shell prompt, provided that the job does not catch and then ignore the signal. Other forms of **kill** are also available (see p. 200).

5.3.7 File Name Expansions

You can use wildcards (see Section 2.11.1) within a file name to represent a sequence of characters. The process of expanding wildcards is called *file name expansion* or, in C shell parlance, *globbing*. Csh provides two abbreviations in addition to the usual wildcards:

- The character '~' at the beginning of a file name, used by itself, stands for the home directory of the user who called this copy of csh (see Section 2.8.3 for a discussion of home directories). Followed by a name of some other user, it stands for that user's home directory.

- A string within a file name of the form

    $a\{x_1,x_2,\ldots,x_n\}b$

stands for the list of file names

    $ax_1b\ ax_2b\ \ldots\ ax_nb$

Either a, b, or both can be empty. However, an occurrence of '{', '}', or '{}' surrounded by whitespace is taken literally and is not treated by csh as an abbreviation. For example, the command

    echo {} a{bb,caci,rmad}a

produces the output

    {} abba acacia armada

More usefully, the command

    cp ~noah/fauna/{terns,gerbils,lemurs,zebras} .

copies four files from user **noah**'s directory **fauna** to your current directory. Lacking the '{}' notation, you would have to repeat the reference to '~noah/fauna' four times.

**5.3.8
History
Substitutions**

A history substitution enables you to reuse a portion of a previous command as you type the current command. History substitutions save typing and also help reduce typing errors.

A history substitution normally starts with '!'. A history substitution has three parts: an *event* that specifies a previous command, a *selector* that selects one or more words of the event, and some *modifiers* that modify the selected words. The selector and modifiers are optional. A history substitution has the form

> !*[event][[:]selector[:modifier]* ...]

The event is required unless it is followed by a selector that does not start with a digit (see "Special Conventions" on page 189). The ':' can be omitted before *selector* if *selector* does not begin with a digit. You can change the character '!' used in history substitutions to another character by changing the value of `histchars` (see p. 196).

History substitutions are interpreted by `csh` before anything else—even before quotations and command substitutions. The only way to quote the '!' of a history substitution is to escape it with a preceding backslash. Be particularly careful to escape the '!' when you call a mailer with a UUCP network address on the command line (see Section 10.1.1).[24] A '!' need not be escaped, however, if it is followed by whitespace, '=', or '('.

See "History-related Variables" on page 196 for information about intrinsic variables that affect history substitutions.

Events and Their Specifications.   `Csh` saves each command that you type on a history list provided that the command contains at least one word. The commands on the history list are called *events*. The events are numbered, with the first command that you issue when you enter `csh` being number one. For complex commands such as `for` that consist of more than one line, only the first line makes its way to the history list. The `history` variable (see p. 196) specifies how many events are retained on the history list. You can view the history list with the `history` command (see p. 199).

These are the forms of an event in a history substitution:

`!!`	The preceding event. Typing '`!!`' is an easy way to reissue the previous command.
`!`*n*	Event number *n*.
`!-`*n*	The *n*th previous event. For example, '`!-1`' refers to the immediately preceding event and is equivalent to '`!!`'.
`!`*str*	The unique previous event whose name starts with *str*.
`!?`*str*`?`	The unique previous event containing the string *str*. The closing '?' can be omitted if it is followed by a newline.

Selectors.   You can select a subset of the words of an event by attaching a *selector* to the event. A history substitution without a selector includes

---

24. This inconvenience might not exist had UUCP-style addressing been used more heavily in the original BSD UNIX environment.

all the words of the event. These are the possible selectors for selecting words of the event:

`:0`	The command name
`[:]^`	The first argument
`[:]$`	The last argument
`:n`	The nth argument ($n \geq 1$)
`:n_1-n_2`	Words n_1 through n_2
`[:]*`	Words 1 through $
`:x*`	Words x through $
`:x-`	Words x through ($\$ - 1$)
`[:]-x`	Words 0 through x
`[:]%`	The word matched by the preceding '?*str*?' search

The colon preceding a selector can be omitted if the selector does not start with a digit.

Modifiers. You can modify the words of an event by attaching one or more modifiers. Each modifier must be preceded by a colon.

The following modifiers assume that the first selected word is a file name:

`:r`	Removes a trailing '.*str*' component from the first selected word.
`:h`	Removes a trailing path name component from the first selected word.
`:t`	Removes all leading path name components from the first selected word.

For example, if the command

```
ls -l /usr/elsa/toys.text
```

has just been executed, then the command

```
echo !!^:r !!^:h !!^:t !!^:t:r
```

produces the output

```
/usr/elsa/toys /usr/elsa toys.text toys
```

The following modifiers enable you to substitute within the selected words of an event. If the modifier includes 'g', the substitution applies to the entire event; otherwise it applies only to the first modifiable word.

`:[g]s/l/r`	Substitutes the string r for the string l. The delimiter '/' may be replaced by any other delimiting character. Within the substitution, the delimiter can be quoted by escaping it with '\'. If l is empty, the most recently used string takes its place—either a previous l or the string *str* in an event selector of the form '!?*str*?'. The closing delimiter can be omitted if it is followed by a newline.
`:[g]&`	Repeats the previous substitution.

The following modifiers quote the selected words, possibly after earlier substitutions:

`:q`	Quotes the selected words, preventing further substitutions.

`:x`   Quotes the selected words but breaks the selected text into words at whitespace.

The following modifier enables you to see the result of a substitution without executing the resulting command:

`:p`   Shows ("prints") the new command but doesn't execute it.

Special Conventions.   The following additional special conventions provide abbreviations for commonly used forms of history substitutions:

- An event specification can be omitted from a history substitution if it is followed by a selector that does not start with a digit. In this case the event is taken to be the event used in the most recent history reference on the same line if there is one, or the preceding event otherwise. For example, the command

      `echo !?quetzal?∧ !$`

  echoes the first and last arguments of the most recent command containing the string 'quetzal'.

- If the first nonblank character of an input line is '∧', the '∧' is taken as an abbreviation for '!:s∧'. This form provides a convenient way to correct a simple spelling error in the previous line. For example, if by mistake you typed the command

      `cat /etc/lasswd`

  you could re-execute the command with 'lasswd' changed to 'passwd' by typing

      `∧l∧p`

  You can replace '∧' with a different character by changing the value of `histchars` (see p. 196).

- You can enclose a history substitution in braces to prevent it from absorbing the following characters. In this case the entire substitution except for the starting '!' must be within the braces. For example, suppose that you previously issued the command

      `cp accounts ../money`

  Then the command '!cps' looks for a previous command starting with 'cps' while the command '!{cp}s' turns into the command

      `cp accounts ../moneys`

5.3.9
Aliases

You can define an *alias* as an abbreviation for a command that you commonly use. You can create, display, and destroy aliases with the `alias` and `unalias` commands (see p. 197). Csh keeps a list of your aliases; each alias in the list associates a command word with the text of its definition.

When csh reads a command line, it tests whether the first word of the line has an alias. If it does, csh replaces the word by the definition of the alias as follows:

- If the definition contains no history substitutions, the command name is directly replaced by its definition.

- If the definition contains any history substitutions, the substitutions are applied as though the entire text of the command were the previous input line. The result replaces the *entire* command line. Such history substitutions enable the alias definition to utilize the arguments on the command line.

You can defeat an alias by putting a backslash in front of it, thereby giving the alias word its original meaning.

If an alias substitution leaves the first word on the command line unchanged, then the substitution is complete. Otherwise, csh makes further substitutions until no more alias substitutions apply or it detects a loop.[25] An alias substitution such as

```
alias who 'who;date'
```

is valid: the result of the substitution leaves the first word unchanged, so csh does not process it further.

An alias for 'shell' is treated specially: csh uses its value as the shell to call when it executes a command in a subshell. The alias definition must consist of the full path name of that shell.

Examples.   Here are some examples of the use of aliases:

- If you issue the command

```
alias ls ls -CF
```

then the command 'ls subdir' is transformed into 'ls -CF subdir' but the command '\ls subdir' is executed without change.

- If you issue the command

```
alias locate 'who | fgrep \!^'
```

then the command 'locate igor' is transformed into 'who | fgrep igor', which shows you any terminal where 'igor' is logged in.

5.3.10
Shell Variables

Csh maintains a set of *shell variables*, each containing a list of zero or more words. The shell variables include both predefined variables (see Section 5.3.15) and user-defined variables. You can retrieve the values of these variables and set them to new values. You can also retrieve or set the individual words within a variable. A shell variable is a particular kind of local variable; see Section 2.17 for a general discussion of local variables.

In addition, csh enables you to retrieve and set environment variables. The C shell, unlike the Bourne shell, explicitly distinguishes between environment variables and shell variables and has different commands that apply to them:

- The set and @ commands set shell variables and also display them.

---

25. Csh cannot detect the loop created by a sequence of commands such as

```
alias abc ''def''
alias def ''abc''
echo 'abc'
```

Executing these commands causes csh to run out of memory and produce a core dump.

- The `unset` command removes shell variables.
- The `setenv` command sets environment variables.
- The `env` command displays environment variables.
- The `unsetenv` command removes environment variables.

If a shell variable and an environment variable have the same name, the shell variable takes precedence over the environment variable in any variable substitutions.

5.3.11 Variable Substitutions

A *variable substitution* refers to the value of a shell variable (see Section 5.2.8), a parameter, or one of several other strings tracked by `sh`. The substitution produces text that is then substituted into the command line. *You can omit the braces in these constructs if no ambiguity would result.* Any of the constructs that produce a sequence of words can be modified by the modifiers listed in "Modifiers for Variable Substitutions" on page 192.

Each variable substitution begins with '$'. If you wish a '$' to be taken literally, you must escape it by writing it as '\$'. However, a '$' followed by whitespace need not be escaped.

Named Variables. The following variable substitutions pertain to named variables:

`${`*name*`}`   Produces the words of the variable *name*.

`${`*name*`[`*sel*`]}`

Produces the words of the variable `${`*name*`}` that are selected by *sel*. The selector *sel* selects either a single word or a sequence of words. It has one of the following forms:

n	Selects the nth word.
n_1-n_2	Selects the sequence of words from the n_1th word through the n_2th word.
n_1-	Selects the sequence of words from the n_1th word through the last word.
-n_2	Selects the sequence of words from the first word through the n_2th word.
*	Selects all the words.

The first word of a variable is numbered as 1. The selectors can themselves be the result of variable substitution.

`${#`*name*`}`

Produces the number of words in the variable *name* as a decimal number.

`${?`*name*`}`

Produces 1 if the variable *name* is set and 0 if it isn't.

Command-line Arguments. The following substitutions pertain to the words of the command line:

`${`*n*`}`   Produces the *n*th command-line argument. The predefined variable `argv` (see p. 195) contains the words of the command-line arguments, so this form is equivalent to `$argv[`*n*`]`.

$*	Produces the list of arguments on the command line.

Other Variable Substitutions. The following substitutions provide other kinds of information:

$0	Produces the name of the current input file.
$?0	Produces 1 if the current input file name is known and 0 if it isn't.
$$	Produces the process number of the copy of csh now in control.
$<	Reads a line from standard input and produces it without making any substitutions within it or otherwise interpreting it in any way. This construct is particularly useful for retrieving answers to queries in interactive shell scripts.

Modifiers for Variable Substitutions. The result of a variable substitution can be edited by attaching a modifier to it. If the substitution is written using braces, the modifier must appear within the braces. No more than one modifier can be attached.

The following modifiers have the same meanings as the corresponding modifiers for events (see p. 188) except that the :e modifier applies only to variable substitutions. If a modifier includes 'g', the substitution applies to the entire result; otherwise it applies only to the first modifiable word of the result.

:[g]r	Removes a trailing '.*str*' component.
:[g]e	Removes everything preceding a trailing '.*str*' component.
:[g]h	Removes a trailing path name component.
:[g]t	Removes all leading path name components.
:q	Quotes the substituted words, preventing further substitutions.
:x	Quotes the substituted words but breaks the text into words at whitespace.

5.3.12
Quotation

You can use *quotation* to prevent metacharacters, including whitespace, from being given their normal interpretation (see Section 2.14.2 for a general discussion of quotation). These are the forms of quotation that csh recognizes:

c	Quotes the character *c*. This form of quotation is the only way to quote the history substitution character, normally '!'.
"*text*"	Quotes *text*, except that the characters ($ ' !) within *text* are still recognized as metacharacters. Variable substitutions, command substitutions, and history substitutions are therefore honored. A backslash preceding a bang character or newline escapes and quotes the bang or newline; a backslash in any other context is treated as an ordinary character, even when it precedes another backslash. Since whitespace is taken literally, the entire quoted text acts as a single word. The

only exception is that a newline produced by an embedded command substitution acts as a separator between words.

' *text* '   Like '"*text*"', except that '!' is the only character recognized as a metacharacter within text. As with '"*text*"', bangs and newlines are the only characters that can be escaped with a backslash.

For example, the commands

```
set terrier=rufus
echo \! "[\$terrier; `echo vera`;\\]"\
    '[\$terrier; `echo vera`;\\]'
```

produce the output

```
! [\rufus; vera;\\] [\$terrier; `echo vera`;\\]
```

and each bracketed portion of this output is treated as a single word despite its embedded spaces.

5.3.13 Command Substitutions

You can use a *command substitution* to execute a command and then use its output immediately as part of another command. See Section 2.14.2 for a general discussion of command substitution.

' *text* '   Executes *text* indirectly as a command in a subshell, then replaces *text* within the command line by the standard output of its execution. If the output ends with a newline, that newline is discarded. Whitespace within the output separates words of the resulting command line, although no whitespace is implied at the beginning and end of the command substitution.

If the command substitution occurs within a quotation formed using double quotes, spaces and tabs within its output do not act as word separators but newlines within its output do. Such newlines are the only way that the material between double quotes can consist of more than one word.

For example, the commands

```
set v1 = (X`echo a b c`Y)
set v2 = ("X`echo a b c`Y")
echo \[$v1\] \[$v2\] \[$#v1\] \[$#v2\]
```

produce the output

```
[Xa b cY] [Xa b cY] [3] [1]
```

5.3.14 Expressions

A number of `csh` intrinsic commands accept expressions having nearly the same form as expressions in C. The operands of these expressions are either decimal numbers, octal numbers, strings, or tests. A sequence of digits beginning with zero is taken as an octal number. Tests are described in "Tests" on page 194. The operands can be obtained as the result of variable substitution.

These are the operators recognized by `csh`, in decreasing order of precedence:

(...)	grouping
~	one's complement $(-(n + 1))$
!	negation (0 yields 1, anything else yields 0)
* / %	multiplication, division, remainder
+ -	binary addition, binary subtraction
<< >>	left shift, right shift
< > <= >=	less, greater, less or equal, greater or equal
== != =~ !~	equal, not equal, matches, does not match
&	logical "and"
^	logical difference
|	logical "or"
&&	conditional "and"
||	conditional "or"

Since these operators are intended primarily for use by C programmers, we explain only those that are peculiar to `csh`:

- The '==' and '!=' operators compare strings exactly.

- The '=~' operator matches its left operand against the pattern given by its right operand. The pattern can contain any of the wildcards recognized by file name substitution. The match succeeds if the left operand can be derived from the right operand by making substitutions for the wildcards. The '!~' operator is the negation of '=~'.

The following rules apply to expressions:

- Any two adjacent components, either operators or operands, must be separated by whitespace.

- If an expression uses any of the characters (< > & |), these characters must be made part of a subexpression enclosed in parentheses. That subexpression may be the entire expression.

- Empty operands are permitted. An empty operand of a string comparison is taken as the null string; any other empty operand is taken as 0.

Some versions of `csh` do not support all of these operators.

Tests. Each of the tests described below is an expression that returns 1 if it succeeds and returns 0 if it fails. These tests are chiefly useful in shell scripts.

The following test executes a command and tests if it terminated successfully.

`{cmd}`   Execute *cmd* in a subshell, test if its exit status is zero.

The following tests provide information about a file's status.

`-r` *file*	Tests if *file* has read access.
`-w` *file*	Tests if *file* has write access.
`-x` *file*	Tests if *file* has execute access.
`-e` *file*	Tests if *file* exists.
`-o` *file*	Tests if *file* is owned by the user who called `csh`.
`-z` *file*	Tests if *file* has zero size.
`-f` *file*	Tests if *file* is an ordinary file.
`-d` *file*	Tests if *file* is a directory.

**5.3.15
Predefined Variables**

The variables listed below have predefined meanings for `csh`. Many of them have the same meanings as they do for `sh`; see Section 5.2.15 for further details about them.

Directories and Files.   The following variables indicate where certain files and directories are to be found:

home
:   The home directory of the user who called this shell. It is initialized to the value of the `HOME` environment variable.

cwd
:   The full path name of the current working directory. `Csh` updates this variable whenever you change directories. Not all versions of `csh` provide this variable.

path
:   The list of directories to search for commands. It is initialized to the value of the `PATH` environment variable (see Section 2.11.2).

cdpath
:   The list of directories that the `cd` command uses when it searches for its argument. `Csh` does not use the `CDPATH` environment variable.

mail
:   The list of files where mail might be found. `Csh` checks these files after each command completion to see if the file has been accessed since it was last modified. If not, `csh` notifies you that new mail has arrived. If the first word of `mail` is a number n, `csh` checks for mail every n seconds. The default interval is 600 (ten minutes).

shell
:   The file in which the shell resides. It is initialized to the location of `csh` itself.

The values of `HOME` and `PATH` in `csh`'s inherited environment are updated whenever you change `home` and `path`, so any programs that you call from `csh` see the updated values. However, any changes to these environment variables are lost when `csh` terminates.

Command Interpretation.   The following variables affect the way that `csh` interprets commands:

ignoreeof
:   If set, ignore an end-of-file received from the terminal. If `ignoreeof` is not set, an end-of-file causes `csh` to exit.

noclobber
:   If set, inhibit redirections specified by '>' from sending output to a file that already exists.

noglob
:   If set, inhibit expansion of wildcards in file names ("globbing"). See Section 5.3.7.

nonomatch
:   If set, allow file name expansions that don't match any files. If `nonomatch` is not set, a file name expansion that does not match any files is treated as an error.

Command-line Arguments.   The following variable provides access to the arguments on the command line:

argv
:   List of the command-line arguments (as a sequence of words).

History-related Variables. The following variables affect history substitutions:

histchars
: The pair of characters used in history substitutions. The first character, '!' by default, is the one that introduces a history substitution. The second character, '∧' by default, is the one that you can use at the beginning of a command line as an abbreviation for a substitution into the previous command.

history
: The size of the history list, i.e., the number of commands that csh remembers. By default, savehist is not set and csh remembers just the last command.

savehist
: The number of history entries that csh saves when you log out. (Invocations of csh other than as a login shell are unaffected.) These entries are restored when you log in again. By default, savehist is not set and no history is saved.

Terminal Interaction. The following variables affect how csh interacts with your terminal:

prompt
: The string that csh sends to your terminal before reading a command interactively. If the prompt string includes the character '!', that character is replaced by the current event number, which you can refer to in later history substitutions.

echo
: If set, show each command and its arguments before executing the command.

verbose
: If set, show the words of each command after history substitutions.

notify
: If set, send a notice of any change in the status of a background job immediately instead of waiting for the next command completion.

time
: If set to a value n, any command that requires more than n seconds of processor time to execute causes csh to produce a line of timing information when the command terminates.

filec
: If set, perform file name completion.

fignore
: A list of suffixes to be ignored during file name completion.

Exit Status. The following variable provides information on the exit status of the most recently executed command:

status
: The exit status of the most recently executed command.

5.3.16 Simple Intrinsic Commands

The commands described below are intrinsic to the shell and do not contain other commands.

Variables. The following commands pertain to the definitions of variables:

@ [*name*[[*n*] = *expr*]
: Used by itself, '@' shows the values of all the local variables.

Used with a name but no index n, it sets *name* to the value of *expr*. Used with an index n, it sets the nth word of the variable *name* to *expr*. The expression *expr* is interpreted as described in Section 5.3.14. You must leave whitespace between '@' and *name*.

You can increment or decrement *name* by 1 using the form '@ *name*++' or '@ *name*--'. You can also use operators such as '+=' in place of '='. The effect of

    @ name += expr

is to increase *name* by the value of *expr* (taking *name* as 0 if it is not a number). More generally, any binary operator can be used in place of '+' and *name* can have an index attached to it.

`set`
`set `*name*
`set `*name*`[`*n*`]=`*word*
`set `*name*`=(`*wordlist*`)`

Used by itself, 'set' shows the values of all the local variables and is equivalent to '@'. Used with a name but no index n, it sets *name* to the indicated word *word* or list of words *wordlist*. Used with an index n, it sets the nth word of *name* to the word *word*. The difference between '@' and 'set' is that '@' treats the right side of the assignment as a number, eventually converting it to a string, while 'set' treats the right side as a string to begin with.

`unset `*pat*

Deletes all local variables whose names match the pattern *pat*. The pattern *pat* can contain the same wildcards that are used in file name expansions.

`setenv `*name*` `*val*

Sets the environment variable *name* to *val*. Note that this command does not include an '='.

`unsetenv `*pat*

Deletes all environment variables whose names match *pat*. The pattern *pat* can contain the same wildcards that are used in file name expansions.

`shift `[*var*]

Shifts the words of *var* one word left by deleting the first word. If *var* is omitted it is taken to be `argv` (see p. 195).

Aliases.   The following commands pertain to aliases:

`alias `[*name* [*text*]]

Used by itself, `alias` shows all existing aliases. Used just with a name, it shows the alias if any for that name. Used with a name and some text *text*, it sets *name* to the words of that text.

`unalias `*pat*

Deletes all aliases that match the pattern *pat*. The pattern *pat* can contain the same wildcards that are used in file name expansions.

Control Flow.   The following commands provide exits from certain compound commands and otherwise affect the flow of control within a shell script:

break   Resumes execution after the nearest enclosing `foreach` or `while`.

breaksw   Resumes execution after the nearest enclosing `switch`.

continue   Continues execution of the nearest enclosing `while` or `foreach`.

[*label*]:   Does nothing, but labels this statement with *label* (if present) for use in `goto` and `onintr` commands.

goto *word*
             Executes commands starting with the first available one following the label *word*. The `goto` command is generally useful only in shell scripts.

Directory Management.   In order to make it easy to return to directories that you've previously visited, `csh` provides a stack of directories. You can think of the stack as a list; *popping* the stack removes the first element of the list, while *pushing* a directory onto the stack places that directory at the head of the list. The first element of the stack is numbered 0. The following commands change or display the current directory or the directory stack:

cd [*dir*]
chdir [*dir*]
             Changes the working directory to *dir*. If *dir* is not specified, changes it to the home directory.

dirs   Shows the directory stack.

popd   Pops the directory stack, making the popped directory the current directory.

popd +*n*   Discards the *n*th element in the stack, leaving the current directory unchanged.

pushd   Exchanges the top two elements of the directory stack, then makes the directory at the top of the stack be the current directory. `Pushd` by itself is a convenient way to switch back and forth between two directories.

pushd *dir* Pushes the current directory onto the stack, then makes *dir* the new current directory.

pushd +*n*   Promotes the *n*th element of the stack to the top of the stack by rotating the preceding elements to the bottom of the stack, then makes the directory at the top of the stack be the current directory.

Not all versions of `csh` support `dirs`, `popd`, and `pushd`.

Exiting from csh.   The following commands provide ways of exiting from csh:

logout   Terminates this shell if it is a login shell.

login   Terminates this shell if it is a login shell, then invite a new login.

exit [(*expr*)]

Exits from the shell with *expr* as the exit status. If you call exit from within parentheses, csh does not exit since the exit is only from a subshell.

exec *cmd* Executes *cmd* in place of the current shell. This command is the usual way to switch to a different shell.

Echoing Arguments.   The following commands echo their arguments:

echo [-n] [*word*] ...

Echoes *word* ... to standard output. The -n suppresses the trailing newline.

glob [*word*] ...

Echoes *word* ..., but ignores '\' quotation.

Status Information.   The following commands provide status information and enable you to change certain parameters:

notify [%*job*]

Provides immediate notice when the status of a job changes instead of waiting until the next command completion. If a job *job* is specified (see p. 185), only the status of that job is affected.

history [-r] [-h] [*n*]

Displays the *n* most recent events in the history list. If -r is specified, the events are displayed in reverse order with the most recent events first. If -h is specified, the leading numbers are omitted from the history list, thus making it suitable for saving in a file that can later be re-executed. Each of these options must be surrounded by whitespace.

jobs [-l] Lists the active jobs in the format shown on page 185. If -l is specified, the listing includes the process number of each job.

umask [*n*] If *n* is specified, sets the value of the file creation mask to *n*. Otherwise, shows the file creation mask.

limit [*resource* [*max*]]

Used by itself, this command lists the limits on the consumption of certain resources. If *resource* is also specified, it lists the limit on the consumption of that resource. If *max* is also given, it limits the consumption of that resource by this process and its children to *max*. The particular resources depend on the system.

unlimit [*resource*]

If *resource* is specified, removes the limitation on that resource; otherwise removes the limitations on all resources. Only the superuser may execute this command.

Job and Process Control.   The following commands provide control over processes and jobs (see Section 5.3.6):

`kill` [−*sig*] *id*

> If *sig* is specified, sends that signal to the job or process identified by *id*. A process is specified by its number and a job by its job identifier (see Section 5.3.6). A signal can be specified by name (with 'SIG' omitted) or by number. See Section 2.7.4 for a list of the signal names and numbers. If *sig* is omitted, TERM (signal #15) is assumed.

`kill -l`   Lists all the possible signal names.

`nohup` [*cmd*]

> If *cmd* is specified, runs it with terminal hangups ignored. Otherwise, runs the rest of this process with terminal hangups ignored.

`nice` [+*n*] [*cmd*]

> If *cmd* and *n* are both specified, executes the command *cmd* at priority *n* + 20. If *n* is omitted, priority 24 is used. The higher the number, the lower the priority. If *cmd* is omitted, run the rest of this process at the indicated priority. The intent of this command is to be nice to other users by giving their jobs priority over this one.

`wait`   Waits for all background jobs to complete.

`onintr`
`onintr -`
`onintr` *label*

> Used by itself, this command restores the default interrupt actions. Used with '−', it causes all interrupts to be ignored. Used with a label *label*, it causes csh to transfer control to the command labelled with *label* when an interrupt is received or a child process terminates because it was interrupted.

Miscellaneous Commands.   Here are the remaining csh intrinsic commands:

`rehash`   Recalculates the lookup table for command names. Executing this command causes csh to recognize recently created executable files.

`unhash`   Disables use of the hashed lookup table for commands.

`source` [-h] *file*

> Reads commands from the file *file* and executes them without creating a subshell. If the commands set any local variables, these settings are retained. The commands are not placed on the history list, except that if −h is specified, they are placed on the history list but not executed.

`eval` *arg* ...

> Performs textual substitutions in *arg* ... , then executes the resulting command. You can sometimes use eval to construct

commands that would be difficult to specify otherwise (see p. 174 for an example).

`time [cmd]`

>   If *cmd* is specified, executes it and shows how much time it used. Otherwise, shows how much time this shell has used. See Section 4.6.4 for further discussion.

5.3.17 Compound Commands (Statements)

The following compound commands, also called *statements*, provide conditional tests, case testing, and loops. A command list can occupy several lines and can include nested statements. Generally you should place the parts of a compound command on separate lines as shown in the form of the command. If you execute a compound command interactively, `csh` prompts you for the continuation lines. Only the first line of a compound command appears in the history list.

`if (expr) cmd`

>   Executes *cmd* if *expr* is nonzero (true).

`if (expr) then ...`

>   This variant of the `if` statement has the form

```
if (expr₁) then
    cmdlist₁
[else if (expr₂) then
    cmdlist₂]
...
[else
    cmdlistₙ]
endif
```

>   It tests each *expr* in turn until one is found whose value is nonzero (true), then executes the corresponding command list *cmdlist_i*. If no nonzero *expr* is found and an 'else' part is present, executes its command list.

`switch`

>   The `switch` statement enables you to select commands to be executed according to the form of a string. The form of the `switch` statement is

```
switch(string)
case str: ...
    cmdlist
[default:
    cmdlist]
endsw
```

>   The statement can contain any number of cases. The string *string* at the top is expanded using all applicable substitutions. Each case label is then examined in turn. The string *str* is treated as a pattern and compared with *string*. If *string* can be obtained from *str* by file name expansion, i.e., by expanding wildcards, then that case is selected. Its command list *cmdlist* and any following command lists associated with other cases

are executed until either the 'endsw' is reached or a 'breaksw' command is encountered. Normally each case should be ended with 'breaksw' so that control does not pass to the next case.

If none of the cases match and a default statement is present, its command list is executed. If none of the cases match and no default case is present, execution of the entire statement is considered to be complete.

foreach   The foreach statement has the form

            foreach *name* (*word* ...)
                cmdlist
            end

The command list *cmdlist* is executed once for each word in the list *word* ... , with *name* being set to the current word. Typically, *word* ... is gotten as the result of a file name expansion involving wildcards.

repeat *n cmd*
          Executes the command *cmd n* times. The count *n* must be given by a decimal integer, although that integer can be the result of a substitution.

while   The while statement has the form

            while (*expr*)
                cmdlist
            end

The commands in *cmdlist* are executed repeatedly while the value of the expression *expr* is nonzero (true). The expression *expr* is tested before each execution of *cmdlist*, including the first one.

5.3.18
Calling csh

The form of the csh command line is

        csh [*options*] [*arg*] ...

The arguments *arg* ... are made available through the **argv** shell variable (see p. 195).

Command-line Options.   The following options specify where csh obtains its input:

-c *file*   Read commands from the file *file*.

-s   Read commands from standard input.

-t   Read and execute a single line of input. You can continue the input onto additional lines by ending each line with a backslash.

-i   Issue a prompt whenever a line of input is expected. This is the default if input is from a terminal.

The following options control echoing of commands as they are executed:

-v   Set the **verbose** variable (see p. 196) so that command input is echoed after history substitutions.

-V   Like -v, except that **verbose** is set before the initialization file
            `.cshrc` is executed.

-x   Set the **echo** variable (see p. 196) so that commands are echoed
            before they are executed.

-X   Like -x, except that **echo** is set before the initialization file
            `.cshrc` is executed.

The following options serve other purposes:

-e   Exit if any invoked command terminates abnormally. This op-
            tion is most useful for executing shell scripts.

-f   Don't look for a `.cshrc` initialization file.

-n   Parse commands but don't execute them.

5.3.19
Initialization

When it starts, `csh` looks for a file named `.cshrc` in your home directory
and executes the commands in it. If `csh` was called as your login shell, it
then executes the file `.login` and also executes the file `.logout` when it
terminates.

Execution of `.login` and `.logout` can be useful, but it only happens if
`csh` is your login shell. For example, if `sh` is your login shell you might
switch over to `csh` by ending your `.profile` file (see Section 5.2.18) with
a command

```
exec csh
```

In this case `.login` and `.logout` won't be executed. However, you can
trick `csh` into thinking that it was called as a login shell by creating a syn-
onym '-csh' for `csh` (using the `ln` command) and having your exec command reference '-csh' rather than 'csh'. Csh determines if it's called as
a login shell by checking the first character of the name by which it was
called, which should be '-' for a login shell.

5.4   The Korn Shell `ksh`

The Korn shell, `ksh`, provides a synthesis of the features of the Bourne
shell and the C shell, with a number of useful additions of its own. It was
developed by David Korn at AT&T Bell Laboratories in 1982, with major
improvements released in 1986 and 1988. It is included as a standard
feature of System V Release 4 and in some other systems, and can also be
purchased separately.

The Korn shell closely follows the conventions of the Bourne shell;
nearly all shell scripts written for the Bourne shell also work with the Korn
shell. These are the principal features adopted from the C shell:

- History lists for retrieval of previous commands
- Job control, with the ability to move specific jobs to the foreground
  or background
- Aliases for command names

- Use of '~' to denote the home directory of the current user or, when combined with a user name, of another user
- Ability to compute general numerical expressions and assign the result of the computation to a variable

These are some of the features new to `ksh`:

- Interactive editing of the command line, including file name completion with the same power as that of `csh` and the ability to edit the history list
- Improved function definitions that provide local variables and the ability to write recursive functions
- Extended pattern matching for file names and other constructs, similar to that in `egrep`
- Ability to extract the portion of a string specified by a pattern
- Ability to switch easily between two directories

5.5   The Enhanced C Shell `tcsh`

The `tcsh` shell is a popular enhanced version of the C shell. These are some of the facilities that it adds:

- Ability to edit the command line interactively
- Easy call-up of previously executed commands, which can then be edited
- Interactive completion of file names and command names
- Lookup of documentation of a command as you're typing it
- Ability to schedule periodic execution of a command
- Time stamps in the history list

You can obtain `tcsh` over the Internet via anonymous `ftp` from `tesla.ee.cornell.edu`, IP address `128.84.253.11` (see Section 10.7). It is found in the file `/pub/tcsh-6.03.tar.Z`. You can also obtain it over the `uucp` network from the OSUCIS archive (reference [U3]).

6

Standard Editors

An editor is a program for creating, modifying, or viewing a file of text.
UNIX editors come in two varieties: full-screen editors and line editors.

- A full-screen editor assumes that your terminal has a display screen
and is at least capable of moving the cursor to a specified screen
position. It maintains a model of what the screen should look like
and updates the screen in response to your typed commands. Usually the commands you type are not shown on the screen. If your
terminal is a "smart" terminal that allows lines and characters to be
added and deleted, the editor updates the screen by modifying only
that portion of it whose contents have changed. On the other hand,
if your terminal is a "dumb" terminal that lacks these facilities, the
editor updates the screen by rewriting it completely.

- A line editor is a "lines in, lines out" editor. It expects you to type
some lines; it then types some lines back at you and awaits your next
command. Each line, whether typed by you or the editor, appears
underneath the previous typed line. Most line editors were developed in the days when computer terminals could only display output
by printing it.

Line editors have largely been eclipsed by full-screen editors, which are
far easier to use. Nevertheless you may find a line editor useful or even
essential when you're communicating over a slow or noisy phone line or
when you're working with a crippled system in a maintenance mode for
which most of the usual UNIX facilities are not available.

In this chapter we describe one full-screen editor and two line editors
that come with nearly every UNIX system:

- The full-screen editor vi, sometimes called the Visual Editor, was

205

developed as part of the BSD UNIX project. It was the first popular UNIX full-screen editor and is still very widely used.

- The line editor `ed` is the oldest UNIX editor; under some circumstances it may be the only editor you have. We recommend against using it if you have an alternative, but many people still use `ed` just because they don't want to bother learning a new editor.

- The line editor `ex` is an extended and improved form of `ed`. `Vi` and `ex` are actually the two faces of a single editor. Our main reason for describing `ex` is that you sometimes need to use `ex` commands from within `vi`.

Historically, `ed` led to `ex` and `ex` led to `vi`, but our order of presentation is the reverse since `vi` is likely to be the most useful of the three editors and `ed` the least.

In the next chapter we describe the GNU Emacs editor. Although in our opinion Emacs is far more powerful than `vi`, more flexible, and easier to use, many people still prefer `vi` because it is part of the standard UNIX package.

6.1   The `vi` **Visual Editor**

The visual editor `vi`, pronounced "vee-eye" by Berkeley people, was developed by Bill Joy as part of the BSD UNIX project. It has since been adopted as a standard System V feature. `Vi` is a full-screen editor; it always maintains an image on your screen of a portion of the file that you're editing. It requires a terminal that enables it to control the position of the cursor and place text at an arbitrary position on the screen. In particular, you may not be able to use `vi` if your terminal can only receive and transmit text a line at a time, or if `vi` is unable to access information about your terminal because your system is not fully operational.

`Vi` is an extension to the `ex` line-oriented editor described in Section 6.3 and depends on `ex` for many of its facilities. In fact, `vi` is just `ex` working in *visual mode*. An unfortunate result of that arrangement is that you need to learn certain parts of `ex` in order to use `vi`. For instance, in order to insert another file into the one you're editing, you need to use the `ex` command `r` (which you call from `vi` by typing ':r'). In our description of `vi` we include those `ex` commands that are most likely to be useful; if you need others, you'll have to learn about `ex`.

When you edit a file, `vi` acts on a working copy of the file called the *main buffer*. All of your editing actions apply to the main buffer; the file is not modified until you request it. `Vi` also provides some other buffers that contain text, but when we refer to "the buffer" without qualification we mean the main buffer. The *current file* is the file that you most recently asked `vi` to edit.

**6.1.1
Organization of the
Screen**

As you edit, the screen displays a portion of the buffer. The visual cursor indicates vi's position in the buffer. The *current line* is the line containing the cursor.

If a line of text is longer than the screen width, the part that runs over is placed on one or more additional lines. Commands that move the cursor down or up by lines move by logical lines, not screen lines, so a command that moves down by one logical line may well move down by several screen lines if the logical lines are oversized.

If the portion of the buffer being displayed is too short to fill the screen, vi fills the rest of the screen with lines that contain '~' in the first column and are otherwise blank. When you start to edit an empty buffer, the entire screen is filled with such lines.

The Status Line.   The bottom line of your screen is the *status line*, which vi uses for the following purposes:

- Error messages appear on the status line.

- When vi generates status information such as the name of the current file in response to a command, this information appears on the status line.

- As you type a search pattern or an ex command, vi echoes what you're typing to the status line.

**6.1.2
Meanings of Keys**

Vi assigns specific meanings to many keys on your keyboard. In addition, it recognizes and uses certain assignments of control keys made via stty (see Section 4.4.2):

(Intr)   The interrupt key, which interrupts and cancels whatever you're doing.

(Kill)   The kill key, which erases all the characters you've typed on the current line.

(Erase)   The erase key, which erases the character to the left of the cursor. (If you didn't type the character as part of the current input operation, however, (Erase) won't erase it.)

The (Erase) key is often set to (Ctrl)H; vi treats (Ctrl)H as an additional erase key if you set your (Erase) key to something else. The (Ctrl)D command works as described here whether or not you set your (EOF) key to (Ctrl)D. When vi uses a control key for a particular purpose, that purpose preempts any other vi meaning that the key might have. For instance, if your (Kill) key is set to '@' (the default for printing terminals), the vi commands that use '@' to operate on registers are not available.

Vi is usually configured so that the cursor arrow keys perform the indicated motions. Other directional keys such as (Home) may also work in some systems.[1]

---

1. Vi uses the database of terminal descriptions (see Section 2.19) to establish these meanings.

**6.1.3
Modes**

At any moment, vi is in one of three modes: *command mode, input mode,* or *status-line mode* (called *last-line mode* in most vi documentation). Of these, command mode is the most fundamental since the other two are really excursions from command mode.

- Command mode is the mode for issuing short commands. In command mode, vi treats each character you type as a command to do something or as part of such a command; the character is not echoed to your terminal. The typing conventions for command mode are described in Section 6.1.4 and in Section 6.1.5.

- Input mode is the mode for inserting text into the buffer. In input mode, vi treats each character you type as data and echoes it to the terminal, adding it at the cursor position and moving the cursor one position to the right. The typing conventions for input mode are described in Section 6.1.6.

- Status-line mode is the mode for issuing long commands. As you type characters in status-line mode, vi echoes them to the status line. When you finish typing the command, vi executes it. The typing conventions for status-line mode are described in Section 6.1.7.

The treatments of control characters in input mode and in status mode are similar but not identical.

**6.1.4
Commands**

When vi is in command mode, it interprets every character you type as a command or part of a command. Characters that you type in command mode are not echoed to the screen, so you need to type them carefully. Although most commands are short, you can easily lose track of where you are. If you do, you can always cancel the current command by typing (Intr) .

Nearly all the characters on your keyboard are meaningful commands. If you start typing what you think is input text when vi is in command mode, you'll get a useless and often destructive sequence of actions as a result. This is an easy mistake to make if you're accustomed to using a "modeless" editor in which all the commands are summoned by control characters that are never used in text. If you enable the showmode variable (p. 230), vi will place an indicator on the status line whenever it's in input mode. If the indicator is absent and the cursor is in the buffer rather than on the last line, vi is in command mode.

The effects of most commands are limited to the current line. The exceptions are those commands that search for text, explicitly move across line boundaries, or move the cursor in units of words.

Form of Commands.   Each vi command consists of one or two characters, optionally preceded by a count and possibly followed by various modifiers. In most but not all cases the count specifies a number of repetitions; what is repeated depends on the command. For example, the command '3j' moves the cursor down three lines, while the command '8dd' deletes eight lines starting with the current one.

A command named by a capital letter is usually related to the command named by the corresponding small letter although the nature of the relationship depends on the command:

- The 'f', 'o', 'p', 't', and 'x' commands act at or after the cursor, i.e., forwards; the 'F', 'O', 'P', 'T', and 'X' commands act before the cursor, i.e., backwards.
- The 'i' and 'a' commands act at the cursor position; the 'I' and 'A' commands act at the beginning and end of the current line.
- The 'e', 'w', and 'b' commands act on words; the 'E', 'W', and 'B' commands act on blank-delimited words.

Objects.   Some commands take *objects*. An object is specified by a command that moves the cursor; the object denotes the region of text passed over by the command. A command that takes an object acts on the region it denotes. For instance, the 'w' command moves to the start of the next word, so the 'w' object denotes the text between the cursor and the start of the next word. The 'd' command deletes its object, so the command 'dw' deletes the text preceding the next word.

For a motion command that moves the cursor to a different line, the corresponding object is the set of lines containing the new and old cursor positions. For example, the 'j' command moves to the next line, so the object it specifies consists of all of the current line and all of the next line—even though both the old and new cursor positions may be in the middle of the line. The 'dj' command thus deletes two lines: the current line and the next line. This behavior can be surprising until you get used to it.

Commands That Change the Mode.   Certain commands initiate other modes:

- Commands that expect input text, such as 'i', 'A', and 'o', initiate input mode.

- The ':' command, which introduces an **ex** command, initiates status-line mode. The searching commands '/' and '?' also initiate status-line mode.

**6.1.5
Cancelling and
Interrupting
Commands**

The following keys cancel and interrupt commands:

Esc   Cancels the command you're currently typing. Typing Esc is useful when you're not sure what you've typed, since it lets you start over.

Intr   Cancels the command you're currently typing; if a command is already executing, interrupts it. The cursor returns to where it was before the command was executed. Vi beeps whenever you interrupt it.

Interrupting is a stronger action than cancelling because it works even in input mode and while vi is in the middle of searching for a pattern.

6.1.6
Typing Text in
Input Mode

Several commands expect you to type some text in input mode. The text appears on the screen as you type it. The following keys have special meaning in input mode:

(Enter)	Ends the current line and starts another one.
(Intr)	
(Esc)	Terminates this insertion and returns to command mode. The only difference between (Intr) and (Esc) is that (Intr) beeps at you while (Esc) does not.
(Erase)	
(Ctrl)H	Erases the character preceding the cursor.
(Kill)	Erases all the characters typed on the current line. Typing (Kill) does not affect any characters that were present before you entered input mode, nor does it affect any previously typed lines.
(Ctrl)W	Erases the previous word that you typed.
(Ctrl)V	Quotes the next character, i.e., inserts it into the text verbatim even if it is a control character such as (Esc).

When you back up over characters with (Ctrl)H or (Ctrl)W, the characters you back up over remain on the screen even though they have effectively been deleted. This effect can be confusing at first.

Insert mode is affected by whether vi is in autoindent mode (see Section 6.1.9).

6.1.7
Typing Text in
Status-Line Mode

The ':', '/', and '?' commands initiate status-line mode. The following keys have special meaning in status-line mode:

(Esc)	
(Enter)	Terminates the command you're typing and executes it.
(Intr)	Cancels the command you're typing and returns vi to command mode. If you type (Intr) after issuing a command but before it finishes executing, the execution is interrupted.
(Erase)	
(Ctrl)H	Erases the character preceding the cursor. If you erase the first character on the line, vi returns you to command mode.
(Kill)	Erases all the characters of the command (but not the first character on the line).
(Ctrl)W	Erase the previous word that you typed.
(Ctrl)V	Quotes the next character, i.e., inserts it into the text literally even if it is a control character such as (Esc).

Note the following differences between insert mode and status-line mode in what these keys do:

- In input mode, (Intr) ends the input but does not erase anything. In status-line mode, (Intr) cancels the command you're typing.

- In input mode, (Enter) starts a new line but does not end the input. In status-line mode, (Enter) ends the command you're typing and executes it.

6.1.8
Using ex
Commands

You can issue an ex command from vi by preceding it with a colon. The command is displayed on the status line as you type it. Vi itself doesn't provide commands for file actions such as reading a file or for global actions such as replacing all occurrences of a certain pattern within the buffer; instead it relies on ex for these functions. The descriptions of vi commands below include descriptions of some particularly useful ex commands (see the description of the :s command on page 223 and Section 6.1.27). The only ex commands that you can't issue from vi are those that insert lines of text: 'i', 'I', 'a', 'A', and 'R'.

6.1.9
Autoindent Mode

Autoindent mode is a vi mode of operation that makes it easier to create and modify indented text. Autoindent mode is particularly useful for typing programs. It only affects what you type in input mode. You can activate autoindent mode by typing ':set ai' and deactivate it by typing ':set noai'.

In autoindent mode, vi automatically lines up the beginnings of lines as you type them. It indents each new line by the same amount as the previous line. You can increase the indentation by typing one or more tabs or spaces at the beginning of a line. Vi provides several commands for reducing the indentation either temporarily or permanently. All of them use (Ctrl)D and all of them must be typed at the very beginning of an input line.

(Ctrl)D Decreases the indentation by backing up to the previous shift width interval. The shift width intervals behave like tab stops, so that if the shift width is 3 you back up to the previous column in the set 1, 4, 7, etc. (see the description of the shiftwidth variable on page 231).[2] The shift width interval need not be the same as the tab stop setting, although it ought to be. The (Erase) key won't back up to a shift width interval because it only affects characters that you type explicitly.

0 (Ctrl)D Moves to the left margin, cancelling all indentation. The '0' appears on the line when you type it but disappears along with the indentation when you type the (Ctrl)D.

∧ (Ctrl)D Moves to the left margin but remembers the indentation. The next line you type that does not start with '∧(Ctrl)D' resumes the previous indentation unless you start it with one of the other (Ctrl)D commands. The '∧' appears on the line when you type it but disappears along with the indentation when you type the (Ctrl)D. This facility is useful for putting comments in programs.

If you're in autoindent mode and the lisp variable is enabled (see p. 232), vi inserts extra indentation whenever you type a line that starts with an unmatched left parenthesis.

---

2. Because vi automatically converts leading spaces to tabs, this command may produce unexpected effects if you use it when you're not positioned at a shift width interval.

6.1.10 **The Screen Window**	As you edit, vi displays a portion of the main buffer called the *window*. The window occupies the lower part of your screen. Usually the size of the window is the number of lines on the screen minus one or a smaller number of lines if you're using a slow terminal, but you can change its initial value with the window variable (see p. 233).

You can change the window size as you edit by using the 'z' commands (see p. 214). If you move the cursor to a line not in the window but vi can display that line by enlarging the window, it does so. The next time that vi needs to redraw the window entirely, it reduces the window to the specified size. Reducing the window size is generally not useful on terminals where the time it takes to display a full-screen window is negligible.

6.1.11 **Regular Expressions** **in vi and ex**	The search and substitution commands of vi and ex search for patterns defined by regular expressions. Regular expressions are as defined in Section 2.16, but with certain extensions:

- In a pattern, the sequence '\<' matches the beginning of a word and the sequence '\>' matches the end of a word. For the purpose of this construct, a word is a sequence of letters, digits, underscores, and hyphens.

- In a replacement string, '\U' causes the rest of the replacement string to be converted to all uppercase and '\l' causes the rest of the replacement string to be converted to all lowercase. Similarly, '\u' causes the next character to be converted to uppercase and '\L' causes the next character to be converted to lowercase. If these commands appear in the middle of a replacement string, they affect only the remaining part.

6.1.12 **Calling vi**	You can call vi using any of the following three names:

vi	No flags are implicitly set.
view	The –R flag is set and vi edits your files in read-only mode (see –R below).
vedit	The flags are set so as to make the editor easier for beginners to use. The report variable is set to 1 and the showmode and novice variables are enabled. (Not all versions accept this call.)

Whichever name you use, the call has the form

    vi [*options*] [*file*] ...

The files *file* ... can contain wildcards. If you don't specify any files, vi initiates the editing of an unnamed empty file. Within vi you can call for the next file to be edited using the ':n' command or return to the first file in the list with the ':rew' command.

6.1.13 **Command-Line** **Options**	These are the options for the vi command line:

–t*tag*	Edit the file containing *tag* (see Section 6.5). The cursor is initially positioned at the tag. If you also specify a file list, the file containing *tag* is edited first and then the files in the file list

are edited. The relevant tag file, usually the file in the current directory named **tags**, must be available (see the **tags** variable, p. 229).

−r*file*   As **vi** works, it periodically saves the state of the buffer in a recovery file. If the editor or the system crashes during editing, you receive a mail message giving you the name of this recovery file. If you later call **vi** and specify this recovery file with the −r option, **vi** resumes in whatever state it was when it saved the recovery file.

−R   Edit these files in read-only mode (the **readonly** variable is enabled). Setting this flag helps to protect the files from accidental overwriting by inhibiting **vi** from writing to them unless special commands such as ':**w**!' are used. This flag is irrelevant for **view** since **view** sets it anyway.

−c*cmd*
+*cmd*   Execute the **ex** command *cmd* before starting to edit the first (or only) file in the file list. For example, the command line

```
vi -c:122 krumhorn
```

starts editing the file **krumhorn** at line 122 since the **ex** command ':122' jumps to line 122. The −c form is better because it's consistent with the general UNIX conventions for command lines, but some systems may recognize only the + form.

**6.1.14
Quick Exit**

If you're stuck and need to get out of **vi** quickly, there are two sure ways to do it:

- If you want to save the file you're working on, type '(Esc)ZZ'. If that fails to work, type '(Intr)ZZ'. The (Intr) may cause your most recent changes to be lost.

- If you don't care about saving the file, type '(Intr):q!(Enter)'. Any changes you've made since the file was last written are discarded.

Under unusual circumstances you may need more than one (Intr) to get these to work.

If your shell provides job control (see Section 2.7.1), you can suspend **vi** by typing (Ctrl)Z. See Section 6.1.27 for more information about exiting from **vi**.

**6.1.15
Initializing** vi **or** ex

You can provide a set of initialization commands that the editor, be it **vi** or **ex**, executes whenever it starts up. Initialization commands are useful for setting variables and for defining macros that you want to have available whenever you use the editor. You can provide these commands in either of two ways:

- You can record the commands in the environment variable EXINIT (see Section 2.7.5).

- You can store the commands in an .exrc file.

Here's how the editor looks for preset variables:

(1) It checks the environment variable EXINIT. If EXINIT is nonempty, the editor executes the commands in it.

(2) If EXINIT is empty but a file named .exrc exists in your home directory, the editor executes the commands in that file.

(3) If the commands thus executed cause the exrc variable to be enabled (it's disabled by default), the editor then executes the commands in the .exrc file in the current directory (if it exists).

By placing different .exrc files in different directories you can adjust the editor's behavior to the nature of the files in the directory.

**6.1.16
Adjusting the Screen**

The following commands adjust what is displayed on the screen.

Scrolling Commands. The scrolling commands change what is displayed on the screen while changing your position in the file as little as possible. The cursor usually doesn't appear to move.

Ctrl F   Scrolls down (forward) one screen.

Ctrl B   Scrolls up (backward) one screen.

Ctrl D   Scrolls down (forward) by half a screen. If you specify a count n, vi scrolls down by n lines. Subsequent Ctrl D's and Ctrl U's then scroll by the same amount.

Ctrl U   Scrolls up (backward) by half a screen. If you specify a count n, vi scrolls up by n lines. Subsequent Ctrl D's and Ctrl U's then scroll by the same amount.

Ctrl E   Scrolls down (forward) by one line. The form n Ctrl E scrolls down by n lines. It differs from n Ctrl D in that it does not affect subsequent commands.

Ctrl Y   Scrolls up (backward) by one line. The form n Ctrl Y scrolls up by n lines. It differs from n Ctrl U in that it does not affect subsequent commands.

Orienting the Screen. The following commands are useful for placing the current line or a line containing a particular pattern at a specified position on the screen:

z Enter
z+   Regenerates the screen with the current line as the top line of the screen and the cursor positioned at the beginning of that line.

z-   Regenerates the screen with the current line as the bottom line of the screen and the cursor positioned at the beginning of that line.

z.   Regenerates the screen with the current line as the middle line of the screen and the cursor positioned at the beginning of that line.

/*pat*/z (Enter)

> Regenerates the screen with the next line containing the pattern *pat* as the top line of the screen and the cursor positioned at the beginning of that line. Other forms of '/*pat*/z' such as '/*pat*/z-' behave analogously.

z*n* (Enter)

> Uses a window of *n* lines and positions the cursor at the top of that window. Combinations using 'z*n*' such as '/*pat*/z*n*-' behave analogously. A 'z*n*' command sets the default value of *n*; subsequent 'z' commands without *n* gives you a window size of that default value.

Restoring the Screen.   The following commands for restoring your screen are useful when your screen has become scrambled. This can happen if you interrupt vi with (Intr), if some other program writes to your screen in the middle of editing, or if you're using vi over a noisy line.

(Ctrl) L   Regenerates the screen.

(Ctrl) R   Regenerates the screen, eliminating any lines that have no characters at all, not even spaces. Normally this command is equivalent to (Ctrl) L, except for dumb terminals.

6.1.17
Moving by Direction

The following commands move the cursor horizontally or vertically:

(Space)
l
> Moves right one character, but not past the end of the line.

(Erase)
h
(Ctrl) H
> Moves left one character, but not past the beginning of the line. Note that h works only when you're in command mode.

(Ctrl) N
(Ctrl) J
j
> Moves directly down one line. Vi tries to maintain your horizontal position. (Ctrl) N is a mnemonic for "next".

(Ctrl) P
k
> Moves directly up one line. Vi tries to maintain your horizontal position. (Ctrl) P is a mnemonic for "previous".

0
> Moves to the first character on the current line. This command is unaffected by a repetition count.

^
> Moves to the first *nonwhite* character on the current line. (The "white" characters are space, end of line, tab, and formfeed.) This command is unaffected by a repetition count.

$
> Moves to the last character on the current line. This command is unaffected by a repetition count.

(Enter)
+
> Moves to the first nonwhite character on the following line.

−
> Moves to the first nonwhite character on the previous line.

n|	Moves to column *n* of the current line. The first column is numbered 1. You can omit the count; it defaults to 1.
H	Moves to the beginning of the first line on the screen. If you precede this command with a count *n*, you move to the *n*th line from the top of the screen.
M	Moves to the beginning of the middle line on the screen. A count with this command has no effect.
L	Moves to the beginning of the last line on the screen. If you precede this command with a count *n*, you move to the *n*th line from the bottom of the screen.
G	Moves to the first character on line *n*, where *n* is the count preceding 'G'. If you omit *n*, `vi` moves to the last line of the buffer. The '1G' command is the simplest way to move to the beginning of the buffer. You may find it convenient to use the ':map' command (see p. 227) to define the otherwise unassigned 'g' command as '1G'.

**6.1.18
Moving by
Syntactic Units**

For the purposes of the commands that follow, a *word* is either (a) a sequence of letters, digits, and underscores, or (b) a sequence of characters none of which are either whitespace or word characters. A *blank-delimited word* is a sequence of characters surrounded by whitespace. *Whitespace* is a sequence of the following "white" characters: space, end of line, tab, formfeed. Generally speaking, a word doesn't include punctuation while a blank-delimited word does.

Moving by Words.   The following commands move the cursor by words:

e	Moves to the last character of the current word (or the next word, if the cursor is on whitespace).
E	Moves to the last character of the current blank-delimited word (or the next word, if the cursor is on whitespace).
w	Moves forward to the beginning of the next word.
W	Moves forward to the beginning of the next blank-delimited word.
b	Moves back to the beginning of the current word (or to the beginning of the previous word, if the cursor is on whitespace).
B	Moves back to the beginning of the current blank-delimited word (or to the beginning of the previous blank-delimited word, if the cursor is on whitespace).

Moving by Sentences.   The following commands move the cursor by sentences:

)	Moves forward to the end of the current sentence and then to the first nonwhite character of the next sentence. If the cursor is within the last sentence in the buffer, this command moves

the cursor to the end of the buffer. Vi considers a sentence to be ended by any of the following:

- An end-of-sentence character (. ! ?) followed by two spaces

- An end-of-sentence character followed by a blank line

- A blank line

Vi also treats the characters ( )] ') following punctuation at the end of a sentence as part of the sentence. A repetition count causes vi to move forward several sentences. In LISP mode, this command moves the cursor past the next S-expression.

(Moves backward to the first character of the current sentence as defined just above. A repetition count causes vi to move backward several sentences. In LISP mode, this command moves the cursor to before the previous S-expression.

Moving by Paragraphs and Sections.   The following commands move the cursor by paragraphs and sections:

}   Moves forward to the next paragraph boundary. Vi considers a paragraph boundary to be (a) a blank line, or (b) one of the nroff requests listed in the paragraphs variable (see Section 6.2), or (c) the end of the buffer. A repetition count causes vi to move forward several paragraphs. In LISP mode, this command moves the cursor past the next S-expression that isn't an atom.

{   Moves backward to the previous paragraph boundary as defined just above (the beginning of the buffer acts as a paragraph boundary). A repetition count causes vi to move backward several paragraphs. In LISP mode, this command moves the cursor to before the first previous S-expression that isn't an atom.

]]   Moves forward to the next line that marks a section boundary. The following lines mark section boundaries:

- An nroff section command, namely, one of the nroff requests listed in the sections variable (see Section 6.2)

- A line that starts with a left brace at the left margin, e.g., the beginning of a C function definition

When this command is combined with a command for deleting, altering, or copying text (see Section 6.1.22), it treats a line starting with '}' as a section boundary. You can't use a repetition count with this command. In LISP mode, this command moves the cursor to the beginning of the next line that starts with a '(' .

[[Moves backward to the nearest previous line that marks a section boundary as defined just above. You can't use a repetition count with this command. In LISP mode, this command moves the cursor to the beginning of the nearest previous line that starts with a '('.

The commands below search for specified textual items.

Searching for Characters.   The following commands search for particular characters. None of them move beyond the current line.

f*c*   Moves to the next occurrence of the character *c* on the current line.

F*c*   Moves to the previous occurrence of the character *c* on the current line.

t*c*   Moves to the character just before the next occurrence of the character *c* on the current line.

T*c*   Moves to the character just after the previous occurrence of the character *c* on the current line.

;   Repeats the last 'f', 'F', 't', or 'T' command. Note that if the last command was 't' or 'T', the ';' command has no effect unless you precede it with a count (since the cursor is already positioned just before or just after a *c*).

,   Repeat the last 'f', 'F', 't', or 'T' command, but reverse the direction.

The following command finds the mate to a delimiter:

%   Moves the cursor to the delimiter that matches the character under the cursor. The delimiters are (( ) [ ] { }). For example, if the cursor is on a '(', this command moves it to the matching ')'; if the cursor is on a '}', this command moves it to the matching '{'. If the cursor is not on a delimiter, you receive an error warning. This command can move to another line.

Searching for Patterns.   The following commands search for patterns:

/*pat* Enter
/*pat*/
/*pat*/+*n*
/*pat*/-*n*   Moves forward to the first character of the next portion of text that matches the pattern *pat*. The pattern appears on the status line as you type it.

The pattern is given as a regular expression (see Section 6.1.11). If you've enabled the `wrapscan` variable and the pattern isn't found in the rest of the buffer, `vi` continues the search at the beginning of the buffer. You must quote any use of the character '/' within the pattern by typing it as '\/'. You can disable the special interpretation of regular expression characters by turning off the `magic` variable.

The forms '/*pat*/+*n*' and '/*pat*/-*n*' indicate the first nonwhite character on the *n*th line after or before the place where *pat* is found, or the end of that line if it contains only whitespace. The form '/*pat*/+0' works and is sometimes useful since it forces the object specified by the motion to be line-oriented. **Note:** You cannot use a count with this command.

?pat (Enter)

?pat?

?pat?+n

?pat?−n   These commands are like the corresponding '/pat/' commands except that they search backward rather than forward. The new cursor position is at the first character of the matching text.

/   Searches again for the pattern you most recently searched for in the forward direction (no matter what the direction of the previous search). In other words, an empty search pattern means "repeat the search".

?   Searches again for the pattern you most recently searched for in the backward direction (no matter what the direction of the previous search).

n   Searches again for the pattern you most recently searched for, in the same direction as the most recent '/' or '?' command. For the purpose of determining the direction, a search with an empty pattern still counts. The advantage of this command and the next one over '/' and '?' is that they are just single keystrokes.

N   Searches again for the pattern you most recently searched for, but in the opposite direction from the most recent "/" or '?' command. For the purpose of determining the direction, a search with an empty pattern still counts.

6.1.20
Setting and Moving
to Placemarks

The following commands enable you to put *placemarks* in the buffer and to move the cursor to those placemarks. The placemarks are denoted by a letter or digit, indicated as *c* in the descriptions below. Uppercase and lowercase letters are equivalent.

m*c*   Attaches placemark *c* to the current cursor position.

'*c*   Moves the cursor to placemark *c*.

'*c*   Moves the cursor to the beginning of the line containing placemark *c*.

''   Moves to the previous *context*, determined as follows:

  • Initially, the context is at the top of the buffer.

  • An insertion sets the context to the beginning of the insertion.

  • A pattern search sets the context to the beginning of the text that matches the pattern.

  • A deletion sets the context to the cursor position after the deletion.

  • A '' or '' command sets the context to the cursor position.

You can conveniently use this command to move back and forth between two places in the buffer.

`'`   Moves to the beginning of the line containing the previous context.

**6.1.21
Inserting Text**

Whenever you type one of the commands in this group, `vi` enters input mode and expects you to type the text to be inserted.

`a`   Inserts (appends) text after the cursor.

`A`   Inserts (appends) text at the end of the current line.

`i`   Inserts text before the cursor.

`I`   Inserts text before the first non-white character at the start of the line (or at the start of the line if the line is empty).

`o`   Opens up a blank line under the current line, then starts inserting text there.

`O`   Opens up a blank line above the current line, then starts inserting text there.

You can put a count in front of 'a', 'A', 'i', or 'I'; a count of n causes n copies of the text to be inserted. (`Vi` silently ignores a count in front of 'o' or 'O'.[3]) But beware of this anomaly in some versions of `vi`: if the text includes an (Enter), only the text preceding the (Enter) is repeated; the text on the following lines appears only once.

**6.1.22
Deleting and
Altering Text**

The commands in this section delete or alter text. You can think of altering text as consisting of two operations: deleting the text and then inserting some new text. We first describe the commands that take objects and then the commands that do not.

Conventions for Commands That Take Objects.   The following conventions apply to commands that take objects:

- An object is specified by a motion command, which can be any command that moves the cursor other than one that scrolls the screen or inserts text. The commands in Sections 6.1.17 through 6.1.20 all qualify as motion commands. The action of a command taking an object applies to the region denoted by the object (see "Objects" on page 209). For example, 'dW' deletes the next blank-delimited word.

- If the command is preceded by a count n, its motion is performed n times. For example, '4yt; (Enter)' yanks the text from the cursor up to but not including the fourth following semicolon on the current line. (You receive an error warning if there aren't four more semicolons on the line.) The forms '4yt;' and 'y4t;' are equivalent, as are other analogous pairs of forms.

- A line-oriented motion command defines a region that consists of whole lines. The region includes the line containing the starting cursor position, the line containing the ending cursor position, and

---

3. In early versions of `vi`, a count n in front of 'o' or 'O' caused n lines to be opened up. This was useful only for slow terminals.

all lines in between. For example, the 'j' command defines a region consisting of the line containing the cursor and the next line. The line-oriented motion commands are

        j k + - H M L G

A command using line-oriented motions may operate on a region bigger than you'd expect. For instance, 'dj' deletes the current line *and* the next one, while '3yk' yanks *four* lines, the current line being the last of them.

- If you double the command character, the command applies to all of the current line (and does not take an object). For example, 'dd' deletes the current line, while '3dd' deletes the current line and the next two lines.

Commands That Take Objects.   Each of the following commands takes an object m:

dm Deletes the region of text from the cursor to m and puts it into the anonymous buffer.

cm Changes the region of text from the cursor to m by deleting it and then inserting new text. The replacement text is typed in input mode and can include newlines. The deleted text is placed in the anonymous buffer.

ym Yanks the region of text into the anonymous buffer (see Section 6.1.24), leaving it undisturbed.[4] The contents of the anonymous buffer can then be put somewhere else, giving you the effect of a copy action.

>m Indents the region from the current line to the line containing m by one shift width (see p. 231). Note that a preceding count affects the search for m and does not produce multiple indenting. A convenient way to get multiple indenting is to follow this command by the '.' (dot) command.

<m Outdents the region from the current line to the line containing m by one shift width. If the line is already at the left margin it is unaffected. Note that a preceding count affects the search for m and does not produce multiple outdenting. A convenient way to get multiple outdenting is to follow this command by the '.' (dot) command.

!m *cmd*   Executes *cmd*, transmitting the region of text from the cursor to m as the standard input for *cmd*. The standard output of *cmd* then replaces the text in this region. For example, if fmt is a program for formatting a paragraph, the command '!}fmt' causes the lines of the next paragraph to be formatted.

---

4. The term "yank" is misleading since it suggests that the yanked text no longer remains where it was; but the use of the term has a long tradition among people who write editors—probably because 'y' doesn't naturally stand for anything else.

=*m*   Realigns the lines in the region of text from the cursor to *m* as though they had been typed in using the LISP autoindent conventions. If the `lisp` variable isn't on, you get an error warning.

Commands That Do Not Take Objects.   The commands below for deleting and altering text do not take objects.

The following commands replace existing text. For each of them, the replacement text is typed in input mode. You can type beyond the end of the current line and even start new lines; the effect is as though the additional text was appended at the end of the current line. In particular, new lines are *inserted* after the current line and do not overwrite lines below the current line.

s   Substitutes for the character under the cursor by erasing the cursor character and then inserting new text. With a count of *n*, substitutes for *n* characters starting with the character under the cursor (or the rest of the line if fewer than *n* characters remain). This command is equivalent to 'cl'.

S   Substitutes for the current line by erasing the current line and then inserting new text. With a count of *n*, substitutes for *n* lines starting with the current line. This command is equivalent to 'cc'.

C   Changes the rest of the line. A count given with this command is ignored. The 'C' command is equivalent to 'c$'.

R   Overwrites ("replaces") characters with input text starting with the character under the cursor. The overwritten characters are *not* copied to the anonymous buffer. You can't use a count with this command.

The following commands delete or replace characters within a line:

x   Deletes the character under the cursor. Used with a count of *n*, this command deletes *n* characters starting with the character under the cursor and going to the right. It is equivalent to 'dl'.

X   Deletes the character preceding the cursor. Used with a count of *n*, this command deletes *n* characters starting with the character before the cursor and going to the left. It is equivalent to 'dh'.

r*c*   Replaces the character under the cursor with the character *c*. If you give a count *n* with this command, the next *n* characters on the line are replaced with copies of *c*. The count must not exceed the number of characters remaining on the line.

D   Deletes the rest of the line. A count given with this command is ignored. The 'D' command is equivalent to 'd$'.

The following commands reinsert yanked or deleted text:

p   Puts the contents of the anonymous buffer (the one that 'y' and 'd' write to) just after the cursor character. If the anonymous buffer contains whole lines, it is put just after the current line. The anonymous buffer is lost when you change files, so you should use named buffers when you're transferring text from one file to another.

P   Puts the contents of the anonymous buffer (the one that 'y' and 'd' write to) just before the cursor character. If the anonymous buffer contains whole lines, it is put just before the current line.

The following commands perform other operations:

Y   Yanks the current line into the anonymous buffer. With a count of n, this command yanks n lines starting with the current line. The 'Y' command is equivalent to 'yy'.

J   Joins the current line with the next line. With a count of n, joins n lines, that is, joins the current line with the next $(n - 1)$ lines. When two lines are joined, the junction is created as follows:

 (1) If the first character of the second line is ')', all whitespace at the junction is eliminated.

 (2) If the first line ends with a period, question mark, or bang, the junction and any adjacent whitespace are replaced by two spaces.

 (3) In all other cases, the junction and any adjacent whitespace are replaced by a single space.

:g /*pat*/s//*repl*/g
                     Replaces *pat* by *repl* throughout the buffer. The 's' in this form invokes the ex command substitute; the preceding ':g /*pat*/' causes the substitution to take place globally, i.e., throughout the buffer, on all lines containing *pat*. The trailing 'g' indicates that the command applies to all occurrences within the line rather than just to the first occurrence. The substitute command is explained in Section 6.3.17; global execution of commands is explained in Section 6.3.23. See those explanations for variations on this form.

&   Repeats the previous replacement command (applied to the first occurrence only).

~   Changes the case of the letter under the cursor and moves to the next character. Nonalphabetic characters are unaffected.

See Section 6.1.24 for additional commands that delete, alter, or copy text, and the '.' command for repeating actions (p. 225).

**6.1.23
Moving and
Copying Text**

Vi does not have any explicit commands for moving and copying text. Instead, you move text in two steps: deleting it from its original location and putting the deleted text in the new location. Similarly, you copy text by "yanking" it from its original location and putting it in its new location. Here are two examples:

- To move the next two lines to another place, type '2dd', move to the place you want to put the lines, and type 'p'.

- To copy an arbitrary block of text to an arbitrary place, go to one end of it, type '`a' (to mark that end), go to the other end, and type 'y`a'. Then go to the place you want to put the text and type 'p'.

**6.1.24
Named Buffers**

Vi has a set of twenty-six named buffers for holding text, named by the letters of the alphabet. You can transfer text between these buffers and the main buffer. When you transfer text *to* a named buffer, the nature of the transfer depends on whether you specify the buffer with a lower-case letter or with an uppercase letter. For a lowercase letter, the transferred text replaces the previous buffer contents; for an uppercase letter, the transferred text, preceded by a newline, is appended to the previous buffer contents. When you transfer text *from* a named buffer, however, lowercase and uppercase buffer names are equivalent.

A named buffer contains either lines or characters, depending on whether it was filled by a line-oriented command or a character-oriented command. This distinction affects the behavior of commands that insert the contents of a named buffer into the main buffer. Appending text to a named buffer makes it a line-oriented buffer.

With the exception of the ⓺*b* command, each of the named-buffer commands is gotten from a corresponding command for the anonymous buffer by prefixing the corresponding command with '"*b*'. These are the commands for operating on named buffers:

"*bdm*   Deletes the region of text from the cursor to *m* and stores it in buffer *b*. In this command, '*dm*' has the same meaning as it does in the deletion commands of Section 6.1.22. For example, '"*x*dw' deletes the next word and stores it in buffer X. The '"*b*dd' command deletes the current line and stores it in *b*, while the '"*b*D' command deletes the rest of the current line and stores it in *b*. You can also precede 'd' with a count; the conventions of Section 6.1.22 apply. An example of such a command is '"R3dj', which deletes the next three lines and appends them to buffer R.

"*bym*   Yanks the region of text from the cursor to *m* and stores it in buffer *b*. In this command, '*ym*' has the same meaning as it does in the deletion commands of Section 6.1.22. For example, '"Ay0' copies the text from the beginning of the line up to and including the character under the cursor into buffer A. The '"*b*yy' command deletes the current line and stores it in *b*. You can also precede 'y' with a count; the conventions of Section 6.1.22 apply.

"*b*p   If buffer *b* contains characters, inserts those characters after the cursor. If it contains lines, inserts those lines just after the current line. Usually this *isn't* what you want; for inserting lines, the '"*b*P' command just below is more likely to give you the right result. If you provide a count with this command, vi ignores it.

"*b*P   If buffer *b* contains characters, inserts those characters before the cursor. If it contains lines, inserts those lines just before the current line. If you provide a count with this command, vi ignores it.

"*b*⓺   Treats the contents of buffer *b* as a sequence of vi commands and executes them.

@   Treats the contents of the anonymous buffer as a sequence of vi commands and executes them. On most systems this command won't work if '@' is your (Kill) character.

@*b*   Treats the contents of buffer *b* as a sequence of vi commands and executes them. On most systems this command won't work if '@' is your (Kill) character.

6.1.25
Undoing or
Repeating Actions

Vi provides two commands for recovering from a mistake:

u   Undoes the most recent change, insertion, or macro-defined command. Two 'u's in a row cancel each other. If you undo a command defined by a macro (see Section 6.1.29), *all* the actions of the macro are undone.

U   Restores the current line to the state it was in when you most recently started editing it. The restoration may undo several individual changes.

"*n*p   Retrieves the *n*th most recently deleted block of text and inserts it into the buffer following the cursor. Up to ten blocks can be retrieved. This command is useful for recovering from accidental large deletions.

"*n*P   Like p, except that the text is inserted preceding the cursor.

.   Repeats the last action that modified the buffer. As a special case, vi increments the deletion number if the action was '"*n*p' or '"*n*P'. Thus the sequence '"1pu.u.u.', continued as long as necessary, causes vi to insert successively older deletions. If you're not sure which deletion you want to retrieve, this sequence is a good way to find the right one.

6.1.26
Checking the Status

The following command reveals vi's status:

(Ctrl) G   Displays on the status line the name of the current file, the number of the current line, and how far down in the buffer the current position is (as a percentage).

6.1.27
Reading Files,
Writing Files,
and Exiting

We discuss reading and writing files along with exiting from vi because the actions of writing the buffer to a file and exiting are often combined.

Vi has only one file command, 'ZZ', of its own. It relies on ex for all other operations on files. We list the most useful such ex commands below, writing them with the preceding colon that you need in order to use them from vi.

:wq
ZZ   Saves the buffer you're editing and exits from vi. The buffer is saved in the current file.

:[*r*]w [*file*]   Here *r* is a range as defined by ex (see Section 6.3.5). If *r* is omitted, the command writes the buffer to *file*, then continues editing it. If you specify *r*, just those lines are written to *file*. If you omit *file*, it is taken to be the current file. By using ':w' with both *r* and *file*, you can write a portion of the buffer to a different file than the one you're editing. The portion must consist of entire lines. Here is the method:

(1) Type 'ma' to mark the beginning of the region you want to write out (see the 'm' command in Section 6.1.20).

(2) Move to the end of the region, i.e., the beginning of the next line.

(3) Type ':'a,.w *file*' to write out the region.

There are many variations on this method.

:q   Quits vi, abandoning the buffer. Vi rejects this command if you've changed the current file since the last time you wrote it and the warn variable is enabled.

:q!   Quits vi, abandoning the buffer even if you've changed the current file. Vi rejects this command if you've changed the current file since the last time you wrote it and the warn variable is enabled.

:e *file*   Abandons the buffer and starts editing *file*.

:r *file*   Reads in (inserts) the file *file*, inserting it just after the current line.

:ta *tag*   Opens the file containing the tag file entry *tag* and moves the cursor to that tag within the file. The tags are searched for in the list of tag files given by the tags variable (p. 229). By default, the file named tags in the current directory is searched first. See Section 6.5 for more information about tag files.

6.1.28 Setting Local Variables

You can use the following ex command to set the values of the local variables that modify vi's behavior. The local variables are enumerated and explained in Section 6.2.

:set   Specifies or queries a variable using the set command of ex (see Section 6.3.21).

6.1.29 Defining Macros

Vi includes a very useful facility for defining *macros*. Although the commands for defining and undefining macros are all ex commands, they are of no use in ex since macros are recognized only in visual mode. You issue them in vi by preceding them with a colon.

A macro definition has two parts: a left side and a right side. Both parts are sequences of keystrokes. When you type the keystrokes on the left-hand side, vi translates them into the keystrokes on the right-hand side. The left-hand side consists of a sequence of one or more characters. If the sequence contains more than one character, the first character must be a nonprinting character.[5]

---

5. This restriction is a safeguard against defining macros that you are likely to type unintentionally.

Macros are most often used to create definitions for special keys such as function keys and arrow keys on your keyboard, but you can also use them to associate commands with single characters that don't already have a meaning. You can override a built-in vi command with a macro definition; that is sometimes convenient when you've run out of command letters and there are some vi commands you never use. You can make a collection of macro definitions available whenever you use vi by including the definitions in your initialization commands (see Section 6.1.15).

Vi starts out with a set of precompiled macro definitions for the arrow keys and possibly a few others if your keyboard has them. Vi extracts the key definitions from the data base of terminal descriptions (see Section 2.19). You can see them by issuing the map command by itself.[6]

The way that vi responds to a multi-character macro can be affected by the timeout variable (see p. 232). It usually makes no difference for macros that you call by pressing just one special key, but it may affect macros that you call by explicitly pressing several keys in sequence.

The following commands enable you to create and remove macro definitions:

:map [*lhs rhs*] (Enter)

> The map command defines a macro as a "map" of one sequence of keystrokes into another sequence. Macros defined using :map only affect command mode; vi ignores them when it is in input mode. In the map command, *lhs* is the sequence you want to type and *rhs* is the sequence you want vi to execute. For example, typing
>
> :map v :%subst /∧/> / (Ctrl) V (Enter) (Enter)
>
> defines the 'v' key, which is otherwise unused, to mean the same thing as
>
> :%subst /∧/> / (Enter)
>
> Typing 'v' then puts the sequence '> ' in front of each line in the buffer—a handy thing to do when the buffer contains a mail message that you wish to respond to. (See Section 6.3.17 for an explanation of the substitute command). The (Ctrl) V quotes the (Enter) following it; it is needed because otherwise the first (Enter) would appear to end *lhs* instead of being part of it. The final (Enter) ends the map command itself. In general, you need to put a (Ctrl) V in front of any whitespace character (space, tab, (Enter)) that is part of *lhs* or *rhs*. The left-hand side *lhs* is limited to 10 characters and the right-hand side *rhs* is limited to 100 characters. Contrary to the information in many vi documents, one (Ctrl) V always suffices except for one peculiar case: a '|' in a macro definition needs two (Ctrl) V's in front of it (so that the definition contains the sequence '(Ctrl) V |').

---

6. The map listing shows three columns: a key name, the characters transmitted by the key, and the definition. Although the first and second columns are different for the precompiled definitions, you can't create such named definitions yourself; any definition you create will have the same information in the first two columns.

Unless the `remap` variable has been disabled, the editor attempts to map the result of a macro mapping repeatedly until there are no more changes. For example, if you map '`q`' to '`#`' and '`#`' to '`a`', '`q1`' maps to '`a1`'. With `remap` off you can, for example, map Ctrl L to '`1`' and Ctrl R to Ctrl L without having Ctrl R map to '`1`'.

`Vi` has a special notation for associating macros with the function keys on your terminal. If *lhs* has the form '`#n`', where *n* is a digit between 0 and 9, the definition is associated with function key *n*. (The notation '`#0`' generally refers to function key 10, not function key 0.)

If you type `map` without *lhs* and *rhs*, you get a listing of all the existing macros.

`map!` *lhs rhs* Enter

This form of `map` is like the previous one, except that the macro thus defined is interpreted in input mode rather than in command mode.

`unm[ap][!]` *lhs*

Deletes the mapping you've defined for *lhs*. This command affects input-mode macros if the '`!`' is present and command-mode macros if the '`!`' is not present.

**6.1.30
Switching to** ex

The following command enables you to switch from `vi` to `ex`:

`Q`   Switches from `vi` to `ex` and enters line editing mode.

6.2   Local Variables for `vi` and `ex`

The local variables listed here affect the behavior of both `vi` and `ex`. You can set or query their values from `vi` with `:set` and from `ex` with `set` (see Section 6.3.21). Some of them are either enabled or disabled; others have numbers or strings as their values. It is often useful to include commands for setting these variables among your initialization commands (see Section 6.1.15).

**6.2.1
Search Control**

The following variables affect the way that search and motion commands work:

`magic`   If this variable is enabled, the editor gives special meaning to the regular expression characters (`.\ [ *`) in patterns. If this variable is disabled, those characters are treated as ordinary data characters when left unquoted but are treated as metacharacters when quoted with a preceding backslash—just the opposite of the usual convention for regular expressions.

The '∧' and '$' characters represent the beginning and end of the line as usual whether magic is enabled or disabled.

Default: magic (for most systems)

wrapscan

ws   This variable indicates that when the editor is searching for a pattern and reaches the end of the buffer, it should continue the search at the beginning of the file, i.e., it should "wrap around" the end of the buffer.

Default: nowrapscan

ignorecase

ic   If this variable is enabled, the editor ignores the case of the letters in a search pattern so that, for example, the string 'digital' matches the string 'Digital' (no matter which one is the pattern and which one is in the file text).

Default: noignorecase

paragraphs

para   This variable contains a string giving the names of the troff or nroff macros that are assumed to start a paragraph (see the '{' and '}' commands in vi).

Default: IPLPPPQPbpP LI

sections

sect   This variable contains a string giving the names of the troff or nroff macros that are assumed to start a section (see the '[[' and ']]' commands in vi).

Default: NHSHH HU

tags   This variable contains a sequence of files to be used as tag files by the ta (or :ta) command. The files in the sequence are separated by spaces.

Default: tags /usr/lib/tags

taglength

tl   If this variable has a nonzero value n, the tags processed by the :ta command are significant only to n characters. If n is zero, all characters in a tag are significant.

Default: 0

edcompatible

ed   This option causes certain suffixes on substitute commands (:s in vi) to behave as they normally do in the ed editor rather than as they normally do in ex:

• The 'g' and 'c' suffixes act as toggles, initially off, that control whether global searching within a line is done and whether you are asked to confirm each substitution. Each appearance of 'g' or 'c' reverses the state of the corresponding toggle.[7]

---

7. These conventions are from the BSD UNIX version of ed, not from the original Seventh Edition version still used in System V.

- The 'r' suffix (repeated substitution) recognizes '%' rather than '~' as the character that stands for the most recent preceding substitution.

Default: `noedcompatible`

6.2.2
Warnings and Status Information

The following variables control what the editor does in order to protect you from losing your work:

`writeany`
`wa`   When this variable is enabled, the editor does not make any safety checks before writing to a file.
Default: `nowriteany`

`warn`   If this variable is enabled, the editor prevents you from leaving the editor or switching files if you have not saved your latest changes. It issues a warning when you attempt such an action.
Default: `warn`

`autowrite`
`aw`   If this variable is enabled and you've changed the buffer since you last saved it, the editor writes out the current file before executing a command (!, n, or `ta`) that switches to another file.
Default: `noautowrite`

`report`   If the value of this variable is n, the editor tells you whenever it modifies, removes, or yanks more than n lines as the result of a single operation. The message, which appears on the status line, tells you the number of lines affected.
Default: `5`

The following variables control how the editor warns you of a potential problem:

`errorbells`
`eb`   If this variable is enabled, the editor sounds the bell (Ctrl G) before every error message.
Default: `noerrorbells`

`flash`   If this variable is enabled and your terminal provides a visual warning signal such as flashing the screen that supplants the error bell, the editor uses the visual warning instead of the error bell.
Default: `flash`

`terse`   If this variable is enabled, the editor's error diagnostics are given in their terse, shortened form.
Default: `terse`

The following variable tells the editor to put an indicator on the status line whenever you are in input mode:

`showmode`
`smd`   If this variable is enabled, `vi` places an indicator on the status line whenever you are in input mode. The indicators are

'INSERT MODE', 'APPEND MODE', 'OPEN MODE', and 'CHANGE MODE'.
This variable has no effect in ex.

Default: noshowmode

**6.2.3
Tabbing and
Word Wrap**

The following variable enables or disables autoindent mode, described in
Section 6.1.9:

autoindent
ai   If this variable is enabled, the editor indents each line by the
           same amount as the previous nonempty line. Enabling this
           variable is particularly useful for editing computer programs.

           Default: noautoindent

The following variables affect the number of columns that tabbing commands move backward or forward:

shiftwidth
sw   The value of this variable specifies the shift width, which defines
           the number of spaces in the shifts produced by the '<' and '>'
           commands and the tab stops used by Ctrl D when backing up
           during textual input in autoindent mode.

           Default: 8

tabstop
ts   The value of this variable is an integer n. The editor assumes
           that there is a tab stop every n spaces across the line. When it
           prints or displays a TAB character, it converts that character to
           the number of spaces needed to position the cursor at the next
           tab stop. (The variable has no effect on the buffer itself—only
           on the way that it is displayed.) Note that although shiftwidth
           and tabstop should usually be set to the same value, the editor
           does not require that they be.

           Default: 8

The following command affects the treatment of long input lines:

wrapmargin
wm   If this variable has a nonzero value n, the editor automatically
           starts a new line when you're in input mode and fewer than n
           characters remain on the line that you're typing (not when the
           length of the line exceeds n characters, as you might expect).
           This feature is called "wordwrap" in many editors. Wordwrap
           is disabled if the value of wrapmargin is zero.

           Default: 0

**6.2.4
Input Interpretation**

The following variables affect how the editor interprets your input:

beautify
bf   If this variable is enabled, the editor discards any nonprint-
           ing characters that you type in input mode, except for Ctrl I
           (⟨tab⟩), Ctrl J (⟨linefeed⟩), and Ctrl L (⟨formfeed⟩).

           Default: nobeautify

lisp If this variable is enabled, vi interprets the (( ) { }) commands as operating on LISP S-expressions. It also adds extra indentation to unclosed lists when you're inserting text in input mode and autoindent mode is on.

Default: nolisp

6.2.5
Macro Expansion and Definition

The following variables affect macro expansion and definition:

remap If this variable is enabled, the editor repeats the macro mapping process until no more characters are mapped (see Section 6.1.29). If it is disabled, the editor does not apply macros to the result of a macro expansion.

Default: remap

timeout This variable affects how vi behaves when you type a character that begins a multi-character macro. If it is enabled, vi assumes that any further characters you type after about a second has elapsed are *not* part of a macro call. If timeout is disabled, vi waits indefinitely for more characters to see if they are part of a macro call. See Section 6.1.29 for a discussion of macros.

The purpose of this variable is to ensure that macros associated with special keys on your keyboard work properly. These keys usually transmit a sequence of characters starting with (Esc) when you type them. You can associate an action with a special key by defining its sequence as a macro. Ordinarily the character sequence for a special key is transmitted very quickly—well within the timeout interval—so vi recognizes the sequence in any case. But if you're working with vi over a network, the network may impose arbitrary delays between the characters in the sequence, preventing vi from recognizing it. By disabling timeout you enable vi to recognize the sequence in any case.

For example, some keyboards have a (Meta) or (Alt) shift key. Typing '(Meta) c' for any key c usually produces the sequence '(Esc) c'. Suppose you define the (Meta)W key as a macro that searches for the next occurrence of the string '*/' using the command

        :map (Ctrl)V (Meta)W /*\/\ctl-v(Enter) (Enter)

Typing (Meta)W produces the sequence '(Esc)w'. You can now observe the following behavior, assuming no line delays:

- If you type '(Esc)w' quickly, the search is performed in any case.

- If you type '(Esc)w' slowly and timeout is disabled, the search is still performed.

- If you type '(Esc)w' slowly and timeout is enabled, the current command is terminated in response to the (Esc) and the cursor moves forward one word in response to the 'w'.

The timeout interval is system-dependent but is usually about a second. A few versions of `vi` provide a separate command for changing it. The value of `timeout` has no effect on anything you type when you're not in visual mode.

Default: `timeout`

6.2.6	The following variables affect how the editor displays or types lines:
Display Control	

`list`   If this variable is enabled, the editor prints or displays each line with tabs shown explicitly as '∧I' and the end of each line shown explicitly as '$'.

Default: `nolist`

`number`
`nu`   If this variable is enabled, the editor places a line number in front of each line that it prints or displays.

Default: `nonumber`

`autoprint`
`ap`   If this variable is enabled, the current line is shown after each `ex` command that modifies text. This variable has no effect on `vi`.

Default: `autoprint`

`prompt` This variable tells `ex` to display the prompt character ':' when it's waiting for a command. This variable has no effect on `vi`.

Default: `noprompt`

The following variable affects the distance that scrolling commands move:

`scroll` This variable specifies the number of lines that (Ctrl)U and (Ctrl)D initially scroll up or down. Using these commands with a count changes the scroll amount thereafter.

Default: half the number of lines on the screen, or 11

The following commands affect the window size:

`window` This variable sets the number of lines in `vi`'s working window.

Default: the number of lines on the screen minus one

`w300`
`w1200`
`w9600`   These variables have the same effect as `window`, but only apply when your terminal is operating at the specified baud rate. For example,

```
:set w300=12 w1200=23
```

indicates that you want a 12 line window at 300 baud and a 23 line window at 1200 baud.

Default: not used

When you type a ')' or '}' character, you can have the editor show you the matching '(' or '{' by enabling the following variable:

showmatch
sm   If this variable is enabled, vi shows you the corresponding '(' or '{' whenever you type a ')' or '}', provided that the matching symbol is on the current screen. This variable has no effect on ex.

Default: noshowmatch

6.2.7
Novice Mode

The following variable enables you to configure ex to run in a mode more suitable for novices:

novice   This command changes the behavior of ex to make it more suitable for novices. It is only available on a few systems.

Default: nonovice

6.2.8
Editor Commands in Documents

The following command enables the editor to recognize and execute editor commands that appear in a document that you're editing:

modelines
           If this variable is enabled, you can embed commands in the first five lines and/or the last five lines of a file, and the editor executes them whenever it starts editing that file. The command lines must have one of the forms

                 ex:*cmd*:
                 vi:*cmd*:

           You should leave this option disabled unless you are editing a specific file that requires it.

Default: nomodelines

6.2.9
Inhibiting Messages

The following variable enables you to control whether your terminal can receive messages from other users:

mesg   If this variable is enabled, other programs can send messages to your screen while you're editing. If it's disabled, messages from other programs are rejected. If you disable mesg, enabling it again has no effect.

Default: mesg

6.2.10
Environmental Information

The following variables tell the editor about your environment:

directory
dir   This variable contains the name of the directory where vi puts its temporary file.

Default: /tmp

exrc   If this variable is enabled, the editor looks for an .exrc file in the current directory before starting to edit your file. Since exrc is disabled by default, exrc can only have an effect if it is enabled by commands in the environment variable EXINIT or by commands in an .exrc file in your home directory. Not all systems provide this variable—if your system doesn't, you should assume that it behaves as though exrc is enabled.

Default: noexrc

shell   This variable gives the name of the shell that the editor uses for commands such as those in Section 6.4.14 that either execute a command in a subshell or call a subshell interactively.

Default: the value of the SHELL environment variable

ttytype
term   These variables contain the name of your terminal type.[8] You cannot set it from within vi.

Default: the value of the TERM environment variable

6.2.11
Terminal Control

The following variables enable you to control how the editor transforms the output sent to your terminal. Most of them have no effect on smart terminals.

hardtabs
ht   If the value of this variable is n, vi assumes that tab stops on your terminal occur every n spaces. This spacing can either be built into your terminal or implemented in system software. If your terminal supports hard tabs you can set them with the tabs program (see Section 4.4.4). Vi uses the value of hardtabs to condense sequences of spaces to tabs whenever it can before sending them to your terminal. The condensation does not affect the contents of the buffer.

Default: 8

optimize
opt   If this variable is enabled, automatic carriage returns are inhibited in multi-line output sequences for terminals that lack direct cursor addressing. These are carriage returns generated following each ⟨linefeed⟩. Optimization speeds up the output of indented lines at the cost of losing typeahead on some older systems. Typeahead is the ability to type characters that the system is not yet ready to interpret.

Default: optimize

redraw   If this variable is enabled, vi always keeps the screen up to date even if it must redraw the screen entirely (and therefore transmit the entire contents of the screen). It makes a difference

---

8. Although ttytype and term are generally described in vi documents as different variables, they always have the same value.

only for dumb terminals. For **ex**, enabling **redraw** causes lines to be shown again whenever characters are inserted, deleted, or changed.

Default: noredraw

slowopen If this variable is enabled, **vi** does not update your screen when you're in insert mode. Instead, it delays the update until you've finished the insertion. **Vi** still shows you what you're typing, but it overwrites lines on the screen that will later be restored. This mode is useful if you're working with a slow terminal.

Default: slowopen

6.3   The Extended Editor ex

The **ex** line editor is so named because it extends the **ed** editor. The **ex** line editor and the **vi** visual editor (see Section 6.1) are integrated into a single program.

6.3.1
Calling ex

The call to **ex** has the form

   ex [*options*] [*file*] . . .

The items in the list of files can contain wildcards. Within **ex** you can call for the next file to be edited using the **next** command. When you call **ex**, it prompts you for commands. The possible commands are described below. You can also provide the input to **ex** from a file by redirecting standard input from that file.

The following are the options for the **ex** command line. You can give them in any order.

–   Suppress all interaction with the terminal. This option is intended for processing editor scripts provided on **stdin**.

–v   Invoke **ex** in *visual mode*. The call 'ex –v' is equivalent to calling **vi** and accepts the same additional options that **vi** does.

–t*tag*   Edit the file containing *tag* (see Section 6.5). The cursor is initially positioned at the tag. If you also specify a file list, the file containing *tag* is edited first and then the files in the file list. The relevant tag file, usually the file in the current directory named **tags**, must be available (see the **tags** variable, p. 229).

–r*file*   As **ex** works, it periodically saves the state of the buffer in a recovery file. If the editor or the system crashes during editing, you receive a mail message giving you the name of this recovery file. If you later call **ex** and specify this recovery file with the –r option, **ex** resumes in whatever state it was when it saved the recovery file.

-R   Edit these files in read-only mode (the `readonly` flag is set). Set-
            ting this flag helps to protect the files from accidental overwrit-
            ing by inhibiting ex from writing to them unless special com-
            mands such as `w!` are used.

+*cmd*
-c*cmd*   Execute the ex command *cmd* before starting to edit the first
            (or only) file in the file list. Some systems may recognize only
            one or the other of these forms.

6.3.2
Initializing ex

When ex starts up it executes a set of initialization commands before reading any input from your terminal. These commands are gotten just as they
are for vi. The procedure is described in Section 6.1.15.

6.3.3
The Main Buffer

The material you're editing is kept in a place called the *main buffer*. The
same main buffer is used for ex and vi. All editing commands apply to
the main buffer, sometimes just called "the buffer". A typical editing cycle
consists of reading a file into the main buffer, editing it, and writing it back
to the same file.

The focus of editing is a particular line in the main buffer called the
current line. An empty file has, in effect, a single current line numbered
zero. Whenever you operate on a line, say by finding some text in that line
or changing that line, that line becomes the current line. If you operate
on a sequence of lines as a group, for example by showing them, the last
line in the sequence becomes the current line.

The main buffer has a file associated with it called the *current file*. When
you start editing a file, that file becomes the current file. A number of ex
commands change the current file (see Section 6.3.19).

6.3.4
Form of a Command

An ex command has one of the following forms:

> [*lineset*] *cmd* [`!`] [*params*] [*count*] [*flags*]
> *lineset*
> Enter

In the first form, the allowable components depend on the command. The
second form is equivalent to

> *lineset* `print`

The third form is equivalent to '`+print`'. It advances the current line to
the next line and prints that line.

Here is what the items in the first form mean:

lineset   The address of a single line or a range of consecutive lines (see
            Section 6.3.5). Most commands, if given an extra address, ig-
            nore it.

cmd   The name of the command to be executed.

!   A modifier that changes the meaning of the command. You
            should not type a space between *cmd* and '`!`'. There are two
            commands, however, for which a space is required: '`write !`'

and 'read !'. There is also a 'write!' command having a very different meaning than 'write !': 'write!' writes a region of text to a file without overwrite protection while 'write !' applies a command to a region of text and writes the standard output of that command to a file.

params　　The parameters expected by the command. File names and regular expressions are examples of such parameters.

count　　The number of lines that the command displays or operates on. An omitted count defaults to 1.

flags　　A set of flags that affect the operation of the command (see Section 6.3.7).

For example, the command

```
3 join 2 #
```

joins two lines beginning with line #3 and shows the resulting line. The # flag causes the displayed line to be preceded by a line number.

Except for the requirement that a command be immediately followed by its modifier,[9] spaces between the components of a command are optional. For example, the join command above could also be written more compactly as

```
3j2#
```

The j here is an abbreviation of join.

Multiple Commands on a Line.　You can put several commands on a single line by separating them with '|'. Commands prefixed by global and commands that use '!' to call a UNIX program must appear last on a line.

6.3.5
Line Addresses and
Line Ranges

Some ex commands operate on a line or on a range of lines. You can specify a line in a number of ways:

.　　　The current line.

$　　　The last line of the file.

n　　　The *n*th line of the file, where *n* is a decimal number.

'*c*　　　The line marked with the letter *c* (see the ma command below).

''　　　The line that you most recently moved to with a non-relative motion of any kind. A relative motion is one that you obtain with a count such as '+5'. A motion with ''' itself is non-relative, so you can switch between two locations by using this form of address.

/*pat*/　　The next line containing the pattern *pat*. The pattern is given by a regular expression. See Section 6.1.11 for a description of the particular kinds of regular expressions accepted by ex and vi.

?*pat*?　　The nearest previous line containing the pattern *pat*.

---

9. Some versions of ex relax this requirement.

$a+n$
$a-n$
$a\,n$ The address a plus or minus n lines, where n is a decimal number. You can omit the '+ 'as shown in the third line. For example, '`/reg/+4`' denotes the fourth line after the next line containing the string '`reg`'.

$+n$
$-n$ The nth line relative to the current line either forward ('+') or backward ('-'). For example, if the current line is line 27, '-5' denotes line 22.

$a+$
$a-$
$+$
$-$ The line after ('+') or before ('-') the line with address a. If a is omitted it is taken as the current line. Note that you can generate addresses such as '--', which means the second previous line, by using '+' and '-' repeatedly.

An address of zero, whether computed or given explicitly, refers to the very beginning of the main buffer. Such an address is valid only for commands that append text *after* a given line. For example, the command '`0 append`' is valid but the command '`0 insert`' is not.

A line range can have one of three forms:

a_1,a_2 The group of lines starting with a_1 and ending with a_2. For example, '`/whit/,$`' designates the range starting with the next line containing '`whit`' and continuing to the end of the file.

$a_1;a_2$ Like a_1,a_2 except that the current line is set to a_1 before a_2 is evaluated. For example, the command '`+,+p`' shows the next line while the command '`+;+p`' shows the next two lines.

%   Equivalent to '`1,$`' (the entire file). This abbreviation is particularly useful.

If a line range is used in a context where only a single address is expected, the second address of the range is used. If a single address is used in a context where a line range is expected, the line range consists of the single line specified by the address.

6.3.6 Specifying Groups of Lines

Many ex commands operate on groups of lines. All of these commands let you specify a line range r, a count n, or both. The lines affected by the command are determined as follows:

(1)   If r is missing, it is taken as the address of the current line.
(2)   If n is given, r is interpreted as a line address and the command affects n lines starting with line r.
(3)   If n is not given, the lines in r are shown.

Here are a few examples:

p3   Show ("print") three lines starting with the current line.
/fault/d2   Delete two lines starting with the next line containing 'fault'.
-,+j   Join the preceding line, the current line, and the next line.

6.3.7
Command Flags

Certain commands can have the following *print flags* attached to them. The following flags cause a line to be shown ("printed") after the command is executed:

p   Show ("print") the last line affected by the command. Used by itself, this flag usually makes no difference since the last line affected would be shown anyway.

l   Show the last line affected by the command, showing tabs and the end of line as they would be shown with the `list` option (p. 233) enabled.

\#   Show the last affected line, preceded by a line number as it would be with the `number` option (p. 233) enabled.

\+   Increase the line number by 1 before showing a line. Multiple uses of '+' increase the line number by 1 for each use. For example, '++' increases the line number by 2.

\-   Decrease the line number by 1 before showing a line. Multiple uses of '-' decrease the line number by 1 for each use.

These flags can be used in any combination and in any order. The effect of the 'l' and '#' flags persists until the next command that changes text. If you use '+' or '-' without any other flags, the last line affected by the command is still printed.

6.3.8
Abbreviations

You can abbreviate the names of most of the **ex** commands. The description of each command indicates the shortest abbreviation that **ex** recognizes, but you can use longer abbreviations too. For instance, the so[urce] command can be written as 'so', 'sour', or 'source'. You'll almost always want to use the shortest abbreviation you can, although the longer forms are sometimes helpful when you're writing an editing script.

You can also create your own abbreviations for useful phrases using the **abbreviate** command (see Section 6.3.22). These abbreviations are only recognized in input text.

6.3.9
Comments

When you have a prepackaged file of editor commands, it's often useful to include comments in it. A comment begins with '"'. It can be on a line by itself or come at the end of a command line. The editor ignores everything from the comment character to the end of the line.

6.3.10
Typing Conventions

The following keys have special meanings as you type commands:

[Enter]   When you're typing a command, ends the command and issues it. When you're typing input text, ends the current line and starts another one.

[Intr]   Terminates this command and prompts for another one. If you press [Intr] while typing textual input for a command such as insert, the current line is discarded but previously typed lines are retained.

(Erase)
(Ctrl) H   Erases the character preceding the cursor.

(Kill)   Erases all the characters typed on the current line.

(Ctrl) V   Quotes the next character, i.e., inserts it into the text verbatim
              even if it is a control character such as (Esc).
                  In addition, if autoindent is enabled, the (Tab) and (Ctrl) D
              characters behave as they do in vi (see Section 6.1.9).

**6.3.11
Special Buffers**

In addition to the main buffer, ex keeps twenty-six named buffers, one for
each letter of the alphabet, and an anonymous buffer. You can use these
special buffers to move text from one place to another using the yank,
delete, and put commands.

Each of these commands accepts a buffer name as a parameter. If you
omit the buffer name, the command uses the anonymous buffer. For yank
and delete, the command replaces the contents of a named buffer if you
specify the buffer name with a lowercase letter. If you specify a buffer
name to yank or delete with an uppercase letter, the command appends
to the existing contents of that named buffer. For example, the command

> .,+y A

appends the current and next lines to named buffer A, while the command

> d

deletes the current line and places it in the anonymous buffer.

The @ command also operates on a buffer, executing its contents as a
sequence of ex commands.

**6.3.12
Showing Lines**

The following commands show one or more lines on your terminal:

(CR)   Shows the next line and sets the current line to that line.

r [*flags*]
[r] p[rint] [n] [*flags*]
              Shows ("prints") a group of lines, specified as described in Sec-
              tion 6.3.6. As particularly simple cases, typing '.' shows the
              current line and typing '+' shows the next line. Typing a line
              range by itself shows that range.
                  The command can include print flags, indicated as *flags*.
              These behave as described in Section 6.3.7.
                  After the lines are shown, the current line is set to the last
              line shown.

r l[ist] [n] [*flags*]
              Like print, except that tab characters are shown as '∧I' and the
              actual end of the line is indicated by '$'. The effect is equivalent
              to print with the '#' flag.

r # [n] [*flags*]
r nu[mber] [n] [*flags*]
              Like print, except that a line number is displayed in front of

the text of each line. The effect is equivalent to `print` with the '1' flag.

[a] (Ctrl)D Scrolls down the file to line *a*, then shows a sequence of lines. The number of lines shown is given by the `scroll` variable (p. 233). The default for *a* is the current line.

[a] z [t] [n]

Shows a window of *n* lines with the line at *a* placed in the window according to *t*:

+	Shows a window starting with line *a*. Successive 'z+' commands display successive windows of text.
-	Shows a window ending with line *a*.
^	Shows a window ending with the line two windows back from line *a*. Successive 'z^' commands back up through the buffer.
.	Shows a window with line *a* at its center.
=	Like '.', except that the indicated line is surrounded by lines of dashes and is made the current line.

The default for *a* is the current line. The default for *n* is twice the value of the `scroll` variable (p. 233).

6.3.13
Status Information

The following commands provide various kinds of status information:

[a]= Shows the address of the line at *a*, but doesn't change the current line. The default for *a* is the current line.

ve[rsion] Shows the version number of the editor.

ar[gs] Shows the file arguments that were on the command line. These are the files that you can access using the `next` command. It is chiefly useful when these files were specified using wildcards.

6.3.14
Inserting Text

The following commands insert text into the buffer. The inserted text is ended by a line containing a period and nothing else. If you want the text to include a line that appears to contain a period and nothing else, you can put a blank after the period—or if that is unacceptable, insert some other text and change it to a period later.[10]

[a] a[ppend][!]

Appends input text after line *a*. If you omit *a*, it defaults to the current line. The current line becomes the last line appended.

  If '!' is present, the `autoindent` variable (p. 231) is toggled from its current state to the opposite state for the duration of the input. The next command that reads input will revert to the old state.

---

10. This situation isn't entirely theoretical—it comes up all the time in writing documentation for programs such as `ex`, `ed`, and `mail`.

[*a*] i[nsert][!]

> Inserts input text before line *a*. If you omit *a*, it defaults to the current line. The current line becomes the last line appended. The '!' modifier does the same thing as for append.

6.3.15
Modifying Text

The following commands enable you to delete or change text by groups of lines:

[*r*] d[elete] [*buf*][*n*][*flags*]

> Deletes a group of lines, specified as described in Section 6.3.6. The deleted lines are sent to a special buffer according to the rules described in Section 6.3.11. If you specify a named buffer *buf*, you need to put a space in front of its name.
>
> The command can include print flags, indicated as *flags*. These behave as described in Section 6.3.7. After executing this command, the editor shows the line following the last line it deleted.
>
> For example, the command '/rug/d e3#' deletes three lines starting with the next line containing the string 'rug'. The deleted lines replace the contents of buffer e. After the deletion, the editor shows the next line preceded by a line number (because of the '#' flag).

[*r*] c[hange][!][*n*]

> Deletes a group of lines, then inserts input text in their place. The lines in the group are specified as described in Section 6.3.6. The replacement text is ended by a dot on a line by itself as it is for the insert and append commands.

The following command enables you to join two or more lines into one:

r j[oin][!][*n*]

> Joins a group of lines. The group is specified as described in Section 6.3.6, except that if both *r* and *n* are missing the current line is joined with the next line. When two lines are joined, the junction is created as follows:
>
> (1)   If the first character of the second line is ')', all whitespace at the junction is eliminated.
>
> (2)   If the first line ends with a period, question mark, or bang, the junction and any adjacent whitespace are replaced by two spaces.
>
> (3)   In all other cases, the junction and any adjacent whitespace are replaced by a single space.

The following commands enable you to shift groups of lines right or left:

[*r*] > [*n*] [*flags*]

> Shifts a group of lines right by one shift width (see p. 231). The group is specified as described in Section 6.3.6. Typing '>>' shifts by two shift widths, typing '>>>' shifts by three, etc. The current line is set to the last line in the affected region.
>
> The command can include print flags, indicated as *flags*. These behave as described in Section 6.3.7.

[r] < [n] [flags]
>   Like '>', except that leading indentation is deleted rather than
>   inserted. A line with no leading indentation is unaffected.

6.3.16
Moving and Copying Text

The following commands enable you to move and copy text:

r m[ove] [a]
>   Moves the lines in region r to the location after address a. If a
>   is zero, the lines are moved to the beginning of the file. If you
>   omit r, it defaults to the current line. After ex moves the lines,
>   it sets the current line to the last line it moved. Line a must not
>   fall within r.

[r]t a
[r]co[py] a [flags]
>   Copies ("transfers") the lines in range r to address a. If a is
>   zero, the lines are copied to the beginning of the file. If you
>   omit r, it defaults to the current line. After ex copies the lines,
>   it sets the current line to the last line it copied.
>
>   The command can include print flags, indicated as flags.
>   These behave as described in Section 6.3.7.

[r] y[ank][buf][n][flags]
>   Copies ("yanks") a group of lines into a special buffer. The
>   group is specified as described in Section 6.3.6. The lines are
>   copied into or appended to a special buffer according to the
>   rules described in Section 6.3.11. If you specify a named buffer
>   buf, you must put a space in front of its name. If you omit r, it
>   defaults to the current line. After ex copies the lines, it sets the
>   current line to the last line it copied.
>
>   The command can include print flags, indicated as flags.
>   These behave as described in Section 6.3.7.
>
>   You can use this command, together with pu, as an alternate
>   way of copying lines. It is particularly convenient when you
>   want to copy the lines to several places.

[a] pu[t][buf]
>   Copies ("puts") the lines from a special buffer into the main
>   buffer following address a. The special buffer can be either the
>   anonymous buffer or a named buffer (see Section 6.3.11). If
>   you omit a, it defaults to the current line.

6.3.17
Substitutions

The following commands enable you to perform substitutions, also known
as "search and replace" operations:

[r] & [opts] [n] [flags]
[r] s[ubstitute] [/pat/repl/] [opts] [n] [flags]
>   Substitutes the replacement text repl for the pattern pat in each
>   line of a specified group of lines. Unless the g option described
>   below is specified, only the first occurrence of the pattern on a

particular line is affected. The group of lines eligible for substitution are determined as described in Section 6.3.6. The pattern is given by a regular expression (see Section 6.1.11 for an explanation of the particular regular expressions accepted by ex and vi).

The following options can be specified individually or in combination as *opts*:

c   Ask for confirmation of each substitution. If you type 'y' the substitution is made; if you type anything else it is not.

g   Perform the substitution throughout the line.

Following the substitutions, the current line becomes the last line where a substitution took place. If you omit *r*, it defaults to the entire buffer. If you specify any flags, the editor shows you the last line where it made a substitution (see Section 6.3.7).

A replacement consisting only of '~' denotes the replacement that was used in the most recent substitute command. An '&' within the replacement is replaced by the first subexpression of the pattern within the markers '\(' and '\)'. More generally, an occurrence of '\n' in the replacement, *n* being a single digit, is replaced by the *n*th such subexpression (see p. 51). You can cancel the special meanings of '%' or '&' by escaping these characters with a preceding backslash. Within the replacement text, a newline escaped by '\' turns into a real newline, causing the replacement text to be split into two lines at that place.

The edcompatible variable (see p. 229), if set, modifies the way that g and c work and also changes the character that denotes the most recent replacement from '~' to '%'.

Note that there isn't a "search" command corresponding to the "replace" command, but you can search for a pattern *pat* by using the command '/*pat*/p'.

6.3.18
Marking Lines

The following command attaches a mark to a line so that you can go back to that line later:

[*a*] k *c*
[*a*] ma[rk] *c*

        Marks the line at *a* with the letter *c*, which you can later use in the address ''*x*' to refer to this line. This command does not change the current line.

6.3.19
File Operations

The commands that follow enable you to read from a file, write to a file, or start editing a different file.

Reading a File.   The following commands enable you to read a file:

ex[!] *file* +*cmd*
e[dit][!] *file* +*cmd*

        Discards what is in the buffer, then starts editing *file*. The file *file* must already exist; you cannot edit an empty nonexistent file. If `autowrite` is enabled (see p. 230), the buffer is saved automatically before the new file is edited. If you attempt to execute this command and the current file has been modified but not saved (either explicitly or automatically), the editor issues an error message and aborts the command. If '!' is present, the editor executes the command without complaint in any case.

If '+*cmd*' is present, the editor executes the command *cmd* immediately upon starting to edit the file. In particular, if *cmd* is a line address such as a number or pattern, the editor starts editing at that line address. The command *cmd* must not contain any spaces.

Note that this and the following commands require a blank between the command and the file name that follows it.

a r[ead] *file*
Reads the contents of *file* into the buffer, inserting them after line *a* in the manner of `append`. If you omit *file*, it defaults to the current file.

ta[g] *tag*   Opens the file containing the tag file entry *tag* and moves the cursor to that tag within the file. The relevant tag file, usually the file in the current directory named `tags`, must be available (see the `tags` variable, p. 229). See Section 6.5 for more information about tag files.

The 'read !' command (p. 249) also provides a form of reading.

Writing to a File.   The following commands enable you to write to a file:

[*r*] w[rite][!] [>>] *file*
Writes the lines in region *r* to *file*. The following rules apply:

- If you omit *r*, it defaults to the entire buffer.

- If you omit *file*, ex writes the contents of the buffer to the current file.

- If *file* already exists but its name does not match the name of the file being edited, the editor gives you an error message and aborts the command. If '!' is present, however, the command is executed without complaint in any case.

- If '>>' is present, the text is appended to the file instead of replacing its contents.

This command does not change the current line.

[*r*] w[rite][!] [>>] *file*
Writes the buffer to *file*, then quits. This command behaves exactly like the corresponding form of `write` followed by `quit`.

The 'write !' command also provides a form of writing.

Editing Another File.   The following commands enable you to start editing a different file:

n[ext][!] [+*cmd*] [*file*] ...
If the files *file* ... are omitted, discards the buffer and edits the next file in the current file list. Otherwise, replaces the current

file list by *file* ... and edits the first file in the new file list. If the current file has not been written out, the editor behaves as it does with the `edit` command.

If '+*cmd*' is present, the editor executes the command *cmd* immediately upon starting to edit the first file in the file list. In particular, if *cmd* is a line address such as a number or pattern, the editor starts editing at that line address. The command *cmd* must not contain any spaces.

This command is useful when the file list is specified with wildcards and contains more than one file, since otherwise `edit` would be the natural way to switch files.

rew[ind][!]
Resets the list of files to be edited to its beginning and edits the first file as you would with the `next` command.

f[ile] *file* Changes the name of the current file to *file* and marks it as "not edited", indicating that this file was not the original one edited. If you omit *file*, `ex` tells you the name of the current file and its status.

Changing Directories.   The following command enables you to change to another directory:

cd *dir*   Changes the current directory to *dir*. Executing '!cd *dir*' does not have this effect because the change is lost when the subshell exits.

6.3.20 Exiting from the Editor

The following commands enable you to exit from the editor:

q[uit][!] Quits the editor without writing out the buffer. If the buffer has been modified since it last was written or initialized, the editor issues an error message and aborts the command. The behavior in this case is similar to the `edit` command; the '!' modifier silences the error message.

x[it] [*file*] Exits from the editor, writing out the buffer if it contains any unsaved changes. The buffer is written to *file* if specified, otherwise to the current file (the one being edited).

st[op][!] Stops the editor and suspends the process under which it's running, returning to the shell from which it was initiated. The editing process can be resumed later on. If the buffer has been modified and the `autowrite` variable is enabled, the buffer is saved before the editor is stopped. This command only works in systems that support job control (see Section 2.7.1).

6.3.21 Setting Local Variables

The `set` command enables you to set the value of a local variable. The local variables are described in Section 6.2. These are the forms of the `set` command:

set *x*   Enables variable *x*, i.e., turns it on.

set no*x*   Disables variable *x*, i.e., turns it off. For example, 'set nomagic' disables the magic variable, thus disabling the interpretation of certain characters in regular expressions.

set *x=val*

    Sets the value of variable *x* to *val*.

set   Shows those variables that have been changed from their default values.

set all   Shows the values of all the variables. An important use for this command is finding out what variables are available on your system.

set *x*?   Shows the value of variable *x*.

You can include several settings in a single command such as

    `set ai wm=6 nomesg`

You can preset the variables to suit your taste by putting them in initialization files (see Section 6.1.15).

6.3.22
Abbreviations and
Macros

The following commands enable you to create and remove abbreviations:

ab[breviate] *lhs rhs*

    Makes the single word *lhs* an abbreviation for the keystroke sequence *rhs*. The abbreviation *lhs* can contain digits as well as letters, but it must start with a letter. Thereafter when you type *lhs* in input mode, vi replaces it by *rhs*. If *lhs* isn't surrounded by spaces or punctuation, vi won't recognize it. For example, suppose you type the command

    `ab clm the Computer Liberation Movement` Enter

    Thereafter whenever you type 'clm' as a word in input mode, vi replaces it by 'the Computer Liberation Movement'. The replacement would not apply to 'clm1', however, since in this case 'clm' isn't surrounded by blanks or punctuation.

una[bbreviate] *lhs*

    Removes the abbreviation *lhs*.

Macros.   Ex also includes map and unmap commands for creating and removing macro definitions (see Section 6.1.29). However, these commands are of no use within ex since ex never recognizes macros.

6.3.23
Performing
Commands
Globally

The following commands enable you to perform some other command for each line in the buffer that matches a pattern:

[*r*] g[lobal][!] /*pat*/ *cmds*

    Performs the list of commands *cmds* globally for each line containing text that matches the pattern *pat*, where *pat* is given by a regular expression (see Section 2.16). Any '/' in *pat* must be quoted by writing it as '\/'. If a region *r* is specified, only the lines in *r* are examined; otherwise all lines in the buffer are examined.

Each command of *cmds* must appear on a line by itself. Each line in turn must be ended by a backslash except for the line containing the last command in the list. The **insert**, **append**, and **change** commands are permitted and should be followed by their input, ending with a line containing only a dot and a backslash (.\). An empty line ends both the input and the command list (the dot isn't needed in this case). The command list can be empty; in this case ex simply shows the lines containing text that matches the pattern.

For example, here is a command that gets rid of 'cholesterol' by deleting each line containing it:

```
g /cholesterol/d
```

[*r*] **g**!/*pat*/*cmds*
[*r*] **v**/*pat*/*cmds*

The two forms of this command are like the **g** command, except that the editor performs the indicated commands on those lines in the region *r* that *don't* meet the search criterion.

6.3.24
Calling Programs
from within
the Editor

The following commands enable you to execute UNIX commands in a subshell and to apply them to portions of text in the buffer:

sh[ell]   Runs an interactive subshell, with control returning to the editor when the shell exits.

[*r*] **!** *cmd*   Executes the command *cmd* in a subshell, taking the standard input for *cmd* from the lines specified by the range *r* and replacing those lines by the standard output of *r*. If *r* is omitted, both standard input and standard output are taken from your terminal; the editor waits for you to provide the input. For example, the command '%!sort' sorts the contents of the entire buffer.

[*a*] **r[ead]** **!** *cmd*
Executes *cmd* in a subshell, inserting its standard output after line *a*. The default for *a* is the current line.

[*r*] **w[rite]** **!** *cmd*
Executes *cmd* in a subshell, passing the lines in region *r* to *cmd* as its standard input. If *r* is omitted it is taken to be the entire buffer. This command does not change or show the current line.

!!   Executes the most recent shell escape command again. A shell escape command is a command following '!' in any of the commands above. The terminal is used as the standard input and output for the re-executed command even if the previous execution was requested by 'read !' or 'write !'.

6.3.25 **Saving and** **Recovering**	The editor periodically saves its state so that you can recover if the editor or the system crashes. The following commands recover the state and save the state explicitly:

rec[over] *file*

> Recovers the state of **ex** from *file* after a crash. In the event of a crash, you receive a mail message giving you the name of the recovery file to use with this command.

pre[serve]

> Saves a copy of the buffer to a special "preserve" area for use by the editor's recovery procedure. This command can be useful when a **write** command has failed and you don't know how else to save your work. You can later recover the buffer using the -r command-line option.

6.3.26 **Entering Visual** **Mode**	The following commands enable you to enter visual mode or its variant, open mode:

vi

> Enters visual mode and enables full-screen editing according to the **vi** conventions (see Section 6.1). Typing 'Q' returns you to **ex**.

open [*pat*] Enters *open mode* at the current line or at the next line matching *pat* if *pat* is specified. Open mode is like visual mode except that only one line is displayed at a time. It is sometimes useful when you're running **ex** on a terminal of an unknown type. A **vi** command that would move you to another line under **vi** causes that line to be displayed. For example, typing 'j' causes the next line to be displayed. Just as with visual mode, the 'Q' command returns to **ex**.

6.3.27 **Undoing the** **Previous Action**	The following command enables you to undo a previous action:

u[ndo]

> Undoes the most recent change or insertion. If the previous action was carried out with the **global** command, all the consequent changes are undone. Two u's in a row cancel each other.

6.3.28 **Executing** **Commands from a** **File**	The following command enables you to execute commands that are in a file:

so[urce] *file*

> Reads the lines in the file *file* and executes them as though they had been typed at the terminal.

6.3.29 **Executing** **Commands in a** **Buffer**	The following command enables you to execute commands from a named buffer:

*buf

> Interprets the text in named buffer *buf* as a sequence of commands and executes those commands.

6.4   The ed **Line Editor**

The ed line editor is the oldest and simplest of the UNIX editors. It was originally designed when UNIX was mostly used with slow teletypewriters and its design reflects that fact. Ed has been widely imitated; for example, the MS-DOS edlin editor is based on ed. Despite its age, some people still prefer it. You are likely to find small variations from one implementation of ed to another.

6.4.1
The Command Line

The form of the ed command line is

   ed [*options*] [*file*]

where *file* is a file to be edited. If you omit *file*, ed starts editing an un-named empty file.

When you call ed, it first shows you the number of characters in the file you're editing. It then expects you to type a sequence of commands. The possible commands are described below. Ed does not explicitly prompt you unless you ask it to with the P command or by specifying the -p option on the command line. You can also provide the input to ed from a file by redirecting standard input from that file.

There are two possible options for ed:

-p *string*   Use *string* as the interactive prompt string.

-s   Suppress the messages that give information about character counts, and also suppress the '!' prompt after a subshell call. If this option is set, ed does not produce any output that you do not request explicitly. Setting this option is usually desirable when you are providing an editing script as the standard input to ed. An example of such a script might be the output of diff (see Section 3.10.2).

6.4.2
The Buffer

The material you're editing is kept in a place called the *buffer*. All editing commands apply to the buffer. A typical editing cycle consists of reading a file into the buffer, editing it, and writing it back to the same file.

The focus of editing is a particular line in the buffer called the *current line*. The buffer has a file associated with it called the *current file*. When you start editing a file, that file becomes the current file. Two ed commands change the current file: the e command, which starts editing a different file, and the f command, which explicitly changes the current file. The r (read) command sets the current file if it was undefined, as it would be if you called ed without a file name.

6.4.3
Form of a Command

A command has one of the forms

   [*lineset*] *cmd* [!] [*params*] [*sfx*]
   address
   (Enter)

All command names consist of a single character, usually a letter. For example, the command '2,5p' shows ("prints") lines 2 through 5 of the buffer on your terminal. Spaces between the parts of a command are optional, except that a space is required between an alphabetical command and a bang or parameter that follows it.

- The *lineset* or *address* part specifies the group of lines or single line affected by the command. In the form above, *lineset* is a line address or a line range as described below and *address* is a line address.

- The *params* part contains any addresses, file names, commands, or other information required by the command.

- The suffix *sfx* is one of the command names (l n p). A suffix can be attached to any command that does not expect a file name or UNIX command as a parameter. A suffix causes the current line to be shown after the command to which it is attached has been executed. The line is shown as it would be by the command appearing in the suffix. For example, the command 'dn' deletes the current line and shows the following line with a line number. Here 'd' is the command and 'n' is the suffix.

If you type an illegal command, ed notifies you by responding with '?'. You can get a more explicit error message by using the commands described in Section 6.4.16.

Line Addresses and Line Ranges. The notations for specifying a line address are as follows:

$ The last line of the file.

.   The current line.

n   The *n*th line of the file.

'*c*   The line marked with the letter *c* (see the k command below).

/*pat*/   The next line containing the pattern *pat*. The pattern is given by a regular expression. See Section 2.16 for a description of the regular expressions accepted by ed. You may find some variations among different versions of ed in what regular expressions they accept.

?*pat*?   The nearest previous line containing the pattern *pat*.

a n   The address *a* plus or minus *n* lines, where *n* is a decimal number. You can omit the '+' as shown in the third line. For example, '/mao/-3' denotes the third line before the next line containing the string 'mao'.

+*n*

−*n*   The *n*th line relative to the current line either forward ('+') or backward ('−'). For example, if the current line is line 103, '+7' denotes line 110.

a+

a−

+

−   The line after ('+') or before ('−') the line with address *a*. If *a* is omitted it is taken as the current line. Note that you can generate addresses such as '++', which means the second line after the current line, by using '+' and '−' repeatedly.

An address of zero, whether computed or given explicitly, refers to the very beginning of the buffer. Such an address is valid only for commands that append text *after* a given line. For example, the command '0a' is valid but the command '0i' is not.

A line range can have one of the following forms:

a_1, a_2 The group of lines starting with a_1 and ending with a_2. For example, '1,/catafalque/' designates the range starting with line 1 and continuing to the first line containing 'catafalque'.

$a_1; a_2$ Like a_1, a_2 except that the current line is set to a_1 before a_2 is evaluated. For example, the command '+,+p' shows the next line while the command '+;+p' shows the next two lines.

,   The entire file.

;   The pair '.,$'.

If a line range is used in a context where only a single address is expected, the second address of the range is used. If a single address is used in a context where a line range is expected, the line range consists of the single line specified by the address.

6.4.4
Showing Lines

The following commands show one or more lines on your terminal:

[*r*]p   Shows ("prints") the group of lines in the line range *r*. The current line is set to the last line shown. The default for *r* is the current line.

CR   Shows the next line.

a   Shows the line at address *a*.

[*r*]n   Shows the group of lines in the line range *r*, putting a line number at the beginning of each line. The current line is set to the last line shown. The default for *r* is the current line.

[*r*]l   Shows the group of lines in the line range *r*, showing nonprinting characters explicitly as octal numbers and tabs as '> '. The current line is set to the last line shown.

6.4.5
Showing the
Line Number

The following command shows you the line number of a specified line.

[*a*]=   Shows the address of the line at *a*. If *a* is omitted it is taken to be the last line of the buffer, so typing '=' is a convenient way to see how many lines are in the buffer. The form '/*pat*/=' shows you the address of the next line containing the pattern *pat*. This command does not change the current line.

6.4.6
Inserting Text

The following commands insert text into the buffer. The inserted text is ended by a line containing a period and nothing else. If you want the text to include such a line, you can put a blank after the period—or if that is unacceptable, you can insert some other text and change that text to a period later.

[a]a   Appends input text after line *a*. If you omit *a*, it defaults to the current line. The current line becomes the last line appended.

[a]i   Inserts input text after line *a*. If you omit *a*, it defaults to the current line. The current line becomes the last line appended.

6.4.7
Modifying Text

The following commands delete or change text by groups of lines:

[r]d   Deletes the lines in range *r*.

[r]c   Changes the lines in range *r* by deleting them and then inserting input text. The input text is ended by a line containing just a dot, as it is for the a and i commands.

[r]j   Joins the lines in *r* into a single line by deleting the newlines between them. Any whitespace at the beginning or end of a joined line is unaffected, and no additional whitespace is added. The default for *r* is '., .+1', i.e., the current line and the next one.

6.4.8
Moving and
Copying Text

The following commands move and copy text:

[r]m*a*   Moves the lines in range *r* to the location after *a*. The default for *r* is the current line.

[r]t*a*   Copies ("transfers") the lines in range *r* to address *a*. The default for *r* is the current line.

6.4.9
Substitutions

The following command performs substitutions, also known as "search and replace" operations:

[r]s/*pat*/*repl*/[*opts*]
[r]s*c pat c repl c* [*opts*]

Replaces the pattern *pat* by the text *repl* within each line in the line range *r*, which defaults to the current line. The pattern is given by a regular expression (see Section 2.16). The options *opts* determine which occurrences of *pat* are replaced:[11]

- If *opts* is omitted, just the first occurrence is replaced.

- If *opts* is an integer *n* ($1 \leq n \leq 512$), the *n*th occurrence is replaced.

- If *opts* is **g** (for "global"), all occurrences are replaced.

Although the pattern and replacement are customarily delimited by '/' as shown in the first form, you can use any character other than space or tab as the delimiter as shown in the second form.

An '&' character appearing in the replacement stands for the text matched by the pattern unless the '&' is quoted with '\'. The

---

11. The BSD UNIX version of **ed** uses different conventions for *opts*.

'\(...\)' notation described in Section 2.16 can also be used. A replacement consisting of the single character '%' stands for the most recent previous replacement. An escaped newline, i.e., a newline preceded by '\', can appear in the replacement provided that this command is not part of a global execution specified by a **g** or **v** command.

6.4.10
Marking Lines

The following command attaches a mark to a line so that you can go back to that line later:

[*a*]k*c*   Marks the line at *a* with the letter *c*, which you can later use in the address ''*x*' to refer to this line. This command does not change the current line.

6.4.11
File Operations

The following commands enable you to read from a file, write to a file, or change the name of the current file:

[*a*]r [*file*]   Reads the file *file* into buffer after line *a*. The default for *file* is the current file; the default for *a* is the end of the buffer. After reading a file, **ed** shows you the number of characters that it read. This command does not change the current file unless the current file is undefined, as it is when you start editing the empty file.

The 'r !' command (p. 257) also provides a form of reading.

[*r*]w [*file*]   Writes the lines in the line range *r* to *file*. If *file* does not exist, it is created. The default for *file* is the current file; the default for *r* is the entire buffer. After writing a file, **ed** shows you the number of characters that it wrote. If *file* is omitted, **ed** writes to the current file. This command does not change the current file unless the current file is undefined, as it is when you start editing the empty file.

The 'w !' command (p. 257) also provides a form of writing.

e [*file*]   Discards the contents of the buffer, reads *file* into the buffer, makes it the current file, and starts editing it. When **ed** reads *file* it shows you how many characters it read. If the buffer has not been written out since it was last modified, **ed** warns you and leaves the buffer unchanged. If you type 'e' a second time, however, the command is executed. The default for *file* is the current file.

The 'e !' command (p. 257) enables you to edit the standard output of a UNIX command.

E [*file*]   Like **e**, except that **ed** unconditionally executes the command without complaint.

f [*file*]   Changes the name of the current file to *file*. If you omit *file*, **ed** shows you the name of the current file.

6.4.12 Exiting from the Editor

The following commands enable you to exit from the editor:

q   Quits the editor. If the buffer has not been written out since it was last modified, ed warns you and lets you continue editing. A second q at this point does take effect.

Q   Like q, except that ed unconditionally quits without complaint.

6.4.13 Performing Commands Globally

The following commands enable you to perform some other command for each line in the buffer that matches a pattern:

$[r]$g/pat/$[cmds]$

Performs the commands in *cmds* for those lines in r that match the regular expression *pat*, i.e., performs them "globally". The default for r is the entire buffer. The command list *cmds* can contain multiple commands, provided that each command except the last one is on a line by itself ended with a backslash. The a, i, and c commands are permitted, with their input becoming part of the command list. The input lines must also be ended by a backslash.

As usual, the input for one of these commands is ended by a line containing just a dot (and its backslash). If the last command in the list is an input command, however, the dot line ending its input can be omitted. An empty command list is equivalent to a command list containing just p. The command list cannot contain any g, G, v, or V commands.

Ed executes this command by looking for the next line l in r that contains *pat*. It then executes *cmds* with the current line set to l. It continues this cycle until no more lines containing *pat* remain in r. For example, the command

```
g s/loser/winner/g\;
a
Hooray!
```

causes ed to go through the buffer replacing each occurrence of 'loser' by 'winner'. At each line where it makes a replacement, ed adds a line containing 'Hooray!'.

You can terminate this command with (Intr) if it starts to run away.

$[r]$G/pat/   Like g, except that the commands are gotten interactively. For each matching line in r, ed shows you the line and then awaits a *single* command. The command cannot be an a, c, i, g, G, v, or V command. It then executes the command that you type. Typing just (Enter) acts as a null command; typing '&' executes the previously entered command for this line.

$[r]$v/pat/$cmds$

Like g, except that the selected lines are those in r that do *not* contain a match for *pat*.

$[r]$V/pat/   Like G, except that the selected lines are those in r that do *not* contain a match for *pat*.

6.4.14
Calling Programs
from within
the Editor

The following commands execute UNIX commands in a subshell and apply them to portions of text in the buffer:

!*cmds*   Executes the UNIX commands *cmds* in a subshell. Any un-quoted occurrence of '%' within *cmds* is replaced by the name of the current file. If the first character of *cmds* is itself a bang, that bang is replaced by the text of the most recently executed subshell commands. Thus '!!' provides an easy way of executing one command several times.

e !*cmds*   Executes the UNIX commands *cmds* in a subshell and edits their standard output as though that output were a file brought in with the **e** command. Ed shows you the number of characters that it read into the buffer. The 'e !' command does not change the current file.

[*a*]**r** !*cmds*

Executes the UNIX commands *cmds* in a subshell and reads their standard output into buffer after line *a*, which defaults to the current line. Ed shows you the number of characters that it read into the buffer.

[*r*]**w** !*cmds*

Executes the UNIX commands *cmds* in a subshell, using the lines in range *r* as the standard input to *cmds*. The default for *r* is the entire buffer. Ed shows you the number of characters that it passed to *cmds*.

6.4.15
Undoing the
Previous Action

The following command enables you to undo a previous action:

u   Undoes the most recent change or insertion. If the previous action was carried out with the global command, all the consequent changes are undone. Two u's in a row cancel each other.

6.4.16
Prompts and Error
Messages

The following commands control the prompts and error messages that you get from ed:

P   Toggles prompting for subsequent commands.

h   Gives help on the most recent error diagnostic.

H   Toggles error messages for '?' diagnostics.

6.5   Tag Files

A *tag file* is a kind of index file that gives the location of each definition appearing in a set of files. An example of such a definition is a C function definition. Each line of a tag file specifies the name of a definition, the file containing that definition, and the line within that file where the definition is to be found. The vi and ex editors use the information in a tag file to enable you to edit files containing C programs and similar text conveniently.

The **ctags** program reads a collection of C source programs and constructs a tag file from them. For example, the command

```
ctags *.c
```

creates a tag file named **tags** in the current directory that you can use to conveniently edit all the '.c' files (which presumably contain C programs) in that directory. We won't discuss the **ctags** program further in this book.

The Emacs editor can create and use tag files (see Section 7.23), but Emacs tag files are in a format incompatible with that of the tag files created by **ctags** and utilized by **vi**.

7

The GNU Emacs Editor

The GNU Emacs editor is an extensible, customizable, self-documenting full-screen editor written by Richard Stallman as part of the GNU project and made available through the Free Software Foundation.[1] Unlike vi, Emacs is a *modeless* editor. Commands for operations such as moving the cursor or deleting some text are all assigned to special keys; when you type an ordinary printable character, it is inserted into the text of your document.

Emacs is a working environment by itself—besides its document editing facilities, it provides a mailer, a directory editor, a LISP debugger, and other services. It also provides modes for handling several classes of specialized text, including TeX documents, outlines, programs in any of several programming languages, and pictures made out of text characters.

Emacs is written in a dialect of LISP called Elisp. You can customize Emacs in simple ways without becoming involved in LISP programming or customize it more extensively by modifying its source code. Modifying the source code, which is freely available, requires specialized knowledge and usually is not a small project.

The material in this chapter should suffice for most editing tasks, but Emacs has too many specialized commands and facilities and too many details for us to cover it completely here. We don't describe the commands and modes associated with specific programming languages, nor do we explain every aspect of each command's behavior. Moreover, we describe but a few of the many variables that you can use to customize Emacs. You'll

---

1. In our references to Emacs we follow the convention of the Emacs manual in calling the editor "Emacs" rather than "emacs".

find these details in the Emacs manual, which you can view on-line in hypertext form with the (Ctrl) H (Ctrl) I command (see Section 7.6).

You can obtain Emacs over the Internet via anonymous `ftp` from `prep.ai.mit.edu`, IP address 18.71.0.38 (see Section 10.7). It is found in the file `/pub/gnu/emacs-18.57.tar.Z`. You can also retrieve it over the `uucp` network from the OSUCIS archive (reference [U3]).

7.1 Calling Emacs

The form of the Emacs command line is

> `emacs` [*options*]

where *options* are the command-line options listed below. One possible option is a file name; in this case the specified file is edited. The other options are generally of interest only to advanced users. Calling Emacs without options causes it to display a screen of introductory information; typing any key makes that information go away.

7.1.1
Command-Line
Options

The Emacs command-line options do not follow the standard UNIX conventions described in Section 2.14.3. Options can be specified either with single letters or with full words as indicated below, but options cannot be combined. A blank is needed between the name of an option and its argument. A file name on the command line is treated as a particular type of option rather than as a separate argument following the options.

The options fall into two groups. The following options may appear in any order, but must follow the options in the second group. These options may appear more than once.

file   Initially visit *file* using `file-find`. If you specify several files, the last one is brought to your screen. The others are brought to additional Emacs buffers (see Section 7.4.1).

+*n file*   Initially visit *file*, go to line *n*.

-l[oad] *file*
            Load LISP code from *file* with `load`.

-f[uncall] *func*
            Call LISP function *func* with no arguments.

-i[nsert] *file*
            Insert *file* into the current buffer.

-kill   Exit from Emacs without asking for confirmation.

The following options must come first and must appear in the order listed:

-t *dev*   Use *dev* as the terminal device.

-d *disp*   Use *disp* as the display under X.

-batch   Run Emacs in batch mode. The text being edited is not displayed; the standard interrupt characters have their usual

meanings. This option is normally used only with the -l or -f
options.

```
-q
-no-init-file
```
> Don't load the Emacs initialization file (the file .emacs in your
> home directory).

```
-u[ser] user
```
> Load the Emacs initialization file .emacs from *user*'s home di-
> rectory.

7.2 Interacting with Emacs

Emacs is a modeless editor; unlike editors such as vi, it does not have
distinct command and input modes. When you type an ordinary printable character such as the letter 'U', it is inserted into your document;
when you type a control character such as '[Ctrl]C' or '[Esc]', it is taken
as a command (or the beginning of a command) to perform an operation such as deleting the previous character, moving to the next line, or
saving the file you're editing. For example, to erase the next character,
you type '[Ctrl]D'; to start editing a new file named fiddleheads, you type
'[Ctrl]X [Ctrl]F fiddleheads'. Ordinary printable characters are commands
also; typing a 'U' summons the self-insert command whose effect is to
insert a 'U'.[2]

7.2.1
Keyboard
Conventions

Emacs uses the capabilities of your keyboard more intensively than any
other program we describe in this book. It recognizes three kinds of shift
keys: ordinary, control, and meta. Most commands start with either a
control-shifted key such as [Ctrl]C or a meta-shifted key such as [Meta]X.
Many of these shifted keys are commands by themselves. The three shift
keys can be used individually or in combination.

- The ordinary shift key is the one that changes 'a' to 'A'.

- The control shift key is the one that produces control characters.

- How you produce a meta shift depends on your particular keyboard;
  on some keyboards it's not possible at all.[3] For those keyboards that
  don't have a meta shift, you can obtain the same effect by preceding
  the meta-shifted character with [Esc]; for example, typing '[Esc]x' is
  one way to produce the [Meta]X character. On keyboards that do
  have a meta shift, you can still use [Esc] to "meta"-ize a character.

---

2. The vi emulation provided by Emacs redefines the printable characters so that, for example, 'j' becomes a command to move down by one line.

3. On the PC-type keyboards that we work with ourselves, the [Alt] key acts as a meta shift—
but only under X.

In the description below, we use (Meta)C to indicate the letter 'c' with meta shift and (Meta)(Ctrl)C to indicate the letter 'c' with both meta and control shift. ((Meta)c is equivalent to (Meta)C and (Ctrl)c is equivalent to (Ctrl)C, and similarly for the other letters.) For some other characters, the ordinary shift can modify the other shifts. For instance, the (Ctrl)_ character (control underscore) is usually generated by holding down the ordinary shift and the control shift at the same time while pressing the '-' key. That's because the standard typewriter keyboard has the '_' character on the same key as the '-' character.

Unlike most UNIX programs, Emacs assigns the (LnFd) (linefeed) key a different meaning than the (Enter) key; (LnFd) starts a new line but also, under some circumstances, indents that new line. If your terminal doesn't have a (LnFd) key (most don't), you can obtain its effect by typing '(Ctrl)J'.

The Emacs *key bindings* specify the action caused by a particular key or key sequence. You can modify them if you wish (see Section 7.26.1); Emacs will update the help information where it can to account for the change. A disadvantage of changing the key bindings is that much of the Emacs documentation (including the description in this book) won't reflect your changes.

7.3   Hints on Getting Started

Emacs offers an extensive help system—in fact, the screen you first see when you call Emacs tells you how to start the Emacs tutorial. The (Ctrl)H key activates the help menu (see Section 7.6); in particular, typing '(Ctrl)Ht' starts the tutorial at any time.

The tutorial provides an excellent guided tour of the most important Emacs features and concepts, but it isn't of much use for retrieving information on how to do something in particular. The other options of the help system can be difficult to use until you've already gained some familiarity with Emacs. The hints that follow are intended to aid you in using the help system before you've gained that familiarity.

To display the help options, type (Ctrl)H three times. Emacs displays a window listing the options and providing a brief explanation of each one. Some options replace the window by a window of help information; some others split the screen into two windows. The screen always contains at least one window; the window containing the cursor is called the *selected window*.

The following commands provide the window operations that you'll need in order to use the help system and escape from it when you're done:

- To switch windows when the screen contains more than one window, type '(Ctrl)X o'.
- To scroll the selected window forward (down), type '(Ctrl)V'.
- To scroll the selected window backward (up), type '(Meta)V'.
- To scroll the other window forward, type '(Meta)(Ctrl)V'. (There's no command for scrolling the other window backward.)

- To make all windows disappear except for the selected window, type '⌈Ctrl⌉ X 1'.
- To remove help information from the selected window, type '⌈Ctrl⌉ X k ⌈Enter⌉'.

All these commands are described again later in this chapter.

Probably the most useful form of help when you're first starting out is "apropos" help, which you can use to find out all the commands relating to a particular topic. You can get "apropos" help by typing '⌈Ctrl⌉ H a'. Emacs then asks you for some text that might appear in the names of the commands you are interested in. For instance, if you respond with 'delete', Emacs lists all the commands that have 'delete' in their names along with their explanations. If the listing is too long to fit in the window, you can use the scrolling and window-switching commands listed above to view the entire list and to make the help window go away when you're done with it. Some of the keywords commonly used in command names are the following:

```
char line word sentence paragraph region page sexp
list defun buffer screen window file dir register mode
beginning end forward backward next previous up down
search goto kill delete mark insert yank fill indent
case change set what list find view describe
```

7.3.1 Quick Exit

If you're stuck within a command, you usually can get out of it by typing ⌈Ctrl⌉ G one or two times. The sequence ⌈Ctrl⌉ X ⌈Ctrl⌉ C causes Emacs to exit immediately. Before exiting, it gives you an opportunity to save your work. You can also suspend Emacs without actually killing it by typing ⌈Ctrl⌉ Z .

7.4   Emacs Concepts

In the following subsections we explain some of the concepts that are used in the explanations of the Emacs commands.

7.4.1 Buffers

All editing takes place in a *buffer*—a region of computer memory that holds a body of text. The usual way to edit is to read a file into a buffer, modify the buffer, and write the modified buffer back to the file. There are many other ways to use buffers, however. For instance, you can start with an empty buffer and create a file in it, or use a buffer as a scratchpad that you abandon when you're done with it. Emacs often creates buffers for you that hold specialized text. For example, Emacs puts the help information in a buffer when you use the help system and puts the directory list in a buffer when you use the directory editor Dired. See Section 7.15 for a discussion of the commands that apply to buffers.

7.4.2
Treatment of
Newlines

Emacs treats a newline like any other character:

- If the cursor is at the end of a line and you move right by one position, the cursor moves to the first character of the next line.
- If you delete a newline, the line that you're on is joined with the next line. (Pressing Ctrl D at the end of a line deletes the following newline; pressing Del at the beginning of a line deletes the preceding newline.)
- If you insert a newline in the middle of a line (which you can do by typing Enter), the line is split in two.

See Section 7.9.6 for a description of the commands that insert newlines.

7.4.3
Typing Special
Characters

You can insert a control character into your document by preceding it with Ctrl Q, which calls the `quoted-insert` command. For instance, typing Ctrl Q Ctrl X inserts a Ctrl X character.

7.4.4
Windows

As you edit, your screen is divided into *windows*, each containing a buffer. The same buffer can appear in more than one window. Any changes you make to the text in one window are reflected in all the other windows containing the same buffer. The window containing the cursor is called the *selected window*.

At the bottom of each window is a status line called the *mode line* containing the following information:

- The name of the buffer in the window
- The major and minor modes for that buffer (see Section 7.4.6)
- The position of the window relative to the rest of the buffer ('Top', 'Bottom', or some percentage in between)
- Two characters near the left end of the status line that indicate the buffer's modification status: '%%' for "read-only", '--' for "unmodified", and '**' for "modified"

See Section 7.12 for a discussion of the commands that apply to windows. Sometimes a window contains a text line longer than the window's width. In this case Emacs splits the text line into two screen lines, putting a backslash at the end of the first one. Remember that when you move to the end of such a line, you also move down a line. Text lines that require more than two screen lines behave analogously.

The last line of your screen is shared by the *minibuffer*, which displays commands as you enter them (see Section 7.5.1), and the *echo line*, which shows the results of executing commands and also displays error messages. See Section 7.5.1 for a discussion of the commands pertaining to the minibuffer.

7.4.5
The Point, the
Cursor, the Mark,
and the Region

The *point* is the position in the selected window where editing commands take effect. Each window has its own point. The point lies *between* characters, not *on* them.[4] The point can also be at the very beginning or the

---

4. This convention makes it much easier to describe precisely what commands do, particularly in the cases where the point is at the very beginning or the very end of the buffer.

very end of the buffer. The cursor is always on the character just to the right of the point in the window that's currently active.[5]

The *mark* is a position in a buffer that, like the point, is either between two characters or at one end. Each buffer has exactly one mark, although it may have more than one point (since it may appear in several windows).

The *region* of the selected window is the area between the point and the mark. Each window has a region, although the region might include some text that isn't visible in the window (since the mark need not be in the window). When you remove a buffer from a window, Emacs remembers the point position from that window. When you next restore that buffer to a window, the point position in the window is set to the remembered position.[6]

7.4.6 Major and Minor Modes

Each buffer has a set of *modes* associated with it: one major mode and any number of minor modes. These modes serve to adapt Emacs's behavior to the nature of the information in the buffer and to your preferences. The modes in effect at any moment are those of the buffer in the current window.

Major Modes. A *major mode* defines a set of local key bindings that override the global key bindings—the ones that are in effect by default. A major mode usually redefines other aspects of Emacs's behavior as well. The mode line at the bottom of a window indicates the major mode of the buffer in that window. The major mode appears in parentheses near the middle of the line.

Emacs has different major modes for different kinds of information that can appear in a buffer. The major modes fall into three groups:

- Document modes, including ordinary text, outlines, TEX, LATEX, and `nroff`
- Programming language modes, including several varieties of LISP, Fortran, and C
- Internal modes for specialized buffers such as those associated with the directory editor, the buffer list, subshells, and help screens

In this book we don't discuss the modes associated with particular formatters and programming languages. Major modes are mutually exclusive—only one major mode can be in effect for a given buffer at a time. The least specialized major mode is "Fundamental Mode", which gives each key its most general meaning and sets each option to its default value.

Ordinary characters have special meanings in many of the internal modes. For instance, if you type '?' when you're in an internal mode, Emacs usually provides a help screen that shows your alternatives. Typing '?' in an ordinary document or in a computer program merely inserts that character into the edited text.

---

5. If the point is at the end of the buffer, the cursor is on a character that doesn't actually exist in the buffer.

6. The situation is really more complicated since the buffer could have been changed in the meantime by actions in another window.

For reference, here is a list of all the Emacs major modes other than the internal modes:

- `electric-nroff-mode`
- `emacs-lisp-mode`
- `fortran-mode`
- `indented-text-mode`
- `latex-mode`
- `LaTeX-mode`
- `lisp-mode`
- `lisp-interaction-mode`
- `nroff-mode`
- `outline-mode`
- `plain-tex-mode`
- `plain-TeX-mode`
- `text-mode`
- `tex-mode`
- `TeX-mode`
- `vi-mode`
- `vip-mode`

Minor Modes.   A *minor mode* defines a variation in behavior that you can either turn on or turn off. Minor modes, unlike major modes, are independent of each other. Emacs provides the following minor modes:

- **Auto Fill mode.** In Auto Fill mode, Emacs inserts newlines as needed in order to prevent lines from becoming too long (see Section 7.9.2).

- **Overwrite mode.** In overwrite mode, characters that you type replace characters on the screen instead of pushing those characters to the right.

- **Abbrev mode.** In Abbrev mode, abbreviations are activated (see Section 7.26.3).

- **Auto-save mode.** In auto-save mode, Emacs periodically saves a copy of the file in the buffer.

- **Read-only mode.** In read-only mode, Emacs inhibits any modification to the contents of the buffer.

These minor modes are meaningful in all major modes that allow general editing, i.e., all major modes other than internal ones such as directory editing mode.

Emacs could have been set up to provide minor modes that are meaningful only in certain major modes, but it wasn't. However, nothing prevents you from defining such minor modes in your own customized version of Emacs.

Commands for Minor Modes.   These are the commands for turning the minor modes off and on:

(Meta) X `auto-fill-mode`
> Toggles Auto Fill mode.

> Meta X `overwrite-mode`
>> Toggles overwrite mode.
> Meta X `abbrev-mode`
>> Toggles Abbrev mode.
> Meta X `auto-save-mode`
>> Toggles auto-save mode.
> Ctrl X Ctrl Q
>> Toggles read-only mode (`toggle-read-only`).

With a negative or zero argument, these commands turn off the mode; with a positive argument, they turn it on (see Section 7.5.4 for a discussion of arguments to commands). Called without an argument, they toggle the mode, i.e., they turn it off if it was on and turn it on if it was off.

7.4.7 Variables

In Emacs, a variable is a LISP symbol that has a value associated with it. Emacs uses some variables for recordkeeping; the variables of interest to users are those that customize Emacs's behavior, called *options*. The Ctrl H v command (see p. 273) provides documentation on any variable.

The name of a variable usually consists of a sequence of words separated by hyphens, although the syntax for variable names is more permissive. Section 7.21 describes the operations on variables, including how to set and retrieve their values. You can create your own variables with the LISP `defvar` function (type ' Ctrl H f `defvar` Enter ' to get documentation on it).

7.4.8 The Syntax Table

Each major mode has a *syntax table* associated with it that specifies the syntactic role of each character. The syntax table entry for a character specifies the character's syntactic class together with other information about it. The syntactic class is recorded as a single character, chosen in most cases to be a representative of the class. These are the syntactic classes for text:

(space)	Whitespace, e.g., space, tab, newline
w	Word-constituent characters
_	Characters that are part of symbol names but not part of words
.	Punctuation characters that don't belong to any other class
(	Opening delimiters
)	Closing delimiters

The syntax table for a program mode usually has additional syntactic classes. The Ctrl H s command displays the syntax table for the current mode. See the Emacs documentation for further information about the syntax table.

7.5   How to Issue Commands

Many commands, including nearly all of the commonly-used ones, have *key bindings*. A command's key binding consists of a sequence of one or more keys and provides a shortcut for executing the command. In addition, every Emacs command has a full name, namely, the name of the LISP function that does its work. You can call a command either by typing the keys bound to it (if it has a key binding) or by typing its full name preceded by (Meta) X .[7] For example, the command for leaving Emacs can be typed either as (Ctrl) X (Ctrl) C or as

> (Meta) X save-buffers-kill-emacs

In the rest of our discussion we assume that you're using the key bindings that come with Emacs. You can modify these bindings using the methods described in Section 7.26.1.

In our descriptions of the commands we denote a command by its key binding if it has one, since that's how you'll usually summon it. In most cases we also show the full name of the command, enclosing it in parentheses and setting it in typewriter type. In the alphabetic summary of the commands (Appendix A) we list the commands according to their full names.

7.5.1 The Minibuffer

The *minibuffer* is a line at the bottom of the screen that displays commands as you type them as well as other status information. When you type a command consisting of more than one key, each key is displayed in the minibuffer as you type it. A one-key command isn't shown in the minbuffer; since the command is executed as soon as you type it, there's nothing to show.

When you enter a command starting with (Meta) X, you may edit the command as you type it. The (Del) command, which erases the character you last typed, is particularly useful. You may also use any of the other editing commands, including those described in "Moving Short Distances" on page 275 and "Erasing Text" on page 278. When you finish typing the command, execute it by pressing (Enter).

7.5.2 Cancelling Commands

The usual way to cancel a command before you've finished typing it (or if you started typing it by accident) is to type (Ctrl) G, the keyboard-quit command. If you don't know what state Emacs is in, typing two (Ctrl) G's halts any ongoing commands. (You need two of them to cancel an interactive search.)

If you're in the middle of a recursive edit (see Section 7.5.6), (Ctrl) G still cancels commands but does not get you out of the recursive edit. The (Ctrl)] command (abort-recursive-edit) gets you out of the recursive edit and also cancels the command that caused the recursive edit.

7.5.3 Command Completion

To make it easier to fill in the information needed to execute a command, Emacs provides a completion feature for the minibuffer. You can type parts of the command's name and use the completion feature to fill in the rest. The following keys support command completion:

(Tab)   Extends the text in the minibuffer as far as possible. A character is added if it is the only possible character. For example, if the text in the minibuffer is a command and you type

---

7. The (Meta) X key is itself bound to the command execute-extended-command.

'fil (Tab)', Emacs extends it to 'fill-' since all the commands whose names start with 'fil' have 'l-' as their next two characters.

(Space)   Extends the last word in the minibuffer as far as possible. This command is like the previous one, except that Emacs ends the completion at a word boundary. If you type (Space) repeatedly, Emacs continues to add words one at a time as long as it can.

(Enter)   Completes the text and acts on it:

- If the text in the minibuffer is a valid value, Emacs uses it and executes the command.

- If the text in the minibuffer has a unique completion, Emacs completes it. For command names or for names of output files, Emacs then executes the command; for names of input files that must exist, Emacs then asks for confirmation.

If you type a buffer name or the name of a visited file followed by (Enter), Emacs always accepts it without attempting further completion. If the buffer or file does not exist, Emacs creates an empty buffer for it.

7.5.4
Arguments to Commands

Most Emacs commands accept arguments. The argument to a command is always a number or something that denotes a number. You type an argument by meta-shifting its digits and sign if any. For instance,

(Meta) 1 (Meta) 3 (Ctrl) F

denotes the command (Ctrl) F with an argument of 13, while

(Meta) – (Ctrl) F

denotes the command (Ctrl) F with an argument of '–', equivalent to -1.

For most commands, an argument of n specifies that the command should be repeated n times. For example, typing

(Meta) 1 (Meta) 3 (Ctrl) F

executes the (Ctrl) F command thirteen times, moving the point forward by thirteen positions. Negative arguments usually specify repetition in the opposite sense, so

(Meta) – (Meta) 4 (Ctrl) F

moves the point backward by four positions. Since an ordinary printable character acts as a command, typing

(Meta) 5 y

inserts 'yyyyy' into the buffer.

Not all commands follow these conventions, however:

- For some commands, the very presence of an argument changes the command's meaning; it doesn't matter what the argument is. For example, the command (Meta) Q with no argument fills out the text of a paragraph; given an argument, it also justifies the text.

- Some commands use an argument as a repeat count but behave differently when called without an argument. For instance, the (Ctrl)K command with an argument of n kills the text up to and including the nth following newline. If you type (Ctrl)K without an argument when the point is before the end of the line, however, it kills the rest of the line but not the newline at the end of it.

- Although (Meta)- is usually equivalent to (Meta)- (Meta)1, a few commands treat it differently.

In the descriptions of the commands below, we mention arguments only when they modify the command's meaning in an unconventional way.

There's another way to specify arguments that's often more convenient. If you type (Ctrl)U in front of a command, that command is repeated four times. You can apply (Ctrl)U to (Ctrl)U itself, giving you 16 repetitions. You can also follow (Ctrl)U by a sequence of digits that specifies an explicit repetition count. For example, '(Ctrl)U 20 (Ctrl)N' repeats the (Ctrl)N command twenty times and moves the point down twenty lines. A few commands give (Ctrl)U a special meaning different from the meaning given to any specific number.

7.5.5 Recalling Complex Commands

Emacs keeps a history of the complex commands (those starting with (Meta)X) that you've recently executed. You can save some typing by recalling these commands, editing them if necessary, and then re-executing them. The following commands recall, execute, and display previous complex commands:

(Ctrl)X (Esc)

> Recalls the complex command you most recently executed (`repeat-complex-command`). The command appears in the minibuffer in its LISP form; an example is

```
Redo: (query-replace "Queeg" "Ahab" nil)
```

(Meta)P   Brings the previous command of the command history into the minibuffer (`previous-complex-command`).

(Meta)N   Brings the next command of the command history into the minibuffer (`next-complex-command`). This command is useful when you want to look at a recent command again.

(Enter)   Executes the complex command in the minibuffer.

(Meta)X `list-command-history`

> Displays the command history in a window. The commands are listed in their LISP form, with the most recent one at the top of the list.

You may only issue the (Meta)P, (Meta)N, and (Enter) commands when the minibuffer contains a recalled command.

7.5.6 Recursive Editing

Sometimes it's useful to interrupt what you're doing in the minibuffer in order to work in another buffer. The most common instance arises during a `query-replace` operation (see "Replacement with Querying" on page 311) when you want to edit the area around a replacement before going on to the next replacement. Typing (Ctrl) R in response to a query executes the `recursive-edit` command (the (Ctrl) R key is bound to that command in the context of a `query-replace`). You can now do any editing you wish, using the (Meta) (Ctrl) C command described below to resume the `query-replace`.

The following commands terminate a recursive edit:

(Meta) (Ctrl) C
> Terminates the recursive edit and returns to the activity underway before you started it (`exit-recursive-edit`).

(Ctrl)]
> Terminates this recursive edit as well as the command that invoked it (`abort-recursive-edit`). This command is stronger than (Ctrl) G (see Section 7.5.2).

(Meta) X `top-level`
> Terminates all currently active recursive edits and returns to the activity underway before you started the outermost one.

As you might guess, recursive edits can be very confusing; generally you should avoid them.

7.5.7 Disabling Commands

A disabled command requires confirmation before it can be executed. By marking a command as disabled, you can prevent it from being executed by accident. The following commands enable and disable other commands:

(Meta) X `disable-command`
> This command asks you interactively for the name of the command *cmd* to be disabled. It then edits your `.emacs` initialization file to include a LISP command that will disable *cmd* in future Emacs sessions. **Note:** This command does not affect the current Emacs session.

(Meta) X `enable-command`
> This command asks you interactively for the name of the command *cmd* to be enabled. You can choose to have the command enabled for the current Emacs session or permanently. If you choose permanent enablement, Emacs inserts an appropriate LISP command in your `.emacs` file.

7.5.8 Undoing Changes

The Emacs undo facility enables you to correct your mistakes by undoing your actions.

(Ctrl) _
(Ctrl) X u
> Undoes the most recent group of actions that changed the text in the current buffer (`undo`). If you enter a sequence of characters without doing anything in between, the sequence is removed by a single undo. Some other sequences of simple actions are also grouped. **Note:** On some keyboards you can type (Ctrl) _ by pressing the '_/-' key while holding down the control and shift keys.

Each buffer has its own undo history. By repeating the `undo` command you can undo any number of actions up to the capacity of the undo history kept by Emacs (about 8000 characters). One way to revert a buffer to its original state is to issue an undo command with a very large argument. You'll know you've succeeded if the stars disappear from the status line.

You can undo an undo if you first perform some simple but irrelevant action such as moving the point forward by a character. That breaks the sequence of undo's, making the previous undo's the most recent actions to be undone. The following experiment illustrates how this works:

(1) Start with an empty buffer.
(2) Type 'abcx'. The buffer now contains 'abcx'.
(3) Type '(Del)'. The buffer now contains 'abc'.
(4) Type '(Ctrl)B def'. The buffer now contains 'abdefc'.
(5) Type '(Ctrl)_'. The insertion of 'def' is undone and the buffer now contains 'abc'.
(6) Type '(Ctrl)_' again. The deletion of 'x' is undone and the buffer now contains 'abcx'.
(7) Type '(Ctrl)B'. The buffer is unchanged but the point moves left by one position.
(8) Type '(Ctrl)_'. The previous undo is undone and the buffer again contains 'abc'.
(9) Another undo yields 'abdefc'.

After you save a file, Emacs marks the file as unmodified. Nevertheless you can undo changes that you made before you saved it (causing the file to be marked as modified again).

7.6   Getting Help

Emacs has an extensive help system, which you can activate by typing (Ctrl)H or (Erase).[8] A second (Ctrl)H (or a '?') causes Emacs to list the help options; a third (Ctrl)H causes Emacs to pop up a window explaining the options. You can also type an option immediately after (Ctrl)H. For example, typing (Ctrl)Hk causes Emacs to bring up the describe-key help option.

Most of the help commands create a window to display the help information. You can make this window go away by typing (Ctrl)X 1 or (Ctrl)X 4b (Enter), depending on how many windows are on the screen when you ask for help. (The help system itself tells you how to do this.)

The help options that you can specify after (Ctrl)H are described below.

---

8. The use of (Erase) as a help key may seem strange. The reason for it is that (Ctrl)H is a natural choice for the help key, and on most keyboards (Erase) and (Ctrl)H generate the same code.

7.6.1 **Information about** **Commands and** **Key Bindings**	The following help options provide information about commands and key bindings.

a *str*   Lists and explains all commands whose names contain the string *str* (`command-apropos`). See p. 263 for a list of words that are useful to include in *str*. The (Meta) X apropos command described below provides a useful extension to this command.

c   Asks you to type a key, then indicates which key you typed and what command is bound to it (`describe-key-briefly`). You can use this command to explore the effects of typing odd key combinations on your keyboard.[9]

k   Asks you to type a key, then indicates which key you typed and what command is bound to it; in addition it provides an explanation of that command (`describe-key`).

b   Lists all key bindings currently in effect (`describe-bindings`). Since the bindings are mode-dependent, you may get different results when you execute this command in different windows.

w   Asks you to type a command, then indicates which keys if any are bound to it (`where-is`).

m   Describes the current mode, indicating those keys that are redefined in this mode (`describe-mode`).

7.6.2 **Information about** **LISP Symbols**	The following help options provide information about LISP symbols that support Emacs.

f   Asks you to type a LISP function, then describes it (`describe-function`). Since all commands are LISP functions, this help option is one way to get information about a particular command. The 'a' option is usually more convenient than the 'f' option but provides fewer details. The 'f' option can query LISP functions that are not Emacs commands.

v   Asks you to type a LISP variable, then describes it (`describe-variable`). See Section 7.4.7 for more information about variables.

s   Displays the syntax table (see Section 7.4.8) that indicates the role of each character in the current mode (`describe-syntax`).

7.6.3 **Information about** **Recently Executed** **Commands**	The following help option shows recently executed commands:

l   Displays the last 100 command characters you typed (`view-lossage`). This command is useful when something has gone wrong and you don't know what you've done.

---

9. For example, we discovered that typing (Ctrl) 7 on our keyboard produced the same effect as (Ctrl) _, providing a particularly convenient way to call the undo command.

**7.6.4
Tutorial and
On-Line Manual**

The following help options provide access to more extended information about Emacs:

t   Starts the Emacs tutorial (`help-with-tutorial`).

i   Runs the `info` program, which provides hypertext-like access to the complete Emacs manual on-line (`info`). Typing 'h' when you start `info` leads you to a tutorial on `info`.

**7.6.5
Information about
Emacs Itself**

The following commands display information about Emacs itself and policies relating to it:

n
(Ctrl) N   Displays documentation on changes to Emacs in chronological order (`view-emacs-news`).

(Ctrl) C   Displays the conditions pertaining to distributing copies of Emacs (`describe-copying`).

(Ctrl) D   Displays information on how to obtain the latest copy of Emacs (`describe-distribution`).

(Ctrl) W   Displays information about the lack of warranty for Emacs (`describe-no-warranty`).

**7.6.6
Other Help
Commands**

The following commands provide help information but are *not* preceded by (Ctrl) H :

(Meta) X apropos
             Like `command-apropos`, except that it lists *all* LISP symbols that match the regular expression.

(Meta) X manual-entry
             Displays the on-line manual pages for a specified UNIX command .

7.7   Exiting from or Suspending Emacs

The following command gets you out of Emacs altogether:

(Ctrl) X (Ctrl) C
             Offers to save any modified buffers that are associated with files (so you don't lose your changes), then terminates Emacs (`save-buffers-kill-emacs`). An argument to this command causes immediate termination.

A less drastic alternative is to suspend Emacs, giving you the opportunity to resume it where you left off. The following command suspends Emacs:

(Ctrl) Z   Suspends Emacs, returning to the shell (`suspend-emacs`). If your shell supports job control (see Section 2.7.1), you can resume Emacs again by typing '%emacs'. For shells that don't support job control, this command creates a subshell that communicates directly with your terminal. The only way to get back to Emacs from this subshell is to terminate the subshell.

7.8   Basic Editing Commands

In the following subsections we describe the editing commands that you're likely to use most often.

7.8.1
Moving the Point

The commands described below move the point.

Moving Short Distances. The following commands move the point by short distances.

(Ctrl)F	Moves forward (right) one character (`forward-char`).
(Ctrl)B	Moves backward (left) one character (`backward-char`).
(Ctrl)N	Moves to the next line (`next-line`). This command and the next one attempt to keep the horizontal position unchanged. Their behavior is also affected by the (Ctrl)X (Ctrl)N command described below.
(Ctrl)P	Moves to the previous line (`previous-line`).
(Ctrl)E	Moves to the end of the line (`end-of-line`).
(Ctrl)A	Moves to the beginning of the line (`beginning-of-line`).
(Meta)M	Moves to the first nonblank character on the line (`back-to-indentation`).
(Meta)F	Moves forward (right) one word (`forward-word`).
(Meta)B	Moves backward (left) one word (`backward-word`).
(Meta)R	Moves to the beginning of the line at the center of the window (`move-to-window-line`). With a positive argument n, this command moves to the nth line from the top; with a negative argument $-n$, it moves to the nth line from the bottom.

You can arrange to have the (Ctrl)N and (Ctrl)P commands always move to the same column whenever possible. The following command enables and disables this behavior:

(Ctrl)X (Ctrl)N

> Sets the current column as the goal column, so that (Ctrl)N and (Ctrl)P attempt to move the point as close as possible to this column (`set-goal-column`). Issuing this command with an argument cancels the use of the goal column.

Moving by Larger Units. The following commands move the point by larger units. Emacs assumes that a sentence ends, as in English, with a '.',

'?', or '!' followed by an end of line or two spaces, with closing parentheses and quotes accounted for properly. A paragraph boundary also ends a sentence. Paragraphs are usually demarcated by blank lines and, for text, by indented lines and formatter commands (but see "Paragraphs" below). Pages are demarcated by ⟨formfeed⟩ characters, which you can produce by typing Ctrl Q Ctrl L .

Meta E   Moves forward to the character following the end of the current sentence (`forward-sentence`).

Meta A   Moves backward to the first character of the current sentence (`backward-sentence`).

Meta]   Moves forward to the character following the end of the current paragraph (`forward-paragraph`).

Meta [Moves backward to the first character of the current paragraph (`backward-paragraph`).

Ctrl X]   Moves forward to the character following the next page marker (`forward-page`).

Ctrl X [Moves backward to the character *following* the previous page marker (`backward-page`). If the point is currently just after a page marker, this command moves back over that page marker and looks for the one before that. Thus two Ctrl X [commands in a row move the point back back two pages.

Paragraphs. In Text mode, the definition of a paragraph is controlled by two variables: `paragraph-separate` and `paragraph-start`, both given by regular expressions (see "Regular Expressions in Emacs" on page 309):

- `Paragraph-separate` matches any line that cannot occur within a paragraph and therefore always separates paragraphs.
- `Paragraph-start` matches any line that either starts a paragraph or separates paragraphs.

By default, `paragraph-separate` matches any line containing only spaces, ⟨tab⟩s and ⟨formfeed⟩s, while `paragraph-start` matches any line that starts with a space, ⟨tab⟩, ⟨formfeed⟩, or newline. (A line that starts with a newline is empty.) Some text modes have values for `paragraph-separate` and `paragraph-start` that match additional patterns; for example, in Nroff mode these variables match certain `nroff` commands.

Moving to One End of the Buffer. The following commands move the point to the beginning or the end of the entire buffer. With an argument, they move part way.

Meta <   Moves to the beginning of the entire buffer (`beginning-of-buffer`). With an argument of n, moves to a point $n/10$ of the way towards the end of the buffer.

Meta >   Moves to the end of the entire buffer (`end-of-buffer`). With an argument of n, moves to a point $n/10$ of the way towards the beginning of the buffer.

Moving to a Character or Line.   The following commands move the point to a specified character position or line:

(Meta) X goto-char

> Moves the point to the left of the nth character in the buffer. Emacs prompts you for n.

(Meta) X goto-line

> Moves the point to the left end of the nth line in the buffer. The first line is numbered 1. Emacs prompts you for n.

7.8.2
Positioning and Scrolling the Window

The following command repositions the selected window around the point:

(Ctrl) L   Repaints the screen and repositions the current window so that the point is at its middle line (recenter). With an argument of n, this command positions the point at line n from the top (or line $-n$ from the bottom if n is negative).

The following commands scroll the text in the window either horizontally or vertically. The horizontal scrolling commands are useful when some of the lines are longer than the width of the window, as often happens when you split a window into two side-by-side windows.

(Ctrl) V   Scrolls the text up, i.e., forward, by one page (scroll-up). With an argument n, scrolls up by n lines.

(Meta) V   Scrolls the text down, i.e., backward, by one page (scroll-down). With an argument n, scrolls down by n lines.

(Ctrl) X <   Scrolls the text left by a little less than the width of the screen (scroll-left). With an argument, scrolls left by n columns.

(Ctrl) X >   Scrolls the text right by a little less than the width of the screen (scroll-right). With an argument, scrolls right by n columns.

7.8.3
Erasing, Moving, and Copying Text

You can erase text either by deleting it or by killing it: Deleted text is not explicitly saved, although you can get it back by undoing the deletion. Killed text is saved in a kill ring from which you can retrieve it later by yanking it (see "Retrieving Killed Text" on page 279). You can also retrieve killed text by undoing the kill, although the capacity of Emacs's undo buffer is smaller than that of its kill buffer; as a result, some kills cannot be undone but can still be yanked.

Deletion applies to small units of text such as a single character or a blank line that aren't worth saving, while killing applies to larger units of text. The name of a command implies whether it kills or deletes.

The usual way to move text ("cut and paste") is to kill the text, move the point to the place where the text should go, and yank the text. The usual way to copy text is to kill it, reinsert it immediately by yanking it, move the point to the place where the text should go, and yank it again. Since yanking leaves the kill ring unchanged, you can use this method to copy text to several places. You can also copy text by using the (Meta) (Ctrl) W command to move the text to the kill ring without erasing it.

In "Moving Text between Buffers" on page 280 below we describe commands for moving text between buffers.

Erasing Text.   The following commands erase small amounts of text by deleting it:

(Ctrl) D   Deletes the character to the right of the point, i.e., the character under the cursor (`delete-char`).

(Del)   Deletes the character to the left of the point, i.e., the character to the left of the cursor (`delete-backward-char`).

The following commands erase larger amounts of text by killing it:

(Ctrl) W   Kills the text in the region (`kill-region`). This is the most general kill command because you can get it to kill any sequence of text by putting the point at one end of the text and the mark at the other end.

(Ctrl) K   Kills the text up to the end of the line, but doesn't kill the newline unless the point is already at the end of the line (`kill-line`). Two (Ctrl) K's in a row kill the rest of the current line and join the beginning of the current line with the beginning of the next line. With an argument of n, (Ctrl) K kills the text up to and including the nth following ⟨newline⟩. The usual way to kill a line entirely is to type (Ctrl) A (Ctrl) K (Ctrl) K.

(Meta) D   Kills the word to the right of the point (`kill-word`). The erased text includes any spaces between the point and the word.

(Meta) (Del)
               Kills the word to the left of the point (`backward-kill-word`). The erasure includes any spaces between the point and the word—note that these are the spaces *after* the word.

(Meta) K   Kills the sentence to the right of the point (`kill-sentence`). The erasure includes any spaces between the point and the first word of the sentence.

(Ctrl) X (Del)
               Kills the text between the point and the end of the previous sentence (`backward-kill-sentence`). Spaces following the end of the previous sentence aren't erased.

(Meta) Z   Kills all characters up to but not including the character c (`zap-to-char`). The command prompts you for c. If the cursor is on a c, nothing happens unless the command has an argument.

The following commands do other kinds of erasures (as deletions):

(Meta) \   Deletes any spaces and tabs surrounding the point (`delete-horizontal-space`).

(Meta) (Space)
               Replaces all the spaces and tabs around the point by a single space (`just-one-space`). If there are no spaces adjacent to the point, this command inserts a single space.

(Meta) ^   Joins the current line with the preceding one by deleting the newline at the end of the preceding line along with any spaces or tabs after it (`delete-indentation`). The deleted newline is replaced by a space unless that space would come after a '(' or before a ')'.

Ctrl X Ctrl O

Deletes blank lines (`delete-blank-lines`) as follows:

- If the point is on an isolated blank line, deletes that line.

- If the point is on a nonblank line followed by one or more blank lines, deletes those blank lines.

- If the point is currently on one of several adjacent blank lines, deletes all but one of those blank lines.

Retrieving Killed Text.   Retrieving killed text is called "yanking" it.[10] Whenever you kill some text, Emacs saves that text in the *kill ring*, from which you can later retrieve it.

You can cycle through the kill ring, examining each fragment of previously killed text, by typing 'Ctrl Y' and then typing 'Meta Y' repeatedly. The cycle always starts with the most recently killed text and proceeds to the oldest text in the ring, then returns to the newest text again. Typing 'Ctrl W' erases the yanked text. Note that retrieving text from the kill ring does not change the information in the kill ring, so you can make several copies of text by yanking it repeatedly.

Ctrl Y   Copies the most recently killed text into the buffer starting at the point, leaving the cursor at the end of the copied text (`yank`). If you type Ctrl U Ctrl Y, the cursor is left at the beginning of the text instead. An argument *n* of any other form retrieves the *n*th most recently killed text. (If *n* is negative, Emacs moves through the kill ring in oldest-to-newest order.)

Meta Y   Replaces the most recently yanked text by the previous text in the kill ring (`yank-pop`). Executing this command repeatedly enables you to retrieve text that is several kills old, since it circulates through the kill ring. An argument has the same effect as it does with Ctrl Y, except that Ctrl U by itself has no special meaning. This command is only meaningful after a Ctrl Y or another Meta Y.

A few other commands besides the ones listed here also do yanking. Note that the commands for killing and yanking rectangles (see Section 7.11) do not use the kill ring.

Copying Text.   One way to copy text is to kill it, reinsert it in its previous place with Ctrl Y, move to the destination, and insert another copy

---

10. Note that Emacs and `vi` use the word "yank" in opposite senses—in `vi`, yanking text copies it *from* the working buffer, while in Emacs, yanking text copies it *to* the working buffer. Neither usage reflects the meaning of the word in English—to yank something ordinarily implies that the thing yanked is no longer there.

with a second (Ctrl) Y. You can avoid the reinsertion by using the (Meta) W command.

(Meta) W   Copies the text from the region to the kill ring without eras-
               ing it (copy-region-as-kill). The effect is like that of (Ctrl) W
               except that the buffer is not modified and the point does not
               move.

(Meta) (Ctrl) W
               If the next command is a kill command (not necessarily
               (Ctrl) W), force it to append the killed text to the last killed text
               instead of making that text a separate entry in the kill ring
               (append-next-kill). This command enables you to collect
               and accumulate text from several locations. It has no effect if
               the following command is not a kill command.

You can also copy text by copying it into a register and then yanking the contents of the register (see Section 7.18.3).

Moving Text between Buffers. The following commands move text directly from one buffer to another. One of the buffers is the current buffer;
the command prompts you for the name of the other buffer (see p. 298).

(Meta) X copy-to-buffer
               Copies the text in the region to the specified buffer, erasing the
               previous contents of the destination buffer.

(Ctrl) X a   Copies the text in the region to just after the position of the
               point in the specified buffer, leaving the point at the end of
               the appended text (append-to-buffer). Successive uses of this
               command cause the successive text fragments to appear in the
               same order that they were copied.

(Meta) X prepend-to-buffer
               Copies the text in the region to just before the position of the
               point in the specified buffer, leaving the point at the beginning
               of the appended text (append-to-buffer). Successive uses of
               this command cause the successive text fragments to appear in
               the *reverse* order that they were copied.

(Meta) X insert-buffer
               Insert the contents of a selected buffer into the current buffer
               at the point.

**7.8.4
Setting the Mark**

The following commands explicitly set the mark to the point:

(Ctrl) - (Space)
(Ctrl) @   Set the mark to the place where the point is (set-mark-
               command). The actual key binding is to (Ctrl) @; (Ctrl) - (Space)
               is merely a convenient way of producing this key on most
               keyboards. If you execute this command with an argument of
               (Ctrl) U, it doesn't set the mark; instead, it moves the mark to
               the previous mark.

(Ctrl) X (Ctrl) X
> Exchanges the point and the mark (exchange-point-and-mark). Executing this command twice is a convenient way of seeing where the mark is.

The Mark Ring.   Each time you set the mark, Emacs saves its location in a *mark ring*. There is one mark ring for each buffer; by default it contains sixteen marks. Repeatedly executing (Ctrl) U (Ctrl) (Space) circulates the point around the mark ring, from the newest mark to the oldest and back again to the newest.

Marking Text.   The following commands set the mark at the end of a unit of text, thereby making that unit the region. The (Meta) @ command sets only the mark; the other commands set both the point and the mark.

(Meta) @   Puts the mark at the end of the next word (mark-word).

(Meta) H   Puts the point at the beginning of the paragraph that surrounds or follows the point and puts the mark at the end of it (mark-paragraph).

(Ctrl) X (Ctrl) P
> Puts the point at the beginning of the page that surrounds or follows the point and puts the mark at the end of it (mark-page).

(Ctrl) X h   Puts the point at the beginning of the buffer and puts the mark at the end of it (mark-whole-buffer).

See also the mark-sexp command (p. 285).

7.9   Additional Editing Commands

The commands described below provide additional editing facilities that are convenient but less essential than the ones described above.

**7.9.1
Filling Regions**

Filling text consists of breaking it up into lines that are as long as possible but still don't exceed a specified length, given by the *fill column*. The fill column is used by Auto Fill mode (see Section 7.9.2). The following commands enable you to specify the fill column, to fill portions of the buffer, and to center one or more lines. See "Paragraphs" on page 276 for the definition of a paragraph.

(Ctrl) X f   Sets the fill column to the column to the right of the point (set-fill-column). With an argument n, this command sets the fill column to n.

(Meta) Q   Fills the paragraph containing the point (fill-paragraph).

(Meta) X fill-region-as-paragraph
> Fills the region, treating it as a single paragraph.

(Meta) X fill-individual-paragraphs

> Fills the paragraphs in the region, treating blank lines as paragraph separators and giving each line of a paragraph the same indentation as its first line.

(Meta) G   Fills all the lines of the region, honoring paragraph boundaries (fill-region).

(Meta) X center-line

> Centers the current line within the line length as given by the fill column. With an argument of n, this command centers n lines.

Suppose that you have a paragraph in which each line starts with the same text, such as a few spaces (for an indented paragraph) or the text '# ' (for a comment that starts a shell script). You can fill the paragraph while excluding that common text from filling by making that common text a *fill prefix* using the following command:

(Ctrl) X .   Sets the fill prefix to the portion of the current line preceding the point (set-fill-prefix). You can make the fill prefix empty by moving to the beginning of a line and issuing this command again.

The fill commands remove the fill prefix from each line before filling and put it back after filling. A line that does not start with the fill prefix is considered to start a paragraph, as does a line that is blank or indented once the prefix is removed.

7.9.2 Auto Fill Mode

Auto Fill mode is a minor mode in which lines are broken at spaces when they exceed a certain width. The width is given by the fill column, which you can set with the (Ctrl) X f (set-fill-column) command (p. 281). Line breaking is triggered when you type (Space), (Enter), or (LnFd). When you type one of these keys, Emacs checks to see if the line is too long; if it is, Emacs breaks it into two or more lines that don't exceed the allowable width, choosing breaks that are as far to the right as possible. You can deliberately create a long line by quoting the triggering character with (Ctrl) Q. For some major modes, Emacs indents the line after an inserted newline if the previous line was indented, or adjusts the indentation in some other way to suit the mode.

Note that turning on Auto Fill mode does not guarantee that all lines will lie within the specified width. If you make a line too long by inserting material in the middle, Emacs doesn't do anything about it. If a paragraph contains lines that are too long, usually the easiest way to fix it is to use one of the fill commands described above.

7.9.3 Selective Display

You can hide lines indented by more than a certain number of columns with Emacs's *selective display* feature. The following command turns it on:

(Ctrl) X $ With argument n, hides all lines indented by at least n columns (set-selective-display). With no argument, reveals all the hidden lines again.

The hidden lines are indicated by '...' at the end of each visible line preceding one or more invisible ones. The (Ctrl)N and (Ctrl)P commands move over invisible lines as though they weren't there, but most other editing commands see them as usual. When the point is on an invisible line, the cursor appears at the end of the previous line after the three dots.

7.9.4 Transposing Textual Units

The following commands transpose textual units:

(Ctrl)T   Transposes the character under the cursor with the character preceding it, i.e., interchanges the two characters surrounding the point (`transpose-chars`). The point moves one character to the right, so you can use this command to move a character across several others.

(Meta)T   Transposes the word following the point with the word preceding it (`transpose-words`). If the point is between words, the two words around the point are affected; if the point is within a word, that one and the next one are affected. The point moves to the beginning of the next unaffected word. With an argument of zero, this command interchanges the word around or after the point with the word around or after the mark.

(Ctrl)X (Ctrl)T

    Transposes the line containing the point with the line above it (`transpose-lines`). The point moves to the beginning of the next unaffected line. With an argument of zero, this command interchanges the line around or after the point with the line around or after the mark.

7.9.5 Changing the Case of Text

The following commands change a sequence of words to all uppercase or to all lowercase, or capitalize a sequence of words:

(Meta)U   Converts the word to the right of the point to uppercase and advances the point to the next word (`upcase-word`).

(Meta)L   Converts the word to the right of the point to lowercase and advances the point to the next word (`downcase-word`).

(Meta)C   Capitalizes the letter to the right of the point, i.e., the letter under the cursor, and advances the point to the next word (`capitalize-word`).

Since these commands advance the point to the next word, you can easily use them to modify a sequence of words. If you provide a negative argument to one of these commands by preceding it with '(Meta)-', the command applies to the preceding word and the point does not move.

The following commands are similar to the previous ones except that they apply to the region and do not move the point:

(Ctrl)X (Ctrl)U

    Converts all the letters in the region to uppercase (`upcase-region`).

(Ctrl)X (Ctrl)L

    Converts all the letters in the region to lowercase (`downcase-region`).

Meta X capitalize-region

> Capitalizes each word in the region. If the region begins in the middle of a word, the first letter of the region rather than the first letter of the word is capitalized.

7.9.6
Commands for
Inserting Newlines

The following commands insert newlines and may have other effects as well:

Enter
> Inserts a newline (newline). If Auto Fill mode is on (see Section 7.9.2), inserting a newline causes the preceding line to be broken if it is too long.

LnFd
> Inserts a newline and indents the next line according to the indentation conventions that are currently in effect (newline-and-indent).

Ctrl O
> Opens up a new line (open-line). This command acts like Enter except that it leaves the point before the newly inserted newline rather than after it.

Meta Ctrl O
> Starts a new line at the point, indenting the new line to the position of the point (split-line). For example, if the point is at the indicated position in the line

```
Exit,. pursued by a bear.
```

and you execute this command, the result is

```
Exit,
      pursued by a bear.
```

7.9.7
Operations on Lists

The following commands move the point around parenthesis-balanced lists. The units of motion are called *sexps*. A sexp is either a word (or similar syntactic unit) or a parenthesis-balanced portion of text that begins with a left parenthesis and ends with a right parenthesis.[11] These commands are useful for nearly all programming languages and sometimes even for ordinary text. For most languages they treat '[' and '{' as equivalent to '(' and ']' and '}' as equivalent to ')'.

Meta Ctrl F
> Moves the point forward (to the right) to just after the next sexp (forward-sexp).

---

11. The term "sexp" is derived from the LISP term "S-expression", which stands for "symbolic expression". More formally, a sexp can be defined as follows:

(1) A single word is a sexp.
(2) A sequence of sexps enclosed in parentheses is a sexp.

Whitespace and punctuation are permitted between components of a sexp and are required between adjacent words.

Meta Ctrl B
> Moves the point backward (to the left) to just before the previous sexp (`backward-sexp`).

Meta Ctrl N
> Moves the point forward (to the right) until it's just after the next *parenthesized* sexp (`forward-list`).

Meta Ctrl P
> Moves the point backward (to the left) until it's just before the parenthesis that starts the previous *parenthesized* sexp (`backward-list`).

Meta Ctrl D
> Moves the point forward (to the right) to just before the next parenthesis that starts a sexp (`down-list`).

Meta Ctrl U
> Moves the point backward (to the left) until it's just before the parenthesis that starts the sexp containing the point (`backward-up-list`). A negative argument moves the point to the right in an analogous way.

The following example shows how these commands work. Suppose that the point is just before the 'o' of 'four' in the following text:

```
(one (two) three f.our five (six) seven)
```

Then the following table shows the effect of the various commands, with the final position of the point underlined:

Meta Ctrl F	`(one (two) three four. five (six) seven)`
Meta Ctrl B	`(one (two) three .four five (six) seven)`
Meta Ctrl N	`(one (two) three four five (six). seven)`
Meta Ctrl P	`(one .(two) three four five (six) seven)`
Meta Ctrl D	`(one (two) three four five (.six) seven)`
Meta Ctrl U	`.(one (two) three four five (six) seven)`

The following commands kill, mark, and transpose sexps:

Meta Ctrl K
> Kills the sexp following the point (`kill-sexp`).

Meta Ctrl T
> Transposes the sexp preceding the point and the sexp following the point by dragging the previous one across the next one (`transpose-sexps`).

Meta Ctrl @
> Places the mark just after the next sexp, which is the place where `forward-sexp` would move to (`mark-sexp`). The point is unchanged.

7.9.8 Sorting

The following commands enable you to sort a portion of the buffer in different ways. All of them apply to the region.

Meta X `sort-lines`
> Rearranges the lines of the region into sorted order. If the command has a prefix, the sort is in reverse order.

(Meta) X sort-paragraphs

> Rearranges the paragraphs of the region into sorted order, comparing the entire text of each paragraph except for leading blank lines. See "Paragraphs" on page 276 for the definition of a paragraph. If the command has a prefix, the sort is in reverse order.

(Meta) X sort-pages

> Rearranges the pages of the region into sorted order, comparing the entire text of each page. Pages are considered to be separated by ⟨formfeed⟩s. If the command has a prefix, the sort is in reverse order.

(Meta) X sort-fields

> Rearranges the lines of the region, sorting them according to the contents of the nth field of each line where n is the argument to the command. If no argument is given, n defaults to 1. A negative argument indicates a decreasing sort of the specified field.
>
> Consecutive fields consist of runs of non-whitespace characters, with whitespace separating the fields. The fields are sorted using the ASCII values of the characters, so for example the field '23' comes before the field '7'. The order of records having the same sort key is preserved, so you can sort on several fields by sorting on the individual fields in *decreasing* (right-to-left) order.

(Meta) X sort-numeric-fields

> Like sort-fields, except that the fields are converted to unsigned integers if possible before sorting and these integers are used to determine the ordering. Fields not containing unsigned integers compare equal.

(Meta) X sort-columns

> Sorts the lines that include the region according to the contents of certain columns of each line. The columns that affect the sort are those between the column containing the point and the column containing the mark. The comparison is done by comparing the strings in those columns of each line. As usual, an argument to the command causes the sort to be in decreasing order.

Another way to sort a region, not using these commands at all, is to apply the UNIX sort command (see Section 8.1) to the region with the (Meta) | (shell-command-on-region) command (see p. 317).

7.9.9
Checking and
Correcting Spelling

You can check and optionally correct the spelling of words in a document of English text. Emacs uses the UNIX spell program to do the checking. When it finds a misspelled word, it asks you to correct the spelling by editing the word in the minibuffer. It then does a query-replace over the entire buffer, giving you the opportunity to make the correction wherever the misspelled word appears. You can accept a correction by typing 'y' or reject it by typing 'n'.

The following commands check and correct spelling over portions of a buffer:

(Meta) $ Checks and corrects the spelling of the word containing the point (`spell-word`).

(Meta) X `spell-region`
    Checks and corrects the spelling of every word in the region.

(Meta) X `spell-buffer`
    Checks and corrects the spelling of every word in the buffer.

(Meta) X `spell-string`
    Prompts for a word, then checks its spelling.

7.9.10
Working with
Outlines

Emacs has a special mode called Outline mode for working with outlines. Facilities in Outline mode include the following:

- Marking heading lines to distinguish them from body lines
- Moving among heading lines at the same level or to heading lines at adjacent levels
- Hiding or revealing body lines and heading lines at lower levels

See the Emacs manual for instructions on how to use Outline mode.

7.10   Indentation

Different major modes have different indentation conventions. For instance, when in Lisp mode Emacs indents code lines according to their parenthesis depth; when in C mode it indents according to the nesting of language constructs such as '{ ... }', conditional statements, and `for` loops.

Emacs has two text modes: ordinary Text mode and Indented Text mode. Indented Text mode is intended for editing text in which most lines are indented. In Indented Text mode, (Tab) is defined to perform relative indentation (see below).

Inserting Single Indentations.   The following commands insert single indentations:

(Tab)   Inserts indentation according to the mode:

- In Text mode, inserts enough spaces and tabs to advance the point to the next tab stop.[12]

- In Indented Text mode, performs a relative indentation (see `indent-relative` below).

---

12. In general, Emacs uses tabs in preference to sequences of more than three spaces. You can force Emacs to use just spaces by setting the variable `indent-tabs-mode` to nil.

- In major modes for programming languages, indents the entire line according to the conventions of the particular language.

If you really want to insert a tab character, type '[Ctrl] Q [Tab]'.

[Meta] I   Inserts enough spaces and tabs to advance the point to the next tab stop, no matter what the mode (tab-to-tab-stop). In Text mode, [Tab] and [Meta] I are equivalent.

[Meta] X indent-relative

Performs a relative indentation, in which the point is advanced until it is under an *indentation point*, namely, the end of a sequence of whitespace or the end of the line, in the following manner:

- If the point is to the left of or under the last indentation point of the previous line, Emacs advances it to be under the next indentation point.

- If the point is to the right of the last indentation point of the previous line, Emacs tries deleting any whitespace before the point and then uses the next indentation point of the previous line.

- If that doesn't work, Emacs simply advances the point to the next tab stop.

Relative indentation is particularly useful for tabular material, since a relative tab at the end of an item usually causes that item to line up with the item in the same column of the table in the previous row.

Following an empty line, absolute and relative indentation are equivalent. In Indented Text mode, [Tab] and [Meta] X indent-relative are equivalent.

Indenting Lines of a Region. The following commands indent all the lines in the region. A line is considered to be in the region if it begins in the region.

[Meta] [Ctrl] \

Indents each line as it would be indented by [Tab] typed in the middle of the line (indent-region). With an argument n, this command causes the first nonblank character of each line to be positioned at column n.

[Ctrl] X [Tab]

Indents each line in the region by one column (indent-rigidly). With an argument n, this command indents each line by n columns. This command, unlike the previous one, preserves relative indentation.

Tab Stops. The tab stops are stored in the variable tab-stop-list. For text, the default tab stops are in columns 1, 9, 17, ... Changes

to the tab stops affect all buffers unless you've made a local copy of the
`tab-stop-list` variable. The following command sets the tab stops.

[Meta] X `edit-tab-stops`
> Creates and selects a buffer containing a description of the tab
> stop settings. Assuming tab stops every three spaces, the buffer
> looks like this:

```
       :   :   :   :   :   :   :   :   :   :   :   :   :
       0           1           2           3           4   ...
       0123456789012345678901234567890123456789012345678901
       To install changes, type C-c C-c
```

> You can then set the colons to the positions you want. While
> editing this buffer, the key sequence '[Ctrl] C [Ctrl] C' is bound to
> the command `edit-tab-stops-note-changes`, which kills the
> buffer and saves your changes.

The positions of the tab stops are independent of the way that Emacs actually displays a tab character embedded in the text. For display purposes,
Emacs assumes that tab stops are in columns $1, n + 1, 2n + 1, \ldots$, where
n is the value of the variable `tab-width`. The default value of `tab-width`
is 8. When Emacs is deciding how to translate a [Tab] that you type into a
combination of spaces and recorded ⟨tab⟩ characters, it takes the value of
`tab-width` into account. If you change `tab-width`, the appearance of the
buffer is likely to change if the buffer contains any actual tab characters.

Converting between Tabs and Spaces. The following commands convert
tabs to spaces and vice versa:

[Meta] X `untabify`
> Converts all tabs to sequences of spaces so as to preserve the
> appearance of the text.

[Meta] X `tabify`
> Converts all sequences of three or more spaces to tabs so as to
> preserve the appearance of the text.

7.11 Operations on Rectangles

The Emacs rectangle commands operate on a rectangular region of a
buffer. They are particularly useful for working with multicolumn or tabular information.

You define a rectangle by placing the point at one corner of it and the
mark at the other corner. For instance, if the point is to the left of line 3,
column 7, and the mark is to the left of line 26, column 17, the rectangle
consists of columns 7–16 of lines 3–26. If any lines within the rectangle
don't already extend to the right edge of the rectangle, they are extended
as necessary with spaces.

The following commands operate on rectangles:

(Meta) X delete-rectangle

> Deletes the text in the rectangle, moving the text that was to the right of the rectangle leftward so that it occupies the vacated space.

(Meta) X kill-rectangle

> Like (Meta) X delete-rectangle, except that the rectangle is saved as the "last killed rectangle". Emacs remembers only a single killed rectangle.

(Meta) X yank-rectangle

> Inserts the last killed rectangle into the text with its upper left corner at the point. Existing text in the area occupied by the rectangle is moved rightward so that it starts just to the right of the newly inserted rectangle.

(Meta) X clear-rectangle

> Replaces all the text in the rectangle by spaces.

(Meta) X open-rectangle

> Like (Meta) X clear-rectangle, except that the text in the region occupied by the rectangle is moved rightward rather than blanked out.

In addition there are commands for copying a rectangle to or from a register (see Section 7.18.3).

7.12   Operations on Windows

This section describes commands that operate on windows. See Section 7.4.4 for a general discussion of windows.

7.12.1 Splitting Windows

The following commands split the selected window into two windows. Initially, each of the windows contains the same material as the parent window.

(Ctrl) X 2   Splits the selected window vertically into two windows (split-window-vertically). The new windows are one above the other and have the same width as the old one.

(Ctrl) X 5   Splits the selected window horizontally into two side-by-side windows (split-window-horizontally). The new windows have the same height as the old one and are separated by a column of vertical bars. It's usually better to force the text in a narrow window to be truncated rather than wrapped. You can get this effect by setting the variable truncate-partial-width-windows to 't' (see "Examining and Setting Variables" on page 312). The horizontal scrolling commands (see Section 7.8.2) are often useful with narrow windows.

7.12.2
Operations on
Other Windows

The windows on your screen have a particular order, generally from top to bottom and from left to right. By default, a window command applies to the next window; with an argument n, it applies to the nth window. For example, an argument of '-2' causes a next-window command to apply to the second previous window.

The following command enables you to select the next window:

(Ctrl) X o   Makes the next window the selected window (other-window). In the common case when there are just two windows, this command switches to the other window.

The following commands start a particular activity in the next window. If there is only one window, they create another one. The commands all start with (Ctrl) X 4—without the '4', they start the same activity in the selected window.

(Ctrl) X 4 (Ctrl) F
(Ctrl) X 4f   Visits a file in the next window (see p. 293).

(Ctrl) X 4b   Brings a particular buffer to the next window (see p. 298).

(Ctrl) X 4d   Starts Dired in the next window (see p. 297).

(Ctrl) X 4m   Starts composing a mail message in the next window (see p. 327).

(Ctrl) X 4.   Starts searching for a tag in another window (see p. 315).

The following commands perform other operations on the next window.

(Meta) (Ctrl) V
      Scrolls the next window down by one page, i.e., does a (Ctrl) V in that window (scroll-other-window).

(Meta) X compare-windows
      Compares the selected window with the next window, starting at the point. After the comparison, the point in each window is positioned at the first differing character.

7.12.3
Deleting and
Resizing Windows

The following commands remove a window or change its size:

(Ctrl) X 0   Deletes the selected window, redistributing the space that it occupies among the other windows (delete-window). Deleting a window does not kill the buffer associated with the window; the buffer remains available to be recalled to a window later.

(Ctrl) X 1   Deletes all windows other than the selected one (delete-other-windows).

(Ctrl) X ^   Makes the selected window taller by one line (enlarge-window). With an argument of n (n positive), enlarges the window by n lines; with an argument of n (n negative), reduces the window by n lines.

(Ctrl) X }   Makes the selected window wider by one column (enlarge-window-horizontally). With an argument of n (n positive), widens the window by n columns; with an argument of n (n negative), narrows the window by n columns.

7.13   Operations on Files

To edit a file, you must bring it into a buffer by *visiting* it. You can visit a file that doesn't exist in order to create it. When you've finished editing the copy of a file in a buffer, you can update the file by saving the buffer.

7.13.1 Specifying File Names

When you issue an Emacs command that requires a file name, Emacs displays a default directory in the minibuffer and prompts you for the rest of the name. If the file you want is in that directory, you can specify it by completing the name. If not, you can specify a different directory by editing the path name of the default directory. Often the simplest way to do that is to type the full path name of the file you want. Emacs will not be confused if the edited path name contains '//' or '~' somewhere in the middle as in

        /usr/genghis//etc/passwd

or

        /usr/mikhail/~boris/comrades

The first path name refers to /etc/passwd, the second to ~boris/ comrades. These path names would not be accepted by the usual UNIX shells.

You can type (Enter) in response to a request for a file name, asking Emacs to use the default file name. If the current buffer is associated with a file, Emacs uses the name of that file as the default. Otherwise it uses the current directory and either gives you a Dired (directory editor) buffer for that directory or complains.

You can insert the value of an environment variable *var* into a file name by typing '$*var*'. To refer to a file whose name includes '$', replace the '$' with '$$'.

Default Directory.   Each buffer has a default directory, which you can set or query with the following commands:

(Meta) X cd Sets the current directory to the pathname *dir*. Emacs prompts you for *dir*. You can use '~' to start the pathname with your home directory.

(Meta) X pwd
        Shows the pathname of the current (working) directory.

Whenever Emacs prompts you for a file name, it takes the default directory from the current buffer. If the current buffer happens to be, say, a help window, the current directory will be somewhere in the middle of the system Emacs files, not in your own files—a nuisance but not a disaster.

**7.13.2
Visiting Files**

The following commands visit a file:

⟨Ctrl⟩ X ⟨Ctrl⟩ F

> Visits a file, loading it into the selected window (`find-file`). Emacs prompts you for the name of the file. If a buffer doesn't already exist for the file, Emacs creates one and names it after the file, appending '[21~<2>', '<3>', etc. to the name if necessary to make it unique. If you visit a directory, Emacs starts the directory editor Dired for that directory in the selected window (see Section 7.14).

⟨Ctrl⟩ X 4 ⟨Ctrl⟩ F
⟨Ctrl⟩ X 4f   Visits a file and brings its buffer to the next window (`find-file-other-window`). Emacs prompts you for the file name.

⟨Ctrl⟩ X ⟨Ctrl⟩ R

> Visits a file in read-only mode, loading it into the selected window (`find-file-read-only`). Changes to the window are inhibited. You can turn off the read-only status with ⟨Ctrl⟩ X ⟨Ctrl⟩ Q, the `toggle-read-only` command (p. 267).

⟨Ctrl⟩ X ⟨Ctrl⟩ V

> Kills the current buffer, then visits a file as with `find-file` (`find-alternate-file`). If the current buffer contains unsaved modifications to a file, Emacs asks you for confirmation before killing the buffer. This command is useful when you've just visited the wrong file by accident.

In addition, the `find-file-other-window` command visits a file in the next window.

**7.13.3
Saving Regions and
Buffers to Files**

The following commands save part or all of a buffer in a file and perform related operations:

⟨Ctrl⟩ X ⟨Ctrl⟩ S

> Saves the contents of the current buffer in the file associated with that buffer (`save-buffer`). If no file is associated with the buffer, Emacs prompts you for one.

⟨Ctrl⟩ X s   Goes through the list of buffers that have been modified but not saved, asking you for each one if you want to save it (`save-some-buffers`).

⟨Meta⟩ X set-visited-file-name

> Associates the current buffer with a specified file, usually different from the one it's currently associated with. Emacs prompts you for the new file name. The buffer need not currently be associated with any file.

⟨Ctrl⟩ X ⟨Ctrl⟩ W

> Saves the current buffer to a specified file and associates the current buffer with that file from now on just as with the `set-visited-file-name` command (`write-file`). Emacs prompts you for the new file name.

(Meta) X `write-region`

> Writes the region to a specified file. Emacs prompts you for the file name. The file associated with the buffer is not changed.

(Meta) X `append-to-file`

> Like `write-region`, except that the region is appended to the specified file instead of replacing it.

(Meta) ~

> Marks the current buffer as "not modified", thus inhibiting Emacs from saving it automatically or complaining if you abandon it (`not-modified`). This command is useful when you've modified a file but don't want to save the modifications.

7.13.4
Inserting a File

The following command enables you to insert the contents of a file into a buffer:

(Ctrl) X i

> Inserts the contents of a specified file into the current buffer following the point (`insert-file`). Emacs prompts you for the name of the file.

7.13.5
Miscellaneous File Operations

The following command provides a listing of a directory or a set of files:

(Ctrl) X (Ctrl) D

> Creates a buffer containing a brief listing of a directory or a set of files (`list-directory`). Emacs prompts you for the name of a directory or a file name possibly containing wildcards. With an argument, this command gives you a verbose listing, by default the same one you obtain from '`ls -l`' (see Section 3.1.2).

Generally only the brief listing form is useful since you can obtain the verbose form just as easily with Dired (see Section 7.14).

The following commands provide various operations on files, unrelated to the contents of the Emacs buffers (although `view-file` uses a buffer temporarily). Most of these commands are also available through Dired.

(Meta) X `view-file`

> Scans a file without modifying it. The file is brought to a temporary buffer whose major mode is View. In View mode, certain keys are rebound as follows:

> | (Space) | Moves down by one screenful. |
> |---|---|
> | (Del) | Moves up by one screenful. |
> | (Ctrl) C | Exits from viewing, kills the view buffer. |

> Most other keys have their usual meanings, except that you can't modify the view buffer.

(Meta) X `copy-file`

> Copies the contents of a specified file to another file. Emacs prompts you for the names of both files.

(Meta) X `delete-file`

> Deletes a specified link to a file, just as you would with `rm` (see Section 3.9.1).

(Meta) X rename-file

> Renames a specified file, just as you would with mv (see Section 3.7.2). Emacs prompts you for the names of both files.

(Meta) X add-name-to-file

> Provides an additional name for a specified file, just as you would with ln (see Section 3.7.1). Emacs prompts you for the names of both files.

(Meta) X make-symbolic-link

> Provides an additional symbolic link to a specified file, provided that your system supports symbolic links (see p. 27). Emacs prompts you for the names of both files.

7.13.6 Automatically Saving, Recovering, and Backing Up Files

Emacs has two mechanisms for protecting you from accidentally losing files that you're working on: automatic backup and auto-saving.

- When you save a file and an older copy of that file already exists, Emacs saves the older copy in a backup file. You can create a series of numbered backup files if you wish.
- Periodically, Emacs saves all of the files you've visited in auto-save files, distinct from the backup files.

Either of these mechanisms may be disabled.

Backup Files. By default, Emacs makes a single backup file whenever you save a file and discards the previous backup file. If you save a buffer more than once, however, only the first save causes the backup file to be made—though if you kill the buffer and reread the file, you'll get a new backup. The backup file is named by adding a '~' to the name of the original file, so the backup file for stilton would be stilton~. Setting the variable make-backup-files to nil inhibits the creation of backup files (see "Examining and Setting Variables" on page 312).

You can also arrange to back up files more extensively by using numbered backup files. The backup files for the file ricotta would be named ricotta.~1~, ricotta.~2~, etc. You can activate numbered backups by setting the version-control variable. Its possible values are as follows:

t   Make numbered backups.

nil   Make numbered backups only for files that already have them; make single backups for all other files. (This is the default.)

'never   Never make numbered backups, but always make single backups.

Emacs does not reuse version numbers for backup files—the newest numbered backup always has a version number one higher than the highest existing one.

When Emacs creates a new numbered backup, it normally keeps the oldest two versions (usually '.~1~' and '.~2~') and the newest two, deleting any in the middle after asking you. The following variables affect which versions Emacs keeps:

kept-old-versions

> How many of the oldest versions to keep (default 2).

`kept-new-versions`
> How many of the newest versions to keep (default 2).

`trim-versions-without-asking`
> If non-`nil`, middle versions are deleted without a confirmation query.

You can restore a file from one of its backups either by renaming the backup to the original file name using the `rename-file` command or by visiting the backup file with the Ctrl X Ctrl F command and saving it under the original name.

Auto-Saving.   Auto-saving provides protection against disasters such as killing Emacs by mistake and power failures. Periodically, Emacs saves the contents of each file you edit in an auto-save file. The auto-save file is independent of any backup files. The name of the auto-save file for `camembert` is `#camembert#`. By default, auto-save takes place every 300 keystrokes. The default interval is recorded in the variable `auto-save-interval`. You can also auto-save a file explicitly with the Meta X `do-auto-save` command.

You can recover an auto-save file with the `recover-file` command (type Meta X `recover-file`), which visits a file and then restores it (after confirmation) from its auto-saved version. Saving the current buffer with Ctrl C Ctrl S then causes the recovered file to become the current version of the file in question. In addition, the `revert-buffer` command (see p. 299) offers to revert to the auto-save file rather than the original file if the auto-save file is newer than the original file.

Auto-saving is a minor mode, controlled by the `auto-save-mode` command (see p. 267).

7.14   Directory Operations with Dired

Emacs provides a directory editor called Dired that you can use to operate on files. When you start Dired, it asks you to specify the directory you wish to edit according to the usual conventions for specifying file names (see Section 7.13.1). You may provide a file name instead of a directory name; the file name may contain wildcards.

Once started, Dired lists the files in that directory or set of files, using the same "long" format as the '`ls -l`' command (see Section 3.1.2). You can then operate on one or more listed files, selecting a file by moving the cursor to the line where it appears.

Several Dired buffers can be active at the same time. Viewing a directory with the Dired '`v`' command creates a new Dired buffer for that directory; you cannot, however, switch an existing Dired buffer to a different directory.

Note: If you change the contents of the directory in a Dired buffer from outside Emacs, the information in the buffer will not reflect the change. To update the buffer, issue the Meta X `revert-buffer` command.

7.14.1 Starting Dired

The following commands start Dired, either in the selected window or in another window:

Ctrl X d — Creates a Dired buffer in the selected window (`dired`).

Ctrl X 4d — Creates a Dired buffer in the next window (`dired-other-window`).

For each of these commands, Emacs prompts you for the directory name.

In addition, visiting a directory causes Emacs to start up Dired for that directory.

7.14.2 Getting Help

The following command provides help on Dired:

`?` — Provides a brief listing of Dired commands on the echo line. This listing is not complete.

7.14.3 Moving Around the Listing

The following commands move you to the next or previous line in the listing:

Space
Ctrl N
`n` — Moves to the beginning of the file name on the next line.

Ctrl P
`p` — Moves to the beginning of the file name on the previous line.

You can also use any of the usual commands for buffer navigation, including search commands.

7.14.4 Deleting Files

To delete a file, you first flag it for deletion and later delete all flagged files. The following commands provide for the flagging and for the actual deletion:

`d` — Flags this file for later deletion.

`u` — Removes the deletion flag on this line.

Del — Removes the deletion flag on this line, if any, and moves up one line.

`#` — Flags all auto-save files. An autosave file has a name that starts and ends with '`#`' (see "Auto-Saving" on page 296).

`~` — Flags all backup files. A backup file has a name that ends with '`~`' (see "Backup Files" on page 295).

`.` — Flags excess numbered backup files (see "Backup Files" on page 295). The excess files are those that are neither oldest nor newest.

`x` — Deletes all flagged files.

7.14.5 Other File Operations

The following commands provide other operations on files. They all apply to the file on the current line.

`f` — Visits this file. If you visit a directory, Emacs creates another Dired buffer for it. For instance, if you visit the '`..`' file, Emacs creates a Dired buffer for the parent directory of the one you're now examining.

o	Visits this file in another window.
v	Views this file using the `view-file` command described above.
c	Copies this file. Emacs prompts you for the destination file.
r	Renames this file. Emacs prompts you for the new name.

7.15   Explicit Operations on Buffers

Nearly all Emacs operations affect buffers in one way or another. In this section we describe Emacs operations that explicitly relate to buffers. Section 7.16 describes the buffer menu, a facility for operating on a list of buffers in a window.

7.15.1 Specifying a Buffer Name

When Emacs prompts you for a buffer name, the default is the buffer that was previously in the selected window. If you specify a buffer that doesn't already exist, Emacs creates a new empty buffer by that name (in Fundamental mode). You can type a prefix of a buffer name followed by a tab or space to get Emacs to complete the name automatically (see Section 7.5.3). But if you just type the prefix of a name and then press (Enter), Emacs takes the prefix as the entire name of the buffer—usually not what you want.

7.15.2 Bringing a Buffer into a Window

The following commands bring a specified buffer into a window:

(Ctrl) X b   Brings a specified buffer into the current window (`switch-to-buffer`). Emacs prompts you for the buffer name.

(Ctrl) X 4b   Brings a specified buffer into the next window (`switch-to-buffer-other-window`). Emacs prompts you for the buffer name.

7.15.3 Killing Buffers

The following command kills a specified buffer:

(Ctrl) X k   Kills a specified buffer (`kill-buffer`). Emacs prompts you for the buffer name; the default is the current buffer. If the current buffer is associated with a file and has been modified, Emacs asks you for confirmation before performing the kill.

You can also use the (Meta) X `kill-some-buffers` command to kill buffers (see p. 298).

The following command provides a convenient way of getting rid of buffers you don't want, as an alternative to calling up a buffer menu.

(Meta) X `kill-some-buffers`

Goes through the list of buffers, asking you for each one if you want to kill it. Emacs tells you if a buffer has been modified; if you kill it anyway, your changes will be lost (although you still may be able to recover most of them from an auto-save file).

<table>
<tr><td>

**7.15.4
Positions and
Counts**

</td><td>

The following commands enable you to find your position in the buffer:

</td></tr>
</table>

(Ctrl) X =   Shows the position of the point (as a character number) on the echo line (`what-cursor-position`).

(Meta) X `what-line`
  Shows the current line number on the echo line.

(Meta) X `what-page`
  Shows the current page number, and line number within the page, on the echo line. For the purposes of this command, pages are considered to be delimited by ⟨formfeed⟩ characters.

The following related commands count the lines in the region or in the current page:

(Meta) =   Counts the number of lines in the region (`count-lines-region`).

(Ctrl) X l   Counts the number of lines in the current page, which is delimited by ⟨formfeed⟩s (`count-lines-page`). This command also shows the number of lines before and after the point.

**7.15.5
Narrowing a Buffer**

Narrowing a buffer is useful when you want to work with only a portion of it, e.g., for restricting the scope of a search and replace operation. When you narrow a buffer, only the narrowed portion is visible and motion commands are restricted to that portion. However, the invisible portion is not lost; if you ask to save a buffer when it's narrowed, Emacs saves the entire buffer, not just the visible part.

(Ctrl) X n   Narrows the buffer to the region between the point and the mark (`narrow-to-region`).

(Ctrl) X w   Widens the buffer to its full extent (`widen`).

The `narrow-to-region` command is normally disabled (see Section 7.5.7). If you try to use it, you're given the opportunity to enable it either temporarily or permanently.

**7.15.6
Other Operations**

The following commands provide other operations on buffers:

(Meta) X `revert-buffer`
  Restores the contents of the buffer from its associated file, discarding all changes. If an auto-save file newer than the associated file exists, Emacs asks you if you want to revert to the auto-save file instead, thereby keeping all but your most recent changes.

(Meta) X `rename-buffer`
  Gives the current buffer a new name. Emacs prompts you for the new name. Renaming a buffer does not change the name of the file associated with the buffer, so saving the buffer saves to the same file as before.

(Meta) X `view-buffer`
  Changes the major mode of the current buffer to View mode.

In View mode the buffer becomes read-only, but a few keys are
rebound to make it easier to scan through the buffer:

Space	Moves down one page.
Del	Moves up one page.
Ctrl C	Reverts to the previous major mode, preserving the position of the point.
?	Displays a list of available commands.

7.16   The Buffer Menu

A buffer menu lists all the buffers and enables you to perform operations
on them. Here is an example of what a buffer menu looks like:

```
MR Buffer          Size  Mode           File
-- ------          ----  ----           ----
.  % shrink.c      1974  C              /usr/alice/shrink.c
   % *info*        50661 Info
*    cheshire.tex  109585 Text          /usr/alice/cheshire.tex
     *scratch*     0            Lisp Interaction
*    *Buffer List* 351          Buffer Menu
```

Here is what the indications in the first three columns mean:

.	The buffer selected before the buffer menu itself.
*	File has been modified.
%	File is read-only.

A buffer containing a buffer menu is in the Buffer Menu major mode and
is named '`*Buffer List*`' unless you forcibly change its name. Ordinarily
at most one buffer contains a buffer menu.

7.16.1 Creating or Selecting a Buffer Menu

The following commands create a buffer menu and select a buffer menu
if it already exists:

Meta X buffer-menu

Displays a buffer menu in another window and selects it. The
buffer menu is created if it doesn't already exist.

Ctrl X Ctrl B

Displays a buffer menu in another window but doesn't select it.
The buffer menu is created if it doesn't already exist.

7.16.2 Operations on a Buffer Menu

When you select a buffer menu, Emacs puts you into Buffer Menu mode
in which certain ordinary keys are bound to commands as described below. Typing '?' causes Emacs to display explanations of the buffer menu
commands in another window. The window goes away when you type a
command.

Vertical Motions.   The following keys provide vertical motions:

(Space)   Moves down one line.

(Del)   Moves up one line.

Deleting and Saving Buffers.   The following commands enable you to flag buffers for deletion or saving, to remove the flags, and to carry out the operations specified by the flags. A buffer flagged for deletion is marked with 'D', while one flagged for saving is marked with 'S'. Flagging a buffer does not cause Emacs to delete or save it immediately; Emacs postpones these actions until you call for them with an 'x' command.

    The following commands are available from a buffer menu:

(Ctrl) K
d
k   Flags this buffer for deletion and moves down one line.

(Ctrl) D   Flags this buffer for deletion and moves up one line.

s   Flags this buffer for saving.

u   Removes all deletion and save requests from this line and moves down one line.

x   Performs all outstanding deletion and save requests.

~   Marks this buffer as unmodified. This marking is not a request for action; its effect is to prevent the buffer from being saved in its current state (since Emacs doesn't carry out a save action on an unmodified buffer).

Assigning Buffers to Windows.   The following commands enable you to choose which buffers occupy windows. All of them except 'm' cause the buffer menu to be deselected. In each case the buffer referred to as "this buffer" is the one on the line containing the cursor.

1   Selects this buffer in a full-screen window.

2   Sets up two windows, one containing this buffer and the other containing the buffer that was replaced by the buffer list (so the buffer displaced by the buffer list returns to the screen).

f   Replaces the buffer list by this buffer.

o   Selects this buffer in another window, leaving the buffer list visible.

q   Selects this buffer and displays any buffers marked with 'm' in other windows. If no other buffers are marked with 'm', this buffer is displayed in a full-size window.

m   Marks this buffer so that the 'q' command will display it. The mark appears as an 'm' in the buffer list.

7.17   Printing

The following commands print either a buffer or a region. You can attach page headings to the printed output or print it as is.

(Meta) X print-buffer
> Prints the entire buffer with page headings.

(Meta) X print-region
> Prints the region with page headings.

(Meta) X lpr-buffer
> Prints the entire buffer as is, without automatically attaching page headings.

(Meta) X lpr-region
> Prints the region as is.

Printing is done with the 'lpr -p' command if you ask for page headings and with the 'lpr' command otherwise. The command doesn't actually cause the printing to happen—it merely places the output on the print queue. You can add other options to the 'lpr' command by assigning them to the variable lpr-switches (see "Examining and Setting Variables" on page 312). The 'lpr' commands work on almost any system, but the print commands may not work on systems that use 'lp' as their print spooler.[13]

7.18   Registers and Their Operations

A *register* is a place where you can store a position, a portion of text, or a rectangle. A particular register can hold only one of these at a time. Each register has a name, which can be any printable character. Retrieving the contents of a register does not disturb the register's contents.

7.18.1
Viewing Register
Contents

The following command shows you what is in a register:

(Meta) X view-register (Enter) r
> Displays the contents and type of register r.

7.18.2
Saving and
Retrieving Positions

The following commands save a position in a register or move to a position specified by a register. The position includes both a buffer and a point location within that buffer.

(Ctrl) X / r   Saves the location of the point from the selected window in register r (point-to-register).

---

13. The reason for this strange state of affairs is that the Emacs implementation translates 'lpr' to 'lp' when necessary, but it doesn't account properly for the '-p' option, which 'lp' doesn't recognize.

(Ctrl) X j *r*   Restores the location recorded in register *r* (`register-to-point`). If the stored location is from a different buffer, that buffer is brought to the selected window.

7.18.3
Saving and
Retrieving Text
Using Registers

The following commands save text in a register or restore text from a register. The text can be either ordinary text or a rectangle (see Section 7.11).

(Ctrl) X x   Copies the text contained in the region into register *r* (`copy-to-register`). If you provide an argument, the copied text is deleted from the buffer.

(Ctrl) X r *r*   Copies the rectangle defined by the point and the mark into register *r* (`copy-region-to-rectangle`). If you provide an argument, the copied rectangle is deleted from the buffer.

(Ctrl) X g *r*   Inserts the text or rectangle stored in register *r* into the text (`insert-register`). The type of the register's contents determine the nature of the insertion. The effect is the same as `yank` or (Meta) X `yank-rectangle`.

7.19   Composing and Editing Pictures

Emacs has a special major mode, Picture mode, for editing pictures made out of text characters. In Picture mode, the buffer is treated as an area with its upper left corner at the beginning of the document, extending indefinitely to the right and downward. Lines are extended by adding spaces at the right end whenever they are needed. In Picture mode you cannot tell where the right end of a line is; you only know where its rightmost nonblank character is.

To fit this model, Picture mode rebinds a number of keys to commands appropriate to the mode. For instance, (Ctrl) F always moves one position to the right—if you move past the actual end of the line, Emacs assumes that the positions you pass over contain spaces. In contrast, in an ordinary mode (Ctrl) F moves to the beginning of the next line when you reach the end of a line. In Picture mode, tab characters within the text are treated as though they were expanded to spaces.

Picture mode is designed so that you can edit a picture as part of a larger document, leaving the rest of the document undisturbed. You can restrict the effects of Picture mode, however, by using the (Ctrl) X n command to narrow the document to the region of interest (see Section 7.15.5).

7.19.1
Entering and
Leaving Picture
Mode

The following commands enable you to enter and leave Picture mode:

(Meta) X `edit-picture`
    Enters Picture mode, remembering the mode that you were previously in .

(Ctrl) C (Ctrl) C
    Leaves Picture mode, restoring the major mode previously in

effect (`picture-mode-exit`). This command also strips trailing spaces from the end of each line, even if the spaces were there before you entered Picture mode.

7.19.2
Moving around a Picture

The following commands have very similar effects to the corresponding commands in non-Picture mode s. Whenever a horizontal motion command encounters a tab character, it converts the tab to a sequence of spaces.

[Ctrl] F   Moves one column to the right (`picture-forward-column`). This command never moves to a new line.

[Ctrl] B   Moves one column to the left (`picture-backward-column`). If the left end of the line is reached, no further motion takes place.

[Ctrl] N   Moves down one line (`picture-move-down`). This command preserves the columnar position no matter what the actual length of the line that it moves to.

[Ctrl] P   Moves up one line (`picture-move-up`). This command preserves the columnar position no matter what the actual length of the line that it moves to.

[Enter]   Moves to the beginning of the next line (`picture-newline`).

7.19.3
Inserting New Lines

The following commands insert new lines into the picture.

[Ctrl] J
[LnFd]   Makes a copy of the current line underneath the current line and moves down to the same column position on that line (`picture-duplicate-line`). This command is not affected by arguments.

[Ctrl] O   Inserts an empty line immediately below the current line (`picture-open-line`).

7.19.4
Erasing Parts of a Picture

[Del]   Replaces the preceding character with a space (`picture-backward-clear-column`). The point moves left by one position.

[Ctrl] D   Replaces the character under the cursor with a space (`picture-clear-column`). Unlike the previous command, *the point does not move.* With an argument of n, this command clears out n characters—but the point still remains in the same place.

[Ctrl] K   Erases the portion of the current line to the right of the point (`picture-clear-line`). Unlike the usual `clear-line` command, this one never erases newlines.

[Ctrl] C [Ctrl] D
   Deletes the character under the cursor (`delete-char`). This command has the same meaning as usual; it's just bound to a different key sequence.

In addition to these commands, the [Ctrl] W (`delete-region`) command works as usual.

**7.19.5
Linear Motions**

The following commands set the direction of motion after an insertion. For instance, if you type '(Ctrl)C***' you produce a sequence of stars moving diagonally down and right. Note that motion to the right or down is unbounded.

(Ctrl)C<   Moves left after each insertion (`picture-movement-left`).

(Ctrl)C>   Moves right after each insertion (`picture-movement-right`).

(Ctrl)C^   Moves up after each insertion (`picture-movement-up`).

(Ctrl)C.   Moves down after each insertion (`picture-movement-down`).

(Ctrl)C'   Moves up and to the right after each insertion (`picture-movement-ne`).

(Ctrl)C`    Moves up and to the left after each insertion (`picture-movement-nw`).

(Ctrl)C\   Moves down and to the right after each insertion (`picture-movement-se`).

(Ctrl)C/   Moves down and to the left after each insertion (`picture-movement-sw`).

The following commands move in the current direction of motion without changing anything. They provide a convenient way of moving along a line drawn with the commands above.

(Ctrl)Cf   Moves by one unit along the direction of motion (`picture-motion`).

(Ctrl)Cb   Moves by one unit backwards along the direction of motion (`picture-motion-reverse`).

**7.19.6
Tab-based
Operations**

In Picture mode, Emacs recognizes a context-based form of tabbing in which tab stops are assumed at each position occupied by an "interesting" character. By default the interesting characters are the nonblank printing characters, but you can change this set by assigning a character string containing the desired characters to the variable `picture-tab-chars` (see "Examining and Setting Variables" on page 312). You must be in Picture mode when you make the assignment.

These are the tab-based operations:

(Tab)   Moves to the next tab stop (`picture-tab`). With an argument, blanks out the text that it moves over. The value of the argument is irrelevant. Initially the tab stops are at the positions that they had when you entered Picture mode, but you can reset them with the (Ctrl)C (Tab) command below.

(Ctrl)C (Tab)   Sets a tab stop at each position occupied by an "interesting" character on the current line (`picture-set-tab-stops`). These tab stops remain in effect even when you move to a different line.

(Meta) (Tab)   Moves to the position underneath the next "interesting" character that follows whitespace in the previous nonblank line (`picture-tab-search`). With an argument, moves to the next "interesting" character in the current line. The value of the argument is irrelevant. This command never modifies the buffer.

7.19.7 Rectangle-based Operations

The following commands that operate on rectangles are analogous to their non-rectangle counterparts, which are also available and sometimes useful (see Section 7.11):

[Ctrl] C [Ctrl] K

> Kills and clears the rectangle defined by the region, leaving the rest of the picture undisturbed (`picture-clear-rectangle`). With an argument, deletes the rectangle and moves the material to its right leftward.

[Ctrl] C [Ctrl] W *r*

> Clears the rectangle defined by the region as in the previous command, but saves its contents in register *r* (`picture-clear-rectangle-to-register`).

[Ctrl] C [Ctrl] Y

> Copies the last killed rectangle into the picture, aligning its upper left corner with the point and overwriting whatever was previously in the picture (`picture-yank-rectangle`). With an argument, moves the material previously in the area occupied by the rectangle to the right so that it isn't lost.

[Ctrl] C [Ctrl] X *r*

> Copies the rectangle from register *r* as in the previous command (`picture-yank-rectangle-from-register`).

7.20   Searching and Replacing

Emacs has two types of search commands: incremental and nonincremental. Incremental search is usually more convenient, although you can't use it in conjunction with replacement. You can search for a regular expression as well as for a specific string. You can also use a regular expression when you're doing a replacement. You can perform a replacement with or without querying each occurrence of the string you're replacing; you have this option both when replacing strings and when replacing regular expressions.

Searches are normally case-insensitive, so for example the search string 'hermes' matches 'Hermes', 'HERMES', and 'HerMes'. You can make searches case-sensitive by setting the variable `case-fold-search` to `nil` (see "Examining and Setting Variables" on page 312). Setting this variable in one buffer does not affect any other buffer.

The search commands all start at the point and continue to the end of the buffer. They don't provide any method of restricting the search to just a portion of the rest of the buffer. However, you can get that effect easily enough with the (Ctrl)X n (narrow-to-region) command (see Section 7.15.5).

7.20.1
Incremental Search

In an incremental search, Emacs starts searching as soon as you type even a single character in the search string. These are the commands for ordinary incremental search:

(Ctrl)S   Searches forward incrementally (isearch-forward).

(Ctrl)R   Searches backward incrementally (isearch-backward).

As soon as you type one of these commands, Emacs prompts you for the search string. In addition to these commands, you can perform an incremental search for a regular expression (see Section 7.20.4).

The most striking property of incremental search is that you often find the string you're searching for before you've typed the entire search string. Suppose you are searching for the next occurrence of the string 'schlock.' You start the search by typing '(Ctrl)S s'. Emacs immediately positions you just after the next 's'. You now type 'c', and Emacs positions you just after the next 'sc'. If the first 's' was immediately followed by a 'c', the point moves by just one character. Typing 'h' causes Emacs to look for the next 'sch', and so forth. When you've typed enough letters to locate the next 'schlock', you end the search by typing (Esc).

The effects of typing various characters in the search string are as follows:

(*any printable or other non-command character*)
    Adds this character to the search string and looks for the next occurrence of the search string.

(Esc)   Terminates the search. The mark is set to the point, which is at the end of the matched string. Typing (Esc) as the first character of the search string gives you a nonincremental search (see Section 7.20.2).

(Ctrl)S   Searches for the next occurrence of the search string so far. If your search finds a different occurrence than the one you're looking for, (Ctrl)S enables you to get to the right one. If you type (Ctrl)S after a failed search, Emacs performs a wrapped search, starting at the beginning of the buffer.

    If you type (Ctrl)S as the very first character of the search string, Emacs searches for the string from the previous search. In this case you can't edit the search string.

(Ctrl)R   Searches for the previous occurrence of the search string (as typed so far).

(Del)   Deletes the last character of the search string. Emacs moves the point back to the previous string that it found. When you repeat a search using the previous search string, however, attempting to delete part of that search string deletes all of it.

(Ctrl)G   The effect of (Ctrl)G depends on the context:

    • If you've just found the search string, it cancels the search.

- If the search string has not been found, it deletes all characters in the search string that you've typed since the last successful match—or all characters in the search string if there hasn't yet been a successful match. There are two reasons why the search string might not have been found: it doesn't exist, or it exists but Emacs is still looking for it. (Ctrl) G produces the same effect in either case.

It follows from the description above that (Ctrl) G (Ctrl) G always cancels the search. A cancelled search reverts the point to where it was before the search.

(Ctrl) W   Adds the word (or the rest of the word) following the point to the search string.

(Ctrl) Y   Adds the rest of the line following the point to the search string.

To search for a character such as (Ctrl) S or (Del), quote it with (Ctrl) Q.

7.20.2 Nonincremental Search

The following commands perform nonincremental searches:

(Ctrl) S (Esc)

    Performs a forward nonincremental search for a specified string (`search-forward`). Emacs prompts you for the string.

(Ctrl) R (Esc)

    Performs a backward nonincremental search for a specified string (`search-backward`). Emacs prompts you for the string.

In either case, if you type (Ctrl) W as the first character of the search string, you get a word search (see Section 7.20.3).

The nonincremental search commands don't include a feature for repeating a search, but you can conveniently repeat a search with the (Ctrl) X (Esc) (`repeat-complex-command`) command.

7.20.3 Word Search

A word search searches for a sequence of words. The words may be separated by single spaces, newlines, tabs, punctuation, or sequences of these characters. For instance, the command

    (Ctrl) S (Esc) (Ctrl) W `fat.cat\enter`

finds any of the following:

```
fat cat
fat   cat
fat-cat
Fat, Cat
```

These are the word search commands:

(Ctrl) S (Esc) (Ctrl) W

    Searches forward nonincrementally for a specified sequence of words (`word-search-forward`). Emacs prompts you for the string.

(Ctrl) R (Esc) (Ctrl) W

    Searches backward nonincrementally for a specified sequence of words (`word-search-backward`). Emacs prompts you for the string.

**7.20.4
Regular Expression
Search**

The following commands perform a search for a regular expression (see "Regular Expressions in Emacs" below). You can search either incrementally or nonincrementally.

(Meta) (Ctrl) S
> Searches incrementally in the forward direction for a regular expression (isearch-forward-regexp).

(Meta) X isearch-backward-regexp
> Searches backward incrementally for a regular expression.

(Meta) X re-search-forward
> Searches forward nonincrementally for a regular expression.

(Meta) X re-search-backward
> Searches backward nonincrementally for a regular expression.

Emacs prompts you for the characters of an incremental search expression or for the entire expression string of a nonincremental search in the same way that it does for the versions of these commands that work with plain strings. Adding characters to the regular expression of an incremental search does not cause the cursor to move in the opposite direction, even though a match might be found earlier (since adding characters to a regular expression can enlarge the set of matching strings).

You can repeat an incremental search for a regular expression. Having found one occurrence, you can find another one by typing '(Ctrl) S' (not '(Meta) (Ctrl) S'). To repeat an earlier incremental search for a regular expression, type '(Meta) (Ctrl) S (Ctrl) S'.

Regular Expressions in Emacs.   Regular expressions in Emacs are an extension of the basic UNIX set (see Section 2.16), although the Emacs regular expressions don't include the '\{...\}' notation described there. The following characters act as metacharacters with special meanings when they appear unquoted in a regular expression:

.	Matches any single character.
*	Matches the preceding regular expression repeated zero or more times.
+	Matches the preceding regular expression repeated one or more times.
?	Matches the preceding regular expression zero or one times.
[*str*]	Matches any character in the set of characters specified by *str* according to the usual conventions (see p. 51).
∧	At the beginning of a regular expression, matches an empty string at the beginning of a line; in any other context, matches a '∧' character.[14]
$	At the end of a regular expression, matches an empty string at the end of a line; in any other context, matches a '$' character.
c	Matches the character *c* unless it is one of the special constructs listed below. The characters that need to be quoted with '\\' are (. * + ? [\\ ).

---

14. A regular expression such as 'a?∧Q' does not match a 'Q' at the beginning of a line.

A regular expression can also include the following "quoted" constructs:

$a\backslash|b$ Matches either *a* or *b*. '\|' applies to the largest possible expressions *a* and *b*.

\(*expr* \)

Matches the regular expression *expr*. The parentheses provide grouping. Parenthesized expressions can be referred to later using the '\n' notation.

\n Matches the *n*th parenthesized expression, which must come earlier in the regular expression. The variable *n* must be a single decimal digit.

\' Matches an empty string at the beginning of the buffer.

\' Matches an empty string at the end of the buffer.

\b Matches an empty string at the beginning or end of a word. For example, the regular expression '\bfa\(cts\|x\)' matches either of the words 'facts' and 'fax'.

\B Matches an empty string that is *not* at the beginning or end of a word.

\< Matches an empty string at the beginning of a word.

\> Matches an empty string at the end of a word.

\w Matches any character that can be part of a word.

\W Matches any character that cannot be part of a word.

\x*code* Matches any character whose syntax code is *code* (see Section 7.4.8).

\X*code* Matches any character whose syntax code differs from *code*.

**7.20.5
Replacement**

The replacement commands search for a string and replace it with another string. The replacement starts at the point and continues to the end of the buffer. You can carry out the replacement unconditionally or with querying. The `narrow` command, Ctrl X n, is often very convenient in conjunction with the replacement commands in order to restrict the search and replacement to a particular part of the buffer (see Section 7.15.5).

If the replacement string for a replacement command is entirely in lowercase, the replacement preserves case: if a word is entirely in uppercase its replacement is translated to full uppercase, while if a word starts with an uppercase letter its replacement also starts with an uppercase letter. For instance, if the search string is 'cheddar' and the replacement string is 'tilsit', then 'CHEDDAR' is replaced by 'TILSIT' and 'Cheddar' or 'ChedDar' is replaced by 'Cheddar'. Setting the variable `case-replace` to nil inhibits the case conversion (see "Examining and Setting Variables" on page 312).

Unconditional Replacement. These are the commands for an unconditional replacement:

Meta X replace-string

Replaces each occurrence of a specified string with another specified string. Emacs prompts you for both strings. The search for occurrences begins at the point and continues to the end of the buffer.

[Meta] X replace-regexp

> Like replace-string, except that it searches for a regular expression rather than for a string. Within the replacement expression you can use the following notations:

\&	The entire string matching the regular expression.
\n	The string matching the nth parenthesized expression in the regular expression.
\\	The character '\'.

Replacement with Querying.   These are the commands for replacement with querying:

[Meta] %   Replaces each occurrence of a specified string with another specified string, querying each replacement (query-replace).

[Meta] X query-replace-regexp

> Like the previous command, except that this one searches for a regular expression rather than for a string. The notations described above for replace-regexp apply to this command also.

These are the possible responses to the query:

[Ctrl] H
?   Displays a list of the possible responses.

y
[Space]   Performs the replacement.

n
[Del]   Skips this occurrence.

,   Replaces this occurrence and displays the result. If you now type [Ctrl] R, you can edit the replacement. After this command, [Space] and [Del] respectively accept and reject the replacement.

[Esc]   Exits without doing any more replacements.

.   Performs this replacement, then exits.

!   Replaces all remaining occurrences without asking.

^   Returns to the previous occurrence (but doesn't undo it). You can then edit that occurrence with [Ctrl] R. This command only remembers the immediately preceding occurrence, so you cannot issue it twice in a row.

[Ctrl] R   Enters a recursive edit, enabling you to edit the text in the neighborhood of the text that matched the search string. (see Section 7.5.6). You can exit from the recursive edit with [Meta] [Ctrl] C.

[Ctrl] W   Like [Ctrl] R, except that the replacement string is not inserted before the recursive edit starts.

[Ctrl] L   Redisplays the screen, then asks again.

**7.20.6
Searching for
Matching Lines**

The following commands search from the point to the end of the buffer, looking for lines that match a specified regular expression. Emacs prompts you for the regular expression.

(Meta) X occur
(Meta) X list-matching-lines

> Opens an Occur buffer and lists in it each line in the current buffer matching a specified regular expression. Each line in the listing is preceded by its line number. The search for matching lines starts at the point and runs to the end of the buffer.

(Meta) X count-matches

> Counts the number of lines following the point that include a string matching a specified regular expression.

(Meta) X delete-matching-lines

> Deletes each line between the point and the end of the buffer that contains a match for a specified regular expression.

(Meta) X delete-non-matching-lines

> Deletes each line between the point and the end of the buffer that does *not* contain a match for a specified regular expression.

7.21   Operations on Variables

A variable can be either local (particular to a single buffer) or global (common to all buffers). A reference to a variable looks first for a local copy and then for a global one. A variable may have different values in different buffers and may be local to some buffers but not to others. Option variables provide adjustments to Emacs's behavior; other variables are used for internal recordkeeping (see Section 7.4.7).

Examining and Setting Variables. You can use the following commands to examine or set the value of a variable. You can also use the (Esc) (Esc) command for these purposes (see p. 314) and the help command (Ctrl) H v (see p. 273) to see the value and documentation of a variable.

(Meta) X set-variable

> Sets a specified variable to a specified value. Emacs prompts you for both the variable and the value. The effect is local if the current buffer has a local variable by that name, global otherwise.
>
> You can use the LISP operator `setq-default` to set the global value of a variable independently of its local value. For example, typing
>
> (Esc) (Esc) `(setq-default fill-column 60)`

sets the fill column to 60 globally, leaving the local value undisturbed. Section 7.22 discusses the evaluation of LISP expressions such as this one.

(Meta) X list-options
> Displays a buffer giving the name, value, and documentation of each option variable .

(Meta) X edit-options
> Creates a List Options buffer and edits it in Options mode. The editing commands make it easy to change and set values. The "nearby" variable is the one that the point is in or near.

n	Moves to the next variable.
p	Moves to the previous value.
s	Sets the nearby variable to a specified value, which Emacs prompts you for.
0	Sets the nearby variable to nil.
1	Sets the nearby variable to t (the canonical non-nil value).
x	Toggles the nearby variable between nil and t.

Creating and Removing Local Variables. The following operations relate to creating and removing local variables in the current buffer:

(Meta) X make-local-variable
> Reads the name of a variable and makes that variable local to the current buffer.

(Meta) X kill-local-variable
> Reads the name of a variable and removes its local copy so that references to the variable within the current buffer become references to the global variable.

(Meta) X make-variable-buffer-local
> Reads the name of a variable and arranges for it to become local when it is next set. Until then, Emacs uses the value of the global variable. If the variable is already local, this command has no effect.

7.22 Evaluating LISP Expressions

In this section we explain a few basic aspects of LISP. A full discussion of LISP is outside the scope of this book,

7.22.1
LISP Expressions

A LISP expression, also called a *sexp*, is either an *atom* or a parenthesized list. An apostrophe (') in front of an expression quotes that expression; the value of a quoted expression is the expression itself.

Certain atoms stand for themselves. Evaluating such an atom yields the atom again. The following kinds of atoms stand for themselves:

- String literals in double quotes, e.g., `"rock 'n roll"`.
- Numbers.
- The special atoms 't' (true) and 'nil' (false).

Evaluating a quoted atom such as `'never` yields that atom, unquoted. Other atoms are *symbols*; a variable is one kind of symbol.

A parenthesized list contains a function name or other LISP operator followed by the arguments of the function. Since the arithmetic operators are functions, the value of the LISP expression

```
(+ (* 8 4) (* 3 5) 5)
```

is 52. A particularly useful operator is `setq`; evaluating the form '(setq *var expr*)' evaluates the expression *expr* and assigns its value to the variable *var*. For example, evaluating

```
(setq case-fold-search nil)
```

sets the variable `case-fold-search` to `nil` and causes string searches to be case-sensitive (see p. 306).

You can quote a parenthesized list as well as an atom. The value of the quoted list is the unquoted list. A quoted list is data and thus need not start with the name of an operation.

7.22.2
Commands for Evaluating LISP Expressions

The following commands evaluate one or more LISP expressions:

Esc Esc   Interactively evaluates a LISP expression (`eval-expression`). Emacs prompts you for the expression. This command provides an easy way to retrieve or set the value of an Emacs variable. If you respond to the prompt with a variable, you see its value; if you respond with a 'setq' expression as described above, you assign a value to a variable.

Ctrl X Ctrl E
          Evaluates the LISP expression preceding the point (`eval-last-sexp`). That expression is either an atom or a parenthesis-balanced portion of text.

LnFd   In Lisp Interaction mode, evaluates the LISP expression preceding the point and inserts its value in front of the point (`eval-print-last-sexp`).

Meta X `eval-region`
          Evaluates all the expressions in the region, discarding the results.

Meta X `eval-current-buffer`
          Evaluates all the expressions in the current buffer, discarding the results.

7.23 Tags and Tag Tables

A *tag table* is a file that describes and locates definitions of textual units within a set of files. The nature of the definitions depends on what is in the files: for example, for C or LISP programs, the definitions include C or LISP functions, while for LATEX text they are LATEX commands such as \section or \cite. You can create an Emacs tag table with the UNIX command

　　　　etags *file* ...

where *file* ... is a list of files to be analyzed. This command creates a file named TAGS in the current directory that contains the tag table. **Note:** Tag tables produced by Emacs do not have the same form as those produced by ctags (see Section 6.5) even though they serve the same purpose. Emacs cannot handle ctags tag tables; the vi editor, which understands ctags tag tables, cannot handle Emacs tag tables.

**7.23.1
Operations on
Tag Tables**

Emacs has at most one tag table selected at a time. All the tag table commands work with the selected tag table.

Selecting a Tag Table.　The following command selects a tag table that you have created with etags:

(Meta) X visit-tags-table
　　　　Makes a specified file be the selected tag table. Emacs prompts you for the file name.

Finding a Definition.　Once a tag table has been selected, you can use the following commands to find any definition named in that table. You can specify a tag by giving just the beginning of its name. If the first tag you find isn't the one you want, you can look for another one.

(Meta) .　　Locates the definition named by the specified tag, then visits the file containing that definition and positions the point at the definition (find-tag). Emacs prompts you for the name of the definition. With an argument of (Ctrl) U, this command searches for another match to the specified tag.

(Ctrl) X 4 .　Locates the definition named by the specified tag as with (Meta) ., but visits the file in another window (find-tag-other-window).

Regular Expression Search.　The following commands enable you to search for a regular expression (see "Regular Expressions in Emacs" on page 309) in the files listed in the selected tag table. You can replace the regular expression once you've found it. For these commands, only the files matter; they pay no attention to the tags themselves.

(Meta) X tags-search
　　　　Searches for a regular expression within the files listed in the tag table. Emacs prompts you for the regular expression.

(Meta) X tags-query-replace

> Performs a query-replace on each file listed in the tags table. Emacs prompts you for the search expression and the replacement.

(Meta) ,

> (tags-loop-continue). Restarts one of the commands above, beginning the search at the point. You can use this command to continue a search without having to respecify the regular expression.

Visiting Files Containing Definitions.   You can advance through the files explicitly with the following command:

(Meta) X next-file

> Given an argument, this command visits the first file listed in the selected tag table. Without an argument, it visits the next file.

Information about Tags.   The following commands provide information about the tags in the selected tag table:

(Meta) X list-tags

> Lists all the tags in one of the files named in the selected tag table. Emacs prompts you for the file name.

(Meta) X tags-apropos

> Lists all the tags in the selected tag table that match a specified regular expression. Emacs prompts you for the regular expression.

7.24   Executing UNIX Commands from Emacs

You can execute UNIX commands from within Emacs, either singly or in a subshell. Many Emacs users find the Emacs command execution facilities so convenient that they issue all their UNIX commands from within Emacs. Another way to execute UNIX commands from Emacs is to suspend Emacs with (Ctrl) Z (see p. 274), execute the commands, and resume Emacs again.

7.24.1
Executing a Single Command

The following commands execute a single command in a subshell. Emacs chooses the shell to use by looking in the variable shell-file-name, which it initializes from the SHELL environment variable. In each case Emacs prompts you for the command.

(Meta) !

> Executes a specified command in a subshell with standard input taken from the null device \dev\null (shell-command). If the command produces any output, Emacs creates a buffer called '*Shell Command Output*' for it.

Meta | Executes a specified command in a subshell with standard in-
put taken from the region (`shell-command-on-region`).

- If the command is called without an argument, any
output that it produces is placed in a '`*Shell Command
Output*`' buffer as it is with the previous command.

- If the command is called with an argument, the old region
is deleted and any output produced by the command replaces the old region.

7.24.2
Running a Subshell
in a Buffer

Emacs provides some very powerful facilities for working within a subshell,
while at the same time disabling some of the facilities that are normally
there. You may therefore find it better to use a simple shell such as the
Bourne shell rather than a more powerful one such as the Korn shell.
Emacs looks in the variable `explicit-shell-file-name` for the name of
the shell to use. If that variable contains `nil`, Emacs then first looks in
the environment variable `ESHELL` and finally in the environment variable
`SHELL`.

Initiating a Subshell.   The following command initiates a subshell and creates a buffer to hold its input and output:

Meta X shell

Creates a buffer called '`*Shell*`' in Shell mode and initiates a
subshell in that buffer, which then becomes the current buffer.
If you execute this command a second time, you are returned
to the same buffer. To create a second shell buffer, rename the
first one to something else such as '`shell1`' and then issue this
command.

When you issue a command in a shell buffer, you don't have to wait for it
to finish—you can switch to another buffer and edit that buffer while the
command is executing.

Executing and Editing Subshell Commands.   You can freely edit the contents of the shell buffer, so it's easy to construct new commands from frag-
ments of old ones or even from the output of commands. The Enter key
has a special binding in a shell buffer:

Enter | Sends the current line as input to the shell (`send-shell-input`).
If the point is on the last line in the buffer, that line is sent;
otherwise the current line is copied to the end of the buffer
and then sent. In either case, any text at the beginning of the
line that matches the shell prompt is removed from the line
that is sent to the shell. Positioning yourself at a previously
executed command and pressing Enter is therefore an easy
way to execute that command again, possibly after editing it. To
insert a newline into the edited text, use the Ctrl O command.

The following key combinations are also bound to shell commands and
provide convenient editing facilities.

Ctrl C Ctrl Y

Makes a copy of the line that you most recently typed as

shell input and inserts it into the buffer following the point (`copy-last-shell-input`). This is the easiest way to re-execute a command. Typing (Ctrl)C (Ctrl)Y doesn't actually cause the command to be executed, so you can edit it and then, after editing it, execute it by typing (Enter).

(Ctrl)C (Ctrl)W
> Kills the word preceding the point (`backward-kill-word`).

(Ctrl)C (Ctrl)R
> Arranges the shell window so that the first line of output from the most recently executed command is the first line of the window (`show-output-from-shell`).

Subshell Control Keys. The following key combinations consist of (Ctrl)C followed by the key that usually produces the desired effect outside of Emacs.

(Ctrl)C (Ctrl)D
> Sends an end-of-file to the shell (`shell-send-eof`).

(Ctrl)C (Ctrl)C
> Interrupts the shell or the command that the shell is currently executing (`interrupt-shell-subjob`).

(Ctrl)C (Ctrl)O
> Discards any further output from the command that the shell is currently executing, but allows the command to finish executing (`kill-output-from-shell`). This command may not work in some environments.

(Ctrl)C (Ctrl)\
> Sends a quit signal to the shell or the command that it is currently executing (`quit-shell-subjob`). This command, unlike the previous one, produces a memory dump (in a file named core in the current directory.)

(Ctrl)C (Ctrl)Z
> Sends a stop ("suspend") signal to the shell or the command that it is currently executing (`stop-shell-subjob`). It only works if executed under a shell that supports BSD UNIX job control (see Section 2.7.1).

7.25   Environmental Inquiries

Emacs has two commands for inquiring about your environment:

(Meta)X `display-time`
> Causes the time and on some systems the system load to be displayed on each mode line.

(Meta)X `emacs-version`
> Displays the current version of Emacs on the echo line.

7.26   Customizing Emacs

In this section we discuss several methods of customizing Emacs: changing key bindings, defining macros and abbreviations, and setting up a `.emacs` initialization file in your home directory.

7.26.1
Key Bindings

The following commands enable you to bind a key to a command either globally or when you're in the current major mode:

(Meta) X `global-set-key`

> Globally binds a specified key to a specified command.

(Meta) X `local-set-key`

> Binds a specified key to a specified command, but for the current mode only. The key binding remains in effect for all uses of that mode in the current Emacs session, but does not affect future sessions.

For both of these commands, Emacs prompts you for the key you wish to bind and for the command you wish to bind it to.

If you rebind a key, remember that the explanations in this book and in the Emacs manual assume the standard key bindings. However the Emacs help system is quite clever about this—if you rebind a key, the information displayed by help commands such as 'w' and 'k' reflect the new binding (see Section 7.6).

In order to bind a key, you must know what characters are generated when you type it. For function keys and for keys pressed with various shift combinations, that may not be obvious. An easy way to find out is to select a scratch buffer, type (Ctrl) Q followed by the key, and then type (Ctrl) H l (`view-lossage`). That displays the characters most recently received by Emacs. This method is particularly useful when the first generated character is (Esc), as it often is.

Key Maps.   Emacs keeps the information about key bindings in LISP data structures called *key maps*. There's a global key map, stored in the variable `global-keymap`, that defines the default mappings for all the single-character commands. In addition, each major mode has its own local key map for single-character commands. For the major mode *mode*, the local key map is stored in the variable *mode*-`mode-map`; thus `text-mode-map` contains the key map for Text mode. When you rebind a key, either locally or globally, Emacs effects the rebinding by modifying one of these key maps.

Prefix keys also have key maps. A *prefix key* is a key or key sequence that has no meaning by itself as a command but can be followed by other keys to form a command. For example, (Ctrl) X and (Ctrl) X 4 are both prefix keys. The entry in a key map for a prefix key is a LISP symbol that denotes another key map; the second key map gives the bindings of the keys that can follow the prefix key. These bindings can in turn denote further key maps. For example, the entry in `global-keymap` for (Ctrl) X is a LISP symbol, ctl-x-4-map, that contains the key bindings for keys that can follow [Ctrl] X 4. Note that [Ctrl] X 4 is not a valid command by itself, and couldn't be; you have to type something else after it.[15]

A key map can have either of two LISP forms: an array of length 128 that lists the binding for each key, or a list of pairs, each containing an ASCII code and its associated binding. If you know the name of a key map, you can examine it by typing [Ctrl] H v followed by the name.

7.26.2 Keyboard Macros

A *keyboard macro* is an abbreviation for a sequence of keystrokes. Emacs enables you to define your own keyboard macros. Once you've defined a keyboard macro, you can either use it without naming it or give it a name, making it available even after you've defined other keyboard macros.

Emacs's macro-defining facilities are simple and convenient, but they aren't adequate for defining complex commands. To define a command that isn't expressible as a macro, you'll have to write a LISP program.

Defining Keyboard Macros. These are the commands for defining keyboard macros:

[Ctrl] X (Starts defining a keyboard macro (start-kbd-macro). If you precede this command with [Ctrl] U, it re-executes the most recently-defined macro and then adds the keys you type to its definition.

[Ctrl] X)   Ends the definition of a keyboard macro (end-kbd-macro).

These are the steps in defining a keyboard macro:

(1) Type '[Ctrl] X (' to start the definition.
(2) Type the sequence of commands that you want to define as a keyboard macro. These commands are executed as you type them. If you make a mistake, you can correct it as long as the mistake combined with the correction still leaves you with a workable definition.
(3) Type '[Ctrl] X)' to end the definition.

The keyboard macro has now been defined, although it does not have a name. For example, to define a keyboard macro that replaces the current line by the text '*Deleted*' no matter where you are within the line, leaving you positioned at the beginning of the next line, type

[Ctrl] X ([Ctrl] A [Ctrl] K Deleted*ctl-f [Ctrl] X)

Calling The Most Recently Defined Keyboard Macro. After you've defined a keyboard macro, you can call it with the following command:

[Ctrl] X e   Calls the keyboard macro that you've most recently defined (call-last-kbd-macro). Calling a keyboard macro causes the commands associated with it to be executed. Preceding the macro call by an argument n causes the macro to be repeated n times.

---

15. That's because all Emacs commands are required to be self-delimiting—when you've typed the last character of the command, Emacs knows it.

Only one macro at a time is available to be called by this command, since defining a new macro causes the new one to replace the previous one as the most recently defined macro.

Naming and Saving Keyboard Macros.   In order to save the definition of a keyboard macro, even within a single Emacs session, you must name it using the following command:

(Meta) X `name-last-kbd-macro`

> Assigns a name to the most recently defined keyboard macro. Assigning a name makes the macro available to be called as a command under that name. Emacs prompts you for the name. For example, if you define a keyboard macro as above for deleting and labelling a line, you can call it `label-deleted-line` by typing

---

(Meta) X `name-last-keyboard-macro` (Enter) `label-deleted-line` (Enter)

Command completion works for commands defined by macros just as it does for predefined commands. You can also bind a macro-defined command to a key using the methods described in Section 7.26.1.

To make a macro-defined command available in subsequent sessions, you must save its definition in your initialization file, `.emacs` (see Section 7.26.4). The usual way to do that is to visit the `.emacs` file and execute the following command:

(Meta) X `insert-kbd-macro`

> Inserts some LISP code into the buffer to define a specified keyboard macro. Emacs prompts you for the name of the macro. The code, which starts with '`(fset ...`', is inserted at the point. This command is primarily useful for inserting macro-defining commands in your initialization file.

Note that you must name a macro before you can save it for later sessions.

Executing Keyboard Macros with Variations.   By including the following query command in a macro definition, you can have the macro ask you whether to make a particular change:

(Ctrl) X q

> Inserts a query into the ongoing macro definition (`kbd-macro-query`). If you execute this command with an argument, it behaves differently:
>
> - During definition, it initiates a recursive edit (see Section 7.5.6) that enables you to do editing that does not become part of the definition.
>
> - During execution, it enters a recursive edit that enables you to make arbitrary changes.
>
> You can get out of these recursive edits with (Meta) (Ctrl) C. This command is only meaningful when you're defining or executing a keyboard macro.

When Emacs is executing a macro definition and it encounters a (Ctrl) X q command, it offers you five responses:

(Space)	Continues execution.
(Del)	Aborts this execution.
(Ctrl) D	If the macro call had no argument, aborts this execution as with (Del). If it had an argument, aborts this execution and all remaining executions.
(Ctrl) L	Redraws the screen and asks again.
(Ctrl) R	Enters a recursive edit (which you can abort with (Meta) (Ctrl) C). The recursive edit gives you the opportunity to make arbitrary changes. The effect of executing (Ctrl) U (Ctrl) X q in a macro definition is equivalent to executing (Ctrl) X q and generating an automatic (Ctrl) R response.

Typing anything else aborts the execution of the macro.

7.26.3 Abbreviations

An *abbreviation* is a word that expands into some different text when you insert it. For instance, if you define 'phd' as an abbreviation for 'piled higher and deeper', then whenever you type 'phd', Emacs automatically replaces it by 'piled higher and deeper'. Expansion is triggered by typing a word terminator, so if you create an abbreviation by editing existing text, the abbreviation is never expanded (unless you later type a space, period, etc. after it).

The expansion of an abbreviation is capitalized if you capitalize the abbreviation itself when you type it, so typing 'PhD' (or 'Phd') yields 'Piled higher and deeper'. Fully capitalized abbreviations produce fully capitalized expansions. You can turn off the capitalization by setting the variable abbrev-all-caps to nil.

Emacs expands abbreviations only when the minor mode Abbrev is enabled.

Defining Abbreviations.   You can define an abbreviation either globally or for the current major mode. **Note:** A mode abbreviation applies to all buffers having that mode for the rest of your editing session.

When you define an abbreviation, the word before the point becomes the expansion of the abbreviation; Emacs prompts you for the abbreviation itself. You can also define an abbreviation inversely; in this case the abbreviation is taken from the buffer and Emacs prompts you for the expansion.

The following commands define abbreviations and remove the definitions:

(Ctrl) X +	Defines a global abbreviation (add-global-abbrev). With argument *n*, takes the *n* words preceding the point as the expansion. For example, typing '(Meta) 4 (Ctrl) X +phd' defines 'phd' as an abbreviation for the preceding four words.
(Ctrl) X (Ctrl) A	Defines an abbreviation for the current mode only (add-mode-abbrev).
(Ctrl) X -	Inversely defines a global abbreviation (inverse-add-global-abbrev). The abbreviation is taken from the buffer and Emacs

prompts you for the expansion. An argument of n indicates the nth preceding word.

Ctrl X Ctrl H
: Inversely defines an abbreviation for the current mode only (`inverse-add-mode-abbrev`).

Meta X `kill-all-abbrevs`
: Removes all abbreviations, whether mode-specific or global.

Further Expansion of Abbreviations. The following commands enable you to expand abbreviations even under circumstances when they would not ordinarily be expanded:

Meta '
: Indicates the beginning of a possible abbreviation (`abbrev-prefix-mark`). For instance, if 'sgl' abbreviates 'signal' and you type 're Meta ' sgl', what you typed turns into 'resignal'. This command provides a convenient way of expanding an abbreviation with an attached prefix.

Ctrl X '
: Expands the abbreviation, if any, that precedes the point (`expand-abbrev`). This command is effective even if Abbrev mode is off.

Meta X `unexpand-abbrev`
: Undoes the most recent abbreviation.

Meta X `expand-region-abbrevs`
: Expands all unexpanded abbreviations in the region. This command is useful when you've typed some text that uses abbreviations but you've forgotten to turn Abbrev mode on.

Editing Abbreviations. You can change or even add abbreviations by editing the list of abbreviations. A typical entry in this list looks like this:

```
"rtb"     7      "rock the boat"
```

Here 'rtb' is the abbreviation, 'rock the boat' is its expansion, and the '7' indicates that the abbreviation has been expanded seven times during the current editing session. These are the commands for editing abbreviations:

Meta X `list-abbrevs`
: Creates a buffer listing the current abbreviations. The buffer's name is '`*Abbrevs*`' and its major mode is Edit Abbrevs.

Meta X `edit-abbrevs`
: Creates a buffer listing the current abbreviations and makes it the current buffer.

Meta X `edit-abbrevs-redefine`
: Redefines the current set of abbreviations according to the `*Abbrevs*` buffer. In Edit Abbrevs mode this command is bound to Ctrl C Ctrl C.

Saving and Restoring Abbreviations. The following commands save the current set of abbreviations in a file and read them back in. The default file name for each of these commands is `$HOME/.abbref_defs`.

(Meta) X `write-abbrev-file`

>   Saves the current set of abbreviations in a file. Emacs prompts you for the file name.

(Meta) X `read-abbrev-file`

>   Reads a file containing a set of abbreviation definitions and makes those definitions effective.

(Meta) X `quietly-read-abbrev-file`

>   Like the previous command, except that no message is displayed. This command is mainly useful in your initialization file.

The following commands enable you to save and restore abbreviations using a buffer:

(Meta) X `insert-abbrevs`

>   Inserts a description of all current abbreviations into the current buffer at the point.

(Meta) X `define-abbrevs`

>   Treats all of the current buffer as a set of abbreviation definitions and makes those definitions effective.

Dynamic Abbreviations. Emacs's *dynamic abbreviation* facility enables you to type part of a word you've typed before and have it completed automatically. The following command indicates a dynamic abbreviation:

(Meta) /

>   Expands the word in the buffer preceding the point as a dynamic abbreviation (`dabbrev-expand`). For instance, if you type the word 'Millard' and later type 'Mil (Meta) /', Emacs replaces what you typed by 'Millard'.
>
>   The search order is backward from the point to the beginning of the buffer and then forward from the point to the end of the buffer. An argument n with this command specifies that the nth expansion found should be used; a positive value indicates backward search and a negative value indicates forward search.

**7.26.4
The .emacs
Initialization File**

When Emacs is called, it looks for a file named `.emacs` in your home directory and executes the LISP commands in it. The principal method of customizing Emacs is placing appropriate LISP commands in this file. You can inhibit Emacs from executing `.emacs` or have it execute someone else's `.emacs` file with the `-q` and `-u` command-line options (see p. 261).

Although any serious discussion of LISP is beyond the scope of this book, we can point out a few of the most common cases of LISP commands in the initialization file:

- To define a key globally, use the `global-set-key` command. For example, the command

    ```
    (global-set-key "\C-x\C-y" 'buffer-menu)
    ```

globally binds the key combination '[Ctrl]X[Ctrl]Y' to the buffer-menu command.

- To define a key for a particular mode, use the define-key command. For example, the command

  ```
  (define-key text-mode-map "\C-xz" 'lpr-region)
  ```

  binds the key combination '[Ctrl]Xz' to the lpr-region command in text mode only.

- To set the global variable *var* to the value *val*, use the command

  ```
  (setq-default var val)
  ```

- To use a LISP symbol as a value, prefix it with an apostrophe. Thus the command

  ```
  (setq default-major-mode 'text-mode)
  ```

  causes the default major mode of a newly created buffer to be Text mode. To use a string *str* as a value, enclose it in double quotes.

- To include a macro definition in an initialization file, use the insert-keyboard-macro command (p. 321).

- To include a set of abbrevations, save them to a file and read them with the command

  ```
  (quietly-read-abbrev-file file)
  ```

  where *file* is the file containing the abbreviations (see "Saving and Restoring Abbreviations" on page 324), written as a string enclosed in double quotes.

- To set a variable *var* to the value *val* in the mode *mode*, use the command

  ```
  (setq mode-hook
     '(lambda () (setq var val)))
  ```

  If you want to set several variables or execute other commands whenever you enter a mode, you must collect them in a sequence following the 'lambda ()', as a given mode can have only one listing hook.

An easy way to see the LISP form of a command is to execute it and then bring the LISP form to the echo line with the [Ctrl]X[Esc] command (repeat-complex-command, p. 270).

Example of an Initialization File.   Here is an example of an initialization file, heavily stripped down. It is designed to work with a PC keyboard in a particular environment, so you should take it as an example of method rather than as a piece of code that you can transcribe and use without mod-

ification. You'll need to consult the Emacs documentation to understand
how some of it works.

```
; Provide for non-unique key combinations starting with ESC
; by extending 'esc-map'.

(defvar cursor-map-1 (make-keymap)
  "Keymap for cursor commands with ESC-O")
(fset 'Cursor-Map-1 cursor-map-1)
(define-key esc-map "O" 'Cursor-Map-1)

(defvar cursor-map-2 (make-keymap)
  "Keymap for cursor commands with ESC-[")
(fset 'Cursor-Map-2 cursor-map-2)
(define-key esc-map "[" 'Cursor-Map-2)

; Now define keys whose representations start with ESC.
; For example, typing Right generates ESC OC on this keyboard.

(define-key esc-map "OC" 'forward-char)          ; Right
(define-key esc-map "OD" 'backward-char)         ; Left
(define-key esc-map "OA" 'previous-line)         ; Up
(define-key esc-map "OB" 'next-line)             ; Down
(define-key esc-map "O\O" 'beginning-of-line)    ; Home
(define-key esc-map "O$" 'end-of-line)           ; End
(define-key esc-map "[5~" 'scroll-down)          ; PgUp
(define-key esc-map "[6~" 'scroll-up)            ; PgDn
(define-key esc-map "[[" 'backward-paragraph)

; Map 'help' to function key 1, backward delete to backspace,
; forward delete to DEL.

(define-key esc-map "[11~" 'help-command) ; Function key 1
(define-key esc-map "[20~" 'undo)         ; Function key 9
(define-key esc-map "[21~" 'other-window) ; Function key 10

(global-set-key "\C-h" 'backward-delete-char-untabify)
(global-set-key "\177" 'delete-char)

; The following commands are needed so that changes to the
;  global map to redefine DEL don't get overridden locally.

(define-key lisp-interaction-mode-map "\177" nil)
(define-key emacs-lisp-mode-map "\177" nil)
(define-key c-mode-map "\177" nil)

; Now reset the backspace to do what DEL used to do

(define-key lisp-interaction-mode-map
  "\C-h" 'backward-delete-char-untabify)
```

```
(define-key emacs-lisp-mode-map "\C-h"
  'backward-delete-char-untabify)
(define-key c-mode-map "\C-h" 'backward-delete-char-untabify)
(setq search-delete-char ?\b)

; Set the tab stops every 3 columns

(setq-default tab-stop-list
  '(3 6 9 12 15 18 21 24 27 30 33 36 39 42 45 48 51 54
    57 60 63 66 69 72 75 78 81))
(setq-default tab-width 3)

; Other useful key bindings

(global-set-key "\eG" 'goto-line)

; We don't want to disable narrowing

(put 'narrow-to-region 'disabled nil)
```

7.27   The Emacs Mailer

Emacs has a rich set of commands for handling mail. Rmail is the Emacs subsystem for reading mail. Emacs doesn't have a name for the group of commands that handle outgoing mail, so we call them "Smail". See Chapter 9 for a discussion of mail in general and the relevant terminology.

Emacs uses its own format, called "Rmail format", for mail files. Although Rmail format is incompatible with the standard UNIX format for mail files, Emacs provides commands for converting between Rmail format and UNIX format.

7.27.1
Sending Mail with Smail

These are the Smail commands for composing an outgoing mail message:

[Ctrl] X m   Prepares to accept a mail message in the current window (mail). If you provide an argument to this command and a *mail* buffer already exists, Smail selects that buffer.

[Ctrl] X 4 m   Prepares to accept a mail message in the next window (mail-other-window). If you provide an argument to this command and a *mail* buffer already exists, Smail selects that buffer.

These commands create a *mail* buffer for your message if one doesn't already exist, fill it with a skeletal message, and put you into Mail mode (an internal mode), ready to compose the message. If you use one of these commands without an argument and a *mail* buffer does already exist, Smail gives you the option of discarding it or returning to it.

After composing a message, you can send it with the [Ctrl] C [Ctrl] S or the [Ctrl] C [Ctrl] C command. These commands are described below. If you edit a message and then decide not to send it, you can kill or simply abandon the mail buffer.

Form of a Mail Message. An outgoing mail message has the following form:

```
headers
--text follows this line--
message text
```

You can edit a message freely before you send it, but if you attempt to send a message that doesn't contain the 'text follows this line' line exactly, Smail complains about an unsuccessful search and proceeds no further.

Smail knows about the following header fields:

To	The recipients of the message.
Subject	The subject of the message.
CC	Additional "carbon copy" recipients to whom the message is not primarily addressed.[16]
BCC	Additional "blind carbon copy" recipients who should receive the message but who should not be listed in the header.
FCC	The name of a file (in UNIX mail format) to which the message should be appended after it has been sent.
From	Your own mailing address, if you're sending the message from someone else's account.
Reply-To	The sender of the message, if the automatically generated return address for the message is not usable as a reply address. From and Reply-To differ only in what they mean to a person reading the message.
In-Reply-To	Text describing a message you're replying to. Normally Rmail fills in this field automatically when you're replying to mail.

The following rules apply to the header fields:

- The name of each field ends with a colon and is followed by optional whitespace and the contents of the field.
- Field names are case-insensitive.
- Recipient names in fields are separated by commas. The commas can be preceded or followed by whitespace.
- A field can be continued on additional lines. The continuation lines must start with whitespace.
- If recipients are listed in two fields of the same type, the lists are combined.
- There must be at least one To field.
- If you have a .mailrc initialization file for mailx in your home directory (see Section 9.3.7), any aliases contained in it are used when the names of recipients are interpreted.

You can also include other header fields that Smail doesn't know about. Smail passes them to the mail transport agent unmodified.

---

16. According to bureaupolitical tradition, however, it matters less to whom you send a memo than to whom you send the carbon copies.

Commands for Mail Mode. The following commands are available in Mail mode (the mode you're in when Smail is active):

Ctrl C Ctrl S
> Sends the message in the buffer but leaves the buffer selected (`mail-send`).

Ctrl C Ctrl C
> Sends the message in the buffer and reverts to the previously selected buffer in this window (`mail-send-and-exit`).

Ctrl C Ctrl F Ctrl T
> Moves to the first To field, creating one if it doesn't exist (`mail-to`).

Ctrl C Ctrl F Ctrl S
> Moves to the first Subject field, creating one if it doesn't exist (`mail-subject`).

Ctrl C Ctrl F Ctrl C
> Moves to the first CC field, creating one if it doesn't exist (`mail-cc`).

Ctrl C Ctrl W
> Inserts the file `.signature` from your home directory at the end of the message text (`mail-signature`).

Ctrl C Ctrl Y
> When sending mail as a result of the Rmail commands for composing responses (see "Creating Responses to Messages" on page 332), inserts the original message into the outgoing message at the point (`mail-yank-original`). The original message is the one that was current in Rmail. Most header fields are deleted.
>
> - With no argument, the command indents the inserted message by four spaces.
>
> - With an argument of n, it indents by n spaces.
>
> - With an argument of Ctrl U alone, it doesn't indent at all and doesn't remove any of the header fields from the original.

Ctrl C Ctrl Q
> Fills all the paragraphs of the inserted message (`mail-fill-yanked-message`).

7.27.2
Receiving Mail
with Rmail

Rmail is the Emacs subsystem for reading and processing mail. The following command starts Rmail:

Meta X rmail
> Create or select a buffer for reading mail and enter Rmail mode, an internal mode. The name of the buffer is 'RMAIL'.

When you start up Rmail, it reads any new mail that has arrived in your primary mailbox (see Section 9.2), appends it to the mail that you've already received, and positions you at the first new message. You can operate on the messages either directly or via a message summary (see Section 7.27.3). As you process your mail, you can mark messages for deletion. Deleted messages remain in the buffer until you expunge them or until you quit Rmail—but if you merely save the buffer with the Ctrl X Ctrl S (`save-buffer`) command, the deleted messages are saved along with the others.

Rmail Files. Rmail keeps your mail in mailboxes called "Rmail files". Your secondary mailbox—the one that Rmail uses by default—is the file RMAIL in your home directory.[17] You can also store mail in other auxiliary mailboxes. Rmail uses its own format for these mailboxes, different from the UNIX mailbox format. Within an Rmail file, messages are arranged in order of receipt, oldest first.

When you call Rmail, it automatically saves newly arrived messages in your secondary mailbox. Furthermore, if you're exiting from Emacs and you've abandoned an Rmail buffer, Emacs asks you if you want to save it. You can check for new mail while you're within Rmail with the 'g' command (p. 333).

Arguments to Rmail Commands. When you're in Rmail, the buffer is normally in a read-only state in which ordinary characters that you type are not inserted into the text. Therefore you don't need to "meta"-ize an argument to a command when you type it. For example, you can supply the argument '3' to the 'j' command by typing '3j' (although 'Meta 3 j' still works). If you explicitly make the buffer modifiable with the 'w' command, however, the meta shift is necessary (see "Editing Received Messages" on page 332).

Saving the Buffer or Exiting from Rmail. The following commands save the Rmail buffer and exit from Rmail. Executing either of them expunges deleted messages.

s   Saves the Rmail buffer in the secondary mailbox (`rmail-save`). If you want to save the buffer without expunging deleted messages, use the Ctrl X Ctrl S (`save-buffer`) command.

q   Saves the Rmail buffer in the secondary mailbox, then exits from Rmail (`rmail-quit`).

Creating a Message Summary. The following commands create either a complete or a selective summary of the messages in the buffer. The summary appears in another window and has its own set of key bindings defined for it (see Section 7.27.3).

h
Meta Ctrl H
           Makes a summary of all messages (`rmail-summary`).

---

17. The Emacs manual calls this file your "primary mail file", a usage that conflicts with the terminology we use elsewhere in this book.

(Meta) (Ctrl) L *labels*
> Makes a summary of the messages with a label from the set of labels *labels* (`rmail-summary-by-labels`).

(Meta) (Ctrl) R *names*
> Makes a summary of all messages with a recipient in *names* (`rmail-summary-by-recipients`). The recipient's name can appear in any header field, so you can use this command to select messages by author—although you'll also get those sent to you by other people with copies to that author.

Selecting a Message to Read. The message that you're reading at any moment is the *current message*. The following commands enable you to select a particular message as the current message:

n
> Selects the next nondeleted message (`rmail-next-undeleted-message`).

p
> Selects the preceding nondeleted message (`rmail-previous-undeleted-message`).

(Meta) N
> Selects the next message whether or not it has been deleted (`rmail-next-message`).

(Meta) P
> Selects the preceding message whether or not it has been deleted (`rmail-previous-message`).

j
> Selects the first message (`rmail-show-message`). With an argument *n*, selects the *n*th message (whether deleted or not).

>
> Selects the last message (`rmail-last-message`).

(Meta) S
> Selects the next message matching a specified regular expression (`rmail-search`). Preceded by '-', this command moves to the preceding message matching a specified regular expression. Emacs prompts you for the regular expression.

Scrolling within a Message. The following commands enable you to scroll through the current message:

(Space)
> Scrolls the current message forward (`scroll-up`).

(Del)
> Scrolls the current message backward (`scroll-down`).

.
> Scrolls to the beginning of the current message (`rmail-beginning-of-message`).

Deleting and Undeleting Messages. The following commands enable you to delete or undelete a specified message.

d
> Deletes the current message (`rmail-delete-forward`).

(Ctrl) D
> Deletes the current message and moves to the nearest preceding undeleted message (`rmail-delete-backward`).

u
> If the current message was deleted, undeletes it; otherwise undeletes the nearest preceding deleted message (`rmail-undelete-previous-message`).

x

e   Expunges the Rmail buffer by removing all deleted messages (`rmail-expunge`). Unlike 's', this command does not save the buffer; if you kill the buffer without saving it, the expunged messages remain in the mailbox.

Creating Responses to Messages.   After reading a message, you may wish to respond to it by replying to the person who sent it, by sending a message to someone else, or by forwarding the message to some other recipients.   The following commands provide these facilities, calling Smail for you so that you can create the response.   Within Smail, you can use the Ctrl C Ctrl Y (`mail-yank-original`) command (p. 329) to copy the original message into the one you're composing.

r   Prepares for a reply to the current message (`rmail-reply`) by activating Smail in another buffer and filling in the header fields of the reply message, using the information in the header of the message you're replying to.

m   Starts editing a new message (not a reply) with Smail in another buffer (`rmail-mail`). The difference between using this command and using Ctrl X 4m is that if you use this command you can insert the current (received) message with Ctrl C Ctrl Y .

c   Resumes editing an outgoing message (`rmail-continue`). This command is useful when you were creating a reply but switched back to Rmail to look at, and possibly copy, another message. You need this command to create a reply that incorporates two different messages from your Rmail buffer.

f   Forwards the current message to other recipients (`rmail-forward`).   This command activates Smail in another buffer and initializes that buffer with the text of the current message and appropriate header information. You can then fill in the new recipients and send the message.

Editing Received Messages.   Normally the Rmail buffer is read-only and cannot be modified. The following two commands enable you to modify it:

t   Toggles the full header display (`rmail-toggle-headers`). Normally this toggle is off, and header fields that Rmail presumes to be uninteresting are not shown. With this toggle on, all fields are shown.

w   Enables modification to the current message (`rmail-edit-current-message`). Executing this command disables all the other Rmail commands, since ordinary characters now become self-inserting. The following key combinations have special meaning in this mode, called Rmail Edit mode:

Ctrl C Ctrl C

                                Returns to Rmail, making the buffer read-only again and re-enabling the usual key bindings.

[Ctrl] C [Ctrl]]

Like [Ctrl] C [Ctrl] C, except that the editing changes you made are discarded.

Some messages have the form of a message digest (a sequence of messages collected into a single message). The following command decomposes a message digest:

[Meta] X undigestify-rmail-message

If the current message is a message digest, separates it into its component messages.

Reading Mail from Other Mailboxes. You can use Rmail to read and process mail in auxiliary mailboxes as well as in your primary mailbox. The mail in these mailboxes can be in UNIX mail format. The following commands enable you to read mail from other mail files:

i *file*   Runs Rmail on the messages in *file*, treating it as an auxiliary mailbox (rmail-input). When you exit from Rmail with 'q' or a similar command, the current buffer is saved to *file*. Other mailboxes are unaffected by anything you do to the mailbox in *file*.

[Meta] X set-rmail-inbox-list

Specifies a list of input mailboxes for the current Rmail file. The file names in this list should be separated by commas. If the list is empty, this Rmail file will have no input mailboxes. The list is stored in the Rmail file when you save it; when you next process the Rmail file, these input mailboxes will be checked for new mail.

g   Checks the input mailboxes of the current Rmail file for new mail and appends it to the mail in the buffer (rmail-get-new-mail). This command works both for secondary mailboxes and for auxiliary mailboxes.

Copying Messages to Other Mailboxes. The following commands enable you to copy a message from the current Rmail buffer to a specified file:

o *file*   Appends a copy of the current message in Rmail format to *file* (rmail-output-to-rmail-file).

[Ctrl] O *file* Appends a copy of the current message in UNIX format to *file* (rmail-output).

Labelling Messages. A message can have a set of labels attached to it. You can make up your own labels and attach or remove them. In addition, Rmail attaches and removes certain predefined labels, called *attributes*, automatically. Attributes are not displayed either as part of the message or as part of the message summary, but user-defined labels do appear in the message summary. These are the Rmail attributes:

unseen   This message has never been current.

deleted   This message has been deleted (indicated by the 'D' flag).

filed   This message has been copied to a file.

answered This message has been answered using the r command.

forwarded

This message has been forwarded to other recipients.

edited   This message has been edited.

These are the commands for attaching and removing labels:

a *label*   Assigns the label *label* to the current message (rmail-add-label).

k *label*   Removes the label *label* from the current message (rmail-kill-label).

These are the commands for selecting labelled messages:

Meta Ctrl N *labels*

Moves to the next message with a label from the set of labels *labels* (rmail-next-labeled-message).

Meta Ctrl P *labels*

Moves to the preceding message with a label from the set of labels *labels* (rmail-previous-labeled-message).

For each of these commands, the labels are separated by commas. You can also use the Meta Ctrl R (rmail-summary-by-labels) command to locate those messages that have a particular label. Message selection commands can be used with attributes as well as with user-defined labels.

7.27.3 Rmail Summary Commands

You can operate on a message either by working with the message itself or by working with the header summary. The following key bindings are available when you select the buffer containing the header summary. When you select a message using the header summary, the Rmail buffer is selected and the message you've chosen is displayed in that buffer.

j   Selects the current message (rmail-summary-goto-msg).

Ctrl N   Moves to the next line and selects its message (rmail-summary-next-all).

Ctrl P   Moves to the preceding line and selects its message (rmail-summary-previous-all).

n   Moves to the next line containing a nondeleted message and selects its message (rmail-summary-next-msg).

p   Moves to the preceding line containing a nondeleted message and selects its message (rmail-summary-previous-msg).

d   Deletes the current message, then moves to the next line containing a nondeleted message (rmail-summary-delete-forward).

u   Undeletes and selects this message or the nearest preceding deleted message (rmail-summary-undelete).

Space   Scrolls the message window forward (down) (rmail-summary-scroll-msg-up).

Del   Scrolls the message window backward (up) (rmail-summary-scroll-msg-down).

x   Removes the summary from its window (`rmail-summary-exit`). The Rmail buffer is reselected.

q   Exits from Rmail (`rmail-summary-quit`). The Rmail buffer is saved and both the summary window and the Rmail window are killed. (The buffers themselves still remain.)

7.28   Amusements

The following commands call for one of Emacs's amusements:

Meta X doctor
        Executes the Eliza program. You end each input line by typing Enter twice.

Meta X yow
        Displays a strange saying.

Meta X hanoi
        Runs the towers of Hanoi. An argument if present specifies the number of discs.

Meta X dissociated-press
        Scrambles a buffer of text in an amusing way. Killing the Dissociated Press buffer restores the previous buffer, so you can try this command without destroying what you're working on.

8

Data Manipulation Using Filters

A *filter* is a program that modifies or transforms its input in order to obtain its output. By convention, a filter reads its input from standard input and writes it to standard output, so it's easy to connect several filters as a pipeline (see Section 2.12.1). Such combinations of filters are one of the best-known and most useful methods of using UNIX effectively, since they enable you to build complex transformations out of simple components. Most filters are also able to take their input from one or more explicitly specified files.

In this chapter we discuss the following filters:

- The `sort` program, which sorts its input
- The `tr` program, which translates characters from one set into characters from another set
- The `cut` and `paste` programs, which extract fields from input lines and paste them together again in a different arrangement
- The `uniq` and `comm` programs, which eliminate repeated lines and extract lines common to two files
- The `sed` script editor, which enables you to edit a file according to a predefined script
- The `grep`, `egrep` and `fgrep` programs, which extract lines that match a predefined pattern
- The `awk` program, which provides the full power of a programming language for specifying data transformations

We also briefly describe the Icon and `perl` programming languages, which offer alternatives to `awk`.

8.1 Sorting Files with sort

The sort command sorts a single file or a sequence of files, either treating each line as a single record or basing the order of the output on keys extracted from each line. Used without any options or file specifications, sort sorts standard input, writes the result to standard output, sorts by lines, and compares individual characters according to their ASCII positions. Sort is limited to sorting records that occupy a single line, although the line can be very long if necessary. You can sort a file in place with the −o command-line option.

The form of the sort command line is

sort [*options*] [*keyspec*] ... [*file*] ...

The specified files *file* ... are concatenated and sorted. If no files are specified, standard input is sorted. Within the list of files, '−' denotes standard input treated as a file.

The *keyspecs* define the sort keys (see below). If no *keyspecs* are present the entire line is treated as a single sort key.

The *options* contain options that govern the entire sort. Some of them pertain to how keys are interpreted; these options can be applied either to all keys or to individual keys. If they appear before the *keyspecs*, they apply to all keys.

8.1.1 Key Specifications

By providing *keyspecs* on the command line, you can base the order of sort's output on a sequence of *keys* extracted from each input record (line). Output records are ordered by the first key; for records having the same first key, by the second key, and so forth. Records having all keys equal are further sorted by comparing the records byte for byte.

Each *keyspec* specifies the location of a single key within the record and how that key is to be interpreted. A *keyspec* has the form

[+*pos*$_1$ [−*pos*$_2$]]

where *pos*$_1$ indicates where within the line the key starts and *pos*$_2$ where it ends. If *pos*$_2$ is missing, the key continues to the end of the line. You can also include flags in *pos*$_1$ or *pos*$_2$ that change the interpretation of the key from the default, which is to interpret it as a sequence of ASCII characters.

To define the locations of keys within a record, the record is partitioned into a sequence of fields bounded by delimiters. By default the delimiters are the space and tab characters; the spaces and tabs are themselves considered part of the field that they begin. For example, the input record

cruel gruel

is partitioned into two fields, 'cruel' and ' gruel'; the second field begins with two spaces. You can override the default delimiters by specifying a single delimiter character with the −t option. In this case the delimiter character is not considered part of a field, and two delimiter characters in a row define an empty field.[1] (Although the delimiter set contains two characters by default, it can only contain one delimiter character if you specify it explicitly.) Fields are always ended by the end of the line, so missing fields are effectively empty.

Each *pos* in a key specification has the form

$$f[.c][flags]$$

Here *f* specifies a field and *c* a character within the field, *with fields and characters numbered starting with zero*. The ending position is the first position *not* in the key. If you omit '.*c*', it defaults to zero. For instance, the key specification

```
+2.1 -5.3
```

specifies a key that starts with the second character of the third field and is ended by but does not include the fourth character of the sixth field. The key specification

```
+1 -2
```

specifies a key that begins with the first character of the second field and is ended by but does not include the first character of the third field—in other words, the second field exactly.

The flags, listed below in Section 8.1.3, are specified as letters only (no dashes). For instance, the key specification

```
+2r
```

indicates a key that starts with the third field, runs to the end of the line, and is to be sorted in reverse order. You can attach keys either to *pos₁* or to *pos₂*—it makes no difference. Any flags appearing in options that precede the first *keyspec* apply to all keys.

An example showing these facilities used in combination is

```
sort -t: +2 -2.2 +0n -1
```

In this case there are two sort keys. The input (taken from standard input) is first sorted according to the first two characters of the third field. Within each group of records with identical first keys, the input is sorted numerically (because of the n) according to the contents of the first field.

8.1.2
Options Affecting the Entire Sort

The options that precede the first *keyspec* apply to the entire sort.

General Options.   The following options generally affect how `sort` operates:

-o *outfile*   Send the output to *outfile* rather than to standard output. The file *outfile* can be one of the input files; if it is, that input file is replaced by the result of the sort.

-c   Check that the input is already sorted. No output is produced unless the file is not sorted. If `sort` finds a record to be less

---

1.   Thus there is a subtle difference between the default case and the effect of the option '-t" "', which specifies a space as the delimiter. Aside from the fact that tabs no longer serve as delimiters with this option, the record in the example just above would have one space at the beginning of the second field, not two.

than the preceding one, it sends an error message to standard output indicating the record that was out of order and exits.

-m   Merge the input files, assuming them to be already sorted.

-u   Produce unique keys only, i.e., when several lines have equal keys, produce only one of the lines. The extra lines are suppressed even when the complete lines are not identical.

-t *c*   Use *c* as the field delimiter.

Capacity and Performance.   The following options affect the capacity and performance of `sort`. They are not available in the BSD UNIX version of `sort`.

-y [*n*]   Use *n* kilobytes of main memory, enlarging this space as necessary. If *n* is 0, `sort` starts with a minimum amount of memory; if *n* is omitted, `sort` starts with a maximum amount of memory. Adding memory may reduce sorting time but increases the load on your system.

-z *n*   Assume *n* to be the longest record size. If you don't specify *n*, `sort` uses a default value, typically 1024. This option has an effect only if you've specified -c or -m, since otherwise `sort` determines the longest record size when it's first passing through the input. If the longest record is longer than the assumed maximum, `sort` terminates abnormally.

Flags Applying to All Keys.   The flags that apply to individual keys can also be applied (as options) to all keys. For example, a '-b' option is equivalent to attaching 'b' to each key specification.

8.1.3
Flags Applying to Individual Keys

As noted above, these flags can also be used as options.

Ignoring Initial Whitespace in Keys.   By default, leading whitespace in a non-numeric key is significant. The following flag enables you to ignore it:

-b   Ignore leading whitespace in determining character positions within a non-numeric key. In other words, position 0 of the key is the first *nonwhite* character of the key.

Reversing the Sort Order.   The following flag reverses the sort order:

-r   Reverse the sense of comparisons for the indicated key, causing keys that would normally come first to come last.

Interpreting Keys.   The following options provide different ways of interpreting keys. By default, a key is interpreted as a sequence of ASCII characters.

-d   Use dictionary order, ignoring characters other than letters, digits, and whitespace in making comparisons. Note that all uppercase letters still precede all lowercase letters, so 'Z' precedes 'a'.

-f   Fold lowercase letters to uppercase, i.e., convert every lower-
        case letter to its uppercase counterpart.

-i   Ignore nonprinting ASCII characters (those whose decimal val-
        ues are less than 32 or greater than 126).

-M   Treat the key as a three-letter case-insensitive month name.
        Whitespace preceding the month name is ignored, as is the part
        of the key after the first three letters. Thus 'jan' precedes 'feb',
        'feb' precedes 'MAR', and so forth. A key that is not a month
        name precedes 'jan'; all such keys compare equal. This option
        is not available in the BSD UNIX version of sort.

-n   Treat the key as a number. If the key contains a number fol-
        lowed by whitespace and other text, sort considers only the
        number part. The number can include a plus or minus sign
        and a decimal point. Sort ignores initial whitespace within a
        numeric key field but does not ignore initial whitespace at the
        beginning of a line when performing a numeric sort on entire
        lines. For example, the command 'sort -n' with the input

            2
          1

produces output consisting of these two lines in the original
order. For the command 'sort +0n', the whitespace preceding
the '2' is ignored and the order of the output lines is reversed.

8.2   Simple Data Transformations

The programs described in this section perform relatively simple transformations of their input:

- Tr translates from one character set to another, deletes characters,
  or eliminates repetitions of certain characters.
- Cut extracts specified portions of each input line.
- Uniq eliminates or reports adjacent repeated lines in its input.
- Paste pastes together corresponding lines from several files into one
  long line or concatenates all the lines of a single file into one long
  line.
- Comm selects or rejects lines that are common to two sorted files.

8.2.1
Translating or
Deleting Characters
with tr

The tr command enables you to edit a file by replacing certain characters by other characters, by deleting certain characters, or by removing
repeated sequences of certain characters. The form of the tr command
line is

        tr [*options*] [*str*$_1$ [*str*$_2$]]

where *str*$_1$ specifies a string of characters to be replaced or deleted and
str$_2$ specifies a string of characters to be substituted or condensed. Tr

reads from standard input and writes to standard output. The following conventions apply to str_1 and str_2:

- A backslash quotes the following character unless that character is an octal digit.
- A backslash followed by one, two, or three octal digits represents the ASCII character whose character code is given by those digits. (If this construct is to be followed by an octal digit that isn't part of it, you should write the octal number using all three digits.)
- The notation $[c_1-c_2]$ represents the sequence of characters in the ASCII code starting with the character c_1 and ending with the character c_2.
- The notation $[c*[n]]$ represents n repetitions of the character c. If n starts with 0 it is taken as an octal number, otherwise as a decimal number. If n is missing or zero it is taken as indefinitely large.

If no options are specified, `tr` replaces each occurrence of the nth character of str_1 by the nth character of str_2. If str_1 is longer than str_2, the excess characters of str_1 are ignored. The –d option causes `tr` to delete the characters in str_1; the –s option causes it to condense the characters in str_2 if –d is present and str_1 if –d is absent.

A simple and useful example of `tr` is

```
tr "[a-z]" "[A-Z]"
```

This command replaces each lowercase character in standard input by the corresponding uppercase character and sends the result to standard output.

Command-line Options.   The `tr` command has the following options, which can be used in combination:

-d   Delete the characters in str_1 instead of replacing them. If the –s option is not also present, str_2 is irrelevant.

-s   Squeeze repetitions of characters in str_2 (if –d is present) or str_1 (if –d is absent) to single characters. For instance, if str_i contains the space character, sequences of several spaces are condensed to a single space (independently of whether substitutions are taking place). Sequences of different characters from str_i are *not* squeezed.

-c   Use the complement of str_1 instead of str_1. The complement consists of all non-null ASCII characters that are not in str_1, taken in their ASCII order. This option is usually useful only if you also specify –d; in this case the characters in str_1 are retained and all others are deleted.

8.2.2 Extracting Portions of Input Lines with cut

The `cut` command extracts specified portions of each line of its input. You can define the portions either by specifying the character positions that they occupy or by specifying the fields that they occupy and the delimiter character that separates the fields. The form of the `cut` command line is

```
cut options [file] ...
```

where the input consists of the concatenation of the files *file* . . . . If no files are specified, `cut` takes its input from standard input. A *file* given by '–'

specifies standard input. The `-c` option specifies extraction by characters; the `-f` options specifies extraction by fields. Exactly one of these options must be present.

In either case, the argument of the option specifies the portions to be extracted as a list (denoted in the rest of this description as *list*). A list is written as a sequence of single numbers and ranges. The first character or field is numbered as 1. The numbers should be in increasing order.[2] A range is indicated as a pair of numbers separated by '-'. Within a range, you can omit the first number (implying the first item) or the last number (implying the last item). For example, the command

    cut -c2,5-8,14-

extracts characters 2, 5 through 8, and 14 through l from each line, where l is the line length.

Extracting Characters.   The following command-line option applies when you are extracting characters:

-c*list*   Extract the characters specified in *list*. No space can appear between `-c` and *list*.

Note: If the length of an input line is less than the largest character number specified on the command line, `cut` simply ignores the missing characters.

Extracting Delimited Fields.   The following command-line options apply when you are extracting fields separated by delimiters. The default delimiter is ⟨tab⟩.

-f*list*   Extract the fields specified in *list*. No space can appear between `-f` and *list*. The fields are concatenated and sent to standard output.

-d*c*   Use the character *c* instead of ⟨tab⟩ as the field delimiter.

-s   Suppress lines containing no delimiter characters. By default, such lines are included in the output. The `-s` option can sometimes be useful for suppressing header lines in a tabular file.

A sequence of several delimiters in a row defines a sequence of several fields; empty fields are permitted and recognized. If the delimiter is a space, this may not be what you want. Cut inserts the delimiter character between consecutive fields of the output, even if they are empty. For example, the command

    cut -f1,3-4 -d:

specifies that fields 1, 3, and 4 should be extracted from each line with ':' as the field delimiter. Applied to the input line

    I:say::what:I:mean

---

2. Cut doesn't complain if the numbers aren't in increasing order. However, its output always contains the included portions of the input line in the order that they appear in the line from left to right. Specifying the list items in a nonincreasing order doesn't increase the power of cut—it just creates confusion as to what the output will be.

this command yields the output

```
I::what
```

Note: If the number of fields on an input line is less than the largest field number specified on the command line, cut ignores the missing fields and produces no delimiters for them.

**8.2.3
Pasting Fields from
Several Files
with** paste

The paste command pastes together corresponding lines from several files, sending the result to standard output. If there are just two input files, each output line contains a line from the first file followed by a separator character and a line from the second file. If there are more than two input files the output is analogous. By default, the separator character is a tab. You can also use paste with the -s option to paste together the lines of a single file into one long line.

The paste command line has the form

```
paste [options] [file] ...
```

The files *file* ... contain the lines that are to be pasted together, with the usual convention that '-' indicates standard input. If no files are specified, standard input is pasted by itself (interesting only if -s has been specified). For example, if the file beach contains

```
walrus
oysters
carpenter
```

and the file party contains

```
dormouse
hatter
Alice
white rabbit
```

then the result of the command paste beach party is

```
walrus      dormouse
oysters     hatter
carpenter   Alice
            white rabbit
```

where the spaces preceding the second column indicate a single tab character.[3]

Paste is sometimes used with cut (see Section 8.2.2) to rearrange the fields of a file.

Command-line Options.   The options for paste are as follows:

-d*list*   Use the characters in *list* circularly as separators. You must not leave a space between d and *list*. For instance, if you specify '-d, ;' and have four input files, a line might look like this:

```
tweedledum,tweedledee;egg,fall
```

---

3. If you actually display this result, the columns probably won't line up as neatly as they do here.

-s   Merge lines serially from one file, combining them into one long line. If you specify more than one input file you'll get a useless and confusing result.

8.2.4
Eliminating
Repeated Lines
with uniq

The uniq command processes a file, eliminating or reporting consecutive lines that are identical. You can optionally cause initial parts of the lines to be ignored in the comparison; in this case the first line in a group of equal lines is the one that is retained.

The form of the uniq command line is:

    uniq [*options*] [*infile* [*outfile*]]

where the input comes from *infile* and is written to *outfile*. As usual, *infile* and *outfile* default to standard input and standard output respectively. If none of the -u, -c, or -d options are specified, uniq produces each nonrepeated line and the first line of each sequence of repeated lines. This effect is equivalent to the -u and -d options together.

Command-line Options.   The following options affect which lines appear in the output:

-d   Produce just the first copy of each repeated line.

-u   Produce just the lines that are not repeated.

-c   Precede each output line by a count of how many times it occurs. This option implies the -d and -u options.

The following options enable you to ignore initial parts of lines when comparing them:

+n Ignore the first n fields. For the purposes of the comparison, fields are assumed to be separated by whitespace. Whitespace preceding any of the first n fields (but not the $(n + 1)$st field) is ignored.

-n Ignore the first n characters. If both +n and -n are specified, fields are skipped first, then characters.

8.2.5
Listing Common
Lines
with comm

The comm command enables you to compare two *sorted* files, listing the lines that are common to both of them and sending that listing to standard output. The default listing has three columns:

(1)   The lines that only occur in the first file.
(2)   The lines that only occur in the second file.
(3)   The lines that occur in both files.

You can suppress one or more of these columns by specifying flags on the command line, which has the form

    comm [-*flags*] *file*$_1$ *file*$_2$

Here *flags* consists of one or more of the digits 123. Each digit in *flags* indicates that the corresponding column of the listing should be suppressed. The command arguments *file*$_1$ and *file*$_2$ are the two files being compared; either one can be given as '-', indicating standard input.

8.3   Using sed to Edit from a Script

The sed editor applies a fixed set of editing changes to a file or a sequence of files. A typical application of sed is to rearrange the output of a UNIX utility such as who. Historically, sed is derived from the ed editor—but it isn't "just like" ed, despite statements to that effect in the UNIX literature.

Sed is particularly good for simple changes such as uniform substitutions. You can also use it for more complex editing tasks, although its one-pass approach limits what it can do and awk is usually easier to use for such tasks (see Section 8.5). Sed almost always runs faster than awk.

An application of sed consists of applying a fixed "editing script" to a sequence of files. The form of the sed command line is

    sed [options] [file] ...

where *file* ... is a list of files to be edited. You can supply the script by giving it explicitly as part of the command as in

    sed -e 's/knave/jack/g' cardgame

This command replaces each occurrence of 'knave' in the file cardgame by 'jack' and sends the result to standard output. The original cardgame file is unaffected. You could also put the text of the script in a file deknave and issue the command

    sed -f deknave cardgame

A command equivalent to the first one is

    sed 's/knave/jack/g' cardgame

since if there is just one -e option and there are no -f options, the -e option is implicit. See Section 8.3.4 below for further discussion of these options.

8.3.1
The Editing Cycle

Sed makes use of two buffers that can hold text: the *input buffer* and the *hold buffer*. These are called the "pattern space" and "hold space" in the sed manual pages. For most edits, the hold buffer isn't needed; it only becomes active if you use a command that refers to it. Initially the hold buffer contains a single empty line.

Editing proceeds irrevocably in the forward direction—a constraint that you can often overcome with some cleverness in using the hold buffer. Sed repeats the following cycle until the input is exhausted. If you specify several files as input, they are effectively concatenated.

(1)   If the input buffer is empty, sed reads the next input line and places it into the buffer. The input buffer might not be empty if the previous cycle was terminated by a 'D' command; in this case sed doesn't read another line, but it does perform the rest of the steps below.

(2)   It examines in sequence the commands in the command script, performing those that are currently selected (see Section 8.3.2).

(3) If the command script wasn't terminated by a 'd' or 'D' command and if output hasn't been suppressed by the −n option, it writes the contents of the input buffer to standard output and empties the input buffer. For some editing tasks it is convenient to suppress the normal output and to produce the output explicitly with 'p' or 'P' commands instead.

In the explanations below, we use the term "produce" to mean "send to standard output".

**8.3.2
Form of an
Editing Script**

An editing script consists of a sequence of commands separated either by newlines or by semicolons.[4] Each command is denoted by a single letter or other character. Most commands can be preceded by a selector, either an address or a pair of addresses. A command is executed only if it is selected, i.e., its selector is satisfied. Ordinarily an address selects a set of individual lines, while a pair of addresses selects a set of ranges of lines. For example, the command

```
/jam/,/jelly/d
```

specifies that whenever sed finds a line containing the pattern 'jam', it deletes that line and all others up to and including the next line containing the pattern 'jelly'. (If 'jam' and 'jelly' occur on the same line, just that line is deleted.) Any number of line ranges may be deleted in this way. A command without any addresses applies to all lines. This description is a slight oversimplification since patterns are actually matched against the input buffer (see below).

A sed script can contain groups of commands enclosed in curly braces. You can label particular points in the script with the ':' command and transfer to a labelled point with the 'b' and 't' commands.

Sed recognizes two kinds of addresses: line numbers and regular expressions.

- A line number address is a single integer or '$', which denotes the last line. Each time sed reads a line, it advances the line number (the first line is line #1). A line number address is satisfied if the line most recently read has that number.

- A regular expression address usually has the form

    /*regexpr*/

    where regular expressions are as defined in Section 2.16. Alternatively you can write a regular expression address as

    c regexpr c

    where *regexpr* is a regular expression and *c* is any single character. (The spaces surrounding '*regexpr*' are for clarity only and are not part of the form.) For example, the pattern

    \\#quince#

---

4. The manual pages for sed don't mention that semicolons also work as command separators—but they do.

matches any line containing the string 'quince'.

A regular expression address is satisfied if it matches the input buffer. Ordinarily the input buffer contains a single input line, but it can contain additional text as a result of the 'G', 'H', or 'N' commands. In checking for a match, sed assumes '\n' matches a newline and dot (.) matches any character except a newline at the end of the input buffer.

When a selector is a range, i.e., it consists of a pair of addresses, the first address starts selection and the second one ends it. If the first address is a regular expression, it can be reselected any number of times. Here are some examples:

- The range '3,5' selects lines 3 through 5.
- The range '/walrus/,/oyster/' selects groups of lines that start with a line containing 'walrus' and end with the next line containing 'oyster'. A single line containing both 'walrus' and 'oyster' is a group by itself.
- The range '3,/oyster/' selects line 3 and all lines up to and including the next line containing 'oyster', or the rest of the input starting with line 3 if 'oyster' does not appear.
- The range /walrus/,5 consists of the first line containing 'walrus' and continues through line 5. If the first line containing 'walrus' is later than line 5, the range consists of just one line.

You can apply a command to those addresses not in a range with the '!' command (see "Miscellaneous Commands" on page 350).

8.3.3 Commands

In the commands discussed below, *r* indicates an address range and *a* indicates a single address. A range can be replaced by an address or omitted; a single address can also be omitted. A command is executed either if its selector (range or address) applies or if it has no selector.

Textual Substitutions. The following commands enable you to perform textual substitutions. Many applications of sed use a script consisting of a single 's' command.

s/pat/repl/[flags]

Substitutes *repl* for the pattern *pat*, where *pat* is a regular expression having the same form as a regular expression used in an address (see Section 8.3.2). By default, sed substitutes for the first occurrence of the pattern in the input buffer only.[5]

---

5. The regular expression notation doesn't provide any way of writing nonprinting characters in a printable notation, either within the pattern or within the replacement. But the following Bourne shell script shows how you can sometimes get around this limitation:

```
CR=`echo \\015`
add_cr () { sed -e "s/${CR}*$//g; s/$/${CR}/"; }
remove_cr () { sed "s/${CR}*$//g"; }
```

The shell functions add_cr and remove_cr perform the transformations needed to convert UNIX files to MS-DOS files and vice versa.

The following flags modify how **sed** does the substitution:

g	Substitute for all occurrences rather than for the first occurrence.
n	Substitute for the *n*th occurrence rather than for the first occurrence. (*n* must be less than 512.)
p	Produce the input buffer if any substitutions were made.
w *file*	Append the input buffer to *file* if any substitutions were made.

Note carefully that the notation '\n' has different meanings in the pattern and in the replacement. In the pattern, it indicates a newline; in the replacement, it simply indicates the letter 'n'. To include a newline in the replacement, use a backslash at the end of a line as in the following example:

```
s/cut here/cut\
here/
```

This command replaces the blank between **cut** and **here** by a newline.

r y/*string*₁/*string*₂/

   Substitutes characters in *string*₂ for the corresponding characters of *string*₁.

Deletions.   The following commands perform deletions:

r d
   Deletes the input buffer and starts another cycle, ignoring the rest of the script.

r D
   Deletes the first line of the input buffer and starts another cycle, ignoring the rest of the script. This command is unique in that it can leave the input buffer nonempty; if it does leave the input buffer nonempty, a new line is not read in on the next cycle. When you've collected a group of lines in the input buffer—using, for instance, the commands involving the hold buffer—you can use D to process the lines one at a time.

Inserting and Changing Groups of Lines.   The following commands insert and change groups of lines. Their input consists of lines of text, with the command itself and each line other than the last one ended by a backslash. For example, the input

```
$a\
Your manuscript is both good and original,\
but the part that is good is not original,\
and the part that is original is not good.\
\
-- Samuel Johnson
```

appends the indicated five lines of text after the last input line. **Note:** It is not possible to transfer the text introduced by one of these commands into either the input buffer or the hold buffer.

a i*text*   Produces *text* immediately. Although this command and the next one expect at most one address, you can get them to work with a range by enclosing them in braces and applying the range to the braces.

a a*text*   Produces *text* before reading the next line. Note that the effect of this command is postponed until all other commands in the script have been executed. Multiple 'a' commands take effect in the order that they are executed.

r c\\ *text* Changes the lines in *r* to *text* and start another cycle, ignoring the rest of the script. Equivalent to 'a' followed by 'd'.

Using the Hold Buffer.   The hold buffer is useful for accumulating sequences of lines, either to move them to another location later in the input or to compare them to a pattern that spans several lines. The following commands provide operations that transfer information to or from the hold buffer:

r g   Replaces the input buffer by the hold buffer.

r G   Appends the hold buffer to the input buffer.

r h   Replaces the hold buffer by the input buffer.

r H   Appends the input buffer to the hold buffer.

r x *file*   Exchanges the input buffer with the hold buffer.

The following commands illustrate the use of the hold buffer:

    4h; 5,10H; $G

These commands taken together move lines 4 through 10 of the input file to the end of the file. The command '4,10H' doesn't work correctly for this purpose because it introduces an extraneous blank line (the original contents of the hold buffer) at the start of the transferred material.

Other Input and Output Operations.   The following commands enable you to produce the contents of the first line of the input buffer or all of it, to read the next line into the input buffer, and to show the contents of the input buffer unambiguously (almost):

r n   Produces the input buffer, then replaces it with the next input line. The line number is advanced. This command does not start a new cycle; after executing it, sed continues with the rest of the script.

r N   Appends the next input line to the input buffer. The line number is advanced. This command does not start a new cycle; after executing it, sed continues with the rest of the script.

r p   Produces the input buffer. This command is useful in conjunction with the −n option, since it enables you to replace implicit output (the default action at the end of a cycle) by explicit output. Explicit output is often more convenient than implicit output in complex scripts.

r l	Produces the input buffer in a representation that accounts for control characters and long lines.[6] Lines that exceed the line length of your terminal are folded so that they don't exceed that length. Nonprinting character are replaced by '*dd*', where *dd* is the octal representation of the character.
r P	Produces the first line of the input buffer. This command is often followed by 'D'.

The following command enables you to produce the line number:

a=	Produces a line containing the current line number. This command does not affect the input buffer.

Reading and Writing Files Explicitly.   The following commands enable you to read from and write to files not named on the command line:

r r *file*	Produces the contents of *file* before reading the next line. Like the 'a' command, this command does not have its effect until the end of the editing cycle.
r w *file*	Appends the input buffer to *file*. This command is like the 'p' command, except that it affects a named file rather than standard output.

Labels and Branches.   The following commands enable you to label a place in the script and to branch to a label either unconditionally or conditionally:

: *label*	Places the label *label*.
r b [*label*]	Branches to the point in the script bearing the label *label*.
r t [*label*]	Branches to the point in the script labelled *label* if any substitutions have been successfully made by an 's' command since sed most recently either read an input line or executed a 't' command.
a q	Quits editing. No more commands are executed, no more lines are read, and no more output is produced.

Miscellaneous Commands.   The following commands don't naturally fall into any of the groups above:

#	Indicates a comment (first line only). If the line starts with '#n', the default output is suppressed just as it is with the −n option. This command enables you to cause output suppression from within a script.
(*empty*)	Does nothing.
r ! *cmd*	Applies the command *cmd* to all lines not selected by *r*.
r { [*cmd*] ... }	
	Executes the commands *cmd* ... . If any commands within

---

6. The manual pages for sed state that this command produces the line in an unambiguous representation, but that isn't quite true—for example, the lines 'a*c*b' and 'a\13b' both produce the output 'a\13b' if *c* is the character whose octal representation is 13.

the braces have addresses or ranges attached to them, those addresses or ranges act as selectors just as they do outside of braces. The commands are separated by newlines or semicolons.

8.3.4 Command-line Options

The following options can appear on the command line:

-e *script* Edit the files according to *script*. The script usually needs to be enclosed in single quotes so that special characters such as ';' and '\' are interpreted by sed rather than by the shell. If a command line contains a single -e option and no -f options, you can omit the -e and provide *script* only. You can provide a multiple-line script with this option; if you do, pay careful attention to the shell conventions about quoting newlines and backslashes. These conventions are not the same for all shells.

-f *sfile* Edit the files according to the script found in *sfile*. Since sed itself reads the script, shell conventions about quoting backslashes and newlines do not apply.

-n Don't produce the input buffer after processing a line. You can also produce the effect of this option by beginning a script with a line that starts with '#n'.

A command line may contain several -e and -f options—if it does, the various scripts are concatenated.

8.4 Finding Patterns with the grep Family

The grep family of programs enables you to search through a set of files for all lines that match a specified regular expression (see the definition of a regular expression in Section 2.16). The name grep stands for "Global Regular Expression Print". You can also use these programs as filters to extract the matching lines from standard input and send those lines to standard output.

The three members of the family differ in the generality of the expressions that they search for and in the speed of search:

- The grep program searches for ed-style regular expressions exactly as defined in Section 2.16. It is the original member of the family. Grep uses a compact nondeterministic algorithm for the search.

- The fgrep (fast grep) program searches for a fixed string, although it does treat lowercase and uppercase letters as equivalent if the -i option is specified. Fgrep uses a search algorithm that is both fast and compact.

- The egrep (extended grep) program searches for a generalized regular expression as defined in Section 2.16.1. Egrep uses a fast deterministic search algorithm. This algorithm can require huge amounts of space in pathological cases, but these cases almost never arise.

Generally you should use `fgrep` to search for a single string and `egrep` otherwise—unless you're searching for a pattern with repeated parts that `grep` handles but `egrep` doesn't.

The regular expressions used by `grep` use quoted parentheses ('\(' and '\)') to define groups, sometimes called *tagged regular expressions*. They allow explicit checking for repeated groups. The regular expressions used by `egrep` use unquoted parentheses ('(' and ')') for grouping but do not provide for checking repeated groups. This difference is an important incompatibility between `grep` and `egrep`, and shows that there are certain patterns that can be found with `grep` but not with `egrep`.

8.4.1

The Command Line

The command lines for the three commands have the forms

```
grep [options] pat [file] ...
egrep [options] [pat] [file] ...
fgrep [options] [pat] [file] ...
```

where *pat* is a regular expression to be searched for and *file* ... is a list of files to be searched. If no files are specified, the program searches standard input. The results of the search are sent to standard output. The *pat* component is omitted if the `-e` or `-f` option is present.

Usually you should quote the pattern in apostrophes in order to prevent any of the characters within it from being interpreted as shell metacharacters (see Section 2.14.2).

For example, the command

```
egrep 'idol|adultery' KingJames
```

searches the file `KingJames` for each line containing either the string 'idol' or the string 'adultery' and sends each such line to standard output.

Command-line Options. The following options affect the pattern match itself:

-w   Search for the pattern as a word. Any character other than a letter or digit counts as a word delimiter. This option is only recognized by the BSD UNIX version of `grep`.

-x   Match entire lines only (BSD UNIX version of `grep` only).

-v   Select the lines that *don't* match.

-i   Ignore the case of letters in making comparisons, i.e., treat uppercase and lowercase letters as equivalent.

The following options affect the form of the output:

-n   Precede each line by its file name and line number.

-b   Precede each line by its disk block number.

-c   Only show a count of matching lines.

-l   Only show the names of files containing matching strings— don't show the strings themselves.

-s   In System V this option suppresses error messages and applies only to `grep`. In BSD UNIX it applies to all three programs and causes the program to suppress the normal output and only show error messages.

For any of these options other than -s, the output also includes the name of the file being examined if the input contains more than one file.

The following options provide alternate ways of providing the pattern. They are only recognized by fgrep and egrep.

-e *pat*   Use *pat* as the search pattern. If you specify this option, then the command line must not include an additional pattern. The purpose of this option is to provide for patterns that begin with '-'.

-f *file*   Read the pattern list from *file*.

8.5   The awk Programming Language

The awk programming language provides a convenient way of doing many data manipulation tasks. Some awk programs are so short and simple that you can easily write them on a single command line, yet awk is expressive enough so that you can use it for general programming. Stylistically awk is much like C, but it also incorporates ideas from other languages such as Snobol and PL/I. Awk was named after its authors Alfred Aho, Peter Weinberger, and Brian Kernighan.

In presenting awk, we cannot avoid assuming that you have had some programming experience—though not necessarily very much. But even lacking that experience, you can write awk programs for many simple tasks. Awk is thoroughly described in a book by its authors (see reference [B2]).

8.5.1
Calling awk

The form of the awk command line is

    awk [*option*] [*program*] [*file*] . . .

You must provide the program either on the command line or via the -f option described below. If you give it on the command line, you should enclose it in apostrophes (see the discussion of quotation in Section 2.14.2) to prevent metacharacters and whitespace in the program from being misinterpreted as shell metacharacters. The program you write (not awk itself) takes its input from the concatenation of *file* . . . if present and from standard input otherwise. However, an awk program can use the information on the command line for a different purpose if it chooses. The lines that awk reads in are called *input records*.

On some systems the program named awk may be an older version; the current version is then usually named nawk (new awk). If that is the case we recommend that you either make awk an alias for nawk (if your shell lets you) or create a link to nawk under the name awk, setting your PATH environment variable so that the link to nawk is seen before the link to the older version of awk.

Command-line Options. These are the options that can appear on the awk command line:

-F*s*   Set the field separator to *s* (see "Input Field Separators" on page 359).

-f *file*   Read the program from the file *file* instead of taking it from the command line. This option is usually needed for awk programs of more than a line or two.

Command-line Variable Assignments. You can assign values to awk variables from the command line. An argument of the form '*var=val*' assigns the value *val* to the variable *var* using the usual rules for the assignment operator (see "Assignment Operators" on page 364).

8.5.2
Simple awk
Programs

To illustrate how to write simple programs in awk, we assume that the file products contains the following data on products, their prices, and their sales:

```
knapsacks    22.00     11
knickers     44.95      0
knishes       1.29    193
knives       11.98     57
knobs          .27     35
```

By default, an awk program reads its input either from standard input or from a sequence of files specified on the command line. As it reads each input record, it decomposes the record into a sequence of *fields* separated by whitespace. The fields are named $1, $2, etc.; the entire line is named $0. A line of an awk program has the form of a *pattern-action statement*, where the pattern selects some set of input records and the action, enclosed in braces, specifies what is to be done for each of those lines. For example, the command

```
awk '{print $1, $2, $2 * $3}' products
```

produces the following list of products and the amounts of their sales:

```
knapsacks 22.00 242
knickers 44.95 0
knishes 1.29 248.97
knives 11.98 682.86
knobs .27 9.45
```

In the command the '*' indicates multiplication, the pattern is omitted since all input records are selected, and the action is enclosed in braces. Here is a more elaborate version of the same program:

```
awk '$3 > 0 {print $1, $2, $2 * $3; sum += $2 * $3}
    END {print "\nTOTAL:", sum}' products
```

This version omits lines for products with zero sales, thanks to the pattern '$3 > 0', and produces a total after all lines have been read. The 'END' indicates actions to be performed after all input has been read. In this case the action is to produce a total. The variable sum, like all awk variables, is implicitly initialized to the empty string. It is then converted to 0 since the context requires that conversion.

8.5.3
Form of an awk Program

An awk program consists of a sequence of pattern-action statements and user function definitions. User function definitions are discussed in Section 8.5.21. A pattern-action statement may contain a pattern (see "Patterns" below), an action (see "Actions and Statements" on page 356), or both. A pattern-action statement has one of the following forms:

BEGIN { *action* }

> Executes *action* once, before any data is read in. If an awk program consists of a single pattern-action statement having this form, the action is executed and no data is read in except as requested explicitly by the action. Awk programs consisting of a single 'BEGIN' action are very useful since you can use them to carry out any computations whatsoever without your being bound by awk's normal method of reading and processing data.

END { *action* }

> Executes *action* once, after awk has read in all the input data and encountered an end of file. If awk never sees an end of file, the 'END' actions are not executed.

{ *action* } Executes *action* for each input record.

pattern [{ *action* }]

> Executes *action* for each input record that satisfies *pattern*. The default action is 'print $0', so if no action is specified, each input record satisfying *pattern* is shown.

*pattern*₁ , *pattern*₂ [{ *action* }]

> Executes *action* for each input record starting with the first one matching *pattern*₁ and continuing through the next one matching *pattern*₂. If a subsequent input record matches *pattern*₁, the process is repeated. If no match is found for *pattern*₂, execution continues to the end of the data. The default action is 'print $0', so if no action is specified, each input record within the pattern range is shown.

Note that several different actions may apply to a single line of input data.

Patterns.   A *pattern* is either an expression or a regular expression enclosed in slashes:

- An ordinary expression used as a pattern is evaluated for its logical value, either truth or falsity (see "Truth Values" on page 357). Usually a pattern is given by a comparison such as '$2 > 0', which tests if the second field of the input line is greater than zero, or by a combination of such comparisons. Conventionally, a successful comparison returns 1 (true) and an unsuccessful comparison returns 0 (false).

- A regular expression enclosed in slashes and used as a pattern matches an input record if a match for the regular expression can be found within the input record.

The regular expressions recognized by awk are the generalized regular expressions described in Section 2.16.1. The escape sequences described on page 358 can appear in the regular expression. For example, a pattern '/unc.+ble/' would match any input record containing the word 'runcible'.

Actions and Statements.   An *action* is a sequence of zero or more *statements*. A statement carries out an action such as producing some output text or conditionally executing another statement depending on the result of a test. Since certain kinds of statements contain other statements, a single action can be quite complex. We classify the kinds of statements as follows:

- Expressions as statements (see Section 8.5.19)
- Printing statements (see Section 8.5.15)
- Control-flow statements (see Section 8.5.20)
- Miscellaneous statements: the `close` statement (see Section 8.5.16), the `delete` statement (see Section 8.5.8), and the `return` statement (see "Returning from a Function" on page 374)

8.5.4
Program Format

An `awk` program is formatted according to the following rules:

- A pattern and the opening left brace of its action must appear on the same line. This rule also applies to `BEGIN` and `END`.

- Statements are separated by newlines or semicolons. A statement can be continued onto additional lines by ending all but the last line with a backslash. A newline (with or without a backslash) can be inserted after any of the following elements:

    ```
    ,   {  &&  ||  do  else  if(...)  for(...)
    ```

    A basic `awk` element such as a number, a string, or a variable, however, must appear entirely on one line.

- Comments start with '#' and extend to the end of a line. Comments and blank lines are ignored.

- Spaces and tabs can be used around basic `awk` elements but are not required unless running two elements together could cause those elements to be interpreted as a single element. `Awk` is generally permissive about omitting spaces; for example, the program

    ```
    BEGIN{a=94 + 3;print"abc"2a}
    ```

    produces the output 'abc297'.

- A left parenthesis that introduces an argument list, either for a user-defined function or for a statement such as `print` or `close`, must be immediately adjacent to the function or statement name, with no intervening whitespace. For example, you must write

    ```
    print($1, $2)
    ```

    rather than

    ```
    print ($1, $2)
    ```

**8.5.5
Values and
Expressions**

Awk recognizes two kinds of values: numbers and strings.

- Numbers are represented internally in floating-point form.   In output, however, integer values normally appear as integers; other numbers normally appear as decimal fractions.

- Strings are sequences of characters.

If you use a number in a context where awk is expecting a string, awk converts the number to a string and vice versa (see "Coercions between Strings and Numbers" below).

An *expression* is a formula for computing a value. The awk statement

```
print expr
```

illustrates a particularly simple use of an expression; it sends the value of the expression *expr* to standard output. An expression can be used as a statement by itself.

An expression is built up from three kinds of primary elements: constants (numeric or string), variables (user-defined, predefined, or field), and regular expressions. (The awk documentation uses the term "built-in" rather than "predefined".) Constants and variables are expressions in their own right and are discussed in Section 8.5.6. Regular expressions are used as the right operands of the '~' and '!~' pattern-matching operators and as arguments of certain predefined functions.

Awk also provides three kinds of elements in addition to the primary ones: array elements (see Section 8.5.8), function calls (see Section 8.5.11), and parenthesized expressions. Array elements and function calls can themselves contain expressions.

In general, an expression consists of a sequence of elements and operators (see Section 8.5.10), with the operators specifying how the elements are to be combined. For example, the expression

```
($2 + 17) * saxify(3, a + 9)
```

is formed by combining two elements, a parenthesized expression and a function call, using the multiplication operator '*'.

Truth Values.   Certain awk constructs such as the if statement test the value of an expression for truth or falsity. Awk treats a nonzero numerical value or a nonempty string value as being true and a zero numerical value or an empty string value as being false.

Coercions between Strings and Numbers.   You can coerce a string to a number in an expression by writing

```
+ str
```

This expression forces awk to treat the string *str* as a number but leaves the numerical value unchanged. When awk treats a string as a number, it produces the number represented by the string; if the string does not represent a number, awk produces zero. For example, the expression

```
("4." "92") + "abc"
```

evaluates to 4.92. (Juxtaposing two strings causes awk to concatenate them.) Similarly, you can coerce a number *n* in an expression to a string by writing

> *n* ""

This subexpression concatenates a null string onto *n*, forcing awk to convert *n* to a string but leaving the string unchanged.

Awk converts a number to a string by formatting it according to the format specification contained in the OFMT predefined variable. The default value of OFMT is '%.6g' (see "Output Formats" on page 369). This format usually yields the most natural representation of a number.

8.5.6
Constants and Variables

As mentioned earlier, awk represents numbers internally in floating-point form. A numeric constant can be written as an integer such as '747', a decimal fraction such as '2.718', or a number in scientific notation such as '69e-7' or '6.9E-6'. The last two of these numbers both represent the decimal value .0000069; 'e' and 'E' are equivalent here.

You write a string constant by enclosing it in double quotes. Within a string constant you can use the following escape sequences to denote certain special characters:

\b	⟨backspace⟩
\f	⟨formfeed⟩
\n	⟨linefeed⟩ (newline)
\r	⟨return⟩
\t	⟨tab⟩
ddd	Octal number *ddd*, where *ddd* contains one to three digits
c	The character *c*, where *c* is none of the above

If the *ddd* form is followed by a digit you must provide all three digits of *ddd*, using leading zeros if necessary. **Note:** You can include a double quote within a string by writing it as '\"'.

Awk provides three kinds of variables: user-defined, predefined, and field:

- A *user-defined variable* is named by a sequence of letters, digits, and underscores starting with a letter. User-defined variables are never declared; they simply come into existence when you start using them. The initial value of a user-defined variable is the null string.

- A *predefined variable* is a variable such as RLENGTH (p. 366) whose meaning is defined by awk. All predefined variables have names written entirely in upper case.

- A *field variable* is a variable whose value ordinarily is a portion of the text of the current input record. Field variables are discussed below in Section 8.5.7.

8.5.7
Fields and Field Variables

When awk reads an input record, it splits the record into *fields* and assigns the text of those fields to the field variables $1, $2, and so forth. It assigns the entire input record to $0. By default, the fields are separated by whitespace, the same convention used in analyzing arguments to an ordinary command. The predefined variable NF is set to the number of fields;

field variables with numbers greater than NF are set to the null string. For example, suppose awk reads the input record

    Karl and Groucho Marx

Awk sets the field variables as follows:

$0:   Karl and Groucho Marx
$1:   Karl
$2:   and
$3:   Groucho
$4:   Marx
$5, $6, . . . :   (empty string)
NF: 4

You can change the value of a field variable by assigning something else to it.

A field whose text represents a number is treated as a number rather than as a string in any context where it makes a difference. For instance, in the comparison '$3 < 7', the field $3 is treated as a number rather than as a string if it contains text such as '29'. In this case the comparison yields a false result even though a string comparison would yield a true result.

Input Field Separators.   By default, successive input fields are separated by whitespace, a sequence of one or more spaces or tabs. Newlines also act as whitespace characters if they are not record separators (see "Input Record Separators" below). You can specify the input field separator by assigning a string value to the predefined variable FS (input field separator). The default value of FS is a single space. If FS has this specific value, awk ignores whitespace at the beginning of a record and treats *both* spaces and tabs as separators. If FS has any other value, a separator at the beginning of an input record indicates that the first field of the record is an empty string.

If the value of FS is a single character other than a blank, that character acts as the input field separator. Otherwise the value of FS is a regular expression that specifies the set of all possible input field separators. Usually you should specify FS either on the command line, using the –F option (see p. 354), or in a BEGIN action. For example, starting an awk program with

    BEGIN { FS = "[, \t][\t]*" }

causes either a comma, a comma followed by whitespace, or whitespace alone to act as a separator between input fields. **Note:** If you want the separator to be a single blank, you must write it as '[ ]' or the equivalent.

Input Record Separators.   Just as you can specify input field separators with the FS predefined variable, you can specify the input record separator with the RS predefined variable. The input record separator marks the boundary between input records. For example, if you set RS to ';', awk finds successive input records by scanning up to the next semicolon. The record separator itself can never be part of a record. The record separator, unlike the field separator, is always either a single character or a null string; if you set RS to a longer string, awk uses only the first character of it.

The default value of RS is '\n', i.e., a single newline. Setting RS to the empty string causes one or more blank lines to act as the record separator and thus provides one way of treating several lines as a single record. If you change RS, newlines will act as field separators no matter what value FS has.

<table>
<tr><td>

**8.5.8
Arrays**

</td><td>

An *array* is a kind of lookup table that consists of a set of *elements*. Each element acts as a variable; you can use its value in an expression or change its value in an assignment. The values you use to look up the elements of an array are its *subscripts*. An array subscript can be either a number or a string, so awk arrays are more like tables in the Snobol and Icon programming languages than they are like arrays in a language such as Pascal or C. If *a* is an array, the element specified by the subscript *sub* is written as '*a*[*sub*]'.

</td></tr>
</table>

An array comes into existence when you first use it. The same holds true for its individual elements. An array element, like any other variable, has the empty string as its initial value. The statement

        delete *a*[*sub*]

deletes the element of the array *a* with subscript *sub*. This is the *only* way to delete an array element.

For example, the effect of the assignment expression

        pulchritude["brigitte"] = 97

is to create a pulchritude array if it doesn't already exist and to place an element with subscript 'brigitte' and value 97 in that array. A subsequent use of 'pulchritude["brigitte"]' in an expression yields the value 97 (unless you meanwhile assign a different value to that array element).

There are two special constructs for operating on arrays:

- The in operator tests whether an array has an element indexed by a particular subscript (see p. 363).

- The for statement has a form that iterates through the subscripts of an array (see p. 373).

Multidimensional Arrays. A multidimensional array is an array with more than one subscript. Although awk does not support multidimensional arrays directly, it does provide a method of simulating them. When you write an array reference of the form

        arr[*sub*$_1$, *sub*$_2$]

awk translates the subscript pair '*sub*$_1$, *sub*$_2$' into the string

        sub$_1$ *sep* *sub*$_2$

where *sep* is the value of the predefined variable SUBSEP (subscript separator). For example, if you set SUBSEP to ':::', the subscript pair

        "lemur", 17

is translated into the string

        lemur::17

The default value of SUBSEP is a one-character string consisting of the character with ASCII code 28, which you obtain by typing ⌈Ctrl⌉ \ .[7] Arrays of more than two dimensions are handled analogously. You can even construct an array that has some one-dimensional subscripts and some two-dimensional subscripts. When you iterate through a multidimensional array using a for statement (see p. 373), the iteration values are strings that include the subscript separator.

8.5.9
Input-related
Variables

The following predefined variables are related to reading input records:

FS	The specification of the input field separator (see "Input Field Separators" on page 359).
RS	The specification of the input record separator (see "Input Record Separators" on page 359).
NF	The number of fields in the current record (see p. 359).
FNR	The number of records read so far from the current input file, counting the current one.
NR	The total number of records read so far from all input files.
FILENAME	The name of the current input file. If the current file is standard input, the value of FILENAME is '−'.

8.5.10
Operators

The following subsections describe the operators you can use to combine elements into larger expressions. Their relative precedence is described in "Precedence of Operators" on page 364. You can use parentheses within expressions to group subexpressions in the usual way, thus overriding the normal precedences.

Ordinary Arithmetic Operators. The arithmetic operators operate on numbers. A string appearing as an operand of an arithmetic operator is converted to a number (see "Coercions between Strings and Numbers" on page 357). The binary arithmetic operators are:

+	Addition.
−	Subtraction.
*	Multiplication.
/	Division. The value of x/y is a decimal fraction if x is not evenly divisible by y.
%	Remainder. The result has the same sign as the first operand.
∧	Exponentiation. The value of $x \wedge y$ is x to the power y. If the result is not mathematically well-defined, awk issues an error diagnostic.

In addition, the + and − operators can be used as unary operators. The only effect of the unary + operator is to convert its operand to a number if it isn't one already.

---

7. This value was chosen because it is relatively unlikely to appear in a subscript string.

Incrementing and Decrementing Operators. The incrementing and decrementing operators can be applied only to a variable. Here they are:

v++   Returns the value of the variable v and then adds 1 to v. For instance, suppose the value of x is 5. Evaluating the expression '`x++`' then yields the value 5 and changes the value of x to 6.

++v Adds 1 to the variable v and returns the result. For instance, suppose the value of x is 5. Evaluating the expression '`++x`' then yields the value 6 and also changes the value of x to 6.

v--   Like v++ except that 1 is subtracted from v rather than added to it.

--v Like ++v except that 1 is subtracted from v rather than added to it.

Concatenation. Concatenation is an *implicit* operator. You concatenate two strings by writing them one after another. If you concatenate a number with a string or even with another number, the number is converted to a string. For example, evaluating the expression

```
"meow"(2*8)"arf""oink" "moo"
```

yields the value

```
meow16arfoinkmoo
```

Note that the concatenated operands can be written with or without whitespace between them.

Comparisons. You can use the `awk` comparison operators to compare either numbers or strings. Strings are compared character by character from left to right until a differing character is found or one string is exhausted. If a differing character is found, the string with the lesser character according to the ASCII sequence is the lesser string; if one string is exhausted, that one is the lesser. In a comparison in which one operand is a number and the other is a string, the number is converted to a string.
    These are the comparison operators:

==   Equal. Don't confuse this with the assignment operator '='.
!=   Not equal.
<   Less than.
>   Greater than.
<=   Less than or equal to.
>=   Greater than or equal to.

A true comparison yields 1 and a false comparison yields 0.

Pattern-matching Operators. The following pattern-matching operators check whether a string contains a match for a regular expression. Using them, you can perform the same kinds of tests within an expression that you can using the pattern part of a pattern-action statement.

~   The expression '*str~pat*' is true if the string *str* contains a match for the regular expression *pat* and false otherwise.

!~   The expression '*str*!~*pat*' is true if the string *str* does *not* contain a match for the regular expression *pat* and false if it does.

Here as elsewhere, truth is represented by the number 1 and falsity by the number 0.

In expressions using these operators, the second operand of *pat* can be given as a string rather than as a regular expression. Thus you can store the regular expression in a variable. A string used in a pattern match is like a regular expression, but with one critical difference: any backslashes within the string must be quoted with a backslash, even if they are themselves used for quotation. For example, the expressions

```
sep ~ /\.|\?/
sep ~ "\\.|\\?"
```

are equivalent; they both are true if sep contains either '.' or '?'.

Array Membership Operator.   The array membership operator in tests whether an array contains an element corresponding to a certain subscript (see Section 8.5.8). The form of the test is

$$sub \text{ in } arr$$

where *arr* is an array and *sub* is a possible subscript for *arr*. If *arr* contains an element with subscript *sub*, the test is true and yields 1; otherwise it is false and yields 0.

Logical Operators.   The logical operators are usually used to combine the results of comparisons and other tests, although their operands can be any expressions at all. These are the logical operators:

&&   The expression 'x&&y' is true and yields 1 if both x and y are true, i.e., have nonzero values. If x is false, however, the expression yields 0 immediately and y is never evaluated. For example, the expression

```
y > 0 && x / y > t
```

does not cause a division by zero even if y is zero. In this case the logical combination yields false as soon as 'y > 0' is evaluated, so the division 'x / y' is never performed.

|| The expression 'x||y' is true and yields 1 if either x or y is true. If x is true, y is never evaluated.

!   The expression '!x' yields the logical negation of x: its value is 1 if x is zero or an empty string and 0 otherwise.

Conditional Expressions.   A conditional expression is analogous to a conditional statement. The form of a conditional expression is

$$expr_1 \text{ ? } expr_2 : expr_3$$

It yields the value of $expr_2$ if $expr_1$ is true and the value of $expr_3$ otherwise. Only one of the expressions $expr_2$ and $expr_3$ is ever evaluated.

Field Selection Operator.   The field selection operator '$' (see Section 8.5.7) is a unary operator that takes a single numeric operand. Its operand is normally an integer or a variable but can be a more general expression. For example, the expression '$(NF-1)' refers to the next to the last field of an input record.

Assignment Operators. An assignment operator sets a variable to a value. An assignment expression is one whose main operator is an assignment operator. Like any expression, an assignment expression also can be used as a statement.

The most straightforward kind of assignment expression is a *direct assignment* of the form

    var = *expr*

where *var* is a variable and *expr* is an expression. The effect of evaluating the assignment expression is to evaluate *expr*, obtaining a value *val*, and then to make the value of *var* be *val*. The value of the assignment expression is *val*.

If *var* and *expr* have different types (one has a string value and the other a numeric value, for example), the type of *var* is changed to agree with that of *expr*. For example, if the variable `falafel` has the value 7 and the variable `pita` has the value 0, the effect of the assignment

    `pita = (falafel = "hum") "mus"`

is to set the value of `falafel` to 'hum' and then, since the value of the inner assignment expression is 'hum', to set the value of `pita` to 'hummus'.

The other form of assignment is a *modifying assignment*. There are five modifying assignment operators:

    `+=` `-=` `*=` `/=` `%=`

The effect of the assignment expression

    var `+=` *expr*

is to evaluate *expr*, obtaining a value *val*, and then to add *val* to *var*. The value of the entire expression is the new value of *var*. For example, suppose the value of `macaw` is 12. Then the assignment expression

    `macaw += 18`

sets the value of `macaw` to 30. The value of the expression is also 30. The other modifying assignment operators have analogous meanings.

Precedence of Operators. When several operators appear in an expression, they are grouped according to their relative precedence: an operator with greater precedence is applied before one with lesser precedence, and operators having the same precedence are applied in order from left to right. Here is a list of the `awk` operators in order of decreasing precedence:

(...)	(grouping)
$	(field selection)
++ --	(increment and decrement)
^	(exponentiation)
!	(logical "not")
+ -	(unary additive)
* / %	(multiplicative)
+ -	(binary additive)
juxtaposition	(concatenation)
< <= == != > >=	(relational)
~ !~	(pattern matching)

in	(array membership)
&&	(logical "and")
||	(logical "or")
? ... :	(conditional)
= += -= *=	(assignment)
/= %= ^=	

8.5.11 Function Calls

A function call is a type of expression. The value of that expression is determined by the function's definition. If a function does not explicitly return a value when it is called, the value of the function call is undefined.

Most calls on predefined functions and all calls on user-defined functions have the form

$$f(a_1, a_2, \ldots, a_n)$$

where f is the name of the function and the a_i are its *arguments*. No space is permitted between the function name and the left parenthesis that encloses its argument list.

The arguments of an ordinary function call are given by expressions. When the function is called, awk evaluates the expressions and passes their values to the function by assigning them to the function's *parameters*. The argument list can be empty; an empty argument list is written as '()'.

A few predefined functions extend the form of a function call:

- Certain predefined string functions expect one of their arguments to be a regular expression delimited by slashes.

- The getline predefined function does not take an argument list but can have a redirection attached to it (see Section 8.5.14).

8.5.12 Predefined String Functions

Awk provides a number of predefined functions for operating on strings. They all follow the convention that the first character has position 1 and succeeding characters have successively higher position numbers.

Basic String Analysis.   The following predefined functions perform basic string analysis:

length(s)
> Returns the number of characters in the string s.

index(s,t)
> Returns the position of the first place in the string s where the string t occurs. If t does not occur within s, index returns 0.

substr($s,p[,n]$)
> If n is not specified or if $p + n - 1$ is less than the length of the string s, returns the substring of s starting with the pth character; otherwise returns the substring of s that starts with the pth character and is n characters long. For example, the value of 'substr("bullock",2,4)' is 'ullo' and the value of 'substr("bullock",4,5)' is 'lock'.

Pattern Matching and Substitution. The following predefined functions perform pattern matching and substitution. Some of them take a regular expression as an argument; such a regular expression is enclosed in slashes. Alternatively, a string can be provided in place of the regular expression (see p. 355).

match(s, r)

>Tests whether the string s contains a match for the regular expression r.

>- If it does, match returns the position of the character that begins the leftmost matching substring and sets the predefined variable RLENGTH to the length of the longest matching substring that starts at that position.

>- If it does not, match returns 0 and sets RLENGTH to -1.

>In either case the predefined variable RSTART is set to the value returned by match. For example, the value of

>```
>match("sitzmark", /[ratzk]+/)
>```

>is 3; evaluating this expression sets RSTART to 3 and RLENGTH to 2.

sub($r, s[, t]$)

>If the string t is specified, substitutes the string s for the first occurrence of the regular expression r in t. If t is not specified, it is taken to be $0. An occurrence of '&' within s is replaced by the substring of t that matches r. Sub is usually evaluated for the sake of its side effect, which is to change t. Therefore t is usually a variable. The value returned by sub is 1 if a substitution was made and 0 otherwise. For example, the output of the program

>```
>BEGIN {
>    var = "chalcedony"
>    print sub(/l.*n/, "nc", var), var
>    }
>```

>is

>```
>1 chancy
>```

gsub($r, s[, t]$)

>Like sub, except that the substitution is made globally, i.e., for all occurrences of r in t. Each substitution is made to t as modified by previous substitutions and is made at the first occurrence of r to the right of where the previous substitution if any ended. The value returned by gsub is the number of substitutions made.

split($s, a[, fs]$)

>Splits the string s into fields using the separator fs, then puts those fields into elements of the array a with subscripts '1', '2', etc. If fs is not specified it is taken to be FS. The string s is split in the same way that an input record would be (see Section 8.5.7). Note that the subscripts are strings, not numbers,

so the subscript '10' comes before the subscript '2' when you iterate through the subscripts of the array.

Formatting a Sequence of Values.   The following function formats a sequence of values:

sprintf(*fmt*, *expr*, ...)

Formats *expr* ... according to the format *fmt* and returns the string containing these formatted values. The formatting is done in the same way that it is by the print statement (see Section 8.5.15).

8.5.13
Predefined
Numerical
Functions

The following functions provide various numerical operations.

Integer Part.   The following function provides the integer part of a number:

int(*x*)   Returns the integer part of x, i.e., truncates x towards zero to an integer. For example, the value of 'int(-2.7)' is -2.

Elementary Functions.   Awk provides the following elementary mathematical functions:

sin(*x*)   Returns the sine of x radians.

cos(*x*)   Returns the cosine of x radians.

exp(*x*)   Returns e^x, the exponential function of x.

log(*x*)   Returns $\log x$, the natural logarithm of x.

atan2(*y*,*x*)

Returns the arctangent of y/x. The result r is chosen so that $-\pi \le r \le \pi$.

sqrt(*x*)   Returns the square root of x.

Random Number Generation.   The following functions support random number generation:

rand()   Returns a random number r, $0 \le r < 1$.

srand([*x*])

Uses x as a new seed for rand. The seed provides a starting value for the sequence of random numbers produced by rand. If you call srand with a particular argument k, then k determines the ensuing sequence of rand values. If you later call srand again with the same argument k, rand will produce the same sequence of values.

The value of the seed x should be a nonzero integer.[8] If you omit x, awk uses the time of day as the seed.

---

8. Note that although the seed is an integer, the values produced by rand are not integers. Rand actually computes the random numbers as integers and then converts them to floating-point numbers before returning them. Each integer is derived from the previous one unless it is specified by a call on srand.

**8.5.14
Reading Input
Explicitly**

The `getline` predefined function reads an input line from a specified source, either a file or the output of a UNIX command. The `getline` function provides more precise control over reading than does `awk`'s default reading mechanism and also enables you to read from files other than standard input.

Although `getline` is considered to be a function, the conventions for calling it are entirely different from those of other functions. A call on `getline` has one of the following forms:

`getline [`*var*`]`

> Reads the next record from standard input into the variable *var* if *var* is specified and into $0 otherwise. As a side effect, the predefined variables NR and FNR (see Section 8.5.9) are both incremented. If *var* is specified, the input line is not split into fields and the predefined variable NF is left unchanged. If *var* is not specified, the input line is split just as though it had been read implicitly and NF is set to the number of fields. The value returned by `getline` is 1 if a record was read successfully, 0 if an end of file was encountered, and -1 if an error occurred on the attempted read.

`getline [`*var*`] <` *file*

> Like the previous form, except that `awk` reads the record from *file* instead of from standard input. The variable *file* must be specified as a string-valued expression giving the name of the file. A '<' operator following `getline` is interpreted as specifying a file rather than as a comparison operator unless the `getline` happens to be preceded by '|'. Successive `getline`s specifying the same file read successive lines of that file unless you close the file with `close` (see Section 8.5.16).

cmd `| getline [`*var*`]`

> Like the first form, except that `awk` executes the UNIX command *cmd* in a subshell and sends the lines of its standard output to `getline`. The variable *cmd* must be specified as a string-valued expression giving the name of the command. Repeated calls on `getline` with the same command do not cause the command to be executed repeatedly. Instead, the command is executed once and its output is passed to `getline` one line at a time, so successive `getline` calls retrieve successive output lines. You can cause *cmd* to be executed again by using the `close` statement (see Section 8.5.16).

Because the `getline` call has such an odd syntax, it's wise to enclose it in parentheses if it's part of a larger expression.

**8.5.15
Producing Output**

The `print` and `printf` statements produce output. By default this output is sent to standard output, but you can redirect it by attaching a redirection to the statement. A redirection is indicated by *redir* in the statement forms below (see "Redirecting Output" on page 369). Here are the forms of the `print` and `printf` statements:

`print`   Sends $0 to standard output.

```
print expr [, expr] ... [redir]
print(expr [, expr] ... ) [redir]
```
> Evaluates each expression *expr* in turn, converts its value to a string if necessary, and sends that string to standard output. Successive values are separated by the output field separator, whose value is given by the predefined variable OFS. The last value is followed by the output record separator, whose value is given by the predefined variable ORS. The default value of OFS is a single space; the default value of ORS is a single newline.

```
printf fmt, expr [, expr] ... [redir]
printf(fmt, expr [, expr] ... ) [redir]
```
> Evaluates each expression *expr* in turn and sends the values of these expressions to standard output, formatting them according to the output format *fmt* (see "Output Formats" below). To format a list of expressions and send the result to a string instead of to a file or pipe, use the sprintf function (see "Formatting a Sequence of Values" on page 367).

A use of '>' in a print or printf statement is interpreted as a redirection operator rather than as a comparison unless either the '>' and its operands or the expression list of the statement is enclosed in parentheses. In the parenthesized forms of print and printf, no whitespace is permitted between the left parenthesis and the 'print' or 'printf'.

Note the difference between the following two statements:

```
print 1 2 3
print 1, 2, 3
```

The first one contains a single expression that is the concatenation of three numbers and produces '123'. The second one contains three expressions and therefore produces three numbers separated by the output field separator, namely, '1 2 3'.

Redirecting Output.   The *redir* components of the print and printf statements have one of the following forms:

> *file*   Sends the output to *file*. The variable *file* is a string that names a file. The first such redirection for a particular file erases the contents of the file; subsequent redirections accumulate output in that file.

>> *file*   Appends the output to *file*. The variable *file* is a string that names a file. Unlike '> *file*', this form does not erase the previous contents of the file.

| *cmd*   Pipes the output to the UNIX command *cmd*, making it part of the standard input to *cmd*. The variable *cmd* is a string that names a UNIX command. The command is called only once unless it is closed by a close statement (see Section 8.5.16). Successive outputs from print and printf are passed as successive lines of input to *cmd*.

Output Formats.   An output format specifies how a list of values is to be represented as a string. The format is a string that acts as a template, with fixed and variable parts. The fixed parts are reproduced literally; successive variable parts, called *format specifications*, specify how successive values are to be represented. The format specifications are always introduced by '%', with '%%' indicating a literal '%'. For example, the format in the print statement

```
printf("The current value of %s is %03d.\n", "lemming", 29)
```

has two format specifications, '%s' and '%03d', that format the values 'lemming' and 29. The '%s' specifies string formatting and the '%03d' specifies three-digit decimal formatting with leading zeros. The resulting output is

```
The current value of lemming is 029.
```

In general, a format specification has three parts: the '%' that introduces the format specification, a sequence of up to three modifiers, and a format character. The format character specifies the general form of the result, called a *field*, while the modifiers provide additional details. The format characters are as follows:

c	The ASCII character with this numerical code
s	String
d	Decimal integer
o	Octal integer (unsigned)
x	Hexadecimal integer (unsigned)
f	Decimal fraction in the form [-]d ... d.dddddd with as many digits as necessary preceding the decimal point
e	Scientific notation in the form [-]d.ddddddE[+-]dd
g	Either e or f format, whichever is shorter, with extra zeros suppressed

The modifiers, which must appear in the indicated order if they appear at all, are as follows:

-	Left-justify the output string within its field.
w	If the field is less than *w* characters wide, pad it out to *w* characters. If *w* is written with a leading zero, pad with zeros; otherwise pad with blanks.
.*prec*	For a string, truncate the string after *prec* characters; for a number with a decimal fraction part, use *prec* digits in that part.

The following examples show how values are formatted according to various specifications, with spaces indicated by '␣':

Format	*Value*	*Result*
%c	68	D
%d	-68	-68
%4d	68	␣␣68
%-4d	68	68␣␣
%04d	68	0068
%x	68	44
%f	68.1	68.100000
%7.2f	68.1	␣␣68.10

```
%e      68.1    6.810000e+01
%g      68.1    68.1
%s      shark   shark
%.4s    shark   shar
%-5.2s  shark   sh␣␣␣
```

8.5.16
Closing Files and Pipes

When output is redirected to a file, the file is ordinarily opened only once. Successive output lines are sent to the file, so its final contents become the concatenation of all the lines sent to it. Similarly, when input is redirected from a file, the file is ordinarily opened only once and successive input lines are read from it. Input and output piped to or from commands behave analogously.

You can in effect reinitialize a file or pipe by closing it with the following command:

close(*str*)

> Closes the file or piped command whose name is *str*. Subsequent input from or output to a file causes it to be reopened. Subsequent reads or writes start again from the beginning. Subsequent input to or output from a piped command causes it to be executed again.

8.5.17
Executing System Commands

The following function enables you to execute a UNIX command from within an awk program:

system(*cmd*)

> Executes the UNIX command *cmd* in a subshell. The value of the function is the exit value of *cmd* (see Section 2.7.3).

8.5.18
Command-line Arguments

The awk command line can contain zero or more arguments, according to the general conventions for command lines (see Section 2.14.3). Certain items on the command line don't count as arguments: the -f and -F command-line options, the program itself, variable assignments, and redirections. Usually the arguments are names of input files but in fact they can be arbitrary strings (quoted if necessary). You can retrieve the command-line arguments via the following two predefined variables, which are set by awk when it starts up:

ARGV
> An array containing the command-line arguments. The first argument, ARGV[0], is the name of the command itself, normally 'awk'.[9] The remaining ones, ARGV[1], ARGV[2], ... , contain the actual arguments.

ARGC
> The number of command-line arguments, including ARGV[0]. This number is equal to the subscript of the last actual argument.

For example, the command line

```
awk -f kvetch ketch yawl
```

---

9. If awk is called via a differently named link, ARGV[0] contains the name of that link.

leads to the following values for `ARGV` and `ARGC`:

```
ARGV[0]: awk
ARGV[1]: ketch
ARGV[2]: yawl
ARGC: 3
```

8.5.19 Expressions as Statements

An expression can be treated as a statement. An expression appearing in the context of a statement is evaluated and its value discarded. Expressions whose main operator is an assignment operator are often used as statements (see "Assignment Operators" on page 364).

8.5.20 Control-Flow Statements

The control-flow statements relate to the grouping of statements and to statements that affect what is executed next.

Grouping and Empty Statements. The following two constructs provide grouping and an empty statement:

`{ stmt ... }`

> Executes a group of statements. A group of statements enclosed in braces can be used in any context requiring a single statement. The statements must be separated by semicolons or newlines.

`;`

> Does nothing. This construct is called an *empty statement*. You can provide an empty statement by writing nothing at all in any context where a semicolon would not be required after some other kind of statement. For example, a group containing a single empty statement can be written as '`{}`'.

Conditional Statement. Using a conditional statement, you can test the value of an expression and use the result to select a statement to be executed:

`if (expr) stmt₁ [; else stmt₂]`

> Executes the statement $stmt_1$ if the value of the expression *expr* is true; otherwise executes the statement $stmt_2$. For nested `if`'s, each `else` is paired with the nearest unpaired `if` to its left. Although $stmt_1$ and $stmt_2$ are single statements, you can execute any number of statements as $stmt_1$ or $stmt_2$ by making the statements into a group.

Iteration Statements. The following statements provide various forms of iteration. Wherever a single statement is required you can put several statements by enclosing those statements in a group.

`while (expr) stmt`

> Executes the statement *stmt* while the expression *expr* is true.

`do stmt while (expr)`

> Executes the statement *stmt* once, then executes it repeatedly while the expression *expr* is true. The expression *expr* is tested before each execution of *stmt* except the first one.

```
for (expr₁; expr₂; expr₃) stmt
```
Evaluates the expression $expr_1$, then performs the following steps repeatedly:

(1)   Evaluates $expr_2$. If the value is false, terminates the iteration.

(2)   Executes *stmt*.

(3)   Evaluates $expr_3$.

For example, the awk program

```
BEGIN {
    n = ARGV[1]
    for (i = 1; i <= n; i++)
        print i, sqrt(i)
}
```

produces a sequence of lines listing the integers from 1 to n and their square roots, with n being provided as the command-line argument.

Any of the expressions in a for statement may be omitted; if $expr_2$ is omitted it is taken to be true. Thus the form

```
for (;;) stmt
```

causes awk to execute *stmt* repeatedly until the iteration is somehow interrupted, e.g., by a break statement.

```
for (var in array) stmt
```
Executes the statement *stmt* with *var* set to each subscript of the array *array* in turn.

Breaking Out of Iterations.   The following statements break out of iterations:

break   Leaves the innermost while, for, or do statement containing the break, then terminates execution of the containing statement.

continue   Starts the next iteration of the innermost while, for, or do statement containing the continue, skipping any statements remaining in the current iteration.

next   Reads a new input record and starts the next iteration of the main input loop. The next statement cannot be used within the action of a BEGIN or END statement-action pair.

exit [*expr*]
If awk is currently executing the action of an END statement-action pair or if there is no END statement-action pair, exits from the program with exit status *expr*. The default for *expr* is 0. Otherwise, goes immediately to the action of the END statement-action pair.

8.5.21
User-Defined
Functions
	A user-defined function has the form
	
	``
	function name(param [, param] ...) {
	    [stmt] ...
	}
	``

and may appear wherever a pattern-action statement may. When the function is called, the parameters *param* ... are initialized to the corresponding arguments. The calling protocol passes copies of numerical or string arguments ("call by value") but passes array arguments without copying the array elements ("call by reference"). Therefore the effect of an assignment to a numerical or string parameter is not visible at the point of call, but an assignment to an element of an array parameter *is* visible at the point of call. The nature of a particular parameter is determined only when the function call actually takes place.

A function call can have fewer arguments than there are parameters in the corresponding function definition. The excess parameters act as local variables for the function definition, and in fact the only way to create local variables is to make them extra parameters. Changes to local variables (aside from changes to array elements) are not visible upon return from a function call. Any variables that are not local are global. Global variables are accessible throughout the awk program except when they are obscured by a parameter with the same name. Awk functions can be recursive.

Returning from a Function. You can return from a function to the calling context either by running off the end of the list of statements in the function definition or by executing a `return` statement of the form

```
return [expr]
```

If *expr* is given, its value becomes the value of the function at the point of call. If *expr* is not given, the value of the function is undefined—which is not a problem provided that the function call appears in the context of a statement. Running off the end of the list of statements is equivalent to executing `return` without an expression.

8.6   Other Data Manipulation Languages

You may be interested in knowing of two other languages commonly used on UNIX systems for the same purposes as awk: Icon and perl. Neither is part of any UNIX vendor's standard distribution, but they are widely available nonetheless.

8.6.1 **The Icon** **Programming** **Language**	Icon is a general-purpose high-level language with a large repertoire of operations for processing strings and other symbolic data. Icon has a C-like syntax and borrows many ideas from C, but its principal ancestor is the string processing language Snobol. Designed by Ralph Griswold at the University of Arizona, Icon is one of the most elegant and powerful programming languages now available. The program used to generate the index of this book was written in Icon.

You can obtain Icon over the Internet via anonymous `ftp` from `cs.arizona.edu`, IP address `192.12.69.1`, in the directory `/icon` (see Section 10.7), or by dialing into the Icon bulletin board (1-602-621-2283). You can send electronic mail to `icon-project@cs.arizona.edu` over the Internet or to `{uunet,allegra,noao}!arizona!icon-project` over the UUCP network.

Central to Icon is the notion of a *generator*, a procedure that yields a sequence of values rather than a single value. When the generator has no more values to yield, it fails. Control structures are driven by the failure of generators rather than by the more usual true and false boolean values. Generators lead naturally to the notion of goal-directed evaluation, in which alternatives in a pattern match or other similar construct are tried until a combination is found that succeeds.

Icon provides a variety of high-level data structures including strings of arbitrary length, records, tables (like `awk` associative arrays), sets, and lists. These are supported by a large collection of useful intrinsic operations. String scanning is provided by string-analysis functions and a pattern-matching operator '?' rather than by regular expression matching. Like `awk`, Icon uses no declarations; a variable can contain a value of any type. Conversions among data types are automatic but can also be requested explicitly.

Icon has been implemented for UNIX as well as for many other operating systems. The most popular implementation as of this writing is based on an interpreter, but a compiler for Icon has recently been developed. A noteworthy feature of the UNIX version of Icon is its ability to open a UNIX command as a pipe. For example, the Icon expression

```
datfiles := open("ls *.dat", "p")
```

assigns a pipe to the file object `datfiles`. A subsequent expression

```
while write(read(datfiles))
```

sends the list of the files whose names end with '`*.dat`' to standard output.

8.6.2
The `perl` Language

The `perl` Practical Extraction and Report Language is a language for manipulating text, files, and processes designed by Larry Wall and Randal L. Schwartz. You can obtain `perl` over the Internet via anonymous `ftp` from `jpl-devvax.jpl.nasa.gov`, IP address `128.149.1.143`, in the directory `/pub/perl.4.0/` (see Section 10.7) or over the UUCP network from the OSUCIS archive (reference [U3]).

Stylistically eclectic, `perl` borrows from C, `awk`, and shell programming. It is free of arbitrary limitations—lines can be of any length, arrays can have any number of elements, variable names can be as long as you wish, and binary data will not cause problems. Perl provides all the capability of `awk` but in addition provides convenient access to the facilities of UNIX itself. Using `perl`, you can move files, rename them, change their permissions, and so forth. You can create and destroy processes, control the flow of data among processes, and use sockets to communicate with processes on other machines. Perl has become particularly popular among UNIX system administrators.

9

Sending and Receiving Mail

Sending and receiving messages by electronic mail is a major activity on most UNIX systems. You can use electronic mail to communicate with users at your own site as well as at other sites. Electronic mail is also the medium for participating in newsgroups and bulletin boards.

A *mailer* is a program for sending and receiving electronic mail. In this chapter we focus on mailers and how to use them. In the next chapter we discuss remote addressing and also discuss other forms of communication with remote sites.

In order to handle your electronic mail you need to know which mailers are available on your system and what their names are. That may not be as easy as it seems. Many different UNIX mailers are in use, and at least two of them are often named `mail`—the original Seventh Edition mailer and the Berkeley mailer. BSD UNIX systems call the Berkeley mailer `Mail`, while modern System V systems retain the name `mail` for the Seventh Edition mailer and use the name `mailx` for their adaptation of the Berkeley one, which they usually provide because it is far superior. The Seventh Edition mailer is often referred to as 'binmail' because it resides in the /bin directory, even on BSD UNIX systems.[1]

In this chapter we cover the Berkeley `Mail` mailer and the Seventh Edition `mail` mailer, calling them by the names used in System V: `mailx` for the Berkeley mailer and `mail` for the Seventh Edition mailer. If your mailer is a variant of Berkeley `Mail`, our description of `mailx` should apply to it. You can see which mailer you have by typing '?'—most mailers

---

1. On BSD UNIX systems the default path gives you the Berkeley mailer, but you can get the Seventh Edition one by explicitly specifying /bin/mail as the command name.

recognize this as a request for help—and comparing the list of commands you see with those of the mailers we describe in this chapter.

Technically, the mailers you work with as a user are *mail user agents.* Most of them use other, more primitive, mailers to handle the actual transmission of mail. These other mailers, known as *mail transport agents,* go by names such as `smail`, `rmail`, `delivermail`, and `sendmail`. You'll probably never need to deal with a mail transport agent directly.

In this chapter, besides `mail` and `mailx`, we briefly cover the MH and `elm` mailers. The emacs editor also includes its own mailer, which we discuss in Section 7.27.

9.1   What's in a Message?

Here is an example of a message, sent using `mailx`:

```
From gkc  Wed Feb 27 21:35:13 1991
Received: by booker (5.61/1.35)
    id AA00406; Wed, 27 Feb 91 21:35:13 -0500
Date: Wed, 27 Feb 91 21:35:13 -0500
From: gkc (Gilbert K. Chesterton)
Message-Id: <9102280235.AA00406@booker>
To: gbs
Subject: A shocking observation
Status: RO

To look at you, Shaw, one would think
there was a famine in England.
```

And here is the reply to it:

```
From gbs  Wed Feb 27 21:36:01 1991
Received: by booker (5.61/1.35)
    id AA00413; Wed, 27 Feb 91 21:36:01 -0500
Date: Wed, 27 Feb 91 21:36:01 -0500
From: gbs (George Bernard Shaw)
Message-Id: <9102280236.AA00413@booker>
To: gkc
Subject: Re:  A shocking observation
Status: RO

To look at you, Chesterton, one would think
you were the cause of it.
```

As these examples show, a message consists of a *header* that contains information about the message followed by the text of the message. The header starts with a *postmark* that says who sent the message and when it was delivered to you. The postmark for the first message above is

```
From gkc  Wed Feb 27 21:35:13 1991
```

The postmark is attached as part of local mail delivery and is not part of the header. A postmark is not attached to messages sent to remote systems such as those sent over the Internet.

The rest of the header consists of a sequence of *fields*. (Observe that the 'From' in a postmark is followed by a space, not a colon; the lack of a colon distinguishes it from the 'From' field below it.) Each field starts with a field name followed by a colon. Which fields are present in a message header depends in part on which mailer first sent the message and which other mailers have processed it afterwards. It should be obvious what most of the header information means, but a few points are worth explaining:

- The (5.61/1.35) in the 'Received' field indicates the version of the mail transport agent—sendmail in this case—that handled this message.

- The date indicates when the message was sent. The '-0500' in the 'Date' field indicates that the time at the receiving machine is five hours ahead of Greenwich Mean Time.

- The 'Re:' in the subject of the second message indicates that this message is a response to the previous one. Most mailers automatically create the subject of a response by putting 'Re:' in front of the subject of the original message.

- The 'RO' in the 'Status' field indicates that you have read this message and that it is an "old" one (see Section 9.3.10). A message can be old even if you haven't read it. This use of the 'Status' field is peculiar to mailx.

Some messages have other fields in their headers in addition to the ones shown here; for example, a message from a newsgroup may have an 'Article-Id' field.

When a mailer processes a message, it places the message in an *envelope* that bears a description of the message for routing purposes. Any mailer can then process the message just by looking at its envelope—even if the message itself has been encrypted.

**9.1.1
Recipients**

A *recipient* of a message is the person or entity to whom the message is sent. You can send a message to any number of recipients. A recipient can be a user in your own system or a user at a remote computer linked to your system over a network or telephone line (see Section 10.1). Most newer mailers and mail facilities also allow a recipient to be a file or a program. Mail sent to a file is appended to that file; mail sent to a program is used as the standard input of that program.

Some mailers enable you to denote a set of recipients by a single name called an *alias*—see, for example, the alias command of mailx (p. 394). You may have your own set of aliases, and in addition your system may provide some. System-wide aliases are listed in /etc/aliases or /usr/lib/aliases.

Although a message has only one sender, it may have many recipients. The primary recipients are listed in the 'To' field. You can send "carbon copies" of a message to other recipients. These recipients are listed in a 'Cc' field. You can also send "blind carbon copies", which are listed in a

'Bcc' field that does not show up on the copies of the message received by any of its other recipients.

9.2 Mailboxes

A *mailbox* is a place where messages are stored. Each UNIX user has at least two mailboxes, a *primary mailbox* for new mail and a *secondary mailbox* for old mail:

- When a mailer receives a message addressed to you, it stores the message in your primary mailbox, also known as your *system mailbox*.[2] If your user name is zog, your primary mailbox is a file named /usr/mail/zog, /usr/spool/mail/zog, /var/spool/mail/zog, or a similar name assigned by your system. You can locate it by typing

  ```
  echo $MAIL
  ```

  Although you have write permission for your primary mailbox, you have no control over its location; it isn't even in a subdirectory of your home directory.

- Once you've read a message, the mailer normally puts it into your default secondary mailbox, a file named mbox in your home directory (and sometimes referred to as your *mbox*). Thus if your user name is zog, your default secondary mailbox is /usr/zog/mbox. You can have the mailer put your mail in a different file if you choose.

In addition to your primary and secondary mailboxes, you can have other mailboxes, which we call *auxiliary mailboxes*. Auxiliary mailboxes are useful for sorting mail by category or according to the person who sent it.

When you read your mail, the mailer by default shows you each message in your primary mailbox and adds it to your secondary mailbox after you've read it. These are some of the alternative dispositions you can request:

- Leave the message in your primary mailbox.
- Delete the message altogether.
- Save the message in a mailbox other than the usual one.

9.2.1 Forwarding Mail

You can arrange to have your mail forwarded to one or more recipients. Forwarding your mail to yourself under another name or at a different site can be particularly useful when you're away.[3] How you arrange forwarding depends on which mail transport agents your system uses.

Forwarding Mail with a .forward File.   For systems such as BSD UNIX, SunOS, and AIX that use sendmail as the first step in mail transport, you

---

2. Zog was the last king of Albania.

3. BSD UNIX systems have a vacation program that you can use to notify people who send you mail that you are away. The vacation program makes use of your .forward file.

have your mail forwarded by placing a file named `.forward` in your home directory that lists the recipients to whom your forwarded mail should be sent. A recipient can be a user name (local or remote), a file, or a program:

- A file name must be specified using an absolute pathname. Each forwarded message is appended to the specified file.

- A program is written in the form '`"|`*cmd*`"`'. Whenever a message is forwarded, the command *cmd* is called with the message as its standard input. The double quotes are usually needed to prevent the shell from misinterpreting the '`|`'.

You can keep a local copy of forwarded mail by employing this undocumented trick: include yourself as one of the recipients in `.forward` but put a backslash in front of your name. You'll continue to receive a copy of your mail in your primary mailbox as usual. Another method is to forward your mail to a file, where it will accumulate.

The recipients listed in the `.forward` file are separated by commas, optionally followed by whitespace or newlines. Assuming your user name is `duchess`, you can set up a `.forward` file by typing something like

```
cat > .forward
mhare, dodo, dormouse@tparty
\duchess
EOF
```

(see Section 3.4). Your mail will be forwarded to these people and also will be saved in your own mailbox.

If you don't know whether your system supports `.forward` files, you can find out by typing

```
cd
cat > .forward
"|cat"
EOF
```

and sending yourself a message. If the message appears on your terminal, `.forward` works in your system. Don't forget to delete `.forward` after you've done this experiment!

Forwarding Mail from Your Primary Mailbox. Some systems, notably Xenix, use the Seventh Edition mailer (the one we call `mail` in this book) rather than `sendmail` as their principal mail transport agent. In these systems you have your mail forwarded by setting the contents of your primary mailbox to the single line

```
Forward to person
```

You can do this with the `mail -F` command, provided that `mail` actually refers to the System V mail program (see Section 9.4). Alternatively you can just copy the necessary line into the file by typing

```
cat > $MAIL
Forward to person
EOF
```

To forward your mail to several people, replace *person* by a list of those people, separating their names by commas or whitespace.

Note: You should empty your primary mailbox by reading whatever is in it before you set it up to forward your mail.

A number of systems use `sendmail` for network mail and Seventh Edition `mail` for local mail. These systems honor both forms of forwarding—but if you build a `.forward` file, it takes precedence over any forwarding notice in your primary mailbox.[4]

9.3   The `mailx` (Berkeley `Mail`) **Mailer**

The `mailx` mailer is the System V adaptation of the `Mail` mailer developed at Berkeley. You can use `mailx` either to send mail or to read it. `Mailx` is a mail user agent that acts as a "front" for the mail transport agents that actually deliver mail. It moves mail among your mailboxes and mail files, shows you your incoming messages and their headers, and passes your outgoing mail to the transport agents. It has nothing to do with putting mail into your primary mailbox—it just handles your mail once it arrives there.

**9.3.1
Sending a Message**

The command for sending a mail message has the form

> `mailx` [*options*] *namelist*

where *options* is a sequence of options taken from those listed below and *namelist* is a list of recipients. The names of the recipients are separated by whitespace or commas. After you've given the command, `mailx` asks you for the subject of your message. It then puts you into *input mode* (see Section 9.3.21), expecting you to type the text of your message followed by an end-of-message indicator, usually [EOF]. You can interrupt the composition of your message to give any of the input mode commands described in the subsections following Section 9.3.21. An input mode command starts with a tilde (~) and appears on a line by itself. You can use input mode commands for such tasks as including a message you've received in the text of the message you're sending or adding "carbon copy" recipients to an outgoing message.

**9.3.2
Reading Your Mail**

The command for reading your mail has the form

> `mailx` [*options*]

---

4. How all this works is unpleasantly complicated. To make matters worse, it varies from one kind of system to another and can also depend on how an individual system is configured.

where *options*, again, is a sequence of options taken from those listed below. Mailx first gives you a summary of the headers of the messages you've received (unless you tell it to do something else) and then puts you into *command mode*. In command mode you can give any of the commands listed below in the subsections following Section 9.3.11, including commands that let you switch over to sending mail. It would be convenient if you could call mailx in a way that would put you into command mode even when you don't have any mail, but unfortunately mailx doesn't provide for that.

When you exit from mailx after reading some messages in your primary mailbox, it transfers those messages to your secondary mailbox. The messages you haven't read remain in your primary mailbox. When mailx transfers a message to your secondary mailbox, it puts that message at the beginning, not the end, of the secondary mailbox. The secondary mailbox therefore has the newest messages first if they were put there by mailx itself. However, some of the commands listed below also transfer messages to mailboxes; these commands always append the messages to the *end* of the mailbox.

The simplest way to retrieve messages with mailx is to type (Enter) in response to every query and to type 'q' when mailx tells you that it's reached the end of the file. Mailx shows you all of your incoming messages and transfers each one to your secondary mailbox after you've read it. You can review the messages in your secondary mailbox by typing

```
mailx -f
```

and then typing (Enter) after each one. To delete a message from any mailbox, type 'dp' after you've read it. That deletes the message and shows you the next one.

9.3.3
Quick Exit

You can exit from mailx when you're at a mailx prompt by typing 'q' or 'x' (see Section 9.3.18). If mailx is showing you a long message and you don't want to see any more of it, you can get back to the mailx prompt by typing (Intr).

9.3.4
Recipients for
mailx **Messages**

A recipient of a mailx message may be any of the following:

- A user registered in your system.
- A user at a remote site (see Section 10.1).
- A file for which you have write permission. You need a '/' somewhere in the file name so that the mailer knows you're referring to a file rather than a user. You can designate a file in your current directory by putting '. /' in front of its name.
- A shell-level command with the message used as standard input, denoted by '|*cmd*'. You should quote this form to prevent the shell from interpreting the '|' as a pipe symbol, for example writing it as '"| noteit"'. Mailx does not allow you to use redirection within *cmd*.

The recipients you can specify to `mailx` are very similar to those you can specify in a `.forward` file (see "Forwarding Mail with a `.forward` File" on page 379). These are the main differences:

- A file name in `.forward` must be absolute, but a file name as a recipient for `mailx` can be relative, either to your current directory or to your home directory.
- You can use redirection in a command appearing as a recipient in `.forward`, even though you cannot use redirection in a command appearing as a recipient in a call on `mailx`.

**9.3.5
Naming Files after
Recipients**

Certain commands such as `Save` save a message in a file named after the message's sender, providing a convenient way of sorting your mail. When `mailx` stores a message in a file named after its sender, it derives the actual file name by stripping off all network addressing from the sender's name and prefixing it by '+' if the `outfolder` variable (p. 401) is enabled. The treatment of '+' is in turn determined by whether the `folder` variable (p. 401) is enabled; if `folder` isn't enabled, the '+' simply becomes part of the file name.

To illustrate, suppose that the current directory is `$HOME/stash` and that `mailx` is saving a message sent by `amherst!emily` (user emily at remote computer `amherst`) in a file named after her. The file where `mailx` stores the message is determined by `folder` and `outfolder` as follows:

`outfolder` *disabled*	`$HOME/stash/emily`
`outfolder` *enabled*, `folder` *disabled*	`$HOME/stash/+emily`
`outfolder` *enabled*, `folder`=`mail`	`$HOME/mail/emily`

The same rules apply when a message is saved in a file named after the first recipient of the message, an effect you can obtain with the `-F` command-line option.

**9.3.6
Command-line
Options**

The command-line options for `mailx` depend on whether you're sending a message or reading your mail.

Options for Sending a Message.   When you call `mailx` to send a message, the options on the command line are as follows:

`-s` *string*   Set the subject of the message to *string*. If you specify this option, you don't get a 'Subject' prompt.

`-i`   Ignore any interrupts that occur while you're composing mail. This option is often useful when you're working with a noisy phone line that can generate spurious interrupts.

`-F`   Save each message of your mail in a file named after the first recipient of that message rather than in your secondary mailbox (see Section 9.3.5). This option overrides any setting of the `record` variable (p. 401). It's useful for sorting mail according to whom you've sent it to.

The following options are, to quote the Berkeley manual, "not for human use". They are intended to support scripts and programs that employ `mailx` to transmit mail over networks. They affect only the envelopes of messages, not the messages themselves, and their effects are not visible to ordinary users of `mailx`.

-h *n*	Set the number of network hops so far to *n*. This option would be used by a script that retransmits messages to another site. The hop count is used by mail transport agents to prevent messages with defective addresses from cycling endlessly around a network; messages whose hop count exceeds a certain maximum (usually 17) are returned to the sender or, if that isn't possible, to a postmaster.
-r *addr*	Cause *addr* to appear to network delivery software as the sender of the message, and disable '~' commands. Such a substitute address is rejected by `sendmail`, the underlying mail transport agent, unless the sender is known to be trustworthy.
-U	Convert path-style UUCP addresses to domain-style Internet addresses (see Section 10.1). Uses of '!' are removed where possible and '.UUCP' is appended to the address.

Options for Reading Your Mail.   When you call `mailx` to read your mail, the options on the command line are as follows:

-e	Test for presence of mail and exit immediately. The status code on exit is 1 if you have mail and 0 if you don't.[5] You can use this option in initialization files such as `.profile` and `.login` to test for the existence of mail without actually processing it.
-H	Just show a summary of the headers and exit.
-N	Go into command mode immediately without showing a summary of the headers.
-f [*file*]	Read mail from *file* instead of from your primary mailbox. If *file* is omitted, read the mail from your secondary mailbox.
-u *user*	Read mail from *user*'s mailbox instead of from your own. This option will work only if you have read access to that mailbox.

The following options are sometimes useful for reading messages sent by newsgroups:

-I	In the header summary, treat the first newsgroup in the 'Newsgroups' field as the sender of the message. This option can only be used if the -f option is also present. It's useful for scanning mail that comes from several newsgroups at once.
-T *file*	Extract the 'Article-Id' field of each message containing such a field and list these fields in *file*, one per line. This option is intended for use in shell scripts that use `mailx` to read mail sent by newsgroups. Mailx does not accept the -T option unless you also specify an explicit input file with the -f option.

---

5. The usual convention for status codes is that 0 indicates success and any other value indicates failure. You can think of these status codes as indicating success or failure in testing for the *absence* of mail.

Option for Suppressing Initialization. The following option can be applied either when you're sending mail or when you're receiving it:

-n   Don't execute the commands in the initialization file for this mailer (see Section 9.3.7). The commands in this file are intended to be appropriate for all users. `Mailx` executes these commands, if at all, before it does anything else. Specifying -n does not stop `mailx` from executing the commands in your local initialization file.

9.3.7 Initialization Files for `mailx`

When `mailx` is called, it executes the commands in two initialization files before it does anything else—in particular, before it asks you for any input. It executes these commands whether you're sending mail or reading it.

*   The first initialization file is global (common to all users). It is named either `/usr/lib/mailx/mailx.rc` or `/usr/lib/Mail.rc`, depending on your system. This file contains commands that are expected to be useful to anyone. You can suppress its execution with the -n option described above.

*   The second initialization file is local (particular to each user). By default it is named `.mailrc` and resides in each user's home directory. You can specify a different local initialization file by putting its file name into the environment variable `MAILRC` (see p. 399). You can tailor the initialization file to suit your own needs.

When `mailx` is called, it first executes the global initialization file and then the local initialization file of the user who called it if these files exist.

Here is an example of an initialization file:

```
set PAGER=less
set crt=24
alias jekyll cellar!hyde
group mates wynken blynken nod
```

The settings for `PAGER` and `crt` cause long messages (those of at least 24 lines) to be shown using the `less` paging program. The `alias` lets you substitute the short name `jekyll` for the longer network address `cellar!hyde`. The `group` lets you give a name to a set of people so that you can easily send a message to all of them at once. Initialization files often contain long lists of aliases and groups. The `set`, `alias`, and `group` commands are all explained below.

9.3.8 Using a Folder Directory

You can keep your secondary and auxiliary mailboxes in a separate directory that you use for all your saved mail. The mailboxes in that directory are called *folders*, and the directory itself is called your *folder directory*.[6]

When you specify a file name to `mailx` and that name starts with '+', `mailx` takes that name to be relative to your folder directory (if you have

---

6. The `mailx` documentation from Berkeley is inconsistent in its use of the term "folder", sometimes taking it to mean a single mailbox and sometimes taking it to mean the directory that contains your mailboxes.

one). For instance, if your folder directory is `$HOME/mymail`, `mailx` takes the file name `+aaron` to mean `$HOME/mail/aaron`. You can use this convention for file names that you specify for `mailx` internal commands. You can also use it on the `mailx` command line provided that `folder` is set in your `mailx` initialization file. If you haven't specified a folder directory, a '+' at the start of a file name is not treated specially by `mailx`.

You can set up a folder directory by including commands in your initialization file that take the following actions:

(1) Set the `folder` variable to your mail directory (which must already exist).
(2) Enable the `outfolder` variable.
(3) Set the `MBOX` variable to `+mbox`.
(4) Optionally, set the `DEAD` variable to '`+dead.letter`' (see p. 401).

See Section 9.3.33 for a description of these variables and "Setting the Values of Variables" on page 394 for the commands that set variables..

The `followup`, `Followup`, `Save`, and `Copy` commands save a message in a file named after the sender of the message. The first two steps above cause `mailx` to keep these files in your folder directory. The third step ensures that your secondary mailbox is in your folder directory rather than in your home directory.

9.3.9
Message Lists

Many commands use *message lists* to designate a subset of the messages you've retrieved. The numbers in a message list are those that appear in the header summary. The notation for message lists is as follows:

n	Message number *n*.
.	The current message. Whenever you read a message, that message becomes the current message.
^	The first (undeleted) message.
$	The last (undeleted) message.
m-n	The messages numbered from *m* to *n*, where *m* and *n* are any of the single message specifiers given above.
*	All the messages in the message list.
name	All messages from the user *name*.
/string	All messages with *string* in the subject. For the purposes of this test, the case of the letters in *string* is ignored.
:*c*	All messages of type *c*, where *c* is given as follows:

d	deleted messages
n	new messages (from your primary mailbox)
o	old messages
r	messages that you've read
u	messages that are unread

In the commands below, an omitted *msglist* or *msg* is taken as referring to the current message. The ':d' message specifier works only with the `undelete` command described below.

**9.3.10
Header Summary
and Status Codes**

When `mailx` is called, it gives you a summary of the headers in your primary mailbox. You can get an updated header summary at any time when you're in command mode.

Here is an example of what a header summary looks like:

```
    1 empor!slick        Mon Apr 29 15:18   56/2257  What a deal!
    3 curie@pasteur.fr   Sat May 18 14:20   90/3595  Glowing reports
U   4 empor!slick        Wed May 22  9:07   44/1786  Sales analysis
N   5 dvorak             Wed May 22 16:32   17/452   Re: Keyboard layout
N   6 hst                Thu May 23 10:31   21/496   Election results
N   7 To gorgon          Thu May 23 15:19   10/302   Dinner invitation
```

Here is how to interpret it:

- The first column gives the status code for each message.
- The second column gives the message number. In this case message 2 is missing because it's been deleted.
- The third column gives the sender of the message. Generally, a name with '!' in it indicates a UUCP network address while a name with '@' in it indicates an Internet address (see Section 10.1). The sender information is obtained from the 'From' line in the header (the one with the colon) rather than from the postmark. A 'To' in this column indicates a message that you've sent; for such messages, the recipient rather than the sender (you) is shown if you've enabled the `showto` variable (p. 399).
- The next four columns give the date and time when the message was received.
- The next column gives the number of lines and number of characters in each message.
- The last column gives the subject of the message.

These are the status codes that can appear in a header summary:

N   A new unread message, i.e., one that has arrived since you last called the mailer but that you haven't read.

U   An old unread message, one that was in your primary mailbox when you last called the mailer.

P   A preserved message, one that you've explicitly requested `mailx` to leave in your primary mailbox.

M   A message that `mailx` will move to your secondary mailbox when you exit even if you haven't read it.

*   A message that `mailx` has copied to an auxiliary mailbox. Such a message won't be saved when you leave `mailx` (since it's already saved in the auxiliary mailbox).

A blank code indicates a message that you've read.

The status codes stored in a message within a mailbox appear in the `Status` field of a message header and are different from those that appear in the header summary. There are just two of them:

O   An old message., i.e., one that isn't new. A new message is one that arrived in your primary mailbox since you last called `mailx`.

R   A message that you've read but haven't yet moved out of your primary mailbox.

'R' and 'O' can appear either separately or together. A message with no 'Status' field is new and unread, but `mailx` never shows you a message without an 'R' status since the very act of showing it to you gives it 'R' status. (You can verify this by reading your primary mailbox as a file.)

9.3.11
Command Mode

Command mode is the mode you're in when reading mail. The commands you can issue from command mode are listed below. `Mailx` prompts you for a command when it first starts up (after showing you the list of message headers) and after it's finished executing the most recent command. Pressing ⟨Enter⟩ in response to a prompt is equivalent to giving the `next` command—it tells `mailx` to show the next message.

Most commands can be abbreviated by typing just the first letter or so of the command. The part that can be omitted is shown in brackets. Thus the `copy` command, indicated as 'c[opy]', can be typed as 'c', 'co', 'cop', or 'copy'.

9.3.12
Commands for General Information

The commands below give you information about `mailx` itself and enable you to control the content and form of the visible part of the header summary.

Information about `mailx`.   The following commands give you information about `mailx` itself.

?
hel[p]   Shows a summary of the most commonly used commands. Not all commands are included in this summary.

l[ist]   Shows the available commands but omits their explanations.

ve[rsion] Shows the version number and release date of the version of `mailx` you're using.

Controlling the Header Display.   The following commands control the header display (see Section 9.3.10).

.

=   Shows the current message number.

h[eaders] *msg*
    Shows the page of the header summary that includes *msg*.

f[rom] [*msglist*]
    Shows the header summary for *msglist*. This command is helpful when you want to select the messages that were sent by a particular person or that refer to a particular subject. You can select these messages using the *name* or '/*string*' forms of message specifier (see Section 9.3.9).

to[p] [*msglist*]
    Shows the top few lines of the messages of *msglist*.

z
z+
z−   Scrolls the header display. The z and z+ commands scroll it
               one screen forward; the z− command scrolls it one screen back-
               ward.

di[scard] *header-field-list*
ig[nore] *header-field-list*
               Causes the specified header fields to be omitted from now
               on when messages are being shown. For example, 'ignore
               Path' causes mailx to omit the 'Path' field whenever it shows a
               message—convenient if the routing information given in that
               field is just visual clutter to you.

Listing Your Mail Folders.   The following command is useful for keeping
track of your mailboxes if you keep them in a folder directory:

folders   Shows the names of the files in the directory specified by the
          folder variable (see p. 401).

**9.3.13
Showing Messages**

The commands in this group enable you to read your messages, check
their sizes, or mark them as though you've read them. If the crt variable
is enabled (p. 399), long messages are sent to the pager specified by the
PAGER variable (p. 399) instead of being shown directly.

[Enter]   Shows the next message.

n   Shows message number *n*.

−[*n*]   Shows the *n*th previous message. If you omit *n* (the usual case),
           this command shows the previous message.

p[rint] [*msglist*]
t[ype] [*msglist*]
           Shows the messages of *msglist*.

P[rint] [*msglist*]
T[ype] [*msglist*]
           Shows the messages of *msglist*, including all header fields—
           even those that you earlier asked to have ignored by using the
           ignore command described above.

si[ze] [*msglist*]
           Shows the length in characters of each message in *msglist*. This
           command is redundant since the headers command also gives
           you this information.

n[ext] *msg*
           Goes to the next message matching *msg* and shows it. Unlike
           Type, next shows only a single message even if you give it a
           message list. It's useful, for example, if you want to retrieve
           the next message from a particular user.

tou[ch] [*msglist*]
           "Touches" the messages of *msglist* so that they appear to have

been read. This command is useful when you want some messages to be moved to your secondary mailbox even though you haven't read them, perhaps because you already know what they say. Touching a message does not affect its status as shown in the header summary.

9.3.14 Responding to Messages

The following commands enable you to send responses to mail you've received. Each of them places you into input mode.

m[ail] *namelist*
> Enters input mode to compose a message, then mails that message to the people in *namelist*.

M[ail] *name*
> Enters input mode to compose a message, then mails that message to *name* and records a copy of the message in a file named for that person.

r[espond] [*msg*]
r[eply] [*msg*]
> Enters input mode to compose a response to *msg*, then mails that response to the sender of *msg* and to all other recipients of *msg* other than yourself. The subject line is gotten by putting 'Re:' in front of the subject of the first message in *msglist* (if 'Re:' isn't there already).

R[espond] [*msglist*]
R[eply] [*msglist*]
> Enters input mode to compose a response to the messages in *msglist*, then sends the response to the sender of each message in *msglist*. The subject line is obtained by putting 'Re:' in front of the subject of the first message in *msglist* (if 'Re:' isn't there already).
>
> The difference between respond and Respond is that respond responds to a *single* message, sending copies of your response to the sender *and all recipients* of that message, while Respond responds to a *set* of messages, sending copies of your response to the senders of all messages in the set but *not to the recipients* of those messages.

fo[llowup] [*msg*]
> Like respond, except that a copy of the message is saved in a file named after the sender of *msg* (see Section 9.3.5).

F[ollowup] [*msglist*]
> Like Respond, except that a copy of the message is saved in a file named after the sender of the first message (see Section 9.3.5).

Forwarding Messages.   Suppose you've received a message from miller and want to forward that message to monroe. Mailx doesn't have an explicit command for this, but you can do it in three steps:

(1)   Use the mail command described above to compose a message to monroe.

(2)   Within that message, use the ~f input mode command to include the message from `miller` in the message you're composing.

(3)   Send the message you've just composed to `monroe`.

Including Messages in Responses.   When you respond to a message you can include parts of that message, distinctively marked, in your response. Use the `reply` command or one of its variants, immediately inserting the text of the current message into your response with ~f or ~m (see Section 9.3.21). Then enter your editor with the ~e or ~v command. If, for instance, you want to put '> ' in front of each line of the original message, use the editor to replace the beginning of each line with '> '.

Your response now consists of the original message with each line preceded by '> '. By further editing you can delete the parts you don't want to respond to and put your own comments after the other parts. Now exit from the editor. Your response is ready to send—just transmit it by typing (EOF) or '~.' (or '.' if the `dot` variable has been enabled).

9.3.15
Saving and Deleting
Messages

Ordinarily, messages are saved in your secondary mailbox after you've read them. The commands in this group let you save messages in other files as well.

mb[ox] [*msglist*]

Marks the messages of *msglist* for saving in the secondary mailbox. Whenever you issue a `quit` or `file` command, all messages so marked are then saved there. A message marked by this command is indicated by an 'M' status in the header summary. If `mailx` is terminated by an interruption or by `exit`, all messages have the same status as when `mailx` started and the special saving indicated by 'M' does not take place.

ho[ld] [*msglist*]
pre[serve] [*msglist*]

Causes the messages of *msglist* to be left in your primary mailbox when `mailx` terminates or when you switch files with the `file` command.

s[ave] [*file*]
s[ave] *msglist file*

Saves the messages of *msglist* in *file*. When `mailx` terminates or when you switch files, a second copy of these messages will not be saved to your secondary mailbox. You can force that second copy to be saved by enabling the `keepsave` variable (p. 400). The default for *file* is your secondary mailbox. **Note:** If you specify a message list but fail to specify a file, `mailx` will misinterpret the message list as a file name.

S[ave] [*msglist*]

Saves each message of *msglist* in a file named for the sender of the first message (see Section 9.3.5). This command is useful for filing messages according to who sent them to you. It behaves like `save` except that it puts the messages in a different place.

c[opy] [*file*]
c[opy] *msglist file*

> Copies the messages of *msglist* to *file* without marking them
> as saved. If you save a message with copy, it appears in your
> secondary mailbox as well as in the file that you specify with
> copy. If you don't specify *file*, *file* defaults to your secondary
> mailbox. **Note:** If you specify a message list but fail to specify
> a file, mailx will misinterpret the message list as a file name.

C[opy] [*msglist*]

> Saves each message in *msglist* in a file named for the sender of
> the first message in *msglist* (see Section 9.3.5). The messages
> are not marked as saved. Copy behaves like copy except that
> it puts the messages in a different place. Alternatively, you can
> think of Copy as behaving like Save except for the fact that Copy
> doesn't mark the messages as saved.

w[rite] [*msglist*] *file*

> Writes the messages of *msglist* to *file*, omitting headers and the
> trailing blank line. This command is otherwise equivalent to
> save.

When these commands save messages to a file, they always put those messages at the end of the file. In contrast, when messages are implicitly transferred from your primary mailbox to your secondary mailbox, those messages go at the beginning of the secondary mailbox (so the newest mail is first).

The files named in the save and copy commands are taken to be in the current directory unless you explicitly designate another directory. A common way to designate another directory is to use the '+' notation described in connection with the file command (p. 393). Note that the current directory is the one from which you called mailx and isn't necessarily your home directory.

Deleting and Undeleting Messages. The following commands delete messages and recover deleted messages:

d[elete] [*msglist*]

> Deletes the messages of *msglist* from the mailbox. If the auto-
> print variable is set, the message following the deleted one is
> shown.

dp [*msglist*]
dt [*msglist*]

> Deletes the messages in *msglist* from the mailbox and shows the
> message after the last one deleted. This command produces the
> same effect as delete with autoprint set.

u[ndelete] [*msglist*]

> Undeletes the messages of *msglist*. You can only undelete mes-
> sages that you've deleted in the same mailx session. When you
> undelete a message, it is marked as having been read even if
> you did not read it before you deleted it.

**9.3.16
Editing Messages**

The following commands enable you to edit or otherwise manipulate the messages in a set of messages. When you edit a message that is later saved, the edited version is saved.

e[dit] [*msglist*]

> Edits the messages in *msglist* using the editor specified in the `mailx` variable `EDITOR` (p. 402). The default value of `EDITOR` is the line editor `ed`.

v[isual] [*msglist*]

> Edits the messages in *msglist* using the editor specified in the `mailx` variable `VISUAL` (p. 402). The default value of `VISUAL` is the visual editor `vi`.

Note: There is no *requirement* that `edit` call a line editor and `visual` call a visual (full-screen) editor. You can, for instance, define one of these "editors" to be a shell script that reformats the messages so that you can easily reply to them. Whatever editor you specify is called with a single argument that names a temporary file containing the messages in *msglist*. `Mailx` puts the text of the messages into this file before it calls the editor and expects to find edited messages in this file when the editor returns.

**9.3.17
Switching Files and
Directories**

The following commands pertain to switching files and directories:

ch[dir]*dir*
cd *dir*   Changes the current directory to *dir*.

fold[er] *file*
fi[le] *file* Stops processing the current set of messages and takes a new set from *file*. You can specify *file* by name or by using one of the following notations:

> %   Your primary mailbox
> %*user*   The primary mailbox of *user*
> #   The previous file
> &   Your secondary mailbox (as specified by the `MBOX` variable)
> +*file*   File *file* in your folder directory (see p. 401)

> When you issue this command, the files in your current mailbox are saved just as though you had given the `quit` command. Note that `mailx` understands these notations (except for +*file*) *only* in the context of the `file` command.

so[urce] *file*

> Reads and executes the commands in *file*. Afterwards, `mailx` returns you to command mode.

**9.3.18
Quitting** `mailx`

The following commands let you get out of `mailx`.

q[uit]   Quits `mailx`, saving all the messages you've read in the secondary mailbox. This is the usual way to exit from `mailx`.

x[it]
ex[it]   Exits from `mailx`, leaving your primary mailbox unchanged. The messages there retain the status they had before you called

mailx. In particular, any messages you deleted will still be there.

9.3.19
Shells and Pipes

The following commands enable you to call shells and other programs from within mailx, possibly using those other programs to process a set of messages. Mailx chooses the shell to use for executing these commands as follows:

(1)   If the SHELL variable (see p. 402) has a value, mailx uses that value.
(2)   Otherwise, if the environment contains a SHELL variable, mailx uses the value of that variable.
(3)   Otherwise, mailx uses your login shell.

| [*msglist*] [*cmd*]
pi[pe] [*msglist*] [*cmd*]

> Passes the messages in *msglist* as standard input to *cmd*. For example, if *cmd* is lp or lpr the messages are printed on your system's printer. You can omit *cmd* if you've given it a default value with the cmd variable (p. 400).

! *cmd*   Executes *cmd* in a subshell.

sh[ell]   Starts a subshell. You can use this subshell just as you would your login shell. You'll probably find job control or some other form of process switching more convenient than using the shell command if your environment provides it (see Section 2.7).

9.3.20
Commands Useful
for Initialization

The commands below are primarily useful for adapting mailx to your requirements and tastes. To have them executed each time you start mailx, put them in your initialization file (see Section 9.3.7).

Defining Alternate Names.   The following commands let you introduce alternate names for people you send mail to and for your own login name:

a[lias] *name namelist*
g[roup] *name namelist*

> Treats *name* as an alias for each name in *namelist*. This command is particularly useful for naming groups of people you send mail to and for providing shortened forms of long addresses.

alt[ernates] *namelist*

> Treats the names in *namelist* as alternates for your login name. This command is useful when you have accounts on more than one system to avoid having automatically generated mail sent to another system.

Setting the Values of Variables.   The following commands let you control the internal variables of mailx (see Section 9.3.29). These variables and the commands that set them generally follow the conventions described in Section 2.17.

se[t]   Shows all mailx variables and their values.

se[t] *name*
> Enables the `mailx` variable *name*.

se[t] no*name*
> Disables the variable *name*. This form is equivalent to `unset` *name*.

se[t] *name*=*string*
> Sets the variable *name* to the value *string*.

se[t] *name*=*n*
> Sets the variable *name* to the numerical value *n*.

uns[et] *namelist*
> Disables (erases) the `mailx` variables in *namelist*.

You can combine settings of several variables in a single `set` command. Here is an example:

```
set metoo crt=24 noignore
```

Conditional Execution.   The following command executes another command conditionally, depending on whether `mailx` was called to send messages or to receive them:

if s *action*$_1$ [el[se] *action*$_2$] en[dif]
if r *action*$_1$ [el[se] *action*$_2$] en[dif]
> Executes *action*$_1$ or *action*$_2$ depending on whether `mailx` is sending mail (s) or receiving mail (r). The 'if', 'else', and 'endif' must all appear on separate lines. The items *action*$_1$ and *action*$_2$ are sequences of commands, one per line. As the syntax indicates, the 'else' is optional.

Comments and Messages.   The following commands enable you to put comments in an initialization file and send messages to the terminal:

\#   Treats the rest of the line as a comment.

ec[ho] *string*
> Echoes the string *string* to your terminal.

9.3.21
Input Mode

When you specify one or more mail recipients on the `mailx` command line, `mailx` assumes that you're sending a message, first prompting you for a subject and then putting you into input mode. You then compose your message, ending it with ⌷EOF⌷ or '~.'. If you've enabled the `dot` variable (see p. 400), you can also end the message with a dot on a line by itself. `Mailx` also puts you into input mode when you use one of the command-mode commands such as `Forward` to reply to a message.

Input mode has a peculiarity you should be aware of. Because `mailx` usually calls `mail` indirectly for local delivery of messages, a line containing just a dot is likely to cause the rest of the message to be lost. `Mailx` itself, however, processes such a line without comment. If you really want such a line in your message, put a space or two after the dot. This behavior is a good reason for enabling the `dot` variable.

In input mode, a line starting with '~' is taken as an input mode command. These lines are sometimes called *tilde escapes*. To include a text line that starts with '~' in a message, double the '~'. You can change the escape character by assigning a different variable to the `mailx` variable `escape` (see p. 400). The input mode commands are described below.

Interrupting Input.   You can break out of input mode without completing the message you're working on by pressing (Intr). Mailx then returns you to command mode or to your shell, depending on how you entered input mode in the first place. Your incomplete message won't be lost, however—`mailx` stores it in a dead-letter file. By default, that file is $HOME/ dead.letter, but you can choose a different default by setting the DEAD variable (p. 401). The dead-letter file is *not* cumulative—each interrupted message obliterates the previous one.

9.3.22
Getting Help

The following command provides help for the input mode commands:

~?   Shows a summary of the input mode commands.

9.3.23
Showing or Saving the Message

The next two commands let you show or save the text of a partially composed message:

~p   Shows the text of the message composed so far, omitting the header.

~w *file*   Writes the text of the message composed so far to *file*, omitting the header.

9.3.24
Editing the Message

The next two commands let you edit the message you're composing. Because you can't go back to a previous line while composing a message in input mode, these commands provide the best way to construct a message of more than a few lines.

~e   Edits the message text using the editor specified in the `mailx` variable EDITOR (p. 402). The default value of EDITOR is the line editor ed.

~v   Edits the message text using the editor specified in the `mailx` variable VISUAL (p. 402). The default value of VISUAL is the visual editor vi.

Note that there's no requirement that ~e call a line editor and ~v call a visual editor. For instance, in systems that don't support the ~a and ~A commands for generating signatures, ~e is often used to call a shell script or other program that adds a signature to a message.

9.3.25
Inserting Text

The following commands enable you to insert text into a message. The inserted text is always placed at the end of the message you've composed so far.

Inserting the Output of a Command.   The following commands execute
a command in a subshell and insert the standard output of that command
in the message:

~~! *cmd*   Executes *cmd* in a subshell and appends its standard output to
the message text.

~| *cmd*   Pipes the text of the message composed so far through *cmd*,
then replaces the message text with the standard output of *cmd*.

Inserting Files and Messages.   The following commands include the text
of a file or of a received message in a message that you're composing:

~r *file*
~~< *file*   Appends the contents of *file* to the message text.

~d   Appends the contents of the dead-letter file to the message text
(see "Interrupting Input" on page 396).

~f [*msglist*]
Forwards the messages from *msglist* by inserting them into the
message text. You can only use this command when you're
replying to a message. Note that the default for *msglist* is the
first message you're replying to.

~m [*msglist*]
Inserts the messages of *msglist* into the message text, shifting
them to the right by one tab stop. You can only use this command when you're replying to a message. Note that the default
for *msglist* is the first message you're replying to.

The following commands enable you to insert your favorite sequence of
signature lines into a message:

~a   Inserts the signature ("autograph") given by the `mailx` variable
`sign` into the message text.

~A   Inserts the signature given by the `mailx` variable `Sign` into the
message text.

Customarily, ~a is used for an informal signature attached to local mail
while ~A is used for a more formal signature attached to mail sent to other
sites. These commands don't exist in some versions of `mailx`.

Inserting the Value of a Variable.   The following command inserts the
value of a variable into the message:

~i *var*   Inserts the value of the `mailx` variable *var* (see Section 9.3.29)
into the text. If the value of the variable is empty, you just get
a newline.

Inserting a Line Starting with a Tilde.   The following command includes
in a message a line that starts with a tilde:

~~*text*   Appends the line '~*text*' to the message.

9.3.26
Specifying Header Fields

The following commands enable you to specify or modify the header fields of the message you're composing. In each case, *namelist* is a list of recipients separated by whitespace. If you type one of these commands without a *string* or *namelist*, mailx prompts you for the information.

~s *string* Sets the subject line to *string*, discarding the current subject.

~t *namelist*
> Adds the names in *namelist* to the 'To' (recipient) list of the message.

~c *namelist*
> Adds the names in *namelist* to the 'Cc' (carbon copy) list of the message.

~b *namelist*
> Adds the names in *namelist* to the Bcc (blind carbon copy) list of the message.

~h
> Prompts for the header fields ('Subject', 'To', 'Cc', and 'Bcc') of the message. You can interactively edit the previous contents of these fields.

9.3.27
Issuing Other Commands

You can issue a command-mode command from input mode with the following input-mode command, which you can only use if you originally called mailx in receive mode.

~: *cmd*
~_ *cmd*   Performs the command-mode command *cmd*.

  The following command calls a subshell from input mode:

~! [*cmd*] Performs the command *cmd* in a subshell. The shell that is used is the one given in the SHELL variable (see p. 402). The default is the Bourne shell sh. If *cmd* is absent, the subshell is given control of your terminal so that you can issue a sequence of UNIX commands.

9.3.28
Quitting mailx

The following commands provide alternative ways of leaving mailx. You can also leave it, abandoning the message you're composing, by pressing (Intr) twice.

~.
> Terminates the message you're composing, sends it, and exits from mailx.

~q
> Quits, saving the message text in the dead-letter file (see "Interrupting Input" on page 396).

~x
> Quits, abandoning the message text.

If you use these commands in send mode, they terminate the message you're composing but don't terminate mailx itself.

**9.3.29
Local and Imported
Variables**

`Mailx` has a collection of local variables that you can enable, disable, or set (see Section 2.17 and "Setting the Values of Variables" on page 394). These variables are described below. `Mailx` lets you set and erase any variable, not just those it recognizes. An extra variable can be useful, for example, if you set it to some canned text and later use the `~i` input mode command to insert the text into a message (see p. 397).

`Mailx` imports the following two variables from its environment:

HOME   Your home directory.

MAILRC   The name of the file of commands that `mailx` executes when it starts up (see Section 9.3.7).

You cannot modify the values of these variables from within `mailx`.

**9.3.30
Controlling What
`mailx` Shows You**

The following variables affect the information that `mailx` shows you and the format of that information:

header   Shows the header summary when starting up. (Enabled by default.)

quiet   Don't show the opening identification line (the one that contains the version number) when starting up in send mode. (Disabled by default.)

toplines=n
          Cause the `top` command (p. 388) to show n lines of the header summary. (The default value is 5.)

showto   When `mailx` is showing a message in the header summary and you're its sender, show the first recipient's name rather than yours. The recipient's name is preceded by 'To'. (Disabled by default.)

autoprint
          Whenever messages are deleted, show the text of the message following the last one that was deleted. Similarly, after messages are restored by `undelete`, show the last of the restored messages. (Disabled by default.)

screen=n Set the number of lines in a full screen of headers to n. (The default is 20 if your transmission rate is 2400 baud or greater, 10 if your transmission rate is 1200 baud, and 5 otherwise.)

crt=n Send messages of more than n lines to your pager (as selected by PAGER) instead of simply showing them on your screen. The message text is the standard input to the pager. (Disabled by default, i.e., don't use a pager.)

PAGER=cmd
          Use cmd as the pager for showing long messages. (The default is `pg` (see Section 3.13.2) or `more`, depending on your system.)

prompt=$string$
          Set the command mode prompt to *string*. (The default is '?'.)

debug   Turn on verbose diagnostics, but suppress the actual delivery of messages. (Disabled by default.)

`sendwait` Wait for the background mailer to finish before returning from `mailx`. (Disabled by default.)

9.3.31
Input Interpretation

The following variables affect the way that `mailx` interprets what you type.

`asksub` In send mode, prompt for a subject if a subject isn't given by the `-s` option on the command line. (Enabled by default.)

`bang` Enable the special casing of '!' in shell escape commands so that typing '!!' causes the previously executed command to be repeated. With this variable disabled, '!!' executes '!' as an ordinary shell command. (Disabled by default.)

`escape=`*c* Use *c* as the escape character when in input mode. (The default is '~'.)

`cmd=`*cmd* If a `pipe` command (p. 394) is given without an explicit command, use *cmd* as the default. (Disabled by default.)

`dot` When you're composing a message, cause a dot on a line by itself to end the message. Although this option is disabled by default, we strongly recommend enabling it—see page 395 for the reasons.

`ignore` Ignore interrupts while entering messages.[7] Setting this variable can be helpful when you're working with a noisy telephone line, since the line noise can generate spurious interrupts. (Disabled by default.)

`ignoreeof`
Ignore end of file during message input. If this variable is enabled, you need to end your message either with '~.' or, if you've enabled `dot`, with a dot on a line by itself. (Disabled by default.)

`metoo` Prevent your name from being deleted from an automatically generated list of recipients for a message that you're sending. Normally your name *is* deleted from such a list. (Disabled by default.)

9.3.32
Message Processing

The following variables affect the way that `mailx` processes messages after you've created or saved them.

`append` Append rather than prepend messages sent to the secondary mailbox when you quit, i.e., put them at the end rather than at the beginning. (Disabled by default.)

`keep` Don't remove a mailbox when it becomes empty. Normally a mailbox is deleted when `mailx` removes all the messages in it. (Disabled by default.)

`keepsave` When a message is saved to a specific file using a command such as `save`, save it to your secondary mailbox as well. Normally

---

7. Don't confuse the `ignore` variable with the `ignore` command.

such a message isn't saved to your secondary mailbox when you quit. `Keepsave` has no effect if you're reading messages from any mailbox other than your primary one. `Keepsave` is disabled by default.

hold
Preserve messages that you've read in your primary mailbox rather than in your secondary mailbox. (Disabled by default.)

save
Cause interrupted messages to be saved in the dead-letter file (see "Interrupting Input" on page 396). If `save` is disabled, such messages are discarded. (Enabled by default.)

sign=*string*
Use *string* as the "signature" for the ~a command. (Empty by default.)

Sign=*string*
Use *string* as the "signature" for the ~A command. (Empty by default.)

page
Put a ⟨formfeed⟩ after each message passed through the `pipe` command (p. 394). When the collected messages are displayed on a screen, the ⟨formfeed⟩s make them easier to read. (Disabled by default.)

record=*file*
Record all outgoing mail in *file*. If `outfolder` is enabled, *file* is taken as relative to your folder; otherwise it is taken as relative to your home directory (see the explanations of `folder` and `outfolder` below). (Disabled by default.)

allnet
Treat network names as identical if their last components match, e.g., treat `mars!alien`, `lune!alien`, and `alien` as all referring to the same person. Enabling this variable avoids having a message sent to the same person at several locations. (Disabled by default.)

9.3.33
Mailbox Locations

Using the `followup`, `Followup`, `Save`, and `Copy` commands, you can save a message in a mailbox named after its sender or first recipient. You can also save a message in a mailbox named after its sender by specifying the −F option on the command line. Normally `mailx` looks for these mailboxes in your current directory, (the directory you were in when you called `mailx`), but you can have `mailx` look for them in a folder directory instead (see Section 9.3.8). The following commands enable you to define a folder directory:

folder=*dir*
Define the directory for your mail folders to be $HOME/*dir*, i.e, *dir* relative to your home directory. Enabling `folder` causes the '+' notation for file names to be defined. If `folder` is disabled, no substitution is made for a '+' at the beginning of a file name. You need to create the folder directory yourself; `mailx` won't make it for you. (Disabled by default.)

outfolder
Keep outgoing messages in the directory specified by `folder`.

Outgoing messages that you create explicitly are saved in the file designated by the `record` variable; those saved in files named after message senders or recipients follow the rules below. (Disabled by default.)

The following variables specify the location of your secondary mailbox and of the mailbox where `mailx` puts partially completed messages:

MBOX=*file* Use *file* as your secondary mailbox. The location of your secondary mailbox is unaffected by `folder` and `outfolder`, but you can place it in your mail folder by setting `MBOX` to '+mbox'. (The default value of `MBOX` is 'mbox'.)

DEAD=*file* Save partial messages that were interrupted in the dead-letter file *file* (see "Interrupting Input" on page 396). (The default is `dead.letter`.)

9.3.34 Command Interpreters

The following variables determine the executable UNIX commands that `mailx` calls upon for certain services:

LISTER=*cmd*

Use *cmd* to list the contents of the folder directory. (The default is `ls`.)

SHELL=*cmd*

Use *cmd* as your shell. (The default is the value of the `SHELL` environment variable in effect when `mailx` was called or from your login shell if that environment variable doesn't exist.)

EDITOR=*cmd*

Use *cmd* as the editor for the ~e command. (The default is the line editor `ed`.)

VISUAL=*cmd*

Use *cmd* as the editor for the ~v command. (The default is the visual editor `vi`.)

sendmail=*cmd*

Use *cmd* as the mail transport agent that actually delivers the messages you send. (The default is usually either /usr/lib/sendmail or /bin/rmail.)

9.3.35 Network Addressing

The following variables affects how `mailx` interprets network addresses (see Section 10.1):

onehop Disable alterations to remote recipients' addresses in the case where you're responding to a message that was sent to several remote recipients. If `onehop` is disabled, `mailx` adds additional components to the addresses of these recipients so as to get your response from your machine to the machine from which the original message was sent.[8] Enabling `onehop` may improve

---

8. If you think this explanation is complicated and hard to understand, you're right.

efficiency in a network where any node can send messages directly to any other node, but it may also cause messages not to be delivered. (Enabled by default.)

`conv=`*style*

Convert UUCP network addresses to the form of *style*. The only value of *style* that `mailx` currently recognizes is 'internet'. If you set 'conv=internet', an address such as `vienna!freud` will be recast to `freud@vienna.UUCP`. (Disabled by default.)

9.4   **The Seventh Edition** `mail` **Mailer**

The mailer we are discussing in this section is the one known as `mail` in System V, an inheritance from Seventh Edition UNIX. The mailer called `mail` on your system may be a different one, perhaps `mailx`. If `mail` prompts you with 'Subject:' when you attempt to send a message, you've probably got `mailx` or one of its variants rather than Seventh Edition `mail`. Seventh Edition `mail` is sometimes referred to as `binmail` because it resides in the `/bin` directory. You'll probably find it there even if an unadorned `mail` command calls a different mailer.

Compared with `mailx`, `mail` is a very primitive mailer.[9] In particular, it doesn't process headers in any special way—it just treats them as part of the message text. This can be an advantage if you're trying to find out why your mail is going askew, since you can construct any header you wish and make it part of the message you're sending. It's usually inadvisable to use `mail` to read your mail if you have any choice, but `mail` can sometimes be convenient for sending very short messages. The `mail` program also enables you to send messages with customized headers that your usual mailer can't create.

9.4.1
Sending Mail

To send mail to one or more recipients, use the command line

`mail` [*options*] *namelist*

where *namelist* is a list of recipients. The names of the recipients must be separated either by commas or by whitespace. Typing this line puts you into `mail`'s input mode. The `mail` program now expects you to type the text of the message, ending it either with (EOF) or with a line containing just a dot. If you really want your message to include a line with just a dot, put a space or two after the dot. If you want the message to include a subject header, you must insert it yourself.

---

9. In fact, `mail` is both a mail user agent and a mail transport agent for local mail. This dual role goes back to the early days of UNIX when network connections weren't a consideration and there wasn't any need for the distinction. Often a second link to `mail` is created under the name `lmail`, and the name `lmail` is used when `mail` is called to deliver local mail. The `mail` program can check which name it was called with and act appropriately.

The `mail` program puts a 'From' line followed by an empty line at the top of the message before delivering it. The 'From' line does *not* have a colon. You can suppress the empty line after the 'From' line with the -s option described just below.

Command-line Options.   The following options can appear on the command line when you're sending mail:

-o   Don't optimize addresses. Without this option, `mailx` checks path-style addresses to see if any components appear more than once (see Section 10.1.1) and removes any that it finds. (People never write addresses like that but programs sometimes do.)

-s   Don't put an empty line between the From line and the text of the message.

-w   When sending a letter to a user on another computer, don't wait for the actual transfer before exiting.

-t   Cause a To: line to be inserted after the From line, indicating the recipients.

**9.4.2
Reading Mail**

To read your mail, use the command line

    `mail [`*options*`]`

The absence of a list of recipients indicates that you're receiving rather than sending mail.

Command-line Options.   The following options can appear on the command line when you're sending mail:

-e   Exit immediately with value 0 if there's mail in your primary mailbox and value 1 if there isn't. You can use this option to test for the existence of mail without processing it.

-h   Shows a window of message headers before prompting for a command.

-p   Show all messages without prompting for commands.

-r   Process the messages in order from oldest to newest, rather than the default which is newest to oldest.

-f *file*   Take the incoming mail from *file* rather than from your primary mailbox.

-q   If `mail` is interrupted, terminate it entirely instead of just terminating the processing of the current message.

Commands for Reading Mail.   When you use `mail` to read your mail, it prompts you for commands with '?'. The simplest way to read your mail using `mail` is to press ⌷Enter⌷ at each prompt. The `mail` program then steps you through your messages and exits when it's shown you the last one. The other commands you can use are described below. The `mail` program, unlike the `mailx` program, leaves the messages that it reads in your primary mailbox (referred to in the `mail` documentation as the "mailfile").

The list of headers shown by `mail` is similar to that shown by `mailx` (see Section 9.3.10), but with some important differences:

- The message numbers are in reverse order, so the oldest messages appear first in the list. You can get the opposite order with the `-r` option.
- No subjects are shown.
- Deleted messages are marked with a d but are not removed from the list.

The current message is indicated with a '>' symbol. In the descriptions below, the terms "next" and "previous" refer to the order in which the messages are listed.

Quitting `mail`.   The following commands provide for terminating the `mail` program:

EOF	
q	Quits the mail program, leaving all undeleted mail in the primary mailbox.
x	Quits the mail program, leaving the primary mailbox unchanged. Deleted messages remain there.

See also the `dq` command below.

Getting Help.   The following command provides a "help" facility:

?	Shows a summary of the `mail` commands.

Showing Headers.   The following commands show a selected header or set of headers:

h	Shows a window of headers, centered around the current message.
h *n*	Shows the header of message number *n*. As a side effect, this command sets the current message to *n*.
h a	Shows the headers of all messages in the primary mailbox.
h d	Shows the headers of those messages that have been deleted. (Until you exit from `mail`, deleted messages still exist in the primary mailbox.)

Showing Messages.   The following commands provide for showing a selected message or set of messages. Showing a message causes it to become the current message.

+	
Enter	Shows the next message.
p	Shows the current message again.
-	Shows the previous message.
a	Shows the message that arrived most recently during the current `mail` session. (If more than one has arrived, 'a' will not help you get the others.)
n	Shows message number *n*.

Sending Messages.   The following commands provide for sending messages, either in response to the current message or independently of it:

r [*namelist*]

> Enters input mode for composing a reply to the current message. The reply is sent to the sender of the message and to the people listed in *namelist* (if *namelist* is present).

m *namelist*

> Sends the current message to the recipients named in *namelist* and marks it for deletion with 'm'. The message received by these recipients will not bear any explicit indication that you forwarded it, although it will have an extra 'Received by' header line. Remailing a message is one of the few things that's much easier to do with mail than with mailx.

Deleting and Undeleting Messages.   The following commands provide for deleting and undeleting messages. The number of the current message becomes undefined when you delete a message.

d	
dp	Deletes the current message.
d *n*	Deletes message number *n*.
dq	Deletes the current message and quits.
u [*n*]	Undeletes message number *n*. If you omit *n*, the current message is undeleted. Undeleting a message that wasn't deleted in the first place has no effect.

Saving Messages.   The following commands provide for saving messages:

y [*filelist*]	
s [*filelist*]	Saves the current message in *each* of the files in *filelist* (by appending it at the end). The message is then removed from the message list (and cannot be recovered via 'u'). If *filelist* is absent, mbox (the usual secondary mailbox) is assumed.
w [*filelist*]	Like 's', except that the first header line is omitted from the saved message.

Shell Escape.   The following command provides for executing a command in a subshell:

! *cmd*   Executes the command *cmd* in a subshell. Mail always uses the Bourne shell sh here.

9.4.3
Forwarding Mail
with mail

You can use mail to set up forwarding of your mail, provided that your primary mailbox is empty. The command

```
mail -F namelist
```

causes a forwarding message to be placed in your primary mailbox. Thereafter, all of your mail will be forwarded to the people specified in *namelist*. If *namelist* contains any whitespace, you should enclose it in quotes as in this example:

```
mail -F "antlers!nick, nick@pole.com, msklaus"
```

To cancel mail forwarding, call `mail` with the `F` option and an explicit empty string as argument:

```
mail -F ""
```

The `""` is necessary, since `mail` won't accept `-F` without an argument.

9.5 Other Mailers

We briefly discuss two other popular mailers, MH and `elm`.

9.5.1
The MH Message
Handling System

The MH message handling system is a collection of programs originally developed at the Rand Corporation and subsequently adapted as part of BSD UNIX. As the MH manual states, "the list of 'MH immortals' is too long to list here." We briefly summarize the major features of MH.

The approach of MH is very different from that of `mailx` and `mail`. Instead of providing a single program for all mail functions, it provides a set of independent programs for particular functions that you can call from an ordinary shell prompt. MH keeps track of the mail context in a context file in your home directory, so a sequence of calls on different MH programs maintains the same continuity that is found in unitary programs such as `mailx`. For example, after you've read a message, you can read the next one with a simple `next` command at the shell level; no further specification is needed. MH also maintains profile information in a file named `.mh_profile` in your home directory containing the name of the directory where folders and special files are kept, default arguments for each MH program, and other information for customizing MH to your tastes.

Viewing New Mail. The principal command for viewing new mail is `inc`. It transfers newly arrived messages from your primary mailbox to your secondary mailbox and provides a summary of those messages.

Folders. MH keeps messages in UNIX directories called *folders*. Each message is kept in its own file; the files within a folder are named by the message numbers. Using the UNIX directory structure, you can have folders within folders. You can also include a message in several folders by creating a link to that message from each folder. This arrangement makes the full power of UNIX available for working with messages, but it has the disadvantage that the messages kept in MH folders cannot be read by other mailers.

Operations on Folders and Messages. There are four commands for examining the messages in a folder:

`show`	Displays a message or a set of messages.
`prev`	Shows the message preceding the current message.
`next`	Shows the message following the current message.
`scan`	Provides a summary of the messages in the folder.

You can rearrange and examine the messages in folders with the following commands:

rmm   Removes a message from a folder.

pick   Selects a set of messages based on their contents and assigns that set a sequence name.

mark   Modifies a message sequence by adding or deleting messages.

refile   Moves a message from one folder to another.

folder   Optionally changes to a different folder. It then shows the name of the current folder and summarizes its contents.

folders   Summarizes the contents of all the folders.

rmf   Removes a message folder.

anno   Adds an annotation to a message in a folder. It can also be used to add an annotation to a message after you create it.

burst   Breaks up a digest of messages into its individual messages.

Creating and Sending Messages.   The following commands provide for creating and sending messages:

comp   Enables you to compose a new message.

dist   Redistributes a message to other people.

forw   Forwards a message to other people.

repl   Enables you to compose and send a reply to a message.

send   Retransmits a message or sends the contents of a file as a message.

Aliases.   You can create one or more files of aliases for MH. Each alias associates a name with a group of addresses. A message sent to an alias is sent to all the addresses in its associated group. The ali command shows the addresses associated with a particular alias or, alternatively, shows the aliases associated with a particular address.

9.5.2 The elm Mailer

The elm mailer was written by Dave Taylor and is available in the public domain. Unlike the other mailers discussed in this chapter, elm is screen-oriented rather than line-oriented. It is designed to be used with little or no need for auxiliary documentation since it lists the alternative actions available at any point and provides on-line help on all of its facilities. Like other modern mailers, elm enables you to forward or reply to a message, to group messages into folders, to delete and move messages, and to create aliases for mail addresses or groups of addresses that you often use. Its interactive nature provides additional conveniences. For example, you can move up and down a message summary with cursor motions and then choose a message to read by pressing (Enter). You can also easily create an alias for the sender of a message after you've received the message.

The elm mailer is available electronically from the OSUCIS archives (reference [U3]).

10

Communicating with Remote Computers

Using the power of your own computer to communicate with remote computers provides important benefits:

- You can send mail or files to remote users and receive mail or files from them.

- You can log in on a remote computer and use its facilities.

- Under a windowing system such as X, you can switch back and forth among several remote computers, even using the windowing system to transfer text from one to another (see Chapter 11).

- You can use remote logins as a mechanism for distributing a task among several computers, with the different parts communicating with each other by means of remote procedure calls and similar methods. (A discussion of remote procedure calls is beyond the scope of this book.)

In the first part of this chapter we discuss network addresses, which apply both to sending mail and to other forms of communication with remote computers. In the second part we discuss the programs that you can use to log into remote computers—even ones not running UNIX—and to transfer files to and from those computers.

10.1 Network Addresses

To send a message or a file to someone at another site, you must provide that person's network address to the program that handles the communication. In this section we talk about network addresses in terms of sending messages via mailers—or more precisely, mail transport agents (see p. 377). See Section 10.1.5 for a discussion of sending files rather than messages.

UNIX communications software understands two kinds of network addresses: *path-style addresses* and *domain-style addresses.*[1] A path-style address specifies the transmission route that the message is to take; a domain-style address specifies the destination of the message as though it were a postal address, with each part of the address narrowing down the location. If someone gives you an electronic mail address, you can easily tell which kind it is—if it contains '!'s, it's a path-style address, while if it contains '@'s and dots, it's a domain-style address. Mixed addresses containing both '!' and '@' are also possible.

The two major networks used with UNIX systems are the UUCP network and the Internet:

- The UUCP network is entirely composed of computers running UNIX. It is named for the uucp program (UNIX to UNIX copy) that supports communication from one such computer to another (see Section 10.8.3). The UUCP network originally used point-to-point telephone connections for all its communication, though modern versions of the supporting software can handle other forms of connection as well.

- The Internet, successor to the Arpanet, is an internetwork, i.e., a "network of networks", that interconnects most major networks sponsored by U.S. organizations in the public sector. It also provides connections to the major networks of other countries. Although the networks in the Internet are independently managed, the Internet appears to its users to be a single network. Individual organizations can also belong to the Internet—the Internet structure is indifferent to how big its components are or how much substructure they have.

As a rule, path-style addresses are used within the UUCP network while domain-style addresses are used within the Internet.[2]

When you send mail to a domain-style address, your mailer translates that address into a communication path. A path-style address does not require such a translation since it specifies a route explicitly—the mailer has only to know how to send the message one hop further. However, a smart mailer may revise a path-style address in order to provide a better routing or may recognize aliases for sites that are several links away.

---

1. These are the two kinds of addresses understood by *generic* UNIX software. Particular network handlers may understand other kinds as well. Moreover, an address for a network other than the UUCP network or the Internet can almost always be cast into a path-style or domain-style address. The computer that acts as a gateway for the other network can then reparse the address as necessary.

2. A number of networks, e.g., Telemail and SPAN, use other kinds of addresses but are connected to the Internet through one or more gateway computers. The usual convention for sending mail to a location on one of these networks, e.g., Telemail, is to treat the entire Telemail address as though it referred to a single individual at the gateway site. It may be necessary to transform the Telemail address somewhat in order to get it to work; the rules are network-specific and beyond the scope of this book.

We've spoken of messages being sent to people, but the recipient of a message is really a mailbox rather than a person. A mailbox can belong to any entity that handles mail—a specific individual, someone with a particular responsibility (e.g., `Postmaster`), a mailing list, or even a program.

**10.1.1
Path-Style
(UUCP Network)
Addresses**

In a path-style address—the kind that's used within the UUCP network—you specify the explicit routing that the message is to take in the form '$a_1!a_2!\ldots!a_n!p$'. This notation indicates that the message is first to be sent from your computer to the site a_1, from there to the site a_2, and so on. The final destination is the person p at the site a_n. For example, the address

        `tinker!evers!chance!ruth`

indicates that the message is to be passed first to the site `tinker`, then to the site `evers`, then to the site `chance`, and finally to the person `ruth` at that site.

Suppose you want to send a message to a remote site but don't know of a path to that site. You may be able to get your message there by sending it to a site that has a smart mailer containing a table giving the layout of the UUCP network. The smart mailer can then fill in the rest of the path. For instance, suppose you want to send a message to `moby` at the site `whales`. You don't know of a path to `whales`, but you know that the site `benezra` has a smart mailer. You might be able to get your message to `moby` by sending it to

        `benezra!whales!moby`

possibly with some other path components preceding `benezra`. `Benezra` will then supply the routing needed to get your message to `whales` (assuming that `whales` is a registered UUCP site). A set of maps showing the connections among UUCP computers is available from UUNET (reference [U4]).[3]

Sometimes someone will give you a UUCP address like

        `...{jupiter, saturn, mars}!earth!peoria!oldlady`

or possibly

        `...{jupiter|saturn|mars}!earth!peoria!oldlady`

Such an address means that you can reach the person `oldlady` at any of the addresses

        `...!jupiter!earth!peoria!oldlady`
        `...!saturn!earth!peoria!oldlady`
        `...!mars!earth!peoria!oldlady`

---

3. When a message is sent over a path with intermediate nodes, the intermediate nodes bear the cost of the transmission but gain none of its benefits. UNIX system managers grumble about this but generally have been willing to tolerate it as long as their hospitality is not abused, on the assumption that the externally-imposed costs and the benefits to their own users will eventually even out.

where the ... indicates some sequence of sites that will get you to `jupiter`, `saturn`, or `mars` (which presumably are registered UUCP sites).

Be careful when writing path-style addresses on a command line under the C shell. The '!' character has a special meaning to that shell. If you write something like

```
mailx athens!timon
```

it won't work; the shell will interpret the '!' as referring to the previous command line. Instead you must quote the '!', like this:

```
mailx athens\!timon
```

Double quotes aren't sufficient here to prevent the misinterpretation of the '!'.

The path-style addresses used within the UUCP network, like nearly everything else in UNIX, are case-sensitive.

10.1.2 Domain-Style (Internet) Addresses

Domain-style addresses are the standard addressing form for communication over the Internet. Many local-area networks and uucp-based computers also recognize them. A domain-style address specifies the recipient of a message in the form '$p@l_n. \ldots .l_2.l_1$'. Here p is the person you're sending the message to and l_n through l_1 together form a *domain name* that serves as the person's electronic mail address and identifies a computer where the person can receive mail. The l_i, i.e., the components of the domain name, are called *labels*. The domain name is like a postal address—reading from right to left, it narrows down the destination of the message. The names you obtain by deleting labels from left to right are also domain names, although they usually designate groups of computers rather than individual computers—just as "Montana" contains many towns and cities, "Kalispell, Montana" contains a number of streets, and so forth. To send someone a message you must specify a domain narrow enough to identify a computer where that person is known.

For instance, the address `dduck@orlando.disney.com`[4] would be interpreted as follows: Within the domain of commercial institutions (`com`), look for a particular commercial institution (`disney.com`); within that institution, look for the site `orlando.disney.com`. Send the message to the person `dduck` who receives mail via that site.

The rightmost label in an Internet address is a three-letter code for addresses within the U.S. ('com', 'gov', 'edu', 'org', etc.). For addresses outside of the U.S. it is a two-letter country code ('.uk', '.jp', '.fr', etc.). These labels are called *top-level domains* or *administrative domains*.

Hosts and Name Servers. The term *host* is often used in the computing literature but rarely defined. We take it to mean a computer that renders services to other computers. In the Internet world, the hosts are just the computers that are connected to the Internet. Often any computer connected to a network is called a host, even one connected only to a local-area

---

4. After inventing this example, we were intrigued to discover that Walt Disney International does indeed have an Internet connection under the domain name `walt.disney.com`.

network. Most Internet hosts act as mail delivery agents for a domain or a group of domains. A few hosts provide other specialized services such as looking up addresses. When a host handles mail delivery for a domain, it usually handles mail delivery for the subdomains of that domain as well. However, some subdomains have their own Internet connections; mail addressed to them usually goes to them directly rather than through the host responsible for an outer domain.[5] A few hosts also handle mail for destinations such as computers on other networks that are not part of the Internet.

When a mailer connected to the Internet is given a message to deliver, the mailer sends a query to one or more *name servers* to find out where to send the message. The query specifies the domain appearing in the message's address. The name servers respond with the IP address of the Internet host that handles mail for that domain;[6] the IP address is a physical address that acts like a telephone number (see "IP Addresses" on page 414). The originating mailer then ships the message to the IP address.

A host that receives a message sent via the Internet may in turn need to forward it to some other computer, particularly if the host is responsible for a number of domains. When you see a very long computer-generated domain name, the chances are that the name servers use only the right-most few components of it to select an Internet host—the rest of the components are used by the host itself to effect delivery. Mailers often generate origination addresses that include the label of every domain containing the point of origin, even when many of those labels aren't needed. So if someone gives you a short mail address, use it—even if the return address in the mail you receive from that person is longer.

For instance, suppose that you send a message to

    dduck@fantasy.orlando.disney.com

If a single host is responsible for all subdomains of `orlando.disney.com`, the name servers will probably ignore the `fantasy` component when they look up the host for that domain, leaving it to the `orlando` host to relay the message to the computer called `fantasy` where `dduck` has an account.

Note the following:

- Internet domain names are case-insensitive, unlike UUCP addresses.

- A valid domain may be a subdomain of some other domain, i.e., have the same name but with additional labels. The user names associated with the domain and the subdomain have no necessary relation. For instance, `walt@orlando.disney.com` and `walt@disney.`

---

5. The relation between hosts and domain names is one-to-many, i.e., every domain has a single host responsible for it, but a single host may be responsible for many domains. If the domain is very broad, the responsibility probably won't include actual mail delivery but will include services such as looking up addresses of subdomains.

6. What actually happens is that if the name server for the outermost domain doesn't know the IP address of the appropriate host, it returns the IP address of a more specialized name server that might know it. A mailer thus calls upon a sequence of name servers, each responsible for a narrower domain than the one before, until it finds a name server that does know the IP address.

com might be two different people, or one of those users might exist even though the other one doesn't.[7]

- You may be able to omit extra labels in the domain name, but don't count on it. For instance, you might be able to shorten the address dduck@fantasy.orlando.disney.com to dduck@orlando.disney.com—or you might not. It all depends on how much the responsible host knows about the users in the domains that it handles. If the orlando host knows that dduck receives mail from the computer at the fantasy domain, the fantasy label probably isn't needed.

IP Addresses.   An *IP address* (Internet protocol address) specifies the exact routing to an Internet host. When a name server is given a domain name, it resolves that name to an IP address. Two programs, telnet and ftp, accept IP addresses as alternatives to domain names (see Sections 10.6 and 10.7). If you need to communicate with an Internet site but the programs you are using cannot communicate with a name server, you can use the IP address of the site instead. A disadvantage of using IP addresses is that they sometimes change.

An IP address consists of four numbers, e.g., '126.6.40.93'. The structure is similar to that of a telephone number, with the first number acting as an area code, the second as an exchange, etc. Just as a telephone number tells the telephone switching equipment how to reach the telephones that bear that number, an IP address tells the network software how to reach the host that has that address. The structure of an IP address is more complicated because it accounts for several classes of networks; see page 310 of reference [B12] for one discussion of the structure of IP addresses.

Use of Percents.   You may encounter a domain-style address with extra components for local addressing, marked off by '%'. These components are ignored by Internet mailers, but are used by local hosts for mail delivery. For example, the address

        minnie%fantasy@orlando.disney.com

indicates that fantasy is the name of the computer where Minnie receives her mail (and that the orlando.disney.com host knows how to deliver mail to fantasy). You might also sometimes see this address as

        minnie%fantasy@fantasy.orlando.disney.com

---

7. If you have accounts on several machines, it's a good idea to use the same name for all of them if you can. This may not always be possible—if you have a user name morris on your local machine, you may well find that there's already another morris on a remote machine where you're establishing an account.

There's a good chance that this form won't work, even if it was generated by a mailer. You can often repair it by omitting the '%fantasy' after 'minnie'.

Looking Up Internet Domains.   You can get information about Internet domains with the whois, nslookup, and dig programs if these are available on your system:

- The whois program provides administrative information about a domain such as its full name, location, and the names of the site administrators, but does not list all the lowest-level domains.

- The nslookup program provides the IP address of any domain, even one at the lowest level. It also provides other information about the domain chiefly of interest to network administrators.

- The dig program is similar to nslookup but has a better interface and is easier to use. You can get dig via anonymous ftp from venera.isi.edu (Internet address 128.9.0.32).

10.1.3
Addresses Involving More Than One Network

It's almost always better to send a message using just a single network, be it the UUCP network or the Internet. But when you're on one network and you need to send a message to someone who's only on another, you can't avoid crossing network boundaries. Sending a message over a path involving both the Internet and the UUCP network requires that you route your message through a *gateway*—a computer connected to both networks. You often can send such as message without using a mixed address, but you can use a mixed address if all else fails.

Internet to UUCP.   To send a message from the Internet to the UUCP network, put the UUCP routing from the gateway at the left of the '@'. For instance, suppose that mandelbaum.il is the Internet domain name for a gateway to the UUCP network.[8] Then the message address

        amman!hussein@mandelbaum.il

specifies that the message should first be sent to the Internet node mandelbaum.il. The host in charge of that node forwards the message to the UUCP node amman, which in turn delivers the message to the user hussein. A safer form of the same address—if it works—is

        mandelbaum.il!amman!hussein

Another example of a UUCP address acceptable to an Internet mailer is

        heehaw%barn3.uucp@agri.com

This address tells the host responsible for the domain agri.com to send the message to the person heehaw at the UUCP site barn3 known to the agri.com host. Observe carefully the inversion of order here: with the '%' notation, the UUCP site comes after rather than before the user name. As before, an alternate form is

        agri.com!barn3!heehaw

---

8. The Internet country code for Israel is 'il'; the Mandelbaum Gate was the only crossing point between East and West Jerusalem during the period 1948–1967.

UUCP to Internet.   To send a message from the UUCP network to the Internet, construct a path-style address in which the next to the last component is the Internet domain name for the gateway and the last component is the person you want to send the message to. Assume as above that `mandelbaum` is a UUCP node that serves as a gateway to the Internet. Then an example of such an address is

```
amman!mandelbaum!knesset.il!sharon
```

A message with this address is passed by the UUCP node `amman` to the UUCP node `mandelbaum`, which in turn passes the message to the user `sharon` at the Internet node `knesset.il`.

You may also be able to send the message using the address

```
amman!mandelbaum!sharon%knesset.il
```

An up-to-date UUCP mailer turns the '`%`' into an '`@`' and treats `sharon@knesset.il` as a conventional Internet address. A '`%`' is supposed to be treated as belonging to the local part of an address, not to be interpreted if the address includes any routing information. In this example, `mandelbaum` is the only host entitled to interpret `sharon%knesset.il`.

More on Mixed Addresses.   A hazard of using mixed addresses—and one of the reasons for staying within one network whenever you can—is that different mailers may interpret them differently. The Internet conventions specify that '`@`' has precedence over everything else, but some older UUCP mailers may not follow them. Thus the address

```
garden!alice@wonderland.uk
```

ought to be interpreted by routing the message first to `wonderland` and then to `garden`, where `alice` is. But an older UUCP mailer might instead send the message to `garden`, expecting the mailer there to send it to `alice@wonderland.uk`.

Occasionally you may see an address such as `zeus@olympus.uucp`, a domain-style version of the UUCP address `olympus!zeus` (`olympus` being a registered UUCP site). This address won't work from an Internet site unless your Internet mailer understands the UUCP network. Two possible alternatives are the following:

```
zeus%olympus.uucp@uunet.uu.net
uunet.uu.net!olympus!zeus
```

In these addresses, `uunet` is the name of a specific host that is responsible for relaying messages between the Internet and the UUCP net (see reference [U4]).

Domain-style addresses are also sometimes used for sending mail to other networks such as Bitnet that are connected to the Internet but are not part of it. The addresses have the same form as Internet addresses. An example of such an address is

```
cindy@castle.bitnet
```

The '`bitnet`' label is not the name of an Internet domain, but many mailers will recognize it as a "fake domain" and handle it properly. An Internet mailer may also recognize direct Bitnet addresses such as

```
cindy@castle.bitnet
```

**10.1.4
When Messages
Go Astray**

A message you send to a remote site is handled by at least two mailers, the one at your site and the one at the destination site, and often by several more.[9] The header information on a message that you receive should tell you which mailers have handled it.

A message can go astray in either of two ways: it can be rejected by some mailer on the way or it can be lost entirely. It's unusual for a message to be lost entirely, but it does happen. *Very* rarely, a message will be sent to an inappropriate destination such as an unrelated newsgroup and accepted there. If a message is rejected, a copy of it is sent back to you accompanied by a log of the mailers that handled it. But alas, if a message is lost you may never know it unless you've asked for a return receipt, and very few mailers are able to provide one. You can insert a `Return-Receipt-To:` field into a header with a mailer such as the one in Emacs that allows you to construct your own headers (see Section 7.27). Whether or not a return receipt is actually generated depends on the receiving mailer. A mailer that conforms to the Internet rules generates the return receipt, but some mailers on the UUCP network do not.

When you respond to a message using an automatic reply mechanism such as the `reply` command of `mailx` (p. 390), your response may go astray if the apparent source of the message is not the right address or is not an address acceptable to *your* mailer. Mixed addresses are particularly vulnerable to being mangled, especially by some older mailers. In some cases the apparent source will be in a 'Reply-To' component of the message header; if the header doesn't have such a component, your mailer will probably look for the source in the 'From' component (the one with the colon). If it finds more than one address there, an address enclosed in '< ... >' takes precedence. Unfortunately, most current mailers don't recognize 'Reply-To'—the Emacs mailer is an exception.

A return address will be wrong if the message you're responding to was forwarded and the return address is that of the forwarder rather than that of the original author. Usually a topical forum sends out messages under its own name rather than under the names of the contributors to the forum, so a reply to such a message reaches the original contributor either indirectly or not at all. If you get one of your own messages back from `MAILER-DAEMON` or `Postmaster`, there's little point in using the `reply` mechanism—especially to `MAILER-DAEMON`.

Messages that pass through both the UUCP network and the Internet may be misdirected because UUCP network addresses are case-sensitive ('a' and 'A' are different) while Internet addresses are case-insensitive ('a' and 'A' are the same). Some Bitnet mailers convert addresses to all lowercase or all uppercase; when such an address reaches the UUCP network via the Internet, it is likely to be incorrect. You may be able to cure this problem by replacing the first component *a* of the UUCP address by '*a*.uucp', which tells the mailers how *a* is to be interpreted.

---

9. We emphasize what we mentioned earlier: the mailers involved here are mail transport agents, not mail user agents.

If a message is lost, you may be the victim of an overzealous mailer somewhere on its path. For instance, some mailers attempt to eliminate duplicate addresses and messages that appear to be caught in an endless cycle of retransmissions. If your message appears to be one of those but isn't, it may vanish.

Finally, if you're having a problem getting mail through to a particular location and nothing seems to work, you can send mail to `Postmaster` at that address—or, if that doesn't work, to your local `Postmaster` if you have one. Every Internet site has a person—not just some clever program— who is responsible for handling mail problems involving that site.[10]

10.1.5 Addressing Considerations for File Transmission

Sending a file via the UUCP network is similar to sending a message—a file is always sent to a particular person. Instead of using a mailer, you use `uucp` or one of its relatives. These programs are described later in this chapter. The address you use for sending a file is the same as the one you use for sending a message.

Sending a file via the Internet or another network using the TCP/IP protocols (see p. 419) is fundamentally different from sending a message. These networks don't provide methods of sending files to individuals.[11] Instead, they provide programs for explicitly copying a file from one machine to another (see the descriptions of `ftp` and `rcp` later in this chapter). The implication for addressing is that when you transmit a file you provide the address of a computer, not a person. In terms of domain addresses, you use only the text to the right of the '`@`'. However, the considerations for resolving such addresses are the same as they are for mail messages.

10.2   Local-Area Networks

Perhaps the most common type of UNIX system today is a collection of workstations and servers connected by an Ethernet using the TCP/IP protocols. The servers provide administrative services and network connections and also act as repositories for files, both those shared among users and those private to individual users.

- An Ethernet is a kind of local area network in which the nodes can be connected by simple direct wiring and can communicate with one another just by sending a properly addressed message over the network. The key to the Ethernet technology is its ability to resolve collisions among messages sent at the same time. The Ethernet idea was invented by Robert Metcalf at the Xerox Corporation Palo Alto Research Center.

---

10. Of course, if the program is clever enough, no one will ever know that it isn't a person.

11. People sometimes get around this limitation by putting files into mail messages. That's not a good practice since it tends to overload both mailers and peoples' mailboxes.

- TCP/IP, which stands for "Transmission Control Protocol/Internet Protocol", is a set of rules governing transmission of information between computers (including the case of transmission between a server and a workstation):

  - TCP deals with the assembly and disassembly of data packets, which are the units of information sent over the network. It is responsible for guaranteeing the integrity of the data and will request that a packet be resent if necessary.
  - IP deals with the assembly of data packets into *datagrams* and the delivery of datagrams to a specified IP address (see "IP Addresses" on page 414), and provides network-level services such as choosing a routing for a datagram.

  Users rarely deal with TCP or IP directly, but it's useful to know what they are because references to them appear so frequently in UNIX literature.

10.3   Distributing Files Over Networks

SunOS and similar systems provide facilities for distributing various kinds of files over networks. These facilities were designed so as to be nearly transparent to the operations that you might perform on files. In other words, as a user you rarely either know or care whether the files you're using reside on your own workstation or on a file server. The only time you're likely to be concerned with the location of files is when you want to make files local for efficiency reasons or when something goes wrong. With most modern systems the issue of efficiency rarely arises, since file servers transmit files almost as rapidly as you could access them locally.

Nonetheless it's helpful to be familiar with the two major facilites for distributed files because references to them crop up so frequently in UNIX literature and documentation:

- NIS, the Network Information Service, is a database of system administration information, earlier known as the Sun Yellow Pages. An example of information often provided through NIS is the password file. The NIS database is ordinarily kept on one or more servers, where it can be accessed by any host with the right permissions. This arrangement makes it much easier to maintain the database than it would be if copies of the database were kept in several locations, since it avoids the problem of inconsistent updating.

- NFS, the Network File System, is a facility that allows a file system to be on a different computer than its mount point (see p. 26). Since mount points are the points of connection among file systems, this facility is the key to distributing files over several computers in a way that allows the files to be accessed as though they were local. NFS uses IP, the Internet Protocol, for data transmission. NFS has been implemented under other operating systems besides UNIX, so NFS can even be used to share files among computers that are not running the same operating system.

10.4   Programs for Remote Communications

In the rest of this chapter we describe a number of programs for remote communications. They fall into several groups, reflecting the different forms of connection to remote computers as well as UNIX history—for a long time, the AT&T tradition was to connect computers via dial-up telephone lines or direct wires, while the Berkeley tradition was to connect computers via packet-switched networks. The following table shows how the different programs relate:

Operation	*Dial-up Connections*	*Local Network Connections*	*Remote Network Connections*
Logging in	cu	rlogin, telnet	rlogin, telnet
Copying files	uucp, uuto, uupick	rcp, ftp	ftp
Other operations	uuname	rsh, rwho	—

Generally the goal of the programs that work over local network connections is to make the connection between the local computer and the remote one as transparent as possible. The programs for local network connections assume that all the computers involved are running UNIX and that the computers are aware of each other. Most of the programs that work over dial-up lines and over remote network connections do not make that assumption.

We mention a pair of programs that are often useful for sending a binary file to another computer in the form of a mail message: uuencode and uudecode. The uuencode program transforms a binary file into a sequence of printable ASCII characters; the uudecode program undoes the transformation.

10.4.1
The kermit
File Transfer
Program

A popular program for transmitting files to and from remote computers is kermit, a public-domain contribution from Columbia University. Like uucp, kermit was designed to work over phone lines. Like ftp, it is supported by many different kinds of systems. You can obtain kermit over the Internet via anonymous ftp from watsun.cc.columbia.edu, IP address 128.59.39.2 (see Section 10.7), or over the uucp network from the OSUCIS archive (reference [U3]).

10.5　Remote Operations on "Nearby" Computers

The commands described below provide operations on remote computers that are very similar to operations on your own computer. They have names such as `rlogin` that start with 'r', indicating that they are remote versions of local commands. Except for `rlogin`, they all require that the remote computer be "nearby" in the sense that it recognizes and trusts your local computer—and even `rlogin` works more conveniently if the remote computer is nearby. The notion of a computer being recognized and trusted is quite specific: when data is transmitted to such a computer on a local-area network, the computer can verify that the sending computer is on its own list of trusted computers. That list, in turn, is prepared by a system administrator and ordinarily consists of a group of computers that share account names. Computer systems that share account names are sometimes said to be *equivalent*.

10.5.1
Files Used for
Remote Operations

The remote operations described below make use of certain files, both in system-wide directories and in the directories of individual users. Understanding these files is helpful in understanding how the commands work.

`/etc/hosts`

This file contains a list of other computers (not necessarily trusted ones) known to your computer. A sample line in the `hosts` file might be

---

`183.2.1.12  head.god.net zeus bigshot  # from Olympus`

Here the first item is an Ethernet or Internet address, the second item is the full domain name of the remote computer, and the remaining items are nicknames, or alternate names, of that computer. In this case the network address is '`183.2.1.12`' the full domain name of the computer there is '`head.god.net`', with nicknames '`zeus`' and '`bigshot`'. The material after the '`#`' is a comment. You can use an alternate name whenever you need to refer to a remote computer in a command.

`/etc/hosts.equiv`

This file contains a list of other computers equivalent to your local computer, i.e., that share account names. Computers that are not part of a local-area network usually do not have this file. Each line in the file contains an entry of the form

[-]*host* [[-]*user*]

where *host* is the official name of an equivalent computer and *user* is a user on that computer. An entry without a '-' indicates that access is allowed. A '-' in an entry indicates that access is denied, either to the computer entirely or to a particular user (such as `guest` or `root`) on that computer. Negative entries are intended to override other equivalences that would otherwise be in effect.

`/usr/hosts`

> This directory contains links to the remote shell program `rsh` (see Section 10.5.3). Each link has the name of a remote computer and serves as a command to execute `rsh` on that computer. For instance, if `/usr/hosts` contains a file `hammarfest`, then the command `hammarfest` is equivalent to `rsh hammarfest`. `Rsh` is clever enough to know the name under which it was called.

`$HOME/.rhosts`

> This file, unlike the others listed above, is in *your* home directory and under your control. It enables you to permit a user located on another computer (most likely yourself using an account there) to log in as you on your local computer without providing a password. This permission is essential to using the `rcp` and `rsh` programs from a remote computer.[12]
>
> Each line in the file contains the name of a remote computer and a user name, e.g.,
>
>> `hammarfest gynt`
>
> This line specifies that user `gynt` on the computer `hammarfest` can log in and assume your identity without providing a password. In addition, you can log in as yourself from a trusted remote computer listed in `/etc/hosts.equiv`.
>
> The name that you use in your `.rhosts` file must be the full domain-style name of the remote computer, which may be longer than the name that you ordinarily use to refer to that computer. Here are three ways to find out what the full name is:
>
> (1) If you can connect to the remote computer using `telnet` (by any name), you'll find its full name on the banner line that appears when you make the connection.
>
> (2) Look for the name of the remote computer in `/etc/hosts` on your own computer. The name to use in `.rhosts` is the first one listed on the relevant line of `/etc/hosts` (after the network address).
>
> (3) Look at the first `Received` header line on mail you've received from that computer.
>
> If you have an account on a remote computer that isn't equivalent to your local computer, you can set yourself up to log onto it without a password by making an appropriate entry in your `.rhosts` file under your own user name.[13]

---

12. Careless use of this file can create security hazards, since it enables an intruder who has captured your password on one computer to penetrate all the other computers where you have access. In particular, `.rhosts` should not be used for the `root` user at all except on a system that is isolated from the rest of the world.

13. Although many people use this shortcut, a number of experts advise against it for security reasons.

**10.5.2
Remote Login
with rlogin**

The `rlogin` command enables you to log in to a remote computer via a network. The form of the `rlogin` command line is

> `rlogin` *rhost* [*options*]

For some systems, the order is reversed:

> `rlogin` [*options*] *rhost*

In either case, *rhost* is the name of the remote computer. If you don't provide a user name with the `-l` option, you are logged in under your own name. If the remote computer is equivalent (see Section 10.5.1), you don't need to provide a password. You'll be disconnected from the remote computer when you log out; alternatively you can disconnect by typing '`~.`' (or '`c.`' if you've changed your escape character to *c* with the `-e` option).

If the remote computer is listed in `/usr/hosts`, you can log in just by typing its name. For example, if the remote computer `fakir` is listed there and you type the single command `fakir`, you are logged into `fakir` under your own name without further ado.

When you log into a remote computer, your terminal type is the same on the remote computer as on your local computer; in most respects you can use the remote computer as you would your local computer.

Command-line Options.   The `rlogin` command has the following options:

`-l` *user*   Log in as *user* rather than as yourself. You need not provide a password if you are listed in the `.rhosts` file located in the home directory of the account you are trying to access on the remote computer (see Section 10.5.1).

`-e`*c*   Use *c* as the escape character. There must not be any space between the '`e`' and *c*.

`-8`   Use an eight-bit data path.

**10.5.3
Executing a Shell
Command Remotely
with rsh**

The `rsh` command enables you to execute a command on a remote computer. To use it, the remote computer must be one that you can log onto using `rlogin` without a password. The form of the `rsh` command line is

> `rsh` *rhost* [*options*] [*cmd*]

where *rhost* is the name of a remote computer and *cmd* is a command to be executed on that computer. If you omit *cmd*, `rsh` becomes equivalent to `rlogin`. In this context it supports the `-l` option but not the `-e` or `-8` option.

Just as with `rlogin`, if the remote computer is listed in `/usr/hosts`, you can execute a command on it by typing its name and the name of the command. For instance, if `fakir` is listed there and you type

> `fakir make believe`

the command `make believe` is executed on `fakir`. The result is the same as if you had logged in on `fakir` under your own name (or the name specified with `-l`) and executed the command there.

Remember that shell metacharacters such as '<' are interpreted on the local computer, not on the remote one, unless you quote them. For example, the command

```
rsh fakir make believe \> belfile
```

is the proper way to execute the command `make believe` on the remote computer, redirecting its output to the file `belfile` there.

Rsh is not ordinarily able to execute in the background even if *cmd* expects no input, since `rsh` itself tries to read input in order to pass it to *cmd* and thereby becomes blocked. You can enable `rsh` to execute in the background by using the `-n` option, explicitly indicating that *cmd* expects no input.

Unfortunately, another UNIX program, the restricted Bourne shell (see Section 5.2.21), also has the name `rsh`. If your system includes both programs, the one you get when you type 'rsh' depends on the value of your `$PATH` environment variable: the restricted Bourne shell is usually stored as `/bin/rsh`, while the remote shell program is usually stored as `/usr/ucb/rsh`. The authors of the remote shell program recommend that you provide another link to it under a name such as `remsh`.

Command-line Options. These are the options for the `rsh` command line:

`-l` *user*   Log in as *user* rather than as yourself. If you're listed in the `/usr/`*user*`/.rhosts` file on the remote computer (see Section 10.5.1), you need not provide a password.

`-n`   Take input from `/dev/null`, thus enabling `rsh` to execute in the background.

10.5.4 Remote Copying with `rcp`

The `rcp` command enables you to copy files from one computer to another. For this command to work, you must be able to log onto each remote computer involved in the copy without providing a password (see Section 10.5.2). The form of the `rcp` command line is

```
rcp source ... dest
```

where each *source* is a source file or directory and *dest* is a destination file or directory. Each source and destination has the form

[rhost:]path

where *rhost* is the name of a remote computer and *path* is the path name of the file or directory you wish to use as a source or destination. If you omit *rhost*, `rcp` assumes that the computer is your local computer. For the purposes of the copy, the current directory on a remote computer is assumed to be your home directory there. The copy applies both to directories and files. **Note:** You can use `rcp` to copy files from one remote computer to another as well as to copy files to or from your local computer.

By default, the login implied by `rcp` takes place under your own user name. You can copy files stored under another user name provided that you can log in at the remote computer under that name without a password. To do this, replace *rhost* by '*ruser@rhost*', where *ruser* is the user name on the remote computer *rhost*. For example, the file name

rajiv@fakir:items/ropes

refers to the file `ropes` in the `items` subdirectory of `rajiv`'s home directory on the computer `fakir`.

Command-line Options.   The `rcp` command line has the following options:

-p   Preserve modification times and permissions of source files instead of using the default permissions and the current time.

-r   Recursively copy the subtree rooted at each *source*.

**10.5.5
Listing Users on the
Local Network
with** rwho

The `rwho` command lists all users currently on the local network—or more precisely, all such users whose machines are broadcasting `rwho` data. The form of the command line is

rwho [-a]

Unless you specify the -a option, users who have not typed anything in the last hour are not shown. The form of the listing is similar to the one you get from `who` (see Section 4.1.1).

Since this command requires querying every computer on your local network, you generally should avoid using it unless your network is small or very lightly loaded. In fact, some systems administrators disable `rwho` because it is known to be a resource hog.

You can also get information about users on another computer with the `finger` command (see Section 4.1.2).

10.6   Calling a Remote Computer with `telnet`

The `telnet` program enables you to conduct a dialog with another computer via a network. It is analogous to `cu`, which provides connections to other computers over telephone lines. Communications via `telnet` follow a set of conventions known as the TELNET protocol.

Compared with `rlogin` (see Section 10.5.2), `telnet` provides more control and flexibility but less convenience; in particular, `rlogin` does not work for communicating with computers that are not running UNIX. With `telnet`, you must log into the remote computer explicitly; with `rlogin`, you are usually logged in automatically.

The form of the `telnet` command line is

telnet [*host* [*port*]]

where *host* is the name of the remote computer you wish to connect to and *port* is a particular port on that computer. In this command, *host* can be either a domain name or an IP address (see "IP Addresses" on page 414).

If you omit *host*, `telnet` enters its command mode immediately without attempting to connect you to a particular computer. Once you've made the connection, whatever you type is sent to the remote computer and whatever the remote computer sends back is shown on your screen. If the remote computer breaks the connection, `telnet` exits and returns you to your shell.

You can issue a command to `telnet` by typing the command on a line by itself, preceded by the `telnet` escape character (by default, (Ctrl)]). Telnet issues a 'telnet>' prompt when it's expecting you to type something. You can abbreviate any `telnet` command, variable, etc. to its shortest unique prefix. These unique prefixes are indicated in the descriptions below. The shortest unique prefix may be different from the one given here if your system has a larger set of commands.

Telnet ordinarily translates your interrupt character, kill character, etc. to TELNET signals that are recognized by the remote computer and given the same meaning. The `localchars` toggle described below activates or deactivates this translation. You can send these signals explicitly with the `telnet` command `send`. You can also arrange to use different special characters for remote communication than you use for your own computer (see Section 10.6.3).

Telnet can operate either in character mode or line mode, although some remote computers may support only one of these modes:

- In character mode, each character is sent to the remote computer as you type it.

- In line mode, only completed lines are sent to the remote computer. Each character that you type is echoed locally, although you can turn off local echo by typing the echo-toggle character (by default (Ctrl) E). Turning off local echo is useful for typing passwords.

UNIX systems usually operate in character mode by default but also are able to operate in line mode. The initial mode is determined by the remote computer. You can change modes with the `mode` command if the remote computer supports both modes. It's a good idea to use line mode rather than character mode when communicating with a distant computer since fewer packets need to be sent across the network.

Telnet does not have file transfer capability. If you're using `telnet` and wish to transfer a file, you must exit from `telnet` and call a program such as `ftp` that can perform the transfer.

10.6.1
Quick Exit

To exit from `telnet` quickly, first log out from the remote computer if you can, then type '(Ctrl)] q (Enter)' to close the remote connection and exit from `telnet` itself. If you've set your `telnet` escape character to something other than (Ctrl)] , use that other character instead. See "Connecting and Disconnecting" below for more information about exiting from `telnet`.

10.6.2
Commands

The following commands provide a variety of functions for `telnet` communications. You can issue any of them by preceding the command with the `telnet` escape character.

Getting Help.   The following command provides help information:

? [*cmd*]   Displays help on *cmd*. If you omit *cmd*, you get a help summary.

Connecting and Disconnecting.   The following commands connect you to a remote computer or disconnect you from it:

o[pen] [*host* [*port*]]

>   Opens a connection to *host* at the specified port. If you don't specify a port, `telnet` uses *host*'s default port.

c[lose]   Disconnects from the remote computer but remains in `telnet`.

q[uit]   Disconnects from the remote computer and exits from `telnet`.

z   Suspends `telnet` and returns to the local computer. In some systems that support job control, the `telnet` job is suspended and you are returned to the command line. Other systems treat z as a command to enter a subshell on the local computer.

Showing `telnet`**'s Status.**   The following commands provide information about `telnet`'s state and the values of its variables and toggles:

st[atus]   Shows the current status of `telnet`.

d[isplay] [*var*] ...

>   Shows the value of each variable *var*.

Setting Variables and Toggles.   The following commands affect the state of `telnet`:

m[ode] *type*

>   Enters the specified mode (l[ine] or c[haracter]). Some remote computers are able to work in only one mode and therefore cannot honor this request.

set *var val*

>   Sets the `telnet` variable *var* to the value *val*. An example of what you'd type to issue this command is
>
>   (Ctrl)] set brk (Ctrl)C (Enter)
>
>   Note that when you type the (Ctrl)C you don't see it on your screen.

t[oggle] *var* ...

>   Toggles each variable *var*, changing its state from true to false, or vice versa. The command 'toggle ?' shows a list of the toggles.

See Section 10.6.3 for a list of the variables.

Sending Specific Signals.   The following command provides a way of sending specific signals to the remote computer:

sen[d] *tseq* ...

>   Sends the specified TELNET sequences to the remote computer. The command 'send ?', instead of sending anything, shows a list of the available sequences. The sequences are
>
>   es[cape]   The current character for escaping to command mode

s[ynch]	The TELNET ⟨SYNCH⟩ (Synchronize) sequence
b[rk]	The TELNET ⟨BRK⟩ (Break) sequence
i[p]	The TELNET ⟨IP⟩ (Interrupt Process) sequence
ao	The TELNET ⟨AO⟩ (Abort Output) sequence
ay[t]	The TELNET ⟨AYT⟩ (Are You There) sequence
ec	The TELNET ⟨EC⟩ (Erase Character) sequence
el	The TELNET ⟨EL⟩ (Erase Line) sequence
g[a]	The TELNET ⟨GA⟩ (Go Ahead) sequence
n[op]	The TELNET ⟨NOP⟩ (No Operation) sequence

Usually you can send most of these signals more easily by typing the appropriate control characters (see Section 10.6.3).

10.6.3
Variables with Values

The variables listed below contain the characters you can type to send various signals to the remote computer. They generally correspond to characters you would specify for your local computer with `stty` (see Section 4.4.2).

Characters with Special Meaning to `telnet`. The following variables define characters that have special meaning to `telnet`:

ec[ho]   The character that toggles echoing of locally typed characters in line mode. Its default value is `Ctrl`E.

es[cape]   The character that returns you to command mode. Its default value is `Ctrl`] .

Characters for Sending Control Signals. The following variables specify characters that are intended to send control signals to the remote computer. Typing one of these characters causes the TELNET sequence with the specified meaning to be sent to the remote computer. For instance, if you set the **erase** character to `Ctrl`B, typing `Ctrl`B causes the TELNET sequence ⟨EC⟩ (Erase Character) to be sent to the remote computer. The default value of each of these characters is the local character with the same meaning. For example, the default value of the remote interrupt character is your local interrupt character (as listed by `stty`). If the `localchars` toggle is off, the characters are not given any special interpretation.

i[nterrupt]
     The remote interrupt character.

q[uit]   The remote quit character.

f[lushoutput]
     The character for flushing remote output. Not all systems support this function, which enables you to discard the output of a command without halting its execution. What matters here is whether the remote computer supports the function; it's irrelevant whether your local computer supports it. The default value of this character is the flush character on your local computer; if the local computer doesn't have a flush character, it's usually set to a null character.

er[ase]   The remote erase character.

k[ill]   The remote kill character.

eo[f]   The remote end of file character.

**10.6.4
Toggles**

The `telnet` toggles are either off or on; the command `toggle` *t* reverses the state of the toggle *t*.

Interpretation of Control Characters.   The following toggles affect the interpretation of control characters that you type at your terminal:

l[ocalchars]

If on, transform local control characters to TELNET control sequences that produce the specified effect. If off, local control characters are not given any special interpretation. See "Characters for Sending Control Signals" on page 428 above for a list of the characters affected by `localchars`. The default value of `localchars` is off for character mode and on for line mode.

For instance, if `localchars` is on, typing the interrupt character causes `telnet` to send the TELNET ⟨IP⟩ sequence, which is supposed to cause a process interrupt on the remote computer. With `localchars` off, the local interrupt character is not interpreted by `telnet`—it is treated as an ordinary data character and doesn't interrupt `telnet` itself.

autof[lush]

If on, don't show typed data if an interrupt signal (flush, interrupt, or quit) has been sent to the remote computer but the remote computer has not yet acknowledged it. The initial value is on unless you've issued an 'stty -noflsh' command locally.[14] Autoflushing is deactivated in any case if `localchars` is off.

autos[ynch]

If `autosynch` and `localchars` are both on, typing an interrupt or quit character instructs the remote computer to discard any unprocessed input. `Telnet` achieves that effect by sending a TELNET `synch` signal to the remote computer before sending an interrupt or quit character. Since it may take the remote computer a while to act on this signal, you usually cannot predict how much input, if any, will be discarded.

Treatment of ⟨return⟩ Characters.   The following toggles are useful when communicating with a remote computer that indicates end of line by ⟨return⟩ alone:

crm[od]   If on, map ⟨return⟩ characters received from the remote computer to ⟨return⟩ ⟨linefeed⟩. Turning on this toggle does not affect ⟨return⟩ characters sent from the local computer. By default, `crmod` is off.

---

14. `Telnet` can detect the change of state that results from this command, since it's part of the information yielded by `stty`.

crl[f]   If on, map outgoing 〈return〉 characters to 〈return〉 〈linefeed〉. This toggle is rarely useful since the UNIX newline character is 〈linefeed〉, not 〈return〉; in any event, many systems do not implement the `crlf` toggle. By default, `crlf` is off.

Flow Control.   The following toggle affects the use of the flow control characters 〈DC1〉/〈DC3〉:

f[lowcontrol]

If on, use flow control signals (〈DC1〉/〈DC3〉) to regulate communication between your computer and the remote computer. The state of the `flowcontrol` toggle determines what happens when you type ⌷Ctrl⌷Q (〈DC1〉) or ⌷Ctrl⌷S (〈DC3〉) as follows:

- If on, `telnet` interprets each of these characters immediately and translates it into a signal that it passes to the remote computer (provided that the remote computer is also prepared to interpret these signals).

- If off, `telnet` passes each of these characters to the remote computer as typed.

If you're using a program such as the Emacs editor that assigns meanings to ⌷Ctrl⌷S and ⌷Ctrl⌷Q, you should turn `flowcontrol` off. By default, `flowcontrol` is on.

Debugging Control.   Turning on the following toggles causes debugging information to be generated. These toggles are unlikely to be useful unless you're familiar with the details of the TELNET protocol. All are off by default.

d[ebug]   If on, enable socket-level debugging. This toggle is useful only if you have superuser privileges.

o[ptions] If on, show how `telnet` is processing the TELNET options.

n[etdata] If on, enable display of network data.

10.7   Transferring Files between Computers with `ftp`

The `ftp` program enables you to transmit files to and from a remote computer that understands FTP ("File Transfer Protocol") and to operate on files and directories there. FTP is understood by many different operating systems, not just UNIX. It is built on top of the TELNET protocol—the same protocol used by the `telnet` program (see Section 10.6). Ftp is particularly effective at coping with the variety of conventions used to store files on different computers. Compared with uucp, `ftp` is far more general but also far more complex (see Section 10.8.3). Historically, `ftp` is part of the Berkeley heritage while uucp is part of the AT&T heritage.[15]

---

15. FTP was actually designed at Bolt, Beranek, and Newman—the Berkeley contribution was to integrate it into UNIX.

`Ftp` is a command interpreter—it processes commands that you provide either interactively or from a file and translates them into instructions to the server that handles the lower-level FTP commands. `Ftp` issues an 'ftp>' prompt when it's expecting you to type something. The form of the `ftp` command line is

```
ftp [options] [host]
```

See Section 10.7.16 for a list of the available options.

In this command, *host* can be either a domain name or an IP address (see "IP Addresses" on page 414). If *host* is specified, `ftp` immediately attempts to connect to that computer. Once the connection is completed, `ftp` enters its command interpreter, ready to interpret the commands described later in this section. If *host* is not specified, `ftp` enters its command interpreter immediately.

In either case, once you enter the command interpreter you can issue commands to log in or out, send or receive files from the remote computer, do file maintenance on the remote computer, and carry out several other useful operations. You can abbreviate the name of a command to its shortest unique prefix as indicated for each command. **Note:** The shortest unique prefix may be different if your version of `ftp` has a different or larger command set than the one we list here.

To use `ftp` you must log into the remote computer. As a security measure, `ftp` does not allow you to log into a user account on a remote computer that has no password. If you try, you're prompted for a password anyway—and the login is then rejected (so the fact that the account requires no password is not revealed).

Some of the commands and features described below may not work in your system, particularly if it's running an older version of `ftp`. However, if a given command is implemented at all it should work as we describe.

Remember—`ftp` is a *program* while FTP is a *protocol*—a set of conventions that govern file transmissions. Usually the programs that actually transmit the files are the only ones that care about these conventions.

10.7.1
Anonymous `ftp`

A particularly important application of `ftp`—and the only one that many people ever use—is the so-called "anonymous `ftp`". Several computers, repositories of publicly available files, accept logins under the name `anonymous`. Use your net address as the password when logging in. Available files are typically found in a directory named `pub`. You can use the `dir` command to explore the directory structure of the remote computer and locate the files you're looking for. Having found them, you can retrieve them using the `get` or `mget` command.

10.7.2
Quick Exit

If `ftp` is in the middle of an activity such as transmitting a file or showing a directory, typing (Intr) halts that activity and returns you to the `ftp` prompt. You can then exit from `ftp` by typing 'bye (Enter)' (see "Closing Connections" on page 432).

**10.7.3
Auto-Login**

Ftp provides a facility called *auto-login* for automatically logging onto a remote computer. Auto-login uses the .netrc file in your home directory (if that file exists) to provide the information that the remote computer requires. When you connect to a remote computer, ftp provides the required user name and passwords as long as .netrc exists and auto-login has not been disabled. You can make the connection either by specifying a host name on the command line or by using the open command described below. See Section 10.7.14 for a description of the information in the .netrc file. You can disable auto-login with the −n option (p. 445).

**10.7.4
Opening, Closing,
and Controlling
Remote
Connections**

The commands in this group open a connection with a remote computer, terminate a connection, or control how the connection operates.

Opening Connections. The following commands enable you to open a connection to a remote computer, identify yourself to that computer, or gain access to its resources:

o[pen] *host* [*port*]

        Opens a connection to the computer named *host*. You can use *port* to specify a port number on the remote computer. If you don't specify *port*, ftp chooses a port by default. If your information about the remote computer doesn't include specific port numbers (the usual case), then the default port is almost certain to be the one you want. Auto-login always uses the default port.

us[er] *usrname* [*passwd1* [*passwd2*]]

        Identifies a user to the remote computer. This command expects a user name and optionally, one or two passwords. The first password is associated with the user name, the second with an account that provides access to particular resources on the remote computer. Not all computers make use of accounts; in particular, most UNIX systems don't. If you fail to specify a password that the remote computer requires, you are prompted for it.

ac[count] [*passwd*]

        Verifies a supplemental password that the remote computer requires in order to grant you access to particular resources on that computer. If you don't specify a password, you're prompted for one.

Closing Connections. The following commands enable you to break the connection to a remote computer. After breaking the connection, you can either terminate ftp or continue running it.

EOF

by[e]

qui[t]   Breaks the connection with the remote computer and terminates ftp.

`cl[ose]`
`dis[connect]`

> Breaks the connection with the remote computer without leaving `ftp`. A side effect of this command is that all current macro definitions are erased.

Controlling Connections. The following commands enable you to control the communications link to the remote computer:

`rese[t]`   Resynchronizes communication with the remote computer by clearing the reply queue. This command is useful when the link has gotten into a state where neither computer can understand the other one.

`rest[art]` *marker*

> Restarts the immediately following `get` or `put` at the position given by *marker*. Generally *marker* is a byte offset into the file. This command provides for transmitting just the last part of a file and is useful when a long file transfer has aborted part way through.

`id[le]` [*n*] Sets the inactivity timer of the remote computer to *n* seconds. If you omit *n*, `ftp` shows the current value of the inactivity timer. If the remote computer uses an inactivity timer and no activity takes place under your `ftp` login within the inactivity interval, the remote computer automatically logs you out.

`sendp[ort]`

> Toggles the use of `PORT` commands. `PORT` commands are part of the FTP protocol. Allowing `ftp` to use these commands can speed up transfers of multiple files, but may cause problems if the remote computer does not interpret the `PORT` command correctly.

`quo[te]` *arg* ...

> Sends the specified arguments to the remote computer. This command provides a method of sending specific communications instructions if you know what you're doing and understand the FTP protocol.

`sit[e]` *arg* ...

> Sends the command 'SITE *arg* ...' to the remote computer.

**10.7.5
Getting Help**

Because the `ftp` facilities on the remote computer may not be the same as those on your local computer, `ftp` provides two forms of help, one for each computer:

`? [`*cmd*`]`
`he[lp]` [*cmd*]

> Provides local help information on *cmd*. If you omit *cmd*, you obtain a list of available commands.

`remoteh[elp]` [*cmd*]

> Requests help information on *cmd* from the remote computer.

What happens if you omit *cmd* depends on the help facility on that computer, although you're likely to get a list of commands just as you would from your own computer.

10.7.6
Remote File
Operations

The operations in this group enable you to operate on files and directories residing on the remote computer, but they do not in themselves transmit the contents of those files. You can specify a remote file by using an absolute path name if the remote computer understands absolute path names. However, some computers reinterpret such paths so as to start them at a special directory such as `~ftp` rather than at the true root when you log in using anonymous `ftp`.

Directory Operations.   The following operations show you what the current directory is on the remote computer and change it:

pw[d]   Shows the name of the current (working) directory on the remote computer.

cd *rdir*   Changes the current directory on the remote computer to *rdir*.

cdu[p]   Changes the current directory on the remote computer to its parent. Cdup is equivalent to 'cd ..' for systems with UNIX-like file structures, but not all systems recognize the '..' convention—not even all that have tree-structured directories.

The following operations perform various kinds of directory maintenance on the remote computer. Normally you apply them only to directories that belong to you or over which you have some administrative control.

mk[dir] *dir*

Makes directory *dir* on the remote computer. You can specify *dir* as a path name; thus you can use this command to make directories in places other than the current directory (on most computers).

rm[dir] *dir*

Deletes directory *dir* on the remote computer.

del[ete] *rfile*

Deletes file *rfile* on the remote computer.

mde[lete] [*rfile*] ...

Deletes the specified remote files. If prompting is on (see the `prompt` command above), you're given the opportunity to confirm or reject each deletion. If you don't provide any files, you're prompted for the list.

ren[ame] *name₁* *name₂*

Renames file *name₁* on the remote computer to *name₂*.

ch[mod] *mode rfile*

Changes the permissions of remote file *rfile* to *mode*. The variable *mode* must be given as an octal number. In effect, this command does a `chmod` (see Section 3.12.1) on the remote computer. The remote computer must be running UNIX.

um[ask] [*mask*]
>   Sets the default file permission mask on the remote computer to *mask*. In effect, this command does a `umask` on the remote computer, which must be running UNIX (see Section 3.12.2).

Information About Directories and Files. The following operations enable you to retrieve information about directories and files from the remote computer and store those listings locally. Note that in all cases, using '–' for the local file name causes the listing to be sent to standard output.

dir [*rdir* [*lfile*]]
>   Sends a listing of remote directory *rdir* to the local file *lfile*. The listing is a "long" listing in the style produced by '`ls -l`' (see Section 3.1). If you omit *rdir*, `ftp` takes it to be the current directory on the remote computer. If you omit *lfile*, `ftp` sends the listing to standard output.

ls [*rdir* [*lfile*]]
>   Like `dir`, except that on some systems you may get an abbreviated listing. The difference between an abbreviated and an unabbreviated listing depends on the implementation.

nl[ist] [*rdir* [*lfile*]]
>   Like `dir`, except that the listing is usually in the style of '`ls -a`'; it shows just the names of the files, not their attributes, but includes files whose names start with a dot.

mdi[r] *rfile* ... *lfile*
>   Like `dir`, except that you can provide a list of files instead of a directory. Normally the point of doing so would be to use wildcards in the specification of *rfile*. If *rfile* is a directory, you get a list of its files.

ml[s] *rfile* ... *lfile*
>   Like `mdir`, except that on some systems you obtain an abbreviated listing even if the listing you obtain with `ls` is not abbreviated.

modt[ime] *rfile*
>   Shows the time when remote file *rfile* was last modified.

siz[e] *rfile*
>   Shows the size of remote file *rfile*.

**10.7.7
Transmitting Files**

The commands in this group enable you to transmit either a single file or a group of files from the remote computer to your computer or conversely. The file-naming conventions for the remote computer need not correspond to those on your computer (presumably the UNIX conventions). Ftp therefore enables you to specify a translation from each remote file name to the name of the corresponding local file and vice versa. It also provides a mechanism for creating unique names for received files when those files would otherwise have the same name (see Section 10.7.8).

Transmitting From the Remote Computer. The following commands are used to transmit files from the remote computer to your computer. File names apply to the current directory on each computer unless that directory is overridden by an absolute path name.

ge[t] *rfile* [*lfile*]
rec[v] *rfile* [*lfile*]

> Retrieves remote file *rfile* and stores it in local file *lfile*. If *lfile* is not given, it is obtained by translating the remote file name as described below. Wildcard substitution is not applied to *rfile* since it must be a single file. For example, the command

```
get scoundrels cads
```

> retrieves the remote file `scoundrels` and copies it into your local file `cads`.

reg[et] *rfile* [*lfile*]

> Retrieves the portion of remote file *rfile* that has not already been transferred and stores it in local file *lfile*. The transfer takes place only if *lfile* does not exist or is shorter than *rfile*. If *lfile* is not given, it is obtained by translating the remote file name as described below. The purpose of this command is to complete a transfer of a large file that may have been interrupted by a dropped connection.

ne[wer] *rfile* [*lfile*]

> Retrieves remote file *rfile* and copies it into the local file *lfile* provided that *rfile* is newer than *lfile* or *lfile* doesn't exist. If you don't specify *lfile*, it is assumed to have the same name as *rfile*.

mg[et] *rfile* . . .

> Retrieves the specified remote files. First, wildcards in the *rfiles* are expanded. Then the file names specified by the *rfiles* are translated into local names as described below. Finally, each remote file is transmitted to the corresponding local file, with a prompt preceding each transfer if prompting is turned on.

Transmitting To the Remote Computer. The following commands are used to transmit files from your computer to the remote computer. File names apply to the current directory on each computer unless the current directory is overridden by an absolute path name.

send *lfile* [*rfile*]
pu[t] *lfile* [*rfile*]

> Transmits local file *lfile* to the remote computer, naming it *rfile*. If *rfile* is not given, it is obtained by translating the local file name as described below. The file name *lfile* should not contain any wildcards.[16]

ap[pend] *lfile* [*rfile*]

> Appends local file *lfile* to remote file *rfile*. The file naming and translation conventions are the same as for `put`.

---

16. If *lfile* contains wildcards, the first file in the expansion is used and the others are ignored.

mp[ut] *lfile* ...

> Transmits the specified local files to the remote computer. First, wildcards in the *lfiles* are expanded. Then the file names specified by the *lfiles* are translated into remote names as described below. Finally, each local file is transmitted to the corresponding remote file, with a prompt preceding each transfer if prompting is turned on.

Aborting a Transfer.   If anything goes wrong with a transfer, you can abort it by pressing ⟨Intr⟩. An outgoing transfer is halted immediately, but an incoming transfer may not be. For an incoming transfer, `ftp` sends an FTP `ABOR` sequence to the remote computer—but the remote computer may take a while to respond to it or, in the worst case, may not recognize the `ABOR` command at all. It all depends on what support the remote computer provides for FTP. If the remote computer does not recognize `ABOR`, you won't see the next 'ftp>' prompt until the file has been entirely transmitted.

10.7.8 Translating File Names

The following commands provide translation from remote file names to local file names and vice versa. Note that a single translation is almost certainly not correct for both directions, so if you are transmitting files in both directions during a single use of `ftp`, you must change the translations in between. The commands below are listed in the order in which their translations are applied, so that `case`, for example, is done before `nmap`.

gl[ob]
> Toggles wildcard expansion, called *globbing* in the C shell, for file names. If it is off, no wildcard expansion is done for file names appearing in `mget`, `mput`, or `mdelete`. By default, wildcard expansion is turned on.

ca[se]
> Toggles case mapping for remote file names. Case mapping causes remote file names consisting of all uppercase characters to be translated to all lowercase characters. By default, case mapping is turned off.

nm[ap] *inpat outpat*
> Maps file names according to the input pattern *inpat* and the output pattern *outpat*. Each pattern acts as a template, with up to nine variable parts $1, $2, ... , $9. The entire input file name is available as $0. Each input file name is matched against the input pattern in order to determine the variable parts, which are then substituted into the output pattern. For `get` and `mget` the input file name is the remote name and the output file name is the local name; for `put` and `mput` the relationship is reversed. The pattern need not match completely. Any parts of the input pattern that cannot be matched reading from left to right are simply deleted; the corresponding variable parts are made empty.
>
> Both the input pattern and the output pattern can use '\' as a quoting character. In the output pattern, the construct

'[seq_1,seq_2]' is replaced by seq_1 if seq_1 is not empty, and by seq_2 otherwise.

An example showing the transformation is

```
nmap $1:$2.$3 [$2,FILE].[$3,EXT]:[$1,x]
```

Some input file names and the corresponding output file names are

Input	Output
c:grackle.b	grackle.b:c
starling	FILE.EXT:starling
m:wren	wren.EXT:m

nt[rans] [*inchars* [*outchars*]]

Sets or unsets a translation table for characters in file names. If ntrans is issued by itself it turns off translation. Otherwise a character in the file name that occurs as the *n*th character of *inchars* is translated to the *n*th character of *outchars*. If *n* is greater than the length of *outchars*, the character is deleted from the file name. In particular, if *outchars* is absent all character appearing in *inchars* are deleted. For example, if you issue the command

```
ntrans %![] ..
```

and then transfer a remote file whose name is x1%!q[T], the corresponding local file is x1.Y.qT.

The variable *inchars* should not have any repeated characters.

ru[nique]   Toggles the generation of unique names for files obtained from the remote computer. Suppose that generation of unique names is turned on and a file is received whose (local) name *name* is the name of a file that already exists. Then the new file is stored under the name '*name*.1'. Further duplicates are stored under the names '*name*.2', '*name*.3', etc., with a maximum of 99. By default, unique name generation is turned off.

su[nique]   Toggles the generation of unique names for files sent to the remote computer. Unique generation of remote names works only if the remote server supports it. You receive a report of any files that are renamed as a result of remote generation of unique names. Remotely generated unique names are not necessarily generated by the same rule as local ones.

10.7.9
Interpretation of
Transmitted Files

Although UNIX views a file as a stream of bytes, not all operating systems do. Even among operating systems that take that view of what a file is, conventions differ for representing the end of a line. In order to support file transfer between computers that view files differently, the ftp program provides several parameters that specify the nature of the transfer. In effect, these parameters determine a common language for the sending computer and the receiving computer. Each computer does whatever translation is needed to convert the transmitted stream of data to or from that common language.

The following parameters affect file transfers:

- **Representation type.** The representation type defines how the information content of a file relates to the bits in the file. The two principal representations supported by `ftp` are seven-bit ASCII and image. The former views each group of eight bits as representing a character as defined by the ASCII encoding (with the highest bit ignored); the latter views a file as an uninterpreted sequence of bits that could mean anything at all. You *must* use the image mode (which you can get with `image`) for transferring eight-bit files. `Ftp` also supports the representation used on TENEX computers.

- **Form.** The form applies only to files having a character set (ASCII or EBCDIC) as representation type. It determines whether vertical format controls (newlines, formfeeds, etc.) are to be left uninterpreted, translated to conform to TELNET conventions, or translated to conform to Fortran conventions. `Ftp` currently supports only the uninterpreted form.

- **File structure.** The file structure is either `file` (no internal substructure), `record` (the file is viewed as a sequence of records), or `page` (the file is viewed as a sequence of pages separated by formfeeds). `Ftp` currently supports only `file`.

- **Transfer mode.** The transfer mode is either `stream` (a sequence of bits ended by an end of file), `block` (a sequence of fixed-length blocks of bits), or `compressed` (data compressed by the sender and decompressed by the receiver). `Ftp` currently supports only `stream`.

Setting the Representation.   The following commands choose the representation for subsequent transfers. As a rule you should use `ascii` for any file that isn't explicitly binary. An example of an explicitly binary file would be a compiled C program.

`as[cii]`   Selects seven-bit ASCII as the representation type.

`im[age]`
`bi[nary]`   Selects image as the representation type.

`te[nex]`   Selects the representation type that is appropriate to TENEX computers.

`ty[pe]` [*name*]
              Uses *name* as the representation type. This command merely provides an alternate syntax for the preceding ones.

The following command is meaningful only when the representation type is `ascii`.

`cr`   Toggles stripping of carriage returns for ASCII file transfers from remote computers. This facility is needed because the standard for ASCII file transfers uses the ⟨return⟩⟨linefeed⟩ sequence to represent a newline, while UNIX expects the ⟨linefeed⟩ alone. If this stripping is on, carriage returns are removed from the file as it is received. Some files received from non-UNIX computers may contain single ⟨linefeed⟩s; to use such files you must turn off carriage return stripping and do some local interpretation. By default carriage return stripping is turned on.

Setting Other Transfer Parameters. The following commands set other transfer parameters—but since in each case `ftp` recognizes only one possible value, you should never need to use them. They are included only for the sake of future extensions.

f[orm] [*fmt*]
> Selects 'non-print' for interpreting vertical format controls.

mode [*name*]
> Sets the transfer mode to *name*.

str[uct] [*name*]
> Sets the file structure to *name*.

10.7.10 Local Operations

The following commands enable you to execute commands on your own computer without leaving `ftp`.

! [*cmd*]
> Runs *cmd* locally in a subshell. If you omit *cmd*, you obtain an interactive shell. Ftp looks in the SHELL environment variable to see which shell to use; if SHELL does not exist, `ftp` uses the Bourne shell `sh`.

lc[d] [*dir*]
> Changes the current local directory to *dir*. **Note:** It does no good to execute cd in a subshell because the effect of the change disappears when the subshell terminates.

10.7.11 Controlling Feedback from `ftp`

The following commands affect the feedback that you get during a file transfer:

prom[pt]
> Toggles interactive prompting during multiple file transfers and deletions. By default prompting is turned on, giving you the opportunity to accept or reject any transfer or deletion. If prompting is turned off, all transfers or deletions are performed.

ha[sh]
> Toggles use of a hashmark (#) to indicate that a data block is being transferred. By default the hashmarks do not appear.

be[ll]
> Toggles the sounding of a bell after each file transfer. By default the bell is not sounded.

The following commands provide information about the status of `ftp` and what it is doing.

sta[tus]
> Shows the current status of `ftp`, including which toggles are on and which ones are off. The display looks something like this:

```
Connected to miasma.com.
No proxy connection.
```

```
                        Mode: stream; Type: ascii; Form: non-print
                        Structure: file; Verbose: on; Bell: off
                        Prompting: on; Globbing: on
                        Store unique: off; Receive unique: off
                        Case: off; CR stripping: on
                        Ntrans: off
                        Nmap: off
                        Hash mark printing: off; Use of PORT cmds: on
                        Macros:
                                  ready
                                  groupsend
```

remotes[tatus] [*rfile*]

Shows the current status of remote file *rfile*, or of the remote computer if *rfile* is omitted.

sy[stem] Shows the type of operating system running on the remote computer.

deb[ug] [*n*]

Sets the debugging level to *n* (an integer). If you don't specify *n*, this command toggles debugging on (with a default level) or off. With debugging on, each FTP command sent to the remote computer is shown, preceded by '-->'. Most implementations of `ftp` ignore the value of *n*.

v[erbose] Toggles verbose mode for showing `ftp` responses. In verbose mode, `ftp` shows all responses from the FTP server and reports statistics on the efficiency of each file transfer. By default, verbose mode is turned on if `ftp` is getting its input from a terminal and turned off otherwise.

tr[ace] Toggles packet tracing. This facility is unimplemented; the command exists only for compatibility with future enhancements.

10.7.12
Linking Two Remote Computers

You can use `ftp` for *third party transfers* in which you transfer files from one remote computer to another, using your own computer to control the transfer. The following command makes such transfers possible:

prox[y] *cmd*

Executes *cmd* as an `ftp` command on the remote computer. Ordinarily the first proxy command is an **open** that connects the remote computer to another remote computer. The command 'proxy ?' executes '?' on the remote computer, producing a list of the commands that the version of `ftp` on the secondary computer can execute.

10.7.13
Defining and Using Macros

You can name a sequence of commands by defining a *macro*. Calling the macro then causes those commands to be executed. For instance, typing

```
macdef xfc
mget *.c
```

```
cdup
cd lib
mget *.h
Enter
```

defines a macro `xfc` that you can use as a new command; typing `$xfc` becomes equivalent to typing the sequence of four commands following the `macdef` line. The principal use of macros is in the `.netrc` file; it is rarely worthwhile to type macro definitions as direct commands.

ma[cdef] *mac*

> Defines a macro named *mac*. The definition appears on the lines following the `macdef` and is ended by an empty line.
>
> A macro can have parameters, indicated by `$n` where *n* is a digit. Arguments (which are delimited by whitespace) are substituted for the corresponding parameters: the first argument for '`$1`', the second for '`$2`', and so forth. The special parameter '`$i`' indicates repetition of the macro; its entire sequence of commands is executed once for each argument, with successive arguments substituted for '`$i`' on successive repetitions.
>
> The '`\`' character quotes the following character. It's needed in order to be able to include a literal '`$`' in a macro definition. A '`\`' must itself be quoted, i.e., it must be written as '`\\`'.

$ *mac* [*arg*] ...

> Executes macro *mac* with arguments *arg* ...

When you execute a `close` command, all macro definitions are erased. Executing an '`open` *rhost*' command can cause macros to be defined (or redefined) if the entry in `.netrc` for the computer *rhost* includes macro definitions.

10.7.14
The `.netrc` File

You can provide information in an initialization file, `.netrc`, that enables `ftp` to perform auto-login (see Section 10.7.3). The `.netrc` file is a collection of definitions rather than an initialization file in the usual sense of a file containing more or less arbitrary commands to be executed when a program starts up. It consists of a sequence of machine definitions.

Each machine definition either describes a particular remote computer or provides a default in case no earlier machine definition applies. A machine definition consists of a sequence of items; each item in turn consists of one or more words (called *tokens* in the `ftp` manual pages). Words are separated by whitespace (including newlines), except that special rules apply to a `macdef` item (see below).

The first word in each machine definition is either a `machine` item or a `default` item. When you use `ftp`'s auto-login facility to log into a remote computer named *name*, `ftp` searches for the first machine definition that begins with either '`machine` *name*' or '`default`'. The definition consists of the words up to the next definition or the end of the file. `Ftp` then uses the information supplied in the machine definition to execute the login. If the information is insufficient, `ftp` prompts you for the missing items.

A machine definition may contain the following items:

`machine` *name*

Begins the definition of a machine whose name is *name*. The variable *name* must be a valid network address.

`default` Begins a machine definition to be used in case none of the preceding definitions matches the name of the specified remote computer. Since `default` matches any computer, it should follow all other definitions. Some systems do not yet support `default`.

`login` *name*

Provides the user name *name* when logging onto the remote computer.

`password` *string*

Provides the password *string* when logging onto the remote computer.

`account` *string*

Uses *string* as the account password if the remote computer requires it. If the remote computer does not request an account password when you log onto it but the machine description includes an `account` item, `ftp` executes an `account` command, thus making the account password available later when the remote computer asks for it.

`macdef` *mac*

Defines a macro using the same conventions as the `macdef` command (see Section 10.7.13). The macro definition is given by a sequence of lines; consequently the next word seen by `ftp` after scanning a macro definition in `.netrc` is the one following the empty line that terminates the macro definition. If you define a macro named `init`, `ftp` executes it immediately after a successful login.

Macro definitions are part of a machine definition and have no effect if auto-login is disabled. If you execute a `close` command followed by an `open` for a new machine, the macros for the old machine are erased and the macros for the new machine are installed as a consequence of the fact that `close` erases macros and auto-login defines them.

An example of a short `.netrc` file is

```
machine family.org login grandma
    account kNitting
macdef inmap
nmap $1.$2 $1.[$2,EXT]

default login anonymous password timon@athens
```

If you log into any remote computer other than `family.org`, you'll be set up to do an anonymous `ftp` from that computer.

Security Considerations for `.netrc`. Since the `.netrc` file contains passwords, no one but you should have permission to read it. Many versions of `ftp` refuse to use a `.netrc` file unless its group and other read and write permissions are turned off.

You should also avoid putting real passwords in your `.netrc` file. The reason is that anyone who illegitimately gains access to this file then gains access to the remote computers listed there as well—thus turning a local break-in into a network-wide one. On the other hand, putting a default line for anonymous `ftp` into `.netrc` as shown above is both convenient and innocuous.

10.7.15 Special Forms of File Names

Ftp recognizes certain special file names:

- A file name of '-' specifies standard input in a context that calls for reading a file and standard output in a context that calls for writing a file.

- A file name of the form '|*cmd*' can be used in place of a local file name. It indicates that the command *cmd* is to be executed in a subshell—specifically, the Bourne shell `sh` with the `-c` option.

  - If the '|*cmd*' construct appears in the context of a local file name specifying the *output* of an `ftp` command such as `get` or `dir`, then the actual output of the `ftp` command becomes the standard input of *cmd* and the standard output of *cmd* is sent to your terminal. The actual output of the `ftp` command can be either a file or a directory listing. For example,

    ```
    dir * |pg
    ```

    gives you a paged listing of a remote directory.

  - If the '|*cmd*' construct appears in the context of a local file name specifying the *input* of an `ftp` command such as `put`, then *cmd* is executed with an empty file as its standard input and its standard output is used as the data source for the `ftp` command. For example,

    ```
    put |who herefolks
    ```

    places a listing of the logged-in users on your computer into the remote file `herefolks`. You should avoid allowing the remote file name to be defaulted when you use '|' in that way, since `ftp` treats '|' in a remote file name as an ordinary character—almost certainly not what you want. If you allow the remote file name to be defaulted, it becomes something like '|who'.

  You must either surround the '|*cmd*' construct by double quotes or make sure that it doesn't contain any internal spaces. The first command above could also be written as

  ```
  dir * "| pg"
  ```

In addition to these forms, wildcard substitution according to the usual conventions applies unless you've disabled it with the `-g` option or the `glob` command.

<table>
<tr><td>

**10.7.16
Command-line
Options**

</td><td>

The following options are available on the command line:

</td></tr>
</table>

-d   Enable debugging.

-g   Disable wildcard substitution (globbing) in file names.

-i   Turn off interactive prompting during multiple file transfers .

-n   Don't do auto-login when initially connecting to another computer (see Section 10.7.3). With auto-login turned off, ftp establishes the connection and then waits for you to issue commands. You aren't logged onto the remote computer until you issue a user command.

-v   Show all responses from the remote server and provide statistics on all data transfers. This option is turned on automatically if ftp is receiving its input from a terminal.

-t   Enable packet tracing. This option is as yet unimplemented.

10.8   File Transfers Based on uucp

The easiest way to transfer files between computers running UNIX is to send the files with uuto and retrieve them with uupick. Both of these programs use uucp (UNIX to UNIX copy) to carry out the actual transfer; the UUCP network gets its name from this program. Other useful programs in this group are uustat for checking the status of outgoing files and deleting them if necessary, uuname for finding out which other UNIX systems your computer knows about, and cu for connecting directly to another computer.

The uucp program is part of a group of programs called the "Basic Networking Utilities" (BNU).[17] These utilities were written for store-and-forward communications networks in which messages are held until they can be transmitted and then are sent over direct lines to another station. Ftp and related programs, in contrast, were written under the assumption that they would be used with packet-switching networks in which messages are broken up into packets that are transmitted individually and reassembled at the destination (see Section 10.7).

Although uucp has been extended to work with packet-switching networks and ftp can work with direct connections,[18] they are usually used in these ways only when no alternative exists. Which program you should use depends on the nature of your connection with the remote computer. For a direct connection over a phone line, you'll usually need to use uucp; for a network connection, you'll usually need to use ftp. Most of the time you won't have a choice, since a particular remote computer is likely to be

---

17. These utilities are also sometimes referred to as HoneyDanBer uucp, after their authors Peter Honeyman, Dan Nowitz, and Brian Redman.

18. These connections are constructed using SLIP (Serial Line Internet Protocol).

conveniently accessible only via one type of connection. If you do have the choice, uucp is probably better because you can just issue the request and forget about it—your system will transmit the file at the next opportunity.

The uucp program must be configured before you can use it. A discussion of how to do that is beyond the scope of this book; should you need to do the job yourself, your system manuals together with reference [B21] are your best guide.

10.8.1 Sending Files with uuto

The uuto command sends a set of files or directories to a specified user at a specified computer by generating a request to uucp to send the files. The actual transmission occurs later. Uucp usually transmits the files going to a particular computer in batches, with the uucp scheduling parameters determining when the transmissions take place.

The form of the uuto command is

    uuto [*options*] *source* ... *path* ! *person*

where *path* is a uucp-style path address of the destination computer and *person* is a user known to that computer. If you're calling this command from the C shell, you must quote the '!' character by writing it as '\!'. The first computer name in *path* must be listed in the Systems file on your own computer (see Section 10.8.5) but the remaining computer names need not be. Each source can be either an ordinary file or a directory; if you specify a directory, all files contained in that directory and its subdirectories are sent and the structural information is retained in the transmission. For example, the command

    uuto grammar/adjs grammar/advs handoff!editors!fowler

sends the files grammar/adjs and grammar/advs to the person fowler at the site editors via the site handoff.[19] Only handoff need be known to your computer. Normally, uucp transmits the files from where they reside on your computer rather than making its own copy of them. If a file to be transmitted is deleted before the transmission takes place, it will be lost; if it is modified before the transmission takes place, the modified version will be transmitted. You can change this behavior with the -p option described below.

Command-line Options. Uuto recognizes two options on the command line:

-p   Copy each file to be transmitted to a spooling directory when the transmission is requested. The copied file will be transmitted later; any changes to the original will not affect what is transmitted.

-m   Send mail to the sender indicating when the transmission has been accomplished.

---

19. Many systems disable file transfers that involve multiple computers, however.

**10.8.2
Retrieving Files
with uupick**

The uupick command retrieves files or directories that were sent to you via uucp by a user on a remote computer. When the files arrive, uucp stores them in a special directory, usually

        /usr/spool/uucppublic/receive/*user*/*rsys*

where *user* is your user name and *rsys* is the name of the remote computer from which the files were received. You can then examine them, discard them, or move them to a more convenient place using uupick.

The form of the uupick command line is:

        uupick [-s *system*]

If you specify *system*, the retrieval is limited to files sent from the remote computer *system*. When you call uupick, it goes through the files and directories sent to you, one by one. For each one it sends the appropriate message to standard output:

        from *system*: file *file*?
        from *system*: dir *dir*?

Your response to the message determines what uupick does with the item. These are the possible responses:

?
*   Shows a summary of the commands.

(Enter)   Goes on to the next item.

d   Discards this item.

m [*dir*]   Moves this item to the directory *dir*. If the item is a directory, it and all its subdirectories are moved.

a [*dir*]   Moves all the items received from the computer that sent the current item. If *dir* is not specified, the current directory is assumed.

p   Shows the item, i.e., sends it to standard output. This option does not apply to directories.

(EOF)
q   Quits, exiting from uupick.

! *cmd*   Executes *cmd* in a subshell.

**10.8.3
UNIX to UNIX
Copying with uucp**

The UNIX to UNIX copy program, uucp, copies files from one UNIX system to another. You can use it not just to send files but to fetch them as well as long as you have the necessary permissions.

The uucp command line has the form:

        uucp [*options*] *sfile* ... *dfile*

where each *sfile* is a source file and *dfile* is a destination file. Both *sfile* and *dfile* have the form

        [*system*!] ... *path*

For each source file the sequence of *system*s is a path-style route to the computer where the file is to be found (see Section 10.1.1). The first computer name in *path* must be listed in the Systems file on your own computer (see Section 10.8.5) but the remaining computer names need not be. Similarly, for the destination file the sequence of *system*s is a path-style address of the computer where the files are to be put. For example, the command

```
uucp igloo\!\~/huskies/* .
```

copies all the files from the publicly accessible `huskies` directory on the remote system `igloo` to your current directory. Here the '~' indicates a directory that contains the publicly accessible files on `igloo` (see below). The backslashes preceding '!' and '~' in the command line are escapes that prevent these characters from being interpreted by the C shell. They are not needed for the Bourne shell.

   Note the following points:

- A file name that does not specify a system is taken relative to the current directory unless it is an absolute path name.

- For a transfer to work, the following conditions must hold:
  - Each intermediate computer must be willing to perform the transfer.
  - Each source file must have `r` permission for everyone.
  - Each directory enroute to the source files must have `rx` permission for everyone.
  - Each destination directory must mave `wx` permission for everyone.
  - Each directory enroute to the destination files (except for the destination directories themselves) must have `x` permission for everyone.

  If a transfer fails for any reason, you're sent a mail message telling you of the failure.

- A source file must not be a directory. Although you can transfer all the files in a directory, you cannot transfer the directory itself.

- A source file name can contain wildcards, although the destination file name cannot. If a source file specifies a computer and contains any wildcard characters (`*` `?` `[ ]`), you must quote them to prevent them from being interpreted as shell metacharacters.

- If there is more than one source file after any wildcards have been expanded, the destination is taken to be a directory and the source files are then placed within that directory, using just the last component of each source file's path name.

- To create a destination file it may be necessary to construct additional directories. By default `uucp` constructs these directories, provided that the necessary permissions are turned on. You can stop `uucp` from constructing these directories with the `-f` option.

- The C shell notation '~*user*' designates the home directory of *user*, either on your own computer or on a remote computer. It is recognized by `uucp` even if you are not running `csh`. (In fact, if you're using the C shell you must escape the '~' with a backslash or quote it.) A path name starting with '~/' refers to the directory containing those files that are publicly available for remote access. Usually this directory is /usr/spool/uucppublic.

- You can specify your own computer explicitly just as though it was a remote computer. For example, if the name of your computer is chutzpah, a possible source or destination file on your own computer would be chutzpah!hush.

- If the destination file name does not include any '!'s, the transfer is treated as a request that the source files be sent to you. No external communication is involved. You can also use uucp to move files from one remote computer to another.

- When you ask uucp to transfer a local file, uucp normally doesn't make a copy of that file; instead it transmits the file directly when the time comes. You can force a local copy with the -C option; in this case, changing or deleting the original file will not affect what is transmitted.

- For security reasons, many system administrators only allow files to be transferred to or from the public directory /usr/spool/ uucppublic.

For example, the command

    uucp $HOME/pooch/* mongrels!~hound/infiles

sends the files in your pooch directory to the directory infiles belonging to user hound at remote computer mongrels. The infiles directory must have x permission available to others. The command

    uucp mongrels!~hound/pup .

requests that the file pup belonging to user hound at computer mongrels be sent to you and stored in your current directory under the name pup.

Each request for a file transmission is called a *job*—not to be confused with jobs as sets of processes in the sense of job control.

Command-line Options.   The following options determine whether uucp makes copies of local files and whether it constructs directories at the destination:

-C	Make a copy of each local file when transmission is requested.
-c	Don't make copies of local files.
-d	Make subdirectories at the destination as needed.
-f	Don't make subdirectories at the destination.

The following options affect the messages that result from the job:

-j	Show the job identifier when the job is requested.
-m	Send a mail message to the requestor when the job is done.
-n *user*	Notify *user* on the remote computer that a file was sent.
-s *file*	Send a status report to *file*. You must specify *file* as a full path name because the report is not sent until the uucp command has already terminated.

-x *n*   Turn on debugging at level *n*, where *n* ranges from 0 (no de-
            bugging information) to 9 (maximum debugging information).

The following options affect when the files are actually transmitted:

-r   Queue the job without starting the transfer.

-g *c*   Assign the job a priority of *c*, where *c* is a single letter or digit.
            The priorities are taken in order of the ASCII values of the
            characters—first the digits, then the uppercase letters, and fi-
            nally the lowercase letters.

**10.8.4
Controlling and
Querying** uucp
with uustat

The uustat command enables you to see the status of jobs awaiting transmission by uucp and the status of uucp's communications with other computers. It also enables you to kill the transmission of one of your files.

The uustat command line has the form

        uustat [*options*]

Generally you can use only a single option, although the -s and -u options
can be used together. If you call uustat without any options, you obtain
a list of your files and messages awaiting transmission. The list looks like
this:

gastonC1b68	06/15-17:29	S	gaston	uriah	285	D.booke7c71290
	06/15-17:29	S	gaston	uriah	rmail	uriah
gastonN1b69	06/15-17:41	S	gaston	uriah	21	/usr/uriah/td/osh
liederC00b1	06/15-18:03	S	lieder	uriah	285	D.booke7c72456
	06/15-18:03	S	lieder	uriah	rmail	uriah

Each job occupies one or more lines. Here is what the items in the first
row for each job mean:

- The first item contains an identifier for each file awaiting transmis-
  sion.
- The second item contains the date and time when the file was queued
  for transmission.
- The third item contains 'S' for a message to be sent and 'R' for a
  request for an arriving file. It is almost always 'S'.
- The fourth item contains the destination computer.
- The fifth item contains the user id of the sender of the file.
- The sixth item contains the length of the file to be transmitted.
- The seventh item contains the full path name of a file to be trans-
  mitted or a message identifier (for the first row of a message item).

The job identifier is essential for killing an outgoing transmission.

Command-line Options.   The following command-line options are the
most useful ones:

-a   Output the names of all jobs awaiting transmission.

-k *id*   Kill the job whose identifier is *id*. In order to use this command,
            you must run uustat without options.

-s *sys*   Only report jobs destined for remote computer *sys*.

-u *user*   Only report jobs originated by user *user*.

The -s and -u options can be used together; all other options can only be used by themselves. The following short Bourne shell script provides an easy way of killing all your outstanding uucp jobs:

```
for jn in 'uustat | cut -f1 -d" "'; do
    if [ -n "$jn" ]; then uustat -k $jn; fi
done
```

See Section 8.2.2 for information on what cut is doing here.

The following options are intended for system administrators. Understanding what they do requires an understanding of uucp and the files that it uses. We list them only for the sake of completeness.

-m   Report the status of all remote computers known to uucp.

-p   Execute the command ps -flp for all processes that are in lock files.

-q   List the jobs queued for each remote computer.

-r *id*   Rejuvenate job *id* by resetting its modification time to the current time, thus preventing the cleanup dæmon from deleting it.

Obtaining uucp **Status Information with** uulog.   The uulog command sends a portion of the log of uucp transfers to standard output. Normally it is useful only to system administrators; we mention it only for the sake of completeness. It has the following three options:

-s *system*
             Show only information on transfers involving *system*.

-f *system*
             Do a tail -f command on the log of transfers involving *system* (see Section 3.5).

-x   Look in the uuxqt log rather than the uucico log.

-*n*   Use a tail command with *n* lines.

If you use one of the tail options, you must press (Intr) to terminate the output.

**10.8.5
The** Systems **File**

The Systems file contains the information needed by uucp and its supporting programs to establish a link to a remote computer. Each remote system referenced by uucp or one of its relatives must have an entry in this file. For System V, the full path name of the file is usually /usr/lib/uucp/Systems. On BSD UNIX systems the Systems file is named L.sys; the format is nearly the same. Usually this file is only of concern to system administrators; superuser privileges are required to modify it or even to read it. You can determine which systems are known to your system by typing 'uuname'.

Whenever you wish to establish direct uucp communication with a UNIX system not already listed in Systems, you must add an entry to Systems or have your system administrator do it for you. In our list of electronic resources in Section C.3 we mention a number of remote systems and provide the necessary `Systems` entries for them. For example, one entry for the UNIX system at Ohio State University is

```
osu-cis Any ACU 19200 1-614-292-5112 in:--in:--in: Uanon
```

The parts of this entry are as follows:

- 'osu-cis'. The name of the remote system (to be used on the `uucp` command line).
- 'Any'. The time when the remote computer can be called.
- 'ACU 19200'. The type of communications device used to call the remote system (in this case, an autodialing modem (Automatic Calling Unit) operating at 19200 baud).
- '1-614-292-5112'. The telephone number of the remote system.[20]
- 'in:--in:--in: Uanon'. A sequence of *expect-send* pairs that define the dialog needed to log into the remote computer and establish the connection. The *expect* items are sent by the remote computer; the *send* items are sent by your computer in response. The 'in:' in this example is the end of the string 'login:'; it is repeated several times to allow for the possibility of an initial failure in the communication.

A full discussion of the form of this entry is beyond the scope of this book; see your system manuals for more information about the `Systems` file.

**10.8.6
Identifying Remote
Computers
with** `uuname`

The `uuname` command lists the names of computers known to `uucp`. It has the following options:

`-l`	List the name of the computer you're on.
`-c`	List the names of computers known to the `cu` program (see Section 10.9).

Normally you get the same list with or without `-c`.

10.9   Connecting to Remote Computers with `cu`

Although `cu` stands for "connect to UNIX", you can use the `cu` program to connect to any remote computer over a direct line. Once you've made the connection, your terminal behaves as though it were a terminal on the remote computer. Whatever you type is sent to the remote computer; whatever output the remote computer produces is sent to your terminal. You can still communicate with your local computer by issuing the tilde commands described below, which resemble the input mode commands of `mailx` (see Section 9.3.21). Because `cu` is essentially oblivious to the nature of the remote computer (except for a couple of the commands discussed below), you can even use it for tasks such as explicit control of a modem.

---

20. The dashes are only for readability; omitting them will speed up the dialing slightly.

Cu is analogous to `telnet`, which provides connections to other computers via a network.

The `cu` command line has the form:

`cu` [*options*] [*dest*]

where *dest* is either the name of a remote computer, a telephone number, or `dir` (for "direct"). Some versions of `cu` require that you specify *dest*; others don't recognize `dir` but instead assume `dir` if you omit *dest*.

- If you use a computer name, it must be a computer known to your own computer. You can find a list of such computers by using the '`uuname -c`' command (see Section 10.8.6).

- If you use a telephone number, then your computer must have auto-dialers available. Within the telephone number, '`=`' indicates a wait for a secondary dial tone and '`-`' indicates a four-second delay.

  - If you specify a speed with the `-s` option, then the call is made at that speed or not at all.
  - If you specify a particular line with the `-l` option, then the call is made using the calling unit attached to that line.
  - If you specify a speed but not a line, the call is made on the first available line that operates at that speed.
  - If you specify neither a speed nor a line, the call is made on the first available line, no matter what its speed.

- If you specify `dir` (or omit *dest*, depending on your version of `cu`), then you must either

  - indicate a device name to use as the communication line with the `-l` option; or
  - indicate with the `-n` option that `cu` should prompt you for a telephone number.

  You can communicate directly with a modem on a particular line by using the `-l` option without a computer or telephone number.

The `-l`, `-s`, and `-n` options are described below.

**10.9.1
Quick Exit**

You can exit from `cu` by typing '`~.`' on a line by itself. Before exiting, you should log out from the remote computer if you can. See "Terminating `cu`" on page 454 below for further details.

**10.9.2
Command-line
Options**

The following options determine the communications line and the speed at which it operates:

`-l` *dev*   Use the device *dev* as the communication line. Usually the device is a directly connected asynchronous line whose name has the form '`/dev/tty`*nn*' or simply '`tty`*nn*'; `cu` assumes a prefix of '`/dev/`' if necessary.

`-s` *speed*   Cause the communication line to operate at *speed*. The recognized values of *speed* are 300, 1200, 2400, 4800, 9600, and sometimes higher values such as 19200 and 38400.

You should not use either of these option if you specify a remote computer as the destination of cu since the computer already has a line and speed associated with it.

The following option provides an alternative to specifying a telephone number on the command line:

-n   Prompt the user for the telephone number. Using this option provides a little more security than putting the telephone number on the command line. You should use this option only if you specify neither a telephone number nor a computer name.

The following options specify characteristics of the data transmission:

-e   Send data using even parity.

-o   Send data using odd parity.

-h   Provide local echoing of typed lines (half duplex mode).

-t   Map ⟨linefeed⟩ on the local computer to ⟨return⟩ ⟨linefeed⟩ on the remote computer and vice versa. This option may be necessary for communicating with non-UNIX systems such as MS-DOS.

The following option causes cu to produce debugging information:

-d   Show diagnostic traces.

10.9.3 Tilde Commands for cu

You can issue commands to cu itself while you're running it. These commands, called *tilde commands* or *local commands*, all appear on a line that starts with a tilde (~).

Terminating cu. The following command provides the mechanism for terminating cu:

~.   Terminates the conversation with the remote computer and exits from cu. You should log out from that computer before you issue this command so that you get a clean termination on the remote end. If the remote computer drops the line carrier signal after you log out, cu exits of its own accord and you don't need to issue this command.

The following commands enable you to execute commands on your local computer:

~![*cmd*]   Executes *cmd* in a subshell on the local computer. If you omit *cmd*, you obtain an interactive shell.

~%cd [*dir*]   Changes the current directory on the local computer. You must use this command to change directories because issuing a cd command within a subshell has no external effect. If you omit *dir*, your home directory becomes the current directory as usual.

~$*cmd*   Executes *cmd* in a subshell on the local computer and sends its output to the remote computer.

Controlling the Communication Channel. The following commands provide control over the communication channel:

~%b

~%break   Sends a break signal to the remote computer.

~%nostop   Toggles DC3/DC1 input control. Normally the ⟨DC3⟩ (⟨Ctrl⟩ S)
signal tells the receiver to stop sending output while the ⟨DC1⟩
(⟨Ctrl⟩ Q) signal tells the receiver to start sending output again.
These signals can be used to prevent the remote computer from
sending output faster than the local computer can accept it or
vice versa. If ⟨DC1⟩/⟨DC3⟩ input control doesn't work, you can
turn it off with this command.

Sending Lines That Start with a Tilde.   The following command provides
an escape mechanism for sending a line of text that actually begins with a
tilde:

~~*line*   Sends ~*line* to the remote computer.

This command is particularly useful when the remote computer is running cu to communicate with a third computer, since it enables you to issue tilde commands on the remote computer (by starting them with '~~').
It's also useful for running mailx on the remote computer.

Transferring Files.   The following commands enable you to transfer files
to or from the remote computer:

~%put *rfile* [*lfile*]
Copies remote file *rfile* to local file *lfile*. If you omit *lfile*, cu
takes it to be the same as *rfile*.

~%take *lfile* [*rfile*]
Copies local file *lfile* to remote file *rfile*. If you omit *rfile*, cu
takes it to be the same as *lfile*.

These commands require the remote computer to be a UNIX system that
supports the cat and stty commands. If the erase and kill characters are
not the same on the local computer as on the remote one, the transfer may
not work. These commands don't work for transferring binary files—the
arbitrary control characters that can appear in such files won't be transmitted correctly and are likely to wreak havoc. The uuencode and uudecode
programs mentioned in Section 10.4 can be used to transform binary files
to files containing only printable characters and back again.

We recommend that you avoid using ~%put and ~%take if you can.
They can leave dead processes on the remote computer or even hang
that computer if anything goes wrong. Unfortunately, most versions of
UNIX don't provide any other way of transferring files to or from a remote
UNIX system that you've dialed into—uucp only works if your computer
and the remote computer know each other. The kermit program (see Section 10.4.1) is often a good alternative; whatever communications package
you use must be supported on both ends.

Commands for Debugging.   The following commands enable you to examine line and terminal characteristics for debugging purposes and to
turn debugging output off or on. Using them presumes some knowledge
of UNIX internals as they make use of a particular data structure called
termio. You can usually find a specification of termio in the file /usr/
include/sys/termio.h.

~l   Shows the values of the termio variables for the communication
line.

~t Shows the values of the `termio` variables for your terminal.

~%d

~%debug Toggles diagnostic tracing. Using this command produces the same output that you'd get with the −d option described above.

10.9.4
Output Diversions

Ordinarily, each line received from the remote computer is sent directly to your terminal. You can use an *output diversion* to send these lines to a file instead. An output diversion begins with a line having one of the forms

~> : *file*
~>> : *file*

and ends with a line containing just '~>'. Cu then copies all of the lines between the beginning and end of the diversion to the file *file*. The difference between '~>' and '~>>' is that '~>' erases *file* first while '~>>' appends the diversion to *file*.

11

The X Window System

The X Window System, usually referred to simply as X, is a graphically oriented working environment originally developed at MIT. X has become popular in the UNIX world because it helps to overcome the limitations of the traditional UNIX character-oriented model of computing. It runs under several operating systems besides UNIX and supports the distribution of different parts of a task over a network. Using the `xterm` terminal emulator running under X, you can run any UNIX program under X that you could run otherwise. You can also use X running under UNIX to execute X programs running under non-UNIX operating systems on remote computers.

X is a large and complex system—a system of the same order of complexity as UNIX itself. In this chapter we present the basic concepts and vocabulary of X and describe some of the most useful client programs that run under it; however, space does not permit us to cover X completely. Fortunately, many of the X clients are easy to use even without instructions.

You can obtain the X files over the Internet via anonymous `ftp` from `export.lcs.mit.edu`, IP address `18.24.0.12` (see Section 10.7), or over the uucp network from the UUNET archives (reference [U4]).

11.1 The X Screen

The X screen consists of a set of rectangular *windows* displayed within a background area called the *root window*. Each window contains an ap-

457

plication program called a *client*. The computational effect of running several processes at once is reflected in the visual effect of having several windows on the screen. The screen also contains a cursor whose appearance depends on how the cursor is currently being used. The window that contains the cursor is called the *focus* of the cursor; if the cursor is on the background then the focus is the root window.

The `xterm` terminal emulator (see Section 11.14) is a particularly important client. An `xterm` window appears to be a terminal from which you can run either ordinary UNIX programs such as `ls` or special X programs such as `xclock`. You can run several terminal sessions in parallel by creating several `xterm` windows.

11.2   Getting Started and Quitting

Many systems are set up to start X automatically at your terminal. For these systems, you log in under X as you would at a character-oriented terminal. Normally the `xdm` program, which handles logins and manages X sessions, is called as part of the procedures for initializing your system. Only the superuser can run it. If X has not been started automatically, you can start it with the `xinit` program (see Section 11.18.1). In either case you can set up files that tailor X to your preferences (see Section 11.13).

If X was started automatically, you exit from it by logging out, just as you would from an ordinary shell. If you started it using `xinit`, it will terminate when the last foreground program that you started via `xinit` (usually a window manager) has terminated.

11.3   Window Managers

A window manager is a special client that controls the layout of windows on your machine. A window manager usually provides at least these operations:

- Creating and removing windows.

- Moving windows from one place to another and changing their sizes.

- Converting windows into *icons* and back again. An icon is a small symbol that stands for a particular window that is currently not being displayed.

- Selecting the apparent relative depth of overlapping windows, the top window being completely visible.

A window manager is not logically necessary in order to run X, but without one you would lose most of X's convenience.

The original X window manager `uwm` (universal window manager) is still in common use. An improved version known as `twm` (Tab window manager[1]) is also widely used in the X world. Two commercially important window managers are Motif from the Open Software Foundation and Open Look from AT&T.[2] Many clients can run under any window manager, but some depend on the facilities provided by a particular window manager (see Section 11.5). Because of the variety of window managers in use, we do not attempt to describe them here.

11.4 Servers and Displays

When you use X, your interaction with your computer (or a computer at a remote site) is handled by a program called a *server*. The server controls your screen (or screens, if you have more than one), your keyboard, and your mouse or other pointing device. These are collectively called your *display*. Each server is specialized to the hardware that it controls. For example, different types of video adapters require different servers.

11.4.1 Display Specifications

A display specification informs a client how to connect to the display where the client is running. Display specifications can be given to most clients with the `-display` command-line option. The specification of a display has the form

> [*host*]: *display*[. *screen*]

The parts of the specification are as follows:

- The host name *host* specifies the computer to which the display is physically connected. It is needed because the client can be running on a different computer than the server. For standalone machines it should be the string 'unix'. If *host* is not specified, the server is assumed to be on the same computer.

- The display number *display* is the number of the display with respect to the computer where the server is running. It cannot be omitted. The first (or only) display on a computer is display #0.

- The screen number *screen* is the number of the screen within the display. You can omit it in the usual case where the display has only one screen. For multi-screen displays, the first screen is screen #0.

The default display name is stored in the DISPLAY environment variable; for standalone systems it is usually 'unix:0.0' (same computer, first display, first screen). When you log onto another computer over a network, you must either (a) set DISPLAY on that computer to point back to your own computer or (b) use the `-display` option on the command line to specify the display explicitly to each client program that you call.

---

1. This window manager was originally called "Tom's Window Manager" after its author, Tom LaStrange.

2. The Sun Microsystems version of Open Look is called Open Windows.

11.5   Widgets

X clients are programmed to use predefined software components called *widgets*. The collection of widgets available with the standard version of X is called the X Toolkit. Other widgets may be provided by particular window managers.

Widgets are intended to be used by X application programmers, not by users. Even so, you can customize certain aspects of X clients by customizing the widgets that they use. That's why widgets are significant to users as well as to programmers. When you customize a widget, you affect all the clients that use that widget. Thus, customizing widgets provides a method of customizing clients in a uniform way. If this kind of customization is possible, the client's documentation should tell you about it.

11.6   Properties

A window has a set of *properties* associated with it. A property is a packet of information associated with the window. The properties of a window are available to all clients running under the same server and provide a way for different clients to communicate with each other. In particular, they enable a client to communicate with the window manager. Each kind of property is named by a label called an *atom*. An atom has the form of an ASCII string. The *standard properties* are a minimum set that a client should specify; particular clients may have other properties as well.

11.7   Command-line Options

The command-line options for X applications usually have multi-character names and often begin with '+' rather than '-', so they do *not* follow the command-line conventions given in Section 2.14.3. Usually '-' turns an option on and '+' turns it off—just the opposite of what you'd expect. Most recently written applications let you abbreviate an option to its shortest unique form, e.g., to write '-g' for '-geometry' if no other option starts with '-g'.

11.7.1
Toolkit Options

Certain command-line options are supported by the X Toolkit and therefore are available in those X applications that use the Toolkit. Most of these specify characteristics of the window in which the application will run once it is started.

-display *display*

Use the display specified by *display* (see Section 11.4.1).

-geometry *geometry*

Take the size and placement of the window from *geometry*. See Section 11.10 for the form and meaning of *geometry*.

-fg *color*

-foreground *color*

Use *color* as the foreground color for the window. See Section 11.12 for more information about colors.

-bg *color*

-background *color*

Use *color* as the background color for the window.

-bd *color*

-bordercolor *color*

Use *color* to form a border around the window.

-bw *n*

-borderwidth *n*

Use a border *n* pixels wide.

-fn *font*

-font *font*

Use *font* when displaying text (see Section 11.11). The font *font* can contain the wildcards '*' and '?' with their usual meanings. Wildcards are particularly useful when you specify fonts whose names are given by X Logical Font Descriptions (XLFD's) because these names are very long. You need to quote *font* if it contains any wildcards to ensure that the wildcards are interpreted by the X client rather than by your shell.

-title *string*

Use *title* as the title for this window if the window manager wants a title.

-iconic   When starting up this application, display it as an icon rather than as a full window.

-rv

-reverse Simulate reverse video if possible, usually by swapping the foreground and background colors. Usually this option is used only on monochrome displays.

+rv   Don't simulate reverse video. This option would be specified only if one of the defaults specifies **-rv** and that is not what you want.

-name *name*

Use *name* as the name of the client in determining which resource specifications apply. See page 463 for information on how **-name** is used.

-rxm *resource-spec*

Use the resource specification *resource-spec* to override any defaults. This option can appear any number of times.

In addition to the Toolkit options, most clients accept this one:

-help   Produce a list of the options for this command on standard output.

11.8   Resources

You can adjust the behavior of an X client by providing options on the command line when you call it. These options specify the values of certain attributes of clients and widgets called *resources*.[3] In addition, you can place specifications that establish defaults for resources in *resource files*. The resource specifications available from different sources are interpreted and combined by a program called the *resource manager*.

11.8.1 Resource Specifications

A resource specification specifies a set of resources and assigns a value to each resource in the set. In the simplest case, the resource specification has the form

> *client*[. *widget*] ... . *resource* : *value*

Here the client uses the first widget, the first widget uses the second, and so on. For example, a resource specification

```
xbrowse.scrollbar.foreground : green
```

indicates that the hypothetical client 'xbrowse' uses a widget 'scrollbar' that in turn uses a resource 'foreground'. The value of 'foreground' should be the color 'green'. If several widgets appear, each one makes use of the one to its right.

This notation has several extensions:

- You can use stars to indicate a sequence of zero or more unspecified widgets. This notation is useful when you don't know what the needed widgets might be. For example, you could write the preceding example either as

  ```
  xbrowse*scrollbar*foreground : green
  ```

  or as

  ```
  xbrowse*foreground : green
  ```

  The second specification would affect all widgets that use a 'foreground' resource.

- You can omit the client, causing the specification to apply to all clients for which it is meaningful. For example, the specification

  ```
  *foreground : green
  ```

---

3. The term "resource" reflects a programmer's view of what a resource is, not a user's view.

sets the `foreground` of all clients and widgets that have a `foreground` resource to `green`.

- You can replace the reference to an individual resource, referred to in this context as an *instance,* by a reference to a set of resources, called a *class.* The specification then sets all the resources in the class. By convention, instance names start with lowercase letters while class names start with uppercase letters. Most class names are upper-case forms of their most conspicuous instances. For example, the class 'Foreground' contains instances 'foreground', 'cursorColor', and 'pointerColor'. Thus the three specifications

```
xterm*foreground : orchid
xterm*cursorColor : orchid
xterm*pointerColor : orchid
```

are encompassed by the single specification

```
xterm*Foreground : orchid
```

- If a '-name *name*' option has been specified (see p. 461), the name *name* is used as the client name instead of the actual name. You can use this facility to modify the attributes of a client when you call it. For example, if there is an applicable specification

```
greenterm*background : green
```

then the call

```
xterm -name greenterm &
```

will cause the `xterm` client to have a green background.

Several resource specifications may apply to the same resource of the same widget or client. In that case a specific citation of a resource takes precedence over a more general citation, regardless of order. For example, an instance takes precedence over a class and a specification with '.' takes precedence over a specification with '*'. In a case such as

```
myxterm.vt100.Background : green
myxterm.vt100*background : orange
```

the dot specification ('green') takes precedence over the instance specification ('orange'). When two conflicting specifications have the same precedence, the later one wins.

11.9   The Resource Database

You can provide resource specifications to X clients by placing the specifications in a resource database. By default that database is the file `.Xdefaults` in your home directory. That file is available to clients running on your computer but not to clients running on other computers. However, you can specify the resource database in other ways too:

- You can store resource specifications for particular clients in files within a directory of application defaults, typically named `/usr/lib/X11/app-defaults`. The file for a particular client has the name of that client.

- You can create a global resource database with the `xrdb` program (see Section 11.18.2). That database, unlike `.Xdefaults`, is visible to a client that is using your server even if that client is running on a different computer.[4]

- You can create a set of resource databases in files with names of the form

  `.Xdefaults-`*hostname*

  where *hostname* is the name of a remote computer. Any clients running on that computer will use this database. By this mechanism you can specify the behavior of clients running on a particular remote computer. For example, you could use these databases to cause windows on different remote computers to have different border colors.

Application-specific resource specifications are loaded before the resource databases and thus can be overridden by the databases. If a computer-specific resource database and a global resource database both exist, they are both used. Computer-specific specifications take precedence in case of conflict; in any event, specifications provided via the `-xrm` command-line option take precedence over all others.

11.10   Geometry Specifications

The *geometry* of a window specifies its size and its placement on the screen. The geometry, specified with the `geometry` resource, has the form

  *w*x*h*+*xoff*+*yoff*

Here *w* and *h* give the width and height of the window, measured in either pixels or characters according to the application. (The `xterm` client in particular uses characters.) The values *xoff* and *yoff* give the offset in pixels from the screen's left edge and top edge respectively. Many clients allow the '+' preceding *xoff* or *yoff* to be replaced by a '−'; in this case *xoff* and *yoff* give the offset of the screen's right edge or bottom edge respectively. In addition, either *xoff* or *yoff* can be negative (indicated by two signs in a row), causing the indicated edge to be off the screen. For example, the command

```
xclock -g 75x75-0+0
```

---

4. The `xrdb` program stores the database in the `RESOURCE_MANAGER` property of the root window.

creates a clock that is 75 pixels square, positioned at the upper right corner of your screen.

You can omit any of the elements in the geometry specification. The window manager will use default values for the missing elements.

11.11   Fonts

X provides a collection of fonts that you can use in almost any text-oriented client. The available fonts fall into two groups: miscellaneous fonts that are useful on all systems and contributed fonts provided by several font vendors. Most of the fonts have names given as X Logical Font Descriptions, or XLFD's. Here is an example of one:

```
-bitstream-charter-medium-r-normal--15-140-75-75-p-84-iso8859-1
```

You could specify this font as '*chart*med*-r-*-140-*' in an -fn option, or in a resource specification since this pattern is sufficient to identify the font uniquely. You would need to quote the pattern if it appeared in an option to a command so as to prevent the shell from interpreting the stars.

The description consists of the following fields:

foundry	bitstream
family	charter
weight	medium
slant	r (upright)
set width	normal
additional style	(none)
pixel size	15
point size	140
resolutionX	75
resolutionY	75
spacing	p (proportional)
average width	84
registry	iso8859
encoding	1

We forego further discussion of the meanings of most of these fields. Normally you need not be concerned with them, particularly since your only concern is likely to be to select a font that you like.

A number of the fonts have aliases, notably the fixed-width fonts in the miscellaneous group. For instance, the font

```
-misc-fixed-bold-r-semicondensed--13-120-75-75-c-60-iso8859-1
```

has an alias '6x13'; this font is a fixed-width font six pixels wide and thirteen pixels high. You can refer to a font either by its alias or by its full name. Wildcards work with aliases as well as with full names.

Several programs exist for seeing what fonts are available (see Section 11.17). In addition, you can look directly at certain files that list all the fonts. The command 'xset q' reveals, among other things, the locations of the directories containing the font files. These directories also contain files `fonts.dir` and `fonts.alias`. The `fonts.dir` file lists the font files and their names (you usually care only about the names). The `fonts.alias` file lists a set of aliases and the font name corresponding to each.

11.12   Colors

Several resources such as `foreground` and `background` require you to specify a color, either with a name or with a number that provides intensity values for its red, green, and blue components.

11.12.1
Color Names

X keeps a database that defines a set of color names in a file named `rgb.txt`. A typical full path name for this file is `/usr/lib/X11/rgb.txt`. In any event, you can usually find it by retrieving the font path with 'xset q' and then looking in the X11 directory shown in that path. The colors themselves include the ordinary ones such as 'green' and 'white' as well as more picturesquely named ones such as 'khaki', 'orchid', and 'mediumForestGreen'. The names are case-insensitive. The numbers associated with each color give its red, green, and blue intensities on a scale from 0 to 255. The appearance of the colors varies greatly from one type of color monitor to another. Unfortunately there is no way that you can assign names to your own color choices.

11.12.2
Color Numbers

A color number consists of three hexadecimal numbers (see Section 2.15) that specify the intensity of the red, green, and blue components of the color. The numbers can have up to four hexadecimal digits per color, but most often they have two hexadecimal digits per color. The intensities range from 00 to FF (hexadecimal) or 0 to 255 (decimal), with 0 meaning this color is absent and 255 meaning it has maximum intensity. Encodings for one, two, or four digits are analogous. To illustrate, here are some color values as they appear in `rgb.txt`:

```
000 000 000  black
252 252 252  white
255 000 000  red
000 255 000  green
000 000 255  blue
255 255 000  yellow
000 255 255  cyan
255 000 255  magenta
```

You can specify a two-digit color value by writing it as '#*rrggbb*', where *rr*, *gg*, and *bb* are the hexadecimal values for the three colors. Using this notation, a magenta background would be produced by '-bg "#ff00ff"'. If that's the color you really want, you're better off writing it as '-bg magenta'; however, the numerical notation enables you to create the subtlest shades of color that your monitor can generate.

11.13 Initialization Files for X

You can provide an initialization file containing commands that are executed when X starts up. The name and location of the file depend on whether X has been started automatically or manually.

- If X is in control when you log in, startup is automatic. The arrangements for executing an initialization file are a local option, but the usual convention is that they are found in a file named .xsession in your home directory. The contents of .xsession will be executed *before* the login initialization file associated with your shell (.profile or .login, see Section 2.18.1).

- If X is not in control when you log in, you must start it manually with the xinit program (see Section 11.18.1). In this case the initialization file is $HOME/.xinitrc. At a minimum it should contain commands to call xterm in the background and a window manager in the foreground.

11.14 The xterm Terminal Emulator

The xterm terminal emulator provides a window that acts like a terminal. The terminal associated with the window is sometimes called a *virtual terminal*; the associated device is called. a *pseudo-terminal device*. When xterm creates a virtual terminal, it places that terminal under control of a shell specified by the value of the SHELL environment variable, with /bin/sh as the default. You can use this shell to issue the same commands that you would issue from an ordinary terminal, including calling the various X clients.

The form of the xterm command line is

    xterm [*options*]

See Section 11.7.1 for a list of the Toolkit options and your system manual for those not discussed below.

11.15   Emulation

The `xterm` client emulates two ancient terminals, the DEC VT102 text-oriented terminal and the Tektronix 4015 graphics terminal.[5] Since you are unlikely to have either of them, it is important to understand just what the emulation does and why the characteristics of these terminals will rarely affect you.

Each terminal has certain control sequences that cause it to take special actions. Most of these sequences start with ⟨escape⟩. For example, if a VT102 receives the sequence '⟨escape⟩ [M', it deletes the line containing the cursor. Some of the sequences are useful only on a real VT102, e.g., the '⟨escape⟩#8' sequence that performs a DEC screen alignment test.[6] However, if you type (Esc) at your terminal it will usually be interpreted by whatever program (editor, etc.) that you're using and never be transmitted to the terminal. Thus the chance of issuing one of these sequences by accident is very small.

The terminal emulation built into `xterm` imitates the actions of these control sequences, translating them into the corresponding actions on the material displayed in your X window. For instance, if the emulator receives a VT102 "delete line" sequence, it deletes a line on your screen. The knowledge of these sequences is built into the `terminfo` or `termcap` database of terminal descriptions (see Section 2.19) under the terminal name `xterm`. If a program such as the `vi` editor wants to delete a line, it retrieves the appropriate sequence from the database and sends it to the virtual terminal. When `xterm` sees that sequence in the input to the virtual terminal, it deletes the line.

The VT102 provides many sequences for operating on a screenful of characters while the 4015 provides hardly any. The 4015, on the other hand, provides sequences for drawing lines and plotting collections of points that are not understood by the VT102. By default `xterm` starts in VT102 mode, but you can use the `-t` option on the command line to start it in 4015 mode instead. A single incarnation of `xterm` has two windows, one for the VT102 and one for the 4015; by default, the 4015 window is not displayed.

11.15.1
Using the Mouse

The mouse or other pointing device serves several purposes in `xterm`: copying text, moving within the recently displayed text, and selecting items from menus. Note that there are two independent cursors in the window: the mouse cursor and the text cursor.

---

5. The widgets within `xterm` for the emulations are called `vt100` and `tek4014`, an anachronism from when `xterm` was first written.

6. You can experiment with these sequences by issuing the `cat` command and typing them. Since `cat` transmits its input to the terminal without interpretation (except for newlines), you can see the effect of each one.

Copying Text.   You can select text in one window and copy it to elsewhere in the same window or to another window. For example, you can use the mouse to retrieve a command that you recently executed and execute that command again. The default key and button use described here can be changed by including appropriate specifications in the resource database. Here is what the buttons do:

- The left button saves text into a *cut buffer*. You select the text by moving the mouse cursor to the beginning of the text and holding the button down while moving the mouse cursor to the end of the text. By double-clicking at the beginning of the selection, you can select text a word at a time; by triple-clicking, you can select text a line at a time. The text is highlighted as you select it and remains highlighted after you release the button. To remove the highlighting, click the left button again.

- The right button extends or contracts the selected text at whichever end it is closest to. When you first press the right button, the boundary of the selected (highlighted) text moves to the position of the mouse cursor. If you hold down the button and move the mouse cursor, the text boundary follows it.

- The middle button inserts the text in the cut buffer at the position of the *text* cursor. The position of the mouse cursor is irrelevant except to determine which window receives the text.

Moving within Recently Displayed Text.   You also can use the mouse in the scrollbar at the left edge of the window to move within the recently displayed text:

- The left button moves the text backward.

- The right button moves the text forward.

- The middle button repositions the text, centering it about a position proportional to the position of the cursor within the scrollbar when you release the button. By moving the cursor off the top or bottom of the scrollbar while holding down the middle button, you can move to the bottom or the top of the displayable region.

For the left and right buttons, the lower the position of the cursor within the scrollbar, the greater the movement. You can create a scrollbar with the +sb option and specify the number of extra lines of text to save with the −sl option. These extra lines define the region that you can view by using the scrollbar (64 by default).

Selecting Items from Menus.   You can select one of three menus by holding down the Ctrl shift and pressing a mouse button:

- The left button selects the xterm menu. Items on this menu enable you to initiate logging and to send various signals to the current foreground process. When logging is on, all your input and output are captured to a logging file, by default named XtermLog.n where n is a five-digit decimal number that represents xterm's process number. The log file is kept in the directory from which xterm was started or in your home directory if xterm was started as a login shell.

- The middle button sets various modes in the VT102 or 4105 emulation, depending on which window the mouse cursor is in. Among other things, you can use the middle button to establish or remove a scrollbar for the VT102 window.

The right button is not used with the Ctrl key.

11.16   Informational Displays for X

The xclock program displays a clock and the xbiff program alerts you to incoming mail. These popular clients are almost always run in the background so that their windows are always on the screen.

11.16.1
Displaying a Clock
with xclock

The xclock command displays a clock on your screen. The form of the xclock command line is

    xclock [*options*] &

The '&', while not actually part of the command, indicates that the command should be run in the background. The only way to get rid of the clock is to kill its process (see Section 4.2.3).

Command-line Options.   The following options determine the nature of the clock:

-analog   Display a conventional twelve-hour clock face. This is the default.

-digital   Display a twenty-four-hour digital clock.

   The following options apply to any clock:

-chime   Chime once on the half hour, twice on the hour.

-update *n*
          Update the clock every *n* seconds. A value of *n* less than 60 will cause an analog clock to show a second hand. The default is 60.

-padding *n*
          Use *n* pixels of padding between the window border and the text or picture of the clock. The default is 10 for a digital clock, 8 for an analog clock.

   The following options affect the appearance of the hands of an analog clock:

-hd *color* Use *color* as the color of the hands.

-hl *color* Use *color* as the color of the edges of the hands.

Xclock also supports the Toolkit options (see Section 11.7.1).

**11.16.2
Flagging Mail
with** xbiff

The xbiff client notifies you when new mail arrives.[7] It displays a picture of a mailbox with a flag. The flag is raised when mail arrives and lowered when the mail has been retrieved. You can also lower the flag explicitly by moving the mouse cursor to the mailbox and clicking the left button.

The form of the xbiff command line is

> xbiff [*options*] **&**

The '**&**', while not actually part of the command, indicates that the command should be run in the background. See Section 11.7.1 for a list of the Toolkit options and your system manual for the others.

11.17   Color and Font Information for X

The xcolors program displays a color chart, while the xfd, xlsfonts, and xfontsel programs provide information about fonts.

**11.17.1
Displaying Colors
with** xcolors

The xcolors client, available only in newer versions of X, displays a color chart that shows you what the different named colors look like. The form of the xcolors command line is

> xcolors [*options*]

See Section 11.7.1 for a list of the Toolkit options and your system manual for the others.

**11.17.2
Displaying a Font
with** xfd

The xfd client displays the characters in a specified font. The form of the xfd command line is

> xfd [*options*]

The options must include '**-font** *font*' (or '**-fn** *font*'), where *font* specifies the font to be displayed. See Section 11.7.1 for a list of the Toolkit options and your system manual for the others.

**11.17.3
Listing Fonts
with** xlsfonts

The xlsfonts program lists the available fonts. The form of the xlsfonts command line is

> xlsfonts [*options*]

The '**-font** *font*' (or '**-fn** *font*') option specifies a font name with wildcards that is matched against the available fonts (see Section 11.11). If you omit the option, all fonts are listed. See your system manual for the other options. This program uses none of the X facilities; it merely sends its listing to standard output.

---

7. Legend has it that biff, the ancestor of xbiff, was named by Ken Thompson for his dog Biff, who barked whenever the letter carrier arrived.

11.17.4
Selecting and Displaying Fonts
with xfontsel

The `xfontsel` program, available only in newer releases of X, lists and displays fonts. It works only for fonts named by XLFD's (see p. 465). You can use it interactively to try alternatives for the font fields, seeing which fonts match, and to view any of those fonts. The form of the `xfontsel` command line is

> `xfontsel [options]`

See Section 11.7.1 for a list of the Toolkit options and your system manual for the others.

11.18   Clients for Initializing and Customizing X

The clients described in the following subsections enable you to start X and to customize the appearance of its root window.

11.18.1
Initiating X
with xinit

The `xinit` program starts an X server and a first client program. If your system is not configured to start X automatically, you should start it with `xinit`.

The form of the `xinit` command line is

> `xinit [[client] options] [-- [server] [: display] [options]]`

The information on the command line determines a command or script to be initially executed and a server to be employed. In most cases `xinit` is called without any command-line information and its behavior is determined entirely by default.

The Initial Commands.   When `xinit` is called, it starts the server and then executes a sequence of commands. When these commands have finished executing, the server terminates and X ends. Usually the last command in the sequence is `xterm`, so X remains in control until you exit from your `xterm` shell.

If the command line has no arguments or has '`--`' as its first argument, then all client information is determined by default. In this case `xinit` executes the commands in the `.xinitrc` file of your home directory. This is the simplest and most common case. Usually the `.xinitrc` file includes, at a minimum, commands to start a window manager in the foreground and `xterm` in the background or vice versa. It also often includes commands to start other programs such as `xclock` and `xbiff` in the background.

If client information is specified, the client can either be given by *client* or defaulted. If the first argument of the client information starts with '`.`' or '`/`', indicating a path name, then it is taken as the name of a client program. Otherwise *client* defaults to

> `xterm -geometry +1+1 -n login -display :0`

which sets up a virtual terminal with the string 'login' used to select resources (see p. 461). Any options included in the client information are appended to the client, whether given explicitly or defaulted.

The Server.   Server information is indicated by '--' on the command line. The server program, like the client program, must start with '.' if it is given explicitly. If the first server argument is not such a program or there is no server information, xinit looks for a file .xserverrc in your home directory and executes its commands. If no such file exists, xinit executes the command 'X :0', which calls the default server for the default display. Any other arguments on the command line following '--' are passed as arguments to the server, whether given explicitly or defaulted.

**11.18.2
Specifying Global
Resources with** xrdb

The xrdb program creates and displays a collection of global resources available to all clients that are using your server, even if they are running on other computers (see Section 11.9). The form of the xrdb command line is

> xrdb [*options*] [*file*]

where *file* specifies a file containing a set of resource specifications that replaces standard input in the options described below.

Command-line Options.   Here are the most important options for xrdb:

-query   Send the current contents of the global resource database to standard output.

-load   Load the global resource database from standard input.

-merge   Merge standard input with the global resource database.

-remove   Make the global resource database empty.

See your system manual for descriptions of the remaining options.

**11.18.3
Setting User
Preferences for X**

The xset command sets a number of user preferences including the path name of the font directories, the mouse acceleration, the keyboard auto-repeat adjustments, and the screen saver parameters. The screen saver blanks your screen or displays a moving pattern if your keyboard has been inactive for a while. The form of the xset command line is

> xset [*options*]

The q option (no '-') lists the current settings. See your system manual for descriptions of the remaining options.

**11.18.4
Setting the Root
Window
Appearance
with** xsetroot

The xsetroot client adjusts the appearance of the root window. The root window is the background of all the other windows. Using this client you can specify a one-color or two-color pattern for the window and specify what the colors will be. You can also control the appearance of the cursor when it is in the root window.

The form of the xsetroot command line is

> xsetroot [*options*]

The option '-solid *color*' sets the color of the background to *color*. Other options can be used to fill the background with a two-color pattern. See your system manual for a list of the options.

11.19   Killing an X Client with `xkill`

The `xkill` program forces the X server to close its connection to a client. It is useful for getting rid of unwanted windows, although the clients that it kills may not terminate cleanly. You select the client to be killed by clicking the left mouse button on its window. The form of the `xkill` command line is

>   `xkill` [*options*]

See Section 11.7.1 for a list of the Toolkit options and your system manual for the others.

A

Alphabetical Summary of Commands

In this appendix we provide, in alphabetical order, capsule summaries of the UNIX commands discussed in this book. The purpose of these summaries is to remind you of what each command does and to point you to its full explanation. The first group of summaries lists the commands. The second group of summaries lists the command-line options, flags, and subcommands of each command. The page references are to the full discussions earlier in the book.

Subcommands named by special characters are alphabetized according to their English names (see p. 9).

A.1 List of Commands

The first page reference given with each command is to its description in the main text. The second reference is to the summary of its syntax, options, and subcommands (if any).

at   Schedule a job at a future time (p. 114, p. 477).
awk   Programming language for data manipulation (p. 353, p. 478).
batch   Schedule a batch job (p. 114, p. 480).
basename   Extract base of file name (p. 137, p. 480).
cal   Show a calendar (p. 108, p. 480).
cancel   Cancel printer requests (p. 90, p. 480).
cat   File concatenator (p. 67, p. 480).
cd   Change directory (p. 92, p. 480).
chgrp   Change file's group (p. 82, p. 481).
chmod   Change file permissions (p. 80, p. 481).

475

`chown`   Change file's owner (p. 82, p. 481).
`cmp`   Compare files (p. 77, p. 481).
`comm`   List lines common to two sorted files (p. 344, p. 481).
`compress`   Compress a file (p. 95, p. 482).
`cp`   Copy files (p. 72, p. 482).
`cpio`   Copy file archives (p. 97, p. 482).
`csh`   The C shell (p. 180, p. 482).
`cu`   Connect to a UNIX system (p. 452, p. 486).
`cut`   Extract fields from lines (p. 341, p. 486).
`date`   Display the date and time (p. 107, p. 487).
`df`   Report free disk space (p. 132, p. 487).
`diff`   Find file differences (p. 77, p. 487).
`dircmp`   Compare directories (p. 93, p. 487).
`dirname`   Extract directory from file name (p. 137, p. 487).
`du`   Report disk space in use (p. 133, p. 487).
`echo`   Echo arguments (p. 134, p. 488).
`ed`   Line editor (p. 251, p. 488).
`egrep`   Find regular expression, extended version (p. 351, p. 489).
`emacs`   Emacs extensible text editor (p. 259, p. 489).
`ex`   Line editor, extended version of ed (p. 236, p. 496).
`expr`   Evaluate an expression (p. 136, p. 498).
`false`   Return false (p. 155, p. 498).
`fgrep`   Find regular expression, fast version (p. 351, p. 498).
`file`   Classify files (p. 62, p. 498).
`find`   Find files (p. 62, p. 499).
`finger`   Look up information about a user (p. 105, p. 499).
`ftp`   Transfer files with File Transfer Protocol (p. 430, p. 499).
`grep`   Find regular expression (p. 351, p. 501).
`id`   Show user and group id's (p. 121, p. 501).
`kill`   Signal a process (p. 114, p. 501).
`login`   Log in (p. 117, p. 502).
`ln`   Link file names (p. 71, p. 501).
`lp`   Send files to a printer (p. 86, p. 502).
`lpr`   Berkeley print spooler (p. 88, p. 502).
`lpstat`   Show printer status (p. 89, p. 502).
`ls`   File lister (p. 58, p. 503).
`mail`   Simple mailer (p. 403, p. 503).
`mailx`   Berkeley Mailer (p. 381, p. 504).
`mesg`   Lock out messages (p. 135, p. 507).
`mkdir`   Make a directory (p. 93, p. 507).
`mknod`   Make a special file (p. 74, p. 507).
`mv`   Move files (p. 72, p. 507).
`newgrp`   Change your current group (p. 120, p. 508).
`nice`   Run a command at low priority (p. 116, p. 508).
`nohup`   Ignore hangups (p. 114, p. 508).
`od`   Octal dump (p. 82, p. 508).
`pack`   Pack files (p. 95, p. 508).
`paste`   Paste input fields (p. 343, p. 508).
`pcat`   Unpack and concatenate files (p. 95, p. 509).
`pg`   Page through a list of files (p. 84, p. 509).
`pr`   Format files for printing (p. 90, p. 509).
`ps`   List processes, System V version (p. 109, p. 510).
`ps`   List processes, BSD UNIX version (p. 109, p. 510).
`pwd`   Show working directory (p. 93, p. 510).
`rcp`   Remote copy (p. 424, p. 510).
`rlogin`   Remote login (p. 423, p. 511).
`rm`   Remove files or directories (p. 75, p. 511).
`rmdir`   Remove directories (p. 75, p. 511).
`rsh`   Remote shell (p. 179, p. 511).
`rsh`   Restricted Bourne shell (p. 179, p. 511).
`rwho`   List users on the local network (p. 425, p. 511).
`sed`   Edit from a script (p. 345, p. 512).
`sh`   The Bourne shell (p. 144, p. 513).
`sleep`   Suspend execution (p. 116, p. 515).
`sort`   Sort files (p. 337, p. 515).
`stty`   Set terminal characteristics (p. 125, p. 515).

su   Substitute user (p. 119, p. 516).
tabs   Set tabs on your terminal (p. 131, p. 517).
tail   Extract the end of a file (p. 69, p. 517).
tar   Tape archiver (p. 100, p. 517).
tee   Duplicate input (p. 70, p. 517).
telnet   Call a remote system over a network (p. 425, p. 518).
test   Compare values, test file properties (p. 155, p. 518).
time   Time a command (p. 135, p. 519).
touch   Touch a file (p. 79, p. 519).
tput   Send setup instructions to a terminal (p. 130, p. 519).
tr   Translate or delete characters (p. 340, p. 520).
true   Return true (p. 155, p. 520).
tset   Set terminal information (p. 122, p. 520).
tty   Get the terminal name (p. 107, p. 520).
umask   Mask default file permissions (p. 82, p. 520).
uncompress   Uncompress a file (p. 95, p. 520).
uniq   Eliminate adjacent repeated lines (p. 344, p. 521).
unpack   Unpack files (p. 95, p. 521).
uucp   UNIX to UNIX copy (p. 447, p. 521).
uuname   Get names of remote UNIX systems (p. 452, p. 521).
uupick   Pick up files from UNIX to UNIX transfer (p. 447, p. 521).
uustat   Check uucp status (p. 450, p. 522).
uuto   Send files UNIX to UNIX (p. 446, p. 522).
vi   Visual editor (p. 206, p. 522).
wait   Wait for a process to finish (p. 116, p. 526).
wc   Count words, lines, or characters (p. 94, p. 526).
who   List users and processes (p. 103, p. 522).
write   Write message to terminal (p. 134, p. 526).
xbiff   Mailbox flag for X (p. 471, p. 526).
xclock   Analog/digital clock for X (p. 470, p. 526).
xcolors   Display the X colors (p. 471, p. 527).
xfd   Display an X font (p. 471, p. 527).
xinit   Start the X server (p. 472, p. 527).
xkill   Kill an X client (p. 474, p. 527).
xlsfonts   Display a list of X fonts (p. 471, p. 527).
xrdb   Resource database utility for X (p. 473, p. 527).
xsetroot   Set root window appearance for X (p. 473, p. 528).
xterm   Terminal emulator for X (p. 467, p. 528).
zcat   Uncompress and concatenate files (p. 95, p. 528).

A.2   Summary of Commands and Features

A.2.1
at (Schedule a Job at a Future Time)

The forms of the at command line (p. 115) are

    at *time* [*date*] [+ *increment*]
    at -l [*job* ...]
    at -r *job* ...

The forms for *time* are the following:

- A one-digit or two-digit number specifying an hour
- A four-digit number specifying an hour and minute
- Two numbers (hour and minute) separated by a colon
- One of these followed by 'am', 'pm', or 'zulu'
- 'noon', 'midnight', or 'now'

The forms for *date* are the following:

- A month name followed by a day number, an optional comma, and an optional year number
- A day of the week

- 'today' or `tomorrow`

In the command, *increment* is a number followed by 'minutes', 'hours', 'days', 'weeks', 'months', or 'years', or their singular forms.

Month names and day names can be written in full or with three-letter abbreviations. An omitted *date* defaults to 'today'.

Case is ignored, as are blanks between components.

A.2.2 awk (Programming Language for Data Manipulation)

The form of the awk command line (p. 353) is

    awk [*option*] [*program*] [*file*] ...

The program must be provided either on the command line or via the -f option. If given on the command line, it is almost always enclosed in apostrophes.

Command-Line Options.

-F*s*   Set the field separator to *s* (p. 354)
-f *file*   Read the program from the file *file* (p. 354)

Pattern-Action Statements.

A pattern-action statement (p. 355) has one of the following forms:

BEGIN { *action* }   Executes *action* before reading any data (p. 355)
END { *action* }   Executes *action* after reading all data (p. 355)
{ *action* }   Executes *action* for each line of input data (p. 355)
pattern [{ *action* }]   Executes *action* for each line of input data matching *pattern* (p. 355)
pattern$_1$,*pattern*$_2$ [{ *action* }]   Executes *action* for lines of input data from the first one
        matching *pattern*$_1$ through the next one matching *pattern*$_2$ (p. 355)

In these forms, *action* has the form

    [*statement*] ...

In the last two forms the default action is 'print $0'.

A *pattern* is one of the following:

    expr
    /*regexpr*/

Here *expr* is an expression and *regexpr* is a generalized regular expression.

Expressions.

An expression (see Section 4.6.5) is formed from the following primary elements:

- Numeric constants
- String constants
- Variables
- Function calls of the form $f(a_1, a_2, \ldots, a_n)$
- Array elements of the form $a[i]$.

These elements can be combined using the following operators, listed in order of increasing precedence:

= += -= *= /= %= ^=   Assignment operators
? ... :   Conditional expression operator
|| Logical "or" operator
&&   Logical "and" operator
in   Array membership operator
~ !~   Pattern matching operators (used with /*regexpr*/)
< <= == != > >=   Relational operators
(juxtaposition)   Concatenation operator
+ -   Additive operators
* / %   Multiplicative operators
+ -   Unary arithmetic operators
!   Logical "not" operator
^   Exponentiation operator
++ --   Increment and decrement operators
$ Field selection operator
(...)   Grouping operators

Predefined Variables.

ARGC   Number of command-line arguments (p. 371)

ARGV   Array of command-line arguments (p. 371)
FILENAME   Name of current input file (p. 361)
FNR   Record number in current file (p. 361)
FS   Input field separator specification (p. 361)
NF   Number of fields in current record (p. 361)
NR   Number of records read so far (p. 361)
OFMT   Format used for showing numbers (p. 358)
OFS   Output field separator (p. 369)
ORS   Output record separator (p. 369)
RLENGTH   Length of string matched by match (p. 366)
RS   Input record separator specification (p. 361)
RSTART   Start of string matched by match (p. 366)
SUBSEP   Subscript separator (p. 360)

Predefined Numerical Functions.   All of the following functions return floating-point values except for int.

atan2(y,x)   Arctangent of y/x, result r satisfies $-\pi \le r \le \pi$ (p. 367)
cos(x)   Cosine of x radians (p. 367)
exp(x)   Exponential e^x (p. 367)
int(x)   Integer part of x (p. 367)
log(x)   Natural logarithm of x (p. 367)
rand()   Random number r, $0 \le r < 1$ (p. 367)
sin(x)   Sine of x radians (p. 367)
sqrt(x)   Square root of x (p. 367)
srand([x])   Set new seed for rand (p. 367)

Predefined String Functions.

gsub(r,s[,t])   Substitutes s for r globally in $0 or t (p. 366)
index(s,t)   Returns first position of string t within string s (p. 365)
length(s)   Returns number of characters in string s (p. 365)
match(s,r)   Tests whether string s contains a match for regular expression r (p. 366)
split(s,a[,fs])   Splits s into array a using separator fs (p. 366)
sprintf(*fmt*,*expr*, ...)   Formats *expr* ... according to *fmt* (p. 367)
sub(r,s[,t])   Substitutes s for r once in $0 or t (p. 366)
substr(s,p[,n])   Returns substring of s, or rest of string, starting at position p (p. 365)

Other Predefined Functions.

getline [*var*] [< *file*]   Reads a line into *var* or $0 from *file* or standard input (p. 368)
cmd | getline [*var*]   Reads a line from the standard output of *cmd* into *var* or $0 (p. 368)
system(*cmd*)   Executes the UNIX command *cmd*, return its exit value (p. 371)

Statements.   In the print and printf statements, *redir* has one of the following forms: (p. 369)

> *file*   Sends the output to *file*.
>> *file*   Appends the output to *file*.
| *cmd*   Pipes the output through the UNIX command *cmd*.

These are the awk statements:

expr   Evaluates *expr* and discard its value (p. 372)
{ *stmt* ...}   Executes a group of statements (p. 372)
;   Does nothing (empty statement) (p. 372)
break   Leaves innermost while, for, or do (p. 373)
close(*cmd*)   Breaks the connection between print and *cmd* (p. 371)
close(*file*)   Breaks the connection between print and *file* (p. 371)
continue   Starts next iteration of innermost while, for, or do (p. 373)
delete a[*sub*]   Deletes the element with subscript *sub* from the array a (p. 360)
do *stmt* while (*expr*)   Executes *stmt* once, then repeatedly while *expr* is true (p. 372)
for (*expr*$_1$; *expr*$_2$; *expr*$_3$) *stmt*   Executes *expr*$_1$, then executes *stmt* and *expr*$_3$ while *expr*$_2$ is true (p. 373)
for (*var* in *array*) *stmt*   Executes *stmt* with *var* set to each subscript of *array* in turn (p. 373)
if (*expr*) *stmt*$_1$ [; else *stmt*$_2$]   Executes *stmt*$_1$ if *expr* is true, *stmt*$_2$ otherwise (p. 372)
next   Starts next iteration of main input loop (p. 373)
exit [*expr*]   Goes to the END action, returns *expr* or 0 as program status if within that action (p. 373)

print   Sends $0 to standard output (p. 369)

print *expr* [, *expr*] ... [*redir*]   Sends *expr* ... to standard output, separated by OFS (p. 369)

print(*expr* [, *expr*] ...) [*redir*]   Sends *expr* ... to standard output, separated by OFS (p. 369)

printf(*format*, *expr* [, *expr*] ...) [*redir*]   Sends *expr* ... to standard output, formatted using *format* (p. 369)

return [*expr*]   Returns from a function with value *expr* (p. 374)

while (*expr*) *stmt*   Executes *stmt* while *expr* is true (p. 372)

User-Defined Functions.   A user-defined function (p. 374) has the following form:

```
function name(param [, param] ... ) {
    [stmt] ...
}
```

A user-defined function can appear wherever a pattern-action statement can.

A.2.3
basename
(Extract Base of File Name)

The form of the basename command line (p. 137) is:

    basename *string*₁ [*string*₂]

where *string*₁ is a string that represents a file name and *string*₂ is a suffix of *string*₁.

A.2.4
batch (Schedule a Batch Job)

The form of the batch command line (p. 115) is

```
batch
command file
```

The command file can be taken from a file if redirection is used.

A.2.5
cancel (Cancel Printer Requests)

The form of the cancel command line (p. 90) is

    cancel [*id*] ... [*printer*] ...

where each *id* identifies a printer request and each *printer* identifies a particular printer.

A.2.6
cat (File Concatenator)

The form of the cat command line (p. 67) is

    cat [*options*] *filelist*

The files in *filelist* are concatenated and copied to standard output (p. 67) A '-' in *filelist* denotes standard input.

Command-line Options.

-e   Put '$' at the end of each line (p. 69)
-s   Don't complain about nonexistent source files (p. 68)
-t   Show tabs as '∧I' (p. 69)
-u   Don't buffer the output (p. 68)
-v   Represent nonprinting characters with printable ones (p. 68)

A.2.7
cal (Show a Calendar)

The form of the cal command line (p. 108) is

    cal [[*month*] *year*]

A.2.8
cd (Change Directory)

The form of the cd command line (p. 92) is

    cd [*dir*]

dir becomes the current directory; if *dir* is omitted it is taken as your home directory.

A.2.9 chgrp **(Change File Group)**	The form of the chgrp command line (p. 82) is chgrp *owner file* ...

A.2.10
chmod
(Change File Permissions)

The form of the chmod command line (p. 80) is

    chmod *modespecs filelist*

where *filelist* is a list of file names and *modespecs* is either

- a comma-separated list of permission changes, or
- an octal number of up to four digits.

Each permission change has three parts: one or more "who" letters, an operator, and one or more permission letters.

The "Who" Letters.   The "who" letters (p. 80) are as follows:

g   Group
o   Others
u   User (owner)
a   Everyone (all)

Operators.   The operators (p. 81) are as follows:

-   Take away these permissions
=   Set these permission and no others
+   Add these permissions

Permissions.   The permissions (p. 81) are as follows:

l   Lock during access
r   Read
s   Set user or group ID
t   Sticky bit
w   Write
x   Execute

A.2.11
chown
(Change File Owner)

The form of the chown command line (p. 82) is

    chown *owner file* ...

A.2.12
cmp **(Compare Files)**

The form of the cmp command line (p. 77) is

    cmp [*options*] *file*$_1$ *file*$_2$

The return code is 0 if the files are the same, 1 if the files differ, and 2 if one or both files could not be accessed.

Command-line Options.

-l   Show the byte number and the differing characters for each difference (p. 77)
-s   Show nothing (p. 77)

A.2.13
comm **(List Lines Common to Two Sorted Files)**

The form of the comm command line (p. 344) is

    comm [*-flags*] *file*$_1$ *file*$_2$

where *flags* consists of one or more of the digits 123. Each digit in *flags* indicates that the corresponding column of the listing should be suppressed.

A.2.14
compress
(Compress a File)

The form of the compress command line (p. 95) is

> compress [*options*] [*file*] ...

where *file* ... is a list of files to be compressed. By default each file is replaced by its compressed version *file*.Z.

Command-line Options.

-b *n* Use *n* bits in the compression algorithm (p. 96)
-c   Write the compressed files to standard output (p. 95)
-f   Force compression of a file even if nothing is gained (p. 96)
-v   Show the percentage of reduction for each file compressed (p. 95)

A.2.15
cp (Copy Files)

The forms of the command line are:(p. 73)

> cp [*options*] *ifile ofile*
> cp [*options*] *iname* ... *odir*

where *ifile* is an input file, *ofile* is an output file, each *iname* is an input file or directory, and *odir* is an output directory.

Command-line Options.   These options vary from one system to another.

-i   Ask interactively for confirmation of each copy (p. 74)
-p   Preserve the permission modes and modification time of the original file (p. 74)
-r   Copy subdirectories recursively (p. 74)

A.2.16
cpio
(Copy File Archives)

The forms of the cpio command line (p. 97) are

> cpio [*options*] [*pat*] ...
> cpio [*options*] *dir*

Here *pat* specifies files to be extracted from an archive and is used only with the -i option, while *dir* specifies a destination directory and is used only with the -p option.

Command-line Options.

-6   Read archive in Sixth Edition format (p. 99)
-a   Leave the access times of input files unchanged (p. 98)
-b   Reverse byte order within each word (p. 99)
-B   Use 5120-byte blocks for data transfer (p. 99)
-c   Write header information in ASCII character form (p. 99)
-C *n*   Use *n*-byte blocks for data transfer (p. 99)
-d   Create directories as needed (p. 98)
-f   Copy in those files *not* matching the patterns (p. 98)
-i   Copy archive in (p. 97)
-I *file*   Read the archive from *file* (p. 98)
-k   Attempt to get past bad headers and i/o errors (p. 99)
-l   Link files when possible rather than copying them (p. 98)
-m   Retain previous file modification time (p. 98)
-M *msg*   Issue *msg* when switching media (p. 98)
-o   Copy archive out (p. 97)
-O *file*   Write the archive to *file* (p. 98)
-p   Pass archive to another directory (p. 98)
-r   Interactively rename files (p. 98)
-s   Reverse byte order within each halfword (p. 99)
-S   Reverse halfword order within each word (p. 99)
-t   Show a table of contents of the input, create no files (p. 98)
-u   Copy unconditionally, replacing newer files (p. 98)
-v   List all file names (p. 98)
-V   Show a dot for each file transferred (p. 98)

A.2.17
csh (C Shell)

The form of the csh command line (p. 202) is

> csh [*options*] [*arg*] ...

The arguments *arg* ... are made available through the **argv** shell variable.

Command-line Options.

-c *file*   Read commands from the file *file* (p. 202)
-e   Exit if any invoked command terminates abnormally (p. 203)
-f   Don't look for a `.cshrc` file (p. 203)
-i   Prompt for top-level input (p. 202)
-n   Parse commands but don't execute them (p. 203)
-s   Read commands from standard input (p. 202)
-t   Read and execute a single line of input (p. 202)
-v   Echo command input after history substitutions (p. 202)
-V   Echo all command input, even while executing `.cshrc` (p. 203)
-x   Echo commands before executing them (p. 203)
-X   Echo commands before executing them, even while executing `.cshrc` (p. 203)

Operators.

c& Executes c in the background, then continue (p. 182)
c_1 && c_2 Executes c_1, then c_2 if the exit status of c_1 is zero (p. 181)
c_1 | c_2 Connects the standard output of c_1 to the standard input of c_2 through a pipe (p. 181) .
c_1 |& c_2 Connects the standard output and the standard error of c_1 to the standard input of c_2 through a pipe (p. 181)
c_1 || c_2 Executes c_1, then c_2 if the exit status of c_1 is nonzero (p. 181)
c; Executes c and waits for it to finish, then continues (p. 182)

Redirection.

<*file*   Takes standard input from *file* (p. 183)
<<*word*   Takes standard input from following text (p. 183)
>[&][!]*file*   Sends standard output to *file* (p. 184)
>>[&][!]*file*   Appends standard output to *file* (p. 184)

History Substitutions.   A history substitution has the form

!*event*[[:]*selector*[:*modifier*] . . .]

The *selector* part selects some or all of the words in the event *event*. The ':' can be omitted before *selector* if *selector* begins with one of the characters (^ $ * - %). These are the possible events:

!*n*   Event number *n* (p. 187)
!*str*   The unique previous event whose name starts with *str* (p. 187)
!!   The preceding event (p. 187)
!-*n*   The *n*th previous event (p. 187)
!?*str*?   The unique previous event containing the string *str* (p. 187)

These are the possible selectors for selecting words of the event:

:*n*   The *n*th argument (p. 188)
:*n*:*x**   Words *x* through $ (p. 188)
:*x*-   Words *x* through ($ − 1) (p. 188)
[:]-*x*   Words 0 through *x* (p. 188)
[:]$ The last argument (p. 188)
[:]^   The first argument (p. 188)
[:]%   Word matched by the preceding '?*str*?' search (p. 188)
[:]*   Words 1 through $ (p. 188)
0   The command name (p. 188)

These are the possible modifiers:

:[g]&   Repeats the previous substitution (p. 188)
:h   Removes a trailing path name component (p. 188)
:p   Shows ("prints") the new command but doesn't execute it (p. 189)
:q   Quotes the substituted words, preventing further substitutions (p. 188)
:r   Removes a trailing '.*str*' component (p. 188)
:[g]s/*l*/*r*   Substitutes *r* for *l* (p. 188)
:t   Removes all leading path name components (p. 188)
:x   Quotes the substituted words, but breaks the text into words at whitespace (p. 189)

Variable Substitutions.   In the following forms, the braces can be omitted if no ambiguity would result.

${*n*}   The *n*th command-line argument (p. 191)

${*name*}   The words of the variable *name* (p. 191)
${*name*[*sel*]}   The words of the variable *name* selected by *sel* (p. 191)
${#*name*}   The number of words in the variable *name* (p. 191)
$$ The process number of the parent shell invocation (p. 192)
$<   The next line of standard input, uninterpreted (p. 192)
${?*name*}   The value 1 if the variable *name* is set, 0 if it isn't (p. 191)
$?0   The value 1 if the current input file name is known, 0 if it isn't (p. 192)
$*   List of arguments on the command line (p. 192)
$0   The name of the current input file (p. 192)

Modifiers for Variable Substitutions.

:[g]e   Removes everything preceding a trailing '.*str*' component (p. 192)
:[g]h   Removes a trailing path name component (p. 192)
:q   Quotes the substituted words, preventing further substitutions (p. 192)
:[g]r   Removes a trailing '.*str*' component (p. 192)
:[g]t   Removes all leading path name components (p. 192)
:x   Quotes the substituted words, but break the text into words at whitespace (p. 192)

Quotation and Command Substitution.

c   Quotes the character *c* (p. 192)
"*text*"   Quotes *text*, allows substitutions within it (p. 192)
'*text*'   Quotes *text*, allows no substitutions within it (p. 193)
`*text*`   Executes *text*, substitutes its standard output (p. 193)

Tests.   A successful test returns 1 while an unsuccessful test returns 0 (p. 194)

{*cmd*}   Executes *cmd* in a subshell, tests if exit status is zero.
-d *file*   Tests if *file* is a directory.
-e *file*   Tests if *file* exists.
-f *file*   Tests if *file* is an ordinary file.
-o *file*   Tests if *file* is owned by the user who called csh.
-r *file*   Tests if *file* has read access.
-w *file*   Tests if *file* has write access.
-x *file*   Tests if *file* has execute access.
-z *file*   Tests if *file* has zero size.

Intrinsic Commands.

@ [*name*[[*n*] = *expr*]   Shows or sets a shell variable or the *n*th word of a shell variable (p. 196)
[*label*]:   Does nothing, but label this statement with *label* (p. 198)
alias [*name* [*text*]]   Shows or defines an alias (p. 197)
break   Resumes execution after the nearest enclosing foreach or while (p. 198)
breaksw   Resumes execution after the nearest enclosing switch (p. 198)
case *label*   Attaches a case label to a command within a switch statement (p. 201)
cd [*dir*]   Changes the working directory to *dir* or to the home directory (p. 198)
chdir [*dir*]   Changes the working directory to *dir* or to the home directory (p. 198)
continue   Continues execution of the nearest enclosing while or foreach (p. 198)
default   Labels the default case of a switch statement (p. 201)
dirs   Shows the directory stack (p. 198)
echo [-n] [*word*] ...   Echoes *word* ... to standard output (p. 199)
else   Indicates an alternative for an if statement (p. 201)
end   Marks the end of a foreach or while statement (p. 202, p. 202).
endif   Marks the end of an if statement (p. 201)
endsw   Marks the end of a switch statement (p. 201)
eval *arg* ...   Performs textual substitutions in *arg* ... , then executes the resulting command (p. 200)
exec *cmd*   Executes *cmd* in place of the current shell (p. 199)
exit [(*expr*)]   Exits from the shell with *expr* as status (p. 199)
glob [*word*] ...   Echoes *word* ..., but ignore '\\' quotation (p. 199)
goto *word*   Executes commands starting with the first available one following the label *word* (p. 198)
history [-r] [-h] [*n*]   Displays the *n* most recent events in the history list (p. 199)
jobs [-l]   Lists the active jobs (p. 199)
kill [-*sig*] *id*   Sends signal *sig* or SIGTERM to the job or process identified by *id* (p. 200)

kill -l   Lists all the possible signal names (p. 200)

limit [*resource* [*max*]]   Limits the consumption of a specified resource or shows the limit (p. 199)

login   Terminates a login shell, invites a new login (p. 199)

logout   Terminates a login shell (p. 199)

nice [+n] [*cmd*]   Executes the command *cmd* or the shell itself at a low priority (p. 200)

nohup [*cmd*]   Runs *cmd* or the rest of the script with hangups ignored (p. 200)

notify [*%job*]   Provides immediate notice of changes in job status (p. 199)

onintr   Restores default interrupt actions (p. 200)

onintr -   Ignores all interrupts (p. 200)

onintr *label*   Goes to *label* when an interrupt is received (p. 200)

popd [+n]   Pops the directory stack, discards the *n*th entry if *n* is given (p. 198)

pushd   Exchanges the top two elements of the directory stack (p. 198)

pushd *dir*   Changes to directory *dir*, pushes the old directory onto the directory stack (p. 198)

pushd +n   Rotates the directory stack by *n* items (p. 198)

rehash   Recalculates the lookup table for command names (p. 200)

set   Shows all shell variables (p. 197)

set *name*   Sets the shell variable *name* to the null string (p. 197)

set *name[n]=word*   Sets the shell variable *name* or its *n*th word to *word* (p. 197)

set *name=(wordlist)*   Sets the shell variable *name* to the sequence of words in *wordlist* (p. 197)

setenv *name val*   Sets the environment variable *name* to *val* (p. 197)

shift [*var*]   Shifts the words of argv or of *var* one word left (p. 197)

source [-h] *file*   Reads commands from *file* (p. 200)

time [*cmd*]   Executes *cmd* and shows how much time it used, or shows how much time this shell has used (p. 201)

umask [*n*]   Sets or shows the value of the file creation mask (p. 199)

unalias *pat*   Deletes all aliases that match the pattern *pat* (p. 197)

unhash   Disables use of the hashed lookup table for commands (p. 200)

unlimit [*resource*]   Removes the limitation on the resource *resource* or removes all such limits (p. 199)

unset *pat*   Deletes all variables whose names match *pat* (p. 197)

unsetenv *pat*   Deletes all environment variables whose names match *pat* (p. 197)

wait   Waits for all background jobs to complete (p. 200)

Compound Commands (Statements).

```
foreach name (word ... )
    cmdlist
end
```
Executes commands for each *word*, setting *name* to that word (p. 202)

if (*expr*) *cmd*   Executes *cmd* if *expr* is true (nonzero) (p. 201)

```
if (expr) then cmdlist₁
[else cmdlist₂]
endif
```
Executes *cmdlist*$_1$ if *expr* is true (nonzero) and *cmdlist*$_2$ otherwise (p. 201)

repeat *n cmd*   Executes the command *cmd* *n* times (p. 202)

```
switch(string)
case str: ...
    cmdlist
default:
    cmdlist
endsw
```
Selects the first case *str* that matches the string *string* and executes its command list (p. 201)

```
while (expr)
    cmdlist
end
```
Executes the commands in *cmdlist* while *expr* is true (nonzero) (p. 202)

Predefined Variables.

argv   List of the command-line arguments (p. 195)

cdpath   List of directories to be searched by cd (p. 195)

cwd   Full path name of the current working directory (p. 195)
echo   If set, causes commands and their arguments to be echoed before execution (p. 196)
fignore   Suffixes to be ignored for file name completion (p. 196)
filec   If set, perform file name completion (p. 196)
histchars   Pair of characters used in history substitutions (p. 196)
history   Size of the history list (p. 199)
home   The home directory of the user who called this shell (p. 195)
ignoreeof   If set, ignore end of file received from a terminal (p. 195)
mail   List of files where mail might be found (p. 195)
noclobber   If set, inhibit certain output redirections (p. 195)
noglob   If set, inhibit file name expansion (p. 195)
nonomatch   If set, allow file name expansions that match no files (p. 195)
notify   If set, send notice of changes in status of background jobs immediately (p. 196)
path   List of directories to search for commands (p. 195)
prompt   String to send to your terminal before reading a command interactively (p. 196)
savehist   Number of history entries saved on logout (p. 196)
shell   The file in which the shell resides (p. 195)
status   The exit status of the most recently executed command (p. 196)
time   If set, give timing information on commands that take a long time to execute (p. 196)
verbose   If set, show the words of each command after history substitutions (p. 196)

A.2.18
cu (Connect to a UNIX System)

The form of the cu command line (p. 453) is

> cu [*options*] [*dest*]

where *dest* is either the name of a remote system or a telephone number.

Command-line Options.

-d   Show diagnostic traces (p. 454)
-e   Send data using even parity (p. 454)
-n   Prompt the user for the telephone number (p. 454)
-o   Send data using odd parity (p. 454)
-h   Provide local echoing of typed lines (half duplex mode) (p. 454)
-l *dev*   Use the device *dev* as the communication line (p. 453)
-s *speed*   Cause the communication line to operate at *speed* (p. 453)
-t   Map carriage return to carriage return plus line feed (p. 454)

Tilde Commands.

~![*cmd*]   Executes *cmd* in a subshell on the local system (p. 454)
~$*cmd*   Executes *cmd* in a subshell on the local system and sends its output to the remote system (p. 454)
~%b   Sends a break signal to the remote system (p. 454)
~%break   Sends a break signal to the remote system (p. 454)
~%cd [*dir*]   Changes the current directory on the local system (p. 454)
~%d   Toggles debugging output (p. 456)
~%debug   Toggles debugging output (p. 456)
~%nostop   Toggles DC3/DC1 input control (p. 455)
~%put *rfile* [*lfile*]   Copies remote file *rfile* to local file *lfile* (p. 455)
~%take *lfile* [*rfile*]   Copies local file *lfile* to remote file *rfile* (p. 455)
~.   Terminates the conversation (p. 454)
~~*line*   Sends '~*line*' to the remote system (p. 455)
~l   Shows the values of the termio variables for the communication line (p. 456)
~t   Shows the values of the termio variables for your terminal (p. 456)

A.2.19
cut (Extract Fields from Lines)

The form of the cut command line (p. 341) is

> cut *options* [*file*] ...

where the *files* provide the input.

Command-line Options.   In the following commands, *list* indicates a list of field numbers, with commas separating the fields and - indicating ranges. Either -c or -f, but not both, must be specified.

-c*list*   Extract the characters specified in *list* (p. 342)

-d*c*   Use the character *c* as the field delimiter (p. 342)
-f*list*   Extract the fields specified in *list* (p. 342)
-s   Suppress lines containing no delimiter characters (p. 342)

A.2.20
date **(Display the Date and Time)**

The form of the date command line (p. 107) is

    date [+*format*]

where *format* specifies the format in which the date and time are displayed. BSD UNIX versions of date may not recognize *format*.

A.2.21
df
(Report Free Disk Space)

The form of the df command line (p. 132) is

    df [*options*] [*name*] . . .

where each *name* refers to a mounted file system or a directory.

Command-line Options.
-a   Report on all file systems, even those having no blocks (SunOS) (p. 133).
-f   Count actual blocks in the free list (System V) (p. 133)
-i   Report number of i-nodes free and in use (BSD UNIX, SunOS) (p. 133)
-l   Report only on local file systems (System V) (p. 133)
-t   Report total allocated blocks and i-nodes as well as free ones (System V) (p. 133)
-t *type* Report only on file systems of type *type* (SunOS) (p. 133)

A.2.22
diff **(Find File Differences)**

The form of the diff command line (p. 77) is

    diff [*options*] *file*$_1$ *file*$_2$

The return code is 0 if the files are the same, 1 if the files differ, and 2 if the differences could not be computed.

Command-line Options.
-b   Ignore trailing whitespace, condense other whitespace to a single blank (p. 78)
-e   Produce an editor script (p. 78)
-f   Produce a pseudo-editor script that reads forward (p. 78)
-h   Do a fast but not as effective, i.e., half-hearted, job (p. 78)

A.2.23
dircmp **(Compare Directories)**

The form of the dircmp command line (p. 93) is

    dircmp [*options*] *dir*$_1$ *dir*$_2$

where *dir*$_1$ and *dir*$_2$ are the directories to be compared.

Command-line Options.
-d   Output differences between corresponding files (p. 94)
-s   Suppress all messages pertaining to identical files (p. 94)
-w*n* Set the output line width to *n* characters (p. 94)

A.2.24
dirname **(Extract Directory from File Name)**

The form of the dirname command line (p. 137) is:

    dirname *string*

where *string* is a string that represents a file name.

A.2.25
du **(Report Disk Space in Use)**

The form of the du command line (p. 133) is

    du [*options*] [*name*] . . .

where each *name* is a directory or a file.

Command-line Options.
-a   Produce an output line for each file (p. 133)
-r   Report directories that can't be read and files that can't be opened (p. 133)
-s   Report only the total usage for each *name* (p. 133)

A.2.26
echo (Echo Arguments)

The form of the echo command line (p. 134) is

    echo *arguments*

A.2.27
ed (Line Editor)

The form of the ed command line is (p. 251)

    ed [*options*] [*file*]

where *file* is a file to be edited.

Command-line Options.

-p *string* Use *string* as the interactive prompt string (p. 251)
-s Suppress informational messages (p. 251)

Line Addresses and Line Ranges.   The notations for specifying a line address are as follows:

\$ The last line of the file (p. 252)
.   The current line (p. 252)
n   The *n*th line of the file (p. 252)
'*c* The line marked with the letter *c* (p. 252)
/*pat*/ The next line containing the pattern *pat* (p. 252)
?*pat*? The nearest previous line containing the pattern *pat* (p. 252)
[*a*]*n* The address *a* plus *n* lines (p. 252)
[*a*]+[*n*] The address *a* plus *n* lines (p. 252)
[*a*]-[*n*] The address *a* minus *n* lines (p. 252)

   The notations for specifying a line range are as follows:

a_1,a_2 Lines a_1 through a_2 (p. 253)
$a_1;a_2$ Like the previous form, but the current line is set to a_1 before a_2 is evaluated (p. 253)
,   The entire file (p. 253)
;   The pair '.,\$' (p. 253)

Commands.   The text before the brackets indicates the shortest recognized abbreviation. A line address is indicated by *a* and a line range is indicated by *r*.

a   Shows the line at address *a* (p. 253)
⟨CR⟩ Shows the next line (p. 253)
!*cmds* Executes the UNIX commands *cmds* in a subshell (p. 257)
[*a*]= Shows the address of the line at *a* (p. 253)
[*a*]a Appends input text after line *a* (p. 254)
[*r*]c Deletes the lines in range *r*, then inserts input text (p. 254)
[*r*]d Deletes the lines in range *r* (p. 254)
e [*file*] Starts editing *file*, discards the current buffer (p. 255)
e !*cmds* Edits the standard output of *cmds* (p. 257)
E [*file*] Starts editing *file*, discards the current buffer without checking (p. 255)
f [*file*] Changes name of current file to *file* (p. 255)
[*r*]g/*pat*/ [*cmds*] Performs *cmds* for those lines in *r* that match *pat* (p. 256)
[*r*]G/*pat*/ Interactively performs commands for those lines in *r* that match *pat* (p. 256)
h   Gives help on the most recent error diagnostic (p. 257)
H   Toggles error messages for '?' diagnostics (p. 257)
[*a*]i Inserts input text after line *a* (p. 254)
[*r*]j Joins the lines in *r* (p. 254)
[*a*]k*c* Marks the line at *a* with the letter *c* (p. 255)
[*r*] l Shows a group of lines, showing nonprinting characters explicitly (p. 253)
[*r*]m *a* Moves a group of lines to the location after *a* (p. 254)
[*r*]n Shows a group of lines with line numbers (p. 253)
[*r*]p Shows a group of lines (p. 253)
P   Toggles prompting for subsequent commands (p. 257)
q   Quits the editor without writing the buffer (p. 256)
Q   Quits the editor without checking or writing the buffer (p. 256)
[*a*]r [*file*] Reads *file* into buffer after line *a* (p. 255)
[*a*]r !*cmds* Puts output of *cmds* into buffer after line *a* (p. 257)
[*r*]s/*pat*/*repl*/[*opts*] Replaces the pattern *pat* by the text *repl* (p. 254)

[*r*]s*c pat c repl c*[*opts*]   Replaces the pattern *pat* by the text *repl* (p. 254)
[*r*]t*a*   Copies the lines in range *r* to address *a* (p. 254)
u   Undoes the most recent change or insertion (p. 257)
[*r*]v*/pat/* [*cmds*]   Performs *cmds* for those lines in *r* that do *not* match *pat* (p. 256)
[*r*]V*/pat/*   Interactively performs commands for those lines in *r* that do *not* match *pat* (p. 256)
[*r*]w [*file*]   Writes the lines in region *r* to *file* (p. 255)
[*r*]w !*cmds*   Executes *cmds* as a shell command, *r* is input (p. 257)

A.2.28
egrep
(Find Regular Expression, Extended Version)

The form of the egrep command line (p. 352) is

   egrep [*options*] [*pat*] [*file*] . . .

where *pat* is a regular expression to be searched for and *file* . . . is a list of files to be searched. The *pat* component is omitted if the -e or -f option is present.

Command-line Options.

-b   Precede each line by its disk block number (p. 352)
-c   Only show a count of matching lines (p. 352)
-e *pat*   Use *pat* as the search pattern (p. 353)
-f *file*   Read the pattern list from *file* (p. 353)
-i   Ignore case of letters in making comparisons (p. 352)
-l   Only show the names of files containing matching strings (p. 352)
-n   Precede each line by its file name and line number (p. 352)
-s   Show only error messages (p. 352)
-v   Show all lines that *don't* match (p. 352)

A.2.29
emacs (Emacs Extensible Text Editor)

The form of the Emacs command line (p. 260) is

   emacs [*options*]

Command-line Options.

file   Initially visit *file* using file-find (p. 260)
+*n file*   Initially visit *file*, go to line *n* (p. 260)
-batch   Run Emacs in batch mode (p. 260)
-d *disp*   Use *disp* as the display under X (p. 260)
-f[uncall] *func*   Call LISP function *func* with no arguments (p. 260)
-i[nsert] *file*   Insert *file* into the current buffer (p. 260)
-kill   Exit from Emacs without asking for confirmation (p. 260)
-l[oad] *file*   Load LISP code from *file* with load (p. 260)
-no-init-file   Don't load the Emacs initialization file ~/.emacs (p. 261)
-q   Don't load the Emacs initialization file ~/.emacs (p. 261)
-u[ser] *name*   Load *name*'s initialization file ~*name*/.emacs (p. 261)

Commands.   For each command we indicate in parentheses its default key binding if it has one.

abbrev-mode (p. 267)
abbrev-prefix-mark (Meta ') (p. 323)
abort-recursive-edit (Ctrl]) (p. 271)
add-global-abbrev (Ctrl X +) (p. 322)
add-mode-abbrev (Ctrl X Ctrl A) (p. 322)
add-name-to-file (p. 295)
append-next-kill (Meta Ctrl W) (p. 280)
append-to-buffer (Ctrl X a) (p. 280)
append-to-file (p. 294)
apropos (p. 274)
auto-fill-mode (p. 266)
auto-save-mode (p. 267)
back-to-indentation (Meta M) (p. 275)
backward-char (Ctrl B) (p. 275)
backward-delete-char-untabify (DEL) (p. 278)
backward-kill-sentence (Ctrl DEL) (p. 278)
backward-kill-word (Meta Del) (p. 278)

backward-list (`Meta` `Ctrl` P) (p. 285)
backward-page (`Ctrl` X [) (p. 276)
backward-paragraph (`Meta` [) (p. 276)
backward-sentence (`Meta` A) (p. 276)
backward-sexp (`Meta` `Ctrl` B) (p. 285)
backward-up-list (`Meta` `Ctrl` U) (p. 285)
backward-word (`Meta` B) (p. 275)
beginning-of-buffer (`Meta` <) (p. 276)
beginning-of-line (`Ctrl` A) (p. 275)
buffer-menu (p. 300)
call-last-kbd-macro (`Ctrl` X e) (p. 320)
capitalize-region (p. 284)
capitalize-word (`Meta` C) (p. 283)
cd (p. 292)
center-line (p. 282)
clear-rectangle (p. 290)
command-apropos (`Ctrl` H a) (p. 273)
compare-windows (p. 291)
copy-file (p. 294)
copy-last-shell-input (p. 317)
copy-region-as-kill (`Meta` W) (p. 280)
copy-region-to-rectangle (`Ctrl` X r r) (p. 303)
copy-to-buffer (p. 280)
copy-to-register (`Ctrl` X x) (p. 303)
count-lines-page (`Ctrl` X l) (p. 299)
count-lines-region (`Meta` =) (p. 299)
count-matches (p. 312)
dabbrev-expand (`Meta` /) (p. 324)
define-abbrevs (p. 324)
delete-backward-char (`DEL`) (p. 278)
delete-blank-lines (`Ctrl` X `Ctrl` O) (p. 279)
delete-char (`Ctrl` D) (p. 278)
delete-file (p. 294)
delete-horizontal-space (`Meta` \) (p. 278)
delete-indentation (`Meta` ^) (p. 278)
delete-matching-lines (p. 312)
delete-non-matching-lines (p. 312)
delete-other-windows (`Ctrl` X 1) (p. 291)
delete-rectangle (p. 290)
delete-window (`Ctrl` X 0) (p. 291)
describe-bindings (`Ctrl` H b) (p. 273)
describe-copying (`Ctrl` H `Ctrl` C) (p. 274)
describe-distribution (`Ctrl` H `Ctrl` D) (p. 274)
describe-function (`Ctrl` H f) (p. 273)
describe-key (`Ctrl` H k) (p. 273)
describe-key-briefly (`Ctrl` H c) (p. 273)
describe-mode (`Ctrl` H m) (p. 273)
describe-no-warranty (`Ctrl` H `Ctrl` W) (p. 274)
describe-syntax (`Ctrl` H s) (p. 273)
describe-variable (`Ctrl` H v) (p. 273)
dired (`Ctrl` X d) (p. 297)
dired-other-window (`Ctrl` X 4 d) (p. 297)
disable-command (p. 271)
display-time (p. 318)
dissociated-press (p. 335)
do-auto-save (p. 296)
doctor (p. 335)
down-list (`Meta` `Ctrl` D) (p. 285)
downcase-region (`Ctrl` X `Ctrl` L) (p. 283)
downcase-word (`Meta` L) (p. 283)
edit-abbrevs (p. 323)
edit-abbrevs-redefine (p. 323)
edit-options (p. 313)
edit-picture (p. 303)
edit-tab-stops (p. 289)

```
edit-tab-stops-note-changes   (p. 289)
electric-nroff-mode   (p. 266)
emacs-lisp-mode   (p. 266)
emacs-version   (p. 318)
enable-command   (p. 271)
end-kbd-macro   ( Ctrl X ) ) (p. 320)
end-of-buffer   ( Meta > ) (p. 276)
end-of-line   ( Ctrl E ) (p. 275)
enlarge-window   ( Ctrl X ^ ) (p. 291)
enlarge-window-horizontally   ( Ctrl X } ) (p. 291)
eval-current-buffer   (p. 314)
eval-expression   ( Esc Esc ) (p. 314)
eval-last-sexp   ( Ctrl X Ctrl E ) (p. 314)
eval-print-last-sexp   ( LnFd in Lisp Interaction mode) (p. 314)
eval-region   (p. 314)
exchange-point-and-mark   ( Ctrl X Ctrl X ) (p. 281)
execute-extended-command   ( Meta X ) (p. 268)
exit-recursive-edit   ( Meta Ctrl C ) (p. 271)
expand-abbrev   ( Ctrl X ' ) (p. 323)
expand-region-abbrevs   (p. 323)
fill-individual-paragraphs   (p. 282)
fill-paragraph   ( Meta Q ) (p. 281)
fill-region   ( Meta G ) (p. 282)
fill-region-as-paragraph   (p. 281)
find-alternate-file   ( Ctrl X Ctrl V ) (p. 293)
find-file   ( Ctrl X Ctrl F ) (p. 293)
find-file-read-only   ( Ctrl X Ctrl R ) (p. 293)
find-file-other-window   ( Ctrl X 4f ) (p. 293)
find-tag   ( Meta . ) (p. 315)
find-tag-other-window   ( Ctrl X 4. ) (p. 315)
forward-char   ( Ctrl F ) (p. 275)
forward-list   ( Meta Ctrl N ) (p. 285)
forward-page   ( Ctrl X ] ) (p. 276)
forward-paragraph   ( Meta ] ) (p. 276)
forward-sentence   ( Meta E ) (p. 276)
forward-sexp   ( Meta Ctrl F ) (p. 284)
forward-word   ( Meta F ) (p. 275)
global-set-key   (p. 319)
goto-char   (p. 277)
goto-line   (p. 277)
hanoi   (p. 335)
help-with-tutorial   ( Ctrl H t ) (p. 274)
indent-region   ( Meta Ctrl \ ) (p. 288)
indent-relative   (p. 288)
indent-rigidly   ( Ctrl X TAB ) (p. 288)
indented-text-mode   (p. 266)
info   ( Ctrl H i ) (p. 274)
insert-abbrevs   (p. 324)
insert-buffer   (p. 280)
insert-file   ( Ctrl X i ) (p. 294)
insert-kbd-macro   (p. 321)
insert-register   ( Ctrl X g ) (p. 303)
interrupt-shell-subjob   (p. 318)
inverse-add-global-abbrev   ( Ctrl X - ) (p. 322)
inverse-add-mode-abbrev   ( Ctrl X Ctrl H ) (p. 323)
isearch-backward   ( Ctrl R ) (p. 307)
isearch-backward-regexp   (p. 309)
isearch-forward   ( Ctrl S ) (p. 307)
isearch-forward-regexp   ( Meta Ctrl S ) (p. 309)
just-one-space   ( Meta Space ) (p. 278)
kbd-macro-query   ( Ctrl X q ) (p. 321)
keyboard-quit   ( Ctrl G ) (p. 268)
kill-all-abbrevs   (p. 323)
kill-buffer   ( Ctrl X k ) (p. 298)
kill-line   (p. 278)
```

```
kill-local-variable   (p. 313)
kill-output-from-shell   (p. 318)
kill-rectangle   (p. 290)
kill-region   ( Ctrl W ) (p. 278)
kill-sentence   ( Meta K ) (p. 278)
kill-sexp   ( Meta  Ctrl K ) (p. 285)
kill-some-buffers   (p. 298)
kill-word   ( Meta D ) (p. 278)
latex-mode   (p. 266)
LaTeX-mode   (p. 266)
lisp-interaction-mode   (p. 266)
lisp-mode   (p. 266)
list-abbrevs   (p. 323)
list-buffers   ( Ctrl X  Ctrl B ) (p. 300)
list-command-history   (p. 270)
list-directory   ( Ctrl X  Ctrl D ) (p. 294)
list-matching-lines   (p. 312)
list-options   (p. 313)
list-tags   (p. 316)
local-set-key   (p. 319)
lpr-buffer   (p. 302)
lpr-region   (p. 302)
mail   ( Ctrl X m ) (p. 327)
mail-cc   (p. 329)
mail-fill-yanked-message   (p. 329)
mail-other-window   ( Ctrl X 4m ) (p. 327)
mail-send   (p. 329)
mail-send-and-exit   (p. 329)
mail-signature   (p. 329)
mail-subject   (p. 329)
mail-to   (p. 329)
mail-yank-original   (p. 329)
make-local-variable   (p. 313)
make-symbolic-link   (p. 295)
make-variable-buffer-local   (p. 313)
manual-entry   (p. 274)
mark-page   ( Ctrl X  Ctrl P ) (p. 281)
mark-paragraph   ( Meta H ) (p. 281)
mark-sexp   ( Meta  Ctrl @ ) (p. 285)
mark-whole-buffer   ( Ctrl X h ) (p. 281)
mark-word   ( Meta @ ) (p. 281)
move-to-window-line   ( Meta R ) (p. 275)
name-last-kbd-macro   (p. 321)
narrow-to-region   ( Ctrl X n ) (p. 299)
negative-argument   ( Meta - ) (p. 269)
newline   ( RET ) (p. 284)
newline-and-indent   ( LFD ) (p. 284)
next-complex-command   (p. 270)
next-file   (p. 316)
next-line   ( Ctrl N ) (p. 275)
not-modified   ( Meta ~ ) (p. 294)
nroff-mode   (p. 266)
occur   (p. 312)
open-line   ( Ctrl O ) (p. 284)
open-rectangle   (p. 290)
other-window   ( Ctrl X o ) (p. 291)
overwrite-mode   (p. 267)
picture-backward-clear-column   (p. 304)
picture-backward-column   (p. 304)
picture-clear-column   (p. 304)
picture-clear-line   (p. 304)
picture-clear-rectangle   (p. 306)
picture-clear-rectangle-to-register   (p. 306)
picture-duplicate-line   (p. 304)
picture-forward-column   (p. 304)
```

```
picture-mode-exit  (p. 303)
picture-motion  (p. 305)
picture-motion-reverse  (p. 305)
picture-move-down  (p. 304)
picture-move-up  (p. 304)
picture-movement-down  (p. 305)
picture-movement-left  (p. 305)
picture-movement-ne  (p. 305)
picture-movement-nw  (p. 305)
picture-movement-right  (p. 305)
picture-movement-se  (p. 305)
picture-movement-sw  (p. 305)
picture-movement-up  (p. 305)
picture-newline  (p. 304)
picture-open-line  (p. 304)
picture-set-tab-stops  (p. 305)
picture-tab  (p. 305)
picture-tab-search  (p. 305)
picture-yank-rectangle  (p. 306)
picture-yank-rectangle-from-register  (p. 306)
plain-tex-mode  (p. 266)
plain-TeX-mode  (p. 266)
point-to-register  (Ctrl X /) (p. 302)
prepend-to-buffer  (p. 280)
previous-complex-command  (p. 270)
previous-line  (Ctrl P) (p. 275)
print-buffer  (p. 302)
print-region  (p. 302)
pwd  (p. 292)
query-replace  (Meta %) (p. 311)
query-replace-regexp  (p. 311)
quietly-read-abbrev-file  (p. 324)
quit-shell-subjob  (p. 318)
quoted-insert  (Ctrl Q) (p. 264)
re-search-backward  (p. 309)
re-search-forward  (p. 309)
read-abbrev-file  (p. 324)
recenter  (Ctrl L) (p. 277)
recover-file  (p. 296)
register-to-point  (Ctrl X j) (p. 303)
rename-buffer  (p. 299)
rename-file  (p. 295)
repeat-complex-command  (Ctrl X ESC) (p. 270)
replace-regexp  (p. 311)
replace-string  (p. 310)
revert-buffer  (p. 299)
rmail  (p. 329)
save-buffer  (Ctrl X Ctrl S) (p. 293)
save-buffers-kill-emacs  (Ctrl X Ctrl C) (p. 274)
save-some-buffers  (Ctrl X s) (p. 293)
scroll-down  (Meta V) (p. 277)
scroll-left  (Ctrl X <) (p. 277)
scroll-other-window  (Meta Ctrl V) (p. 291)
scroll-right  (Ctrl X >) (p. 277)
scroll-up  (Ctrl V) (p. 277)
search-backward  (p. 308)
search-forward  (p. 308)
self-insert  (p. 261)
send-shell-input  (p. 317)
set-fill-column  (Ctrl X f) (p. 281)
set-fill-prefix  (Ctrl X .) (p. 282)
set-goal-column  (Ctrl X Ctrl N) (p. 275)
set-mark-command  (Ctrl @) (p. 280)
set-rmail-inbox-list  (p. 333)
set-selective-display  (Ctrl X $) (p. 282)
```

`yank` (Ctrl Y) (p. 279)
`yank-pop` (Meta Y) (p. 279)
`yank-rectangle` (p. 290)
`yow` (p. 335)
`zap-to-char` (Meta Z) (p. 278)

Dired Commands.

DEL   Removes the deletion flag on this line, moves up one line (p. 297)
SPACE   Moves to the beginning of the file name on the next line (p. 297)
Ctrl N   Moves to the beginning of the file name on the next line (p. 297)
Ctrl P   Moves to the beginning of the file name on the previous line (p. 297)
.   Flags excess numeric backup files for deletion (p. 297)
Flags all auto-save files (p. 297)
?   Provides help on Dired (p. 297)
c   Copies this file (p. 298)
d   Flags this file for later deletion (p. 297)
f   Visits this file (p. 297)
n   Moves to the beginning of the file name on the next line (p. 297)
o   Visits this file in another window (p. 298)
p   Moves to the beginning of the file name on the previous line (p. 297)
r   Renames this file (p. 298)
u   Removes the deletion flag on this line (p. 297)
v   Views this file (p. 298)
x   Deletes all flagged files (p. 297)
~   Flags all backup files (p. 297)

Buffer Menu Commands.

Ctrl D   Marks this buffer for deletion, moves up one line (p. 301)
Ctrl K   Marks this buffer for deletion, moves down one line (p. 301)
Del   Moves up one line (p. 301)
Space   Moves down one line (p. 301)
?   Displays explanations of the buffer menu commands (p. 300)
~   Marks this buffer as unmodified (p. 301)
1   Selects this buffer in a full-screen window (p. 301)
2   Sets up two windows with this buffer and the previously selected one (p. 301)
d   Marks this buffer for deletion, moves down one line (p. 301)
f   Replaces the Buffer List buffer by this buffer (p. 301)
k   Marks this buffer for deletion, moves down one line (p. 301)
m   Marks this buffer for display with q (p. 301)
o   Selects this buffer in another window, leaving the buffer list visible (p. 301)
q   Selects this buffer, displays any buffers marked with m in other windows (p. 301)
s   Marks this buffer for saving (p. 301)
u   Removes all requests from this line, moves down one line (p. 301)
x   Performs all deletions and saves requested so far (p. 301)

Rmail Commands.

Space   Scrolls the current message forward (p. 331)
Ctrl D   Deletes the current message, moves to the previous nondeleted message (p. 331)
Ctrl O *file*   Appends a copy of the current message in UNIX format to *file* (p. 333)
Del   Scrolls the current message backward (p. 331)
Meta N   Moves to the next message, deleted or not (p. 331)
Meta P   Moves to the previous message, deleted or not (p. 331)
Meta S   Moves to the next message matching a specified regular expression (p. 331)
Meta X `set-rmail-inbox-list`   Specifies input mailboxes for Rmail (p. 333)
Meta Ctrl H   Makes a summary of all messages (p. 330)
Meta Ctrl L *labels*   Makes a summary of the messages with a label from *labels* (p. 331)
Meta Ctrl N *labels*   Moves to the next message with a label from *labels* (p. 334)
Meta Ctrl P *labels*   Moves to the previous message with a label from *labels* (p. 334)
Meta Ctrl R *names*   Makes a summary of all messages with a recipient in *names* (p. 331)
- Meta S   Moves to the previous message matching a specified regular expression
        (p. 331)
*n*j   Moves to the *n*th message (p. 331)
.   Scrolls to the beginning of the current message (p. 331)

> Moves to the last message (p. 331)
a *label* Assigns the label *label* to the current message (p. 334)
d Deletes the current message (p. 331)
e Expunges the Rmail file (p. 332)
g Merges new mail from input mailboxes (p. 333)
h Makes a summary of all messages (p. 330)
i *file* Runs Rmail on the messages in *file* (p. 333)
k *label* Removes the label *label* from the current message (p. 334)
n Moves to the next nondeleted message (p. 331)
o *file* Appends a copy of the current message in Rmail format to *file* (p. 333)
p Moves to the previous nondeleted message (p. 331)
q Exits from Rmail (p. 330)
s Saves the Rmail file (p. 330)
u Undeletes the current message or the nearest previous deleted message (p. 331)
x Expunges the Rmail file (p. 332)

Rmail Summary Commands.

[Del] Scrolls the other window backward (p. 334)
[Space] Scrolls the other window forward (p. 334)
[Ctrl] N Moves to the next line and selects its message (p. 334)
[Ctrl] P Moves to the previous line and selects its message (p. 334)
d Deletes the current message, then moves to the next line containing a nondeleted
      message (p. 334)
j Selects the current message (p. 334)
n Moves to the next line containing a nondeleted message and selects its message (p. 334)
p Moves to the previous line containing a nondeleted message and selects its message
      (p. 334)
q Exits from Rmail (p. 335)
u Undeletes and selects this message or the nearest previous deleted message (p. 334)
x Kills the summary window (p. 335)

A.2.30
ex (Extended Editor)

Command-line Options.

+ *cmd* Execute *cmd* before editing (p. 237)
- Suppress terminal interaction (p. 236)
-c *cmd* Execute *cmd* before editing (p. 237)
-v Invoke the visual editor vi (p. 236)
-t *tag* Edit the file containing *tag* (p. 236)
-r *file* Recover from file *file* (p. 236)
-R Edit in readonly mode (p. 237)

Line Addresses and Line Ranges.   The notations for specifying a line address are as follows:

$ The last line of the file (p. 238)
. The current line (p. 238)
n The *n*th line of the file (p. 238)
'*c* The line marked with the letter *c* (p. 238)
'' The line you most recently went to with a non-relative move (p. 238)
/*pat*/ The next line containing the pattern *pat* (p. 238)
?*pat*? The nearest previous line containing the pattern *pat* (p. 238)
[*a*]*n* The address *a* plus *n* lines (p. 239)
[*a*]+[*n*] The address *a* plus *n* lines (p. 239)
[*a*]-[*n*] The address *a* minus *n* lines (p. 239)

The notations for specifying a line range are as follows:

a_1,a_2 Lines a_1 through a_2 (p. 239)
$a_1;a_2$ Like the previous form, but the current line is set to a_1 before a_2 is evaluated
      (p. 239)
% The entire file (p. 239)

Flags on Commands.

Show the last affected line with a line number (p. 240)
- Decrease the line number by 1 before showing a line (p. 240)
+ Increase the line number by 1 before showing a line (p. 240)
l Show the last affected line, showing tabs and the end of line (p. 240)

p   Show (print) the last affected line (p. 240)

Commands.   The text before the brackets indicates the shortest recognized abbreviation. A line address is indicated by *a* and a line range by *r*. A count is indicated by *n*.

r [*flags*]   Shows the lines in range *r* (p. 241)
%   Begins a comment.
(CR)   Shows the next line (p. 241)
a (Ctrl) D   Shows a window of lines starting at line *a* (p. 242)
[*r*] & [*opts*] [*n*] [*flags*]   Repeats the most recent substitution command (p. 247)
[*r*] ! *cmd*   Executes the command *cmd* in a subshell, inserts its output just after *a* (p. 249)
! !   Re-executes the most recently executed shell escape (p. 249)
[*a*]=   Shows the address of the line at *a* (p. 242)
[*r*] > [*n*] [*flags*]   Shifts the lines in region *r* right by one tab (p. 243)
Shows lines with line numbers (p. 241)
[*r*] < [*n*] [*flags*]   Shifts the lines in region *r* left by one tab (p. 244)
* *buf*   Executes the commands in named buffer *buf* (p. 250)
ab[breviate] *lhs rhs*   Makes *lhs* an abbreviation for *rhs* (p. 248)
[*a*] a[ppend][!]   Appends input text after line *a* (p. 242)
ar[gs]   Shows the arguments that were on the command line (p. 242)
[*r*] c[hange][!][*n*]   Deletes the lines in range *r*, then inserts input text (p. 245)
cd *dir*   Changes the current directory to *dir* (p. 247)
[*r*]co[py] *a* [*flags*]   Copies the lines in range *r* to address *a* (p. 244)
[*r*] d[elete][*buf*][*n*][*flags*]   Deletes the lines in range *r*, saving them to an anonymous or named buffer (p. 243)
e[dit][!] [+*cmd*] *file*   Starts editing *file*, discards the current buffer (p. 245)
ex[!] [+*cmd*] *file*   Starts editing *file*, discards the current buffer (p. 245)
f[ile] *file*   Changes the name of the current file to *file* (p. 247)
[*r*] g[lobal][!]/*pat*/*commands*   Performs *commands* globally for those lines matching *pat* (p. 248)
[*a*] i[nsert][!]   Inserts input text after line *a* (p. 243)
[*r*] j[oin][!][*n*]   Joins the lines in *r* (p. 243)
[*a*] k *c*   Marks the line at *a* with the letter *c* (p. 245)
[*r*] l[ist] [*n*] [*flags*]   Shows a group of lines, showing tabs and end of line explicitly (p. 241)
map[!] [*lhs rhs*] (Enter)   Defines a macro, i.e., maps a sequence of keystrokes into another sequence (p. 227)
[*a*] ma[rk] *c*   Marks the line at *a* with the letter *c* (p. 245)
[*r*] m[ove] [*a*]   Moves a group of lines to the location after *a* (p. 244)
n[ext][!] [+*cmd*] [*files*]   Edits the next file, optionally replacing the argument list with *files* and executing *cmd* (p. 246)
[*r*] nu[mber] [*n*] [*flags*]   Shows a group of lines with line numbers (p. 241)
open [*pat*]   Enters open mode at the current line or at the next line matching *pat* (p. 250)
pre[serve] Saves copy of buffer to "preserve" area (p. 250)
[*r*] p[rint] [*n*] [*flags*]   Shows a group of lines (p. 241)
[*a*] pu[t][*buf*]   Puts the lines from the anonymous buffer or from a named buffer after address *a* in the main buffer (p. 244)
q[uit][!]   Quits the editor without writing the buffer (p. 247)
[*a*] r[ead] *file*   Reads *file* into buffer after line *a* (p. 246)
[*a*] r[ead] ! *cmd*   Puts output of *cmd* into buffer after line *a* (p. 249)
rec[over] *file*   Recovers **ex** from *file* after a crash (p. 250)
rew[ind]   Resets list of files to be edited to its beginning (p. 247)
se[t]   Lists all variables and their values (p. 247)
se[t] *x*[=*val*]   Enables variable *x*, sets its value to *val* (p. 247)
se[t] no*x*   Disables variable *x* (p. 247)
sh[ell]   Runs a subshell, then returns to the editor (p. 249)
so[urce]\ *file*   Reads and executes the lines in *file* (p. 250)
st[op]   Stops the editor, suspends its process (p. 247)
[*r*] s[ubstitute] [/*pat*/*repl*/] [*opts*] [*n*] [*flags*]   Replaces the pattern *pat* by the text *repl* (p. 247)
[*r*]t *a*   Copies the lines in range *r* to address *a* (p. 244)
ta[g] *tag*   Opens the tag file containing *tag*, moves the cursor to *tag* (p. 246)
una[breviate] *lhs*   Removes an abbreviation (p. 248)
u[ndo]   Undoes the most recent change or insertion (p. 250)
unm[ap][!] *lhs*   Removes a macro definition (p. 228)
[*r*] v/*pat*/*commands*   Performs *commands* globally for those lines *not* matching *pat* (p. 249)

ve[rsion]   Shows the editor's version number (p. 242)
[a] vi[sual] [*type*] [*n*] [*flags*]   Enters "visual mode" (p. 250)
[*r*] w[rite][!] [>>] *file*   Writes the lines in region *r* to *file* or appends them (p. 246)
[*r*] w[rite] !*cmd*   Executes *cmd* as shell command, *r* is input (p. 249)
wq[!][*file*]   Writes the buffer to *file*, then quits (p. 246)
x[it] [*file*]   Exits from the editor, writes the buffer to *file* if it's been modified (p. 247)
[*r*] y[ank][*buf*][*n*][*flags*]   Copies ("yank") the lines in *r* into an anonymous or named buffer
        (p. 244)
[a] z *t n*   Shows a window of *n* lines with the line at *a* placed in the window according to *t*
        (+, -, ., ^, =) (p. 242)

Variables.   Both ex and vi have the same set of variables; see "Environment Variables" on
page 525 for a list of them.

A.2.31
expr (Evaluate an Expression)

The form of the expr command line (p. 136) is

    expr *expr*

where *expr* is composed from the following operators:

    & | =   !=   >   >=   <   <=
    +   -   *   /   %   :   (...)

The : operator denotes matching of a string by a regular expression.

A.2.32
false (Return False)

The form of the false command line (p. 157) is

    false

It does nothing and returns a nonzero exit code.

A.2.33
fgrep (Find Regular Expression, Fast Version)

The form of the fgrep command line (p. 352) is

    fgrep [*options*] [*pat*] [*file*] ...

where *pat* is a regular expression to be searched for and *file* ... is a list of files to be searched.
The *pat* component is omitted if the -e or -f option is present.

Command-line Options.

-b   Precede each line by its disk block number (p. 352)
-c   Only show a count of matching lines (p. 352)
-e *pat*   Use *pat* as the search pattern (p. 353)
-f *file*   Read the pattern list from *file* (p. 353)
-i   Ignore case of letters in making comparisons (p. 352)
-l   Only show the names of files containing matching strings (p. 352)
-n   Precede each line by its file name and line number (p. 352)
-s   Suppress error messages (System V) or suppress output (BSD UNIX) (p. 352)
-v   Show all lines that *don't* match (p. 352)
-x   Match entire lines only (p. 352)

A.2.34
file (Classify Files)

The form of the command line (p. 62) is

    file [*options*] *file*

where *file* ... is a list of files to be classified.

Command-line Options.

-c   Check the magic file (p. 62)
-f *file*   Read files to be classified from *file* (p. 62)
-L   If a file is a symbolic link, test the file
that the link references rather than the link itself (p. 62)
-m *file*   Use *file* as the magic file (p. 62)

A.2.35
find (Find Files)

The form of the command line (p. 62) is

> find *pathlist criterion*

where *pathlist* specifies a set of files and directories to be searched recursively and *criterion* specifies tests applied to each file in the set.

Components of the Criterion. A numerical value *n* in a criterion is interpreted as follows:

- *n* by itself indicates exactly the value *n*.
- *−n* indicates a value less than *n*.
- *+n* indicates a value greater than *n*.

p True if the permissions of the current file are given by the octal number *p* (p. 64)
\(Begin grouped criterion (p. 66)
\) End grouped criterion (p. 66)
! Negate criterion (p. 66)
-atime *n* True if the current file was accessed within the past *n* days (p. 64)
-cpio *file* True for ordinary files, false for others; appends the current file (if ordinary) to *file* in cpio format (p. 65)
-ctime *n* True if the i-node information of the current file was modified within the past *n* days (p. 64)
-depth Always true; processes directory entries before the directory itself (p. 66)
-exec *cmd* Execute *cmd*, return true if the exit status is 0 (p. 65)
-group *gname* True if *gname* is the group of the current file (p. 64)
-inum *n* True if the current file starts with i-node *n* (p. 65)
-links *n* True if the current file has *n* links (p. 64)
-local True if the current file resides on the local system (p. 65)
-mtime *n* True if the current file was modified within the past *n* days (p. 64)
-name *file* True if the current file matches *file* (p. 63)
-newer *file* True if the current file has been modified more recently than *file* (p. 65)
-mount Always true; restricts the search to the file system containing the current pathname from *pathlist* (p. 66)
-o *cmd* Take logical "or" of criteria (p. 66)
-ok *cmd* Like -exec but ask for confirmation (p. 65)
-perm *p* True if the permissions of the current file are given by the octal number *p* (p. 64)
-print Always true, send file name to standard output (p. 65)
-size *n* True if the current file is *n* blocks long (p. 64)
-size *nc* True if the current file is *n* characters long (p. 64)
-type *c* True if the type of the current file is *c*, where *c* is -, d, b, c, or p (p. 63)
-user *uname* True if *uname* is the owner of the current file (p. 64)
-xdev Always true; restricts the search to the file system containing the current pathname from *pathlist* (p. 66)

A.2.36
finger
(Look Up Information about a User)

The form of the `finger` command line (p. 105) is

> finger [*options*] [*name*] ...

where each *name* is a case-insensitive substring of the name of a user.

Command-line Options.

-l Use long output format (p. 106)
-m Match arguments against exact user names (p. 106)
-p Don't show .plan files (p. 106)
-s Force short output format (p. 106)

A.2.37
ftp (Transfer Files with File Transfer Protocol)

The form of the `ftp` command line (p. 431) is

> ftp [*options*] [*host*]

If *host* is specified, `ftp` immediately attempts to connect to that host.

Command-line Options.

-d Enable debugging (p. 445)
-g Disable wildcard substitution (globbing) in file names (p. 445)
-i Turn off interactive prompting during multiple file transfers (p. 445)

-n   Don't do auto-login on initial connection (p. 445)
-t   Enable packet tracing (unimplemented) (p. 445)
-v   Show responses from remote server and statistics (p. 445)

Commands.

(EOF)   Terminates `ftp` (p. 432)
! [cmd]   Runs cmd locally in a subshell (p. 440)
$ mac [arg] ...   Executes macro mac with arguments arg ... (p. 442)
? [cmd]   Provides help information on cmd (p. 433)
ac[count] [passwd]   Supplies a supplemental remote password (p. 432)
ap[pend] lfile [rfile]   Appends local file lfile to remote file rfile (p. 436)
as[cii]   Uses network ASCII as the representation type (p. 439)
be[ll]   Sounds a bell after each file transfer (p. 440)
bi[nary]   Uses image as the representation type (p. 439)
by[e]   Terminates `ftp` (p. 432)
ca[se]   Toggles case mapping for remote file names (p. 437)
cd rdir   Changes the remote directory to rdir (p. 434)
cdu[p]   Changes the remote directory to its parent (p. 434)
ch[mod] mode rfile   Changes the permissions of remote file rfile to mode (p. 434)
cl[ose]   Terminates the remote connection but remains in `ftp` (p. 433)
cr   Toggles stripping of carriage returns for ASCII file transfers (p. 439)
del[ete] rfile   Deletes remote file rfile (p. 434)
deb[ug] [n]   Sets the debugging level to n or toggle debugging (p. 441)
dir [rdir [lfile]]   Sends listing of remote directory rdir to local file lfile (p. 435)
dis[connect]   Terminates the remote connection, remains in `ftp` (p. 433)
f[orm] [fmt]   Uses 'non-print' for interpreting vertical format controls (p. 440)
ge[t] rfile [lfile]   Retrieves remote file rfile, stores it in local file lfile (p. 436)
gl[ob]   Toggles wildcard expansion, called "globbing", for file names (p. 437)
ha[sh]   Toggles use of '#' to indicate when a data block is transferred (p. 440)
he[lp] [cmd]   Provides help information on cmd (p. 433)
id[le] [n]   Sets the inactivity timer of the remote machine to n seconds (p. 433)
im[age]   Uses image as the representation type (p. 439)
lc[d] [dir]   Changes the current local directory to dir (p. 440)
ls [rdir [lfile]]   Sends short listing of remote directory rdir to local file lfile (p. 435)
ma[cdef] mac   Defines a macro named mac (p. 442)
mde[lete] [rfile] ...   Deletes the remote file rfile ... (p. 434)
mdi[r] rfile ... lfile   Sends listing of remote files rfile ... to lfile (p. 435)
mg[et] rfile ...   Gets the specified remote files (p. 436)
mk[dir] dir   Makes directory dir on the remote machine (p. 434)
ml[s] rfile ... lfile   Sends short listing of specified remote files to local file lfile (p. 435)
mode [name]   Sets the transfer mode to name (p. 440)
modt[ime] rfile   Shows the time when remote file rfile was last modified (p. 435)
mp[ut] lfile ...   Transmits the specified local files to the remote machine (p. 437)
ne[wer] rfile [lfile]   Retrieves remote file rfile and copies it to lfile, but only if it's newer (p. 436)
nl[ist] [rdir [lfile]]   Sends listing of remote directory rdir to local file lfile (p. 435)
nm[ap] inpat outpat   Maps file names according to inpat and outpat (p. 437)
nt[rans] [inchars [outchars]]   Sets translation for characters in file names (p. 438)
o[pen] host [port]   Connects to host at the specified port or the default port (p. 432)
prom[pt]   Toggles interactive prompting during multiple file transfers (p. 440)
prox[y] cmd   Executes cmd on a remote machine (p. 441)
pu[t] lfile [rfile]   Transmits local file lfile to the remote machine (p. 436)
pw[d]   Shows the name of the working directory on the remote machine (p. 434)
qui[t]   Terminates `ftp` (p. 432)
quo[te] arg ...   Sends the specified arguments to the remote machine (p. 433)
rec[v] rfile [lfile]   Retrieves remote file rfile, stores it in local file lfile (p. 436)
reg[et] rfile [lfile]   Retrieves remote file rfile, but only if it's longer than the corresponding local file (p. 436)
remoteh[elp] [cmd]   Requests help information on cmd from the remote machine (p. 433)
remotes[tatus] [rfile]   Shows the current status of remote file rfile or of the remote machine (p. 441)
ren[ame] name₁ name₂   Renames file $name_1$ on the remote machine to $name_2$ (p. 434)
rese[t]   Resynchronizes communication with the remote machine (p. 433)
rest[art] marker   Restarts the immediately following get or put at the position given by marker (p. 433)

rm[dir] *dir*　　Deletes directory *dir* on the remote machine.

ru[nique]　　Toggles creation of unique names for files gotten from the remote machine (p. 438)

send *lfile* [*rfile*]　　Transmits local file *lfile* to the remote machine (p. 436)

sendp[ort]　　Toggles the use of PORT commands (p. 433)

sit[e] *arg* ...　　Sends the command SITE *arg* ... to the remote machine (p. 433)

siz[e] *rfile*　　Shows the size of remote file *rfile* (p. 435)

sta[tus]　　Shows the current status of ftp (p. 440)

str[uct] [*name*]　　Sets the file structure to *name* (p. 440)

su[nique]　　Toggles generation of unique names for files sent to the remote machine (p. 438)

sy[stem]　　Shows the type of operating system running on the remote machine (p. 441)

te[nex]　　Uses the representation type appropriate to TENEX machines (p. 439)

tr[ace]　Toggles packet tracing (unimplemented) (p. 441)

ty[pe] *name*　　Uses *name* as the representation type (p. 439)

um[ask] [*mask*]　　Sets the default file permission mask on the remote machine to *mask* (p. 435)

us[er] *usrname* [*passwd*$_1$ [*passwd*$_2$]]　　Identifies yourself to the remote machine (p. 432)

v[erbose]　　Toggles verbose mode for showing ftp responses (p. 441)

A.2.38
grep
(Find Regular Expression)

The form of the grep command line (p. 352) is

> grep [*options*] *pat* [*file*] ...

where *pat* is a regular expression to be searched for and *file* ... is a list of files to be searched.

Command-line Options.

-b　　Precede each line by its disk block number (p. 352)

-c　　Only show a count of matching lines (p. 352)

-i　　Ignore case of letters in making comparisons (p. 352)

-l　　Only show the names of files containing matching strings (p. 352)

-n　　Precede each line by its file name and line number (p. 352)

-s　　Show only error messages (p. 352)

-v　　Show all lines that *don't* match (p. 352)

-w　　Search for the pattern as a word (p. 352)

A.2.39
id (Show User and Group ID's)

The form of the id command line (p. 121) is

> id

A.2.40
kill (Signal a Process)

The form of the kill command is

> kill [-*signum*] *pid*

The signal whose number is *signum* is sent to the process whose number is *pid*. The default signal is #15 (terminate).

A.2.41
ln (Link File Names)

The forms of the ln command (p. 71) are

> ln [*options*] *file*$_1$ *file*$_2$
> ln [*options*] *file* ... *dir*

In the first form, a link is created from *file*$_2$ to the file named by *file*$_1$. In the second form, a link is created from *dir* to each file in *file* ... .

Command-line Options.

-f　　Force confirmation even when overwriting a link lacking write permission (p. 71)

-s　　Make a symbolic link (not all systems) (p. 71)

A.2.42
login (Log In)

The form of the an initial login (p. 117) is

> *name* [*var-setting*] . . .

The form of a replacement login is

> **exec login** [*name* [*var-settings* . . .]]

Each *var-setting* has the form

> [*name* =] *value*

A.2.43
lp
(Send Files to a Printer)

The form of the **lp** command line (p. 86) is

> **lp** [*options*] [*file*] . . .

where each *file* is a file to be printed. Some versions of **lp** allow options and files to be intermixed.

Command-line Options.

-c   Make copies of the files when the command is executed (p. 87)
-d *dest*   Send the job to the specific printer or class of printers named by *dest* (p. 87)
-m   Send a mail message when the job is completed (p. 87)
-n *n*   Make *n* copies of the output (p. 87)
-o *printopt*   Specify a printer option (p. 87)
-s   Suppress messages (p. 87)
-t *title*   Put *title* on the banner page of the output (p. 87)
-w   Write a message to your terminal when all files have been printed (p. 87)

A.2.44
lpr
(Berkeley Print Spooler)

The form of the **lpr** command line (p. 88) is

> **lpr** [options] [*file*] . . .

where the *files* are the files to be printed.

Command-line Options.

#*n text*   Print *n* copies (p. 88)
-C *text*   Use *text* as the system name on the header page (p. 89)
-f   Interpret the first character of each line as Fortran carriage control (p. 88)
-h   Suppress the header page (p. 89)
-i [*n*]   Indent the output by *n* columns (p. 88)
-J *text*   Use *text* as the job name on the header page (p. 88)
-l   Print control characters, suppress page breaks (p. 88)
-m   Send a mail message upon completion (p. 88)
-p   Pass the files through **pr** (p. 88)
-P *printer*   Print the job on the printer named *printer* (p. 88)
-l   Print control characters, suppress page breaks (p. 88)
-r   Remove the file after printing it (p. 88)
-s   Use symbolic links for the files to be printed (p. 88)
-T *text*   Use *text* as the title passed to **pr** (p. 88)
-w *n*   Pass *n* to **pr** as the page width (p. 88)

In addition to these options, **lpr** has options for filtering the output of specific programs. These options depend on the installation.

A.2.45
lpstat (Show Printer Status)

The form of the **lpstat** command line (p. 89) is

> **lpstat** [*options*]

Command-line Options.   In the following commands, *list* is a list of names of printers and classes of printers.

-a [*list*]   Show the acceptance status of each item in *list* (p. 89)
-c [*list*]   Show the names of the printer classes and their members (p. 89)
-d   Show the name of the default printer (p. 89)
-o [*list*]   Show the status of each output request in *list* (p. 89)
-p [*list*]   Show the status of each printer in *list* (p. 89)

-r   Show the status of the request scheduler (p. 89)
-s   Show a summary of the printers known to your system (p. 89)
-t   Show all status information (p. 89)
-u [*ulist*]   Show the status of each output request for each user in *ulist* (p. 89)
-v [*list*]   Show the path names associated with the printers in *list* (p. 89)

A.2.46
`ls` (File Lister)

-a   List all files, including those whose names begin with a dot (p. 59)
-b   Show nonprinting characters in octal (p. 60)
-c   Use time of last i-node modification (p. 60)
-C   Produce multicolumn output, sorted down columns (p. 60)
-d   List directory names only, not contents (p. 59)
-f   List files in directories, not the directories themselves (p. 59)
-F   Put '/' after listed directories and '*' after executable files (p. 60)
-g   List the files in long format, omitting the owner (p. 60)
-i   For each file, print the number of its i-node (p. 60)
-l   List the files in long format (p. 60)
-m   List the files separated by commas (p. 60)
-n   List the files in long format, with user and group numbers (p. 60)
-o   List the files in long format, omitting the group (p. 60)
-p   Put '/' after listed directories (p. 59)
-q   Show nonprinting characters as '?' (p. 61)
-r   List the files in reverse order (p. 60)
-R   List subdirectories recursively (p. 59)
-s   Give the size of each file in blocks (p. 60)
-t   List the files in chronological order (p. 60)
-u   Use time of last access (p. 60)
-x   Produce multicolumn output, sorted across rows (p. 60)

A.2.47
`mail` (Simple Mailer)

The form of the `mail` command line (p. 403) is

mail [*options*] [*namelist*]

where *namelist* is a list of recipients.

Command-line Options for Sending Mail.
-o   Don't optimize addresses (p. 404)
-s   Don't put an empty line between the From line and the text of the message (p. 404)
-w   Don't wait for remote transfer to complete (p. 404)
-t   Put a To: line before the message text (p. 404)

Command-line Options for Receiving Mail.
-e   Exit immediately with status 0 if you have mail, 1 if you don't (p. 404)
-f *file*   Read messages from *file* (p. 404)
-h   Show a window of message headers first (p. 404)
-p   Show all messages, don't prompt for commands (p. 404)
-q   Terminate `mail` entirely on interrupt, not just one message (p. 404)
-r   Process messages in oldest to newest order (p. 404)

Commands.
(Enter)   Shows the next message (p. 405)
(EOF)   Quits, leaving undeleted mail in the primary mailbox (p. 405)
n   Shows message number *n* (p. 405)
!*cmd*   Executes *cmd* in a subshell (p. 406)
-   Shows the previous message (p. 405)
+   Shows the next message (p. 405)
?   Shows a summary of the `mail` commands (p. 405)
a   Shows the most recently arrived message (p. 405)
d   Deletes the current message (p. 406)
d *n*   Deletes message number *n* (p. 406)
dp   Deletes the current message (p. 406)
dq   Deletes the current message and quit (p. 406)
h   Shows a window of headers (p. 405)

h *n*   Shows the header of message number *n* (p. 405)
h a   Shows the headers of messages in the primary mailbox (p. 405)
h d   Shows the headers of deleted messages (p. 405)
m *namelist*   Send the current message to *namelist*, mark it for deletion (p. 406)
p   Shows the current message again (p. 405)
q   Quits, leaving undeleted mail in the primary mailbox (p. 405)
r [*namelist*]   Composes a reply to the current message (p. 406)
s [*filelist*]   Saves the current message in each file of *filelist* and expunges it (p. 406)
u [*n*]   Undeletes message number *n* (p. 406)
w [*filelist*]   Like **s**, but doesn't save the first header line (p. 406)
x   Quits, leaving the primary mailbox unchanged (p. 405)
y [*filelist*]   Saves the current message in each file of *filelist* and expunge it (p. 406)

A.2.48
`mailx`
(Berkeley Mailer)

The command line for sending mail via `mailx` has the form

> `mailx` [*options*] *namelist*

The command line for retrieving mail via `mailx` has the form

> `mailx` *options*

In these forms, *options* is a sequence of options taken from those listed below and *namelist* is a sequence of intended recipients for the message.

Command-line Options.   The command-line options for sending mail are as follows:

-F   Save mail in a file named after the first recipient (p. 383)
-i   Ignore interrupts (p. 383)
-n   Don't initialize from `mailx.rc` (p. 385)
-s *string*   Set message subject to *string* (p. 383)

The command-line options for retrieving mail are as follows:

-e   Just test for presence of mail (p. 384)
-f *file*   Read mail from *file* (p. 384)
-h *n*   Set number of network hops so far to *n* (p. 384)
-H   Show header summary only (p. 384)
-I   Take message authors to be newsgroups, not individuals (p. 384)
-n   Don't initialize from `mailx.rc` (p. 385)
-N   Don't show initial header summary (p. 384)
-r *addr*   Pass the address *addr* to network delivery software, disable '~' commands (p. 384)
-T *file*   Save list of `Article-Id` fields in *file* (p. 384)
-u *user*   Read mail from *user*'s mailbox (p. 384)
-U   Convert uucp addresses to Internet addresses (p. 384)

Notation for Message Lists.

n   Message number *n* (p. 386)
^   The first message that you haven't deleted (p. 386)
$ The last message (whether deleted or not) (p. 386)
.   The current message (p. 386)
*   All the messages in the message list (p. 386)

Commands for Command Mode.   An optional *msglist* is taken as referring to all messages in the current message set. An optional *msg* is taken as referring to the current message.

(Enter)   Shows the next message (p. 389)
n   Shows message number *n* (p. 389)
! *cmd*   Executes *cmd* in a subshell (p. 394)
| [*msglist*] [*cmd*]   Passes the messages in *msglist* as standard input to *cmd* (p. 394)
-[*n*]   Shows the *n*th previous message (p. 389)
.   Shows the current message number (p. 388)
=   Shows the current message number (p. 388)
Treats the rest of the line as a comment (p. 395)
?   Shows a summary of commands (p. 388)
a[**lias**] *name namelist*   Treats *name* as an alias for each name in *namelist* (p. 394)
alt[**ernates**] *namelist*   Treats the names in *namelist* as alternates for your login name (p. 394)
cd *dir*   Changes the current directory to *dir* (p. 393)
ch[**dir**] *dir*   Changes the current directory to *dir* (p. 393)

c[opy] [*msglist*] [*file*]   Copies messages in *msglist* to *file* without marking them as saved (p. 392)

C[opy] [*msglist*]   Saves each message in *msglist* in a file named by the message's author (p. 392)

d[elete] [*msglist*]   Deletes messages in *msglist* from the mailbox (p. 392)

di[scard] *header-field-list*   Doesn't show the specified header fields when showing messages (p. 389)

dp [*msglist*]   Deletes messages in *msglist* from the mailbox, shows the message after the last one deleted (p. 392)

dt [*msglist*]   Deletes messages in *msglist* from the mailbox, shows the message after the last one deleted (p. 392)

ec[ho] *string*   Echoes the string *string* (p. 395)

e[dit] [*msglist*]   Edits the messages in *msglist* (p. 393)

ex[it]   Exits from `mailx`, leave the mailbox unchanged (p. 393)

fi[le] *file*   Stops processing the current set of messages, takes a new set from *file* (p. 393)

fold[er] *file*   Stops processing the current set of messages, takes a new set from *file* (p. 393)

folders   Shows the names of the files in the directory specified by the `folder` variable (p. 389)

fo[llowup] [*msg*]   Responds to the message *msg* and records the response in a file named for the message's author (p. 390)

F[ollowup] *msglist*   Responds to the first message in *msglist*, sends the response to the author of each message in *msglist* (p. 390)

f[rom] [*msglist*]   Shows the header summary for *msglist* (p. 388)

g[roup] *name namelist*   Treats *name* as an alias for each name in *namelist* (p. 394)

h[eaders] *msg*   Shows the page of the header summary that includes *msg* (p. 388)

hel[p]   Shows a summary of commands (p. 388)

ho[ld] [*msglist*]   Leaves the messages of *msglist* in the mailbox (p. 391)

if (s or r) *action*₁ else *action*₂ endif   Executes *action₁* or *action₂* depending on send or receive mode (p. 395)

ig[nore] *header-field-list*   Doesn't show the specified header fields when showing messages (p. 389)

l[ist]   Lists available commands without explanations (p. 388)

m[ail] *namelist*   Composes and mails a message to the people in *namelist* (p. 390)

Mail *name*   Composes a message to *name* and saves a copy of it in a file named for that person (p. 390)

mb[ox] [*msglist*]   Causes the messages in *msglist* to be saved in the secondary mailbox when `mailx` terminates (p. 391)

n[ext] *msg*   Goes to the next message matching *msg* (p. 389)

pi[pe] [*msglist*] [*cmd*]   Passes the messages in *msglist* as standard input to *cmd* (p. 394)

pre[serve] [*msglist*]   Leaves the messages of *msglist* in the mailbox (p. 391)

P[rint] [*msglist*]   Shows the messages of *msglist*, including all header fields (p. 389)

p[rint] [*msglist*]   Shows the messages of *msglist* (p. 389)

q[uit]   Quits `mailx`, saving messages you've read in the secondary mailbox (p. 393)

R[eply] [*msglist*]   Composes a response to the author of each message in *msglist* (p. 390)

r[eply] [*msg*]   Composes a response to *msg* and sends it to the author and to all other recipients of *msg* (p. 390)

R[espond] [*msglist*]   Composes a response to the author of each message in *msglist* (p. 390)

r[espond] [*msg*]   Composes a response to *msg* and sends it to the author and to all other recipients of *msg* (p. 390)

S[ave] [*msglist*]   Saves messages of *msglist* in a file named for the author of the first message in *msglist* (p. 391)

s[ave] [*msglist*] [*file*]   Saves the messages of *msglist* in *file* (p. 391)

se[t]   Shows all `mailx` variables and their values (p. 394)

se[t] *name*   Sets the `mailx` variable *name* (p. 395)

se[t] *name=string*   Sets the `mailx` variable *name* to *string* (p. 395)

se[t] *name=n*   Sets the `mailx` variable *name* to the number *n* (p. 395)

se[t] no*name*   Disables the variable *name* (p. 395)

sh[ell]   Calls a subshell (p. 394)

si[ze] [*msglist*]   Shows the size, in characters, of the messages in *msglist* (p. 389)

so[urce] *file*   Reads and executes commands from *file* (p. 393)

to[p] [*msglist*]   Shows the top few lines of the messages of *msglist* (p. 388)

tou[ch] [*msglist*]   "Touches" the messages of *msglist* so they appear to have been read (p. 389)

T[ype] [*msglist*]   Shows the messages of *msglist*, including all header fields (p. 389)

t[ype] [*msglist*]   Shows the messages of *msglist* (p. 389)

u[ndelete] [*msglist*]   Undeletes the messages of *msglist* (p. 392)
un[set] *namelist*   Erases the `mailx` variables in *namelist* (p. 395)
ve[rsion]   Shows the version number and release date of this `.mailx` (p. 388)
v[isual] [*msglist*]   Edits the messages in *msglist* using your visual editor (p. 393)
write [*msglist*] *file*   Writes the messages of *msglist* to *file*, omitting headers and the trailing blank line (p. 392)
x[it]   Exits from `mailx`, leaving the mailbox unchanged (p. 393)
z   Scrolls the header summary one screen forward (p. 389)
z+   Scrolls the header summary one screen forward (p. 389)
z-   Scrolls the header summary one screen backward (p. 389)

Commands for Input Mode.   The commands for input mode all start with '~'.

~!   Calls a subshell (p. 398)
~.   Terminates message input (p. 398)
~:*cmd*   Performs the command *cmd* (p. 398)
~_ *cmd*   Performs the command *cmd* (p. 398)
~?   Shows summary of '~' commands (p. 396)
~~< *file*   Inserts the contents of *file* into the message text (p. 397)
~~!*cmd*   Executes *cmd*, inserts its standard output into the message text (p. 397)
~~*text*   Appends '~*text*' to the message (p. 397)
~| *cmd*   Pipes the message text through *cmd*, replacing the text with the standard output of *cmd* (p. 397)
~a   Inserts autograph 'sign' into the message text (p. 397)
~A   Inserts autograph 'Sign' into the message text (p. 397)
~b *namelist*   Adds names in *namelist* to 'Bcc' (blind carbon copy) list (p. 398)
~c *namelist*   Adds names in *namelist* to 'Cc' (carbon copy) list (p. 398)
~d   Inserts the contents of the `dead.letter` file (p. 397)
~e   Edits the message text using your designated editor (p. 396)
~f [*msglist*] Forwards the messages from *msglist* by inserting them into the message text (p. 397)
~h   Prompts for header fields (p. 398)
~i *var*   Inserts value of *var* into the text (p. 397)
~m [*msglist*]   Inserts the messages of *msglist* into the text of the message you're composing (p. 397)
~p   Shows the message text (p. 396)
~q   Quits, saving the message text in `dead.letter` (p. 398)
~r *file*   Inserts the contents of *file* into the message text (p. 397)
~s *string*   Sets the subject line to *string* (p. 398)
~t *namelist*   Adds names in *namelist* to 'To' (recipient) list (p. 398)
~v   Edits the message text using your designated visual editor (p. 396)
~w *file*   Writes the message text to *file* (without the header) (p. 396)
~x   Quits, abandoning the message text (p. 398)

Environment Variables.

allnet   Treat network names as identical if their last components match (p. 401)
append   Append rather than prepend messages to `mbox` file (p. 400)
asksub   Prompt for a subject if one isn't given on the command line (p. 400)
autoprint   Enable automatic showing of messages after delete, undelete (p. 399)
bang   Enable '!!' for repeating the previous shell command (p. 400)
cmd=*cmd*   Set default for | (pipe) to *cmd* (p. 400)
conv=*style*   Convert uucp addresses to form of *style* (normally *style* is internet) (p. 403)
crt=*nbr*   Pipe messages of more than *nbr* lines through your pager (p. 399)
DEAD=*file*   Save partial messages that were interrupted in *file* (p. 402)
debug   Turn on verbose diagnostics, don't deliver messages (p. 399)
dot   Take a dot on a line by itself as end of message (p. 400)
EDITOR=*cmd*   Use *cmd* as editor for the ~e command (p. 402)
escape=*c*   Use *c* as the escape character (p. 402)
folder=*dir*   Save standard mail files in directory *dir* (p. 401)
header   Show the header summary when starting `mailx` (p. 399)
hold   Preserve messages that you've read in your primary mailbox, not the secondary mailbox (p. 401)
HOME=*dir*   Use *dir* as your home directory (p. 399)
ignore   Ignore interrupts while entering messages (p. 400)
ignoreeof   Ignore end of file during message input (p. 400)

keep Don't remove an empty mailbox (p. 400)
keepsave Keep messages saved to specific files in mbox as well (p. 400)
MAILRC=*file* Use *file* as the mailx startup file (p. 399)
MBOX=*file* Put messages you've read in *file* (p. 402)
metoo Delete your login from recipient lists (p. 400)
LISTER=*cmd* Use *cmd* to list contents of the folder directory (p. 402)
onehop Disable alterations to remote recipients' addresses (p. 402)
outfolder Keep outgoing messages in the directory specified by folder (p. 401)
page Put formfeed after each message sent through a pipe (p. 401)
PAGER=*cmd* Use *cmd* as the pager for showing long messages (p. 399)
prompt=*string* Set command mode prompt to *string* (p. 399)
quiet Don't show the opening message when starting mailx (p. 399)
record=*file* Record all outgoing mail in *file* (p. 401)
save Enable saving of interrupted messages (p. 401)
screen=*n* Set the number of lines in a screenful of the header summary to *n* (p. 399)
sendmail=*cmd* Use *cmd* to deliver messages (p. 402)
sendwait Don't return until background mailer is finished (p. 400)
SHELL=*cmd* Use *cmd* as your shell (p. 402)
showto Show the recipient's name for messages from you when showing the header summary (p. 399)
sign=*string* Use *string* as signature for *a* command (p. 401)
Sign=*string* Use *string* as signature for *A* command (p. 401)
toplines=*n* Show *n* lines for the top command (p. 399)
VISUAL=*cmd* Use *cmd* as editor for the ~v command (p. 402)

A.2.49 mesg (Lock Out Messages)

The form of the mesg command line (p. 135) is

 mesg *options*

If no options are specified, mesg reports the message status.

Command-line Options.

-n Don't allow others to write to your terminal (p. 135)
-y Allow others to write to your terminal (p. 135)

A.2.50 mkdir (Make a Directory)

The form of the mkdir command line (p. 93) is

 mkdir [*options*] *dir* ...

Here each *dir* is the absolute pathname of a directory you want to create.

Command-line Options. The following options apply to mkdir:

-m *n* Set the permissions of each created directory to *n* (p. 93)
-p Create intermediate empty directories if necessary (p. 93)

A.2.51 mknod (Make a Special File)

The form of the mknod command line (p. 74) is

 mknod *file option*

where *file* is the name of the file to be constructed and *option* specifies its type:

-b n_1 n_2 Block special file with major number n_1, minor number n_2
-c n_1 n_2 Character special file with major number n_1, minor number n_2
-p Named pipe

A.2.52 mv (Move Files)

The forms of the mv command (p. 72) are

 mv [*options*] *file*$_1$ *file*$_2$
 mv [*options*] *file* ... *dir*

In the first form, *file*$_1$ is renamed to *file*$_2$. In the second form, each file in *file* ... is renamed to a file in *dir* having the same file identifier.

Command-line Options.

-f Don't ask for confirmation even when overwriting a link lacking write permission (p. 72)
-i Ask for confirmation when overwriting any link (p. 72)

A.2.53
newgrp (Change Your Current Group)

The form of the newgrp command line (p. 120) is

    newgrp [-] [*group*]

where *group* is the name of the group that you want to join. – indicates that the effect should be as though you had just logged in as a member of *group*.

A.2.54
nice
(Run a Command at Low Priority)

The form of the nice command line (p. 116) is

    nice [-*n*] *cmd* [*arg*] . . .

where *n* is a decrease in priority and the *arg*s are the arguments of *cmd*.

A.2.55
nohup (Ignore Hangups)

The form of the nohup command line (p. 114) is

    nohup *command* [*argument* . . .]

A.2.56
od (Octal Dump)

The form of the od command (p. 83) line is

    od [*options*] *file offset*

options, *file*, and *offset* are all optional. *offset*, the starting byte, has the form (p. 83)

    [+] *n* [.] [b]

n Offset value.
. Take offset value in decimal, not octal.
+ Optional separator from *file*.
b Take offset in 512-byte blocks, not single bytes.

Command-line Options. The options indicate the display modes and units:

-b Show bytes in octal (p. 83)
-c Show bytes as ASCII characters (p. 83)
-d Show words in signed decimal (p. 83)
-o Show words in octal (p. 83)
-x Show words in hexadecimal (p. 83)

A.2.57
pack (Pack Files)

The form of the pack command line (p. 95) is

    pack [*options*] *file* . . .

Command-line Options.

- Show a report on the encoding (p. 95)
-f Force packing of a file even if nothing is gained (p. 95)

where *file* . . . is a list of files to be packed.

A.2.58
paste
(Paste Input Fields)

The form of the paste command line (p. 343) is

    paste [*options*] [*file*] . . .

Command-line Options.

-d*list* Use the characters in *list* circularly as separators (p. 343)
-s Merge lines serially from one file (p. 344)

A.2.59
pcat **(Unpack and Concatenate Files)**

The form of the pcat command line (p. 95) is

   pcat *file* ...

where *file* ... is a list of files to be unpacked and sent to standard output.

A.2.60
pg **(Page Through a List of Files)**

The form of the pg command line (p. 84) is

   pg [*options*] *file* /dots

Command-line Options.

-*n*   Use *n* as the window size (p. 85)
+*n*   Start examining the file at line *n* (p. 85)
+/*pat*/   Start examining the file at the line containing *pat* (p. 85)
-c   Clear the screen before showing each page (p. 85)
-e   Don't pause at the end of examining a file (p. 85)
-f   Don't split lines longer than the screen width (p. 85)
-n   Don't wait for (Enter) at the end of a command (p. 86)
-p *str*   Use *str* as the command prompt (p. 85)
-s   Show messages in inverse video or the equivalent (p. 86)

Commands.   In the following commands, *n* indicates a signed or unsigned integer.

[*n*] (Enter)   Shows the *n*th page (p. 84)
[*n*] (SPACE)   Shows the *n*th page (p. 84)
[*n*] (Ctrl) D   Scrolls down (or up) by half a page (p. 84)
(Ctrl) L   Shows the current page again (p. 85)
! *cmd*   Executes *cmd* in a subshell (p. 85)
^*pat*^   Searchs backwards for the pattern *pat* (p. 84)
$ Shows the last windowfull of the file (p. 84)
.   Shows the current page again (p. 85)
?*pat*?   Searches backwards for the pattern *pat* (p. 84)
/*pat*/   Searches forward for the pattern *pat* (p. 84)
[*n*]d   Scrolls down (or up) by half a page (p. 84)
h   Shows a help list (p. 84)
[*k*]n   Examines the *k*th next file (p. 85)
[*k*]p   Examines the *k*th previous file (p. 85)
q   Quits the program (p. 85)
Q   Quits the program (p. 85)
s *file*   Saves the file now being examined in *file* (p. 85)
[*k*]w   Moves forward one window, set the window size to *k* (p. 85)
s *file*   Saves the file now being examined in *file* (p. 85)

A.2.61
pr
(Format Files for Printing)

The form of the pr command line (p. 90) is

   pr [*options*] [*file*] ...

Command-line Options.

+*n*   Start formatted output at page *n* (p. 92)
-*n*   Format using *n* columns (p. 91)
-a   Format columns across the page (p. 91)
-d   Format with double spacing (p. 92)
-e[*c*][*k*]   Replace tabs by spaces up to every *k*th position, with *c* as tab character (p. 91)
-f   End pages with formfeeds rather than linefeeds (p. 92)
-h *text*   Use *text* as the page header text (p. 91)
-i[*c*][*k*]   Replace spaces by tabs to every *k*th position, with *c* as tab character (p. 91)
-l *n*   Set the page length to *n* lines (p. 91)
-m   Merge and format files, one file per column (p. 91)
-n[*c*][*k*]   Provide *k*-digit line numbers followed by tab character *c* (p. 92)
-o *n*   Offset each line by *n* spaces (p. 91)
-p   Pause before starting each page (p. 92)
-r   Don't issue messages about files that can't be opened (p. 92)
-s [*c*]   Use *c* as the separator character between columns (p. 91)
-t   Don't set aside space for top and bottom margins (p. 91)
-w *n*   Set the line width to *n* characters (p. 91)

A.2.62
ps (List Processes, System V Version)

The form of the ps command line (p. 109) is

     ps [*options*]

Command-line Options.   In the following options, a *list* is a sequence of items separated by spaces or commas.

-a   Produce information about every process except for process group leaders and
       processes not associated with a terminal (p. 109)
-d   Produce information about every process except for process group leaders (p. 109)
-e   Produce information about every process (p. 109)
-f   Produce a full listing (p. 110)
-g *grouplist*   Produce only output pertaining to the specified process groups (p. 110)
-l   Produce an extended (long) listing (p. 110)
-n *name*   Produce output for the processes running on system *name* (p. 110)
-p *proclist*   Produce only output pertaining to the specified processes (p. 110)
-t *termlist*   Produce only output pertaining to the specified terminals (p. 110)
-u *userlist*   Produce only output pertaining to the specified users (p. 109)

A.2.63
ps (List Processes, BSD UNIX Version)

The form of the ps command line (p. 111) is

     ps [-] [*options*] [*pid*]

where *pid* is a process id. See your system manual for other information that can appear on the command line.

Command-Line Options.

a   Produce information about all processes with terminals (p. 111)
c   Show the internally stored command name (p. 112)
e   Show the environment as well as the command (p. 112)
g   Produce information about all processes (p. 111)
k   Use the /vmcore file (p. 113)
l   Produce a long listing (p. 112)
n   Show information numerically rather than symbolically (p. 113)
s   Show the kernel stack size of each process (p. 113)
t*term*   Show only processes running on terminal *term* (p. 111)
u   Produce information in a user-oriented format (p. 112)
v   Show virtual memory statistics (p. 112)
w   Use a wide output format (p. 112)
x   Show information about processes not associated with a terminal (p. 111)
U   Update the private database of system information (p. 113)

A.2.64
pwd (Show Working Directory)

The form of the pwd command line (p. 93) is

     pwd

A.2.65
rcp (Remote Copy)

The form of the rcp command line (p. 424) is

     rcp *source* ... *dest*

where each *source* is a source file or directory and *dest* is a destination file or directory.

Command-line Options.

-p   Preserve modification times and permissions of source files (p. 425)
-r   Recursively copy the subtree rooted at each *source* (p. 425)

A.2.66
`rlogin`
(Remote Login)

The form of the `rlogin` command line (p. 423) is

        `rlogin` *rhost options*

For some systems, the order is reversed:

        `rlogin` [*options*] *rhost*

In either case, *rhost* is the name of a remote system.

Command-line Options.

`-8` Use an eight-bit data path (p. 423)
`-e`*c* Use *c* as the escape character (p. 423)
`-l` *user* Log in as *user* rather than as yourself (p. 423)

A.2.67
`rm`
**(Remove Files
or Directories)**

The form of the `rm` command line (p. 75) is

        `rm` [*options*] *file* \dots

where the files in *file* . . . can include directories if the `-r` option is present.

Command-line Options.

`-f` Don't ask for confirmation of files lacking write permission (p. 75)
`-i` Ask interactively for confirmation of each removal (p. 75)
`-r` Remove directories and all indirectly contained files and subdirectories (p. 75)

A.2.68
`rmdir` **(Remove
Directories)**

The form of the `rmdir` command line is

        `rmdir` [*options*] *dirlist*

where *dirlist* is a list of directories.

Command-line Options.

`-p` Remove empty parent directories (p. 76)
`-s` Suppress messages (p. 76)

A.2.69
`rsh` **(Remote
Execution of a Shell
Command)**

The form of the `rsh` command line (p. 423) is

        `rsh` *rhost* [*options*] [*cmd*]

where *rhost* is the name of a remote system and *cmd* is a command to be executed on that system.

Command-line Options.

`-l` *user* Log in as *user* rather than as yourself (p. 424)
`-n` Take input from `/dev/null` (p. 424)

A.2.70
`rsh` **(Restricted
Bourne Shell)**

The `rsh` command line (p. 179) follows the same rules as `sh`, except that certain operations are inhibited.

A.2.71
`rwho` **(List Users on
the Local Network)**

The form of the `rwho` command line (p. 425) is

        `rwho` [`-a`]

The `-a` option indicates that users who have not typed anything in the last hour are also to be included.

A.2.72
sed (Edit from a Script)

The form of the sed command line (p. 345) is

    sed [*options*] [*file*] . . .

where the *files* are files to be edited. In the explanations below, the term "produce" means "send to standard output".

Command-line Options.

-e *script*   Edit the files according to *script* (p. 351)
-f *sfile*   Edit the files according to the script found in *sfile* (p. 351)
-n   Don't produce the input buffer after processing a line (p. 351)

Addresses.

/*regexpr*/   Any line that matches the regular expression *regexpr* (p. 346)
\c *regexpr* c   Any line that matches the regular expression *regexpr* (p. 346)
n   Line number *n* (p. 346)
a_1, a_2 Lines a_1 through a_2, where a_1 and a_2 are any of the forms above (p. 346)

Commands.   In the following list of commands, *r* indicates an address range and *a* indicates a single address. A range can be replaced by an address or omitted; a single address can also be omitted. A command is executed only if the range or address applies, or if it has no range or address.

empty   Does nothing (p. 350)
r !*cmd*   Applies the command to all lines not selected by *r* (p. 350)
r{ [*cmd*] . . .}   Executes the commands *cmd* . . . (p. 350)
: *label*   Places the label *label* (p. 350)
a=   Produces a line containing the current line number (p. 350)
Indicates a comment (first line only) (p. 350)
a a*text*   Produces *text* before reading the next line (p. 349)
r b [*label*]   Branches to *label* (p. 350)
r c\ *text*   Changes the lines in *r* to *text* (p. 349)
r d   Deletes the input buffer, recycle (p. 348)
r D   Deletes the first line of the input buffer, recycle (p. 348)
r g   Replaces the input buffer by the hold buffer (p. 349)
r G   Appends the hold buffer to the input buffer (p. 349)
r h   Replaces the hold buffer by the input buffer (p. 349)
r H   Appends the input buffer to the hold buffer (p. 349)
a i*text*   Produces *text* immediately (p. 348)
r l   Produces the input buffer in a representation that folds long lines and shows non-printing characters (p. 350)
r n   Produces the input buffer, then replace it with the next input line (p. 349)
r N   Appends the next input line to the input buffer (p. 349)
r p   Produces the input buffer (p. 349)
r P   Produces the first line of the input buffer (p. 350)
a q   Quits editing (p. 350)
r r *file*   Produces the contents of *file* before reading the next line (p. 350)
s/*pat*/*repl*/[*flags*]   Substitutes *repl* for the pattern *pat*, applying the flags listed below (p. 347)
r t [*label*]   Branches to *label* if any substitutions have been made (p. 350)
r w *file*   Appends the input buffer to *file* (p. 350)
r x *file*   Exchanges the input buffer with the hold buffer (p. 349)
r y /*string*₁/*string*₂/   Substitutes characters in $string_2$ for the corresponding characters of $string_1$ (p. 348)

Flags for the s Command.

n   Substitute for the *n*th occurrence (p. 347)
g   Substitute for all occurrences (p. 347)
p   Produce the input buffer if any substitutions were made.
w *file*   Append the input buffer to *file* if any substitutions were made (p. 347)

A.2.73
sh (The Bourne Shell)

The form of the sh command line (p. 177) is

    sh [*options*] [*cmd* [*arg*] . . .]

Command-line Options.

-a Automatically export modified or created variables (p. 177)
-c *string* Use *string* as input to sh (p. 178) .
-e Exit sh on nonzero exit status of command (p. 178)
-f Turn off the interpretation of wildcards (p. 178)
-h Enter commands of function definition into lookup table when the function is defined
    (p. 178)
-i Expect interactive input (p. 178)
-k Treat all local variables as exported (p. 178)
-n Don't execute commands, just read them (p. 178)
-r Make this shell restricted (p. 178)
-s Read input from standard input, write output to standard error (p. 178)
-t Exit sh after first command list (p. 178)
-u Treat unset variables as erroneous (p. 178)
-v Show each input line as it is read (p. 177)
-x Show each simple command and its arguments as it is executed (p. 177)

Operators.

c& Executes c in the background, then continues (p. 147)
c_1 && c_2 Executes c_1, then c_2 if the exit status of c_1 is zero (p. 147)
c_1 | c_2 Connects the standard output of c_1 to the standard input of c_2 through a pipe
    (p. 147)
c_1 || c_2 Executes c_1, then c_2 if the exit status of c_1 is nonzero (p. 147)
c; Executes c and waits for it to finish, then continue (p. 147)

Variable Substitutions.

$@ Substitutes entire argument list, spaces are not quoted (p. 159)
$* Substitutes entire argument list, spaces are quoted (p. 159)
$*var* Substitutes value of $*var* (p. 159)
${@} Substitutes entire argument list, spaces are not quoted (p. 159)
${*} Substitutes entire argument list, spaces are quoted (p. 159)
${*var*} Substitutes value of $*var* (p. 159)
$*var*-*word* Substitutes for $*var* if it exists, otherwise uses *word* (p. 159)
$*var*:-*word* Substitutes for $*var* if its value is non-null, otherwise uses *word* (p. 159)
$*var*=*word* Substitutes for $*var* if it exists and assigns *word* to *var*, otherwise uses *word*
    (p. 160)
$*var*:=*word* Substitutes for $*var* if its value is non-null and assigns *word* to *var*, otherwise
    uses *word* (p. 160)
$*var*?[*word*] Substitutes for $*var* if it exists and assigns *word* to *var*, otherwise issues error
    message *word* (p. 160)
$*var*:?[*word*] Substitutes for $*var* if its value is non-null and assigns *word* to *var*, otherwise
    issues error message *word* (p. 160)
$*var*+*word* Substitutes *word* for $*var* if $*var* exists, otherwise substitutes nothing (p. 160)
$*var*+*word* Substitutes *word* for $*var* if $*var* is non-null, otherwise substitutes nothing
    (p. 160)

Special Variables.

$! The process number of the most recent asynchronously executed command (p. 161)
$- The flags supplied to sh when it was called (p. 161)
$$ The process number of the current shell invocation (p. 161)
$# The number of arguments, as a decimal number (p. 161)
$? The exit code of the most recent synchronously executed command (p. 161)

Quotation and Command Substitution.

c Quotes the character *c* (p. 162)
"*text*" Quotes *text*, allows substitutions within it (p. 162)
'*text*' Quotes *text*, allows no substitutions within it (p. 162)
`*text*` Executes *text*, substitutes its standard output (p. 163)

Redirection.

<file   Takes standard input from *file* (p. 149)
<<[-]word   Takes standard input from following text (p. 150)
>file   Sends standard output to *file* (p. 150)
>>file   Appends standard output to *file* (p. 150)
<&n   Copies file descriptor *n* to standard input descriptor (p. 150)
>&n   Copies file descriptor *n* to standard output descriptor (p. 150)
<&-   Closes standard input (p. 150)
>&-   Closes standard output (p. 150)
n redir   Applies redirection *redir* to descriptor *n* (p. 151)

Intrinsic Commands.

(EOF)   Exits the shell with exit status 0 (p. 170)
[*test*]   Performs the indicated test (p. 175)
: [*text*]   Does nothing; *text* is ignored (p. 171)
.*file*   Executes commands in *file* directly (p. 170)
break [*n*]   Breaks out of *n* enclosing loops (p. 171)
cd [*path*]   Changes the current directory to *path* (p. 175)
continue [*n*]   Restarts the *n*th enclosing loop (p. 171)
echo [*word*] ...   Echoes the arguments (p. 175)
eval [*word*] ...   Evaluates words, then uses their values (p. 174)
exec *cmd* [*arg*] ...   Executes *cmd*, replacing this shell (p. 170)
exec *redir* ...   Uses the redirections *redir* from now on (p. 172)
exit [*n*]   Exits the shell with exit status *n* (p. 170)
export [*name*] ...   Exports named variables (p. 172)
getopts *text name* [*word*] ...   Parses options of a command (p. 172)
hash [-r] *name* ...   Specifies or shows hashing of command names (p. 173)
newgroup [*arg*] ...   Changes group identification (p. 175)
pwd   Shows the current (working) directory (p. 175)
read [*name*] ...   Reads values of variables from standard input (p. 174)
readonly [*name*] ...   Makes named variables read-only (p. 172)
return [*n*]   Returns from function with exit status *n* (p. 170)
set [*options*] [*word*] ...   Enables or disables options and sets numbered parameters (p. 172)
shift [*n*]   Renumbers parameters by shifting them left by *n* (p. 172)
test *test*   Performs the indicated test (p. 175)
times   Shows time usage (p. 174)
trap [[*cmdtext*] *n* ...]   Associates commands with signals (p. 171)
type [*name*] ...   Shows interpretation of commands (p. 173)
ulimit [*n*]   Limits child processes to *n* disk blocks (p. 175)
umask *n*   (p. 175) Reduces the default permissions for file creation by subtracting *n* (see Section 3.12.2).
unset *name* ...   Deletes named variables (p. 172)
wait [*n*]   Waits for process *n*, or all processes, to finish (p. 175)

Compound Commands.

{ *list*;}   Executes foreground commands in-line (p. 154)
{ *list*&}   Executes background commands in-line (p. 154)
(*list*)   Executes commands in a subshell (p. 154)
name () { *list*; }   Defines a shell function (p. 154)

case *word* in *casetest* [*casetest*] ... esac
where each *casetest* has the form
pattern [| *pattern*] ...) *list*;;
   Selects commands by matching a word against patterns (p. 153)

for *name* [in *word* ... ;] do *list* done
   Executes commands once for each word in a list (p. 152)

if *list* then *list* [elif *list* then *list*] ...
     [else *list*] fi
   Executes commands conditionally (p. 152)

until *list* do *list* done
   Executes commands until a command returns nonzero exit status (p. 153)

while *list* do *list* done
  Executes commands while a command returns zero exit status (p. 153)

Predefined Variables.

CDPATH The sequence of directories searched by the cd command (p. 168)
HOME   Your home directory (p. 167)
IFS   The input field separators (p. 168)
MAIL   File checked for mail (p. 169)
MAILCHECK   Value of *n*, mail checked every *n* seconds (p. 169)
MAILPATH   Sequence of files checked for mail (p. 168)
PATH   The sequence of directories searched for commands (p. 168)
PS1   The primary command prompt (p. 168)
PS2   The secondary command prompt (p. 168)
SHACCT   Place to write accounting records for commands (p. 169)
SHELL   Location of command for child shells (p. 170)

A.2.74
sleep (Suspend Execution)

The form of the sleep command line (p. 116) is

  sleep *n*

where *n* is the number of seconds for which execution is to be suspended.

A.2.75
sort (Sort Files)

The form of the sort command line (p. 337) is

  sort [*options*] [*keyspec*] ... [*file*] ...

where *options* contains options applying to all keys. and the *files* are the files to be concatenated and sorted. Each *keyspec* has the form

  [+*pos*$_1$ [-*pos*$_2$]]

pos$_1$ indicates where a key starts and *pos*$_2$ where it ends. Each *pos* in turn has the form

  f[.*c*][*flags*]

Here *f* specifies a field and *c* a character within the field, with fields and characters numbered starting with zero. The flags are specified as letters only (no dashes).

Options Applying to All Keys.

-c   Check that the input is already sorted (p. 338)
-m   Merge the input files, assuming them already sorted (p. 339)
-u   For sets of lines having equal keys, produce only one of them (p. 339)
-o *outfile*   Send the output to *outfile* (p. 338)
-t *c*   Use *c* as the field delimiter (p. 339)
-y [*n*]   Use *n* kilobytes of main memory (p. 339)
-z *n*   Assume *n* to be the longest record size (p. 339)

The flags applying to individual keys can also be applied to all keys by indicating them as options.

Flags Applying to Individual Keys.

-b   Ignore leading whitespace in determining character positions within a key (p. 339)
-d   Use dictionary order, ignoring characters other than letters, digits, and whitespace (p. 339)
-f   Fold lowercase letters to uppercase (p. 340)
-i   Ignore nonprinting ASCII characters (p. 340)
-M   Treat the key as a three-letter case-insensitive month name (p. 340)
-n   Treat the key as a number (p. 340)
-r   Reverse the sense of comparisons (p. 339)

A.2.76
stty (Set Terminal Characteristics)

The form of the stty command line (p. 125) is

  stty [*options*] [*setting*] ...

The options and settings vary considerably among systems.

Command-line Options. These are the System V options. Other systems may not have them.

-a   List all settings (p. 126)
-g   List current settings in a form that can be used as input to stty later (p. 126)

Settings for Control Characters.

eof *c*   Set the eof character to *c* (p. 127)
erase *c*   Set the erase character to *c* (p. 127)
flush *c*   Set the flush character to *c* (p. 127)
intr *c*   Set the interrupt character to *c* (p. 127)
kill *c*   Set the kill character to *c* (p. 127)
quit *c*   Set the quit character to *c* (p. 127)
start *c*   Set the start character to *c* (p. 127)
stop *c*   Set the stop character to *c* (p. 127)
susp *c*   Set the job suspension charater to *c* (p. 127)
swtch *c*   Set the job switch character to *c* (p. 127)
werase *c*   Set the "erase last word" character to *c* (p. 128)

Other Settings. These are some of the more commonly used settings. This is not an exhaustive list. A '-' in front of a setting negates it.

speed   Set the line to the indicated speed (baud rate) (p. 128)
term   Set all settings to values appropriate for the terminal *term* (p. 129)
0   Hang up the phone line (p. 128)
cooked   Enable processing of special characters (p. 129)
[-]echo   Echo each typed character (p. 129)
[-]echoe   Echo erase characters as ⟨backspace⟩⟨space⟩⟨backspace⟩ (p. 129)
[-]echok   Send a newline after eack kill character (p. 129)
ek   Set the erase and kill characters to # and @ (p. 129)
[-]evenp   Enable even parity (p. 128)
[-]hup   Hang up the phone line upon logout (p. 128)
[-]icanon   Enable the erase and kill characters (p. 128)
[-]icrnl   Map ⟨return⟩ to ⟨newline⟩ on input (p. 128)
[-]igncr   Ignore ⟨return⟩ on input (p. 128)
[-]inlcr   Map ⟨newline⟩ to ⟨return⟩ on input (p. 128)
[-]isig   Enable the interrupt, quit, switch, and flush characters (p. 128)
[-]iuclc   Map uppercase alphabetic characters to lowercase on input (p. 128)
[-]ixon   Enable the start and stop characters (p. 128)
[-]lcase   Enable conversion of lowercase alphabetic characters to uppercase ones (p. 129)
[-]nl   Disable special processing of ⟨newline⟩ and ⟨return⟩ (p. 129)
[-]ocrnl   Map ⟨return⟩ to ⟨newline⟩ on output (p. 129)
[-]oddp   Enable odd parity (p. 128)
[-]olcuc   Map lowercase alphabetic characters to uppercase on output (p. 129)
[-]onlcr   Map ⟨newline⟩ to ⟨return⟩ on output (p. 129)
[-]opost   Post-process the output (p. 129)
[-]parenb   Enable parity generation and detection (p. 128)
[-]parity   Enable even parity (p. 128)
[-]raw   Disable processing of special characters (p. 129)
sane   Set all settings to reasonable values (p. 129)
[-]tabs   Replace tabs by spaces when showing text (p. 129)
[-]xcase   Indicate uppercase characters with backslash (p. 129)

A.2.77
su (Substitute User)

The form of the su command line (p. 119) is

su [-f] [-] [*name* [*arg*]]

The arguments are as follows:

-f   Inhibit csh from executing the .cshrc file.
-   Produce login environment if present, preserve current environment if absent.
name   Name of new user.
arg ...   Arguments passed to the newly created shell.

A.2.78
tabs **(Set Tabs on Your Terminal)**

The form of the tabs command line (p. 131) is

> tabs *options*

Command-line Options.

$n_1,n_2, \dots$ Set tab stops at positions n_1, n_2, etc. (p. 131)
−*code*   Use the correct tabs for the programming language designated by *code* (p. 131)
−*n*   Set tab stops every *n* spaces (p. 131)
−−*file*   Use the tab stops given in the format specification in *file* (p. 131)
+m[*n*]   Use a left margin of *n* (p. 132)
−T *term*   Send the tab-setting sequence for a terminal of type *term* (p. 131)

A.2.79
tail **(Extract the End of a File)**

The form of the tail command line (p. 69) is

> tail *sign*[*n*][*unit*][f] [*file*]

The components of the first argument are as follows:

sign   Start from beginning of file if +, from end if −.
n   Number of units to extract.
unit   Lines (1), 1024-byte blocks (b), or characters (c).
f   Continuous monitoring of *file*.

A.2.80
tar **(Tape Archiver)**

The form of the tar command line (p. 100) is

> tar *key* [*arg*] ... [*file*] ...

The *key* consists of a sequence of key letters. The number of *arg*s is equal to the number of letters in *key* that require arguments. The *files* are the files to be written to the archive or extracted. The form and key letters for this program vary greatly, even among System V-style or Berkeley-style systems.

Key Letters.   The key letters that follow are the most common ones:

n   Use drive #*n* for the archive (p. 101)
b   Take the blocking factor for raw magnetic tape from the next argument (p. 101)
c   Create a new archive containing the files (p. 101)
−C *dir*   Change directory to *dir* before writing more files (p. 101)
f   Take archive device name from the next argument (p. 101)
k   Take the capacity of the archive device (in kilobytes) from the next argument (p. 101)
l   Don't complain about files that can't be found (p. 101)
m   Don't restore modification times (p. 101)
o   Disregard ownership information when reading a file (p. 101)
p   Assign original permissions to extracted files (p. 101)
r   Write the files at the end of the archive (p. 100)
t   List the contents of the archive (p. 100)
u   Add the files to the archive if they are newer (p. 100)
v   Show the name of each file processed (p. 101)
w   Wait for confirmation of each action (p. 101)
x   Extract the files from the archive (p. 100)

A.2.81
tee **(Duplicate Input)**

The form of the tee command line (p. 70) is

> tee [*options*] [*file*] ...

Command-line Options.

−i   Ignore interrupts (p. 70)
−a   Append the output to each file instead of overwriting the file (p. 70)

A.2.82
telnet (Call a Remote System Over a Network)

The form of the telnet command line (p. 425) is

    telnet [*host* [*port*]]

Commands.

? [*cmd*]   Gets help on *cmd* (p. 427)
c[lose]   Disconnects from the remote host but remains in telnet (p. 427)
d[isplay] [*var*] ...   Shows the value of each variable *var* (p. 427)
m[ode] *type*   Enters the specified mode (line or character) (p. 427)
o[pen] [*host* [*port*]]   Opens a connection to *host* at the specified port (p. 427)
q[uit]   Disconnects from the remote host and exit from telnet (p. 427)
sen[d] *tseq* ...   Sends the specified TELNET sequences to the remote host (p. 427)
set *var val*   Sets the telnet variable *var* to the value *val* (p. 427)
st[atus]   Shows the current status of telnet (p. 427)
t[oggle] *var* ...   Toggles each variable *var* (p. 427)
z   Suspends telnet, returns to the local system (p. 427)

TELNET Sequences.

?   Show help information for send (p. 427)
ao   The TELNET ⟨AO⟩ (Abort Output) sequence (p. 428)
ay[t]   The TELNET ⟨AYT⟩ (Are You There) sequence (p. 428)
b[rk]   The TELNET ⟨BRK⟩ (Break) sequence (p. 428)
ec   The TELNET ⟨EC⟩ (Erase Character) sequence (p. 428)
el   The TELNET ⟨EL⟩ (Erase Line) sequence (p. 428)
es[cape]   The current character for escaping to command mode (p. 427)
g[a]   The TELNET ⟨GA⟩ (Go Ahead) sequence (p. 428)
i[p]   The TELNET ⟨IP⟩ (Interrupt Process) sequence (p. 428)
n[op]   The TELNET ⟨NOP⟩ (No Operation) sequence (p. 428)
s[ynch]   The TELNET ⟨SYNCH⟩ (Synchronize) sequence (p. 428)

Variables with Values.

ec[ho]   The character that toggles echoing of locally typed characters (p. 428)
eo[f]   The remote end of file character (p. 429)
er[ase]   The remote erase character (p. 428)
es[cape]   The character that returns you to command mode (p. 428)
f[lushoutput]   The character for flushing remote output (p. 428)
i[nterrupt]   The remote interrupt character (p. 428)
k[ill]   The remote kill character (p. 429)
q[uit]   The remote quit character (p. 428)

Toggles.

?   Show the names of the available toggles (p. 427)
autof[lush]   Don't show typed data until remote interrupt is acknowledged (p. 429)
autos[ynch]   Cause the remote system to discard input preceding an interrupt (p. 429)
crl[f]   Map ⟨return⟩ sent by local system to ⟨return⟩ ⟨linefeed⟩ (p. 430)
crm[od]   Map ⟨return⟩ received from remote system to ⟨return⟩ ⟨linefeed⟩ (p. 429)
d[ebug]   Enable socket-level debugging (for superuser only) (p. 430)
f[lowcontrol]   Use flow control signals to regulate communications (p. 430)
l[ocalchars]   Transform local control characters to TELNET control sequences (p. 429)
n[etdata]   Enable showing of network data (p. 430)
o[ptions]   Show internal protocol processing (p. 430)

A.2.83
test (Compare Values, Test File Properties)

The test command line (p. 155) has two forms:

    test *expr*
    [*expr*]

String Comparisons.

s_1 True if s_1 is nonempty (p. 155)
s_1 = s_2 True if strings s_1 and s_2 are identical (p. 155)
s_1 != s_2 True if strings s_1 and s_2 are not identical (p. 155)

-n s_1 True if s_1 is nonempty (p. 155)
-z s_1 True if s_1 is empty (p. 155)

Numerical Comparisons.

n_1 -eq n_2 True if $n_1 = n_2$ (p. 156)
n_1 -ge n_2 True if $n_1 \geq n_2$ (p. 156)
n_1 -gt n_2 True if $n_1 > n_2$ (p. 156)
n_1 -le n_2 True if $n_1 \leq n_2$ (p. 156)
n_1 -lt n_2 True if $n_1 < n_2$ (p. 156)
n_1 -ne n_2 True if $n_1 \neq n_2$ (p. 156)

File Tests.

-b *file*   True if *file* exists and is a block device file (p. 156)
-c *file*   True if *file* exists and is a character device file (p. 156)
-d *file*   True if *file* exists and is a directory (p. 156)
-f *file*   True if *file* exists and is an ordinary file (neither a directory nor a device) (p. 156)
-g *file*   True if *file* exists and its set-gid bit is set (p. 156)
-k *file*   True if *file* exists and its sticky bit is set (p. 156)
-p *file*   True if *file* exists and is a named pipe (p. 156)
-r *file*   True if *file* exists and is readable (p. 156)
-s *file*   True if *file* exists and its size is greater than zero (p. 156)
-t [*n*]   True if the file associated with file descriptor *n* is a terminal (p. 156)
-u *file*   True if *file* exists and its set-uid bit is set (p. 156)
-w *file*   True if *file* exists and is writable (p. 156)
-x *file*   True if *file* exists and is executable (p. 156)

Combinations of Tests.

! *expr* True if *expr* is false and false otherwise (p. 156)
(*expr*)   True if *expr* is true (p. 157)
expr$_1$ -a *expr*$_2$ True if *expr*$_1$ and *expr*$_2$ are both true (p. 156)
expr$_1$ -o *expr*$_2$ True if either *expr*$_1$ or *expr*$_2$ is true (p. 156)

A.2.84
time (Time a Command)

The form of the `time` command line (p. 135) is

> `time` *cmd*

where *cmd* is the command to be timed.

A.2.85
touch (Touch a File)

The form of the `touch` command line (p. 80) is

> `touch` [*options*] [*date*]

The date, recognized only under System V, has the form *mmddhhmm*[*yy*], where *mm* is the month, *dd* is the day, *hh* is the hour, *mm* is the minute, and *yy* is the year.

Command-line Options.

-a   Change the access time (p. 80)
-c   Don't create the file if it doesn't already exist (p. 80)
-f   Force the touch no matter what the file permissions (p. 80)
-m   Change the modification time (p. 80)

A.2.86
tput (Send Setup Instructions to a Terminal)

The form of the `tput` command line (p. 130) is

> `tput` [-T *term*] *cmd*

where *term* is your terminal type and *cmd* is one of the following:

name [*param*] . . .   Set the `terminfo` capability *name* as indicated by the *params* (p. 130)
`init`   Send the terminal initialization string (p. 130)
`longname`   Produce the full name of the terminal on standard output (p. 130)
`reset`   Send the terminal reset string (p. 130)

A.2.87
tr (Translate or Delete Characters)

The form of the tr command line (p. 340) is

> tr [*options*] [*str*₁ [*str*₂]]

where *str*₁ contains characters to be replaced or deleted and *str*₂ contains characters to be substituted or squeezed.

Command-line Options.

-c Use the complement of *str*₁ rather than *str*₁ (p. 341)
-d Delete the characters in *str*₁ (p. 341)
-s Squeeze repetitions of characters in *str*₂ to single characters (p. 341)

A.2.88
true (Return True)

The form of the true command line (p. 157) is

> true

It does nothing and returns a zero exit code.

A.2.89
tset (Set Terminal Information)

The form of the tset command line (p. 122) is

> tset [*options*] [*term*]

where *term* is the name of a terminal type.

Command-line Options.

-     Produce the terminal type on standard output (p. 124)
-e[*c*] Set the erase character to *c* (p. 124)
-E[*c*] Set the erase character to *c* if the terminal can backspace (p. 124)
-h   Use the terminal type found in the /etc/ttytype table (p. 123)
-I   Don't initialize the terminal, just reset it (p. 124)
-k[*c*] Set the kill character to *c* (p. 124)
-m[*itype*][*test speed*]:[?]*type*   Match terminal type *itype* according to *speed*, conditionally set it to *type* (p. 123)
-Q   Suppress "Erase set to" and "Kill set to" messages (p. 125)
-r   Produce a message identifying the terminal type on standard error (p. 125)
-s   Produce commands for setting TERM on standard output (p. 124)
-S   Produce value for setting TERM on standard output (p. 125)

A.2.90
tty (Get the Terminal Name)

The form of the tty command line (p. 107) is:

> tty [*options*]

Command-line Options.

-l Show the line number of the terminal if it's a synchronous line (p. 107)
-s Suppress the printing of the terminal's path name (p. 107)

A.2.91
umask (Mask Default File Permissions)

The form of the umask command line (p. 82) is

> umask [*n*]

where *n* is the three-digit octal number specifying permissions to be masked out.

A.2.92
uncompress (Uncompress a File)

The form of the uncompress command line (p. 96) is

> uncompress [*options*] [*file*] ...

where *file* ... is a list of files to be uncompressed. By default each file, whose name must have the form '*file*.Z', is replaced by its uncompressed version.

Command-line Options.

-c Write the uncompressed files to standard output (p. 95)

A.2.93
uniq (Eliminate Adjacent Repeated Lines)

The form of the uniq command line (p. 344) is

> uniq [*options*] [*infile* [*outfile*]]

where the input comes from *infile* and is written to *outfile*.

Command-line Options.

+*n* Ignore the first *n* fields, and any blanks preceding them (p. 344)
−*n* Ignore the first *n* characters (p. 344)
−c Precede each output line by a count of how many times it occurs (p. 344)
−d Produce just one copy of each repeated line (p. 344)
−u Produce just the lines that are not repeated (p. 344)

A.2.94
unpack (Unpack Files)

The form of the unpack command line (p. 95) is

> unpack *file* . . .

where *file* . . . is a list of files to be unpacked.

A.2.95
uucp (UNIX to UNIX Copy)

The form of the uucp command line (p. 447) is

> uucp [*options*] *sfile* . . . *dfile*

where each *sfile* is a source file and *dfile* is a destination file of the form *system*!*path*.

Command-line Options.

−c Don't make a copy of local files (p. 449)
−C Make a copy of local files (p. 449)
−d Make subdirectories as needed (p. 449)
−f Don't make subdirectories (p. 449)
−g *c* Assign the job a priority of *c* (p. 450)
−j Show the job identifier (p. 449)
−m Send a mail message to the requestor when the job is done (p. 449)
−n *user* Notify *user* on remote system that a file was sent (p. 449)
−r Queue the job without starting the transfer (p. 450)
−s *file* Send a status report to *file* (p. 449)
−x *n* Turn on debugging at level *n* (p. 450)

A.2.96
uuname (Get Names of Remote UNIX Systems)

The form of the uuname command line (p. 452) is

> uuname *options*

Command-line Options.

−l List the name of the machine you're on (p. 452)
−c List the names of systems known to the cu program (p. 452)

A.2.97
uupick (Pick Up Files from UNIX to UNIX Transfer)

The form of the uupick command line (p. 447) is

> uupick [−s *system*]

If you specify *system*, then you'll only get to retrieve files sent from that remote system.

Responses for Each Item.   For each item retrieved, uupick asks for a response. The possible responses are as follows:

(Enter)   Go on to the next item (p. 447)
(EOF)   Quit, exit from uupick (p. 447)
!*cmd*   Execute *cmd* in a subshell (p. 447)
*   Show a summary of the commands (p. 447)
a [*dir*]   Move all the items received from the system that sent the current item (p. 447)
d   Discard this item (p. 447)
m [*dir*]   Move this item to the directory *dir* (p. 447)
p   Show the item, i.e., send it to standard output (p. 447)
q   Quit, exit from uupick (p. 447)

A.2.98
uustat (Check uucp Status)

The form of the uustat command line (p. 450) is

    uustat *options*

Command-line Options.

-a   Output the names of all items awaiting transmission (p. 450)
-k *id*   Kill the item whose identifier is *id* (p. 450)
-m   Report the status of all machines known to uucp (p. 451)
-p   Execute the command ps -flp for all processes that are in lock files (p. 451)
-q   List the items queued for each remote machine (p. 451)
-r *id*   Rejuvenate item *id* by resetting its modification time (p. 451)
-s *sys*   Only report items destined for remote system *sys* (p. 451)
-u *user*   Only report items originated by user *user* (p. 451)

Except for -s and -u, only one option can be used at a time.

A.2.99
uuto (Send Files UNIX to UNIX)

The form of the uuto command line (p. 446) is

    uuto [*options*] *source* ... *path*!*person*

Command-line Options.

-p   Copy each file to be transmitted to a spooling directory (p. 446)
-m   Send mail notification to the sender (p. 446)

A.2.100
who (List Users and Processes)

The forms of the command line (p. 103) are

    who [*options*] *file*
    who am i
    who am I

The file *file* is optional; if it is given, who looks for its data there. The second and third forms produce your login name and the name of the terminal you're currently using.

Command-line Options.

-a   Turn on all other options except -T (p. 105)
-b   Indicate when the system was last rebooted (p. 105)
-d   List dead processes started by init (p. 105)
-H   Put a heading above each column.
-l   List only those terminals currently not in use (p. 104)
-p   List all active processes started by init (p. 105)
-r   Indicate the current run level of init (p. 105)
-q   Show only the names and count of logged-on users (p. 104)
-s   List only the name, terminal, and login time of each user (p. 104)
-t   Indicate when the system clock was last changed (p. 105)
-T   Indicate the "write state" of each terminal (p. 104)
-u   List only those users currently logged in (p. 104)

A.2.101
vi (Visual Editor)

The form of the vi command line (p. 212) is

    cmd [*options*] [*file*] ...

where *cmd* is one of the following:

vi   No flags are implicitly set (p. 212)
view   Set the -r (read only) flag (p. 212)
vedit   Set the novice-mode flags (p. 212)

Input Mode Commands.

(Erase)   Erases the previous character (p. 210)
(Enter)   Ends the input line, starts a new one (p. 210)
(Esc)   Ends the insertion, returns to command mode (p. 210)
(Intr)   Ends the insertion, returns to command mode (p. 210)
(Kill)   Deletes all characters typed on the current line (p. 210)
(Ctrl) D   Backs up over a tab at the start of a line (p. 211)

(Ctrl) V   Takes the next character literally (p. 210)
(Ctrl) W   Erases the word just typed (p. 210)
∧ (Ctrl) D   Starts this line at the left margin in autoindent mode (p. 211)
0 (Ctrl) D   Cancels all indentation in autoindent mode (p. 211)

Status-Line Mode Commands.

(Erase)   Erases the previous character (p. 210)
(Enter)   Executes the command, then returns to command mode (p. 210)
(Esc)   Executes the command, then returns to command mode (p. 210)
(Intr)   Interrupts whatever is happening, returns to command mode (p. 210)
(Kill)   Deletes all but the first character of the status line (p. 210)
(Ctrl) V   Takes the next character literally (p. 210)
(Ctrl) W   Erases the word just typed (p. 210)

Cancelling and Interrupting Commands.

(Esc)   Cancels the command you're typing (p. 209)
(Intr)   Interrupts the command that's executing (p. 209)

Command-line Options.

+*command* Executes *command* before editing (p. 213)
-c *command* Executes *command* before editing (p. 213)
-r *file*   Recovers the editor state from *file* (p. 213)
-R   Edits in readonly mode (p. 213)
-t *tag*   Edits the file containing *tag* (p. 212)

Commands for Command Mode.
Most commands can be preceded by an integer n, which indicates a repetition count. In the list of commands that follows, n is shown only when it is explicitly mentioned in the command's description.

(Erase)   Moves left one character (p. 215)
(Enter)   Moves to the first nonwhite character on the following line (p. 215)
(SPACE)   Move right one character (p. 215)
(Ctrl) B   Scrolls up (backward) one screen (p. 214)
(Ctrl) D   Scrolls down (forward) by half a screen or n lines (p. 214)
(Ctrl) E   Scrolls down (forward) by one line (p. 214)
(Ctrl) F   Scrolls down (forward) one screen (p. 214)
(Ctrl) G   Shows status information (p. 225)
(Ctrl) J   Moves directly down one line (p. 215)
(Ctrl) H   Moves left one character (p. 215)
(Ctrl) L   Regenerates the screen (p. 215)
(Ctrl) N   Moves directly down one line (p. 215)
(Ctrl) P   Moves directly up one line (p. 215)
(Ctrl) R   Regenerates the screen, eliminating null lines (p. 215)
(Ctrl) U   Scrolls up (backward) by half a screen or n lines (p. 214)
(Ctrl) Y   Scrolls up (backward) by one line (p. 214)
&   Repeats the previous global replacement command (p. 223)
'*c*   Moves to the beginning of the line containing mark c (p. 219)
''   Moves to the beginning of the line containing the previous context (p. 220)
@   Executes commands in the anonymous buffer (p. 225)
@*b*   Executes commands in buffer b (p. 225)
'*c*   Moves to mark c (p. 219)
''   Moves to the previous context (p. 219)
!*m cmd*   Executes *cmd* with the region to m as standard input, replaces that region by standard output (p. 221)
n| Moves to column n of the current line (p. 216)
{   Moves backward to the previous paragraph boundary or non-atomic LISP S-expression (p. 217)
}   Moves forward to the next paragraph boundary or non-atomic LISP S-expression (p. 217)
[[Moves backward to the previous section boundary (p. 217)
]]   Moves forward to the next section boundary (p. 217)
∧ Moves to the first nonwhite character on the current line (p. 215)
:*cmd*   Executes the ex command *cmd* (p. 211)
, Repeats the last f, F, t, or T command in the reverse direction (p. 218)

− Moves to the first nonwhite character on the previous line (p. 215)
$ Moves to the last character on the current line (p. 215)
. Repeats the last action that modified the buffer (p. 225)
"*b*@ Executes commands in buffer *b* (p. 224)
"*b*d*m* Deletes the region of text from the cursor to *m* and stores it in buffer *b* (p. 224)
"*b*p Inserts contents of buffer *b* after the current character or line (p. 225)
"*n*p Puts the *n*th most recently deleted block of text after the cursor (p. 225)
"*b*P Inserts contents of buffer *b* before the current character or line (p. 225)
"*n*P Puts the *n*th most recently deleted block of text before the cursor (p. 225)
"*b*y*m* Yanks the region of text from the cursor to *m* and stores it in buffer *b* (p. 224)
=*m* Realigns the lines from the cursor to *m* using LISP autoindent conventions (p. 222)
>*m* Indents the region from the current line to the line containing *m* (p. 221)
<*m* Outdents the region from the current line to the line containing *m* (p. 221)
(Moves backward to the first character of the current sentence or the previous LISP S-expression (p. 217)
) Moves forward to the first nonwhite character of the next sentence or the next LISP S-expression (p. 216)
% Moves to the matching delimiter (p. 218)
+ Moves to the first nonwhite character on the following line (p. 215)
? Searches backward for the most recent search pattern (p. 219)
?*pat* (Enter) Moves backward to the next text matching *pat* (p. 219)
?*pat*? Moves backward to the next text matching *pat* (p. 219)
?*pat*?+*n* Moves backward to the beginning of the *n*th line before the next text matching *pat* (p. 219)
; Repeats the last f, F, t, or T command (p. 218)
/ Searches forward for the most recent search pattern (p. 219)
/*pat* (Enter) Moves forward to the next text matching *pat* (p. 218)
/*pat*/ Moves forward to the next text matching *pat* (p. 218)
/*pat*/+*n* Moves forward to the beginning of the *n*th line after the next text matching *pat* (p. 218)
/*pat*/z (Enter) Regenerates the screen with the next line containing *pat* at the top (p. 215)
~ Changes the case of the letter under the cursor (p. 223)
0 Moves to the first character on the current line (p. 215)
a Appends text after the cursor (p. 220)
A Appends text at the end of the current line (p. 220)
b Moves back to the beginning of the current word (p. 216)
B Moves back to the beginning of the current blank-delimited word (p. 216)
c*m* Changes the text from the cursor to *m* (p. 221)
cc Changes the current line (p. 221)
C Changes the rest of the current line (p. 222)
d*m* Deletes the text from the cursor to *m* (p. 221)
dd Deletes the current line (p. 221)
D Deletes the rest of the current line (p. 222)
e Moves to the last character of the current word (p. 216)
E Moves to the last character of the current blank-delimited word (p. 216)
f*c* Moves to the next occurrence of *c* (p. 218)
F*c* Moves to the previous occurrence of *c* (p. 218)
*n*G Moves to the first character on line *n* (p. 216)
h Moves left one character (p. 215)
H Moves to the beginning of the first line on the screen (p. 216)
i Inserts text before the cursor (p. 220)
I Inserts text before the first non-white character on the line (p. 220)
j Moves directly down one line (p. 215)
J Joins the current line with the next line (p. 223)
k Moves directly up one line (p. 215)
l Moves right one character (p. 215)
L Moves to the beginning of the last line on the screen (p. 216)
m*c* Places mark *c* at the current cursor position (p. 219)
M Moves to the beginning of the middle line on the screen (p. 216)
n Searches in the same direction for the most recent search pattern (p. 219)
N Searches in the opposite direction for the most recent search pattern (p. 219)
o Opens a line under the current line (p. 220)
O Opens a line above the current line (p. 220)
p Puts the contents of the anonymous buffer just after the cursor (p. 222)
P Puts the contents of the anonymous buffer just before the cursor (p. 223)
Q Switches over to ex (p. 228)

r*c*   Replaces the character under the cursor with *c* (p. 222)
R   Replaces characters with input text (p. 222)
s   Substitutes for the character under the cursor (p. 222)
S   Substitutes for the current line (p. 222)
t*c*   Moves to the character just before the next occurrence of *c* (p. 218)
T*c*   Moves to the character just after the next occurrence of *c* (p. 218)
u   Undoes the most recent change or insertion (p. 225)
U   Restores the current line (p. 225)
w   Moves forward to the beginning of the next word (p. 216)
W   Moves forward to the beginning of the next blank-delimited word (p. 216)
x   Deletes the character under the cursor (p. 222)
X   Deletes the character before the cursor (p. 222)
y*m*   Yanks the text from the cursor to *m* (p. 221)
yy   Yanks the current line (p. 221)
Y   Yanks the current line (p. 223)
z Enter   Regenerates the screen with the current line at the top (p. 214)
z*n* Enter   Regenerates the screen with an *n*-line window and the current line at the top
        (p. 215)
z-   Regenerates the screen with the current line at the bottom (p. 214)
z.   Regenerates the screen with the current line in the middle (p. 214)
z+   Regenerates the screen with the current line at the top (p. 214)
ZZ   Saves the buffer you're editing and exit (p. 225)

ex **Commands Commonly Used in** vi.

:e *file*   Abandons the buffer and starts editing *file* (p. 226)
:q   Quits vi, abandoning the buffer (p. 226)
:q!   Quits vi unconditionally, abandoning the buffer (p. 226)
:r *file*   Reads and inserts the file *file* (p. 226)
:s/*pat*/*repl*/g   Globally replaces the pattern *pat* by *repl* (p. 223)
:set   Specifies or queries a variable (p. 226)
:ta *tag*   Opens the file containing *tag*, move the cursor to *tag* (p. 226)
:[*r*]w [*file*]   Writes region *r* of the buffer to *file*, continue editing (p. 225)
:wq   Writes the buffer to the current file and quits (p. 225)

Environment Variables.   The bracketed commands indicate abbreviations.

autoindent [ai]   Enable automatic indentation (p. 231)
autoprint [ap]   Show line whenever modified (p. 233)
autowrite [aw]   Write changed file before switching to another file (p. 230)
beautify [bf]   Discard nonprinting characters from input (p. 231)
directory [dir]   Specify directory for vi temporary file (p. 234)
edcompatible [ed]   Follow ed conventions, not ex (p. 229)
errorbells [eb]   Sound bell before every error message (p. 230)
exrc   Look for .exrc file before editing (p. 235)
flash   Use visual warning instead of error bell (p. 230)
hardtabs [ht]   Specify tab spacing assumed by your environment (p. 235)
ignorecase [ic]   Ignore case of letters in search pattern (p. 229)
lisp   Interpret ( ) { } to operate on LISP S-expressions (p. 232)
list   Show tabs as '∧I', newlines as '$' (p. 233)
magic   Recognize regular expression characters (. \ [*) in patterns (p. 228)
mesg   Accept messages from other programs (p. 234)
modelines   Recognize editor commands in the first five lines and/or the last five lines of a
        file to be edited (p. 234)
novice   Edit in "novice" mode (p. 234)
number [nu]   Prefix each output line with a line number (p. 233)
optimize [opt]   Inhibit automatic carriage returns (p. 235)
paragraphs [para]   Specify nroff macros that start a paragraph (p. 229)
prompt   Show the prompt character :when waiting for a command (p. 233)
redraw   Keep screen current even if it must be redrawn (p. 235)
remap   Repeat macro mapping until no more characters are mapped (p. 232)
report   Specify *n* for reporting changes of more than *n* lines resulting from a single
        operation (p. 230)
scroll   Specify number of lines that Ctrl U and Ctrl D initially scroll up or down
        (p. 233)
sections [sect]   Specify nroff macros that start a section (p. 229)

shell   Specify shell for "escaped" commands (p. 235)
shiftwidth [sw]   Specify tab spacing for < and > commands and for (Ctrl) D in input (p. 231)
showmatch [sm]   Show '(' or '\{' matching typed ')' or '\}' (p. 234)
showmode [smd]   Put insert indicator on status line (p. 230)
slowopen   Don't update screen in insert mode (p. 236)
tabstop [ts]   Specify tab stop interval for showing text (p. 231)
tags   Specify list of files to be searched for tags (p. 229)
taglength [tl]   Specify the number of significant characters for tags (p. 229)
term   Specify terminal type (p. 235)
terse   Give error diagnostics in terse form (p. 230)
timeout   Allow one second for typing left-hand side of macro definitions (p. 232)
warn   Issue warning when leaving editor or switching files when current file is unsaved (p. 230)
window   Set number of lines in vi's working window (p. 233)
w300, w1200, w9600   Same effect as window, but only at specified baud rate (p. 233)
wrapscan [ws]   "Wrap around" the end of the buffer during a search (p. 229)
wrapmargin [wm]   Specify input line length for wrapping to a new line (p. 231)
writeany [wa]   Inhibit safety checks before writing to a file (p. 230)

A.2.102
wait (Wait for a Process to Finish)

The form of the wait command line (p. 116) is

    wait [n]

where *n* is the number of the process being waited for.

A.2.103
wc (Count Words, Lines, or Characters)

The form of the wc command line (p. 94) is

    wc [options] [file] . . .

Command-line Options.
\-c   Count characters (p. 94)
\-l   Count lines (p. 94)
\-w   Count words (p. 94)

A.2.104
write (Write to Terminal)

The usage of the write command (p. 134) is

    mesg *user line*
      . . .*text of the message*
    (EOF)

The message is sent to *user*. The terminal name *line* is necessary only if *user* is logged in at more than one terminal.

A.2.105
xbiff (Mailbox Flag for X)

The form of the xbiff command line (p. 471) is

    xbiff [options]

See Section 11.7.1 for a list of the Toolkit options and your system manual for the others.

A.2.106
xclock (Analog/Digital Clock for X)

The form of the xclock command line (p. 470) is

    xclock [options]

Command-Line Options.
-analog   Display a conventional twelve-hour clock face (p. 470)
-chime   Chime once on the half hour, twice on the hour (p. 470)
-digital   Display a twenty-four-hour digital clock (p. 470)
-hd *color*   Use *color* as the color of the hands on an analog clock (p. 470)
-hl *color*   Use *color* as the color of the edges of the hands on an analog clock (p. 470)
-padding *n*   Pad the edges of the clock with *n* pixels (p. 470)
-update *n*   Update the clock every *n* seconds (p. 470)
See Section 11.7.1 for a list of the Toolkit options for xclock.

A.2.107
xcolors **(Display the X Colors)**

The form of the xcolors command line (p. 471) is

>   xcolors [*options*]

See Section 11.7.1 for a list of the Toolkit options and your system manual for the others.

A.2.108
xfd **(Display an X Font)**

The form of the xfd command line (p. 471) is

>   xfd [*options*]

The options must include -fn *font*, where *font* specifies the font to be displayed. See Section 11.7.1 for a list of the Toolkit options and your system manual for the others.

A.2.109
xfontsel **(Select and Display X Fonts)**

The form of the xfontsel command line (p. 472) is

>   xfontsel [*options*]

See Section 11.7.1 for a list of the Toolkit options and your system manual for the others.

A.2.110
xinit **(Start the X Server)**

The form of the xinit command line (p. 472) is

>   xinit [[*client*] *options*] [-- [*server*] [:*display*] [*options*]]

Here *client* is a program to be started initially, *server* is the server program to be used, ':*display*' is the display to be used, and the second set of *options* are appended to the command line for *server*.

A.2.111
xkill **(Kill an X Client)**

The form of the xkill command line (p. 474) is

>   xkill [*options*]

See Section 11.7.1 for a list of the Toolkit options and your system manual for the others.

A.2.112
xlsfonts **(Display a List of X Fonts)**

The form of the xlsfonts command line (p. 471) is

>   xlsfonts [*options*]

The -fn *font* option specifies a font name with wildcards that is matched against the available fonts. See your system manual for the other options.

A.2.113
xrdb **(Resource Database Utility for X)**

The form of the xrdb command line (p. 473) is

>   xrdb [*options*] [*file*]

where *file* specifies a file containing a set of resource specifications.

Command-Line Options.
-load   Load the global resource database from standard input (p. 473)
-merge   Merge standard input with the global resource database (p. 473)
-query   Send the current contents of the global resource database to standard output (p. 473)
-remove   Make the global resource database empty (p. 473)

See your system manual for a description of the remaining options.

A.2.114
xset **(Set User Preferences for X)**

The form of the xset command line (p. 473) is

>   xset [*options*]

The q option (no '-') lists the current settings. See your system manual for a list of the remaining options.

A.2.115
xsetroot (Set Root Window Appearance for X)

The form of the xsetroot command line (p. 473) is

> xsetroot [*options*]

See your system manual for a list of the options.

A.2.116
xterm (Terminal Emulator for X)

The form of the xterm command line (p. 467) is

> xterm [*options*]

See Section 11.7.1 for a list of the Toolkit options and your system manual for the others.

A.2.117
zcat
(Uncompress and Concatenate Files)

The form of the zcat command line (p. 96) is

> zcat [*file*] ...

where *file* ... is a list of files to be uncompressed by uncompress. By default each file, whose name must have the form '*file*.Z', is replaced by its uncompressed version. The uncompressed files are written to standard output.

B

Comparison of
MS-DOS and UNIX

If you're accustomed to working with the MS-DOS operating system for the IBM PC family of computers, you'll find a lot of resemblance between MS-DOS and UNIX; in fact, much of the structure of MS-DOS is derived from UNIX. In this appendix we correlate features of MS-DOS with similar features of UNIX.

B.1   Treatment of Files

These are some of the differences between the treatment of files in MS-DOS and in UNIX:

- The directories in a MS-DOS path are separated by '\', while those in a UNIX path are separated by '/'.

- In MS-DOS, file names are case-insensitive; in UNIX they are case-sensitive.

- The dot in a MS-DOS file name separates the name part from the extension. Every MS-DOS file name has a eight-character name and a three-character extension, even though the extension may be blank. In UNIX, a dot is like any other character in a file name, so a UNIX file name can have any number of dots or none at all. Some UNIX programs, however, do adopt the convention of suffixing file names with an extension such as '.c'. The division of a name into a name part and an extension is a convention adopted by particular programs, not a property of UNIX itself. A UNIX file name may have any

529

length up to the maximum permitted by the implementation you're using (at least 14 characters).

- In MS-DOS, each file system resides on its own drive, designated by 'd:' where d is the drive letter. In UNIX, all file systems are part of a single hierarchical tree descending from the root directory '/'.

- In MS-DOS, an executable file is one with an extension of .exe, .com, or .bat. In UNIX, any file whose execute permission is turned on is executable, regardless of its name.

- In MS-DOS, a sequence of commands may be collected into a batch file with an extension of .bat. In UNIX, such a sequence of commands would be treated as a shell script. The file containing the script must have execute permission but need not have any special name.

- A MS-DOS file has only one name; a UNIX file may have several names, each represented by a different link.

- Both in MS-DOS and in UNIX, a file name can include the wildcards '?' and '*'. The '?' stands for any single character and the '*' for an arbitrary sequence of characters.

  o In MS-DOS, a file name to be matched against a name with wildcards is first padded with blanks to extend the name part to eight characters and the extension to three characters. Wildcards are matched independently within the name part and within the extension. A star matches everything up to the end of the part containing it, so characters after a star have no effect. The construct '*.*' matches all files, while the construct '*' matches just those files with an empty or blank extension.

  o In UNIX, a file name to be matched against a name with wildcards is treated as a single string.[1] Characters after a star are considered in the match and can affect the result. UNIX file names can also include wildcards of the form '[*cset*]' (see Section 2.11.1). The construct '*.*' matches file names containing one or more dots, while the construct '*' matches all file names (except those whose names start with a dot).

  As another example, a file name 'agley.c' would be matched by the constructs 'agl*z.c*' and 'agley.c??' under MS-DOS but not under UNIX. It would be matched by the construct 'agl*c' under UNIX but not under MS-DOS.

- In a MS-DOS text file, the end of a line is indicated by the two-character sequence ⟨linefeed⟩ ⟨return⟩ (ASCII 13 followed by ASCII 10). In a UNIX text file, the end of a line is indicated by a single newline character, represented as ⟨linefeed⟩. Some MS-DOS and UNIX programs are affected by this difference, while others are not. When

---

1. Wildcard matching, also called "file substitution", is done by the various UNIX shells, not by the kernel. Nevertheless, all shells follow essentially the same conventions for wildcard matching. In MS-DOS, wildcard matching is handled by MS-DOS itself in response to low-level system requests.

you need to use a file created under one system within the other one, you may need to do a format conversion. The utility programs for this conversion vary from system to system, but typical names for them are dtou (MS-DOS to UNIX) and utod (UNIX to MS-DOS).

- The information about a file kept by MS-DOS differs somewhat from that kept by UNIX. For instance, there is nothing in a UNIX directory entry corresponding to the MS-DOS archive bit, which MS-DOS uses to keep track of whether a file has been backed up. On the other hand, UNIX has a more extensive set of file permissions.

- In MS-DOS, you can make a file read-only by setting its read-only attribute or make it invisible to most programs by setting its system or hidden attribute. These permissions apply to any program that accesses the file. In UNIX, a file has independent sets of "read", "write", and "execute" permissions for its owner, the other members of its owner's group, and the rest of the world. The only way to make a file invisible is to deny read permission for the directory containing the file.

- When you create a pipeline under MS-DOS, the operating system creates a temporary file to contain the output of the first program. The second program then reads that file. The second program cannot start until the first one has finished. Under UNIX, no file is created; the data passed through the pipeline is passed through memory and the two programs run in parallel.

B.2   MS-DOS Commands and Their UNIX Equivalents

These are some of the most common MS-DOS commands and the UNIX commands that perform approximately the same functions:

MS-DOS	UNIX	*Function*
attrib	chmod, ls -l	Sets or displays file attributes.
cd, chdir	cd, chdir, pwd	Sets or displays current directory.
command	sh, csh	Calls a subshell.
comp	cmp	Compares files byte by byte.
copy	cp,cat	Copies files.
date	date	Shows or set the date.
del, erase	rm	Removes files.
dir	ls	Lists files in a directory.
exit	exit	Exits from the command processor.
fc	cmp,diff	Compares files.
find	fgrep	Searches for a string in a set of files.
md, mkdir	mkdir	Makes a directory.
more	more, less, pg	Displays output by screenfuls.
path	set PATH	Sets search path for commands.
print	lp,lpr	Prints files.

`prompt`	`set PS1, set prompt`	Sets shell prompt .
`rem`	`echo`	Displays a comment.
`ren`	`mv`	Renames files.
`rd,rmdir`	`rmdir,rm -r`	Removes directories.
`set`	`set,setenv`	Sets or displays environment strings.
`sort`	`sort`	Sorts data in files.
`time`	`date`	Shows or sets the time.
`type`	`cat`	Displays the contents of a file.
`xcopy`	`cp,cpio -p`	Copies files and subdirectories.

B.3   Other Related Features

These are some other correspondences between MS-DOS and UNIX:

- In MS-DOS, you are automatically connected to your system when you turn on the computer; in UNIX, you must log in and provide a password (unless explicit provision has been made to the contrary).

- In MS-DOS, the `autoexec.bat` file contains commands that are executed when you start the system. The corresponding UNIX files are `.profile` for the Bourne shell and `.login` for the C shell. The MS-DOS `config.sys` file has no direct analogue in UNIX.

- In both MS-DOS and UNIX, your interaction with the system is controlled by a shell. In MS-DOS, your primary shell is specified as part of the `config.sys` file or defaulted to `command.com`. In UNIX, it is set by the system administrator and recorded in `/etc/passwd` or defaulted. The UNIX default is a local option; usually it is chosen to be either `/bin/sh` or `/bin/csh`.

- In MS-DOS, you can turn a sequence of commands into a command *name* by placing the commands in a file '*name*.bat'. In UNIX, you would place such a sequence of commands in an executable file '*name*', making it into a shell script with the command

    `chmod +x` *file*

- Both MS-DOS and UNIX provide for a set of environment variables to be associated with a shell. In UNIX, the variables are associated with a process, which need not be a shell; in MS-DOS, there are no processes other than shells in execution. Environment variables are referenced as '%*name*%' in MS-DOS but as '$*name*' in UNIX.

C

Resources

In this appendix we list a number of books on UNIX and a collection of resources available electronically via the UUCP network and the Internet.

C.1 Books

While in our more sanguine moments we may believe that we've written the most useful book about UNIX, we certainly wouldn't claim that we've written the only useful book about UNIX. Here are some of the others that we recommend:

[B1]   Abrahams, Paul; Berry, Karl; and Hargreaves, Kathy. *TEX for the Impatient*. Reading, Mass.: Addison-Wesley, 1990.

A TEX handbook for technically-oriented users who are not TEX experts.

[B2]   Aho, Alfred V.; Kernighan, Brian W.; and Weinberger, Peter J. *The AWK Programming Language*. Reading, Mass.: Addison-Wesley, 1988.

The definitive book on `awk`, written by `awk`'s authors. It includes a tutorial, many examples, and a reference manual.

[B3]   Anderson, Gail, and Anderson, Paul. *The C Shell Field Guide*. Englewood Cliffs, N.J.: Prentice-Hall, 1986.

A detailed tutorial on the C shell, including shell scripts. This book has been called the C shell bible.

[B4]   AT&T. *UNIX System V: System Manuals.* Englewood Cliffs, N.J.: Prentice-Hall, 1987.

A collection of several volumes containing all the manual pages for System V and some tutorials as well. The User's Reference Manual is particularly useful.

[B5]   Bach, Maurice J. *The Design of the UNIX Operating System.* Englewood Cliffs, N.J.: Prentice-Hall, 1986.

An excellent reference source on UNIX internals. Topics include the buffer cache, internal representation of files, process scheduling, memory management (swapping and paging), and the I/O subsystem.

[B6]   Bolsky, Morris I., and Korn, David G. *The KornShell: Command and Programming Language.* Englewood Cliffs, N.J.: Prentice-Hall, 1989.

The definitive guide to the Korn shell, including both a tutorial and a reference manual.

[B7]   Computer Systems Research Group, University of California, Berkeley, Cal. *4.3 Berkeley Software Distribution: Manual Set, Virtual VAX–11 Version.* User's Manual Set (3 vols.), Programmer's Manual Set (3 vols.), System Manager's Manual (1 vol.). Berkeley, Cal.: Dept. of Electrical Engineering and Computer Science, University of California, Berkeley, 1986. Available through USENIX Association, Manual Order Dept., 2560 Ninth St., Ste. 215, Berkeley, CA 94710, tel. (415) 528-8649.

An exceedingly useful collection of documents even for those who are not using BSD UNIX. The Supplementary Documents include nearly all the classic UNIX papers from Bell Telephone Laboratories, tutorials on many UNIX programs, and information on the internals of BSD UNIX. Much of this information is very difficult to locate elsewhere.

[B8]   Comer, Douglas E. *Internetworking with TCP/IP: Volume 1.* 2nd ed. Englewood Cliffs, N.J.: Prentice-Hall, 1991.

A detailed technical discussion of the architecture of the Internet and its protocols. The presentation does not assume a knowledge of programming.

[B9]   Dougherty, Dale, and O'Reilly, Tim. *UNIX Text Processing.* Indianapolis, Ind.: Hayden, 1987.

A tutorial on UNIX editors and formatters. Its coverage includes `nroff`, `troff`, `tbl`, `eqn`, `pic`, `vi`, `ex`, `sed`, and `awk`.

[B10]   Griswold, Ralph E., and Griswold, Madge T. *The Icon Programming Language*. 2nd ed. Englewood Cliffs, N.J.: Prentice-Hall, 1990.

The authoritative tutorial and reference manual for Icon, written by Icon's authors.

[B11]   Hewlett Packard. *The Ultimate Guide to the VI and EX Text Editors*. Redwood City, Cal.: Benjamin/Cummings, 1990.

A guide to `vi` and `ex` that includes many details not found elsewhere.

[B12]   Hunter, Bruce H., and Hunter, Karen B. *UNIX Systems: Advanced Administration and Management Handbook*. New York, N.Y.: Macmillan, 1991.

A guide to system administration that includes a lot of information on systems internals of interest to ordinary users.

[B13]   Kernighan, Brian, and Pike, Rob. *The UNIX Programming Environment*. Englewood Cliffs, N.J.: Prentice-Hall, 1984.

The classic overview of Seventh Edition UNIX by two of its major contributors. It covers both the user's view and the essentials of the implementation.

[B14]   Kernighan, Brian W., and Ritchie, Dennis M. *The C Programming Language*. 2nd ed. Englewood Cliffs, N.J.: Prentice-Hall, 1988.

The classic book on the C programming language. The second edition has been updated to describe the ANSI standard version of C.

[B15]   Kochan, Stephen G., and Wood, Patrick H. *UNIX Shell Programming*. Indianapolis, Ind.: Hayden, 1985.

A tutorial on shell programming using the Bourne shell. It also includes sections on the C shell and the Korn shell.

[B16]   Knuth, Donald E. *The TEXbook*. Reading, Mass.: Addison-Wesley, 1986.

The ultimate source of information on TEX, written by TEX's designer and implementor.

[B17]   Lamport, Leslie. *LATEX: A Document Preparation System*. Reading, Mass.: Addison-Wesley, 1986.

The authoritative user's guide and reference manual for LATEX.

[B18]   Leffler, Samuel J.; McKusick, Marshall Kirk; Karels, Michael J.; and Quarterman, John S. *The Design and Implementation of the 4.3 BSD UNIX Operating System*. Reading, Mass.: Addison-Wesley, 1989.

The authoritative description of the design of BSD UNIX.

[B19] Libes, Don, and Ressler, Sandy. *Life with UNIX: A Guide for Everyone.* Englewood Cliffs, N.J.: Prentice-Hall, 1989.

An excellent source for material on the history and culture of UNIX. It includes a lot of information about the USENET.

[B20] O'Reilly, Tim; Quercia, Valerie; and Lamb, Linda. *X Window System User's Guide, Vol. 3.* 3rd ed. Newton, Mass.: O'Reilly & Associates, 1990.

A guide to X from the user's viewpoint, including the structure of the system, major X clients, the `twm` window manager, and the procedures for configuring X on your system. Other volumes in this series deal with programming conventions for X.

[B21] O'Reilly, Tim, and Todino, Grace. *Managing UUCP and USENET.* Newton, Mass.: O'Reilly & Associates, 1989.

One of the few books to completely explain how to set up `uucp`. It even explains how to wire a null modem. Particularly useful to new system administrators.

[B22] Stoll, Clifford. *The Cuckoo's Egg.* New York: Doubleday, 1989.

A popular bestseller with a fascinating true story about an attempted break-in on a UNIX system and how it was foiled. In passing, it explains much about UNIX systems and networks.

[B23] Wall, Larry, and Schwartz, Randal L. *Programming Perl.* Newton, Mass.: O'Reilly & Associates, 1990.

The authoritative description of Perl, written by Perl's authors.

[B24] Zlotnick, Fred. *The POSIX.1 Standard: A Programmer's Guide.* Redwood City, Cal.: Benjamin/Cummings, 1991.

A guide to the conventions for writing C programs that will work on nearly all UNIX systems.

C.2 Electronic Resources (the UUCP Network)

The resources described below are available from sites on the UUCP network (see Section 10.1.1). Some sites allow you to pick up files with the `uucp` program (see Section 10.8.3) but don't allow you to log in and use the system interactively. This type of access is called *anonymous* `uucp` (see Section 10.7.1). Other sites do allow interactive access. A few of these also permit any logged-in user to perform a `uucp` file transfer; most of the rest permit it only with explicit permission from the site administrator.

To use `uucp` you need an appropriate entry in your `Systems` file (see Section 10.8.5); our listings indicated those entries. For interactive access you can use `kermit` (see Section 10.4.1) or any other communications program. You can also use cu (see Section 10.9), but cu is not suitable for transferring binary files and often misbehaves even when transferring text files.

[U1]   USENET (User's Network).

The USENET is a network of computers, most running UNIX, that provides newsgroups on a wide range of topics as well as other services such as file transfer and conferencing. The USE-NET is also available from many Internet sites. The comp.unix. questions newsgroup is particularly useful for exchanging information about UNIX. The rn ("read news") program provides a convenient way of browsing through newsgroups; many other programs for participating in newsgroups are also available. To participate in USENET, locate a site that is connected to it such as one of the public access sites listed below. Once you have logged in, just type rn, or use the help facilities provided by the site.

[U2]   List of UNIX systems that are available for public access.

A number of sites provide dial-up public access to UNIX systems. Through these sites you can reach the USENET and the UUCP network. Some are free; others charge a small fee. Both short and long lists of these sites are available. The short list, named nixpub.short, contains only the sites; the long list, named nixpub, contains information about each site. Both lists can be retrieved from the following sources:

- Lagniappe Systems, Doylestown Pa., site lgnp1. The commands to transfer the lists to your current directory are

```
uucp lgnp1\!\~nuucp/nixpub   .
uucp lgnp1\!\~nuucp/nixpub/short .
```

  The Systems entry is

```
lgnp1 Any ACU speed 1-215-348-9727 "" "" login: nuucp
```
---

  where *speed* is 2400 or 19200 depending on your modem.
  You can also log in at lgnp1 interactively using the same telephone number and the name bbs.

- USENET. The lists are regularly posted to the newsgroups comp.misc and alt.bbs.

- Anonymous ftp from uop.uop.edu (IP address 138. 9.200.1) under ~/pub/nixpub.{short,long}.

- Anonymous ftp from gvl.unisys.com (IP address 128. 126.220.102) under ~/pub/nixpub/{short,long}.

If you have an electronic mail address accessible from the Internet, you can place yourself on the nixpub electronic mailing list by sending mail to nixpub-request@ls.com.

[U3]   File repository at OSUCIS (Ohio State University Computer and Information Science Department).

The file repository contains a very large collection of publicly available software, documents, and databases. The first files you should retrieve are these:

`ls-lR.Z`   List of the available files in compressed form (about 60KB). See Section 3.17.2 for how to decompress it.

`GNU.how-to-get`
Information on how to get the GNU files from the Free Software Foundation (about 35 KB).

The command to transfer these files to your current directory is

```
uucp osu-cis\!\~/ls-lR.Z osu-cis\!\~/GNU.how-to-get .
```

The `Systems` entry for a modem using the PEP protocol is

```
osu-cis Any ACU 19200 1-614-292-5112 in:--in:--in: Uanon
```

The `Systems` entry for any other modem at 1200, 2400, or 9600 bps is

```
osu-cis Any ACU n00 1-614-292-31n "" \d\r\c Name? osu-cis
nected \c GO \d\r\d\r\d\r in:--in:--in: Uanon
```

In this entry, replace n with '12', '24', or '96' (in both the speed and the telephone number). This text must be supplied on a single line without line continuations; we show it on two lines because it won't fit on one line in this book.

Because the OSUCIS facility is very heavily used, you may have difficulty in making a connection to it. If so, you may prefer to use UUNET (see reference [U4]).

The OSUCIS facility is also available via the Internet (reference [I5]).

[U4]   UUNET (USENIX Communications Service).

UUNET provides anonymous uucp access via a 900 number. As of this writing, the cost is 40 cents per minute. The first file you should retrieve is `help`, about 6KB long. The command to retrieve it to your current directory is

```
uucp uunet\!\~/help .
```

The file `ls-lR.Z` is a compressed listing of all files available from UUNET. It is much longer (about 450KB). See Section 3.17.2 for how to decompress it. The UUNET archive contains material similar to that in the OSUCIS archive but is generally more up-to-date.

UUNET supports the PEP and V.32 9600 bps protocols as well as all standard modems operating at speeds of 2400 bps or less. The `Systems` entry is

    uunet Any ACU *speed* 1-900-468-7727 "" "" login: uucp

where *speed* is 9600, 2400, 1200, or 300.

Here are the address and phone number of UUNET:

> UUNET Technologies Inc.
> 3110 Fairview Park Drive, Suite 570
> Falls Church, Virginia 22042
> Tel: (703) 876-5050
> Fax: (703) 876-5059

You also can access UUNET via the Internet (reference [I6]).

[U5]   Registering a site on the UUCP network.

For information on registering a site on the UUCP network, send email to any of the following addresses:

- `rutgers!uucpmap`
- `uucpmap@rutgers.edu`

C.3   Electronic Resources (the Internet)

The resources described below are available from sites on the Internet (see Section 10.1.2). To obtain them you must be a registered user at an Internet site; mail access to the Internet is not sufficient. You can transfer files from an Internet site with `ftp` (see Section 10.7). In some cases you may need to log in at a site to use its resources. You can do this with `telnet` (see Section 10.6).

We provide the IP address (see "IP Addresses" on page 414) of each site we mention. These addresses are correct as of this writing but may change in the future. "Looking Up Internet Domains" on page 415 describes some programs that retrieve information about Internet domains.

[I1]   Internet archive searching service from McGill University.

The `archie` program performs an interactive search for material available via `ftp` from Internet sites. To access `archie`, use `telnet` to call `quiche.cs.mcgill.ca` (IP address `132.206.2.2` or `132.206.51.1`) and log in under the name `archie`. No password is required. A short help screen will come up explaining how to use the system.

[I2]   List of sites that provide information via anonymous `ftp`.

This list is available by anonymous `ftp` from `pilot.njin.net` (IP address `128.6.7.38`), directory `/pub/ftp-list/`. The relevant files are `ftp.list`, `ftphelp`, and `archie`.

[I3]   USENET (User's Network).

See [U1] for a description of USENET.

[I4]   Internet Resource Guide.

This guide lists major resources available from the Internet, including: supercomputer centers, library catalogs, data archives, databases listing individual users ("White Pages" service), gateways to other networks, network information centers, and other miscellaneous resources. It is available by anonymous `ftp` from `nnsc.nsf.net` (IP address `128.9.0.32`) under the file name `resource-guide.tar.Z` and also from UUNET.

[I5]   File repository at OSUCIS (Ohio State University Computer and Information Science Department).

See [U3] for a description of this repository. It is reachable via anonymous `ftp` from `tut.cis.ohio-state.edu` (IP address `128.146.8.60`). The first files to retrieve are `ls-lR.Z` and `GNU.how-to-get` in the `/pub` directory.

[I6]   UUNET (USENIX Communications Service).

See [U4] for a description of the material available from UUNET. UUNET is reachable via anonymous `ftp` at the address `uunet.uu.net`, IP address `137.39.1.2`.

[I7]   The UNT list of on-line bibliographic databases.

Many libraries now provide Internet access to their bibliographic databases. The University of North Texas maintains a list of these databases, including many outside the United States. The entries in the list include explicit instructions on how to reach each database and retrieve information from it. You can retrieve the list by anonymous `ftp` from `vaxb.acs.unt.edu`, IP address `129.120.1.4`. Enter the following commands at successive '`ftp>`' prompts:

```
cd library
get libraries.txt
```

The file is about 100KB long.

[I8]   List of Internet interest groups.

This file contains a list of Internet interest groups to which you can subscribe. When you join a group, you are placed on its mailing list and receive all items sent to the group. You can retrieve the list from `ftp.nisc.sri.com`; the file to retrieve is `netinfo/interest-groups`.

D

Glossary

absolute path name A file name given relative to the root of the file system. An absolute path name starts with '/'.

archive A file containing the contents of a collection of other files, chiefly used for backup.

argument A word following the name of a command in a call on that command that specifies input information to the command. When a shell script is called, the arguments of the call become available as parameters within the script.

ASCII A standard character set whose full name is "American Standard Code for Information Interchange".

background process A process initiated by a shell as a background activity. When a shell executes a command as a background process, the shell does not wait for that command to complete but continues to execute commands from the command list it is working on.

block A unit of storage allocation, particularly used with respect to disk storage.

buffer (a) A region of computer memory that holds a portion of the data in a file after that portion has been read from the file or before that portion is written to the file. (b) A place where an editor stores text that is being edited.

byte A unit of data, usually corresponding to a single character and consisting of eight bits.

cache A set of buffers, usually in main memory, that is used to hold data from a block device or from another source such as a name server so that the data does not need to be read again when a program asks for it.

child process With respect to a parent process, one of the processes it has spawned.

541

client   (a) A terminal or workstation connected to a server. (b) A program run under the auspices of a server, as in the X system.

command mode   A mode of interpretation in which a program expects its input to consist of executable commands such as to delete a range of lines (in an editor) or to respond to a message (in a mailer).

command substitution   A construct that enables you to execute a command and then use its output as part of another command. A command substitution is enclosed in backquotes (' ').

concatenate   To combine two or more sequences of characters into a single sequence. For example, the concatenation of 'fat' and 'her' is 'father'.

cooked mode   The mode of reading from or writing to a terminal in which the incoming and outgoing streams of characters are preprocessed in order to put them into the form convenient for most programs. The opposite of *raw mode*.

core dump   A listing showing the contents of memory and other aspects of the state of the machine, produced by the kernel in cases of errors that might indicate program or machine malfunctions. The name is quaint, since magnetic cores have not been used as memory devices in computers for more than two decades.

current directory   The directory that is used as the starting point for path names that do not begin with '/'. In particular, a file name by itself is assumed to refer to a file in the current directory. The current directory is also called the *working directory*.

dæmon   A process that resides in a running UNIX system more or less permanently and performs some ongoing task such as collecting files to be printed and routing them to printers.

device   A piece of equipment used to store or communicate data.

device driver   A program associated with a special file that performs input and output for its associated device. Device drivers are also called *interfaces*.

directory   A file that contains links to other files.

disabled   Not in existence, with respect to a local variable.

dump   A listing of the contents of a file or a region of memory, usually showing each byte in octal or hexadecimal notation.

editor   A program for creating, modifying, or viewing a file of text.

enabled   In existence, with respect to a local variable.

envelope   An electronic container for a message that contains a description of the message for routing purposes.

environment   The set of environment variables associated with a process.

environment variable   A variable associated with a process that can be queried or set by any program running within the process.

erase character   The character that, when typed, erases the previously typed character.

escape   A character, most often a backslash but sometimes a tilde, that gives a special meaning to the character or characters after it. Also, the ASCII ⟨escape⟩ character.

escaped character   A character following an escape character that is effectively quoted by the escape character.

exit status   A number returned by a process to its parent process that indicates whether or not it succeeded at its task. Conventionally, zero indicates success and nonzero indicates failure.

field   An identifiable portion of a line of text, record of data, header of a message, etc.

FIFO file   See *named pipe.*

file   A collection of data stored on a disk or similar storage medium. A UNIX file can be an ordinary file, a special file, or a directory. UNIX views a file as a sequence of bytes.

file descriptor   An entity provided by the kernel that enables a program to refer to a file. Each file descriptor has a number; the first three file descriptors are standard input, standard output, and standard error.

file identifier   The name of a file within a directory.

file name   The name of a file, given either as an absolute path name or as a relative path name.

file permissions   A binary number associated with a file that specifies who can do what to the file.

file substitution   The process of substituting for wildcards in filenames. See *wildcard.*

filter   A program that modifies or transforms its input in order to obtain its output.

folder   A directory designated for containing mailboxes and files of messages.

foreground process   The process that currently has control of your terminal.

gateway   A computer that is connected to two or more networks and is willing and able to relay messages and other communications from one network to another.

globbing   The Berkeley term for *file substitution.*

group   A set of users recognized by the file system. Each file in the file system has a group id associated with it; members of the group can be given permissions to operate on the file that are not given to other users.

header   (a) A block of information at the beginning of a message that gives information about the message such as who its sender is and when it was delivered. (b) A descriptive block of information at the beginning of an archive file.

HOME   The environment variable containing the full path name of your home directory.

home directory   The directory that is the starting point for a user's directory structure.

host   A computer that renders services to other computers. A computer connected to a network, particularly a network using the TCP/IP communications protocols, is often called a host.

initialization file   A file containing commands that a program executes before it does anything else. Most initialization files reside in a user's home directory and therefore can be constructed to meet the user's requirements and preferences.

initialization string   A string sent to your terminal to make it behave as expected when you start using it.

i-node   A data structure that stores the essential information about a file—where the actual contents of the file are stored, how long it is, how many links there are to it, when it was created, and so forth. Each i-node in a file system has a unique identifying number. The term *i-node* stands for *information node*.

input mode   A mode of interpretation in which a program expects its input to be general text, e.g., the contents of a document (for an editor) or of a message (for a mailer).

interface   See *device driver*.

interrupt   An external event that interrupts the normal execution of a program, such as the signal generated when a user presses the (Intr) key.

IP address   A set of four numbers that specifies the exact routing to an Internet host.

job   A group of processes that behaves as a unit with respect to job control.

job control   A facility that allows jobs to be started, stopped, killed, or moved between the foreground and the background.

kernel   The program at the heart of the operating system that controls access to the computer and its files, allocates resources among the various activities taking place within the computer, maintains the file system, and manages the computer's memory.

kill character   The character that when typed causes the contents of the current line to be deleted.

link   An entry in a directory, consisting of a file identifier that names a file within the directory and an i-node number.

local variable   A variable in a program that is capable of holding a value and is not visible outside that program.

logging in   The process of establishing a connection to a UNIX system.

login name   The name that you use when logging into a UNIX system.

login shell   The shell that is called on your behalf when you log in.

macro   A named sequence of commands, possibly containing parameters. A macro definition associates the sequence with the name; a macro call causes the commands to be executed, with macro arguments substituted for macro parameters.

magic number   A number appearing at the beginning of a file that helps to identify what kind of file it is.

mail transport agent   A program that handles the transportation and delivery of mail.

mail user agent   A program that provides a user interface for sending and receiving mail.

mailbox   A file where messages are stored by a mailer.

mailer   A program for sending and receiving electronic mail.

major number   A number that characterizes the type of a device. Devices with the same major number all use the same device driver.

mask   A binary number (usually written in octal notation) used to remove bits from another binary number such as a set of file permissions.

mbox   See *secondary mailbox.*

message of the day   A message that is sent to all users when they log in, containing information such as the status of the system and announcements of newly installed software.

metacharacter   A character used in a regular expression or in a shell command that has a special meaning rather than standing for itself. For example, '.' is a metacharacter in a regular expression that stands for an arbitrary character and '>' is a metacharacter in a shell command that stands for output redirection.

minor number   A number that identifies a particular device within a group of devices of the same type, e.g., the number of a particular tape drive.

mount point   A directory in a file system that corresponds to the root directory of some other file system.

named pipe   A kind of file that behaves much like a pipe and exists independently of any process. Any number of different processes can read from it and write to it. Also called a *FIFO file* (first in, first out).

newline   The character that marks the end of a line. It corresponds to the ASCII ⟨linefeed⟩ character (code 10). You can usually produce a newline at your terminal by typing either (Enter) or (Ctrl) J , although a few programs such as Emacs differentiate between the two in certain contexts.

null character   The character whose binary representation is all zeros. By UNIX convention it is used to mark the end of a string.

null string   A string with no characters in it, synonymous with the empty string.

octal   The base 8 numbering system, in which the digits range from 0 to 7. Each octal digit consists of three bits, so the octal number 175 would be 001_111_101 in the binary number system (and 125 in the decimal number system). Octal numbers are used throughout UNIX, but they must be regarded as an anachronism.

option   An indicator that can be attached to a command in order to modify or control what the command does. Options are ordinarily indicated by single letters.

packet   A portion of a message that is transmitted as a unit over a network such as an Ethernet or the Internet.

pager   A program that breaks up its input into screen-size chunks and sends these chunks to your terminal, waiting for confirmation after each one. Some pagers such as pg allow you to move around a file as you view it.

parameter   A variable within a shell script that corresponds to an argument passed to the script.

parent directory   The directory that lies above a given directory in the file system.

parent process   With respect to a child process, the process that spawned it.

password A sequence of characters that you type when you log in in order to verify your identity.

path A sequence of directories that indicates how to locate a particular file.

pipe A connection between two processes that passes the output of the first to the input of the second.

pipeline A sequence of two or more processes connected by pipes.

pixel A picture element, namely, a dot on a screen.

port A connection between a machine and the outside world, usually identified by a port number.

postmark An item in the header of a message that says who sent the message and when it was delivered to you.

primary mailbox The mailbox where mailers put your mail originally, before you have looked at it. Also called *system mailbox*.

process An activity or thread of execution taking place within UNIX that is recognized as such by the kernel. The state of a process contains all the information that the kernel needs to know about it.

process group A group of processes that behaves as a unit for certain purposes such as control of the terminal. Under job control, each job forms a process group; without job control, the processes associated with a terminal form a process group.

process group leader A process in a group whose process number serves as an identifier for the entire group, typically the first process in a pipeline.

quotation A collection of syntactic devices for marking single characters or sequences of characters so that the characters are taken literally and their meanings as metacharacters are ignored.

raw interface An interface to a block device that transfers data between the device and memory without using a cache (another name for *character interface*).

raw mode The mode of reading or writing a terminal in which input/output operations transfer data directly between the terminal and memory without interpreting the data in any way.

recipient The person or entity to whom a message is sent.

recursive Pertaining to a process or action that is applied to an entity and its directly or indirectly contained subparts.[1]

redirection A shell construct for causing a program to take its standard input from a specified file or to send its standard output to a specified file. Other file descriptors can also be redirected in some shells.

regular expression An expression used to specify a set of strings being searched for. Regular expressions use metacharacters to specify variable parts of the expression.

relative path name A file name taken relative to your current directory. A relative path name does not start with '/'.

---

1. The mathematical definition of a recursive process is more general than this definition.

reset string	A string that can be sent to your terminal when it is in an unknown mixed-up state in order to restore it to sanity.
restricted shell	A shell that restricts its user to a limited, well-understood set of facilities, for example by preventing that user from changing the current directory.
root	(a) The directory in the file system that is at the top of the tree and of which all files are descendents. (b) The name of the superuser (root).
secondary mailbox	A mailbox where your mailer puts messages after you've read them. Also called the *mbox*.
server	A computer in a local area network that provides administrative services and network connections, and also act as a file repository.
set-uid bit	A bit within the permissions of an executable file that gives the file the permissions of its owner rather than the permissions of the user who called it.
shell	A program that controls your interaction with UNIX by reading input from your terminal and sending output to it. It is also possible to provide input to a shell from a source other than a terminal or to send the output of the shell to another destination.
shell script	A sequence of commands to a shell, written in the form of an input file for that shell, that can be called as though it were a command in its own right. A shell executes a shell script by passing it to a subshell; the subshell need not use the same shell program as the outer shell.
signal	An indication sent to a program of an unusual event such as disconnection of the terminal, timeout, or forced termination of the program by the user.
special file	A file that provides access to a device.
standard error	The file descriptor, normally associated with the terminal, to which programs usually send error messages.
standard input	The file descriptor, normally associated with the terminal, from which programs usually read their input.
standard output	The file descriptor, normally associated with the terminal, to which programs usually write their output.
sticky bit	A bit within the permissions of a file that enables a program to be retained in memory so that many users can share a single copy of it.
string	A sequence of zero or more characters.
subcommand	A command that provides a particular facility of a program, i.e., a specialized command that you call from within that program. Subcommands are often referred to as commands—occasionally a source of confusion.
subshell	A process, constructed as a child of the current process, that starts up a shell and executes a specified command or list of commands within that shell.
superuser	A person logged in under the special name root who is automatically granted permission to access any file and to carry out other operations not permitted to ordinary users. The purpose of having a superuser is to provide a mechanism for carrying out essential maintenance activities that ordinary users are not permitted to carry out for security reasons.

system administration	A collection of tasks whose purpose is to make the UNIX system available to its users in an orderly and secure manner.
system mailbox	See *primary mailbox.*
tag file	A file that acts as an index for a set of textual definitions such as C function definitions by giving the location of each definition in the set. Each line of the tag file specifies the definition's name, the file containing that definition, and the line within that file where the definition is to be found.
TCP/IP	Transmission Control Protocol/Internet Protocol, the communications protocol developed at Berkeley that serves as the basis for BSD UNIX communications software and is used for most communications over the Internet.
terminal	A device, including a keyboard and a screen (or printer), used to send data to and receive data from a computer.
toggle	To turn on a switch or flag that is turned off, and vice versa.
tree	A data structure that visually looks like an upside-down arboreal tree and consists of nodes. The top node of the tree is the root, and the nodes under any node are its branches. The UNIX file system is organized as a tree.
umask value	An octal number that specifies the permissions to be masked out when a file is created.
UNIX	The operating system that is the subject of this book.
user	A person or entity registered within a system and permitted to use that system. Ordinarily a user is able to log onto the system and send and receive mail.
virtual terminal	A simulated terminal that behaves logically as an independent connection to your computer but physically shares the same keyboard and screen.
whitespace	A sequence of characters that produce only empty space: spaces, horizontal or vertical tabs, and newlines. Whitespace is used to separate parts of commands and other syntactic entities.
wildcard	A character or sequence of characters appearing in a filename that stands for a set of possible characters or sequences of characters. The wildcards are '?' (any single character), '*' (any sequence of characters), and '[...]' (any character from a specified set of characters). The process of substituting for wildcards is called *file substitution* or, in Berkeley-derived programs, *globbing.*
window	An area on a display screen devoted to an activity or process.
window manager	A program that controls windows and provides services such as creating and destroying windows, moving windows around the screen, and changing the appearance of windows.
word	A syntactic unit, typically forming the argument of a command. A word consists of a sequence of characters; the successive words of a command are separated by whitespace.
working directory	See *current directory.*

Index

Within this index, special characters are ordered according to their English names (see p. 9). Terms such as .profile are listed under 'p' rather than under '.'. Page references in *italics* are places where the index term is defined. (Some index terms are defined in several places.)

Subcommands and options for the various commands are generally not listed in this index, since you can easily look them up in Appendix A. Including them in the index would have been redundant and would have made the index more cluttered and difficult to use.

About the Authors

Paul W. Abrahams, Sc.D., CCP is the author of *TeX for the Impatient*, a book whose success inspired *UNIX for the Impatient*. A consulting computer scientist and past president of the Association for Computing Machinery, he specializes in programming languages, design and implementation of software systems, and technical writing. In 1963 he received his doctorate in mathematics from the Massachusetts Institute of Technology, where he studied artificial intelligence under Marvin Minsky and John McCarthy. He is one of the designers of the first LISP system and also the designer of the CIMS PL/I system, which he developed while a professor at New York University. Currently he is working on the design of SPLASH, a Systems Programming LAnguage for Software Hackers. A member of the Authors Guild, Paul resides in Deerfield, Massachusetts, where he writes, hacks, hikes, hunts wild mushrooms, and listens to classical music. He can be reached by electronic mail as `abrahams@mts.cc.wayne.edu`.

Bruce R. Larson is the founder of Integral Resources, a systems integration and UNIX consulting firm. A mail and security specialist whose expertise includes System V, BSD UNIX, and SunOS, he has been administering UNIX installations since 1986. His experience includes configuring and administering an Internet domain and connecting UNIX systems to X.25 networks; his current interests include building an X.400 UNIX mail gateway. From 1979 to 1981 he did software modelling for the Federal Aviation Authority under a grant from the U.S. Department of Transportation; in 1988 he received his bachelor's degree in pure mathematics from the University of Massachusetts at Boston. A nominated member of the American Mathematical Society and a member of the American Helicopter Society, Bruce resides in Milton, Massachusetts. He can be reached by electronic mail as `blarson@ires.com`.